Reflections on Men and Ideas

The M.I.T. Press
Massachusetts Institute of Technology
Cambridge, Massachusetts, and London, England

Reflections on Men and Ideas

Giorgio de Santillana

Set in Monophoto Bembo
and printed by Halliday Lithograph Corporation.
Bound in the United States of America by The Colonial Press, Inc.

Library of Congress catalog card number: 68–14450

Foreword

GIORGIO DE SANTILLANA IS—IF ONE COULD CONFINE SO AGILE A mind within any definition—a historian of scientific ideas. He has written on the origin of such ideas, and his best-known book describes, in a novel way, one of the most famous episodes in their history; the long-delayed frontal collision, in 1633, between the "new" conception of a heliocentric system, which had been advanced a century before by Copernicus, and the "old" geocentric system which was approved by the Church. That collision, so accidental in form, so dramatic in impact, between two old friends—both scholars, virtuosi, academicians—Galileo and Pope Urban VIII, who nevertheless found themselves the representatives of opposing world systems, the one backed by reason, the other by authority, has never been so well told as in de Santillana's book, *The Crime of Galileo*: a book to read and reread, for both the drama that it contains and the thought that it provokes.

It provokes thought because Professor de Santillana is himself a thinking man, and it is dramatic because he is also a man of imagination. Whatever problem he faces in the long history of human ideas, he never sees it in isolation. He sees it as a moment in an unending process; and he sees the process, too. We speak naturally of the "new" heliocentric, the "old" geocentric ideas. But the "new" ideas of Galileo—as ideas—were as old as the Greeks, and the "old" ideas of the Church were only sanctified by medieval innovations. Aristotle was condemned as an innovator in the thirteenth century, while behind Galileo there was a tradition as ancient as any to which the Pope and the Jesuits could appeal. If they went back to the Church Fathers and the book of Joshua, he went back to Aristarchus and to the pre-Socratic philosophers: those ancients whom the genius of Plato and Aristotle had so long outglared and whose primacy, in Galileo's own time, Francis Bacon sought to restore.

Giorgio de Santillana goes back to the pre-Socratics, too. Like few other historians of science, he is also a classical scholar, equally at home among ancients and moderns, and thus able to see, in its fullness, the classical inheritance that the great scientific innovators of the Renaissance and the seventeenth century took for granted but which we, who have severed ourselves from it and hardly look back beyond the hither end of the "Middle Ages," too easily ignore.

What damage was done to intellectual history by the famous, if unreal, battle, at the end of the seventeenth century, of the "Ancients" and the "Moderns." The idea of progress, which grew out of the victory of the "Moderns," was no doubt a noble and a fertile idea. But it has grossly simplified the problems of history. Thanks to it, we tend to look back at the complex tissue of past thought and extract from it only those elements that we recognize as "progressive," as leading toward us. Indeed, in the eighteenth century, in the flowing tide of the Enlightenment, in a moment of what de Santillana would call "illuministic arrogance," d'Alembert proposed that, by a periodic burning of books, all the irrelevant matter of the past—all that did not look "forward" to the *Grande Encyclopédie*—should be destroyed. In such a wholesale spring-cleaning, who knows what would have disappeared? The Platonism, the hermeticism, the magic of the Renaissance; the astrology of Campanella or Kepler; the alchemy and chronology of Newton . . . for the sake of a temporary "modern" thesis, the indivisible personality of the past would have been surgically altered, and true history, which must see that personality whole, would have been fatally distorted.

Professor de Santillana is a humane historian who insists on seeing that personality whole. Like Ranke, he will not allow one age to judge another. He recognizes that "ancient" and "modern," "progress" and "reaction," are arbitrary categories, imposed retrospectively from without. In the long span of intellectual history he sees not only that human situations repeat themselves but also that the various strands of human thought, which for analytical purposes we must distinguish, are in fact inextricably, organically, mixed. The astrology of the Renaissance, he insists, is not "vapid chatter": it "lent a helping hand to science." Metaphysics and science do not exclude each other: Parmenides must be "restored to the world of science, without removing him from metaphysics." Indeed, metaphysics is never absent from the scientific spirit that it inspires and shapes: "the metaphysical accent is never lifted, it only shifts according to time." Alchemy and hermeticism are not "irrelevant" to us: they are at the base of the scientific revolution of the seventeenth century, at the base even of the complex mind of Newton himself—that Newton whom the eighteenth century saw as the embodiment of sovereign reason but whom Lord Keynes, more penetrating, could see as "the last magician." In this, as in other respects, the world has come round to the views of Keynes. Nor are progress and retrospection to be crudely distinguished, for the god of science is Janus-faced. Newton believed that in discovering the law of gravitation he was restoring the ancient knowledge of the Greeks. "Allow me to think it significant," says de Santillana, "that a man who sparked so many new ideas in his own time"—he is referring to Toscanelli—"should be the one in whom the most ancient frame of ideas has been reborn: that the new scientific thought should have as its precondition the rebirth of a cosmology going back to the gray dawn of antiquity." And further back, toward that gray dawn, he tells us, of the Pre-Socratics, that "it is those ancients who have dealt out all the ideas that Western thought has played with ever since."

But if de Santillana, with his profound philosophy, looks widely and deeply over the history of scientific ideas, he has also the great gift of imagination, the power to see and illuminate the dramatic moment, the conjuncture that makes old ideas suddenly fertile and brings an infant new cosmology to conception. These moments are easy to see once they have been pointed out, but it takes both scholarship and imagination to discover them. Sometimes they can be seen simply, in the striking apposition of dates. Such was the philosophical reversal that took place between 323 and 313 B.C., between the flight of Aristotle from Athens, when the death of his pupil Alexander the Great exposed him to danger from the orthodox, and the arrival there of the new Phoenician teacher, Zeno of Citium. In those years the philosophy of Aristotle, of the time-honored Greek city-state, suddenly departed with its founder, and the new philosophy of Zeno, of stoicism, quietly replaced it for centuries of monarchical rule. Another such moment is singled out by Gibbon, in one of those unforgettable footnotes to his great work. The astronomical observations made, for two thousand years, by the priests and astronomers of Babylon were, he remarks, captured by Alexander the Great at his conquest of that city. By him "they were communicated, at the request of Aristotle, to the astronomer Hipparchus. What a moment in the annals of science!" A similar moment is illuminated by de Santillana at Florence in the decade between 1428 and 1438, between the state visit of Prince Pedro of Portugal and the meeting of the Ecumenical Council of the Church. The first of these events caused the passage to Portugal of the cartographic science of Italy; the second "brought together, for the last time, eastern and western Christendom and ensured the passage of Greece into Europe"; and they coincided in time with "a wonderful conjunction" of personalities, of Brunelleschi and Toscanelli, the architect and the geometrician who, together, recreated the works of Hipparchus for the modern world.

How few these seminal moments are in the long history of slowly changing human thought! Francis Bacon himself, who saw the disclosure of truth as "the inseparable propriety of time," nevertheless, looking back, saw only three periods of positive enlightenment, of which his own age was the third; and later generations have not, in this, corrected him. Professor de Santillana also sees three great moments, at least until the mid-seventeenth century, and to them, in these essays, he continually recurs. His learning may range over vast tracts of time. He is sensitive to stimulus in many fields. He is at home in Babylon, in China, in Snorri Sturluson's Iceland, in untouched Polynesia, in pre-Columbian America. He will quote Hrabanus Maurus and Bertolt Brecht as effortlessly as Metrodorus or Athanasius Kircher, and carry us with him, a little breathless perhaps, and dizzy with his throw-away allusions and polyglot versatility, from Anaximander and Parmenides to Einstein and Oppenheimer, from Hesiod and the Epic of Gilgamesh to Kafka, Auden, Salvemini, and Simone Weil. But three points of time and place always catch him as he skims over them and bring him down to draw out their dramatic quality and wrestle with their problems. These three points are the Greece—or rather the Greek Dispersion—of the Pre-Socratics, the Florence of Brunelleschi and Toscanelli, and Galileo's battle with Rome.

Each of these three subjects has special essays in this book devoted to it, but none of them can be confined within the limits of a single essay: all overflow into the others. The reason, I think, is clear. It is not only the views of these men, or of their generations, that fascinate de Santillana, it is also the permanent problem of their emergence, their success, the revolutionary breakthrough which they achieved; for the real revolutions, he more than once insists, are not the blind *jacqueries* of economically oppressed classes but the revolutions of thought that occur "when a group of individuals arises in whom the community recognizes in some way the right to think legitimately in universal terms."

This problem of the emergence of such generations is a challenge not only to scholarship but also to the imagination. In order to appreciate the work of the pre-Socratics, it is not enough to consider it, however profoundly, in itself. We have to imagine the cosmology that they had received from their predecessors. In order to recognize the greatness of Brunelleschi and Toscanelli, we must envisage a world in which geometrical space was unimagined, or had been forgotten. And in order to appreciate the true significance of Galileo's contest with authority, "to disengage the great struggle from the clichés of conventional history," we must be aware of the cosmological agreement in which Pope and scientist were united—the view that the universe is "a whole, finite and perfect, indeed the most perfect work of art"—as well as of the great mathematical or methodological gulf that separated them. It is in his power to recreate, by imagination, these situations that de Santillana's great gift lies; and it is thanks to the same gift, as well as to the erudition and scholarship on which it plays, that he is able to bring out the significance of these great moments in the annals of science and history.

"There is more in a culture," says Giorgio de Santillana, "than is inscribed in its rational decisions." These words might serve as an epigraph to this volume of essays. They penetrate, at carefully chosen points, below the skin of history and touch, sometimes, a sensitive nerve. For de Santillana is never content with received opinions, with those "rational decisions" that are publicly recorded in formal literature. He is always looking deeper, at the totality of the human mind, not yet dissociated by specialization, or into "the no-man's land between art and science," or at the psychological underside of history, or at the unexpressed assumptions of a past age, which the ideas of the great innovators, now absorbed, once had to undermine and overturn. This is the constant, unifying quality that runs through all these essays and lectures which, to a superficial view, might seem scattered and miscellaneous. Thanks to it, we can deduce a general philosophy: it is the philosophy by which history itself is sometimes gradually changed.

H. R. Trevor-Roper
Oxford, March 1968

Preface

I SHOULD HAVE LIKED TO CALL THIS BOOK *Thoughts in Three Languages* because this is the way these articles took shape over the years, and it corresponded to their true nature, often divided against itself. Thus, my "Aftermath to Galileo" was conceived and written for the French edition, and it turned, notwithstanding my love of French culture, into a scornful denunciation of the role that France had played in the suppression of the Galilean heritage, first at the hands of Descartes, then of the Encyclopedia. I could not have thought and written it so unsparingly except in French for a French public. The piece on Bruno and Leibniz is inspired by the same desire to right a too-current evaluation of those great men in the light of their true intentions and the actual greatness of their effort. I felt driven to use the actual language in which the strongest criticisms were leveled at them by people I knew well.

It is the same attachment to minds that were truly great and original which prompted my defense of the true Leonardo, "Man without Letters," against the debunkers of the Duhem variety, and it also encouraged me in outlining (against Lynn Thorndike) that lovable, self-effacing, and admirable figure, Paolo Toscanelli. The great Brunelleschi himself has not escaped the picayune criticism of certain historians, and that was the origin of my paper on "Science and Art in the Renaissance."

When I come to think of it, even my major undertaking, "The Crime of Galileo," had its early origin not only in the ancient historical iniquity but in the modern spectacle of cruel injustice visited on the free scientific mind, of which we were all witnesses in the trial of Oppenheimer. May I add that the original piece on the Oppenheimer Affair was written in Italian (omitted here, as it would be too long) and was prefaced by a spirited defense of the American judicial procedure of the adversary trial as opposed to the Latin abuse of the *instruction de procès*, although the piece itself, as it appears here abridged in English, was of course a protest against the disgraceful and un-American behavior of the Special Tribunal run by Admiral Strauss and his colleagues in power.

On other occasions my spirit of protest ran away with me, and I have prefaced here my piece on "Philolaos in Limbo" with a deeply grieving apology for having allowed it to slip into print at a time when Erich Frank had just died, which caused the whole thing to sound like an inconsiderate attack against a master whom we all honored. Yet the polemic idea was surely genuine, turning as it did against the abuse of hypercritical destruction of the great names of Antiquity.

To set the balance right in the matter of the cult of Antiquity, I have inserted an irreverent take-off on Diogenes Laertius, the greatest jackass of ancient tradition, as Flaubert calls him, and on his inane "Lives of the Philosophers," which seems calculated to infuriate where it should inform. I felt I owed a warning to our students on the matter of venerable sources, and I called it "Paralipomena of the Future." I hope it will not be taken as pure frivolity.

My feeling is that history deals with intensely live issues and should remain "current," as the modern saying is. Hence I have taken the liberty of concluding my collection with a piece that is frankly "current"—a reminder to the Italian reader of the many and grave misunderstandings between America and Europe; "The Other Side of the Coin" ("Il Rovescio della Medaglia") is a passionate defense of American civilization against the ideas of their own that Latins like to entertain. There are too many important things to be dealt with to waste our time on erudite trifles. Even my early work on "Eudoxus and Plato," strictly chronological as it is, tries to answer a problem posed by great men and great questions.

The insistent desire to plead for the rights of life and creation against restrictive and stunting interpreters has led me to write on Parmenides, on the seventeenth century, on Newton and Einstein. But here the larger theme takes over, which unifies a great part of my work: the defense of scientific rationalism, of the actual, original, ever-living spirit of cosmology against the present vogue of positivism, operationalism, and their like. My piece on "Necessity, Contingency, and Natural Law" has, I trust, made my meaning clear.

My latest productions are a definite move into a field that had long attracted me, far from ordinary research and the usual tools, remote from the usual documentary material. The few samples that I present ("Riflessioni sul Fato," "Les Grandes Doctrines Cosmologiques") stand for a new approach and a new method which may yet be deemed uninsurable by our more cautious contemporaries: but that it has a point I have no doubt. It is the greatness of the subject that has called me, the prodigious wealth of mythical material gathered over the centuries, immense vistas of lost millenniums, of submerged cultures for which we may have found a key. Judgment must wait for our forthcoming book written in collaboration with Dr. von Dechend, *An Introduction to Archaic Cosmology*. But whatever fate awaits this last enterprise of my latter years, and be it that of Odysseus' last voyage, I feel comforted by the awareness that it shall still be the right conclusion of a life dedicated to the search for truth.

Giorgio de Santillana
Cambridge, Massachusetts, November 1967

Contents

Leonardo, "Man Without Letters"[1]

I HAVE HEARD LEONARDO ACCUSED OF HAVING BEEN A SCIENTIFIC failure because he was a Platonist. Now Leonardo remains for us a strangely ineffectual genius, at times even a perverse nature, but of all strictures that could be leveled at him, that of "Platonism" seems to me the most wildly unfair. I have been wondering why the artist and geometer Leonardo actually had so little of the "Platonist bias" common to the artists and geometers of his day, and with which he has been rather unjustly reproached.

Alexandre Koyré has shown us Galileo the Platonist, and we are entirely in agreement. Galileo was a Platonist, not only in his manner of explaining the concrete by means of the abstract but also in the Socratic method of his *Dialogue*, and especially in his tendency, here and there avowed, toward panmathematicism. But nevertheless there is the fact that Galileo was thought to be a Platonist by order and obedience, so to speak; for the mathematical sciences were under the aegis of Plato, and Galileo's friends and followers were Platonists—much better Platonists, actually, than he ever was. There is no doubt at all that the entire group of the Accademia dei Lincei was Platonistic before it was anti-Aristotelian, and in a vividly militant manner. With Ciampoli, the young prelate who heroically sacrificed his career in order to allow the *Dialogue* to be printed, one glimpses Platonistic insights that border on heresy.

Galileo, then, had good reason to belong to the "sect," as it was called; but more significant is it that he insisted on holding explicit reservations about Platonism as a philosophy. For, as Koyré has very ably proved, he was first and above all an Archimedean. It is Archimedes who was his master in the new science, and Democritus as well; Plato is merely his guarantor, so to speak, in the world of philosophy. What is most "Platonistic" in Galileo is his Pythagoreanism.

But, it might be said, is not Archimedes, again, in the spirit of Plato? I wonder. There is a whole pious tradition, created by Plutarch and other orthodox thinkers, which can be discounted. Archimedes himself was, perhaps, somewhat in Galileo's position. Among the great Greek scientists after Plato, there is actually a visible tension between the accepted philosophy and the necessities of their craft that impels them toward physics, technology, indeed raw operationalism. In the work of Ptolemy, which has been rather fully preserved for us, this struggle is explicit. It is inevitable and as old as time. Daedalus could not, I daresay, be as much of a "Platonist" as Pythagoras (if you don't mind my inverting the times) because he had to manage the Research and Development Center for the National Defense of the Cretan Empire.

[1] From *Léonard de Vinci et l'expérience scientifique au seizième siècle* (Paris: Presses Universitaires de France, 1953), tr. by Starr and Jim Atkinson. Printed by permission of the author.

Well, there you are: Leonardo is much more of a Daedalus than a Pythagoras. If we pause a moment over this idea, we shall see that, despite his technical advancement, his counterparts were not Heron of Alexandria and Polycletus but rather those half-fabulous, Palamedean figures, the first great artist-craftsmen, the *technitai*: Rhoecos and Theodoros of Samos, Harpalos, Hicetas, and Eupalinos. I am well aware that this is not a new idea; it was present in the mind of Valéry when he wrote the dialogue *Eupalinos* and the *Introduction à la méthode de Léonardo de Vinci*. But since I am trying to establish reference points as an historian, I cannot but be happy to find myself at his side. I am well aware, also, that I am making mythic comparisons. But Leonardo is, precisely, an irreducibly mythic personality. That is what he was to his contemporaries; he escaped their understanding in spite of their attention to his work. No one, outside of Shakespeare and possibly Rembrandt, is more mythic than he.

When we come closer to the historical person, the impression persists. At that time, metaphysical Platonism was in sway among artists: consider Paolo Uccello, Piero della Francesca—his direct predecessor—Leon Battista Alberti, Botticelli. Leonardo remains outside of all that: Leonardo, the "man without letters," the solitary man of incomprehensible fantasies, he of whom Michelangelo scornfully said that he had found no one to work his bellows for him.

Similarly, he is far less a Platonist than his teacher of mathematics, Luca Pacioli, whose *Divina Proportione* he nevertheless helped to edit.

And yet, it will be said, what about the Divine Proportion and his studies concerning the symmetries of the human body? But these things were in the air; they came out of Vitruvius and were common parlance. Ictinus, too, had been thinking of them twenty centuries before, when he built the Parthenon; and he could not have borrowed them from the yet-unborn Plato. One might, in that case, think instead of the influence of the Pythagorean Philolaus, whom modern criticism insists upon reducing to the status of a character in some dialogue—for it is well understood among the Right People that there could not have been any truly philosophic ideas before the Academy and the Academicians began giving regular courses in it (for the first time). But that is another story.

The Platonists firmly believed in the mystery of numbers, whereas Leonardo developed a rather special notion of mathematics, one closer to the spirit of his old practical teacher, Benedetto dell'Abaco, than to that of Copernicus. The mathematical instrument that he indefatigably pursued was, for him, really an instrument, a means of construction, a way—as Valéry would put it—of making himself an equerry of his own ideas. It is not the contemplation of a suprasensible world but the study of the geometrical skeleton of the real one.

His style reveals to us the same distance. Had I the time to do so, I could show through stylistic analysis that Leonardo has nothing in common with the robed and lettered brood of his time or even with Leon Battista Alberti. His language is, essentially, spoken Tuscan, such as it continues among the peasants of his region, with its rich pungency, its simplicity, its artlessly graceful turns of phrase, its countless anacolutha. Obviously he knows how to organize it, but then that develops from Machiavelli. It is his friend Machiavelli who is the closest to him as far as style is concerned—Machiavelli, whom elsewhere I have tried to show to be a born physicst, a *physiologos* searching his way among what we call today the social sciences—and also the tough-minded Guicciardini, as he is in the *Ricordi*. In various other places, in some of Leonardo's flights of lyricism, there is a hint of Ariosto, another man of no great learning. That is the intellectual pedigree.

But then, it will be said, all that famous reading, all those authors cited in the Notes, all those influences reconstructed by Duhem and many others? Well, that is the point. I simply ask that one page of manuscript be looked at with an open mind. We are immediately struck by the neat, practiced handwriting, sure and rapid; the handwriting of a notary's son, whose graphic formation fits in so well with the drawings. But when we read, the spelling proves to be a pure chaos, one that far exceeds the irregularities of the day.

The words are severed and broken and also amalgamated. Leonardo writes exactly as the peasants of his century wrote and as they still write today. The spelling is that of the servant maid or the recruit. The phonetization is the same. They, too, cut and combine in the effort of spelling out syllable after syllable, thus breaking the cadence of the spoken word. Leonardo writes rapidly and knows how to retain the cadence, but he remains bound up by his little world's way of writing. He uses archaic verbal forms which had disappeared from contemporary literature: thus *laldare* for *lodare*, *altore* for *autore*. Doubtless he must have spoken in the same way. If Dante shaped the "illustrious vernacular," one might almost say that Leonardo clung to expressing himself in High Demotic, creating the language of learned ignorance. "Savage is he who saves himself." He will never write in the style of *messieurs de la ville*, as Rousseau would say. This is a rejection that extends to their concepts, their logic, and their values.

This man without letters is not illiterate, but as a mistrustful, suspicious, and captious artist-peasant, he examines letters from without. He takes and he leaves. Thus in Pico della Mirandola and his Florentine elders he finds a whole subtle Pythagoreanism which might seem to be cut out for him. His friend Botticelli will let himself be taken up with it; Leonardo rejects it categorically, all the while taking his idea of man from Pico—or perhaps rediscovering it there. His own Pythagorean ideas will be taken from Ovid: the plurality of worlds, the community of the living, even vegetarianism. This is the doctrine of the *Hieros Logos*, the true and the ancient doctrine that he has identified as if by instinct.

It seems to me that the merit of Duhem lies in his having shown, by reconstructing the sources and the intellectual atmosphere which Leonardo certainly knew and made use of, to what extent all of this was actually a foil for his own thought. Assuredly, he read a great deal; he relied even more upon conversation, which so often becomes a spoken, two-way dream.

Long ago Séailles observed that it is the name of Archimedes which most often recurs in Leonardo's notes. Certainly Leonardo frequently sought out the master's texts, and from this Martin Johnson has drawn the conclusion that the best part of Leonardo's science is patterned upon Archimedes.

However, there is little enough in common between the thought of the historical Archimedes and that of Leonardo. And since I have mentioned Machiavelli's name, I might attempt an analogy. No one has reflected more passionately than Machiavelli upon the sources of Roman grandeur; yet Machiavelli's early Romans, as he saw them through Livy, are a myth. They are the unattainable summits blocking off the horizon of his historical vision. This did not preclude his deriving out of that vision a theory of the social man, stamped with the clearest scientific spirit. Leonardo is in rather the same position with respect to the "superhuman" Archimedes. Machiavelli attributes Plutarchian attitudes to the Romans; to Archimedes, Leonardo attributes fantastic machines like his *architrònito*, the "steam cannon." One might almost say that the same mythic distance exists between Archimedes and Leonardo as between Leonardo and Paul Valéry.

The men who have inspired us are not always those we know the best. I am reminded of Diderot, who was always appealing for authority to the ideas of Francis Bacon. Herbert Dieckmann, who knows Diderot as few others do, has recently shown that this man, so enormously well informed, had never read Bacon. Diderot cites only a few sentences of his, always the same ones, and cites them inappropriately. When it came to writing the "Bacon" article for the *Encyclopédie*, he had to resort to one of those little *abbés* who had read everything. We see those *abbés* again with Leonardo. He notes: "Tell Brother Giovanni to show you *De Ponderibus*." Brother Giovanni would explain it to him.

What, then, had he read—really read—from the past? First

of all, obviously, the poets. He was perfectly at home with Dante, the poet of his city. Pulci's *Morgante Maggiore* had a great influence on him. Only too well did he know that strange pot-pourri by Cecco d'Ascoli, the *Acerba*. As for the rest, he drew it from the Pocket Encyclopedias or Popular Sciences of his time: Ristoro d'Arezzo, the *Quadriregio*, Valturius. Only after he was forty did he approach the study of Latin, and then it was Ovid, that treasure-trove of medieval fantasy, whom he absorbed. He got an inkling of the Stoics and through them of Heraclitean intuition. He knew some things from Horace and studied Pliny and Vitruvius. But we need only look at his word lists and his pathetic little grammar exercises during that period to see how foreign a tongue Latin was to him. He draws up study lists of Latin words which he has extracted from his Valturius, to etch them into his memory; and we realize that he is thinking for the first time about their connection with the words that he knows. At the outset he actually takes the trouble to learn the literary Italian of his day, which he had known only at a distance. His Latin remains shaky and rudimentary; he gets lost in its syntax and confuses subject and object in his exercises. This man will never be able to puzzle out a text without the help of a friend. As for Greek, whatever Giovio may say about it, he knew not a word.

What he did do was listen. Books and those who knew books were, for him, a quarry where he sought materials. It is only thus that he treated certain results of Archimedes or the abridgment of Heron of Alexandria published by Giorgio Valla. He took notes on conversations and ideas heard at random. Thus that famous jotting, "The sun does not move," seems surely to be an opinion he picked up somewhere, perhaps listening to people talking about Philolaus, for it has no correspondence at all to the rest of his thought.

This is why he hates summaries. He would have the facts, the results, not the frameworks. He seeks these everywhere in conversations and thus finds himself having unwittingly absorbed massive doses of Aristotle, which will slow down his thought.

One might go on. But in the end we are brought back to Springer's old judgment about his art, a judgment that seems to have been confirmed by modern criticism:

> The role of ancient art in Leonardo's thought is insignificant, and in his painting it is nil.

What if he did study Vitruvius and the Canon of Proportions? What if he did draw, diligently, classical monuments and mythological motifs, if he did exhort the student to imitate the ancient rather than the modern?—all that remains commonplace, the bromides of the day. Once he produces, it is something else again.

A strange man, who by his own opinion put himself in a line with Giotto and Masaccio as masters of the return to nature, while for us he is the first painter to break away from nature and move toward expression. It is true that by "nature" he meant something other than what we mean. And this leads us to the threshold of his scientific thought.

Leonardo, the first of the moderns, "that Italian brother of Faust," as Michelet so rightly said. One imagines him leafing through *De Ponderibus*, Buridan, Albert of Saxony and his anonymous master, and even Themon, "Son of the Jew," consulting his friends, laboriously deciphering here and there wherever his instinct told him that he would gain something by it—with respect, to be sure, sometimes with too much respect.

One single example. Leonardo is meditating upon the flight of birds. He writes (I am quoting from memory):

> And since all movement tends to conserve itself, and in the same direction; or rather, since the *impetus* conserves itself for a time, while exhausting itself . . .

There you have it: the law of inertia was already on the tip of his pen. It was coming to him from that area of nature which might best reveal it to him—but just then he remembers his reading. And also he knows—he believes—that nothing is conserved.

Galileo, who did go through university, who labored over the huge folios of his Pisan professors and the works of his predecessors, will have to spend thirty years of enormous effort to shake off acquired theories (including his own) and to reach the point that Leonardo touched by instinct. Touched: for this man cannot, will not, plumb the abstract to draw out the concrete.

Let us return to the instinct, the labor of the imagination upon a darkly foreign soil. Then . . .

Then my mind returns to those other Leonardos, those Greeks of the little-known years between the twelfth and fifth centuries B.C., scouting around in the towns of Asia Minor or in that strange international port of Ugarit, having texts and processes of calculation explained to them. "We must see . . . ," they were saying; "There are things here. . . ." But actually, they were already seeking something completely different. They were being given devices, but they were searching for science. An arbitrary comparison, it will be said; the *jeu d'esprit* of an historian of science. But listen:

> The shaking of earth pressing upon earth moves a small distance from the point of impact; water, struck by water, makes circles which go far away; the voice goes farther in the air, and even farther goes the spirit in the universe; but since it too is finite, it would not be able to extend to the infinite.

How contemptuous can a man be of what was taught by all the Platonists, Neoplatonists, Peripatetics, Paraperipatetics, and other advocates of the Idea or the Logos; how must he scorn dualism, be ignorant of, or indifferent to, the supernatural; how must he categorically reject all their knowledge down to the very idea they have of knowledge—to write such a passage?

Notice that this is in keeping with the sum total of his thought. Thus he denies the possibility of spirits, for the following reason: in every part of space there is one element or another, and so there is no place anywhere for spirits.

A mechanist? No. Rather, a monist; and it is here that we might suspect him of stoic leanings, for when he is about to define force, he speaks of it as if it were a "spiritual" thing. But it is immediately clear that the "spirit" in force is an *impetus*, which is dissipated like other living forces, "rolling toward its dispersion while it diversifies itself through causes."

If we wish to talk of force before physics, this is not a bad way of talking about it. It is, rather, the successors of Leonardo who remain entangled in this notion, using an idea originating in a vitalistic analogy and trying to give it an abstract status which in the long run could only turn out to be metaphysical.

Leonardo does not get tangled up this way in deductions because he avoids promoting a discovery to the rank of abstraction. This is what keeps him from establishing a science. But *a* science is precisely what he does not wish to establish.

Let me use this subject to give an example of how influences and precedents are discovered. There is no doubt that Nicholas of Cusa influenced Leonardo. The cosmological themes of this remarkable mind are discernible in Leonardo's cosmology; his advocacy of "learned ignorance" was certainly an encouragement; the idea of the synthesis of contraries is perceptible in Leonardo's art and may come, in part, from him.

This is not enough for Duhem: he wants to show that the definition of force, too, comes from the Cardinal of Cusa who, as an orthodox Platonist, speaks of mechanical force as having a spiritual origin in that which moves of itself—that is, the soul. This is the very definition found in the *Phaedrus*. And in fact, remarks Duhem, Leonardo speaks of force as though it originated from spiritual movement: "This spiritual movement, flowing through the limbs of animals, swells their muscles." Hence, etc.

Speak of preconceptions. It takes quite a lot of good will to see orthodox Platonism in that. A force thus described is truly physical. And from other passages we know that Leonardo uses that word "spiritual" as an honorific tag to designate something that resists analysis. Force is *tutta in sè tutta*—almost as we would speak of a photon.

Rather, we see clearly throughout the rest of Leonardo's

thought that the word "spiritual" is *defined* by the notion of force. His entire universe is, so to speak, biological, but within it life is nothing but a form of organization which can mobilize forces, a sort of momentary focus of universal energies constantly in precarious strife with universal dissolution. It is in this, perhaps, that he is the most profoundly modern. For him everything is harmony, rhythm, momentary combination, dispersion; Leonardo's demon, like Maxwell's, is perpetually dying of the very act of creating difference and information, hence life. Its myth is fundamentally that of our present-day physics—the myth of Balzac's *Peau de Chagrin*.

And I shall go further: I shall venture to say that he did not adopt the theory of *impetus* because he read it somewhere else; rather, because his "force" gets dispersed and transformed, he will go to the Parisian scholastics, hoping that they will clarify that idea. His extremely direct intuition of inertia comes up against his rejection of the one sufficient abstraction. It would not suffice for his physics, which is much more complex than that of Descartes. For it is precisely Leonardo's physics that is at cross purposes with his mechanics.

This engineer will not be deceived; he knows that everything cannot be reduced to mechanics, at the cost of ending up with the absurdity of the man-machine. At the same time he remains a physicist, more of a physicist than Descartes, for he avoids the dodge of the *res cogitans*; also he is more modern, more Leibnizian if I may call it that, simply because he remains obstinately close to the real.

What, then is he like?

Leonardo is not at all Epicurean and accepts nothing of that sect. Yet his theory of vision is plainly Democritean. Vision is not an active function, as had been taken for granted by almost everybody; it is the reception of images, *eidola*, which peel off bodies; for "at daybreak, the air is peopled with countless images, which are attracted to the eye as to a magnet." The source of this idea is his theory that geometrical space contains all forms, which is the very source of the pre-Socratic idea, for the theory of *eidola* appears historically before Democritus, in the early Pythagoreans. Let us read on:

> The spirit passes instantaneously from west to east; it is even more rapid than vision, and all the great incorporeal things approximate the spirit in velocity.

This has a very old ring to it, like the words of Dante's Ulysses. And what shall we say of an aphorism like this one:

> Wrongly do men inveigh against experience, and reproach it bitterly for deceiving them. Let them leave it in peace, and turn against their own ignorance, which lets us be carried away by vain and senseless

desires to such a point that we expect of experience what it cannot give us.

Wrongly do men cry out against innocent experience, too often accusing it of trickery and of false demonstrations.

He tries twice, this thinker in "fragments." And it is there already, almost word for word, in a text of Democritus that he did not know. It has the latter's simplicity, his gait, his style, his cadence, his phrasing. And it is most different from the style of the stoic maxims, which he knows and quotes elsewhere.

Actually it is almost impossible to distinguish Leonardo's moral wisdom—in his maxims as well as in his fables—from that of Democritus which is nevertheless so personal. And one cannot say that Leonardo knew it; for it has almost nothing in common with that of Epicurus, so much better known. Democritus' moral texts have been identified only in our own day, by Diels.

What, too, shall we say of this fragment, which might be attributed to Archytas of Tarentum, at the latest:

Flax is consecrated to death and to human corruption: to death, through snares and nets, with which birds, fish, and animals are trapped; to corruption, through the funerary shroud in which the dead are wrapped, for in this garment do they suffer corruption. Moreover, this flax parts from its stem only when it begins to soften and rot; and it is appropriate that we use it to make crowns and ornaments for funeral processions.

If we should begin to wonder whether our imagination is in the process of playing tricks upon us, we would have only to look to Michelangelo for reassurance: to Michelangelo, Leonardo's compatriot and contemporary, that other artist-peasant, whose language was so vigorous and so pungent. In all of Michelangelo's prose, even the most direct, there is absolutely nothing of the pre-Socratic cadence; he is a Tuscan of his own century.

Let us pause at one of Leonardo's strange reflections, which the young Parmenides, too, must certainly have made:

My opponent says that void and non-being are one and the same thing; but void is in space, and non-being is outside of space; space is divisible, and non-being is not.

Surely here is the initial idea of Eleatic non-being, of which Leonardo rightly says that in it everything is contradiction, that it cannot be thought of in any fashion because it is not anywhere:

In the presence of nature, it [non-being] finds its associates among things that are impossible.

And yet when he moves on to other things—to contemplating the total presence of all possible forms and lines in space—he adds:

Among all great things, Nothingness is the greatest. It remains within time, and devours all that is or shall be; but it possesses nothing of the indivisible present, and it does not extend to the essence of anything.

"It remains within time. . . ." That is why, appended Parmenides,

> What men call becoming and perishing, being or being not, change of place and alteration of gleaming colors, are nothing but names.

The essence is elsewhere: in this we see asserted the idea of the truth of the world as an eternal present, as the body of geometric space.

Let us go on further. In his studies of marine fossils found in the mountains Leonardo returns to the path cleared by Anaximander—a path since abandoned (except by Chu Hsi) and one which will remain an object of derision for Voltaire and Buffon. And if the posture of his mind so closely repeats that of the Milesian physicist, it is because they possessed fundamental images in common: the primordial vortex, the separation of the elements, the evolution of the world in the shifting contrast of opposites, the Ionian *ἐπικράτεια*, so different from the categorical contraries of Aristotelianism. And this comes to its conclusion in fire, which again is not the Fire Finale of the Stoics but an actual process:

> The fertile earth, following the law of growth, will eventually lose the water hidden in her breast, and this water, passing through the cold and rarefied air, will be forced to end in the element of fire. Then the surface of the earth will be burned, and that will be the end of all terrestrial nature.

Let us note that this process is merely the natural continuation of that conceived as its origin by Anaximander; it is the third phase, after which the metastable unity that assures life for a time will be broken. It is thus—I quote—that operate

> the hope and the desire to return to one's country, to go back to the original chaos, as with the moth going toward the flame, or the man always impatiently awaiting the next season and the next year, always finding that the anticipated things are too slow to come; and who does not realize that he is aspiring to his own annihilation. But in its quintessence, the desire is the spirit of the elements which, finding themselves imprisoned in the life of the human body, continually aspire to return to their source. And know that this aspiration is the quintessence of nature, and that man is a model of the world.

It is clear; a model in this sense. This is in no way Pico della Mirandola's microcosm with its magical correspondences, its sympathies, its *ἴυγγες*.

Nor is it Stoic. One need only consider the prodigious series of drawings about the Deluge, with the world's return to the primordial vortex; and nothing, absolutely nothing of all the

Christian or semi-Christian Platonism (any more than of the a-Christian Averroism, it might be added). Obviously ideas are not born out of nothing. But at times the "something" is even smaller than the Gospel's mustard seed. Leonardo's whole theory about geological evolution probably springs from Ovid—Ovid again—in a passage that well-read men used to treat as one more of those fantasies:

> . . . Vidi factam ex aequore terram
> Et procul a pelago conchae jacuere marinae.

Ovid attributes it to Pythagoras, although it actually comes from Anaximander. It makes no difference. For Leonardo, who was studying stratifications and who was already headed in that direction, it is enough, just as a few words of Aëtius were enough for Copernicus to set out on his way.

Leonardo's level of thought enabled him to find Anaximander even elsewhere. And it is remarkable to see this cosmologist—this universal man who seeks the "paradise of the mathematical sciences"—refusing to find it where these sciences are most clearly asserted: in the heavens, where the Pythagorean Copernicus will find it at once. He rejects or is unaware of geometric cosmology as a whole; he does not want to "save the appearances": he feels that they do not need saving. Our friend Klibansky, in order to soften the vehemence of Sarton's attack against Leonardo's Platonism, has suggested that even for such as did not follow Plato's doctrine, there were many common sayings of Plato that had irresistibly entered their consciousness. Well, here is one of Plato's common sayings that did not stick.

The cosmology of Leonardo's day is half Platonist and half materialistic. Leonardo is neither one nor the other. And here we have him seeking other reasons—which ones?

In the "F" manuscript of the *Codex Atlanticus*, which fortunately is preserved in its original structure, there is the complete plan for a treatise *On the World and the Waters*, which starts with a wholly unmathematical cosmology and the place of the earth among the celestial bodies; then passes to the effect of the waters upon the earth over the course of time, in order to culminate in hydraulics. Here we clearly see outlined that idea of water, the central and living element, the amniotic fluid, as it were, of the universe, in which the heavenly bodies—themselves, like the moon, covered with oceans—seem to float.

It is a strange theory in defence of which Leonardo feels obligated to take Epicurus as well as Plato to task (for he has no more love for the one than for the other), a theory in which the orbits are not circles nor any other pure geometrical form: a purely pre-Socratic, even a pre-Pythagorean, theory. It is easy to recognize that *physis* of the ancients, which we understand so poorly. This *physis* is Thales' water but also Anaximander's

Boundless, a generative fluid that, we are told, was conceived in imitation of the *gonimon* and does not lend itself to any of our reductive attempts. A theory seemingly originating in the mists of time and yet a purely physical *physis*, a true Ionian universe. Leonardo, like his ancient colleagues, wants to speak—Aristotle would say—"as a *physiologos*."

I had long sensed this affinity with the Ionians, and I discovered that such an idea had previously come up in the sixteenth century. Edgar Wind describes a contemporary Milanese painting representing Heraclitus and Democritus. The man who cries and the man who laughs—a current contrast indeed. But it seems Heraclitus has Leonardo's features, and Democritus, representing someone unknown, has the look of a younger disciple. That was a good guess since Leonardo's notions embrace both men, and in a more profound sense than could be imagined by those humanists who had at their disposal only a half dozen clichés concerning these pre-Socratics. In Leonardo there is the vision of force "living its own death, dying its own life"; there is the hidden harmony of opposites; there is also the serenity and the tireless scientific curiosity of Democritus. Above all—and this has only been apparent since the philologists have assembled the texts—there are the same frame of reference, the same solutions, the same level of attention—and the same strange shiftings of attention that sometimes baffle us.

Unfortunately, only when a man is accustomed to both the Greek of the pre-Socratics and the Italian of Leonardo, does the stylistic resemblance become striking. It is an experience that is not easily communicated. Everything is there: the same stylistic harshness, the choice of words, the turns of speech and foreshortenings, the brusque endings, the ingenuousness, and that prose, inherited from the logographers, which used to make the fourth century say that the "ancients" strung their sentences together instead of organizing them. There is also thought closing itself off in aphorism and those very odd transitions from the particular to the general, those exhibitions of a logic that, although it remains hidden from us, is logical all the same. "If only," he sighs, "real things were to be found in books. . . ."

And he does not mean facts, for there are books that give these —Pliny, for example. A difficult notion, and we can easily see that even his own Italian lets him down in these circumstances. What he wanted to say is something Greek could attain at a single stroke with its peculiar *ex parte objecti* constructions, such as λέγειν τὰ ὄντα. Surely what he wanted to express is the state of mind of a Xenophanes, whom he did not know:

καὶ ει τις τά μάλιστα τύχοι τετελεσμένον ειπών

If it sometimes chanced that someone said what is really accomplished . . .

To say the accomplished, the final statement—actually τετελεσμένον, is not easy to translate. Perhaps we should say, "If only the things they told us were truly and utterly so."

This is not a lawyer's nor even a mathematician's expression; rather it is that of an artist—and one who does not think at that point of being an artist.

Transmission? Only the slightest bit. One might think of Diogenes Laertius, translated by Traversari in 1450. Such as he is, "the greatest imbecile in antiquity" might have been greatly valuable to Leonardo; even through his poor epitomes Leonardo might have re-encountered his thought among the early Ionians. Leonardo mentions Diogenes, but did he really read him? He mentions Anaxagoras, alone, and quotes from him one sentence which must have been repeated to him. Otherwise he would surely quote others, and since he does so nowhere, then perhaps that is the measure of his learning.

It must be more of an encounter or rediscovery. One might speak about parallel mental constellations or subterranean waters enduring under the surface of history. There undoubtedly is a primitive—in the best sense of the word—idea here, rediscovering the same reasons. As Leonardo would say, there are infinite reasons in history that were never in books. There are all kinds of invisible transmissions, all kinds of pickups and amplifications along wavelengths that have almost faded out.

Above all, there is this. As Nietzsche said, every mold for our thought was created in Greece during the earliest centuries. We naturally return to these molds in times of crisis when we sense that developments have gotten out of hand. There is nothing surprising about Bayle's return to them—a third attempt—and this with full awareness of what is involved: the digging of trenches for the vanguard of a new rationalism. With Leonardo, who has only a few elusive inklings, it is more surprising. But that is precisely the point: he has to rediscover a mold along the lines of those previous ones; a mold vaster in scope than those of his day, greater in potentialities that are more implicit, more dormant, if I may venture to say so. He must find a level where objective, analytical, and aesthetic thought are not yet dissociated, where each supports the other; for his mind is creative in each of these spheres, and he cannot think without using all three modes of thought.

This idea of an aesthetically justified science is certainly not peculiar to him. The idea is present in Platonism and still exists in modern science three centuries after Leonardo—particularly in the principle of least action, which is not a discovery of Maupertuis or Voltaire's Dr. Akakia since it was formulated on several occasions, and insistently, by Leonardo and others—the principle Euler still persists in considering heuristic and of eminent domain.

So the idea, in its most abstract form, is not foreign to us. But with Leonardo it is not at all abstract—nor was it so with those living before the abstraction. By means of a few allusions that his successors will dismiss, Leonardo discovers a *φύσις αὐτάρκης*, a universe in which everything is immanent physical clarity, where nothing is fixed or transcendent, where everything is force, life, and movement (an idea, by the way, which will be basic and seminal for Galileo): a universe ruled by a rigorous necessity and an impassive justice, where the hidden harmony and coincidence of opposites subsumes good and evil in an ambivalent duality—a cosmos in which everything is beauty, a beauty which has never known itself. It is this universe that Leonardo feels is fitting for a scientific artist, an artist of the "exact fantasy," as he calls it.

To the Platonists who define art as an inferior and twice-removed copy of Ideas, Leonardo answers sharply: "Painting is a philosophy and a legitimate science of nature." For from it, that which in the universe is unconscious of itself emerges. That is where truth breaks through, provided, however, that this truth has been constructed in depth through the knowledge of all of nature's effects that contribute to the creation of the image.

A man who thinks in such a way is not seeking a method; surely it is useless to reproach him on this account, as if he were an unsuccessful Descartes. As with the pre-Socratics he has to attempt his own *διάκοσμος*; he has to be able to say, "That is the way it is."

He will hardly be able to be an orthodox believer, either. And actually Leonardo's feelings about the Visible Church are lukewarm, nor does he bother to hide them. Leonardo's biographers have made a concerted effort—extending to the official celebrations of his fifth centennial held recently in Rome—to make him out to be orthodox, as Galileo has been made out to be a perverse conspirator. Perhaps they think like the founder of cities in St. John Perse's *Anabase* (again I quote from memory):

> If somewhere there be a hidden prophet, convalescent deep in a cowshed, my advice is that he be killed. If not, there will be revolt.

Says Leonardo (and we wonder what lies behind it),

> I painted God as a child, you imprisoned me. Now that I am painting him as a man, you will do worse.

Leonardo, like Baudelaire, is a little too much the prophet in the cowshed.

Nevertheless, here is what Vasari was writing in 1550 before his pious and sanctimonious 1568 revision:

> He used to philosophize about natural things and their properties; he never ceased to observe the sky, the course of the stars and the intrinsic qualities of living things; such heretical ideas came to him

that he drew near to no religion; he held it in greater esteem to be a philosopher than a Christian.

Need we quote such revealing words as "All our knowledge begins in the senses"; or else these bold pronouncements:

Therefore, reader, observe what we can believe out of the things our ancients have told us, considering that they wanted to define what the soul and life are, things which are not subject to proof; whereas experience continually shows us things about which so many centuries knew nothing, or else it corrects our false beliefs.

Here again is the opening out of the ancient mind with respect to its myths. "We have been taught many false things," said Xenophanes, "but men find better ones with seeking."

Leonardo's originality was all the greater since the recent past is rich with conclusive systems, dogmatic assertions, and subtle controversies. He notes:

For it actually happens that wherever reason is absent, shouting takes its place, something that never happens when things are certain. We shall therefore say that wherever there is much clamor, there is no true knowledge, because truth has one single term which, once it is made known, silences controversy forever.

Obviously all this is modern too. It might be mistaken for Galileo; but let us not forget that Galileo dared openly to say those things only after he had brought to light in the texts, behind the Aristotelian screen, "an older and better school" which reinforced his opinions. With Galileo there is conscious continuity; with Leonardo, instinctive continuity. We shall never know for sure what Giordano Bruno might have been thinking before revealing the secrets of "Pythagoras and Solomon." We know what Leonardo was thinking without having discovered either one or the other: Leonardo, in turn, is the man who will be able to enlighten us about Galileo's original attitudes. For he knows none of the compromises of the "educated man."

In post-Romantic criticism there was sometimes talk of a real "anti-humanist program" on Leonardo's part. That pushes the thesis to absurdity. Leonardo would very much have liked to have the resources of humanism, and it hurts him that he cannot "cite the authorities." But just as he rejected the Platonic *noesis* without thereby scorning Hellenistic philosophy, so what he rejects in humanism is the verbal solution of all physics and metaphysics.

Of all the creative minds in the Renaissance, he is the only one to reject *in toto* the universal consensus of the *docta pietas*, in which humanism, religion, philosophy, and even the more or less diversified heterodoxies found a comfortable niche. And that is done not through indifference or materialism but through a considered and ardent affirmation: the affirmation of a cosmology that is entirely *other*.

Where shall we find this cosmology? In his notes, almost everywhere—but not necessarily in words. It is very much to Berenson's credit, in his studies of Florentine drawing, to have pointed out that Leonardo has a deep distrust for the competency of words and that for him drawing is the form that can carry the most content, even in the region of thought we normally term "abstract."

It is difficult, really, to see the enormous multiplicity of Leonardo's drawings, especially compared with the very small number of finished works, as mere technical exercises and preparatory sketches. Johnson has clearly shown that what we are looking at is the very act of reflection; as Valéry would say, these notebooks are the entire journey of the mind.

Leonardo certainly knows this.

O speculator upon things, do not boast of knowing the things that Nature attends to by herself, according to her order; but be delighted with knowing the end of those things that your mind conceives.

A strange and ambiguous sentence, which could just as easily presage Vico's historicism with its *conversio veri et facti* as modern scientific nominalism at its most extreme. But then, what a contradiction it would be with the rest of Leonardo's notions!

Let us consult the text:

Di quelle cose che son disegnate dalla mente tua.

Watch out. Ravaisson-Mollien, and later MacCurdy, read *disegnate* as "conceives." But Leonardo is not a modern, and he has no pre-Kantian inspirations. He says, "*drawn*, or *designed*, by your mind"—an entirely different matter. This text is a marginal note, very much in place, on a page devoted to the technique for fusing metals. Therefore it is "the drawings of your mind," but consequently in the sense of the *homo artifex*. And it would also be fair, in Leonardo's sense, to understand "which your mind *perceives*" because perception and drawing are the same thing for him. But let us note that he said, "knowing the *end* of those things your mind perceives"; it is clear that he is not thinking merely of the man who knows how to fulfill his craft. This is a metaphysical idea, addressed to the "speculator upon things." The point of departure is an exhortation to be a Daedalus rather than an Aristotle; but in a flash of intuition, since this note is as direct as a drawing, he says that there is a level of reality where the artist creates a universe of discourse that goes beyond man yet is linked to him.

One may then think of those lines, the most argued-about of all, by the enigmatic Parmenides:

καὶ σύ ταῦτα μαθήσεαι, ὣς τα δοκούντα
χρήν δοκίμως εἴναι διὰ πάντός πάντα περώντα.

It is the promise of his deity: "You shall also see how sensory data can furnish a coherent totality for him who is making a general survey of things." A very direct sense, which was unfalteringly seen by Wilamowitz—and which generations of commentators have attempted to skirt by the sheer force of unnatural contortions.

Such a universe is open to the mind. It is a universe of perceptions, and in it perception becomes in some sense normative. The forms are "true."

For Leonardo, delight is the role of the young animal, the smile of creation; he never tires of contemplating it in his children, in his snorting colts, or in his kittens, playing or licking one another—the kittens he puts everywhere in his sacred subjects, to the great dismay of his pious collaborators.

Further on there are action, grandeur, horror, forces hurling themselves toward death, the carefully compared ferocity of those heads of horses, men, and lions caught in the attack. There is effort, tension, monstrosity. There is ugliness and unconscious suffering; above all there is conscious suffering everywhere. A brief annotation:

> The more feeling there is, the more suffering.
> Great agony.

In all of this there is a very beautiful order. There is a logic, the supreme knowledge of the prime mover, elsewhere called "force, divine or other," which was able to allot to all those powers the quality of their effects in the necessary proportion. The universe has no frustration; it operates to its full power, it knows how to express itself. And everywhere the law is, "All power comes of a breaking of balance."

> Lightness is born of weight, and weight of lightness. While paying for the blessing of their creation, their life increases in the measure that their movement does; at the same instant, too, each destroys the other in the mutual atonement of their death.

Anaximander would speak just this way; yet it is not Anaximander but Leonardo who is speaking.

What is man in all this? On this point Leonardo's ideas are nearly the same as Pico's. Man for him is one of nature's greatest variables. He is the center of many possibilities. Angel, animal, and still other things besides, for nature is full of an infinite number of reasons "which never were in experience."

Yet also—and in this he is much more melancholy than Pico—man is a discouragingly unstable variable, one that does not move along a curve prearranged by destiny—for man is his own creator. His themes are supplied from without; it is his job to filter them and to create out of them a being consistent with himself—and this idea, too, came once to Democritus. But here nature is something more than blind necessity: it is the interplay of forms and chance.

To consider a deviation in man that causes him to resemble a wolf is like seeing a manifestation of the same force that will make a rock appear to us in the form of a whale, or that of a whale that has turned rock, "an arrogant form that once used to sow terror among the living," and which the variations of sea and time have transformed into a bleak foundation of other rocks.

A saying from Chateaubriand comes to mind—quite orthodox, as usual:

> Man himself is only a crumbled edifice, the wreckage of sin and death—everything in him is mere ruins.

Leonardo would put it differently. He would say: man is creation's terrible failure. This has to be made good immediately since it is impossible to go on from there.

Let us take a look at his *Prophecies*, which are agreed to be trifling witticisms. Actually they are a list of unnatural things that to us seem natural. *Industrious peoples shall be seen whom brutes deluge to steal their wealth*—these are the bees. *Countless innocents shall be seen slaughtered before their mothers' eyes*—these are young goats. Still clearer:

> On earth creatures shall be seen who are constantly killing one another. Their wickedness shall be limitless; their violence shall destroy the world's vast forests; and even after they have been sated, they shall in no wise suspend their desire to spread carnage, tribulations, and banishment among all living beings. Their overreaching pride shall impel them to lift themselves toward heaven. Nothing shall remain on the earth, or under the earth, or in the waters, that shall not be hunted down and slain, and what is in one country, dragged away into another; and their bodies shall become the tomb and the thoroughfare for all the living things they have ruined. O Earth, what restrains you from opening up and from engulfing them as one, into the deep fissures of your chasms, so that the face of heaven no longer beholds so cruel and abominable a monster!

This relates closely to those drawings of the final period, invoking catastrophe—a genuine figurative expression of an abstract idea.

Perhaps that is the last word of the enigma; just as in the "Last Supper," as carefully constructed as *The Divine Comedy*, the central theme is man betrayed by humanity. For man is a marvel, and yet in a nature where everything is good because it is logical, men alone are cruel and senseless.

With Leonardo there is pure contemplation, fantasy; there is also the sudden shiver of awareness, the *στυγερόν*, the icy Styx. "We are all murderers."

From that point we have the flight toward possibility, all possibilities: those countless machines, and those machines to make machines—the revival of the medieval dream of Alexander conquering kingdoms in the air and in the sea—the redemption of man through creation and intelligence.

Michelangelo, that great hater of Leonardo who constantly accused him of finishing nothing, unwittingly grasped the idea. Michelangelo asks his pardon, as it were, after his death, invoking Leonardo's assistance to finish his own work:

> . . . onde a me non finita verrà meno
> s'or non gli dà la fabbrica divina
> aiuto a farlo, ch'al mondo era solo.

And surely Michelangelo was the man to understand him. Leonardo remains the loneliest man who ever lived.

Newton, the Enigma

ONE DAY, SO THE STORY GOES, SIR ISAAC NEWTON WAS RUSHING from one national committee meeting to another—for he was always driven for time—when his coach broke down. While he was waiting for repairs, he sat under a tree, where an apple fell on his head, and he had time to think about it. So he was able to discover universal gravitation.

This laughing-bitter gibe at the way scientists have to live nowadays underscores the truly ancient dignity and spaciousness in which Newton's mind was allowed to ripen in a quiet, if humble, setting. His father was a poor farmer, yet he was lord of his little manor of Woolsthorpe near Grantham in Lincolnshire, for that was the way the yeomen of England clung to their age-old privileges. Isaac was born on Christmas Day 1642, the year Galileo died, and that conjunction usually marks the year as the beginning of modern science.

Little Isaac was so small at birth that he "could have been held in a quart mug," but he became healthy and durable. His father died before he was born, and his mother remarried. The orphan seemed to be destined to farm labor since in his first school years he seemed retarded, but then suddenly he moved to the top of his class. He was mechanically minded from the first and delighted in frightening the neighborhood with his imitation of a comet made of a lantern fastened to a kite. When he came upon Euclid, he grasped it at once but did not care much for the book, which seemed to belabor the obvious. The true engineering temperament. At the age of eighteen his family found a way to register him in Cambridge University as a "subsizar," which was the polite word for work students who were allowed in on charity. Isaac Barrow was then holding the Lucasian Chair of Mathematics, and it is from him that Newton learned the great and rigorous way of ancient geometry. He quickly became a master of the art; in fact, a purist. We have his notes on the volume of Descartes where he found the great new discovery of analytical geometry. He wrote at times in the margin: "Wrong, wrong, he is no geometer." Archimedes was his model.

The boy had become an earnest, unsmiling young man. His early idyll with his pretty neighbor, Miss Storey, had been left far behind. Over and above his labor, what tormented Newton's mind were religious problems. In the great conflicts of his time he had been from the start on the side of the Puritans. He was after all an East Anglian, which is where our own Puritans come from. Under the suspicious eye of the Establishment and the Church of England, he remained a passionate heretic. This is now too easily forgotten in our happy times of tolerance. As late as 1696, a man was hanged for professing disbelief in the Trinity. Now Newton was not only at heart a Calvinist, an anti-Trinitarian, he was a Unitarian and a humanitarian. These terms today mean only a couple of respectable harmless things, but they meant then that he believed in God the Father alone and that Christ was only a man, the Lamb elected by God. A true Muslim would have recognized in him some kind of brother in the spirit. To confess it publicly under King Charles would have meant, at least, the loss of his career. Newton was, in fact, chosen for his first academic post by preference over a competitor who was not orthodox enough. The promotion must have been a somber day for him, for he knew he owed it to his silence. Later he was to draw on his own great store of scholarship to argue that the Trinitarians misunderstood the Holy text; he did that cagily. But he enjoyed tearing apart Athanasius' reputation until nothing was left. We are reminded of Galileo's predicament in his last days when he insisted daringly that if the Church is always right, still its science drawn from ancient physics remains beneath notice. But Galileo had it better in a way, for his orthodox faith remained untroubled, and what he had battled against was scientific stupidity; he remained to the end, even as a prisoner, the happy warrior; whereas Newton was a true bitter fanatic who would not believe the official articles of faith and could never say so. He was not alone; most of the great names of his time, Milton, Locke, Whiston, Clarke were also nonconformists, but this probably is what made him into the closed, guarded, indirect, lonely, basically unhappy man that he was to remain.

But now came a moment of pure joy. In his twenty-first year he had bought a prism to watch the deflection of images. One day he held the prism in the sunlight coming through a slit in the shutter, and suddenly on the opposite wall appeared in a long strip the colors of the rainbow. "Fortunate Newton," wrote Einstein once, "happy childhood of science! His conceptions seemed to flow spontaneously from experience itself, from the beautiful experiments which he ranged in order like playthings." The light spectrum had been a gift of the gods. The *Opticks*, to be published as late as 1704, remains his most fascinating work.

But meanwhile a much more forbidding challenge was besetting him: it was to work out at last the structure of the universe, to which Copernicus had brought his grand vision of the sun at the center (1543), Galileo had brought the principles of dynamics (1637), and Kepler his own surprising laws about the elliptical motion of planets (1619). These last had passed almost unnoticed—even by Galileo himself to whom Kepler had presented his book—but by great fortune they were dug up just in time by Horrocks, a young English mathematician. Huygens was to provide the theory of centrifugal forces, but Newton meanwhile found it by himself. With this he had most of the pieces laid out for the great construction; but the great idea, the master plan, was missing. He had only a glimmering. Here again fate lent a hand. In 1665, to escape the Great Plague, the college was closed, and Newton went down to his mother's manor of Woolsthorpe. As he sat in his garden in the summer heat, an apple fell on his head, and it set his mind on the fall of heavy bodies. He started wondering how far up this force of heaviness extended. As far up as the heavens? Let us quote the account of his old friend Pemberton:

. . . as this power is not found sensibly diminished at the remotest distance from the center of the earth, to which we can rise, neither at the tops of the loftiest buildings, nor even on the summits of the highest mountains; it appeared to him reasonable to conclude, that this power must extend much farther than is usually thought; why not as high as the moon, said he to himself? and if so, her motion must be influenced by it; perhaps she is retained in her orbit thereby.

The idea was straight as a shaft, but the mathematical difficulties appeared insuperable. In the rush of youthful genius Newton overcame the hurdles. He himself left a fragmentary memoir of those months that has become legendary, couched in the rather difficult language of the times:

In the beginning of the year 1665 I found the method of approximating Series and the Rule for reducing any dignity of any Binomial into such a series [i.e., he had formulated the Binomial Theorem]. The same year in May I found the method of tangents of Gregory and Slusius, and in November had the direct method of luxions [the differential calculus], and the next year in January had the Theory of colours, and in May following I had entrance into the inverse method of fluxions [integral calculus]. And the same year I began to think of gravity extending to the orb of the Moon, and having found out how to estimate the force with which [a] globe revolving within a sphere presses the surface of the sphere, from Kepler's Rule of the periodical times of the Planets being in a sesquialternate proportion of their distances from the centers of their Orbs I deduced that the forces which keep the Planets in their Orbs must [be] reciprocally as the squares of their distances from the centers about which they revolve: and thereby compared the force requisite to keep the Moon in her Orb with the force of gravity at the surface of the earth, and found them answer pretty nearly. All this was in the two plague years of 1665 and 1666, for in those days I was in the prime of my age for invention, and minded Mathematicks and Philosophy more than at any time since.

He was then in his twenty-fifth year. He had his great achievements already blocked out, including the framework of his Principles of Natural Philosophy. The *Principia* is a staggering work. Never has a book understood by so few changed the minds of so many. That it was put recently among the "Great Books" required for undergraduates to read in certain colleges shows only the peculiar mind of those "educators." What could a boy, even very bright, make of that impenetrable towering machinery of a past age? As Whewell wrote once, "We feel we are in ancient armory when the weapons are of a gigantic size." It would take a historian of mathematics versed in the state of the art, *that* art, to appreciate the mastery and resourcefulness with which Newton, like a one-man army or rather like a hundred-armed deity, brings to bear classical geometry as well as the new, invents new ranges of ideas, new techniques, new intellectual tools as the need arises, from theory of conics to infinitesimal analysis, from the expansion of functions into infinite series to ways for interpolations, roots for higher-order equations, and algebraic projective geometry. Worse, he likes to cover up his tracks and plays the purist with theorems in the style of Apollonius without indicating that his means of discovery has been the calculus, or fluxions as he called it, a tool that he rigged for the purpose but did not trouble to pursue or refine further, leaving later a trail of bitter recrimination.

For Newton was not really playing pure mathematics. He was, ever since childhood, what we call a mathematical physicist with a passion for experimental skills and for the construction of instruments. This is what he meant by Natural Philosophy. The word has remained alive in British tradition (the periodical sponsored by the Royal Society still bears the title of "Philosophical Transactions"), and a number of scientists are intent on reviving it now with three centuries of experience and an ampler meaning. It would include, for instance, the thought of that other bewildering genius, Gottfried Wilhelm Leibniz, Newton's contemporary, which is usually passed over in histories of "Science" and yet reveals itself as essential in the new theories on life and perception.

This, then, seems to have been the situation in 1667. The ideas of Newton were practically complete when he came back to Trinity and was made a Junior Fellow. In 1669, he succeeded Barrow as Lucasian Professor. In 1671, he built his reflecting telescope with his own hands. He lectured mostly on optics, but he was chary of publishing. The theory of colors had become in his hands a masterpiece of experimental physics, invincible, easy to understand and enjoy. He wrote to Oldenburg, the great intelligencer of the time, that he would send in an account of a philosophical discovery "being in my judgment the oddest, if not the most considerable detection, which hath hitherto been made in the operation of nature." One feels real warmth in these words. But light had been surrounded by so much speculation and semimetaphysical elaborations that many minds were disturbed by seeing its dazzling and intact purity broken up into a composition of colors. What Newton had communicated to the Royal Society became an object of uneasy speculation abroad. Some asked, in the scholastic manner, "Is light a substance of an accident?" Others tried to go by Aristotle's definition of light: "the actualization of transparency." What he meant in his language was: light is the full achievement in the act of the attribute of transparency. So what, as we would say, for our manners have become deplorably irreverent. There are many ways of standing things on their heads. Those men always wanted to know what light was before examining it. Newton's design was different: "Not to explain the Properties of Light by Hypotheses, but to propose and prove them by Reason and Experiment." It was altogether too modern. Another true modern, Hooke, disagreed on experimental grounds, and Oldenburg who was acting as go-between did his best to spread ill feeling. Hooke was an admirable experimentalist who had become demonstrator at the Royal Society. His skill made him cocksure in his ideas, and self-consciousness over his humble origins made him at times over-assertive. Newton started a correspondence, courteous enough, but soon clammed up. He wrote to Leibniz: "I was so persecuted with discussions arising from the publication of my theory of light, that I blamed my own imprudence for parting with so substantial a blessing as my quiet to run after a shadow." The difficult, jealous, suspicious side of his nature had come out: "I intend to be no further solicitous about matters of philosophy."

In 1684, his faithful friend Halley, who had been speculating hard on the paths of planets but obviously did not know about Kepler's rather cryptic discoveries, asked Newton whether he could guess the orbit of a planet. "Why," said Newton, "it is an ellipse." "Can you prove it?" Yes, Newton had known how to prove it for several years, but when he looked for his papers he found he had mislaid them. After Halley's departure he wrote the proof again and sent it. That was the first inkling that his friends had of a discovery that had taken place eighteen years before. On Halley's urging and begging he eventually gave the Royal Society those parts of his work that relate to central forces. Halley told the Society that there was more, that "Mr. Newton has an incomparable treatise on motion, almost ready for the press." He offered to defray the expenses. Hooke, as soon as he heard, asserted that he had already been in possession of the inverse-square law. But, of course, he did not have the mathematical proofs. Newton went into a cold rage. "Is this not a pretty way of proceeding?" he wrote scornfully and declared he would omit the third book, which was all the application to the solar system. Halley urged and begged again, coaxing him as one would a fractious child, and at last the *Principia* appeared in 1687 containing the mathematical discussion of the laws of solid and fluid motion with their application to the heavenly motions, the tides, the precession of the equinoxes, and so on. Celestial mechanics stood there before the world. The architecture of the universe lay revealed. It was greeted ecstatically, even by those who could understand it but vaguely. Wrote Pope:

Nature and Nature's laws, lay hid in night.
God said: "Let Newton be," and all was light.

But by that time Newton's mind was already elsewhere. He had been plunged for years in his great search for the hidden secrets of alchemy and of the Bible text. That search was to take him darkly, fearfully afar.

But I would like to give here the words of Lord Keynes, the man in our time who certainly knows him best. Keynes was not only the great and revolutionary modern economist that we know, he was also a Fellow of Trinity and a lifelong student and collector of Newton's manuscripts. He had had enough of the thousand-times-rehashed view of Newton as the first truly modern scientist, as the one who taught us to think on the lines of cold and untinctured reason. And this is what he wrote, for the Tercentenary Commemoration, in a somewhat impish vein:

> I do not see him in this light. I do not think that any one who has pored over the contents of that box which he packed up when he finally left Cambridge in 1696 and which, though partly dispersed, have come down to us, can see him like that. Newton was not the first of the age of reason. He was the last of the magicians, the last of the Babylonians and Sumerians, the last great mind which looked out on the visible and intellectual world with the same eyes as those who began to build our intellectual inheritance rather less than 10,000 years ago. Isaac Newton, a posthumous child born with no father on Christmas day, 1642, was the last wonder-child to whom the Magi could do sincere and appropriate homage.

This is profound and clear-sighted, as one would expect of John Maynard Keynes. It is even more clear-sighted historically than would be thought prima facie, for we could extend now his restrained statement "rather less than 10,000 years ago" to further centuries backward and away to other great civilizations all over the world, which brought to their own river valleys what seems to have been actually born in Mesopotamia, not quite from the Sumerians (they are late already) but among those peoples that we still can only designate vaguely as Proto-Elamites, Proto-Hurri, or Proto-Mediterraneans generally, for prehistoric archeology gives only faint clues. What is profound in Keynes is his insight that they saw the world "with the same eyes" as Newton—a quick swat at our pseudo-evolutionary cant. For this archaic aspect in Newton we might also suggest some normal philosophical reasons. His unquestioning Calvinist faith did not attempt any justification by reason. Bowed, like Cromwell, under the power and the glory of God, he did not try to understand, he only tried to decipher the decrees of a Will never to be fathomed. Gravitation had been one of his first clues. He did not imagine, as foolish moderns took to pretending, that it was one more of those forces of nature like magnetism. He was too strict in the rationalist tradition of Galileo and Descartes for that. "No man," he wrote, "endowed with a competent faculty of thinking will grant that a body can act where it is not." Descartes could not have spoken more haughtily. Yet there it was, undeniably, action at a distance between bodies, mathematically clear. "I have not yet been able to find the cause, and I do not feign hypotheses." It remained for him to the end a miracle, not to be explained, a firm manifestation of God's will whereby the universe is kept into place. And indeed, if we take mind, while light and electromagnetism gradually yielded to nineteenth-century physics, gravitation remained outside, a stubborn incomprehensible fact, until Einstein came along, who made it into a strange intrinsic property tied up with the geometry of space itself. This was General Relativity (1915), a splendid synthesis in which matter itself becomes part of that geometry. It has remained esoteric to many, although the magic formula $E=MC^2$ has become a household word ruling in people's minds the awful Mushroom Cloud. But even Einstein could never succeed in his later years in fitting both gravitation and electromagnetism into one true unified theory, and he ended his life in frustration. Heisenberg said this last December: "I am not giving up. Maybe this time I have it."

God remained for Newton an impenetrable Jehovah, somewhat like a saturnine sultan—or rather one of those merciless archaic deities, the stars in their courses—who takes no one into his confidence but manifests his will by signs that have to be humbly interpreted. How different from Kepler's joyous faith that God loved geometry and the music of the spheres as much as *he* did, from the goodness and the fatherhood of God in Platonic Christianity. Newton, although a friend of Henry More's, shared little of his feelings. The bleak statement added to the *Principia* shows little trace of true Christian feeling:

> . . . The Supreme God is a Being eternal, infinite, absolutely perfect; but a being, however perfect, without dominion, cannot be said to be Lord God. . . . It is the dominion of a spiritual being which constitutes a God: a true, supreme, or imaginary dominion makes a true, supreme, or imaginary God. And from his true dominion it follows that the true God is a living, intelligent, and powerful Being; and from his other perfections, that he is supreme, or most perfect. . . . We know him only by his most wise and excellent contrivances of things, and final causes; we admire him for his perfections; but we reverence and adore him on account of his dominion; for we adore him as his servants; and a god without dominion, providence, and final causes, is nothing else but Fate and Nature. . . . And thus much concerning God; to discourse of whom from the appearances of things does certainly belong to natural philosophy.

So Newton's life from his thirtieth year turned into a desperate search for those cryptic signs of power. Keynes goes on in his whimsical way:

Why do I call him a magician? Because he looked on the whole universe and all that is in it as a riddle, as a secret which could be read by applying pure thought to certain evidence, certain mystic clues which God had laid about the world to allow a sort of philosopher's treasure hunt to the esoteric brotherhood. He believed that these clues were to be found partly in the evidence of the heavens and in the constitution of elements but also partly in certain papers and traditions handed down by the brethren in an unbroken chain back to the original cryptic revelation in Babylonia. He regarded the universe as a cryptogram set by the Almighty—just as he himself wrapt the discovery of the calculus in a cryptogram when he communicated with Leibniz. By pure thought, by concentration of mind, the riddle, he believed, would be revealed to the initiate.

He did read the riddle of the heavens. And he believed that by the same powers of his introspective imagination he would read the riddle of the Godhead, the riddle of past and future events divinely foreordained, the riddle of the elements and their constitution from an original undifferentiated first matter, the riddle of health and of immortality. All would be revealed to him if only he could persevere to the end, uninterrupted, by himself, no one coming into the room, reading, copying, testing—all by himself, no interruption for God's sake, no disclosure, no discordant breakings in or criticism, with fear and shrinking as he assailed these half-ordained, half-forbidden things, creeping back into the bosom of the Godhead as into his mother's womb. "Voyaging through strange seas of thought alone," not as Charles Lamb, "a fellow who believed nothing unless it was as clear as the three sides of a triangle."

The earliest section of those manuscripts relates to alchemy —transmutation, the philosopher's stone, the elixir of life. Those papers are still in Cambridge, marked "not fit for printing." Many of them are copies of known alchemical works. Newton seems to have loved his own handwriting, and copying afforded him a diversion. We have at M.I.T. a copy of Nicolas Flamel's well-known effusive autobiography. There are several other copies of that piece in the Papers. But what is minimized by historians is that about 1650 there was a considerable group of serious alchemists in London and Cambridge. There must have been some continuous esoteric tradition, of which we know little, within the University. At any rate, concludes Keynes, Newton was an unbridled addict. He adds with some passion: "It is utterly impossible to deny that [those records] are wholly magical and wholly devoid of scientific value." He might have pondered some remarks from his Magician that give the mind pause. For certainly Newton was not engaged in manufacturing gold and upsetting world trade (as a worldly economist, even if he be Keynes, is apt to suspect): "Because the way that mercury may be so impregnated, has been thought fit to be concealed by others that have known it, and therefore may possibly be an inlet to something more noble, *not to be communicated without immense danger to the world*, if there should be any verity in the Hermetic writers." The italics are ours. But we have it confirmed that it was the Hermetic mysteries that he was after; a huge body of knowledge of which we begin to know at least that it had very little to do with making gold.

The subject of the Hermetic Philosophy (so named after the mythical master, Hermes the Thrice-Greatest) was the cosmos itself and its interlocking forces; not the cosmos of our cosmonauts, to be sure, not even that of Copernicus and Galileo. It was the archaic Universe, which went back to the grey dawn of our civilization, brought forth by powerful minds lost in anonymity, the object of many great thinkers in successive ages—now lost to modern consciousness but deeply studied by Newton in a multitude of texts that no one can even read now, or cares to. Yet a whole that lacked neither depth nor grandeur, a vast polyphony of which Newton could have said in the words of Brunelleschi, the creator of Renaissance architecture: "If it was there, we have dug it up, and if it was not, we have snatched it from heaven." A word of splendid arrogance that he would have deserved to invent himself, for it well expressed Newton's surprising gift of intuition, which made his friends say that even in physics he had the results far ahead of the proofs.

Professor Andrade in his Tercentenary speech reminds us of those last "Queries" from the *Opticks*, so free of the usual meticulous restraint, intent and remote like the last quartets of Beethoven. It is there that Newton speculates about the possible exchange of mass with light, about the existence of small particles endowed with attractive forces of our electrical nature, by the agency of which they act on light and combine with one another. Was he seeing the physics of a later time through a glass darkly? A chancy thought that occurs to us also when we read certain notes of Faraday. In any case those speculations do not bear the imprint of banality. The Pythagoreans in their mathematical mysteries had once warned of immense dangers. So later did Copernicus in his Preface. So have many more. The actual adepts may have thought really of psychic forces and were misunderstood. The idea has been suggested by C. G. Jung. We simply cannot guess. And strange passages occur otherwise in Newton's letters, which are again impenetrable allusions, such as, ". . . but it is plain to me from the fountain that I draw it from, though I will not undertake to prove it to others." We have to leave it at that.

Only here and there can we form a cautionary idea of the trend of his thoughts on tradition, as when he writes that the Greeks must have had some "secret" knowledge of gravitation judging from Plutarch's remarks in the dialogue "on the Face in the Round of the Moon" which could not be accounted for otherwise. He had read his classics when very young, and we suspect that passage was probably more decisive in his early thoughts than the famous apple. Copernicus had been similarly inspired by the Ancients. With all that, in the passage of Plutarch as we read it now and with what we know, there is nothing but some nice play of imagination; the rest is Newton's own genius and his respect for the Greeks who had provided him with such a magnificent geometry—a respect that made him say that we can see farther than the Ancients only because we are perched on the shoulders of giants.

We may get a glimpse of Newton the man in those laborious decades from an account by his relative Humphrey Newton, whom he used as a secretary for preparing a clean copy of the *Principia* for the printer:

His carriage was very meek, sedate and humble, never seemingly angry, of profound thought, his countenance mild, pleasant and comely. I cannot say I ever saw him laugh but once. He always kept close to his studies, very rarely went visiting and had few visitors. I never knew him to take any recreation or pastime either in riding out to take the air, walking, bowling, or any other exercise whatever, thinking all hours lost that were not spent in his studies, to which he kept so close that he seldom left his chamber except at term time, when he read in the schools as Lucasian Professor, where so few went to hear him, and fewer that understood him, that ofttimes he did in a manner, for want of hearers, read to the walls. Foreigners he received with a great deal of freedom, candour, and respect. When invited to a treat, which was very seldom, he used to return it very handsomely, and with much satisfaction to himself. So intent, so serious upon his studies, that he ate very sparingly, nay, ofttimes he has forgot to eat at all, so that, going into his chamber, I have found his mess untouched, of which, when I have reminded him, he would reply—"Have I?" and then making to the table would eat a bite or two standing, for I cannot say I ever saw him sit at table by himself. He very rarely went to bed till two or three of the clock, sometimes not until five or six, lying about four or five hours, especially at spring and fall of the leaf, at which times he used to employ about six weeks in his elaboratory, the fires scarcely going out either night or day; he sitting up one night and I another till he had finished his chemical experiments, in the performance of which he was the most accurate, strict, exact. What his aim might be I was not able to penetrate into, but his pains, his diligence at these set times made me think he aimed at something beyond the reach of human art and industry. I cannot say I ever saw him drink either wine, ale or beer, excepting at meals and then but very sparingly. He very rarely went to dine in the hall, except on some public days, and then if he has not been minded, would go very carelessly, with shoes down at heels, stockings untied, surplice on, and his head scarcely combed.

His elaboratory was well furnished with chemical materials, as bodies, receivers, heads, crucibles, etc. which was made very little use of, the crucibles excepted, in which he fused his metals; he would sometimes, tho' very seldom, look into an old mouldy book which lay in his elaboratory, I think it was titled Agricola de Metallis, the transmuting of metals being his chief design, for which purpose antimony was a great ingredient. He has sometimes taken a turn or two, has made a sudden stand, turn'd himself about, run up the stairs like another Archimedes, with an Eureka fall to write on his desk standing without giving himself the leisure to draw a chair to sit down on. He would with great acuteness answer a question; but would very seldom start one. Dr. Boerhave [the most famous chemist of his time], in some of his writings, speaking of Sir Isaac: "That man," says he, "comprehends as much as all mankind besides."

So here we have Newton the Alchemist, portrayed from life: it sets our mind at rest about the later careless evaluations with which he was dismissed. There is no rambling and dreaming, no flight from reality. Vain his speculations may have been and fruitless his search, but there is nothing mystical or poetic about him; he was "most accurate, strict, exact" as was his nature, and if the object of his search escaped his devoted but not overbright assistant, there was nothing there that he could not have stated clearly if he had cared to. He was fusing metals, experimentally, as he had done to work out that very excellent mirror of his telescope. As he wrote, "We are certainly not to relinquish the evidence of experiments for the sake of dreams and vain fictions of our own devising; nor are we to recede from the analogy of Nature, which is wont to be simple and always consonant to itself." He comes back to the theme again, in his later speculations on the constitution of matter: "Nature in her tenor and course is very consonant and analogous to herself. . . ." His mind moved ever from the known to the unknown by simple procedures with an invincible certainty in the unity of Nature.

He was asked once, the secret of his great discoveries: "Why, Sir," he said, "it was by taking thought all the time." This cold unremitting fire stands out more clearly when Newton tackles the huge field of Church history and of ancient chronology. He writes down everything in order, many times rather than once, and it always makes good sense. But there is no room here for his fulgurating insights and intuitions into Nature. "The history he understands best is plain, practical and Puritanical," as Frank Manuel writes, who made a careful study of it in recent years. Newton has no feeling for psychology and complex motivation: men acted out of vanity and a desire for power. Human nature was again, for him, simple. As his atoms had been. "In the end there are hardly any conscious subjects in Newton's historical world; only objects." And Numbers, of course; for he remained the "last Sumerian" to the end.

His *Chronology of Ancient Kingdoms Amended*, when published, left critics stunned at first with the wealth and rigor of its materials. Gibbon was to remain deeply impressed. With a stroke of genius Newton had used one of those weapons "built by the hands of giants" that only he could handle with ease and with the speed of a computer: the Precession of the Equinoxes, which allowed him to check any date connected with astronomy. With that weapon and an obstinate reduction of mythical material to ordinary events, measurable in time, he was able to cut down the dates of accepted classical history by hundreds of years and to vindicate the pre-eminent antiquity of the Bible stories. To show that the Israelites rather than the heathen were the first founders of the humanity of the ancient world was the one end to which the long historical calculations and the reams of textual analysis were ultimately meant. To cut down the pagans and Papists was the passion that animated this obstinate sectarian. The *Chronology* raised a Battle of the Dates among English and French scholars which filled the air with dust through the eighteenth century. Newton took no literary or artistic nonsense, he cared nothing for the "stone dolls" and "poetical histories" of the ancients, he was a harsh textual critic reconstructing his material with the data at hand, and he did it as well in dating history as in discussing the Prophecies and the Apocalypse:

> It is the temper of the hot and superstitious part of mankind in matters of religion, ever to be fond of mysteries; and for that reason, to like best what they understand least . . . I have for the apostle John that honour as to believe that he wrote good sense. . . . It is only through want of skill therein that Interpreters so frequently turn the Prophetic types and phrases to signify whatever their fancies and hypotheses lead them to. . . .The language wherein the Prophets wrote was one and the same mystical language. It was as certain and definite in its signification as is the vulgar language of any nation.

Even the *Apocalypse*, even the hieroglyph, Egyptian or prophetic, was no mystery; it was a statement of ordinary fact, technically disguised, whose meaning could be shown to be concrete. Newton died with the firm conviction that in the field of ancient chronology he had achieved results as precise as in mechanics. Unfortunately, so many of the dates on which he relied were due to shoddy compilers and lazy officials; others were truly mythical, that is, they could not be reduced to real time in any way. And even the astronomical checks are largely a delusion. Chiron the Centaur, the master of Achilles, is accepted as having been the earliest astronomer and having marked the Colure of the Vernal Equinox where Eudoxus still had it centuries later, at 7° 36′ from the first star of Aries. Whence, extrapolating backward from the position found in the astronomical tables that Newton had for 1960, the Argonautic expedition could be dated about 934 B.C. What boots it, alas, for a great calculator to set the date for those personages, believing them to have been real people, if they were utterly mythical functions from distant ages that only the mirage of myth had turned into living figures for the Greek mind? Yet the method remains utterly correct, and it is helping us today to date back certain truly mythical statements connected with the secular shift in the heavens, such as the Golden Age which seems to have been linked with the station of the Equinoctial Sun in Gemini, about 4500 B.C.

Somewhere about his fiftieth birthday in 1692, Newton suffered what we should now call a severe nervous breakdown. People have spoken of his "madness" and unkindly attributed to a first phase of it the tireless activity that filled hundreds of reams of paper with alchemy and Biblical speculation. But his correspondence with Locke and Bentley shows no sign of derangement. It is simply the exhaustion of an intense and flaming spirit driven beyond endurance for thirty years. So did Faraday's mind yield at one point and leave him a gentle, careful old man with partial amnesia who could undertake only slight efforts. Newton suffered over two years of melancholia, sleeplessness, and fears of persecution. After that he rallied, but his friends set about to move him from his Cambridge isolation and to find him a dignified post in the Establishment. At this point, his successor Whiston was thrown out of the Lucasian Chair for holding his same beliefs. We should like to say that his patience snapped at last; that he denounced the Church of England as a pack of pagans, idolaters, and Jebusites and sailed off to Massachusetts where the Regenerate Saints received him with great honors; that his soul expanded and flowered at last into harmony of thought and belief in a land where his immense scientific prestige was destined to provide a backing for his successors Jefferson and Franklin, helping them make America into a scientific civilization such as they dreamed. We should like to write this, but there is little point in daydreaming. Newton kept his counsel and let his friend go in silence. He was made Master of the Mint in 1696 and President of the Royal Society. One night of 1705 in Trinity after Hall, he was knighted by Queen Anne. He became a great civil servant like Pepys and Lowndes; his shrewd investments made him rich; and for another twenty years Sir Isaac reigned in London as the most famous man of his age. It may be that his breakdown had weakened his iron "consistency of mind" as he called it; although his mathematical and statesmanlike powers seemed unimpaired. Or it may be that, like Galileo, he had seen through the vanity of great gestures and confided in truth to take care of itself.

Paolo Toscanelli and His Friends

THE RENAISSANCE REMAINS A MYSTERIOUS THING. IT IS AN AGE of hazy outlines, illuminated by flashes of passionate affirmation, an epoch of conflict and contradiction, an epoch in which there is the Council of Trent as well as Erasmus and Montaigne, in which the new astronomy comes into collision with the all-powerful, and advancing, astrology, in which the renascence of mathematics allies itself with the resurgence of magic. The sixteenth century is unbelievably far from us by its presuppositions, its mental habits, its superstitious respect for ancient authority, by the very structure of its intelligence which was ready to accept not only belief but knowledge *ex auditu*, from hearsay. Something of this bewildering texture begins to appear in detail when we bring into focus men and activities hitherto barely known.

I should like to discuss an enigmatic personage of the fifteenth century who was called by his contemporaries Master Paul the physician. He was a quiet man. We know so little of his life, his thought, and his personality that we have to reconstruct them by hints and clues. He is, nonetheless, the invisible knot that ties together a number of prodigious personalities—the very men who may be said to have invented the Renaissance and to have started the scientific revolution.

Not too much has been written about him, because so little is known. About fifty years ago, a big book was written about him by Uzielli which contained everything, including what is disputable, and built him up into a very important figure indeed. Then later, in his great *History of Magic and Experimental Science*, Lynn Thorndike undertook rather acidly to cut down to size the "Toscanelli myth," as he called it. And then in 1961, a new study came out by Eugenio Garin, the well-known Florentine scholar, in his *Renaissance Studies*, which is really a brief reappraisal. Garin's authority as a cultural historian stands so high that it is rather chancy to go and revise the question just after him. On the other hand, there is without doubt a slight slant to his thought because he is also an authority on the intellectual history of modern Italy: his strong progressive convictions have developed into a penchant for historical materialism, quite understandable if you have to deal with certain overripe subjects. And so Garin presents Toscanelli the technician and businessman, the healthy representative of the dynamic Florentine entrepreneur class which was reaching at that time its apogee. Surely, in fact, one may wonder why Garin did not bring out a certain episode in his late life in 1469, when he was already more than seventy years old. After the death of his brother, Toscanelli had to pick up the family fortunes and to steer the family firm through the adventures of the Gold Rush of Florence; by which I mean the alum strike in the Tolfa hills which changed so many fortunes around. He did it very successfully. This is the kind of thing that would make a Marxist happy. Garin is far too subtle to let himself be drawn into a trap of that kind: he goes on to characterize his subject in his more old-fashioned interests—but there is no denying that he enjoys setting up Toscanelli's likes, the technicians, against the orators who have adorned and also afflicted Italian culture in the centuries from then till now.

Let us look at Toscanelli, then, first by way of his Florentine friends.

The chief character in that group is, no doubt, Filippo Brunelleschi, the master who brought forth Renaissance architecture. Both as artist and as technologist I have to take him for granted. I should like simply to present him as an innovator, and a radical innovator at that.

With him, as I have tried to show elsewhere, we have for the first time the master engineer of a new type backed by the prestige of mathematics and the "recondite secrets of perspective." (Galileo's slightly tongue-in-cheek description of his own achievements with the telescope is certainly valid here because the man *is* the inventor of perspective.) Brunelleschi is a man whose capacity is not supposed to have been due to long experience and trade secrets but to strength of intellect and theoretical boldness; a man who can speak his mind in the councils of the city and is granted patents for his engineering devices. His judges are no small people either, if you come to think of the group of regents that then ran the cathedral works. The regents and their advisers are men like Niccolò da Uzzano, Niccolò Niccoli, Poggio, Traversari, Palla Strozzi, and, not least, the young Cosimo de' Medici. Men of affairs, most of them, wearers of the "lucco," the red cape of the Council of the Republic, humanists and statesmen all, involved in the European issues of their day, sponsors of the unification of the eastern and western churches, hosts of the last true ecumenic council, when Pope and Patriarch of Byzantium and their retinues, assembled within its walls, made Florence for the time the capital of Christendom.

Certainly we have here, then, something which is reaching world dimensions in general acknowledgment, and new types of men are arising. Donatello may be acquainted with the Latin classics while Brunelleschi is not; but still, it is Brunelleschi who stands as a qualified intellectual of a new type. It is only a century later that the fateful distinction emerges between pure and applied art. By that time the pure artist himself is hardly an intellectual.

Finally, this complex of achievements by a well-known group of great talents—Manetti, Ghiberti, Donatello, Masaccio, Uccello, Luca della Robbia, with Brunelleschi as leader—found a literary expounder of comparable talent in the person of Leone Battista Alberti to give their ideas full citizenship in the robed world of letters and humanism, something that only

Galileo was able later to achieve by himself. It will have been a fragile and fleeting conjunction, no doubt; it will end up in mere academicism, and in theories about art, and just about the time when science breaks forth with its own ideas of method and truth; but as long as it lasts, in the period of creation, it is a true conjunction, two in one. Leon Battista Alberti only paraphrases Filippo's words—we know that—when he says of the new art of architecture, "If it ever was written in the past, we have dug it up, and if it was not, we have drawn it from heaven." (This is a very typical, concisely expressed Renaissance position that leaves both possibilities open.) That "social breakthrough" of the new science of Galileo effected through the telescope, we find here in an early counterpart or rather in its first rehearsal. Everyone in 1450 was aware that a boldly speculative theory had preceded the complex of achievements, until the "cupolone," the great dome of the cathedral, rose unsupported in its greatness; "ample enough," says Alberti, "to hold in its shade all the land of Tuscany."

So there is in Toscanelli's time the feeling of revolution. I have tried elsewhere to characterize such a feeling phenomenologically: it is the resolute assumption of responsibility that forms the criterion. And that is why, in the moment of the Galilean crisis, we know there is a revolution because Galileo assumes the responsibility, in the face of the doctrine of the Church, to consider himself the only authority, or, if you like, the most authorized consultant, in a matter in which that authority has not been formally assigned to him.

To return to our present task: we are trying to define one of those rare points where art and science undeniably join. Brunelleschi created his theory of perspective by experimental means. He built the earliest optical instrument after the eyeglasses, the last one before the telescope—his famous perspective tablet. It had the new element of measurement in it, and it presupposed the establishment of a system of co-ordinates. To quote Krautheimer: "Plans and elevation drawn to scale were fundamental innovations in architectural tooling that he was the first to introduce in Florence." Seen from our point of view, these remarks of the historian of art seem an almost bizarre understatement. The introduction of measurement in its proper place in a theoretical treatment of reality is an innovation in intellectual tooling which is probably the most decisive factor of the scientific revolution. It advances step by step into our own time, and its originality has to be traced in the early stages. The vibrating strings of the Pythagoreans, the angular measurements of the astronomers, the measurements that transfer the study of aesthetic proportion to projective techniques—all are stages that we should work back into. And after that, of course, the way was open for the adventures through the theory of light and for the camera obscura. Here, implicitly, a new theory of space is born and a new geometrization of space and light, the new conception of central perspective which places man in an isotropic, in non-Aristotelian, space. Anyone who has been to visit casually the Pazzi Chapel in Santa Croce in Florence, which is Brunelleschi's most typical work, after having been in a Gothic cathedral, knows that he is facing an entirely different world of space and that the escape in some symbolic direction is denied to him; he is inside central perspective. And Copernicus is, in a way, the one who brings true central perspective to the universe, by placing "the lamp of the universe in the center." All of this implies, indicates, or in various ways announces the moving of the study of reality from imaginary or symbolic into real space.

And now we come to Master Paul the physician. Born in 1397, Paolo dal Pozzo Toscanelli was Brunelleschi's junior by twenty years. He came of a family of rich merchants. Their house was near what is now Palazzo Pitti, on the other side of the Arno. There is a tablet to mark its site. We even have the census that was taken in 1400 of their estate. The Toscanelli family was described as having in town nineteen servants, two horses, and a mule: the three-car garage, so to speak. In other words, they were rich and influential Florentine businessmen.

From his childhood, young Paolo knew Brunelleschi. As soon as he came back (in 1425) from Padua, where he had been studying for the doctorate, he and Brunelleschi were guests at a dinner in the garden of a friend, where they sealed their friendship; and thereafter they became inseparable for the next thirty years. As Toscanelli used to say later when he was an old man, "This was the greatest association of my life." He added, "You should try to understand what Brunelleschi has done because what he did takes great intentness of mind, more knowledge than you think, and also great circumspection." These words are quite significant of both men. Brunelleschi—or Maestro Pippo, as they called him—was (like Leonardo) a "man without letters," that is, he did not know Latin. In fact, his only books seem to have been Dante and the Bible. But he was a scientific and engineering genius, and he readily absorbed the geometry that Toscanelli gave him. Toscanelli had to be sent to Padua to study medicine; he came back with the title of Doctor of Medicine and was generally called "the physician." Actually, the curriculum included mathematics. You may notice that Copernicus went down to Italy and got the title of Doctor of Medicine. And in fact, if Toscanelli stands in the background as a medical man, a cartographer, an astrologer, he is essentially a mathematician; and one of such considerable achievements that the great expert of the time, Regiomontanus, in writing to him calls him a "second Archimedes." This is, of course, a rhetorical or humanist compliment because neither writer nor recipient can be considered in the line of work of Archimedes, but it is a set way of expressing admiration.

It was a wonderful conjunction, that of the architect and the geometrician, so early in the century, planning together the first great feat of modern engineering, the cupola of the cathedral rising unsupported on its base without scaffoldings or centerings toward the sky. And in the lantern of the cathedral, once it was built, Brunelleschi had an aperture made for his friend to project a beam of light down on a sundial on the floor of the cathedral. It was the greatest sundial in the world, then, because the beam was 240 feet long. On that sundial, on that "gnomon" as they called it, Toscanelli measured again with great precision the precession of the equinoxes and the inclination of the ecliptic so as to consecrate, so to speak, the double value of the cathedral.

In those years lies the beginning.

If one were to assign a high point to the Renaissance, one might suggest just those years—the decade, say, between 1428 and 1438, which began with the state visit of Prince Pedro of Portugal to Florence, where he was received with unsurpassed magnificence and a spectacular procession but also was given all the maps and geographical material that he had been asking for, and ended on the ecumenic council which brought together for the last time eastern and western Christendom and insured the passage of Greece into Europe.

It is not without significance that Melanchthon, the representative of the new culture, was to say of Florence a century later, and in carefully measured words, that it was for him the center of world learning. For after all, in a world in which philosophy and theology held such a high place, Paris or even Oxford might have preserved valid claims for the rank. And Florence was not even a university town. It might have been chided as intellectually irregular. Yet it is the center which not only brought to Europe the high and subtle speculations of Neoplatonism but also the texts of Archimedes; it brought forth venture capitalism, and with it a new class of technicians who went ahead in a most venturesome way. It is they who discovered America by mistake, gave it its name by another mistake, built the new cupola, as scholars insisted bitterly, by guess and by God, or as humanists said, "with their false and lying geometry," tried Leonardo's machines, and with the new geometry of space opened the way for that other mad venture whose author was to get at last his richly deserved comeuppance—I mean Galileo himself. If we think of the rigor and prudence of the Paris doctors, we must agree that this is a different view of intellectual leadership.

To return to Toscanelli and the geometrization of space, we should not forget that if in youth he was the junior adviser of Brunelleschi, he became later the senior guide, philosopher, and friend of many, including the great theoretician of perspective, Leon Battista Alberti, the man for whom was coined the title of *uomo universale*. Of them all, Toscanelli was the only one with a real scientific training. He was something, if I may say so, of a quiet Kepler—if a quiet Kepler can be imagined—and it is only when one thinks of it that one is grateful for Kepler's engaging and irrepressible gift of gab.

It is to Toscanelli that Alberti dedicated his dialogues, the *Intercaenales*, or *Table Talks*, those witty conversations which came into so many hands and were to be a model for Erasmus. A singular choice: it is not the treatise on perspective he offers him, but a commentary on society. "As you are a doctor of bodies," wrote Alberti, "so I am trying to be a doctor of souls." The hazy figure of the master is outlined here in the direction of worldly wisdom and knowledge of men, as befits a doctor.

So far we remain within the cultural circle of Florence. But now we have to go far afield.

One of the most commanding figures of the fifteenth century is Nicholas of Cusa, or Cusanus, or the Cardinal of Cusa, the great German prelate. His influence was immense in northern Europe. It sparked the thought of men like Copernicus and Kepler, and, not least, Bruno, for he was the first one to suggest responsibly the infinity of the universe and the mobility—at least some kind of mobility—of the earth. One wonders about this man finding himself such an Italianate German and yet such a misfit at the Court of Rome where he was actually prime minister. One wonders what Aeneas Sylvius, the elegant and worldly man of letters who reigned over the golden age of humanism as Pope Pius II, must have thought of his friend's involved speculations. He may have decided that Nicholas was too good an administrator and diplomat to be wasted on such subtleties, but it apparently enhanced his authority to philosophize thus paradoxically in the obscure manner of the "ultramontanes."

There is no doubt that with Nicholas, German philosophy has entered the scene full-fledged, with some of its powerful characteristics well in evidence, and he makes one think very much of the future continuator of his work, Gottfried Wilhelm Leibniz.

The central fact about Cusanus, which has been too often overlooked because he scored no achievements in science proper, is that he is an imaginative mathematical temperament who has taken up in the raw stage the modern idea of mathematics as a "science of the infinite." This idea, in itself, undercuts radically the conventional and rather simple-minded notion, entertained by the scholastics, of mathematics as the science of magnitude, that is, "of the more and the less." He does not deal simply with irrelevant sizes; he deals with the essence of things, because at the core of things there is understood to be the infinite. If mathematics is the science of the infinite—and this is indeed what the great Greek mathematicians had discovered in their own way and what Aristotle had tried to cover up—why, then, one's metaphysical emotions are apt to respond. To a mind with a medieval training, infinity participates in the divine essence, and should be understood to be somehow at the core of all things. Mathematics ceases to be a science of mere abstractions and becomes a possible avenue to a true knowledge of reality. Yet there is one side to these speculations which strikes any scientific reader as helpless. Anyone, indeed, who reads Cusanus critically will get the curious impression of an inadequately fused intellectual enterprise. There is, no doubt, a creative intuition in the play with mathematical concepts; then there appear new, technically advanced ideas which are not followed up but left to die on the vine. The developments about the relative position and the mobility of the earth around its orbit are one instance. It is as if Cusanus were led on by a thought that he has not fully mastered. We experience such "double takes" in reading Plato, too, but then we know that he was trying to adjust into his speculations the advanced work of contemporary mathematicians like Eudoxus which he had not fully grasped either.

Now who is there back of Cusanus? Philosophers have answered a little too easily by saying the Pythagorean tradition. Surely. It is back of everything and very clearly at the back of such a man. But there is nowhere in Pythagorean tradition this idea of mathematics as the science of the infinite, nor are there those technical developments about relativistic geometry. This is what philosophers have overlooked, and this is also where the historians of science may help.

For Nicholas had one bosom friend of his student days and later, one with whom he had "thought together" during the formative years in Padua, to whom he was to dedicate more than one of his works and in particular his artless little treatise on the squaring of the circle—and that friend was Toscanelli.

It was still Toscanelli who, when his friend Nicholas lay dying a lonely death on the road in the little town of Todi, almost two hundred miles away, hurried to his bedside, at sixty-seven years of age, to share the last vigils.

So those curious seeds of a new mathematical thought, which the cardinal seized upon with his powerful imagination but could not develop adequately, may well have come from Toscanelli himself. From whom else? There was no one else around. And, in fact, there are some significant confirmations.

If the historians of thought have not seen it hitherto, it is because they misread both men. Because the cardinal's mathematics was dismissed disdainfully by Regiomontanus as insignificant—which is a technically correct judgment—they did not see that the man's imagination was that of a creative analyst in the modern sense.

On the other hand, because Toscanelli is etched in history primarily as a doctor of medicine and a practical consultant in so many fields from applied geometry to cartography, because he is kept in the background, because his advice was asked in the matter of buildings and crops and maps and horoscopes and financial computations, because he did not participate in the lofty metaphysics and the luminous transcendental vaporings of Marsilio Ficino nor in the orotund declamations and the golden Platonic eloquence of the Florentine academy; he has been adjudged a modest technician and, at best, an outstanding medical man. And it is very true that Toscanelli gave out results and kept his thoughts to himself, as contemporaries witness. In fact, he wrote nothing at all beyond letters. And those letters are lost—all except the one that Columbus got hold of. But it is quite a letter, as is well known.

And so it was forgotten that he was also a thinker of strange thoughts.

Those thoughts could not very well be grasped by Ficino, the official philosopher, for all that he wrote of Paolo with high praise and indeed adulation. They were very special thoughts. We shall deal with them in a moment. I am trying to see from many angles this constellation of minds which really gives rise to the intellectual Renaissance from Florence to Germany.

There is one feature which has made Toscanelli famous; and although this particular fame is not wholly deserved, it will serve to make up for what he has missed otherwise. I speak of his letter to Portugal concerning the chances of a discovery of a new world.

Here again, we come into one of those high points of a cultural life in which everything seems to tie up with everything, in which the mobile tissue of time becomes almost tangible.

In the year 1474, Marsilio Ficino wrote to Bandini that he had concluded his great book on Platonic theology—which was to come out only later, in 1482, the year of Toscanelli's death. On the twenty-fifth of June of that same year, 1474, at the height of the reign of Lorenzo il Magnifico, in the slightly corrupt splendor of that court which was shooting its last sparklers, Paolo Toscanelli, or Paul the physician as he usually signed, wrote a letter to a Portuguese ecclesiastic called Fernam Martins concerning the possibility of a route to the East by way of the West and joined with it a map he had constructed of the possible route. This Canon Fernam Martins, the recipient of the letter, he had met ten years previously at the bedside of the dying Cardinal of Cusa in Todi. Thus fate works in strange ways.

We have the letter as it was transcribed by Columbus himself on the flyleaf of a book. So he must have given it deep considera-

Paolo Toscanelli

tion. Was it the first cause of his enterprise? Was the underestimated distance of Asia, derived from Strabo's wrong data, an incentive to his voyage? Italian scholars, proud of having this Genoese navigator guided by a Florentine cosmographer, have made a great to-do about it. I myself doubt that it was as decisive as often suggested. Philologists think in terms of classical authors, but technicians have their own sources of information. Columbus had quite reliable maps really—not on the Spanish side, of course: he had that of Fra Mauro of Venice, he had the Genoese map of 1457, the Catalan map of 1375—and they all gave the correct distances within about 10 per cent; so I take it he knew what he was doing. He knew, then, what an adventure it was to set out on a voyage on an unbroken ocean—except for a chain of islands, he hoped—which would take him from Spain to China.

But there is more in a culture than is inscribed in its rational decisions. If Toscanelli acted on Columbus, it was because, as a recognized expert in the stars, he gave him a sense of the urgency of fate. This is the true tension of the Renaissance: this context of political in-fighting and prophetic vision, of heroic vocations and cunning cynicism, of magic, astrology, prophecy, and great new scientific ideas all in one.

In the margin of his own copy of Pierre D'Ailly, Columbus transcribes the lines of Scripture: "The heavens proclaim the glory of God." He is haunted by the power of the cosmos and by a sense of his own calling. Columbus is a man who is quite well inside his own culture; and when he combines Pliny and Pierre D'Ailly and Albumasar, he does exactly what an educated man of his time would have done. For right at the time when Pico della Mirandola wrote so passionately and rationally against astrology and protested against the camouflaging of the Virgin Mary as a constellation, Columbus was transcribing with his own hand a famous text of the Arab astronomer Albumasar: "There ascends in the first aspect a virgin holding two ears of wheat in her hand . . . and she holds a child to her heart."

The great prophetic theme of the return of Virgo, which inspires Virgil's Fourth Eclogue and is echoed through the Middle Ages, reappears here in full force. But how transformed. Witness the Latin lines of John of Garland in his *Stella Maris*:

> Ut Albumasar testatur
> Inter stellas declaratur
> Virgo lactans puerum.

"As Albumasar witnesseth, a virgin is declared among the stars, nursing a child to her heart."

It is a most considerable mix-up.

Albumasar, around this time, had become a name to conjure with. The first printed editions of his *Introductorium* and of his

Great Conjunctions were not to come out until 1489, but there were enough manuscript copies around to spread alarm and despondency in Florence already in 1460, and the talk was all of comets and cataclysms. Albumasar, as they called him, or rather Abu Mashar, for that was his name, was an Arab astrologer who died in 886. He is not accounted technically an astronomer. He shines indeed as an astronomer so little that my friend Willy Hartner, the immensely scholarly and rigorous historian of astronomy, dismisses him as a vapid chatterer and wonders how Tycho Brahe himself could have quoted him at the side of Al Battani. The answer, I dare say, lies right in Hartner's paper which traces this unknown reference. Why did people mention him? Tycho was a great technician of astronomy, but he was also a Renaissance man. So, once he had made, by measuring parallaxes, his epoch-making discovery that comets and novae are in outer space, he thought nothing of quoting Abu Mashar for a confirmation, although the man had no concern with parallaxes. This is not the only time that astrology has lent a helping hand to science. Up to the time of Kepler, astronomy and astrology are so closely intermingled that a man's thought moves freely between them. Allow me to remind you in my turn of that *locus classicus* in *Troilus and Cressida.*

And so here we come to another crucial case. Those lines I have quoted of John of Garland in his *Stella Maris* are part of the new Christian enterprise to refer all constellation properties to the Virgin Mary seen as Virgo, in other words to build up a spiritual astrology inside orthodoxy. And this in turn is due to Abu Mashar, who had announced the exaltation of the Virgin with Child in the heavens. This could not but strike a deep chord in the hearts of a civilization which still believed in Virgil as the prophet of the advent of Christ—the prophet of the Gentiles:

Incipe, parve puer, cui non risere parentes.[1]

That a Moslem should come now bringing Virgil's *nova progenies* explicitly as a child suckling at Virgo's breast is surely one of the more amusing cross-purposes of history. It could have provided a good finale for Comparetti's classic work on *Virgil in the Middle Ages.*

But in truth, the infidel still managed to serve the purposes of infidelity. We should see what he was saying. He is not really announcing, like Virgil, the return of Virgo, or Justice, to earth. This had happened about Anno Domini, with other great signs in heaven: Virgo had come to one of the four crucial points of the ecliptic, the vernal equinox. This was "earth" in the traditional archaic language. The next "return" would be when she reached a solstitial point, a further quarter turn of the precession,

[1] Or maybe Norden is right in reading "qui non risere parenti," the child has not yet laughed to its mother, a great theme in cosmological tradition.

another four thousand years away from us. Rather, Abu Mashar was speaking of Venus coming to a particular aspect in Virgo; and he was using the Oriental symbolism of portraying Venus in this position (for it was Venus who was the protagonist) as a mother with child. This came straight from Babylon: "Inanna with the child in her lap," as the Babylonian hymn puts it; and Inanna is a name for Ishtar. In another symmetrical position, close to Sirius, she was Ishtar the Harlot, *Venus Pandemia*, an abandoned woman. There are some comic repercussions to this so remote theme. Father Kugler, the great historian of Babylonian astronomy who wrote a generation ago, still could not countenance the sea-change of the Lady Ishtar into a woman of loose conduct. It was contrary, he said, to the avowed respect of the Babylonians for moral principles and motherhood to have their chief female deity first impersonate the divine mother with child and then a trot. He suggested the protagonist of this transformation scene must be Sirius the Dog, so essentially associated with Venus in the Sothic cycle, which is marked by their joint heliacal rising. Alas, Fr. Kugler let himself be carried away by his moral fervor. Venus is standing in her own right in both positions.

These things still hurt, apparently: the great feminine principle seen as both mother and demon, the devil himself, the "Frau Venus" of *Tannhäuser*. This it was that came with the expounding of the doctrine by those who knew: dreadful ambiguity in heaven itself, Venus dominant under the cloak of Virgo. This it was that the interpreters of heaven were explaining quietly to some, denying to others. Not the least of the tensions of that strange fifteenth century is laid between the two poles of Venus Anadyomene rising from the sea and the Virgin worshiped in ascetic meditation.

Without those tensions, how could we understand the Church desperately trying to Christianize astrology and hugging this asp to her breast? How could we understand the furious and apocalyptic reaction of Savonarola, the sacking and the burning, Botticelli abandoning his pagan imagery for prayer, Pico della Mirandola forsaking his learning, his esoteric knowledge, his wonderful idea of man in the cockpit of the universe, to attack astrology and end his life in passionate renouncement?

The doctrines of Fate and Freedom were strong drinks to be mixed for an age of transition. Think of Leonardo's great series of drawings of the end of the world in storms of wind and fire, of Columbus' memory of Blessed Joachim of Fiora. Toscanelli, the "cosmographer," as they called him, is doing his part in a wise and statesmanlike way. He refused the astrology of nativities and death signs—we have his own statements on that—but concentrated on cycles of change and renewal, and quietly announced the imminent discovery of a new world. He defines, in a way, the Renaissance itself, in what it has of nascent and renascent. In his letter to Martins, he dreams of wonderful distant cities and unknown civilizations in the spirit of Sir Thomas More. He imagines rivers in that new world with as many as two hundred cities along their banks. But unlike Sir Thomas More, he is writing before, not after, the event. With his authority he is now telling Columbus that something unprecedented is bound to happen—he is giving him a sense of impending fate.

I trust I will not be misunderstood. The historian of science must see what is living and operating at a given time, in order to find the true context of ideas. The main context of the Renaissance is the changing idea of the cosmos, but a cosmos first and last it had to be; and what is there that holds the key to the cosmos except astrology? It stays in that key position until it is replaced by celestial mechanics—and replaced only in a manner of speaking, for the cosmos does not last long without it. Descartes is in the offing. Astrology, then, dominated medicine and physics as the most comprehensive science. Notice the curious relationship you find in Ficino's work; Ficino is officially against astrology, as was his pupil Pico—but he cannot help believing in it all the same. Ficino cannot ignore astrology for the simple reason that Neoplatonism cannot do without it; and Plato himself, the late Plato of astro-theology, had been leading great philosophies back to the Babylonian cocoon. So it is very hard to imagine Ficino not able to believe in astrology, Pico himself not able to believe in astrology. Although Pico attacked it violently, he attacked it as an ambiguous dangerous presence, not as a vain pseudoscience. Astrology tied up heaven and earth in one system, which led men to search for regularities, for the laws of periodicity and change. He who thinks that there is only trash in the books of Albumasar, of Guido Bonatti, of Cardan, of Abu Ezra, of Pietro d'Abano, of al-Kalisi or Cecco d'Ascoli—or, may I add, in the writings of Father Athanasius Kircher himself, although he lived in quite another century—is in for a surprise. Those men were among the first minds of their times. They certainly had more to say than many humanistic philosophers, so called. They were philosophers in the key of a great *techne*, as the Greek would have said, fully formed specialists. In their work we find documents of half-lost religions, remarkable fragments of psychology of the unconscious, important data of geography—for one had to relate exactly places to celestial time—as well as ideas about physiology, about historical cycles, about the character of nations and men, and, of course, some of the best professional astronomy of the time. Kepler is their last offshoot.

It would be well if we could know more about Cecco d'Ascoli. The God-fearing souls have shied away from him because he was burned by the Inquisition, the rationalists have forgotten about him because he believed in astrology. The misunderstanding goes on. We have lost the key to those poems of his which are true cryptograms, and they are certainly not devoid of some important meaning. He did not like Dante; and it cannot be for the reason that he alleges—that Dante was a "man of little faith." But he must have had a singular faith of his own, and a strong one, if it allowed him to face the stake, like Giordano Bruno, instead of submitting. We may get a hint of it in his scornful lines:

> Qui non si canta al modo del poeta
> Che finge immaginando cose vane
> Ma qui resplende e luce onne natura
> Che a chi entende fa la mente leta.

"Here we do not sing after the manner of the poet, who invents, imagining vain things, but here shines in dazzling light every nature [i.e., essence] which fills with joy him who understands."

There could be no clearer statement of the dichotomy between the two cultures—except in certain bitter remarks of Leonardo. What is attacked here, as early as 1325, is not so much the past as what is coming, the literary humanism of the Renaissance, man divorced from the cosmos.

And this in turn should finally give the clue to Toscanelli's philosophical personality. Modern critics have ignored or minimized many remarkable things that were said insistently about him with great respect and veneration—that he was pious and ascetic, that he kept strict chastity and abstained from eating meat. They thought this too goody-goody. They were wrong. For these traits prove Toscanelli to have been a true Pythagorean of the old observance—not simply one of those romantics fascinated by the magic of number, but one in whom there lived again the thought and behavior of the ancient sect. Landino called him a "venerable image of antiquity." He is indeed an original Pythagorean in his strange combination of mathematics, inductive research, practical interests, and a worship of the colossal machinery of cosmic cycles. Where did he get his data? From Arab astronomy, from lost sources, by word of mouth. There is such a knowledge that scholars a little too deliberately ignore. It is seeded here and there by what I have once called the "Jetstream of Time." When we find similar behavior in Leonardo da Vinci—including the vegetarian obsession—and strange bits of information about ancient traditions which are in no text but reappear at odd points in the Renaissance, notably in Jerome Cardan, we have at least some clue as to where they came from.

Men who had those ideas were careful, as was Toscanelli himself, who never talked about his theories. What he gave to the public were results. The only piece of his own that we have is his computation of the comet of 1460. It is an excellent computation, as Celoria has shown, and agrees with the figures of Regiomontanus quite perfectly. Above is written in a shaky hand—probably his, and these are the only words we have in his own hand—"The immense labors and grievous vigils of Paolo Toscanelli on the measurement of the comet." ("Immensi labores et graves vigiliae Pauli de Puteo Toscanelli super mensuram comete.") That is all. It is like an invocation. The measure was the thing. These measures in heaven were for him the important caesuras of the universe, and who should contradict him on that? Professor Bush has quoted Brandes' remark that Voltaire respected very few things in heaven and earth but he respected the uniform caesura. Well, we all love Voltaire—at least, I love Voltaire—but his tragedies are terrible, and you cannot say that the uniform caesura saved him. The master astrologer's caesuras might have still more meaning.

Allow me to think it significant that a man who sparked so many new ideas in his own time should be the one in whom the most ancient frame of ideas had been reborn: that the new scientific thought should have as its precondition the rebirth of a cosmology going back to the gray dawn of antiquity. It is only now that we are beginning to form an idea of the scope and size of the cosmology that was shaped between 5000 and 2000 B.C. and was inherited only in fragments by historic civilizations as we know them. It is hard to imagine the immense intellectual effort it entailed, hard to measure its philosophical scope, which is clothed in myth and only symbolically, technically expressed in its planetary and precessional cycles. It is a lost world coming gradually into view, like a lost continent emerging from the ocean. But Plato still knew about it, at least parts of it, if we are to understand something of his clear technical implications. Nor is Toscanelli the last to have searched for it, for after him comes Johann Kepler, his most legitimate successor and, like him, a passionate defender of astrology, although he was a Copernican. Let me conclude, then, with some words of Kepler that Toscanelli would have signed gladly himself: "The ways in which men came into the knowledge of things celestial appears to me almost marvelous as the nature of those things itself." As Brunelleschi had started out as the earliest archeologist—for that is what he did in his twenties when he and Donatello went to Rome and started digging like men possessed: the Romans thought they were looking for treasures, but they were digging in the ruins of Rome for the secrets of the ancient architects—so Toscanelli had revived remote doctrines of cosmology and found there his inspiration. Nascent or renascent, let us remember Alberti's words: "If they were written, we have dug them up, and if they were not, we have snatched them from heaven."

In the search for the hidden sources of ancient knowledge, for the meaning of "prophetic language," even Isaac Newton himself was to spend the latter half of his life. Who are we, then, to assess casually the "immense labors and the grievous vigils" of the man whom the Florentines called Maestro Pagolo, or Paul the physician?

Alessandro Volta

IT IS DIFFICULT TO APPRECIATE NOW, WHEN ELECTRICITY IS SO commonplace, what a marvel and mystery it was only 200 years ago. By the same token it is not easy to evoke a clear picture of the situation that confronted the early investigators of electrical phenomena. Electricity manifested itself in ways that were sometimes dramatic but that were also somewhat peculiar, for example in lightning or in amber rubbed with wool. Ascertaining the laws that governed its behavior was a process of groping by trial and error aided occasionally by a flash of intuition.

One can recapture some of the mystification of those times and some of the excitement of dispelling it by retracing the intellectual steps of an early investigator of electricity. Such a man was the Italian physicist Alessandro Volta, whose involvement in a major controversy with his countryman Luigi Galvani led him to construct his famous "pile"—the first electric battery and the first source of continuous electricity. With this device he opened the age of electricity, although he himself took little part in the flood of developments that followed quickly on his invention.

Volta was born on February 18, 1745, in the ancient Lombard town of Como. He had four brothers, three of whom became priests, and four sisters, two of whom became nuns. His father, Filippo, had himself been in the Jesuit order for eleven years before deciding at the age of forty-one to marry a girl of nineteen. Filippo Volta was of noble birth, but he was a poor manager of the family funds. Years later Alessandro wrote: "My father owned nothing except a small dwelling worth about 14,000 lire; and he left behind him 17,000 lire of debt."

As a child Alessandro was a source of concern to his family. He seemed dull-witted and was so slow in learning to talk (he said nothing until he was four) that his parents decided he was a mute. At four his mind ignited; by seven he was regarded as being exceptionally bright in school. After Alessandro became famous his father said: "We had a jewel in the house but did not know it."

Because of his family's straitened circumstances Volta received his education through the endeavors of relatives in the church. From them and from his immediate family he was under pressure to enter the priesthood. He was intensely curious about natural phenomena, however, and by the time he was fourteen he knew that he wanted to be a physicist. He also expressed the opinion that there were so many priests, nuns, monsignors, and archdeacons in the family that it was unnecessary for him to aid in sanctifying it.

Volta's early interest in nature did not detract from literary inclinations that he maintained throughout his life. His excellent classical education had made him well versed in Latin poetry. He once composed a long Latin poem on nature and science; it dwelt particularly on the researches of Joseph Priestley and also praised Benjamin Franklin and James Watt. The poem has considerable literary merit; the ear attuned to Latin verse will detect in Volta's lines an echo of Lucretius.

When he was sixteen, Volta was much under the influence of an older friend, the Canon Gattoni, who provided him with his first experimental equipment. Volta did not, however, share Gattoni's orthodox views. He went so far as to write his friend a long dialogue designed to prove the heresy that not only men but also animals have souls.

The same adventurous turn of mind is apparent in Volta's first published scientific paper, *De vi attractiva ignis electrici* (*Concerning the attractive force of electric fire*). Written when Volta was twenty-four, the paper was addressed to Giovanni Battista Beccaria, professor of physics at the University of Turin and a prominent experimenter in electrostatics. In it Volta undertook to show that all electrical phenomena can be attributed to one fluid or force that is akin to, if not identical with, universal gravitation.

That was the last of Volta's flights of speculation. His basic drive was for experimentation, and it soon led him to master the technique of basing conclusions on experimental findings. Even by the time his first paper was published he had been experimenting with electricity for several years. He was eighteen when he began a correspondence with a respected French physicist and investigator of electrical phenomena, the Abbé Antoine Nollet.

Electrical science was of course in its infancy when Volta took it up. Several investigators had discovered during the preceding century that a number of substances behaved like amber when they were rubbed. In 1660 Otto von Guericke had built the first machine for generating an electric charge; it was a sulfur ball turned by a crank and charged by friction. In 1733 this invention, together with the discovery four years earlier that electricity would flow from one place to another through a suitable conductor, led Nollet and Charles François de Cisternay Du Fay to perform an engaging experiment that involved their own bodies. Du Fay was suspended horizontally by silk cords in a dark room and charged up with an electric machine of the von Guericke type; when Nollet touched him, he emitted large sparks. The experiment caught the fancy of the French court, where conducting shocks from one person to another became something of a fad.

Du Fay found in another experiment that objects charged from a glass tube repelled each other but attracted objects charged from a rod of resin. The finding led him to two fundamental conclusions: that there are two kinds of electricity (in this he was not quite correct) and that like charges repel but unlike charges attract. Not long afterward the invention of the

Leyden jar showed that electricity could be stored. Many investigators, accidentally or deliberately discharging Leyden jars by touching them, received numbing shocks. Shocks were routine occupational hazards for the early investigators of electricity; one wonders how they had the courage to persevere.

By this time Franklin had begun his electrical investigations, and he soon became the most important figure among the early theoreticians of electricity. From his experiments with the Leyden jar and other apparatus he concluded that the two kinds of electricity were two aspects of a single force: one was an excess of the force and the other a deficiency. It was he who bestowed the name "positive" on the former and "negative" on the latter; he could not know, of course, that the condition he called positive actually represented a deficiency of electrons and the condition he called negative represented an excess of them. Franklin's famous kite experiment, which led to the development of lightning rods, was conducted in 1752. From then on electrical theory had an almost magical import. Man had controlled lightning.

It was against this background that the youthful Volta began his investigations in 1763. For the next decade, however, he devoted himself mainly to his studies. In 1774 he became superintendent of the Royal School in Como. Soon he was called to the chair of physics at the University of Pavia, thanks to the protection of the Austrian emperor, who was then ruler of northern Italy. By that time he had taken on the personal characteristics often used to describe him. He was a handsome, strapping six-footer; affable and outgoing; fond of the outdoors; not disdainful of ordinary pastimes with ordinary people but very much a notable of his own city, personally acquainted with the foremost men of Europe; carefully conservative in his views and soberly objective in his interests.

In 1774 Volta made his first important contribution to electrical science with his invention of the "electrophorus," which provided experimenters for the first time with a steady, replenishable supply of static electricity. The device worked on the novel principle of electrostatic induction instead of on the direct application of friction required to produce a charge in earlier apparatus. It consisted of a cake of resin or some other non-conducting substance with one plate of metal below it and another plate above it; the upper plate had an insulated handle and could be removed. One removed the upper plate, charged the resin by friction and put the plate back. If one then grounded the upper plate by touching it, the negative charge of the resin would repel the electrons in the plate; they would travel to the ground and the plate would be left with an induced positive charge. Thereafter, by lifting the plate one created an electric potential. If one then touched the plate, it gave off a spark. When the plate was discharged, it could be recharged in the same manner; the process could be repeated indefinitely. Describing the electrophorus in a letter of 1775 to Priestley, Volta wrote: "I present to you a body which, electrified only once for a short time and not strongly, will never more lose its electricity, and will obstinately maintain the live force of its indications, even if it is touched again and again."

It is indicative of Volta's wide-ranging curiosity that his next invention grew out of a fishing trip on Lake Maggiore. He observed the bubbles that rose to the surface of the water in marshy areas, gathered some of this marsh gas (now known to be methane) and found it to be inflammable. He began a series of experiments with the gas and developed his "eudiometer," which was a tube closed at one end. Gases were bubbled into the tube from the water and exploded with an electric spark. The device was to prove valuable in determining the volume of gases that combined. As Volta said later, if he had been able to collect the gases over mercury he would have described the composition of water. He simply did not have enough mercury.

Another of Volta's inventions, announced in 1782, was the condensing electroscope, which was a much more sensitive indicator of the presence of electricity than earlier devices. This invention grew out of work he had done to improve electrometers, the best of which had used the separation of gold leaves to detect electricity. The condensing electroscope resembled the electrophorus except that instead of a slab of resin it used a thinner slab of weakly conductive material; as a result the upper plate could pick up a very small electric charge. This device was a kind of microscope of electricity, and it was what first brought Volta's name to the attention of other men of science. Later Volta used the condensing electroscopes to perfect an early form of the kind of electrometer that determined an electric potential difference by balancing the electric force against the force of gravity.

By this time Volta was making frequent and extended trips abroad, a custom that brought him in contact with many prominent investigators and other figures. On one trip in 1771 he paid his respects to Voltaire, little imagining that not too long afterward Napoleon would stop in front of a wreath inscribed "To the Great Voltaire" and strike out the last letters to make it "To the Great Volta." While on a trip in 1789 Volta wrote home: "I have at last met the great Franklin." The acquaintances Volta made on these tours undoubtedly helped to fortify his reputation against the strains of the long controversy with Galvani.

Galvani, who was a physician and professor of anatomy at the University of Bologna, had begun experimenting with electricity in 1780. His interests included the effects of electric discharges on the nervous system of the frog. He discovered quite by accident in 1786 that the amputated hind legs of a frog would kick convulsively if they were made part of an electrical circuit. (On the occasion of the discovery the circuit was closed by one of Galvani's assistants, who happened to touch the crural nerve of the frog with a scalpel at a moment when an electric machine nearby gave off a spark.)

In many experiments with this phenomenon, extending over several years, Galvani found that it occurred when there was a nearby flash of lightning, and that the frogs' legs would twitch even in good weather if they were hung on an iron fence on a hook made of brass or copper. Pondering the phenomenon, Galvani recognized that it could be explained in one of two ways. Either electricity was a special animal property, in which case the outside influences merely caused the property to manifest itself, or the contact of two metals brought on the kicking, in which case the legs merely acted as an indicator of an outside charge. Galvani decided that it was the former: the animal tissue contained a vital force, which he called "animal electricity."

He published his results in 1791, and they created a sensation. Apparently he had found a key to the mystery of life. Among those impressed by the results was Galvani's friend Volta, to whom Galvani had sent one of the dozen copies of the paper, which he had had printed as a pamphlet.

At first Volta thought, with Galvani, that there was some kind of electrical disproportion between nerve and muscle, and that when metal connected the nerve and muscle of a frog's leg, the balance was restored. As Volta experimented with the phenomenon, however, he began to have doubts. He observed that muscles would contract even when they were not part of an electrical circuit; they did so when electric contacts were merely applied to the nerve. Gradually he came to the view that more attention should be paid to the role of the metals.

The story has been told many times as a beautiful example of nature taking good sense by the hand and guiding it to discovery. This concept, however, does less than justice to the fearfully intricate situation with which the experimenters were confronted. True, there were lucky breaks, such as the discovery that the contact of copper hooks and iron railings gave the best contraction of the frogs' legs. That looks decisive now, but it did not then. The situation remained a jungle of possibilities.

Such was the setting for one of the great decisions of history, a decision that involved nothing less than the turning point of the scientific revolution. Was the new force of the electric current a special aspect of life or did it arrive to found the technological era? To whom was to belong the only form of immortality permitted by fast-rolling oblivion, namely posterity's choice of his name to designate the fundamental electric unit?

It was only historic justice that the decision fell to Volta.

Alessandro Volta

Whereas Galvani stood for the old kind of biological sciences, Volta was the new kind of physicist: quantitatively minded, even if he had no mathematics, and a master of the new experimental approach. He also had the modern ruggedness. Whereas the sensitive, tormented Galvani was a born victim of circumstances, Volta had the gift of impassive adjustment. On the advent of French power in Italy in 1796, Galvani refused the oath of allegiance on conscientous grounds and retired to a silent poverty, from which he was rescued too late by the generosity of the conqueror. Volta, although he resented the invasion, moved into the French orbit as soon as it was prudent to do so. That remained his pattern. Throughout his life storm upon storm of success was to break on that brow and leave it unlined. He went through life unmoved.

In his years of trial after 1792, however, he stood alone and found few to understand him. His opponent had taken ten years to prepare his case, and the case was strong. Nature had even loaded the dice in Galvani's favor, inasmuch as there was in fact more than one electricity involved. There was an artificial electricity that could provide spectacular discharges, comparable to those of the electric eel, whereas it was still difficult to elicit even the smallest shocks and sparks from metallic electricity. There was also the electricity of the tissues that is now recorded by electrocardiographs. It was, to be sure, a feeble kind of electricity, but on the other hand nature had provided the most sensitive electroscopes in the form of frogs' legs; natural, or metallic, electricity did not get the right responses in the usual electrostatic instruments. Finally, the picture was blurred by actions at a distance and induction not yet rightly understood. As soon as Volta thought he had found a secure starting point in the presence of a bimetallic arc, Galvani was able to cut the ground from under him by showing that muscular contractions could be elicited without any metal in the circuit.

It took great firmness and clarity of mind to withstand the onslaught. "I know those gentlemen want me dead," Volta wrote to a friend in those days, "but I'll be damned if I'll oblige them." He had to work out his own electroscopes to detect metallic electricity, namely the sensitive tissues of his tongue and his eye; he had to show that it was the nerves and not the muscles that were stimulated. He concluded his second memoir firmly: "It is the difference of metals that does it."

Pursuing this approach made it necessary for Volta to rebuild the whole structure of electrical concepts. It was here, in particular, that he had to define tension and distinguish it from quantity. "The quantity of electricity," he wrote, "which is put in motion by the contact of metals is not small, it is in fact considerable, but the current has so little tension that it gives no signs on the electrometer, and can be easily stopped by poor conductors. It is an ample flow, but a gentle one." This statement was descriptively perfect.

To Galvani's master argument that removed metals altogether, Volta replied by extending the concept of conductor and motor contact to bodies of the second class as he called them, namely liquids. This concept led him to the problem of adding electromotive forces in chains of conductors. By moving now from electrokinetics to electrostatics, by ingeniously juggling his inadequate instruments and his puny charges, he managed at last to build up his pure contact forces to a tension detectable in the electrometer. Again it was a measuring procedure that led him to his goal. After having searched for two years for a means of multiplying the contact tension of metals by adding up contacts, he hit on his idea of the battery, which he communicated to Sir Joseph Banks, president of the Royal Society, in a letter dated March 20, 1800. The battery was originally a pile of disks: copper-zinc couples, each separated from the next by a disk of cardboard moistened with acidulated water. The ten-year battle had been won: electric power had come into the world.

Volta and Galvani both had their greatness and their limitations. Just as the unfortunate Galvani had invented galvanic electricity and believed its nature to be animal—a misconception that led his followers into the sands of vitalistic quackery and almost killed his discovery—so Volta in saving that discovery had actually discovered electrochemistry without knowing it. He stopped in sight of the promised land. He left it to Anthony Carlisle and William Nicholson of England to achieve within a few weeks the electrolysis of water. They had only to read the letter to Banks and build a battery. Volta never cared to venture into the immense new field. It is strange to think that he was still in his robust fifties when the tide of electrochemical discoveries broke on the world, when Humphry Davy electrolyzed the alkalies and produced the voltaic arc.

It is noteworthy that in a famous demonstration of the pile in Paris in 1801, with Napoleon present, Volta gave an absurd amount of attention to the ways of making his battery assume the appearance of an electric eel by dressing it in a skin. This was not silly gadgeteering, nor was it the cultural lag that made the creators of the railway try to imitate the coach-and-four. It was the final settling of the old quarrel with Galvani about animal electricity. Galvani's articulate nephew Giovanni Aldini had still been defending the cause of galvanism after Galvani's death, so Volta had reason for his attitude. He had knocked down the idea, but he still had to drag it out.

It would be easy to conclude that this last act of the episode is an example of a mind remaining polarized on its moment of creation. Yet nothing in history is as simple as that. One should see that Volta had to go on playing his part in the drama. He had conquered a strongpoint; it then became his business to hold it in the troubled times ahead. That was why his thought continued to have a powerful influence on the next generation. He stood for good method against adventure.

Davy, as early as November, 1800, had concluded that the power of action of the battery is "in great measure proportional to the power of the conducting fluid substance between the double plates to oxydate the zinc." Volta, however, had already taken the position that the mere contact of two metals was enough. In fact, he supplied what seemed to be a convincing proof. Taking a disk of copper and one of zinc, he held each by an insulating handle and applied them to each other for an instant. After the disks had been separated, the electroscope showed that they were electrified with opposite signs. Volta fully understood the phenomenon and explained the impossibility of constructing a pile from disks of metal without making use of moist separators. He showed in 1801 that, in a pile of disks of different metals in direct contact, the disks at the top and the bottom of the pile will be in the same state as disks in direct contact. For him the moist layers only played the part of conductors.

How, then, did he conceive the operation of the pile? Consider first a disk of zinc laid on a disk of copper resting on an insulated support. One may assume, from the single-fluid theory that Volta had learned from Franklin, that electricity will be driven from the copper to the zinc. One may then represent the tension of the copper as $-1/2$ and that of the zinc as $+1/2$, the difference being arbitrarily taken as 1, and the sum, because of the insulation, as 0. In this line of reasoning Volta was using "tension" for an amalgam of two ideas that today are distinct, namely charge and potential.

Now, if one places another disk of copper on top of the zinc, with moist pasteboard between, there will be contact only through the moist conductor, and the copper will receive a charge from the zinc. The states will be represented by $-2/3$ for the bottom copper disk, $+1/3$ for the zinc and $+1/3$ for the top copper disk, giving a sum of 0 as before. If one places another disk of zinc atop the pile, the states will be represented by -1 for the bottom copper disk, 0 for the intermediate pair of disks and $+1$ for the top zinc disk. This is how the tension will increase as the pile is built up.

It is clear that the image behind the theory is that of the Leyden jar, an early form of the condenser. The experimenter will receive the shock of a discharge when he touches the top and bottom disks. The great difficulty that remained (and Volta was aware of it) was that the pile does not discharge itself as a condenser does; it maintains its state. "This endless circulation or perpetual motion of the electric fluid," Volta wrote "may seem paradoxical, and may prove inexplicable, but it is nonetheless real." His neat mind recoiled from the obscurities of chemical action. This was true even when he came to deal with it in explaining that bane of early experimenters: the polarization of batteries. Yet he went on avoiding the thought of any link between chemical change and electric force.

Volta's rigor may appear obdurate and sterile to the modern mind armed with hindsight. No doubt it did bar him from the exciting realm of new discoveries that blossomed during his lifetime. One should consider, however, how bewildering the situation in electricity was then, and what misleading speculations it could prompt in lieu of sound theories. Volta stood for clarity and prudence. The same virtues that had guided him surely through the jungle of galvanism now acted as a brake.

Typically enough, at fifty, when he had completed his work, Volta made up his mind to marry. Even more typically, he went to two of his clerical friends for advice. For twenty-five years he had had a liaison with a well-known singer known as Mademoiselle Paris; should he regularize the situation? One of the clerics thought he should. Volta, however, had habitually followed the advice of a brother who was an archdeacon. Taking the brother's advice, he married a woman of good family; she has been described as ill-favored but implacable in the adminstration of the family estate. Volta now settled down to a new life as a father, a senator and eventually a count of the Napoleonic empire.

One should probably not call him to task for the accommodations of his old age. With the fall of Napoleon, Volta did what everyone else in his region did: he quietly returned to being a good Austrian subject. The Austrians were old protectors, after all, and they were ready to forgive. Volta was not of the stuff that martyrs are made of, and the new time of nations in their birth pangs—with its heroic stands, its exiles, its romantic dreams and its braving of police persecution—was not for him. He was a man of the old order and wanted to live out his time on his country estate in Camnago. It was, perhaps, a not unattractive end. There is poetic symmetry in the fact that the protagonist in the most far-reaching of all revolutions—compared to which the whole Napoleonic adventure was mere sound and fury—should have been a quiet conservative.

Galileo Today

GALILEO HAS NOW MOVED OUT OF HISTORY INTO MYTH. HE IS more than the creator of an era. He has become a hero of our civilization, the symbol of a great adventure like Prometheus or rather like the Ulysses of Dante and Tennyson.

There was in his earlier triumph the note of divine surprise, of an incredible world opening up. There is also, later, darkness closing in on the hero. Let me quote a famous letter of his to Diodati from 1638:

> Alas, honoured Sir, Galileo, your dear friend and servant, has become by now irremediably blind. Your Honour may understand in what affliction I find myself, as I consider how *that* heaven, that world, that universe, that by my observations and clear demonstrations I had amplified a hundred and a thousand times over what had been seen and known by the learned of all past centuries, has now shrunk for me to the space occupied by my person.

"That heaven, that world, that universe." This has the epic ring, the love for the discovery of creation that would well have befitted the Argonauts' enterprise where modesty would hardly have been fitting. At this point, already the prisoner of darkness, compelled to silence, Galileo goes on with the temper of a heroic heart, re-examining, reorganizing, reshaping without cease the vast array of his ideas in a creative impulse that leads to his most powerful achievement, the *Discourses on two new sciences*.

He was establishing the foundations of dynamics, inflexibly bent on the same enterprise that his judges could not stop, short of killing him. Indeed his judges, having humiliated him and debarred him from his main object, had no further concern, incapable as they were of realizing that all science is one and that it will break forth again at any point.

"In this way"—writes Galileo to his dear old friar friend, Fulgenzio Micanzio—"I carry on in my darkness, wondering and dreaming over this or that effect of nature, and I cannot quiet my restless brain which keeps me through the night in tormenting wakefulness." We cannot but be reminded here of the Ulysses of Dante, who carries on forever with his great dream even in the darkness of Hell.

It is not by chance that Galileo has always remained at the core of a great dramatic situation. What more dramatic event than the onset of the greatest revolution in history, than this opening up of thought to the idea of infinity—this soaring off on the powerful wings of mathematics, as Galileo once wrote? The magic circle of a closed world centred on man was broken, and it did not go without alarm and distress among many. In the words of a worthy bishop, there was at the time "an universal Exclamation of the world's Decline and approximation to its Period." But if such was a widespread feeling among the learned, all the more admirable to us is the reckless plunging ahead of the great creative minds. "Oh Nicholas Copernicus," wrote Galileo once, "what must have been thy joy in seeing thy thought confirmed despite so many contrary appearances in nature, and all the learning of past ages." It is this joy that we feel in Kepler announcing his new harmonies, in Galileo's light-hearted bantering and his cutting disregard of the powers leagued against him—even in Bruno's overreaching "heroic frenzies."

Those men felt no reason to be afraid for their souls. As Galileo said, why should we be called innovators and trouble-makers, if what we have been able to prove demonstratively belongs to God's eternal truths that only the ignorance of men could have obscured? There was no fear in the souls of Galileo's own Church friends—those who were able to understand him—but a serene happiness worthy of old medieval Christianity, for they were sure that no discovery of God's works could threaten God's Word but rather enhance it. The "new philosophy," far from putting all in doubt, was a vividly affirmative one and full of great hope. No one had experienced yet the raw reality of what we call progress. On the contrary science had come in to check that strange feeling of decline, of impending social chaos, that we see coexisting so strangely in John Donne together with a disturbed awareness of the new discoveries.

Even more—Galileo discarded the robed Latin of learning and went straight to the people, writing for them in the vernacular, trusting in all those, he said, who had eyes to see and minds to understand. He became thus the initiator of scientific Italian prose, just as Bishop Wilkins stands as the fashioner of English scientific prose.

His thinking is as straight and limpid as his new style. He has concentrated on the problem of motion as providing an essential clue to the mystery of nature and the real decision between Aristotle and Copernicus—that Copernicus himself had not been able to provide. For cosmology always comes first in Galileo's mind. He has chosen the burning issue. The thought of a sphere turning on itself in a void with no reason to stop—a typical Gedanken experiment—gives him the idea of inertia. And why should this not be the earth itself? Then come twenty years of search leading to the laws of fall, which show motion to be subject to mathematics: the great issue is resolved in Galileo's mind. Not quality but quantity rules. Now if the moon can be thought of as moving by the same law that controls the projected stone—and the earth too—namely, inertia, then they are no different in nature from the earthly missile. The earth loses its privileged unique condition and is found to be "in heaven," too. "The Earth is a star." The great prophetic Pythagorean word has fallen. When the discovery of the telescope showed the moon to be made of ordinary rock, the circle of proof was concluded in his mind. The distinction between heavenly and earthly conditions is wiped out, the Aristotelian architecture of the universe has fallen. But this time he has proved his case, not only by the telescope but by the laws of dynamics he has discovered, founded on the new concepts of Galilean relativity, inertial mass, momentum, instant velocity, acceleration. Or at least he feels he has, even without Newton—quite enough for a scientific imagination.

He is ready to face the dramatic issue.

It has now become a commonplace to consider Pope Urban VIII and his court as the oppressors of science who jailed and silenced its first representative. It would be perhaps more correct to see them as ordinary administrators surprised by events beyond their ken. They had come into collision with a new force that they could not evaluate. Both sides, the Pope and Galileo, were profoundly bewildered by their unexpected collision. Galileo could not understand that "they" should not grasp the new power of mathematical physics that he was offering them and walked into his trial still refusing to believe that his judges should prove, as he said, "immovable and unpersuadable." They, on the other hand, were utterly unaware of the mechanism of scientific discovery, which they could stop no more than they could issue a writ against an avalanche. In their minds, schooled in humanistic tradition, they thought they were dealing with *this* particular *Dialogue*, an unique piece of paradoxical ingenuity brought forth by a great writer. They saw it—and Galileo would not have gainsaid it—as a new type of poem. Silence Dante or Virgil, and there would be no Aeneid, no Divine Comedy; literature would take another course. Excellence meant literary excellence. It could also be suppressed.

As for science and wisdom, why that was another thing. It was in gravity and ponderousness akin to the business of lawyers, which the doctors strove to imitate even in their solemn caps and gowns. It went on forever in the way of disputation and classification, co-ordinating all things in a vast verbiage without end. It was law and order itself. Confronted with Galileo's dangerous conclusions, the Aristotelian doctor would indeed lose his head and start clamoring, as he does in the Dialogue: "This manner of thinking tends to the subversion of all natural philosophy and to the disorder and upsetting of heaven and earth and the whole universe!" If Galileo makes gentle fun of this way of identifying his interests with those of the universe as a whole, we still might have a heart for his predicament. Of the heavens, it was understood that man knew little, except their perfection and immutability, a moving image of eternity. They remained inaccessible, it seemed, even with this new gadget, the telescope, for too much had been said about tricky optical effects.

And should we now subvert the vast and documented discourse of the schools—which allows us to account in an orderly manner for nature and life and the soul itself and fits in so handsomely with revealed truth—to launch ourselves in a sea of paradoxes and unnatural conclusions simply because a man has come forward with two lenses in a length of pipe?

It was the professors, and not the clerics, who started the scandal that led to the prohibition of Copernicanism in 1616.

The crisis and the tragedy came later. They have been obscured by so much equivocation that we ought to set the record straight.

Galileo had been authorized by Pope Urban (who had been his friend and protector as Cardinal Barberini) to write a dialogue in which he should examine impartially all the reasons pro and contra the old and the new systems. This was meant by the Pope to be a literary exercise and a further public proof that the question had been maturely weighed before the Church took her decision. For that decision, as I said, had already fallen twelve years before, in 1616, when it was decreed that the Copernican system ran against both philosophy and Scripture, and should be dropped. Still, the Pope now yielded good-naturedly to Galileo's entreaties for a fresh discussion of the problem with the understanding that any system of the universe cannot but remain a pure hypothesis, a "mere" mathematical model. He assumed it was well understood that the actual truth is beyond our reach and that God could have produced the same observable effects in infinitely many ways, for we must not constrain omnipotence within the limits of our particular imagination. In fact, the Pope actually dictated this conclusion in advance and then left his friend Galileo free to display what he was pleased to call his admirable and delectable ingenuity. This has been understood by certain modern positivists as sound scientific prudence *avant la lettre*. It was, of course, nothing of the kind; it was old-fashioned wisdom making sure that nothing should be allowed to disturb it, nor disturb the approved system of teaching. It was still to be Milton's position forty years later, when he said that God allowed men to conjecture without end:

> . . . perhaps to move
> his laughter at their quaint opinions wide
> hereafter . . .

This was the charm of divine philosophy, of God's secrets "to be scanned by them who ought rather admire."

Galileo had to concur respectfully, but needless to say, his intention was vastly different. He hoped to provide under this proper cover such irresistible proofs of the truth of Copernicanism that the Church would quietly drop its veto and move over to new positions, as it had so often done in the past, in time to be spared an acutely embarrassing predicament. There was thus a deep miscomprehension from the start, what I called a collision course. The manuscript was submitted to the Church censors, examined word for word, and came out with official approval. The censors found it good and full of laudable reverence. The *Dialogue of the Great World Systems* came out in 1632; it was an instant enthusiastic success—and then all at once the authorities realized that they had made a frightful mistake. The usual advisors rushed to tell the Pope that, under pretence of following his instructions, the work was really a demolition charge planted by an expert, that it made a shambles of official teaching, and that it was apt to prove more dangerous to Catholic prestige than Luther and Calvin put together.

Actually, Galileo had deceived no one—except maybe himself. He had followed instructions, but his persuasiveness had outrun his prudence. He had laid himself open to his enemies by speaking openly. In his work, style and thought go together. The *Dialogo* is and remains a masterpiece of Baroque style, which knows how to move effortlessly through tight passages of reasoning, unroll with a rustle of silk, sparkle with malice and restrained good humor, maintain its cadence through vast reaches of syntactic intricacy, and rise without break to the solemnity of prophetic invective. It was not only ruthless analysis, it was the magic of the Italian language handled by a master that broke the monopoly of stuffy Latin learning, took the people into camp and revealed to them the new unimagined power of mathematical physics. Copernicus had remained almost unnoticed, by now half-forgotten. Pascal himself was to state: "It will be a good idea not to go any deeper into the opinion of Copernicus." If that was the policy, it had failed already. Here at last heliocentrism had come into its own.

In his triumph Galileo could afford to be generous. His scorn and ridicule are only for the silly pedants who had turned Aristotle into a vested interest and were afraid even of looking through the telescope. "Oh unheard-of baseness of servile minds." Aristotle himself, he insisted, would have been the first to come over to his side if he had learned about the new discoveries. And may I quote here something that I have found, which Galileo never knew but which confirms him utterly. It is a passage from Averroes, surely the greatest of Aristotelians, who had lived 400 years before: "In my youth," he says, "I had hoped that the better scrutiny of the heavens that we need would be achieved by me. In my old age now I despair, but I still hope that my words will induce someone to carry on the search." Is it not a way of begging for the telescope that Galileo was to offer him too late?

The Dialogue is thus a work, truly a poem, of reconciliation. Worldly-wise, it remained terribly dangerous.

If anybody was technically at fault, it was the censors who had been unable to understand. But now the Pope's anger flared high, for he realized that Galileo had only tagged on perfunctorily the profound philosophical ideas that *he*, the Pope, had dictated. There is no fury like a philosopher scorned. Urban wanted now to make a resounding example.

Still the law was on Galileo's side. All the Pope could do by rights was to punish the censors and have the book prohibited administratively. It was frustrating and infuriating.

At this point the Inquisition "discovered" in the file a heaven-sent forgotten document. That document gave out that *when* Galileo was informed of the anti-Copernican decree in 1616, the Commissary-General of the Inquisition had been present and served a stringent personal injunction on the astronomer to cease and desist from ever discussing it verbally or in writing, in any way whatsoever, under the dire penalties of the Holy Office.

This changed the figure of Galileo from that of a harmless respected consultant to that of a man considered by the Inquisition a dangerous suspect and held under surveillance by the thought police. By disregarding the injunction, he had exposed himself to being considered an obdurate heretic, which meant death at the stake. The authorities could try him at last. They had now an airtight case. They could even afford to be lenient and to let Galileo off with a public abjuration and a life sentence, which was further commuted into house arrest.

The trouble is that the famous injunction was a forgery: a false record carefully planted by the Inquisitors in their secret file in case it might come in handy. It did. Galileo had never dreamed of it, and that explains why he did not ask the Pope for explicit clearance before he raised the dangerous subject again.

The forgery, or rather the plant, has been proved beyond doubt by historical research over a century, and the best proof is that when I published the findings in systematic form in 1955, not one authorized voice was raised to contradict me, although a fascinating amount of evasive action has been taken since that time. It might have provided a good occasion to annul at last the old sentence and rehabilitate Galileo, as was done in the case of Joan of Arc, the more so as I had made a good case for pinning down the guilt on a small group of minor officials who had plotted and acted on their own. Pope Urban stood now in the light of history as a chief badly deceived by his subordinates. He was entitled to rehabilitation himself. But the authorities preferred to stand by their ancient decision, as a distinguished cleric recently remarked out of turn, probably because, however faulty juridically, it represented a philosophical decision concerning the *spirit* of modern science from which the Catholic Church still remains unwilling to withdraw. Be that as it may—I would not dare to judge. The reasons on either side are of such majestic import and profound significance for the fate of mankind that we must expect the unresolved tension to last beyond our time. But as far as Galileo went, his personal position remained clear, His recantation, in the civilized language of his times, meant simply that he would not oppose his will to that of his Church and would not separate himself from the communion of the faithful. As for his scientific opinion, it was understood that he would keep it, and in fact he did not refrain from saying so, at considerable risk. What he thought of his judges, he wrote it straight and clear:

> I do not hope for any relief, and that is because I have committed no crime. I might hope for and obtain pardon, if I had erred; for it is to faults that the prince can bring indulgence, whereas against one wrongfully sentenced while he was innocent, it is expedient, in order to put up a show of strict legality, to uphold rigour. . . .

The animosity, which has never abated, shows how much he remains alive and kicking among us to this day. The strangest misrepresentations have found their way even into unsuspecting Protestant sources; witness the writings of Sir David Brewster in the last century.

Again, there have come up writers in our time, acute and modern minds, mark, bound to no confessional obedience, who suddenly saw in Copernicus and Galileo the "sleepwalkers" who moved in to wreck inadvertently the great unity of science and metaphysics that had held our civilization together over many ages. Those writers were inspired, certainly, by a noble cause and by justifiable alarm, but that hardly justifies their attacking Galileo as a vainglorious intellectual adventurer who replaced the absence of proof with "effrontery and illusionism," with "an utter disregard for the intelligence of his readers." Still less does it justify their attempted whitewash of the Inquisition proceedings. Clearly the name of the old man is still potent at conjuring the spirit of hatred and confusion.

This appears more significantly in a work that revives the tragedy on the stage: Bertolt Brecht's famous play, where Galileo is made the hero of scientific civilization as a whole, with its awful contradictions, its revolutionary promises, its human weakness, and its sinister power overshadowed by the cloud of Hiroshima. There is no doubt that Brecht also had in mind the Moscow trials, the conflict of the modern intellectual with totalitarian authority, and that what he denounces is the modern alienation of men's conscience. But in the poetic liberties that he takes with his subject, Brecht reveals all the more clearly the misunderstandings that so many of us harbor concerning science itself. Galileo is shown as the exponent of cold invincible scientific method, a thinker of material thoughts, with a mind that could have led the people to emancipation; but he surrendered miserably once he realized where the real power lay and then wept useless tears of regret. There is a grave misconception here, which goes to the very foundations. No one would deny Galileo's enjoyment of the sensuous side of life, but what is wrong with being a *bon vivant*, in favoring "the newer the idea, the older the wine"? There is no doubt, either, that he dispelled many dreamy, wonderful, and magic aspects of Renaissance imagination by discovering scientific method, the awful art of separation that inexorably divides the true from the false. But his real greatness was not in experimenting with weights, it lay in the power of abstract thinking, in the Pythagorean metaphysical faith that throws a bridge across the chasm between the world of the senses and the realm of pure mathematical abstraction.

In his very language, the greatest Italian prose of the times, Galileo spans the centuries. He is not pushing for a novel philosophy, he is reminding his enemies of theirs, which had been the metaphysical Platonism of the great Middle Ages. In him there lives the ancient ecumenic and conciliar spirit of Christendom with its rights and its freedoms; when he addresses the spiritual rulers, the clauses of submissiveness scarcely veil the power and authority of his speech, which accuses and exhorts with the dignity of the early Fathers. It is he who is going to save Scripture from the incompetence of its guardians. And he solemnly warns: "The greatest detriment for souls would be, if they were to see proved a proposition which it is then made a sin to believe."

In fact, it was easy to see even in his own times that he stood for all that was sound in established law and custom, whereas the authorities were resorting to political expediency and juridical improvisation, as they had become the unwitting tools of the streamlined, the efficient, and the new. "These," he wrote bitterly, "these are the real novelties which have the power of ruining the State and subverting the Commonwealth."

So much should be said, I feel, to disengage the great struggle from the clichés of conventional history, from the terrible simplifiers who see in it only the conflict of free thought against obscurantism. It was, from the start, a conflict among the faithful themselves who disagreed about the correct approach to natural philosophy. On one side were the professors, the administrators, the representatives of ancient tradition, supported by the massive authority of Aristotle, by Greek astronomy itself. This was the house that had been built through the centuries, seemingly on rock. On the other were the new minds who had grasped the possibility that mathematics and physics, hitherto disjoined, should effect an overwhelming conjunction to show us at last a true universe.

They were perforce a minority, but they had the holy fire.

Wrote the good and pious friar, Micanzio, to Galileo during the trial:

> But what kind of men are these, to whom any good effect, and well-founded in nature, should appear contrary and odious . . . if this were now to prevent you from further work, I shall send to the hundred thousand devils these hypocrites without nature and without God.

Here we have the call to insurrection, the true revolutionary cry, already in the name of "Nature and Nature's God," which announces the social breakthrough. And indeed today at four centuries' remove we know that it *was* a revolution, that the split was never healed.

Some of us may wonder whether we are not reading dramatic upheavals into the past, while reality may have been a sequence of slow and unnoticed alluvial effects. Was not the whole Renaissance, in fact, were not the medieval schools of science leading up to this? I suggest that it is best to be coldly phenomenological about it. Revolutionary is as revolutionarily does.

Uprisings, *jacqueries*, justified as they may be, are revolts of the slighted or the oppressed; they are not revolutions. It is only when a group of individuals arises in whom the community recognizes in some way the right to think legitimately in universal terms, that a revolution is on its way. "What is the Third Estate?" said Sieyès. "Nothing. What could it be? Everything. What is it asking to be? Something." This is fair and reasonable, but that "something" has not been granted or taught from above, it is dictated to them by an inner reasoned certainty, and it is that no longer disputable certainty which makes all the difference. Here in the French Revolution are men whose philosophy has grown to impose itself, as it does in the calm utterances of the American Declaration of Independence, men who know they can assume responsibility for the whole body social, not only in the running of its affairs but in its decisions about first and last things. When these decisions sweep even the entrenched opposition off its feet and move it to yield freely its privileges as in the historic night of the Fourth of August, then we know that a real revolution has taken place. It is the resolute assumption of responsibility that forms the criterion. It was *that*, and not, as is currently said, the empirical approach.

As if *that* had not existed before. Galileo was not alone in believing what we see by experience. In fact the scholars of his own time had an exaggerated respect for the raw data of observation and the commonsense physics that goes with those. Let me say more. If there is any dealing with physical nature by trial and error in the Renaissance, it is rather on the side of the magic-mystic materialists and alchemists, of those of the stoic descendance. It is they who tirelessly push, drop, concoct, distil, extract, combine and separate, operate with fire, with acids, with solvents and coagulants—always in the effort to move qualities around experimentally. In their *furor empiricus* they ask Nature to speak to them through its many names, effects, and "signatures," whereas Galileo insisted that the "book of nature is written only in mathematical characters"—by which he meant that out of indubitable premises arising out of number, weight, and measure, we can set the deductive course of our reasoning as geometers do.

More than once Alistair Crombie, one of our most distinguished students of medieval science, has to speak of the strange "irresoluteness" that acutely characterizes the attitude of medieval scientists, even the most advanced, either in equipping themselves with the proper knowledge of mathematics or in their way of attempting experiment. Pierre Buridan himself does not really hope that nature will provide the conditions for mathematical laws to be fulfilled "although it *could* happen that they should be realized through the omnipotence of God." In other words wouldn't it be wonderful, but only a miracle of divine benevolence could free us from the Aristotelian bondage, which emphasizes commonsense. This is exactly the attitude of the submissive traditionalist toward the revolutionary. Yet Buridan is no timid spirit. His work shows him to be a true rationalist, but he has to defer to long-established authority whose dictates become akin in his mind to the Deposit of the Faith or the divine rights of kings. For two centuries this kind of speculation has been going on without much happening. Even in the most daring nominalists, the world of the scholar is too well-knit, spiritually and conceptually, not to keep dangerous deviations in check. Nicole d'Autricourt is free to suggest atomism as a natural philosophy, but once the chips are down, he has to back out or become a heretic.

Here and there the scholar can risk bold theorizing, he can intimate, adumbrate, and prophesy; but he must be prepared for an intervention of authority that tells him to drop his playthings and come back to a correct attitude. This intervention did come at last, brutally, with the anti-Copernican decree of 1616. But this time, however, even if alone and abandoned by the scholars in retreat, there was Galileo. He stated in no uncertain terms that in such grave matters of natural philosophy, his authority was fully equal to that of the Church Fathers themselves. This is what I call the assumption of responsibility. Galileo does not hesitate to denounce the authorities for playing irresponsibly with reactionary subversion. The freedoms granted by tradition, he insists, are his protection, the reason that God gave us to understand His laws is on his side. He makes it clear by his attitude that he will not compromise, that he will not retreat, and that he will be heard.

As we know, Galileo could have gone on establishing the formal science of dynamics without all this fuss. He actually did—by the time he was debarred from writing about cosmology. This would be enough to prove that he did not consider his thought the empiricistic outcome of industrial division of labor or advanced technology or book-keeping or whatever gadget it is that amateur sociologists have devised for his rationale. He felt he had to face the central issue: To the well-worked-out cosmos of his predecessors he opposed another cosmology, another way of knowledge whereby man has to go ahead forever in discovery, trusting Providence that it will not lead him to perdition. This Galileo maintained even when told by the Successor to Peter, the Vicar of Christ, that his doctrine was "pernicious in the most extreme degree." He alone, with very few men of his time, perhaps only Kepler and Castelli, could really know what he was doing. He saw himself not as the depositary of the truth but as the initiator of an unending march of ever-growing cohorts, of the whole of mankind, toward an ever vaster vision of truth, ever receding beyond man's horizon. Here is what I consider Galileo's assumption of responsibility for the whole body social in first and last things. It stands with us to this day.

As for the secularization of thought, it is surely a consequence; it is not the one that Galileo had wished. He still stood for a contemplative natural philosophy in the ancient spirit. He was, as Einstein said of himself, a "gläubiger Physiker." And after all the sound and the fury, there is now at last a glimmer of light on the horizon, a hint of peace. I understand a petition has been introduced in the present Ecumenical Council, by Catholic scientists, suggesting an official rehabilitation of Galileo. The long refusal and the empty words are now at an end. There is some hope for a true reconciliation.

So much for the past.

There is one aspect of Galileo that is undeniably modern and ours. As Aubrey wrote of Bishop Wilkins's father, ". . . he was a very ingeniose man, and had a very Mechanicall head. He was much for Trying of Experiments. . . ." He was indeed, for he himself invented the idea of Experiment as opposed to the old notion of Experience. He even had to invent a word for it: he called it "The *Ordeal* of Experience." This involved extracting a straight yes or no out of nature in answer to a clear theoretical question and not the usual bewildering play of effect and wonders. It puts theory first, as it should, but it provides a way of testing it: to divide the true from the false. This is the ironclad aspect of Galileo's discoveries, which will go on through the aeons.

But with this a great revolution is running its course. It is not so much methodology—a much abused and rather empty word —as the close collaboration between science and technique. The very fact of being content with the *how* instead of the *why* implies the attitude of the man who is concerned with knowing *how*; in turn, he is going to deal with nature in order to obtain the desired result. The physicist operates as a technician. And with Bacon, Galileo was the first who insisted on the role of the arts then called low, vile, sordid, and mechanical in obtaining knowledge. In his famous address to the Venetians, he pointed out that among the men handling machinery in their arsenal, there must come up experts of unparalleled experience and very subtle intelligence. When the scientist puts nature to the ordeal of experience, he has to appeal to the technician to help him—as his equal. The experiment that *works* is, after all, the only way to check his deductions.

This is the way of modern science, and it implies changes that are no less impressive in the social outlook than in the strictly philosophical. For it is the new team of scientist and technician that, by opening up the cataracts of successful results, has freed science from the initial metaphysical mortgage. The scientist needs no longer the philosopher's guarantee about the soundness of his approach; nor will he underlie the philosopher's strictures. Nothing succeeds like success.

But freedom has its price. The magic catchword "research and development" has turned science in the public mind into a handmaiden of technology. Nor would the scientists make much of a stand, bewildered as they are about their own assumptions, caught again, as one of them said, in embarrassing epicyclic expedients as they wait for a true theory.

If we still at least believed with a simple faith in mathematics. But do we really, caught as we are in conventions? A recent paper by Eugene Wigner left me wondering. Its title is "Of the unreasonable success of mathematics in dealing with nature." Such a title would have been unthinkable even fifty years ago.

So many basic ideas are gone that we cannot even put our house in order. The split between the two cultures is widening; the unity of culture of which science was so large a part is shattered. The theoretical freedom that we needed for dealing with quantum phenomena has given us an arbitrariness in physical thinking that goes at the expense of metaphysical consistency, as Einstein ruefully pointed out. When the empiricist suggests that science is a set of operational rules for changing marks on paper, he is obviously overdoing it. Science cannot but remain the search for some kind of being, however elusive. But when we are willing to suppose anything that will "work," when nothing is too farfetched to try, we have surrendered choice of thought and entered a phase that has some of the aspects of intellectual nihilism.

In that sense, we are moving at present out of the era that began with Galileo. We are in search of a new philosophy, for success is not enough. And we must hope that it will be found soon, for otherwise we have a grave crisis in civilization. Inevitably, if science were to insist on presenting itself as an assemblage of devices for pragmatic power and economy of thought, if it were to disguise its poetic objectivity under technological wizardry, then misunderstandings would be found to occur. Outsiders—the other culture—will ask whether such a program could not just as well have fitted Renaissance nigromancy, with its system of recipes.

We have come a long way since Voltaire.

Those who believe intransigently in the right of science to lead may find those signs irrelevant. The researcher's business is simply to go ahead. But what is left of tradition has a way of turning against those who disregard it. Words such as epicycles and nigromancy coming up in the historical consciousness make one doubt and wonder. The scientist has ceased taking part in the great dialogue as a cultural being. The little gusts of revolt blowing through society are the kind that the statesman might find worthy of attention. *Forsitan et Priami fuerint quae fata requiras?*

If it be true that we are really moving out of the Galilean era, then perhaps you will bear with me if I have so insistently dwelt on Galileo's metaphysics; they are his mark and the mark of that era. I would even go farther, and say: it is not perchance that science was born in the epoch that first took metaphysical commitment seriously.

This may sound paradoxical, for the Middle Ages are supposed to be *the* age of metaphysics. But it was a very different thing, based on the inscrutable will of God, operating inductively from hints of that absolute will. What the Pope instructed Galileo to do was correctly medieval: "Surrender to the inscrutable, speculate as you like, but do not believe that we can really *know*." When the Pope rose in fury against him, it was not because of his experimental discoveries, surely not. It was because he spotted the pride of intellect that thinks it can establish a true order deductively.

Let me tell you the story. At one point before the trial, the Pope gave audience to the Florentine Ambassador who had come again to plead desperately for Galileo. "I made free to remark to His Beatitude," reports the Ambassador, "that since God could have made the world in infinitely many ways, it could not be denied that this might be one of those ways, as Il Signor Galileo thought he had discovered." At which the Pope, red in the face and pounding the padded armrest of his pontifical chair, shouted, "We must not necessitate God Almighty, do you understand?"

Necessitating is indeed the fatal word that marks our science. Where there is mathematical deduction of reality, there is necessity itself, that which could not be otherwise. This is what Galileo asserts, powerfully and dangerously, in his Dialogue, where he says that when the mind has deduced a necessary proposition, it perceives it as God himself perceives it. There is an identity at that point between man's mind and God's. The idea of a necessity that is freedom, of a freedom that is necessity, was present in Galileo's metaphysics and not in the Pope's. That is what Sir Thomas Browne had in mind when he spoke of "that mighty exantlation of Truth, in which, against all passions of prescription and prejudice, this century now prevaileth."

The true rationalist instinct is to believe in the reality of what thought is constructing: the Platonist strain will reappear perpetually to breed new scandal. Even to believe in two and two makes four as an eternal verity is to project back archetypes on the mind of God, to limit His absolute will. This is what Descartes realized, and dodged accordingly. But the sound Pythagorean canon of deduction has been re-established, and mathematical physics is on its way, however meagre the results that it can yet show to the public: it may be a shade heretical or at least "offensive to pious ears," as they said, but it is what we are agreed to call science.

When the God of Job displays his heraldry of prodigies, unicorns, and Leviathans brought forth according to his pleasure, he expects Job to break down in uncomprehending wonder. The modern physicist would take it another way. He would say that the arbitrary will of the Deity is a random noise in the system that prevents us from deriving any predictable statements. We cannot try for a science in those conditions.

But if, according to the pious but unhesitating Pythagorean, the holy Number, which is the fountainhead of all things, is an archetype connatural to the divine mind, then the random noise is cut out: our mind is present across the aeons at the stillness of Creation.

Necessity, Contingency, and Natural Law

IN THE LIFE OF BOTH REASON AND IMAGINATION, THERE IS AN irrepressible claim to reality. The realism of imagination was expressed by Keats in a letter to Bailey, in which he stated his creed that what the imagination truly conceives must, somehow, exist. The realism of abstract reason can be, and indeed has been, formulated in exactly the same words. When Metrodorus in 400 B.C. says that a single world in the immensity of space would be as unnatural as a single ear of wheat in a boundless field, he would be hard put to justifying his statement scientifically, but he needs no justification. He relies on that unspoken postulate, the principle of sufficient reason, which underlies all scientific thinking. But the way he puts it reveals a motive axiom which lies even deeper, the principle of fecundity. Through the heroic age of Greek science, the principle is followed with Promethean recklessness. It might be stated in a way parallel to Keats': whatever reason deduces from simple principles without running into contradiction must somehow, somewhere, exist. Parmenides puts it in the most absolute form: "Thinking and that to which thought refers are one and the same, for where else, except in thought from which it receives its name, shalt thou find Being?" Plato's world of Ideas owes its very existence to this type of affirmation. All of the objects of rational thought "exist" in that world beyond space and time. But as Plato has abandoned the attempt at a science of physical reality, there is no "descent" from the world of Ideas, only a confused wriggling and groping of the world of things in the "matrix" as it tries ineffectually to "participate" in what is beyond it. Still, there *is* an order superimposed, there seems to be a selection among all the possibles. Plato gives a striking image of his thought in the myth of the Demiurge when he describes that semi-divine Artisan choosing arbitrarily, among all the essences, those to be brought into existence and, for all his power, having to be content with a poor imitation.

If we were to follow the fate of that Demiurge in late Hellenistic thinking, we would run into Job, but then also into all sorts of weird and grievous developments: for once the Gnostics bring him in as some kind of cosmological necessity to complement the ineffable, infinitely remote and perforce inoperant One of Plotinus, then he becomes also responsible for the evil there is in this world. What Plato had discreetly ascribed to the insufficiency of matter becomes, once it is taken in dead earnest, the kind of activity involved in matter, which "wants" to bring forth matter. If the Gnostic Demiurge does bring forth the real world, it can be only for generally disagreeable reasons, for his aim is to deceive the Soul and involve it in its turn by providing a specious facsimile of the world of Ideas. Having been admitted to the actual vision of the Ideas, he is the Luciferian force who will use them for his purposes. His hasty copying, like that of one admitted to an exclusive fashion show, is only aimed at a discrediting and cheapening of what should be kept for the elect. The world design is the design of a counterfeiter.

Here is the original source of the great heresies, the intellectual temptation which kept Origen himself from the roster of recognized saints: the desire to explain rationally the existence of evil and contingency led to setting up the Adversary in the seat of creation. It was not easy for the orthodox to redefine against this the proper position, for they too felt the presence of some antagonistic principle, and they too had to answer the ever-resurgent questions: "why thus? who is responsible for the wrongness and senselessness in all things?" Their theology, too, was far from simple, since they had to combine the traditional Demiurge of Genesis ("lo, he found his work good") with the transcendent One of neoplatonic theory. If the transcendent Deity can do nothing and take no decisions, and if on the other hand the fatherhood of the Biblical God is an article of faith, then there is no explanation of things as they are except God's impenetrable will, no justification of wrong except in the inscrutability of Divine counsel. Otherwise the image of omnipotence would disintegrate into its components.

This tendency to fall apart into its original elements is always present in medieval Christianity; it is the permanent threat of the great Gnostic heresies like that of the Albigensians, which were repressed with fire and sword. The repressions were pointless as all repressions are; they probably gave the movement its main strength, for there is a perverse nightmarish quality in this idea of a world wholly evil, created by a demon (even if redeemed by the anti-Demon: the New Testament God of Love who sent His Son), which will hardly unfold by itself into a great religion. But it became then a fearsome task for all good orthodox believers to reconcile the soul with the inadequacy and evil of this world; all is not settled when evil has been defined as a mystery. The stress had to be placed on the abyss of divine counsel, on the vanity of our search for reasons. The alternative to gnosticism is a kind of fundamental agnosticism of reason based on faith. The agony of justification *quand même* is what inspires the work of Dante; it is what imparts tension and reality to a structure which otherwise would have nothing for the intellect behind its scholastic façade. The fate of all medieval attempts at theodicy, as can be noted earlier a propos of the other attempts at mathematical rationalism, is to lose themselves in an *o altitudo*. What possibles have been chosen by God for existence, what archetypes, if any, to adorn his universe, is a matter of his arbitrary will. It was so for Job, it will be so for Newton no less than for Duns Scotus: *a posse ad esse non valet illatio*. The reasons must surely be there, but they remain hidden in divine inscrutability.

The last and greatest of the Brethren of the Free Spirit, Jakob

Boehme, will draw the quittance with strong homely sense. "The learned," he wrote, "have rigged up a great quantity of monstrosities concerning the origin of sin, and have scratched themselves therewith . . . They seem to think that God has willed the bad, since he has created such a lot of it." There was nothing in the doctrine that could lift him from "sore trouble and despair," nothing that could be for him "life piercing through the heart of death." He had to find his own way. He had to find some kind of law inside Divine Nature.

On the side of strictly natural explanation, could things fare better? The feeling of relief and reassurance with which Aquinas went through the integral text of Aristotle just translated by his friend William of Moerbeke is not registered in the annals, for these men granted themselves no life history; but it shines through his work. Here at last was a great and organic thought wholly unfolded which made no concessions to *a priori* rationalism and to the pride of the abstract intellect, but proceeded in orderly manner from what we see to what we do not see, from individual objects to the general by sheer induction. The imposing logical architecture of Aquinas has looked to many like the embodiment of reason itself. Few only have troubled to point out that it is inductive procedure which holds it together, and one in which the very possibility of induction is not secured. Nothing else would do in dealing with the order decreed by God, and with existents individually decreed from the same source. Here again, stylistic analysis may give us a clue to Aquinas' impressiveness and effectiveness; for while he is not much more orderly than Aristotle, he spends great effort in making the orderliness and logic palpably explicit in his organization, division, and subdivision. We have at work what Panofsky, in comparing him to the Gothic architects, has called the "postulate of clarification for clarification's sake."

But such formal clarification has little to do with intrinsic clarity of deductive thought. In Aquinas, even more than in Aristotle, the latter is simply not there, nor can it be. The role that was held by Pythagorean Number, by Plato's Ideas in medieval realism ("the only real objects") is held in Aristotle the Naturalist by concrete things. They are there, they are given, and there is an end to it. There is no sense in asking why a thing not in the world is not in the world. *Istae dubitationes stultae sunt*, such questions are silly, Aquinas would remark peaceably. This is no doubt a "scientific" point of view, and indeed the School felt itself well secure in its empiricim. When Pope Urban VIII in 1630 instructed Galileo that we must not try to infer that such and such is the *one* way in which the world laws have to operate, for God might have brought forth the same phenomena in infinitely many ways, and some of them unthinkable for us, he was advocating the "open mind." At least, so it looks to us.

But was he really? If we go back to the decisions of the Lateran Council in 1217, condemning Aristotle when he was first presented to the West in his true aspect, we find that he was condemned because *he* necessitated the Maker. When the Archbishop of Paris in 1270 condemned 219 theses of Aristotelian character, it was for the same explicit reason. It was the other side of Aristotle which was pinned down here, Aristotle the Rationalist, the disciple of Plato, not quite reconciled to the Naturalist, who has to organize Nature according to the great necessities of thought. Apparently, the Church in the thirteenth century knew where it stood with regard to philosophy. They would rather have none than be inconvenienced; Aristotle was inconvenient because he brought in necessity. He made the order of the world necessary, and, as such, eternal. Archbishop Tempier's condemnations overrode the work of Aquinas, and even Aquinas' presence in Paris seems not to have helped. Here we have already the Nominalist groundswell. And if we consider the crisis in this light of fundamentals, then Duhem's thesis that Nominalism freed the scientific imagination appears delusive. It is the metaphysical demonstration itself (without which there is no attempt at true science) which is invalidated and altered by decree from certain to possible. Surely, this implies a corresponding freedom to hold other and new "plausible" opinions without having them sentenced as absurd. Hypotheses can be presented as such, any amount of alternative and even contradictory hypotheses. But Ockham's way of excluding cosmic verities as beyond man's capacity frees the imagination only for ineffectual flights from an irrevelant reality. *Secundum imaginationem* means just that. It is a permissive clause for irrelevancy. Edward Grant quotes a saying of Pierre Ceffons which gives the mind pause: "Nothing prevents some false propositions from being more probable than some true ones."

It may well be, as has been said, that Nominalism is the beginning of modern analytical philosophy. But it can get us nowhere near science. The names of Buridan and Oresme are evoked in vain, empiricism is only an empty word. Induction, which had never been firmed, has been robbed of its last support.

This becomes very clear when we reach the seventeenth century crisis. The Aristotle of Urban VIII had had his teeth drawn, he was the clarifier, the "arranger" of empirical reality according to the most reasonable scheme, subject to higher policy. Urban thought he had both reason and faith coexisting harmoniously beneath his scepter; hence he felt he could lay down high policy in matters of knowledge. But that does not mean "science" as we mean it, nor, certainly, the open mind. While he was quite sure he had both, it was his misfortune that at that point science had already changed hands.

When the crisis came, the bewildered attitude of intelligent lay opinion is well expressed by the Florentine Ambassador, Niccolini, as he stood there in front of the Pope and tried to exculpate Galileo. "I made free to remark to His Beatitude," he reports, "that since God could have made the world in infinitely many ways, it could not be denied that this might be one of those ways, as il Signor Galileo thought he had discovered." At which the Pope, red in the face and pounding the padded armrest of his pontifical chair, shouted that "We must not necessitate the Lord Almighty." Niccolini goes on lightly in his report: "As I saw his temper rising high, I passed on to another subject, for I did not care to run perchance into some heresy, and I wanted to stay clear of the Holy Office."

"Necessitating" is indeed the fatal word which marks our science. Galileo had pointed out that there is no sense in looking for many probable reasons if we can find the mathematical one, for that single reason becomes necessity itself. And this is what the Pope could in no wise accept.

An open world it still was, even in its crystalline enclosure, open towards the Empyrean; a free and multiple world in which individual "natures" spontaneously sought their own good; a trusting world cradled in God's will. If that will once happened to change, it would not be for us to question. But what of the arbitrariness of it all?

> Vanno per l'aere come uccei vagando
> altre spezie di spiriti folletti
> che non furon fedei, nè rei già quando
> fu stabilito il numer degli eletti . . .

The laughing-bitter crack of Luigi Pucci, that most irreverent of poets, a friend of the Magnifico, is aimed straight at preordination, and it shows the inevitable "necessity" of quite another kind of freedom. "There go roaming through the air other kinds of goblins, who did not have the faith, but were not included among the damned when the number of the elect was established. . ."

For is it not written that faith has to be free? This is perfidious paradox, and hardly refutable. If fate comes from arbitrary decrees, then there is bound to be a number of beings who chance to slip through the meshes of the law. They will be, for once, really and totally free. The hydra of rationalism has reared its ugliest head.

It would be absurd to think that Aquinas is not aware of the dreadful issues. His intellectual peace is not provided by the mechanism of pure reason, however subtly and masterfully handled. It comes to him by way of the "intellect," which good medieval usage knew how to distinguish from "reason." It is the intellect which provides the vision by means of its anagogic power leading to the transcendent regions where paradoxes are solved, and impossibilities reconciled. Here is the world of contemplation, which was to Aquinas the true haven just as it was for his Nominalist opponents.

For this way of the intellect there is an essential symbol in the allegorical cosmos: it is Jacob's Ladder. We remember the *Hound of Heaven*:

> . . . Cry unto heaven, and on thy loss
> Will shine the traffic of Jacob's Ladder
> Pitched between Heaven and Charing Cross

This is a profound mystical symbol which can stand unaided by any cosmology. But, as a cosmic element, it was very carefully put in place first by the Pythagoreans, then by Dante in *Par.* 21 and 22. The ladder is pitched from the sphere of Saturn to that of the stars, and loses itself beyond it in the Empyrean, "where place is not," bridging the immeasurable distance between our system and the true heaven. On it, "like the crows warming themselves at dawn" stirs the traffic of none but the souls of the contemplative. The song has ceased, for this is where the harmony of the spheres comes to an end; one has entered as it were the region of ultrasonic silence. This is the point that Dante chooses for having a soul from the heights explain that predestination is such a profound mystery that not the highest ranks of the elect can penetrate it, even while their vision in God can perceive the order of Creation. He has defined thus the incalculable gap between the outer planetary sphere and the constellations as also that between the timeless causes and the world of effects—the gap that only the contemplative minds can cross by an intuitive sweep, "like a flock of birds vanishing into the heights." The ladder, then, is the anagogic way of the intellect leading up to transcendence.

In this hierarchic world, the way up and the way down are not at all one and the same. While the way up goes with the speed of light, the way down is by no means the straight one of deduction. There is, for good reason; no path of descent from the height, only a memory of the ultimate goal as revealed by the intellect. The escalator of understanding can only go up. Once the mystic vision has come to a close, reason finds itself again on earth, beset by all the old contradictions, left to work out its inductive way. And it finds it well that it should be so, and that the difficulties should be unending.

This is how a medieval understood it.

High Scholasticism has been described as the fine art of reconciling the irreconcilables. It solves the contradictions unfolded in Abelard's *Yes and No* with the procedure of disputation, which is really what one might call a technique of subtle incorporation of contradictions. Roger Bacon in the *Opus Minus* pins it down in no uncertain terms: "Division into many parts as do the dialecticians; rhythmical consonances as do the grammarians; and forced harmonizations (*concordiae violentes*) as do the jurists."

Thus, as befits a thought whose true certainties are not of this world, the Scholastic system proceeded towards an organization which implied in ideas coexistence rather than rigor. It showed what "ought to be so" with an indefatigable expenditure of plausibility, presentation, and clarification. It proceeded in orderly manner, as we have suggested, from what we see to what we do not see, from individual objects to the general, by sheer induction. But it is only the procedure that holds it together, and one in which the very possibility of induction is not secured. Nothing else would do in dealing with the order arbitrarily decreed by God, and with existents individually decreed from the same source. To sum up our main contention so far, there is no sense in the scholastic's asking why certain possibles have been realized and others not. It is no doubt a rational point of view; but it does not lead to our science. It discards mathematics because it brings up indiscreetly the fact of intellectual necessity. The fate of all medieval attempts at theodicy, as well as at a mathematical rationalism, always leads to the inscrutability of God's counsels. What possibles have been chosen by God for existence, what archetypes, if any, to adorn his universe, is a matter of his arbitrary will. For suppose—just suppose—that, in the same inscrutable decisions where the Second Coming and the number of the elect are already inscribed, there were also decreed another date, some Annus Mirabilis in which, say, five planets effect a conjunction in quincunx with a comet in the Seventh House; the date of a new deal, when a divine indult will be decreed and a new era will begin, in which animals are granted the gift of speech, the moon rises in the west and the laws of fall are modified. Who can tell us that there is not such a date in the arcana of Divine counsel? There are only a very few things to which the Lord has bound himself by covenant *donec auferatur luna*, but the laws of nature are not included among them. They are by-laws at best, a creational grant. Their learned interpreters had best remember that theirs is an uninsurable business.[1]

If we consider indeed what the medievals defined as "natural law," which had not much to do with nature, we realize it was a set of such creational grants. It was truly a "positive law" as society understands it.

Critical rationalism could thus make a strong case. Blandly

[1] One might no doubt build up a case inside orthodoxy. The Scholastic combination of the omnipotent God of Genesis with the Aristotelian *Analogia Entis* (as the coexistence in the divine *Nous* of all universals in the actualized state) preclude God's interference with Nature on the ground that then God would be departing from his own essence. The possibility of an insured science is always present to the mind, but somehow it is not generally felt compatible with the *Gloria Dei*. Descartes himself has to put in a famous caution: "C'est parler de Dieu comme d'un Jupiter ou Saturne, et l'assujettir au Styx et aux destinées, que de dire que ces vérités sont indépendantes de lui."

presented as above, it would have stood as a conservative estimate of the situation, compelling some kind of assent, the more so as it reaffirmed the proper hierarchy of spiritual values. All strictly intellectual pursuits might lead to pride of intellect; at best they remained, in the terms of that epitaph of the penitent scholar, the croaking of frogs, the cawing of ravens, the vanity of the vain.[2] The Franciscan schoolmen never forgot the point, and impressed it, sometimes discourteously, on their Dominican brethren. But it was there at the back of everyone's mind.

Our thinking is inevitably colored by the present, and tends to show us the early efforts of the Nominalists towards science in today's light. That is because we see what kind of opening was offering itself, we know the road from there; but it could not be seen at the time, and the actual endeavor was much more like advancing in burrows. Science was and remained a "handmaiden of faith"; any real philosophical evolution of knowledge had to be dictated from the vantage point of theology. The further intellectual clarification of Ockhamism only reaffirms the primacy of will over intellect, in accord with what medieval philosophy really implies. The thought of the Middle Ages works itself out in coherent fashion.

However impressive the spectacle of uncompromising and relentless analysis that is presented to us by Ockhamism, we should not forget the principles it stems from that we quoted from Roger Bacon, no mean witness to the spirit of Scholasticism: "Division into many parts as do the dialecticians; rhythmical consonances as do the grammarians; and *concordiae violentes* as do the jurists."

It is the word "violence," so precisely used, which gives one pause. It is borrowed from the law. Much later, Vico, for whom the law has become part itself of the great process of creative mimesis, will define it as "the imitation of violence." Both authors remind us that society is forever based on force, that a philosophy of authority develops force—and is in need of force. When the Pope refused Galileo's metaphysical "necessity," it was not in the name of metaphysical freedom (he reserved that for God alone), it was in the name of intelligently applied constraint which alone could hold irreconcilables together. It was in the name of that classical concept of "method" which leads the mind to preordained conclusions as the artist's method does to an achievement already conceived in the imagination. Under the name of a cosmological science, what he was defending was an art of presentation. That is why, at that point, science had changed hands.

The idea of a necessity which is freedom, of a freedom which is necessity, was present in Galileo's metaphysical and not in the

[2] (1967) This uncomfortable demarcation has been transmuted today, halfway around the world, as that of "red vs. expert," with the Red Guard as the enforcers.

Pope's. The great "clarification" has come to an end, and the offensive rationalists of Pucci's kind had suggested long ago, in strictly private conversation, that it was not going to get anywhere. Buridan's timid wish that God in his goodness might decide sometime to have mathematical laws obtain in reality, does indeed lead nowhere—as a wish. The flight into sheerly analytical reason is after all but a flight. The true rationalist instinct is to believe in the reality of what thought is constructing; the Platonist strain will reappear perpetually to breed new scandal. Even to believe in two and two makes four as an eternal verity is to project back archetypes in the mind of God, to limit his sovereign will. Descartes will prudently discern that this cannot and must not be so, and will trim his sails accordingly. But it is only to save the proper forms. His true way is metaphysical certainty: "Je vous diray que je n'eusse sceu trouver le fondemens de ma Physique, si je ne les eusse cherchés par cette voie."

The sound Pythagorean canon of deduction has been reestablished, and mathematical physics is on its way; it may be a shade heretical, or at least "offensive to pious ears," but it is what we are agreed to call science, and until another one is invented, we have to carry on with it.

Briefly said: any archetype of the Pythagorean or Platonic sort, any immutable intellectual determination and clarity supposed at the divine origin will lead us to the brink of heresy by making it connatural with God. The God of Job has not been Philonized, he sets up his heraldry of prodigies according to his pleasure. If it had been suggested to the pious author that any of those unicorns and Leviathans were archetypes, and hence connatural with the Eternal mind, he would have cried *raka* and veiled his face. This is what the orthodox will call the proper humility of mind in the presence of the supreme mystery. The modern physicist might have another image for that mystery. He would say that the arbitrary will of the Deity is a random noise in the system which prevents us from deriving any predictable statements. Hence, as a matter of strict necessity, no science.

But if, according to the unrepentant Pythagorean, the holy Decad, which is also the Tetraktys and the Fountainhead of all things, is an archetype connatural to the divine mind, then the random noise is cut out; our mind is present across the aeons at the stillness of creation. But then, as Pope Urban would say, God has been in some way "necessitated."

I have been trying to make clear, in this bird's-eye view of centuries, a point which was obvious to the founders of physical science, but which has been obscured to us by a generation of empiricist punditry: that if someone was to create the scientific concept of a law of nature, so utterly at variance wich what previously went under that name, he had to assume a prescriptive link between essence and existence, and let it be established by divine decree, but it must be unalterable. Otherwise it is impossible to reverse the inductive trend, and proceed, as the mathematical mind does, by deducting the real from the theoretically possible. That is why modern science was born, surely not by accident, in the first century that can be said to have again taken metaphysics seriously. This may look at first sight somewhat paradoxical, but we only have to think of the Pope's flaring anger at Galileo's metaphysical stand to realize all that was involved.

Galileo trusted his mathematical metaphysics, as the Pope did not trust his own, fenced in as it was by signs warning of the inscrutability of God. When the signs went down under the Cartesian bulldozer, the ground was open for thoroughgoing rational deduction from first principles. To be sure, this does not mean that all the essences were now to be cataracted into existence; it would have produced only a sorry and monstrous earthly caricature of Plato's heaven. On the other hand, the problem of "descent" of the essences could no longer be evaded artfully as in Plato, nor be screened by suitably disposable parameters like the arbitrary will of God. The real world was going, once and for all, to be really accounted for. From the infinite world of theoretical "possibles," the existent must still be separated by some criterion of choice. But to say that this was the grant of existence itself, as Aquinas suggests, would have been considered in this, the time of Molière, inventing one more *virtus dormitiva*. There must be a clear rule. The essences which come to actual existence must have something in common which may not be part of the essence itself, but is still a fixed rule, and singles them out among the possibles. This is the way for Descartes and his successors.

The kind of rationalist metaphysical faith that I have outlined in the seventeenth-century classics has remained quite alive in our time, in men like Planck and Einstein—the man whom his old friend Michelange Besso called with affectionate and slightly exasperated irony "Don Quixote de la Einsta." In following up Einstein's evolution from early Machian positivism into his late conclusions, Gerald Holton[3] quoted recently from a much-neglected essay:

> Physical theory has two ardent desires: to gather up as far as possible all pertinent phenomena and their connections, and to help us not only to know *how* Nature is and *how* her transactions are carried through, but also to reach as far as possible the perhaps utopian and seemingly arrogant aim of knowing why Nature is *thus and not otherwise*. [This is our prescriptive link!] Here lies the highest satisfaction of a scientific person. . . . [On making deductions from a "funda-

[3] "Mach Einstein and the Search for 'Reality'" (to be published in *Daedalus*, 1968).

mental hypothesis" such as that of the kinetic-molecular theory] one experiences, so to speak, that God himself could not have arranged those connections [e.g., between pressure, volume, and temperature] in any other way than that which factually exists, any more than it would be in His power to make the number 4 into a prime number. This is the Promethian element of the scientific experience. . . . Here has always been for me the particular magic of scientific considerations; this is, as it were, the religious basis of scientific effort.*

* [Preceding two paragraphs added subsequent to publication of original article.]

Prologue to Parmenides

I: The Way of Clarity

THERE HAVE BEEN AS MANY WAYS OF LOOKING AT THE PRESOCRATICS as there have been intellectual generations and changes of attitude in modern times. Prodigious amounts of exact philology and ingenious interpretation have been expended on them, and yet they remain today as mysterious, perhaps more mysterious, than they appeared in the Renaissance. For as our own awareness of history builds up, we cannot help realizing that it is those ancients who have dealt out all the ideas that Western thought has played with ever since—so enticingly near to us in one way, in another remote and incomprehensible beyond retrieve, as they stand out like statues of Memnon in the wastes of the past, each uttering, as it would seem, one note and only one, compared to the tumult and the dialectic of later times.

Of these great ones, the most difficult is Parmenides.

"It is insufficiently known that the philosophy of the Eleatics still forms an obscure chapter in the history of philosophy." Such are the opening words of the latest book on Parmenides, by Dr. J. H. M. Loenen of the University of Leiden, published in 1959. I consider this one of the most engaging understatements of the year. Yes, it may be insufficiently known, let us then proclaim it. The never-ending tangle of successive interpretations, assisted by the most refined philological analysis, by ingenious conjectures and emendations, by all the critical study of the *variae lectiones*, has only made confusion worse confounded. For each point really cleared up (a minor point at best) ten new doubts have arisen. The moment of history defined by Parmenides was described dramatically by Karl Reinhardt forty years ago: "When from the shambles of the past, awesome, spectral, the Sphinx of Metaphysics first reared its head."

The Sphinx is still around, and the shambles still very much in evidence.

Part of the trouble is modern. Since the rescuing of the texts by the great philologists of the nineteenth century, one school after another has tried to inject its preconceptions into their meaning, according to the way in which they read the history of philosophical ideas.

Part is ancient. And it begins very early. Plato, Aristotle, Eudemus, Theophrastus, Proclus, Simplicius are clearly at odds about what Parmenides may really have meant. But he has suffered mostly from Plato's accolade. "August and terrible in his greatness," as Socrates says of him, he stands there as the founder of the doctrine of Being, on which Plato's metaphysics is founded. But surely, it is a very particular doctrine. No one is going to say that the dialogue entitled *Parmenides* is an historical document of the Eleatic's own thoughts. Plato himself is explicitly apologetic about the liberties that he takes with

Parmenides' thought, and speaks playfully of having to commit parricide. But the irresistible effulgence of Platonic thought causes Parmenides to be lost, so to speak, in it. He becomes hardly identifiable as an independent thinker. And indeed the Neoplatonists have completed the work of incorporation, by presenting him as the first step towards a Gnosis of the Divine.

Now it so happens that modern history of philosophy, from Hegel onwards, is mostly written by idealists, who found it natural to preserve the Neo-Platonic scheme, and to present Parmenides as the indispensable link in their intellectual chain, the founder of ontology. A number of such today have extolled him for his "splendid intransigence" towards natural knowledge. And so he has become the banner-bearer of the anti-scientific attitude, however vast the difference may be between our time and reasons, and his.

One should like to ask those bold modernizers: who would imagine Fichte, Hegel, or Heidegger proceeding from cryptic statements on Being and Non-Being to a treatise concerning the mechanism of the planets and the illumination of the moon, or the sterility of mules? For these are subjects in the second part of Parmenides' poem. And if the inattention and the prejudice of commentators had not left us with the pitiful shreds we have of it, no one would have entertained the idea that Parmenides' physics was an insignificant appendix to his doctrine of Truth.

The current interpretation of Parmenides seems to have moved beyond these problems. Carried on in the wake of the Platonic dialogue, armed with the refined apparatus of exact philology, it puts all the stress on the verbal copula *is*, as if this had been at the heart of the epoch-making Eleatic discovery. What sense does it make? Ontological sense, answer the logico-verbalists. But not only in the direction later developed by Plato; Parmenides stands as the originator of logico-verbal Truth, and hence also of sophistic argument. A considerable amount of research has gone into showing the links between Eleatic and Sophistic logic, and that since the times of the ancient pseudo-Aristotelian treatise *De Melisso, Parmenide et Gorgia.* If the tools of reasoning are basically the same, how could there be a basic difference with the Sophists, even if the intentions are admittedly not the same? This seems to be Calogero's view and that of several contemporary authorities.

If the man of Elea had heard this explanation of himself, he might indeed have been, to use his own words, "wondrous hard to convince."

I am going to suggest a very different way of approach. The case has been worked out in a rather substantial essay, as yet unpublished, and the proof cannot be given within the span of a brief lecture. The argument is therefore merely indicated; but in a few key issues, I shall try also to justify my line of reasoning.

Let me start from an old and sound remark of John Burnet:

> Does Parmenides refer to the world of sense or the world of ideas; concrete existence or abstract being; matter or spirit? All these questions would have been absolutely meaningless to an early Greek philosopher, and the system of Parmenides is the best touchstone for our understanding of this fundamental historical truth.

These are words of wisdom. It is pointless to use names like idealism and materialism before object and subject, form and content, matter and spirit have been set up as pairs of well-characterized oppositions.

So we are led back to the neutral ground on which Parmenides had placed himself, a ground where reason and truth about nature were one and the same. Only *that* can be which can be logically; for logic exists "for the sake of what is." Stated thus, in the original words, we cannot but feel that it comes nearer to the spirit of scientific rationalism than to any idealistic or materialistic system. But to keep exactly tuned to Parmenides' own key, we should have to insist on the absence of a higher or lower, or of a difference between abstract and concrete. It is a *conversio veri ac entis*. Thought is coextensive with being, *νοεῖν* and *ἐόν* are only two aspects of the same thing, and that thing is also the one background—what stays forever. It is Anaximander's Unbounded, Pythagoras' Order, Xenophanes' One, Heraclitus' Fire-Logos: *τὸ θεῖον*, the Divine.

When the "ancients," as Aristotle calls them, had meant a primordial substance or a substratum, they had not thought of something present only to the discursive mind, but of something that either meets the eye, or would meet a super-acute eye, if it were refined enough to perceive it right where it is, *in* things. "If we could only say what is exactly so," muses Xenophanes, while Anaxagoras affirms: "The sight of the invisible are the appearances."

With Parmenides instead, and this is undeniable, we have a complete break with the past and a new departure. So far we must agree with those who speak of a radical novelty. But what kind of novelty is it? Let us take an unprejudiced look at the poem—at least at what was preserved of it.

The Proem

The overture is a grandiose and mythical adventure, which is enough to show the text as a *griphos* in the archaic sense—unless we consider it as some do a mere rhetorical exercise, which is hard to suppose. The poet is taken aloft on a divine chariot, beyond the Gates of Night and Day, until he reaches the abode of the Goddess of Truth, who undertakes to explain to him the ways that are open to mortals, that of Truth and that of Opinion. I cannot go here into the intricacies of her initial argument, nor into her violent reprehension of the "akrita phyla," the ordinary speculators, who think that a thing is and is not at the same time, and thus end up by not knowing whether they are coming or going. I am trying to look at the formal and mythical element. The first thing that appears is the Hesiodic model, and it would lead us into a fascinating and most instructive comparison between the two theologies. But then there is another element, too neglected by the commentators, that Diels had brought out seventy years ago, when he described the poem as belonging to the *Epimenideslitteratur*.

This insight, due to Diels' great philological instinct, cuts the ground from under a lot of purely literary criticism of Parmenides as "unpoetical." Parmenides is first and last a mythographer of the "Orphic" kind. When you have to convey a *griphos* your literary capacities do not stand out to their best advantage, and even Dante is not at his most felicitous when he has to work out his vision in Terrestrial Paradise. Such texts are not meant for literary, but for scriptural understanding. Too little is left of the *Epimenideslitteratur* to establish valid parallels, but given the character of the poem, which is eminently an "intellectual purification," and the straight Pythagorean lineage of the author, we might speak of it as of a *Hieros Logos*, a Sacred Discourse.

"How," says Reinhardt, "can Parmenides be credited with any kind of unexpressed theology, he who knows no desire except of knowledge, feels no fetters except of his logic, who is untouched by either god or sentiment?"

It is strange that Reinhardt, who shows such an attentive understanding of Parmenides' personality, should have lent him these traits of illuministic arrogance, in view of the master's obvious and transparent worship of the Female principle. The Pythagoreans had no sex prejudice, contrary to later times, but Parmenides goes much further than they did, further than ever Mr. Robert Graves would dare. His matriarchal absolutism is revealed not only in his Daemon Lady but in all her attendants and epicleses, Dike, Ananke, Moira, Themis, the Heliades, even to the "most intelligent" mares. Even when he speaks of the universal constraint that urges "the female to union with the male, and conversely the male to the female," he opposes the habitual order of thinking which brings the courting male first to the mind: also the word *stygeros* applied to birth strikes one as the woman's point of view. It is usually treated in this case as an ordinary epic epithet, and rendered as "painful" (Diels: *weherfüllt*) but the real meaning is "miserable, wretched, abhorred," which is the connotation it has in Hesiod when applied to Doom and Strife, children of Night. As far as the divine figures go, one might find the consistency in sex easier to understand, since they are all fundamentally aspects of the one feminine power; the Heliads, in fact, may have been originally a college of her priestesses, like the daughters of Neleus, and the mares more sacred to her in her frequent aspect of the Mare-Goddess, which appears in several myths, such as that of Demeter and Erichthonius. But in the strictly physical explanations this line of reasoning does not apply; yet there, too, the feminine element is shown to prevail. We discern here something which cannot be mistaken for an allegorical dressing, which is actually the intrinsic and living form, the "entelechy" in the Aristotelian sense, of Parmenides' thought.

The Way of the Gods

The moment of discovery, the way to the gods, has perforce to be mythological, since it involves that the understanding of the "man who knows" has been rightly guided, and raised above the opinions of mankind. But if the revelation itself has nothing mythological about it, this does not mean a break in style and a change into abstract theory: for that "theoria" itself is the Way of Truth, the Way of the Gods. It is thus that the Pythagoreans had understood mathematical discovery. "Follow the god" was their maxim, or, "Follow in the footsteps of the god." In all early philosophical literature understanding and the Way of the Gods are one. There is no other proper object for the higher awareness. We say understanding, and not explanation: for what the wise man is vouchsafed in this way involves a recognition, a fulfillment, and also a renunciation.

And so we are left to face the Daemon Lady in her absolute, singularly non-Olympian power; just as she is un-Olympian in her personality, ignoring purely and simply the constitutional gods of the Greek cult. Proclus informs us that her name is Hypsypyle, "High Gates" which is strictly a title (cf. Pharaoh, "High House," or the Turkish Sublime Porte). By careful comparison with Hesiod, we can work out her homologues in the Theogony as Themis, Hekate, the Oracle of Night, artfully dispersed by Hesiod, here concentrated in one figure which is also given total cosmic power in the Second Part of the Poem—"The Daemon who steers all things." That the two aspects, the intellectual and the physical, belong to one and the same figure, can hardly be doubted, but has been established conclusively by Rivaud, who identified her as the ancient Aphrodite Urania.[1] It is she that Lucretius invokes as *orbis totius alma Venus*; Lucretius

[1] Aphrodite Urania was an archaic Athenian deity, worshipped with the ancient rites of wineless libation. She was associated in the cult with Mnemosyne, the Dawn, the Sun, the Moon and the Nymphs (schol. ad *Oed. Col.* 100). Hence she belongs to the entities described in the second stage of Hesiod's *Theogony* (1. 265–452). Empedocles reminds us that such deities as Aphrodite Urania came before Kronos and Zeus. In Hesiod, it is Theia who bears Sun, Moon, and Dawn, and Dawn in its turn bears the star Eosphoros "and the gleaming stars with which heaven is crowned" (371–383). Aphrodite Urania was in tradition "the oldest of the Moirai": cf. Parmenides (fr. 8. 37). Hence in the Hesiodic line she would precede even Theia, as the earliest manifestation of Night herself, cf. below.

who ignored the gods, and believed only in atoms and the void, but whose consistency yielded to the poetic feeling engendered by the Parmenidean vision:

> *Quae quoniam rerum naturam sola gubernas*
> *Nec sine te quicquam dias in luminis oras*
> *Exoritur. . . .*

These lines are so close to the exact conception of Parmenides that they may well be a paraphrase of some lost lines of his poem; they have certainly nothing to do with Epicurus. Several such lines appear in Lucretius, taken almost bodily from the *veteres docti poetae* he had chosen as his models.

Another almost exact parallel can be found in the Orphic hymns (n. 27 Abel):

> Holder of the sceptor of famous heaven,
> *Lady of the Many Names, Awful One*
> Who holdest the central throne of the cosmos . . .
> From you has sprung the race of immortals and men

This is indeed the way the Daemon appears in the Second Part of the poem, steering the whirling world from her high seat on the Ecliptic Pole (at least if I read Aëtius right, for critics have put her into all sorts of strange places)—and anyway it cannot be denied, because Aristotle quotes it, that

> First of all things she created Eros

But here she is now, and she turns to her disciple in a sudden movement of intellectual compassion, to teach him about her works:

> Meet it is that you should learn all things, as well the unshaken heart of well-rounded Truth, as also the opinion of mortals, in which there is no certain reliance: but this you shall learn too, how an explanation of things that appear must be considered valid when it goes through all that we know.

This passage is one of the most controversial among philologists, and it has been firmly decided by most that she announces a physical world that can be shown to make no sense (is Parmenides not the "freezer" of all reality, as Plato remarked once?), to the point that Diels went so far as to emend a δοκίμως in the text to square with his preconceptions. But the reading above has been supported by Wilamowitz, and that ought to be safe enough. Dr. Loenen is willing to accept it.

The Way of Men

Then, once she has explained the Way of Truth, the Goddess takes up her earlier promise:

> . . . δόξας δ'ἀπὸ τοῦδε βροτείας
> μάνθανε κόσμον ἐμῶν ἐπέων ἀπατηλὸν ἀκούων.

Now, this is definitely a two-edged proposition. If you begin by translating the perfectly neutral word *doxa* with *Wahngedanken*, as Diels does, you have prejudged the issue: she is going to deal with the "delusions of mortals," and therefore her words are bound to be "deceptive." But in Presocratic usage, *doxa* means "opinion" without any pejorative connotation. It means, barring supernal knowledge, the kind of conclusions a man has been able to reach and is willing to stand by. So, for example, in Xenophanes. In Pythagorean language, it is equivalent to "scientific inquiry" pure and simple. Why should it be here "delusions"? Because of the ἀπατηλόν in the next line, which is commonly understood as "deceptive." Since the Truth has been set up already, the next thing cannot be but deceit and illusion. What a black-and-white notion. When the goddess in the beginning warns her disciple to keep away from ways of inquiry which make no sense, she calls them such in vivid and explicit language. She wastes no words on irrelevant details. Not so here. Nor, on the other hand, does she offer a *gnosis* which should show up all things physical as sick dreams. That kind of *gnosis* had not yet been invented. She is offering a *diakosmos*, and the poet's song rises to Orphic solemnity as he announces it:

> You shall know the origins of things on high, and all the signs in the sky, and the secret works of the glowing sun's clear torch, and whence they arose. And you shall learn likewise of the wandering deeds of the round-eyed moon, and of her nature. You shall know, too, the heaven that encloses round, whence it arose, and how Necessity took it and bound it to keep the limits of the stars . . . .

There is no hint here of meaninglessness, and no one would have started thinking this way if he had had the full text of the Way of Opinion, instead of the few lamentable shreds transmitted to us by doxographers who shared the idealist preconception of modern historians.

Plutarch, who did share idealist preconceptions but had a refreshing sense of reality, brings back things into proportion in his *Adversus Colotem*:

> Parmenides being, as he was, an ancient naturalist, and one who in writing sought to deliver his own and not to destroy another's doctrine, he has passed over none of the principal things of nature.

Let us stand then by this: "he was an ancient naturalist," and his doctrines of nature cannot be a mere exposure of the deceit practiced by such people as naturalists in giving a doctrine of nature. Nor is the Goddess of Truth supposed to utter mere deceit. On this point, I am glad to say, Dr. Loenen finds himself in agreement with me. And we notice that the adjective applies not to the words of her statement, but to the "order of her words." We have then to translate ἀπατηλόν as something else than the too pat "deceitful." We find that the word is used for puzzles, riddling truths, for what seems absurd to the listener and yet turns out to be so. A prime example is Heraclitus fr. 56. There is a whole mythological literature of the difficult saying and the "riddling truth" apt to lead men astray. Amlethus—not Shakespeare's Hamlet, but the age-old powerful personage who appears in Saxo Grammaticus—already bewilders men in this way. We might call it his mark. Let us then take those lines to mean: "Henceforward learn the notions of mortals, lending ear to the cunning order of my words." For it is the *order*, *κόσμος* ἀπατηλός, not the words themselves, which makes the difficulty.

This idea of "cunning" or "tricky" is connected with the next line: "They came to a resolution to name two forms. . . ." It cannot refer to a chance conjecture of some individuals, nor does it refer to the pointless "indiscriminate crowd" against which the poet had been cautioned earlier. The words imply something like a legislative assembly issuing a decree. Caught inside the flux of phenomena, men must work out an acceptable order. One clause however, lends itself to error, that is, we might consider each of those "two forms" separately. This we must not do. We can accept for the present Dr. Loenen's conclusion: "It is clear that Parmenides believes he is bringing something fundamentally new in the *doxa*-part as well, viz. the idea that everything in the world is a combination of 'fire' and 'night'. This is indeed a new idea, at least if 'everything' is really taken very strictly, so that there does not exist a single thing which consists either exclusively of 'light' or exclusively of 'night'." Such a condition makes it very plausible that the Goddess should warn us not to be led astray by the "tricky order of her words."

But *if* the way of Opinion *is* a physics—and it has taken centuries of exegetic blinkering to obscure this obvious fact—then the Way of Truth must make a sense which is correlative to that. We have again to start afresh, looking for a congruence and an integration between both sides of the panel. Indeed, if the discovery of the First Part is simply logical implication, (and surely it is at least that) mankind would have been grateful for a clearer statement. The Way of Truth is, without any doubt, one of the most impressively obscure affirmations in the history of thought. Confronted with the solemn chant of the hexameters, Parmenides' contemporaries must have thought that this man had been granted the sight of things unspeakable, and that he had become intellectually sunstruck. Some, no doubt, must have wondered whether it was the practice to interrupt the ruling deity of the universe at her work, to bespeak the services of "exceeding wise" mares and of a cortege of Daughters of the Sun to carry him aloft, only to come back with a set of oracular tautologies.

Metaphysics, whatever it may be, seems still to lead men astray much more than any physics.

On reading the recent book of Dr. Loenen, which is, as it were, the end point of learned and penetrating decipherment over several decades, I think anyone will be impressed with what little progress has been achieved in solving the riddle of the Sphinx. Dr. Loenen is sound in his approach: he avoids the extreme position, of idealism and logico-verbalism, he does not suppose like some that Parmenides was hypnotized on the verbal copula *is*, or inventing an empty ontological reason. He has come in fact a good part of the way, in presenting the Eleatic doctrine as an epistemological rationalism, and in allowing the Way of Opinion the status of a valid physical theory. And yet, with all his ingenious comments and solicitations, the Way of Truth does not seem to come to life under his hands. Let the reader rather judge by himself. Here we are dealing with a key point of the Way of Truth, the indivisibility of Being: Fr. 8 insists on it in many ways:

> Nor is it separated, since it is all alike, and there is no more anywhere, to prevent it from being continuous, or lesser, but everything is full of Being. Wherefore it is all continuous, for Being presses on Being. . . . But since the last bound is defined on all sides, like the body of a well-rounded sphere, it is equally poised from the center in all directions, for it is necessary that it should not be greater in one direction and smaller in another. Nor is there Non-Being to prevent it from reaching out to its like, nor is it possible for Being to be more here and less there, because it is all inviolable. For it is equal from everywhere, and fits equally in its limits.

The idea of a homogeneous *plenum* seems here to be passionately insisted on. Some modern commentators have even seen a simile for the uniform radiance of spiritual light. Yet this is what Dr. Loenen makes of it:

> (pp. 108–110.) . . . The passage is preceded by the reference to the *image of a ball or a sphere* (the former seems more probable); this implies that Parmenides here considers being from the statical point of view of completeness rather than from the dynamical one of the mental process referred to above; another consequence of this is that a spatial aspect naturally presents itself. The occurrence of this image proves that Parmenides had not yet succeeded in freeing himself entirely from imagination: pure thought is still hampered by it. But in this passage again it will be clear that he intends to transcend all spatiality, which accords with my previous remarks on this subject (I 41 and 44, cf. 45). Being is not a ball, and as a matter of fact Parmenides only says that it is *like* a ball. The only problem is *what exactly is the point of comparison* (see I n. 239). Now it is precisely in connection with this ball-image that he rejects the possibility that the many ideas of being do not fully coincide, that the uniformity might be broken by a greater or smaller idea of being, so that they would not cover each other completely (ll. 44–5). The difference with ll. 23–4 seems

to be that here not only qualitative differences (l. 48, cf. 23ff) but also quantitative differences are denied. One might perhaps think that one idea is greater or smaller than the other, in accordance with the greater or smaller quantity of concrete things which form the regular starting-point for thought. This notion, however, is rejected, and since the ball too is merely an image, one has to assume that he intends to *exclude fundamentally all spatiality from the idea of being*. The passage ll. 46ff. is thus clear: "for there is neither an (idea of) being which might stop its arriving at identity" (because there are no quantitative differences), "nor is it possible for an (idea of) being to be here and there less than an (idea of) being" (because there are no qualitative differences), "since it is all inviolate; for from every side it is identical with itself, uniformly it is within limits." The last line (49), in which we meet with the problem of the πείρατα, forms a suitable transition to the third attribute.

The author seems to find the passage at last clear. I can only envy him. I have always understood that there is a kind of philosophical language which is only accessible to special philosophers. I trust Dr. Loenen will not take it as a personal remark, which would be far from my intention, when I admit that I could not help being reminded of Voltaire's remark: "Quand celui qui parle ne se comprend plus, on appelle cela de la métaphysique."

Let me cite, rather, certain words written by Klaus Reich, the Marburg historian of philosophy, in his 1954 essay on Parmenides:[2]

The most modern interpretations, both philosophical and philological, can only fill the reader with concern. One or the other may also drive him to scorn or ridicule. . . . It seems to me that the fault lies largely with the prejudice which attributes to the so-called archaic period a "structure of thought" different from that of the men of today. Any logical paradox may then appear plausible as the end product of that archaic process, and in fact we must be ready for anything. Empathy is supposed to take the place of clear understanding, as happens in dealing with pathological cases. . . . If a writer today is ready to content himself with that, it is due in my opinion to the insistent trend among philosophers in the last hundred years to equate themselves with literary historians. I fear that this is a way of making the history of philosophy irrelevant to the history of exact sciences, and thus depriving it of what should be its highest distinction.

These are far-reaching remarks, which hold a promise of sound interpretation, and indeed when Reich derives Eleatic Being from an attempt to impose more rigorous conditions on the Anaximandrean Unbounded, one may not agree wholly, and yet accept the cogency of his argument. It is as if the history of ideas were put back upon its feet. Real problems follow upon each other in a way which makes sense to the intellectual imagination. The substrate of all things is found back where it should be—everywhere, rather than nowhere.

[2] Klaus Reich, "Parmenides und die Pythagoreer," *Hermes* No. 82 (1954), 287–294.

I am wondering, with all respect for the learned commentators, whether that shying away from any hint of spatiality is not due to a misunderstanding about the very idea of space—a misunderstanding as old and as hard as the rock of ages. Their main authority is of course Plato, who in the well-known passage (*Parmenides* 150*e*) rejects any connection of Being with the Great and Small, that is, with magnitude. Whatever is not connected with magnitude, so it has been decided *ab antiquo*, can have nothing to do with space. If we take this for a valid critical statement, we forget the depth of the Platonic preconception. The role of extension in Plato is played by that difficult idea, the Receptacle, that which is at the beginning and is the source of all multiplicity as well as concrete magnitude. It is a kind of principle of dispersion, the nearest thing to non-being: it is thus perforce at the other pole from the idea of Being. Plato's denial, then, powerful though it has been in history, has reasons which are not ours.[3] But do they belong to Parmenides? I have noted Socrates' modest disclaimer in the *Theaetetus*, and Klaus Reich comes to my help in this. Plato, he says, implies more than once that he does not wholly understand what Parmenides was really at, and even his quotations from memory are inexact. The logic of implication is there, the imagination that guided it remains hidden.

In Aristotle we find another kind of authority, and another kind of barrier. While he restores Parmenides to his rank as *physikos*, and does not deny the spatial metaphor, he insists that Being must be unconnected with any kind of *topos*, and hence—as we should say—unspatial. Is this straight interpretation, or is it due to the basic Aristotelian preconception about essences? Dr. Loenen is clearly impressed by the argument, as he supports his own interpretation by appeal to the well-known Zenonian paradox on *topos*. If Zeno thus denies "place," because it would in turn have a place, and so on, does it not follow that Parmenides too denied "place" to his Being? Why surely, we make free to answer, and the farthest thing from Parmenides' mind should have been the ordinary idea of space as a collection of places: an idea which stands out in Aristotle but had a long past of commonsense representation. The idea is in fact so commonsensical that we can bring it out easily in cultivated contemporaries of ours who have had the benefit of a strictly classical education, and on whose horizon Descartes has never dawned, let alone what followed. I tried the experiment once on a distinguished philologist and got in all naïveté a startingly Aristotelian definition of what space is. Aristotle, it is well known, refuses geome-

[3] Dr. Loenen has found out, too, that we must assume such grave misunderstandings in antiquity. He manages to make sense of the impenetrable fr. 16 by throwing overboard Theophrastus' official interpretation, and assumes the passage was not only misread but misplaced from Truth into Opinion. The word πλέον is made to mean not "more," but "full," and a possible meaning is restored.

trical abstraction in dealing with physical reality, and his space is nothing but a juxtaposition of qualitatively different loci. The modern idea of space, as I have proved elsewhere, becomes current only about 1400 with the first generation of Renaissance architects. [See "The Role of Art in the Scientific Renaissance," p. 137.] How can the philologist step outside of the circle of ideas if he is unaware of that other world of mathematics?

We are rehearsing here as a scholarly skit what was once a tragedy of misunderstanding at the time of Galileo's contemporaries, the men of the Aristotelian culture who simply could not see what he was driving at. Let me illustrate this tangle with a modern example. We find it in Albertelli's excellent study on the Eleatics, often referred to by Loenen, apropos of Parmenides' sphere of Being. Some authors, says Albertelli, have suggested the possibility of an infinite sphere, but that obviously makes no sense. "To speak of a sphere with infinite radius would be like speaking of a square circle." Now we all deeply respect the mind and personality of Albertelli, the size of his achievement for one who was to die so young in front of a German firing squad: but it is all the more revealing to note this gap between the world of the philologist and that of mathematical ideation. What inner contradiction can anyone find in the concept of an infinite sphere? It is a very natural concept, whose course in time was traced by Dietrich Mahnke, and the *Schriftgelehrten* could well have taken notice of it were it only from the revolutionary influence of Nicholas of Cusa. But the line of mathematical imagination and that of philological critique seem to have faced each other in mutual incomprehension through the centuries.

Metamathematics

Hence, I trust I may be forgiven, if I approach the mysterious text from an entirely new angle—that which Jaeger and Stenzel would have called of mathematical ideation; this is far from implying a denial of the metaphysical content, but it would show us the still unknown underlying intellectual structure, which is metamathematical. I suggest then, that we treat the word "Being" throughout as an undefined term, and replace it in the text with X. It is surely good method to posit our ignorance of a dazzling, familiar and yet unununderstood word, by treating it formally as an unknown term, and trying to define it by context. Now, if we keep our mind "washed clear of preconceptions" as Bacon suggested, and try to define X strictly by context, it will be found that there is one, and only one, other concept which can be put in the place of X without engendering nonsense or contradiction, and that concept is pure geometrical space itself, for which the Greeks did not yet have a technical term (it is known that the early *Elements* were essentially two-dimensional). Moreover, as I think I could show, it was built up by the use of what we would call scientific logic, while Plato and Aristotle discuss Being with different—and far from scientific—logical tools. We shall have to come back to this more explicitly.

So, after Parmenides the physicist, there emerges another, and even less known, Parmenides the mathematician. Why is it strange? It is, I suggest, because we tend to forget that the Master of Elea was considered among the foremost mathematicians and astronomers of his own time.

Yet Proclus mentions him as the author of that negative definition which suits geometrical principles, and elsewhere he is referred to as having first classified figures into rectilinear, curvilinear and mixtilinear. This may sound an unexciting type of activity, until you find in Pythagorean theory all the profound implications of the one vs. the other kind of figure. Kepler spends a passionate page on that, in the *Mysterium Cosmographicum*, and we may be sure that Parmenides, the disciple of Ameinias, undertook the question in very much the same spirit as Kepler. These interests are a kind of intellectual signature.

In the field of astronomy, Parmenides is said to have taught the division of the sphere of the earth into regions corresponding to the celestial circles marked by equator and tropics, and indeed, if we are to believe Theophrastus, it is *he* and not Pythagoras who first taught that the earth is round. He is also said by Diogenes Laertius to have identified the morning and the evening star as one and the same planet. These could hardly have been called discoveries in one or the other region of the Mediterranean World, but in Greece still under the spell of Ionian Physics, they put Parmenides in the forefront of *mathematikoi*. His contemporaries might well have referred to him, as Socrates says of Timaeus, as "the *astronomikotatos* of us all."

Is it the metric song, the mythographic imagery, that have led critics to overlook the scientific background, in favor of the Hesiodic element? It would be again an error of perspective. Images like the gates of Night and Day are defined unequivocally by archaic precedent. Gates, pillars, *nyssai*, *metae*, *portae solis*, always lead back to solstices and equinoxes. The literary *genre* is a superficial guide. Hesiod hardly belongs to a well-set *genre* anyway. We shall find:

1. That Hesiod has written a poem called *Astronomia*—Callimachus claims that it was the model for Aratus;[4]

2. That Hesiod's "Shield of Heracles" with its concentric zones (I. 314) is a cosmographical item as much as the Homeric one.[5]

[4] Pliny *N.H.* 18,213. I transpose "Astrologia" into "Astronomia," because that is what it meant then.

[5] With the significant difference that the Homeric shield was ordered by Tethys, Hesiod's by Zeus (320) and that the latter shield was used by Heracles in his fight against Mars "in" Cygnus.

3. Furthermore, we may note that this shield is contained in Hesiod's "Catalogue of Women," a precedent to Parmenides' feminized imagery.

Do what we will, whatever the line of descent we prefer, call it Hesiodic epic or *Epimenideslitteratur*, we cannot avoid running into the Royal Art, which bore the seal of the scientific knowledge of the time. It is hardly congruent, then, to have issue from that a writer who derives the whole universe of phenomena as vain illusion, and dispenses instead a world of verbal subtleties.

If we add now to these clues what we have right under our eyes, viz. the astronomy of the Way of Opinion, our conclusion will become bodily evidence. Out of the few mutilated fragments, the same type of commentators which is responsible for its perishing sits now in judgment to pronounce it some kind of cosmological fantasy which cannot be made into a physical system. It is clear that even Aëtius, the lone doxographer to whom we owe a partial summary, did not understand what he was writing down. Yet it is enough to presuppose that a pattern of spherical symmetry must be intended, i.e., that the text must make astronomical sense, and it will fall into place, without even need of the emendation suggested by Diels, with the Daemon not in the various impossible places supposed by commentators, but logically seated at a northern pole, and the "crowns" marking an intricate plaited device of tracks over a wide band of heaven. A physics of a rigid geometrical kind, impossibly rigid to be sure, but still in the nature of a kinematic diagram, exactingly precise, with no animation or animism involved. The astronomy is mechanical and geometrical constraints all through, a kind of graphic vision of laws of nature. We have here a perfect example of what I have called the synoptic capacity of archaic astronomy, which is able to grasp the shifting positions of points of light as a complete path on the sphere.

So much I must ask you to take on faith, since I cannot prove it here. But regardless of details which have perforce to remain conjectural, you can verify its main tenets from the only relevant portion of the text that survives: "The narrower (crowns) are filled with pure fire, and those supporting with night, and between these rushes a portion of fire. In the midst of them is the Daemon that steers the course of all things."

Sufficient Reason

Enough evidence has been collected to place Parmenides in the frame of his own concerns, and to dissociate him from the sophistic group who were to occupy the scene two generations later.

The best evidence, in fact, is afforded by his strongest tool of analysis, which depends for the large part, not on the verbal quibbles to be found in Gorgias and Plato's *Parmenides*, but on the fundamental Principle of Symmetry or Indifference, a form of the Principle of Sufficient Reason. This principle states that symmetrical effects, or more generally, that causes which are indistinguishable intrinsically, when considered by themselves, cannot produce distinguishable effects.

At the dawn of scientific philosophy Anaximander applied the principle of symmetry to explain the immobility of the earth. We might paraphrase the argument by saying that a spherically symmetrical system of forces about the earth could cause only a spherically symmetrical motion in it, which excludes the possibility of its moving as a whole in any one particular direction.

We find a somewhat subtler use of it, applied to time, in Parmenides, fr. 6:

> If (Being) came from nothing, what need could have made it arise later or sooner? Therefore it must exist either altogether or not at all.

That is, the points of time have no distinguishing character *per se* that might enable us to pick one and single it out from all the rest; being placed at a given time and nothing else to make reference to, we cannot tell which point of time it is. Therefore, by the Principle of Indifference, the existence of Being must stand in the same relation to all of them; it must either hold at all of them or at none. To speak metaphorically, if Being wanted to come into existence at a definite time, it would have to be able to tell that time absolutely from all the rest, which is impossible.

It is worth noting here that in Aristotle's universe, so lovingly constructed to minimize mathematical symmetry (for all the points are distinguishable), the case of time is the one case where the conditions for the application of the Principle of Indifference are fulfilled, and there he applies the argument in exactly the same way as Parmenides:

> Moreover, why was it destroyed at this particular point of time rather than any other, when up till now it had always existed, or why generated now, when for an infinite time it had not existed? (*de Caelo* 263 *a*).

In fact the Eternity of the World is one of the few points where he applies classical rationalism. But one must note that his argument takes a secondary place in his exposition.

It is, however, in connection with space that the Principle of Indifference finds its greatest scope, as Parmenides well saw when he made it the fundamental instrument in his logic. Euclidean geometry puts three requirements on its space; first, it must have continuity (in a sense somewhat stronger than the mere absence of gaps between points); second, it must be the same, homogeneous throughout, so that we can move figures freely from place to place without altering their geometrical properties; and finally, it must be isotropic, or the same in all direction, so that figures can be turned around without affecting them. In other words, if you are placed in geometrical space, it must be impossible to tell where you are or in what direction you are looking. In modern terms, we say that Euclidean space is invariant under the continuous three-dimensional translation and rotation groups. In fact, from the last two conditions we can derive the first, because of the continuity of the groups. All this is implied by Euclid's axiom affirming the possibility of superposing any two figures, which is known to date from early time, since geometrical algebra depends on it.

Now it is also true that anything satisfying these three conditions must be isomorphic with and intrinsically indistinguishable from Euclidean space. That is the fundamental reason why, when we find Parmenides stating repeatedly and emphatically that his Being satisfies our three conditions, we conclude that it was in fact the space of the mathematician (and physicist) he had in mind:

A. CONTINUITY

> Discern steadfastly with your mind what is at hand and present and what is distant and absent together. For Being does not divide from its connexion with Being, not although dispersed in arrangement everywhere or compacted. (fr. 4)
> Nor is it separated, since it is all alike, and there is no more anywhere, to prevent it from being continuous, nor lesser, but everything is full of Being. Wherefore it is all continuous; for Being adjoins Being. (fr. 8)
> Nor was it ever, nor will it be, for it exists now, all together, a single continuum.

The argument from the principle of indifference is that the presence of gaps in space destroys its homogeneity, in distinguishing between the "points" and the places between them. For completeness it requires the Zenonian procedure, of actually constructing such places in infinite number by successive division; but given that, it is compelling. It is hard not to see a direct criticism of the Pythagorean theory of space in this passage.

B. HOMOGENEITY

. . . In it are very many tokens that Being is uncreated and indestructible, one all through, whole, unmoveable, and without end.
. . . Nor is it separated, since it is all alike . . .
. . . For Being is not permitted to be incomplete; for it is not in want; while if it were, it would miss being all.
. . . Nor is there Not-Being to prevent it from reaching out to its like, nor is it possible for Being to be more here and less there, because it is all inviolable.

The Pythagorean space does not satisfy this requirement either: the diagonal starting out from one corner does not intersect the other: it meets it "between" points. But the diagonal might have started from the other corner.

C. ISOTROPY

> But since there is an ultimate bound, it is limited on all sides, like the body of a well-rounded sphere, equally poised from the center in all directions; for it is necessary that it should not be greater in one direction and smaller in another . . .
> . . . For it is equal from everywhere, and fits equally in its limits.

In the Pythagorean space there is no isotropy, either; there are preferred directions in the lattice. The course of thought that I have outlined, starting from the problems of the discontinuous, is not a matter of mere inference: it comes clearly to light in frs. 5 and 8 which could hardly be referred to anything except formalized Pythagorean theories of discontinuity:

> Nor is it separated, since it is all alike, and there is no more anywhere, to prevent it from being continuous, nor lesser, but everything is full of Being. Wherefore it is all continuous; for Being adjoins Being.

It is further explicitly confirmed by fr. 4:

> Perceive steadfastly with the mind the far and the near together. For Being does not divide in its connexion with Being, not although dispersed in arrangement everywhere, or brought together.

Logico-verbalists have sweated blood over it. "This mysterious fragment," says Calogero, "of which we still lack a satisfactory interpretation." The most common interpretation, he adds, is the idealistic one, but it is also the most far-fetched. For if we understand, e.g. with Diels, "see how now the far is present to your mind reliably," it is difficult to make sense of the following line: "because Being does not divide from its connexion with Being." Fraenkel, in fact, gives up in despair and suggests that the text must be corrupt. But then, he, Diels, Nestle, and Albertelli understand *νόῳ* as *intellectui* tied up with "far" and "near," which inevitably gives, "what is absent and present to the mind" or some such embarrassing sentence; whereas, omitting prejudice, we have the natural translation *νόωι* = *intellectu*, as appears in Burnet and Reinhardt, and suddenly the line makes sense, not only with itself, but with the next one: "Discern steadfastly with your mind the far and the near together; for Being does not divide from its connexion with Being . . ." Calogero, reasonably enough, sees that this is the only way, and concludes that what is meant in fact is extension and spatial contiguity, whence he promptly concludes:

"It is clear that this aspect, so definitely materialistic, of Parmenidian Being, cannot be but the product of the ontologization of the logical requirement of the absolute indifference of Being; a product all the more characteristic because of the effort and the incongruity from which it issues, of a being in its turn all full of being." Calogero is thus back on his feet again, and the arrested pirouette shows him gracefully holding hands with Gorgias; but Albertelli is left on the ground dizzily protesting, "It makes no sense anyway; for if Being does not divide in its connexion from Being, this is no reason for the far to be near."

The difficulty for idealistic interpreters is revealing. We are here at *the* parting of the ways in the history of thought. We perceive the deviation that Aristotle later inflicted on already established terms for his own purposes. His objects of thought are not in nature, they are in an order of discourse constructed on nature. This is how he understands the "unchangeable entities" which are to be the object of understanding and wisdom. It is the discourse which is the ultimate end, for it is supposed to reflect in some way that of the Active Intellect with itself in its eternal process; and that is where the Good is too, which reflects itself down into the articulation of the Discourse. Hence what Aristotle is seeking is not knowledge as we would mean it, but a regularization of the grammatical categories whereby the discourse may flow on in good order, each predicative sentence interlocking with the others in the proper distinction, coordination and context.

But we are here at the point before Plato, where, if the past had to be dropped, the future was still entirely undecided.

Surely, the high abstraction cannot have come in one move to a man thinking in 480 B.C., when everyone before him had been thinking of an organ of the mind that goes by correspondence of similars. Parmenides must have started in his youth from such an assumption, and something of it seems to stick in his ideas about the relation of mind and body. We must not forget that every true naturalistic mind, so long as it was spared the wringer of modern nominalism, has always instinctively assumed what Goethe expressed so well in his own unphilosophical way: "Man knows himself only insofar as he knows the world, of which he can be aware only in himself, as he can be aware of himself only in the world. Each new object, rightly considered, opens up a new organ of perception in us."

Parmenides can no longer understand this in the simple way of imagining a physical super-eye which can see "into the more subtle," the actual grain of things. He has gone beyond it, for he is looking for "that which holds it all together . . ." And this implies no longer visualizing, but an *abstract* representation.

We might say that whereas his predecessors had been projecting symbols of eternity in their element, or life-stuff, or monad, or the like, Parmenides has reached the point where he has to try and project the abstract frame of eternity itself; but such an insight requires a new way of reaching it, a new method; and therein lies his fateful originality. His continuum cannot be visualized as an object; it is of the nature of the mind itself, it is identical to νοεῖν what the mind does. Hence, says Aristotle, Parmenides is the first to speak of the One "according to reason," and he undeniably prepares the ground for the Platonic abstraction.

This, the conversion point in which Truth and Being become interchangeable, contains in itself all future developments of speculative thought. They are not distinct as yet, and can be confused *in fieri* with dangerous ease. But Hegel is quite right in seeing here the transition from the stage of *Vorstellung* to the stage of *Begriff*. This is the illumination which answers the doubts of Xenophanes.

This concept involves no measures, no magnitude, no places, no "great-and-small." Nothing but relations, all-the-relations-there is. It is that new intellectually dazzling Thing, the three-dimensional extension pure and simple. Whenever the mind meets it, as it were, for the first time, it experiences that metaphysical seizure which manifests itself in ontological declarations. It happened again in the seventeenth century: Henry More, Spinoza, Malebranche, Newton himself, express in several ways this ontological experience born of Cartesian space. Says Henry More in the language of his times:

> It is necessary that, because it is a real attribute, some real subject support this extension. This argumentation is so solid that there is none that could be stronger. . . . When we shall have enumerated those names and titles appropriate to it, this infinite, immobile, extended entity will appear to be not only something real but something Divine (which so certainly is found in nature): this will give us further assurance that it cannot be nothing since that to which so many and so magnificent attributes pertain cannot be nothing. Of this kind are the following, such as: One, Simple, Immobile, Eternal, Complete, Independent, Existing in Itself, Subsisting by Itself, Incorruptible, Necessary, Immense, Uncreated, Uncircumscribed, Incomprehensible, Omnipresent, Incorporeal, All-penetrating, All-embracing, Being by its essence, Actual Being, Pure Act.

Some imp would drive one to remark that many such honorific and capitalized adjectives have been often wasted to confer existence on what turned out to be nothing much. But we must sternly repress it. This is the genuine metaphysical experience that can arise out of space conceived as a substrate of all reality, and Henry More's words, as they refer unbeknownst to that very selfsame Eleatic Being, can give us an idea of what Parmenides experienced in the way of intellectual illumination.

There is no doubt that in using this grid everything falls into place. The enumeration of the properties of Being implacably pressing in on the reader of the poem is in no need of the groping justifications worked out by the critics.[6] Fr. 8 does not need a labored exegesis such as we have found in the work. It comes out conceptually as it does from the literary aspect—a single bloc of affirmation poured from the central idea.

"Being" or "that which is," cannot be real, it is a plenum. It is extended, "like unto a sphere" in its intrinsic symmetry. But if it is by itself a plenum, and all of "real body" (we must put these words between strong quotation marks, but they have to be there, for what the senses add is only phenomenological, Light and Night), it is also indistinguishable from isotropic space. A strange kind of "body" indeed, devoid of all concreteness. It might be more adherent to this stage of ideation not to call it "real body" but "body-of-my-thought"; body of Truth, body of reality; not Being, but "Be-er."

Is this, then, the "Truth"? The poem answers with imperatorial absolutism that it is, for no other way is thinkable. Non-Being is "not to be spoken of," for it is, in the strictest sense, nowhere. Being is the same as to say it is. But from this stratospheric peak of logical immediacy there is no going backward; no, nor forward either, except in mathematical theory. In all directions around this point there is an abyss. We can see why young Socrates brings up his question in the beginning of the *Parmenides*: If this is the only point of Truth, or shall we say the one Idea—do we not have an impassable *chorismos*, a separation, between the world and ideas, so that the living mind cannot cross it to reach the ideas, but neither can the gods from there understand the world? Where can be found a *methexis*? How is that very moment of abstraction guaranteed whereby we found the One?

We can put it in our own words, by asking whether this is really an object of the mind's apprehension, and then which is the relation? Or the mind itself, and then surely the mind can proceed further on its own, but where is the object? We have no organ that can be imagined as grasping Being. This is indeed the first time in which thinking has to mean "being aware" in an explicitly different sense than that of perceiving or imagining through *φαντασία*. Taken all at once, the gradient is impassable, it frightens young Socrates into suggesting infinite regression (134a).

There is in our language and our civilization a long experience, going from an implicit and half-realized acceptance of a transcendence between knower and known to modern positivistic resignation, which cushions the impact of such thoughts; but

[6] e.g., Loenen, p. 100: "A much graver problem (is) the question why Parmenides devotes so many additional lines (up to l. 21) to these two attributes (*ἀγένετον καὶ ἀνώλεθρον*)."

to someone living in the fifth century B.C. they well may have been, as is said in Plato, of the kind that will allow a man no peace. Gorgias had shrewdly chosen the subject for his *succès de scandale*.

But—please—let us remember the very real problem which had motivated the quest. Allow me to go back to my *Origins of Scientific Thought* (pp. 96–99):

The great concern for science had been to find the common substrate of all things, the One that unifies the Many. The Pythagoreans had suggested that the substrate is Numbers, that is: points having position. These points, Limit placed in Unlimit, it had been concluded, were the origin and as it were the substance of things. But here begins the difficulties with a doctrine still eminently poetic and magical. What is the single monad but a repetition of identity? Unlimit had been assigned the role of a field, or filling, but it carried within it all the determination of limit, since it was the field of all positions. The Pythagoreans had thought of the power of Number and Limit in a kind of imaginative intuition, but on the very grounds of arithmogeometry the representation would hardly stand scrutiny, because, clearly, it is Unlimit which is the bearer of Position, and hence of Limit. Any logical thought on the idea of number brings forth a continuum underlying it. The Pythagorean School had taken its dualism without investigating it too deeply. But its mathematicians had to.

We know what happened to Pythagorean "number atomism." In the reduction of geometry to numbers, the expression of all the geometric magnitudes which come up in the theory of proportion necessitated a common unit to measure them all that became smaller and smaller. The universal common measure had to shrink to a smallness indeed beyond measure, and yet it had to remain a unit: an uncertain kind of *actual infinitesimal*. Such is the new monad. But the difficulties of defining the line as a row of pebbles remain, however far we shrink the pebbles. Either each monad is separated from next by a tract of Unlimit, or it is not. Either conclusion leads to sacrificing a part of the doctrine. We can sacrifice the discreteness of units, or we can sacrifice precision. A wrongness will remain. Limit and Unlimit are crowded together at every point.

It is curious to note that the Pythagorean movement, which had aimed from the beginning at discovering the principle of form in nature, should have wrecked itself on a rock so much like the one the Ionians had struck. To have order, harmony, and form in the world presupposed a formal substratum which should have no form itself, but be the bearer of all form, exactly as the hydrodynamic universe of the Ionians had been a quest for a material substratum which should be sufficiently neutral in its own intrinsic properties to be modifiable into all the kinds of matter in the world.

It was Parmenides, standing at the confluence of the two traditions, who realized that the two problems were in fact one. The true conception of geometrical space, once formed, is equally well adapted to serve as a substratum for physical form, in view of its rigidity and impassibility, and for matter, if one adopts a view of matter which transforms it into an accidental and contingent property of the space it "occupies." That was the course taken by Parmenides, and later by Newton. It is not surprising that he should have ascribed such a master stroke to the inspiration of the deity. As was natural for one trained primarily as a Pythagorean, it was probably their form of the problem, the analysis of the continuum, which led him to his discovery. That continuum fulfills, then, the same role as the Anaximandrean Unbounded[7]—and also as the Pythagorean numbers. It can no longer be visualized as a great Flow with its eddies, or as points of light in space radiating power. There is nothing to visualize in this kind of substrate; what we put there in imagination falls apart into points, and so on without end, until it becomes clear that what we have to comprehend is the texture, which is that of the continuum. "Grasp firmly with thy mind the near and the far together. . . ." This is truly the "Be-er" (*Eon*, a grammatical construction very similar to that of "filler") since it permeates all things and bears their properties. We have not been able to locate the Many in any "trustworthy" way, and the conclusion is that there are not many separate points of space but only the One. We have moved out of the magic of numbers and entered the realm of pure logical Necessity.

What Parmenides thought he could do to make his position unassailable was to formalize it so as to force total assent from the start. This was later to be the way of the metaphysician. Spinoza asks us to accept the conception of the All, and to deduce consequences therefrom. Parmenides asks: "Would you deny that Being is?" We can not know at that point what is the "Being" he has in mind, hence later ontologists have been tempted again and again to see in it the pure verb *is* of the grammatical copula. The deduction from there can proceed only on the logico-verbal plane. But neither does Descartes, in his *Discourse on Method*, make it clear at the start that his procedure of enumerating and subdividing, by which he hopes to solve all and any difficulty, is described with simple geometrical operations in mind. From all that we have seen, this would seem to be the case with Parmenides.

In that newly conceived continuum, all of mathematics has its native heath and its abode. To it belong the surfaces, lines, figures, numbers, proportions and relations that the mind can bring forth. The realm of Truth is that of mathematics in its amplest formulation as our time has brought it forth: the domain of all the possibilities of rigorous thought. It is unalterable and unmoving, but the mind moves freely in it, for it is of the mind itself. It contains the life of reason. It *is*, even as reason *is*. Such is the true world beyond sense, whose existence has been revealed to Parmenides by something he felt to be divine inspiration.

There is, of course, for us, the difficulty that it is described as a sphere "resting within its bounds." The difficulty persists in whatever interpretation; in fact, the more "unspatial" the worse. But the statements are quite compatible with a sphere imagined

[7] I am glad to note that Klaus Reich has come in, as I have noted earlier, to suggest that the logical origin for the One lies in Anaximander's substrate, but seen as bound and packed in the Bonds of Necessity.

as stretching as far as the mind will go, i.e., of infinite radius, and I am pleased to see that Calogero from the other side comes to agree with me on this. The image of the sphere would then express isotropy ("the same in all directions") as opposite to the uncharacterized Unbounded of Anaximander. And it seems singularly true, thinking of a dense continuum which is "all limit" at every point, that if it lacked a limit it would lack everything.

We should note that Parmenides did not use the already current *peras* for Limit, but the somewhat archaic *peiras*, which indicated "texture" and "design" more than mere "boundary." However it may be, we are following logic into a difficult situation that Parmenides did not have the means to solve. If we have to stand undeviatingly on the principle that the *pampalaioi* did not use reason differently from us, we must still take distance into account. Nor should we try to simplify Parmenides' thought until it meets ours. Or is it ours? More than considerable doubts concerning an infinite kosmos occurred to Kepler and Galileo, for whom yet infinite space was a matter of course. Too few of those doubts came to our Newtonian scientists before they found themselves confronted in our time with Einstein's space and Olbers' Paradox. It is better respectfully to let Parmenides stand there bestriding the unknown—*Achille immobile à grands pas.*

Let us see, finally, how the two parts of the poem complement each other.

Men, caught in the flux of time, themselves part of phenomena, cannot set their life in timeless Truth which is beyond them. They must cope with events and "give them a name," it is a solemn legislative act similar to the foundation of a city. The gods of the city, Parmenides' whole theological position implies, are no less relative, yet they should be considered valid gods. We have to build our own world, we are only asked to *know* what its relation is to the "true faith," and then it becomes wholly legitimate. A very Eleatic character of our time, the man who set up again the Continuum as a substrate of reality—I mean Albert Einstein—has stated it concisely: "If it is certain, it is not physics. If it is physics, it is not certain." Let me talk here in modern terms. Metamathematics, the foundation of the Continuum (Leibniz calls it the Labyrinth of the Continuum) is that on which mathematics itself is founded. Seen from there, the world of physics, that which "takes place" in the Continuum, receives its metaphysical justification. These ought to be the proper terms to talk of these things, since an ethics is engendered therefrom, a clear if one-sided vision of Freedom and Fate.

The Geometer who lays down a theorem partakes at that moment of freedom absolute. He does not aim at sharing or persuading; the Other, and be it his listener, does not exist. Yet he will generate that same freedom in the Other who shares his truth. And the ancient paradox is, that man is free in that he knows himself in the "bonds of Mighty Necessity." That is the way of the gods. But then he must turn to and assume his burden as man among men, he must take on his share of the common relativity, he must be a legislator, a historian, a physicist. He must accept to become a phenomenon, subject to coming-into-being and passing away, to what is positively and implacably decreed, the *stygeron*. His absolute claims are as nil. But he will "receive" (*doxa*) as well as give. The order of his words may be sheer opinion but he will know the power of prestige and persuasion. "Of these things," says the Goddess, "I tell you the whole profitable disposition, in order that no mortal may surpass you in knowledge." His explanation may be valid, in that it brings coherence. The order that sound opinion affirms in the flux of reality is a durable good: things have accepted from man "the seal of a name."

And so at last, man the phenomenon will find himself "at home" (that so significant Greek expression) in a world of phenomena.

These, in sketchy outline, are the reasons that I suggest for restoring Parmenides to the world of science without removing him from metaphysics. There would be much more to say before the ground can be considered clear. I have concentrated on the specifically geometrical fragments. I have not attempted to establish the link of Parmenides with Melissus, nor, further, the filiation of thought which makes of the Eleatics the fountainhead of Sophistic logic. That a new concern with the possibilities of pure reasoning runs through this line is undeniable. The word-play of Zeno is the fateful point when words begin to veer away from the central concern with the kosmos, and to live a life of their own. Inside the Eleatic school itself, there is evidence that some very reckless experimenting went on with the possibilities of the newly discovered verbal instrument, and here we might find the legitimate source of Plato's *Parmenides*. But if the enterprise wandered off into eristics, it also led to Bryson. It was the most adventurous moment of Greek thought, the freest adventure, and it would seem the greatest hope. What the men of those generations saw in the promise of the Goddess is surely incommunicable. All true metaphysical experiences are. By linking the realm of geometry with that of the "logos that is spoken," Parmenides provided a complex of meanings as rich as that of Herakleitos, but lending itself to rigorous deduction at all levels. Nothing in modern thought can provide more than a pale image of that wealth of living meaning: only Plato can show us what a contemporary could hope of it, and in that sense, if in that sense only, his exegesis is valid. For us, dealing with the autopsy of what is no longer an overwhelming truth, the anatomy of logic shows a clear distinction. The logic of the Eleatics is so guided by their object of contemplation as to remain scientifically impeccable; that of their successors is not, and we must assume that the object has changed. On this we rest our case.

We shall get nowhere near Descartes, rather, we shall transform him into the usual caricature of schoolbooks, so long as we do not grasp the *Cogito* for what it is, not a thought but the creative act of the will which discovers at one stroke God, the soul and the real world. It is the act which equates man to eternity. In the same way, for the same reason, we shall lose Parmenides into a set of "Beiträge" to technical philosophy, if we do not grasp his *diakosmos*. It is a word more ancient than "system" and considerably better. The kosmos is of the essence, and if you talk about it you have to be a *physikos*. Idealism, ontology, pure logic are at best consequences, roads taken by others with other aims than his. The two ways of his poem are one whole, needing one another. There is a way of Necessity which is Freedom, there is a way of Law which is uncertainty, limitation, choice, decision, what men can *do*. The kingpin is still archaic Myth, in the figure of the Daemon. The whole structure breaks asunder if we take that figure as a rhetorical device, which is also not good method in any case, since Aristotle would remind us crisply that rhetoric had not yet been invented. The discursive metaphysics of Plato, that first of the moderns, gives itself leeway, built as it is on language, but it is no longer that diamond-hard, impregnable thing based on metamathematics. That is why Plato's *Parmenides* is no good witness to the thought of the Master of Elea; and Socrates talking familiarly with Theaetetus is much more to the point when he modestly admits: "I fear we do not understand him any too well."

II: "Venus Will Now Say a Few Words"

I HOPE I MAY BE FORGIVEN, IF I BORROW FOR THIS LECTURE THE title from a poem by W. H. Auden, which to me is one of the few proofs that modern science is not incompatible with poetic expression.

> . . . That sense of famine, central anguish felt
> For goodness wasted at peripheral fault,
> Your shutting up the house and taking prow
> To go into the wilderness to pray,
> Means that I wish to leave and to pass on,
> Select another form, perhaps your son;
> Though he reject you, join opposing team
> Be late or early at another time,
> My treatment will not differ—he will be tipped,

Found weeping, signed for, made to answer, topped.
Do not imagine you can abdicate;
Before you reach the frontier you are caught;
Others have tried it and will try again
To finish that which they did not begin . . .

In this case the situation is old: man facing nature's harshness in the same timeless context. The power that Mr. Auden brings forward on the scene for a few crisp pitiless statements is surely not the Queen of Heaven, Lady of Truth and Rigor, who appeared in Parmenides' Proem. But she is the other aspect of the Second Part, the Force of Becoming, the ruler of this world, a surely more necessary presence than Lucretius' *Alma Venus*, for Epicurus would not need her but Darwin does: she is exactly Parmenides' dreadful Daemon Lady, the *δαίμων ἣ πάντα κυβερνᾷ,* who now "steers" evolutionary change.

Having once been introduced to this far-from-insignificant Lady through the poem of Parmenides, I realized how often I had met her.

In the catechism for Akousmatics, which belongs to the oldest tradition of the Pythagorean school, we find a number of the "secret names" of things which refer to her: "What are the Bears? They are the Hands of Rhea." "What are the planets? They are the Dogs of Persephone."

The variety of names emphasizes her different aspects. But the hands of Rhea—why they are the very hands of the Daimon of Parmenides, as she keeps the heavens revolving and sends all things to their fate. One sees her turning the celestial sphere by way of those shining handles. So much was clear to me long ago. It was only much later that I learned that those two, the Great and Little Bear, were quite literally the handles of heaven in archaic astronomy. Ursa Major was the key constellation embodying the planets in her seven chief stars; whichever power at a given age held her, held the heavens.[1] She is the Chariot from which Zeus threw Kronos when he succeeded him in the rulership, and it is a relic from far-distant times when we hear that the Norse Kings still held their investiture "from the power of the Bear," although the plumb-line from the Pole to the equinoctial point had long since shifted from the Seven Stars owing to the Precession. Ursa, so to speak, was the great hand on the dial of the year, she was the minute hand while Ursa Minor marked the great hours of the Precession, which stretched each over thousands of years.

Curiously enough, as we all know, the Little Bear was known as Kynosoura, the Tail of the Dog. How many times have we

[1] We still have the ritual formulae spoken by Pharaoh when he staked out the foundations of a temple: "I have seized the peg. I take the measuring line. . . . I observe the progressing motion of the stars. My eye is fixed on the Great-Bear. I count the Time, I check the clock, I establish the corners of my sanctuary." (Brugsch translation).

spoken of cynosures without wondering why this bear should become a dog's tail. But the figure of the Dog is elusive and ubiquitous. It has to do not only with Sirius, but also with the pole of the Ecliptic, with which the Little Bear was associated. While Alcor the Fox sits just above zeta of Ursa Major, she who was once Electra the Pleiad before the fall of Troy. . . . I cannot go now into this prodigious saga of dogs, wolves, coyotes, jackals, foxes *and* their twin brothers, which spring at us from all sides of the archaic jungle of heaven. The tale of Reynard the Fox is only a small chapter of it. I hope our distinguished colleague Dr. von Dechend, the indefatigable searcher, will soon give us some bearings to go by in this primeval landscape. It looks, if I may speak out already, like the most intricate and dynamic symbolism ever devised to do justice both to exactly timed phenomena and to a great eschatological myth. I cannot even indicate it here. Suffice it to say that there is good reason why the planets should be the Hounds of Persephone.

Here are already two different names given to the goddess, but it has been known since ever that they expressed different attributes of the archaic earth-and-sky goddess, called also Hera, Artemis, and other names. Still another name we have met with already—Aphrodite Ourania. From a Pythagorean list of deities we learn something of her role, and it is there also we learn of the great importance of the number Five which belongs to her. She was identified by Rivaud as the same as Parmenides' goddess. There is a list of attributes many lines long concerning her in Nicomachus. We find *ζωναῖα* among others—the Lady of the Girdle—also *κυκλιοῦχος*, owner of the circle, and *ἀξονεδραία*, restored by Delatte, "Steadfast Axis." This makes a fairly consistent set of attributes for the ruler of heavenly revolutions. We retain that her symbol was Five, or the pentagon, whether plain or stellate, the classic Pentalpha.

Why? Plato will answer us. In the *Timaeus* 53C–55B he tells us first about the four elements, requiring the construction of four polyhedra. Then he adds:

> There still remained one construction, the fifth;
> and the god used it for the whole, making a pattern
> of animal figures thereon (*diazographon*).

Cornford (*Plato's Cosmology*, p. 219) explains: "Not requiring a dodecahedron with plane faces for any primary body, the Demiurge 'uses it for the whole'; i.e. for the sphere, to which this figure approaches most nearly in volume, as Timaeus Locrus remarks."[2]

Plato's brevity is rather puzzling. He has dealt amply with the construction of the pyramid (tetrahedron), the octahedron, the

[2] Cf. A. E. Taylor: *A Commentary on Plato's Timaeus* (Oxford, 1928), 377, *Timaeus Locrus* 98e.

icosahedron and the cube; follows the quoted sentence, and off he goes inquiring into the plurality of worlds.

Two points are clearly omitted: a) why should the dodecahedron be used as the frame of the whole; b) why should that frame not be the sphere, whose fitness and nobility (*τὸ πρέπον καί τὸ συγγενές*) has been mentioned already at 33B? We are left with the impression that the Demiurge had one figure left over, and that he did not know what to do with it otherwise. This is a little too disingenuous even for a myth.

Plutarch tries to fill the gap with his questionings:

> . . . is their opinion true who think that he ascribed
> a dodecahedron to the globe, when he says that God
> made use of it in delineating the universe? For
> upon account of the multitude of its bases and the
> obtuseness of its angles, avoiding all
> rectitude, it is flexible, and by circumtension,
> like globes made of twelve skins, it becomes
> circular and comprehensive. For it has twenty
> solid angles, each of which is contained by three
> obtuse planes, and each of these contains one and
> the fifth part of a right angle. Now it is made
> up of twelve equilateral and equiangular quinquangles
> (or pentagons), each of which consists of thirty of
> the first scalene triangles. Therefore it seems to
> resemble both the Zodiac and the year, it being
> divided into the same number of parts as these.[3]

Taylor comments on this dodecahedron with its twelve regular pentagons:[4] "Timaeus does not describe its construction. (Is it just a touch of Pythagorean 'reserve'?)." He answers himself in a footnote: "Perhaps not. His reason for silence may be that he does not know how to construct a pentagon by placing pairs of similar triangles *κατὰ διάμετρον*, a thing which, in fact, obviously cannot be done." Considering that Hippasos was excommunicated just because he had revealed "the construction of the sphere with twelve pentagons," and Plato's reverential attitude towards the Pythagoreans, we need "perhaps" not look for such far-fetched reasons.

Like Plutarch, Proclus, etc., Taylor refers of course, to the *Phaedo* (110 B 6) which

> compares the spherical *earth* with
> balls made by sewing 12 pieces of leather together.
> The pieces of leather would be pentagonal, and, if
> leather were inelastic, the ball would be a dodecahedron;
> owing to the elasticity of leather it can be inflated
> until it is sensibly spherical. Plutarch saw there
> an allusion to the twelve zodia of the Zodiac. This

[3] *Qu. Plat.*, Question 5.1 (1003C).

[4] Taylor, 377, quoting Euclid: *Element.*, XI def. 28: a solid figure composed of 12 equal pentagons with equal sides and equal angles.

> is out of the question as these constellations form a circular band, but the twelve angular points of the dodecahedron inscribed in a sphere do not lie on any such band. Plutarch seems to suppose that the angular points of a regular solid are all in the same plane: Presumably he confused the dodecahedron with a dodecagon in a circle.

I have quoted at some length Taylor's analysis because I feel it shows how easy it is for coldly critical scholarship, even in such a great scholar as Taylor, to defeat itself. A certain Pythagorean reserve is perceived by the philosophical historian; it is hastily withdrawn in a note suggesting an implausible alternative. In the next step, finding a difficulty in Plutarch, he goes so far as to suggest that he confused the dodecahedron with a dodecagon, and imagined that the angular points of a regular dodecahedron are all in the same plane. This is pretending to play croquet with flamingoes. Plutarch is not even one of those archaic thinkers of whom it is rather lightheartedly granted that they lived in a state of perpetual confusion. He was a well-schooled gentleman of Hellenistic culture, and for all his journalistic temperament, a very serious scholar indeed. Rather than dismiss his text as nonsense, it would be better method to keep an open mind about a possible meaning, as Burnet did. We shall now try again, reverting for a start to that *diazographon*, and to what Plutarch adds: "It seems to resemble both the Zodiac and the year."

And to begin with, let us accept resolutely the idea of a "Pythagorean reserve" on the part of Plato. Once you begin to ponder about the dodecahedron with its constituents, its symmetries, its almost-sphericality, you come gradually to understand that *if* mathematical cosmology was deemed classified information at all, then Hippasos' punishment was deserved, and a needed public example.

Behind that Twelve there is a Five, and again, we shall not pass it over as one of those oddities of the mystical mentality that need not be explained, the more so, as it ties up with another oddment, the Pentagram as emblem of the sect. It was supposed, as you know, to stand for the Tetraktys, which is "the root and source of all being," and why, as Lucian wryly remarked, should the Five stand for a Four which is a Three?

When I wrote a book three years ago about the "Origins of Scientific Thought" and had to deal with the Pythagorean system, I could do no more than state the privileged position of the pentagram, and connect it with certain well-known properties, like the presence of the Golden Section throughout, and its links with musical theory. One could figure out other arithmological reasons, but none of them seemed decisive. I still lacked a satisfactory motive for that particular privileged position. I felt sure that the true reason must ultimately be connected with the heavens and I had not forgotten Nicomachus' allusions, but they looked to me far too "mystical" to be taken into account. The prudent critical attitude was the Mighty Necessity which restrained me in its bonds.

Last year, as we were looking into the records of quite other civilizations East and West, we fell to thinking about the insistent recurrence of the eight-year cycle in so many inscriptions and seal cylinders. Dr. Hinze set up for us a chart of the heliacal risings of Venus as morning star over the cycle, and lo, here was the image that Venus drew of herself, a fiery pentagram staked out in eight years along the Zodiac. The figure was almost impeccable, rotating only 2.4 degrees at each successive cycle. Of course, the same pentagon will be given by the planet as evening star—in fact, any synodic position we choose will give it with the proper shift of phase. Anyone could have formed it who had let his curiosity run along Pythagorean lines.

Still later, we found that the diagram had been published by Dr. Manfred Knapp in 1934.[5] Knapp had been inspired by the uninhibited Pythagorean imagination of Johann Kepler, and taken as his model the famous Keplerian time diagram of the Great Conjunction (Fig. 1), where we see the Fiery Trigon (as it was called) formed by successive conjunctions of Jupiter and Saturn slowly shifting on the circle until it closes a complete cycle in 860 years. He tried the same with Venus, and got the pentagram—that is here reproduced. (Fig. 2)

What ancient soul could have resisted this vision? Here is the portrait of the Daimon, a time image of her motion limned in the skies for such as have eyes to see.

Surely, not modern eyes. Knapp's diagram was ignored—at least I had never heard of it until 1960, nor, apparently, did the professional historians of ancient astronomy, who had so expertly and ingeniously interpreted the numbers of the Babylonians. Perhaps the poet was right: *Ne Babylonios temptaris numeros. . . .* Those numbers take your mind away from the arresting moments of geometric fantasy.

What are numbers in the traditional Pythagorean statement? "Points having position." An oracular word. For what gives them position? Here, I felt, I had found one physical meaning of these strange cosmogonic images which leave us wondering. Those points of light in the darkness which cause other points of light to appear in positions prearranged, according to angles dedicated to the several gods—this was no longer an arbitrary fantasy. For this point of light in heaven, shifting position by itself, causing the pentagram to flash forth in the order of time, *was* the physical image. That image had been known and worshipped for many ages. It had now acquired full significance.

[5] *Pentagramma Veneris*, Basel, 1934, that we traced through being quoted in F. C. Endres, *die Zahl in Mystik und Glauben der Kulturvölker, Zürich*, 1935.

We have too often thought of the Pythagoreans as simple-minded. We liked to picture archaic gentlemen like Eurytos arranging pebbles somewhat after the manner of esthetic station-masters in our own time, and forgot how even the *psephismata* could go far and wild in inference. The musical theory is very far from simple. The simple spatial arrangement can tell us little. It gives the bare bones. It is time which is of the essence, represented by that key word, *kairos*. Our image of the pentagram in the sky will tell us how position was divinely given by the order of time, and how points having position could be imagined as generating things in their turn. Time, it has been known from ever, brings all things. But time means essentially rhythm.

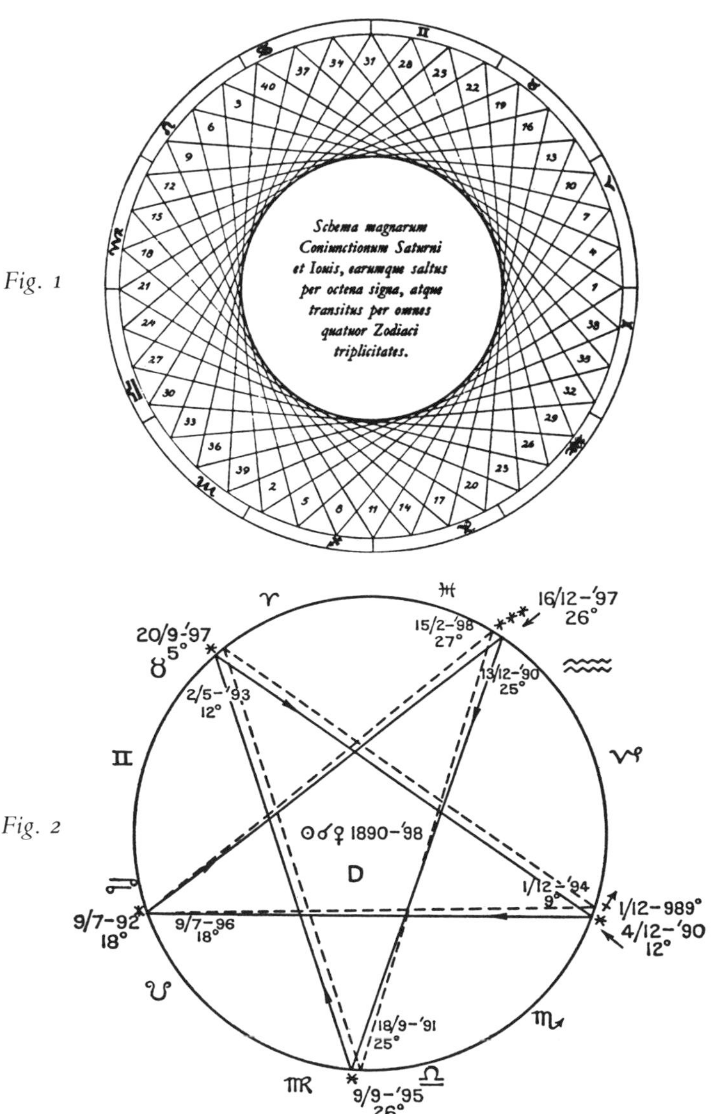

Fig. 1

Fig. 2

Pythagorean theory does not start from notions casually associated. It has a strong conceptual structure which gives meaning to the word "things are numbers"; and however much successive Congresses of the Party may have revised the General Line, as we would say today, the interpretation rests on a firmly held spatiotemporal complex. Time was the preponderant component.

It is to it that we owe the fundamental pattern of our classical physics, based on periodicities. The astronomical model of reality—points without extension in a field of central forces, interacting by oscillation and revolution—has remained central throughout Newtonian mechanics. The continuity of thought is undoubted. Yet, for us moderns, the original complex of thought is very far away. Bergson would remind us that we place rhythm, and the intuition that goes with it, off bounds for our clear awareness, and think in terms of pure amorphous space: "Nous découpons l'espace selon le pointillé de notre action." It is not easy then to fit back into ancient schemes. We see a planet as a point changing positions in the sky, or think of it more abstractly as a track or an orbit. We do not visualize it both synoptically and rhythmically as a fivefold apparition "drawing" a pentagram in its tempo. There is a change in the way of seeing which cuts us off from archaic astronomy.

The space-time complex projects two areas of mathematizable reality, music and the "dance" of planets. The space factor in either is given by the *sectio canonis* and by positional astronomy, the essential factor remaining rhythm: both projections converge in the Harmony of the Spheres. In the complex, Time is firmly set and normative, it gives the *kairos*; space is transformable, it gives room for mapping and symbolism. In the case of our planet, Five will give the original meaning, expressed in the orbital plane by the pentagram, but that five is expressed no less in the "sphere of twelve pentagons." This figure, too, was known as a cult object long before it could be geometrically constructed, as we know from many specimens found all over Europe. It was the three-dimensional image, the frame whereby that same power enfolded the cosmos.

May we then dissent from A. E. Taylor? Plutarch was not talking nonsense. The time-command of the deity over the zodiacal belt, which gives her the name *zonaia*, becomes distributed over the heavens three-dimensionally according to the symmetry of the dodecahedron, and the whole body will appear *diazographomenon*, "inscribed all over with figures."

Once the figure is important, all of its properties are, according to the principle of cosmic inherence.

Let us review some of those properties, beginning with the most obvious, that $12 \times 5 = 60$, the basic unity and unit per se (and the highest "god" Anu) in Cuneiform texts.

There are 30 edges, 20 solid angles, and "360 elements which are produced when each pentagon is divided into 5 isosceles triangles and each of the latter into 6 scalene triangles."

After numbers, intervals. Consider the "golden section," says Burnet:[6] in the scholion on Euclid II, 11 (vol. 5., p. 249, Heiberg) we have what appears to be a Pythagorean way of expressing this. This problem, we are told, "is not to be exhibited by means of pebbles" (**οὐ δείκνυται διὰ ψήφων**). That golden section, as we know, appears as fundamental in the pentagram. It gives the proportion between the two halves of each leg and the whole. Irrationality is thus the kind of essence that is brought under control in the figure.

We might compare to this "problem" the immense efforts of harmonic theory to divide the octave, with its 12 half-steps, into equal parts (stumbling block: the fifth) not only in Antiquity, but in the very same manner in China. The golden section gives for the relevant numbers:

5: 3,1 8: 4,9 12: 7,4 13: 8,0

Does it not look as if the very construction of the dodecahedron by pentagrams, revealed by the "traitor" Hippasos, were meant to give away the whole system? We, as geometric "spacers," are naturally fascinated by the regular "body" without minding the time dimension, although Plato talks enough about time in the *Timaeus*—but even there he does not disclose the moments which really "count": Timaeus ceases to be communicative after having dealt with those times which are produced by Sun and Moon.

What Taylor considers to be "out of the question" turns out to be the case. He is apparently too rigid for the special kind of abstract imagination which distinguished Pythagorean thought: The dodecahedron is a "projection" of time-units into space.

There would be more to say, but I think we have a fairly coherent description of this divine figure, whose dodecahedral "sphere" enfolds the cosmos, and whose name, as we have stated already, is Aphrodite Ourania.

She presents herself here not as a person, not as a "Thou," not even as a force, but as a polyhedron, Pythagorean manner, for she is not so much a force, as an ordering principle.

Once we have her in our sights, we shall discover easily that in her various guises she is a lady of intercontinental standing. It is the figure of the pre-Hellenic, pre-Hesiodic celestial queen of the Ancient Near East: Ishtar/Dilbat. "*Orbis totius alma Venus*" is indeed the Lady of Many Names: from astrological cuneiform tablets we know 31 of these names—she may have had many more; nor was her repertory here and there too different.

If it be felt that I am moving with too much unconcern from

[6] *Greek Philosophy* (London, 1950), 55.

one to the other side of the Mediterranean in the search for "precedents," I should perhaps remind you of a certain historical frame which has never been in fact denied, but is growing ever clearer in the light of contemporary research. It was in a sense ignored by the classical, humanist tradition which took the uniqueness of the Greeks for granted; it still may make certain Hellenic specialists unhappy: but since Frazer revealed once and for all to us the submerged mass of the iceberg, many new data have come to show us the intrinsic links of Greek culture with the Near East, especially in the time that preceded the Persian invasion. Herodotus, being a classic, was himself under no classicist delusion; and when today Neugebauer shows Pythagorean geometry to have sprung directly from Babylonian algebra, he only redefines something which was always accepted by the Pythagorean tradition.

As concerns the goddess figures of Greece and the Orient, we have a morphological test to prove that they are indeed one and the same personage. I shall submit two famous texts in conjunction, whose authenticity has never been doubted. The first is from Pherecydes' *Theogony*, recovered in one of the Grenfell-Hunt papyri. It concerns the wedding of Zas and Chthonie. Three days after the marriage, Zas makes a robe, large and fair, and on it he embroiders Earth and Ogenos. He addresses Chthonie as his wife, saying: "In my desire that your marriage should exist, I honor you with this gift." Whence (it is said in another fragment) "Chthonie acquired the name Ge (Earth) because Zas gives her Earth as a (wedding) present." There is no conflict here with Hesiod, Zas is simply a different (Orphic?) name for Ouranos; but an important new feature is added. It is the mantle that Dionysus/Ouranos gave Ariadne, the Mantle of Hypsipyle.

So much for the Greek side.

The other text is a bilingual one, Sumerian and Babylonian, first published by Thureau-Dangin. We give it in Ebeling's translation:[7] "After Anu, the king, had determined on the exaltation of Innin, had bestowed on her the temple Eanna, his holy mansion, he covered her form with the mantle of divine royalty, the splendor of shining heaven. . . ."

The text is, of course, a thousand years older, but the ceremony and the characters are the same. Anu is the primeval divine principle like the Egyptian Atum. He is written in cuneiform with one wedge = 1 or 60. Ishtar/Innin becomes the Heaven-and-Earth deity by being decked with the starry mantle of cosmic rulership. Her titles are spelled out solemnly in the New Year's festival, the so-called Akitu ritual. Although she is wholly celestial, an awareness of her feral aspects makes the

[7] *Alt-Orientalische Texte*, p. 252.

priest sound like an apprehensive visitor in the den of the Lioness:

> My merciful Lady—My Lady, be calm!
> My Lady, who does not become angry, who is calm,
> My Lady, who gives, My Lady, who is so very good,
> The calm lady, who does not become angry, My Lady, who confers gifts. . . .
> Damkianna,[8] mistress of heaven and earth, whose name is My Lady.

This last name, as Deimel and Zimmern have shown, goes with "Ruler of the Celestial Tiara"—*Zonaia.*

Here we have a case where morphological criteria can overcome difficulties in the literal meaning. In one case the goddess is Chthonie, who acquires the title "Ge" by investiture with the Starry Mantle. In the second it is Ishtar/Innin, who is Venus beyond doubt. The ritual and the conception behind both are certainly the same. We must conclude therefore that in Pherecydes' very specially designed language, Ge becomes a title for Venus, seen here in the role of sky-and-earth goddess, not at all "chthonic" notwithstanding her earthly title. If we trust this logic, we shall be greatly rewarded when we find that in other related cosmologies, the title of "earth-in-heaven" applies to the celestial band of 47° comprised between the two tropics, which is also called the "inhabited earth" because it is where the planet gods move around. With this our interpretation ought to be secured.

What is it that gives Venus this particularly exalted place in mythology? We could give all sorts of reason, which come down to this, that Venus and Sirius are the brightest stars in heaven, each in its category, and are accordingly singled out for dominant roles. But what we have seen of the Pentagram might focus our thoughts on the importance of precision.

"Mother Nature" does not spoil her mathematically minded offspring in dispensing dates that "fit"; but those five synodic revolutions of Venus leave only a minute remainder with respect to eight solar years; the eight-pointed star on countless Mesopotamian seal cylinders, borderstones, etc. means every time Ishtar/Venus, as every Orientalist knows; the Egyptians, laying the accent on the five, have been even more "Venus-minded"; the five revolutions are hers, after all, *she* draws the pentagram. She has, moreover, a unique distinction in her recurrences. There is a simple observational rule which antedates by far all Greek systems, *viz.* that the heliac phases of the planets stand in constant intervals of time to their station points in heaven, before

[8] Sumerian Dam.gal.nun.na. Deimel: *Pantheon Babylonicum* (Roma, 1914), 700, p. 100ff. est nomen antiquissimum uxoris dei Ea, quod semper manebat in usu . . . "mater 'magni filii' (=Marduk/Jupiter)." Deimel quotes Zimmern: "Beachtenswert erscheint . . . dass Damkina als Nin-men-an-na 'Herrin der himmlischen Tiara' bezeichnet wird."

they start on the retrograde loop. (This becomes obvious in Copernican terms, but in the Ptolemaic scheme it remains far from obvious. Ptolemy formulated thence a rule: that the circular motion on the planetary epicycle must be synchronous with the anomaly with respect to the sun.)

The periodic returns of station points to the same region of heaven were taken *ab antiquo* as primary periods, as Böker and Gundel point out.[9] Ptolemy (*Synt.* I,5) calls them the "simple and unmixed motions" from which the other "partial and varied motions" arise.

Now if we concentrate on those primary periods, we shall find a strange variety: Saturn about 59 years, Jupiter 71, Mars 79, *Venus 8*, and Mercury 46 years. That means:[10] the shortest intervals of time, after which the same planetary positions repeat themselves with respect to the fixed stars and, at the same time, with respect to the Sun (in other words: when synodical and sidereal revolutions "fit"), are those mentioned years.

Thus Venus turns out to be a model of reliability, the time-keeper as it were of planetary periods. This fact might help us to understand, why this planet became the Celestial Queen, invested again and again with the "starry mantle"—remember Pherecydes: Zas *presents* Chthonie with the "Earth"—meaning Earth-in-Heaven, i.e., he gives it continuously "all the measures of the whole creation" (that verb *didoi* in Pherecydes is a present tense expressing continuous action). Venus seems to have been a kind of pledge, reassuring the earliest astronomers of the reality of invariable order behind the apparent confusion.

We are moving here admittedly over highly speculative terrain. Historians will discount all such clues which do not belong to their familiar orbit of thought, and hold up against them the vast areas of crude ideas and "primitive" imagery which seem to them to characterize those past millennia.

Yet those other, precise data also exist, and go back to remote antiquity. They might just as well be brought in to characterize a thought which in any case does not resemble ours. It is a risk but a risk worth taking.

Those data are surely not unimportant. It is not unimportant that they should have riveted the attention of lost ages, of those men, as D'Alembert says, who gave us everything except a knowledge of their name and their being. It is difficult for us, who relegate star observations and meridian instruments to a small corner in the scheme of things, to imagine a time when measures of such minute precision entrusted to memory over vast periods occupied such an area of consciousness, as to be held normative for society as a whole.

Beyond the stamping and the screaming and the orgies and the

[9] Cf. Gundel, RE *20*, 2085.

[10] Cf. Ludendorff: Untersuch.Astr.Maya *10* (=SPAW, Phys.Math.Kl. 1935) p. 83.

bloody rites that we instinctively associate with primitive ages it is well that we should perceive the steady work of rigorous abstractive imagination placing the values where we would least have expected them, deriving norms from precise measurement. As the field of ancient metrology is opening up, we can discern a close-woven texture of measure as playing a much higher role than even in our own world, where we pride ourselves on our capacity to telemeter systems with split-second precision millions of miles away.

Those of our scholars who still presume that the unit of length was casually given by thumbs or feet or the "average" size (whatever that may mean) of a grain of barley, are not aware that no unit of length or surface or volume could be considered normative unless it was tied up with cosmic invariants, and this implied a time interval marked by the sun, as Karst and Lehmann-Haupt were first to see, more than fifty years ago. More recently, Erich von Hornbostel has shown how in archaic civilizations the space intervals were tied up with time intervals both in astronomy and in music just as was taught by the Pythagoreans. Why otherwise should the same Egyptian word "Maat" indicate both the standard brick and the standard flute length? When our organ builders designate a tone by such words as "16-foot-tone" they use archaic language. The link between the two areas is the normative link.

Alexander J. Ellis, with his precise measurements on music instruments from the Orient, showed in the 'eighties of the last century that scales and intervals can be multiple and seemingly arbitrary, but that one always discovers in them one or the other norm: he was thus able to show the Near-Eastern origin of the Scottish bagpipe scale. In China the tones of the standard Pan-pipes were checked by inspectors every year at the time of the equinox, when Yin and Yang are supposed to be in proper balance. These inspectors were sent by the "Department of Laws rooted in the Great All." In Egypt and Babylonia the standard measures went back to the authority of Thot and Nabu, the Hermes figures in their Pantheon. It should be expressive enough.

That central concept which is represented by Maat in Egypt, Me in Sumeria, Rta in India, Asha in Iran, and so on, does not so much express a truth-value, as exactness with reference to a norm. The hieroglyph of Maat is the feather, symbol of precise weight in the balance. That feathered precision is everywhere implicit in the accomplishments of what the Greeks called *Mousikē*, a name which far transcends our "music" and is a close equivalent of our "cultured consciousness." Such states of consciousness do not come into being overnight.

When we go back in time—at least for a few millennia—we do not find everywhere, as we would expect, a crude anthropomorphic or theriomorphic representation of the deity. We may run instead into numbers, into a texture of time units projected into space, which bespeaks an astronomical origin. We are reminded then of those strange words of Aristotle at *Metaphysics* 1074b12 (so casually dismissed by Sir David Ross) when he speaks of "ancient heirlooms," *λείψανα,* of high levels of thought in the past, and that the gods must have originally been the planets. Music and time—the time of celestial periods—were *ab antiquo* a moving image of eternity. This remained as the Pythagorean frame, and was inherited together with its original divine rulership by Parmenides and then by Plato.

After so much that has been said, and too often in vain, about the "Archaic Atmosphere" as a source of the strangest and most nonsensical representations, I trust we have here a beginning of a coherent image. Archaic thought is cosmological first and last, it faces the gravest implications of a cosmos in ways which reverberate into later classic philosophy. The chief implication is a profound awareness that the fabric of the cosmos is not only determined, but overdetermined, and such that none of its agents admit of simple location. Be it simple magic or astrology, forces, gods, or number, planetary powers, Platonic Forms, Aristotelian essences or Stoic substances, none of them admit of simple location, if a cosmos has to be thought of. Physical reality cannot be analytical in the Democritean or Cartesian sense, it cannot be reduced to concreteness even if misplaced. Being is change, motion and rhythm, the irresistible circle of time, the incidence of the *kairos*.

We can best appreciate the originality of Parmenides' thought if we consider that he made of geometry the core of reality in an entirely different way from his predecessors. Geometric space itself, no longer numbers and rhythms in space, but three-dimensional extension pure and absolute, became the substrate, the Physis, of things. It seems only right that he should have put such an inspired innovation under the sponsorship of the ruling deity of Time, the holder of the Starry Mantle. She assumes then a double aspect, first revealing the Truth which is unshaken and unmoving, necessary, extraneous to change, and showing herself again as the ruler of time and events, the Daimon who steers all things and drives the living to "dreaded birth and begetting."

Galileo and Oppenheimer

WHEN GALILEO GALILEI WAS BROUGHT BEFORE THE TRIBUNAL OF the Inquisition in Rome in 1633, Pope Urban VIII was determined to break once and for all what to him was the incomprehensible arrogance of the scientific mind. Even after the culprit was found guilty, he was not treated harshly. He was never refused access to the sacraments, and he was allowed to pursue his scientific studies provided he kept away from astronomy. Yet special pains were taken that he should die under imposed penitence and thus be refused burial in hallowed ground as still and forever *vehementer suspectus*.

The Inquisitional trial *de vehementi*—that is, a trial for vehement suspicion of disloyalty, or of heresy as they called it in those days—began with a firm assumption of guilt, or at least of bad judgment, that could not be dispelled by any facts brought in evidence. Under our law, legal proceedings are supposed to begin with an assumption of the defendant's innocence unless or until guilt is proved. Yet many marks of a trial *de vehementi* are to be found in the hearings of J. Robert Oppenheimer before the Atomic Energy Commission's Personnel Security Board in Washington in 1954.

In both trials the accused could not defend himself against the fundamental accusation that was never brought up at the trial. Galileo had no advocates in court, nor was there any discussion of the Copernican theories as such. Galileo was not allowed to defend his scientific work: the only question was, Had he disobeyed the Church or not? Oppenheimer was allowed to have lawyers, but they had no clearance, and security considerations ruled out any adequate discussion of the facts relating to Oppenheimer's controversial views—which were, after all, the basis of the whole trial.

In each case the scientist was shown a good deal of official consideration, although in the public consciousness he was clearly branded as one who was either too clever or too scared to commit himself to the major infamy but whose intentions were sinister from the start. In each case the purpose of the proceedings was to inflict social dishonor on the accused in order to deter others from certain kinds of action that the authorities feared.

There are, of course, many differences between the two cases. In the history of science Galileo is by far the greater figure. Despite all the innuendoes that have been made about him since 1633, his reputation as a "second Archimedes" could not be taken away from him. His ideas were accepted with excitement by the educated public of his times. But in our day the discovery of dreadful powers, for which mankind may not yet be ready, has enveloped science in a climate of fear and even guilt—a fact that no doubt contributed to paralyze Oppenheimer in his defense.

It is permissible to speculate about what would have happened if Oppenheimer, together with Fermi, Bethe, and two or three other authorities in theoretical physics, had stated in 1942, as Heisenberg did in Germany, that the atom bomb was not feasible. No one could have really known except them. On the other hand, supposing the bomb could be made, there was also the troublesome possibility that it might trigger the explosion of our whole planet. Theoretically, it looked all right, but what man of sound practical judgment will trust himself wholly to theory in a matter utterly without precedent, a jump in the dark?

Heisenberg was certainly a patriotic German and a very great physicist, yet, after extensive exploratory work with his colleagues, he gave up—and not even Hitler could say anything.

There is another important difference between the cases to be considered: the Galileo trial concludes with a solemn abjuration; the American trial does not. Rome proceeded on established orthodoxies, hence the final abjuration was in order. But our society is based on the dignity of the individual, and the defendant was permitted to give his recantations right at the beginning as a sort of spontaneous admission. This is what Oppenheimer's pitiful apology in his letter of March 4, 1954, actually amounted to.

Galileo ends up on his knees, but people forget that he started out by challenging his judges, in the name of the law, to tell him what was wrong with his book. Oppenheimer is on his knees at the start—as his legal advisers told him he must be—pouring out in public a tale of his past personal attachments and private beliefs, recounting his insignificant indiscretions, protesting that he has learned his lesson, that he can still be useful. There is, of course, the same ludicrous contrast in both cases—two men with enormous capacities to learn pretending that they had learned their lessons from judges who were by nature "immovable and unpersuadable," as Galileo describes them. Still, Galileo did not have to accuse himself right at the outset of being adolescent-minded, fuzzy-headed, immature, and a liar. He was able to bargain shrewdly with a few such admissions in the course of the trial. He was willing to declare himself rash, vain, ambitious, and somewhat irresponsible, but always in order to exact a concession.

In both cases the object of confession was absolution. Absolution for what crime? Lack of proper "enthusiasm" for directives—Church directives, security directives, H-bomb directives. The equivocation carefully built up is that the "lack of enthusiasm" is taken to refer to the interests of one's country or one's faith, whereas it actually refers to various opinions among ecclesiastics, various types of Pentagonic thought, past, present, and future. "Thou askest us now to believe that thou didst believe that we had maturely considered and finally decided all that is to be seen, considered, and decided in the matter of the survival of the human race. . . ." I apologize for this pastiche out of the 1633 sentence, but it does come awfully close.

In a century as intellectually refined and respectful of forms as the seventeenth, a man knew what was expected of him: it was principally externals. He must not maintain certain opinions "affirmatively"; beyond that he could think as he pleased. He must pretend to be speaking only "academically," or he could resort to the approved dodge of discussing philosophical "probabilities," but he must be sure to point out that they could not be true according to the Faith. A man knew he was writing at his own risk. If the authorities caught up with him, they would compel him to say he had never meant it. This was strictly a formal humiliation, for it was well understood by everyone who counted that he went on thinking every word he had written. A man's condemnation meant only that he had been restored to the community of the faithful, and that was the end of the affair. It was a settlement, at least, in that it came at the end. After the formalities, the man could even be used again if need be.

We, on the other hand, have only this inane notion of "maturity" and that other one of "enthusiasm" to go by, crudely and furtively transferred from pep-talk usage into actual legal standards.

The conclusions of the Gray-Morgan Board (it was really the Gray-Morgan-Evans Board, but Dr. Evans wrote a sharply dissenting opinion) are as follows:

> . . . We have come to a clear conclusion, which should be reassuring to the people of this country, that he [Oppenheimer] is a loyal citizen. . . . We have, however, been unable to arrive at the conclusion that it would be clearly consistent with the security interests of the United States to reinstate Dr. Oppenheimer's clearance and, therefore, do not so recommend.
>
> The following considerations have been controlling in leading us to our conclusion:
>
> 1. We find that Dr. Oppenheimer's continuing conduct and associations have reflected a serious disregard for the requirements of the security system.
>
> 2. We have found a susceptibility to influence which could have serious implications for the security interests of the country.
>
> 3. We find his conduct in the hydrogen-bomb program sufficiently disturbing as to raise a doubt as to whether his future participation, if characterized by the same attitudes in a government program relating to the national defense, would be clearly consistent with the best interests of security.
>
> 4. We have regretfully concluded that Dr. Oppenheimer has been less than candid in several instances in his testimony before the board.

In other words, they admit that Oppenheimer has not disclosed security information. In fact, they themselves stated in an earlier section: "It must be said that Dr. Oppenheimer seems to have had a high degree of discretion reflecting an unusual ability to keep to himself vital secrets." It is about entirely different secrets that they are worried. Oppenheimer had not handed over a person by the name of Chevalier to the police.

Haakon Chevalier, a professor of French literature and a close friend of Oppenheimer, had relayed to him the suggestions of a Communist, George Charles Eltenton, that Americans disclose their discoveries to Russia. Oppenheimer refused sharply, and later warned Security of Eltenton's attempt but made up a false account of the affair to spare Chevalier. This was to become the famous "lie." Oppenheimer later gave Chevalier's name to the authorities, to get out of the tangle.

Oppenheimer was found by the AEC to have exhibited a "persistent and willful disregard for the obligations of security" to a degree that would endanger the common defense and national security. Now both J. Edgar Hoover and General Leslie R. Groves had not taken the charges so seriously when they had first considered them. Hoover's strongest statement was that he "could not feel completely satisfied in view of J. Robert's failure to report promptly and accurately what must have seemed to him an attempt at espionage." General Groves had called Oppenheimer's protection of Chevalier a kind of "schoolboy attitude that there is something wicked about telling on a friend" and had also dismissed as unessential the entire account of Oppenheimer's early leftist associations. When Groves was asked, "Based on your total acquaintance with him and your experience with him and your knowledge of him, would you say that in your opinion he would ever consciously commit a disloyal act?," the general replied, "I would be amazed if he did." These men wanted a job done, and had confidence in Oppenheimer's ability to do it.

When the case went up to the AEC, Commissioner Eugene M. Zuckert raised, and then quickly dismissed, a very pertinent question:

> There have been suggestions that there may be a possible alternative short of finding Dr. Oppenheimer a security risk. One possibility suggested was that the Commission might merely allow Dr. Oppenheimer's consultant's contract to lapse when it expires on June 30, 1954, and thereafter not use his services. I have given the most serious consideration to this possibility and have concluded that it is not practical.

Why wasn't it practical? Because someone else might hire him. In fact, the Science Advisory Committee of the Office of

Defense Mobilization was asking for him. The AEC decided to try to make Oppenheimer unemployable in his own field.

What this action would do to the scientific world was clearly foreseen by Dr. Evans, the dissenting board member, and by Dr. Henry D. Smyth, the dissenting AEC commissioner, who also happened to be the only men on the two boards who were professional scientists. Dr. Evans wrote: "I personally think that our failure to clear Dr. Oppenheimer will be a black mark on the escutcheon of our country. His witnesses are a considerable segment of the scientific backbone of our nation and they endorse him. I am worried about the effect an improper decision may have on the scientific development in our country.

"Nuclear physics is new in our country. . . . I would very much regret any action to retard or hinder this new scientific development."

One example of the scientific community's reaction was contained in the testimony of Dr. Vannevar Bush:

> I feel that this board has made a mistake and that it is a serious one. I feel that the letter of General [K. D.] Nichols which I read, this bill of particulars, is quite capable of being interpreted as placing a man on trial because he held opinions, which is quite contrary to the American system, which is a terrible thing. And as I move about I find that discussed today very energetically, that here is a man who is being pilloried because he had strong opinions, and had the temerity to express them. If this country ever gets to the point where we come that near to the Russian system, we are certainly not in any condition to attempt to lead the free world toward the benefits of democracy.

Time and again the professional Inquisitors had dismissed as not serious, or downright fraudulent, the accusatory material that piled up in their files against Galileo. Accordingly, the scientist had rightly concluded that the traditional directives still stood, and that it was permissible to discuss, at least hypothetically, the dangerous subject of Copernican astronomy. In fact, the Pope himself had told him that he was a most valuable man, and that he should use this opportunity to go on "adorning Christendom with his eloquence." The usefulness of both scientists to society was clearly recognized. Both of them had delivered the goods: Galileo the prestige of his telescopic discoveries, Oppenheimer the atom bomb. The trouble came when the scientists went on to exert their influence, however tentatively and respectfully, on matters of high policy. Galileo's book was a discreet but transparent attempt at getting the Church to change its mind on a fundamental scientific issue. Oppenheimer, too, expressed definite views about the over-all strategy for which his individual contributions formed an important part. Both men acted openly, with full "clearances." But when the authorities woke up to the implications of what the scientists were saying, they decided that these men were dangerous. The stable doors were closed, not quietly but with a crash, to convey the impression that there was still a horse to steal. Both, it was suddenly discovered, had made their great mistakes a decade or more before; both had ignored security injunctions.

Both men were surprised to see how the world changed around them as they faced a procedure *de vehementi*. The late AEC Commissioner John von Neumann described that surprise:

> I would say that all of us in the war years . . . got suddenly in contact with a universe we had not known before. I mean the peculiar problem of security, the fact that people who looked all right might be conspirators and might be spies. . . . This had on anyone a shock effect, and any one of us may have behaved foolishly and inefficiently and untruthfully, so this condition is something ten years later, I would not consider too serious. . . . We were all little children with respect to the situation which had developed, namely, that we suddenly were dealing with something with which one could blow up the world. Furthermore, we were involved in a triangular war. . . . None of us had been educated or conditioned to exist in this situation, and we had to make our rationalization and our code of conduct as we went along. For some people it took two months, for some two years. . . . I am quite sure that all of us by now have developed the necessary code of ethics and the necessary resistance. So if this story is true, that would just give me a piece of information on how long it took Dr. Oppenheimer to get adjusted to this Buck Rogers universe, but no more. I have no slightest doubt that he was not adjusted to it in 1944 or 1945.

In his efforts to be polite, Dr. von Neumann seems to be conceding far too much. He almost takes it for granted that the scientist is bound to be foolish and childish until he is properly trained and housebroken. Maturity is defined in terms of survival in the political jungle. This is pure irony, but it is lost on the board. It is tragic to watch the parade of men who had been associated with atomic power from the beginning coming to testify that Oppenheimer, after all, had done some service to the state and that he was not a subversive:

> James Bryant Conant reiterated his opinion that ". . . a more loyal and sound American cannot be found in the whole United States."
>
> Charles Christian Lauritsen of the California Institute of Technology said that he had less doubt of Oppenheimer's loyalty than he did of "any other person that I know as well."
>
> Oliver E. Buckley, formerly board chairman of Bell Telephone: "I believed and believe that he was loyal to the United States. I just don't recall any event that even raised that issue in my mind."
>
> Even Dr. Edward Teller: "But I have always assumed, and I now assume, that he is loyal to the United States. I believe this, and I shall believe it until I see very conclusive proof to the opposite."

But just as in the Galileo affair, the insistent pleas of scientists and/or prelates from all over Europe were ignored by the cardinals of the board.

Dr. von Neumann's statement seems to come fairly close to the "overall commonsense judgment" that had been set by the AEC itself as a criterion for security procedures. Oppenheimer had never broken security when the Russians had no bomb; now that the Russians have the bomb, what possible justification can there be for getting rid of the man? So we have to dig up a Chevalier case which never existed in any serious sense even in 1943, we refurbish it in 1954, and make of it such a lapse in security as to endanger national safety. It's nothing short of wonderful to see what the final report of the AEC builds up out of this Chevalier business.

Galileo, too, had acted according to standing directives: he had been encouraged, and every sentence of his writing had been cleared and recleared. Then the news came down that he must be gotten rid of. So the Inquisitors dug up an alleged injunction that seventeen years before had forbidden him even to discuss the subject. The judge needed this injunction but obviously did not like it, and his embarrassment is obvious in the way he tried to move on quickly to something else. The chairman of AEC both needed and liked what had been found for him. In fact, he improved on it.

A "susceptibility to influence" is cited by the board. (The parallel is the charge against Galileo of having "corresponded with certain German mathematicians," e.g., Kepler, a Protestant, whom he had also sponsored for his old chair in Padua.) The charge is based upon the Bohm, Peters, and Lomanitz episodes. In brief, Oppenheimer had not refused his help to men who wanted to keep their jobs or were trying to get a job abroad, although they were political suspects at home. But in one case, conscious of his delicate position, Oppenheimer spoke about Dr. Bernard Peters before the House Un-American Activities Committee in such a way as to damage gravely Peters's position at the University of Rochester. He was sternly called to task by a number of other scientists for having hurt Peters unnecessarily. Dr. Edward U. Condon wrote an outspoken rebuke that made Oppenheimer "angry." Oppenheimer then wrote a letter to the Rochester papers, trying to make up for the damage he had done to Peters. The board considers this an example of how Oppenheimer bowed to influence. But there is still worse: "Dr. Condon's letter . . . contained a severe attack on Dr. Oppenheimer. Nevertheless, he now testifies that he is prepared to support Dr. Condon in the loyalty investigation of the latter."

That "Nevertheless" seems a curious word to choose.

Here is another significant aspect of the Buck Rogers universe.

If any susceptibility to influence was shown, it was when Oppenheimer stood before the Un-American Activities Committee and testified against Peters. "Will you step into my parlor, said the spider to the fly. And before I ask you a few simple questions, let me say I trust you are not susceptible to any undue influence." Mindful of his responsibility, Oppenheimer tried to conform to the laws of the political jungle. He thereby lost standing with the scientists, who felt that he was capable of selling out, and his usefulness was thus impaired. He did what he could to regain his standing among his colleagues, and at that point it was Gray and Morgan who ruled that his usefulness had been impaired.

Oppenheimer had been very doubtful in 1949 about committing a great deal of effort and rare materials to a crash program that seemed a wild gamble. He was not alone. Conant said, "I opposed it strongly, as strongly as anybody else . . . ." I. I. Rabi and Enrico Fermi suggested an international agreement to outlaw the bomb before it existed. Hans Bethe testified: "I was hoping that it might be possible to prove that thermonuclear reactions were not feasible at all." Oppenheimer called a meeting of the General Advisory Committee of the AEC about the problem. He remarked: "There was a surprising unanimity—to me very surprising—that the U.S. ought not to take the initiative at that time in an all-out program."

What then was Oppenheimer's crime? Not sticking to his last. There is his famous letter to Conant:

> What concerns me is really not the technical problem. I am not sure the miserable thing will work, nor that it can be gotten to a target except by ox cart. It seems likely to me even further to worsen the unbalance of our present war plans. What does worry me is that this thing appears to have caught the imagination, both of the congressional and of military people, as the answer to the problem posed by the Russian advance. It would be folly to oppose the exploration of this weapon. We have always known it had to be done; and it does have to be done, though it appears to be singularly proof against any form of experimental approach. But that we become committed to it as the way to save the country and the peace appears to me full of dangers.

Is this what the board meant by exercising "highly persuasive influence in matters in which his convictions were not necessarily a reflection of technical judgment, and also not necessarily related to the protection of the strongest offensive military interests of the country"? He goeth about like a roaring lion, seeking whom he may persuade.

Of course, others were discussing these same dangers. George Kennan admits having discussed them with both Oppenheimer and Secretary of State Acheson:

> It seemed to me there was unclarity in the councils of our Government. . . . The unclarity revolved around this question. Were we holding them [our weapons] only as a means of deterring other people . . . or were we building them into our military establishment in such a way that we would indicate that we were going to be dependent upon them in any future war, and would have to use them, regardless of whether they were used against us first? . . . If . . . you were going to regard them as an integral part of forward American military planning and something on which we would be dependent in a future war, then you came up with a different answer. . . .

These were the views of an expert on foreign policy who found himself inevitably invading the province of the military. In the same way, scientists found themselves thinking about both foreign policy and military strategy. They all did. Of this, we have Rabi's confirmation:

> The question was, should it be a crash program, and a technical question: What possibilities lay in that? What would be the cost . . . in terms of the strength of the United States because of the weakening of the effort on which something which we had in hand, namely, the fission weapons, and the uncompleted designs of different varieties, to have a really flexible weapon, the question of the interchangeability of parts, all sorts of things which could be used in different military circumstances. Then there was the question of the military value of this weapon . . . this weapon as promised which didn't exist and which we didn't know how to make, what sort of military weapon was it anyway? What sort of target was it good for? And what would be the general political effect? . . . we felt—and I am talking chiefly about myself—that this was not just a weapon. . . . We felt it was really essential and we discussed a great deal what you were buying if you got this thing.

On April 12, 1633, when Galileo was being interrogated for the first time, he described an audience with Cardinal Bellarmine seventeen years before. The Inquisitor suddenly asked: "Was any other injunction made to you on this subject, in the presence of those Fathers, by them or anyone else, and what?"

Galileo is stunned. He has just presented a document given to him by the late Cardinal Bellarmine stating specifically that there had been no such injunction. Yet the Inquisitor is looking at another document in front of him, and this, after all, is the Inquisition. Galileo tries to retell the story carefully. "It may be that a command was issued to me that I should not hold or defend the opinion in question, but I do not remember it, for it is several years ago."

According to the Inquisitor, the injunction was "that you must neither hold, defend, nor teach that opinion in any way whatsoever."

It has been proved that the "injunction" had been forged into the record by the authorities at a later date. But Galileo is helpless. He stutters: "I do not remember it . . . but it may be that it was."

At this point, he has all but made the concession the Inquisitor wanted to drag out of him. A few days later, Galileo re-established the facts carefully in his written defense, but when the Inquisition summarized it for the judges, it did so in one sentence: "He admits the injunction, but . . . says he has no memory of the clauses 'discussing' and 'in any way whatsoever.' " With effortless efficiency the strongest parts of Galileo's defense have been swept aside.

There would seem to be some foundation for the charge that Oppenheimer was "less than candid," and here, it seems to me, we are coming to the core of the analogy between the two cases. The technical capacity of both Galileo and Oppenheimer was profoundly misunderstood by the authorities. In the 1940's just as in the 1620's, the scientist was thought of as a sort of glorified mechanic. The grumblings at Los Alamos were no louder than those heard at Bellosguardo near Florence three centuries ago.

Galileo was encouraged by the Pope himself to write a book about the two opposing planetary systems, the Ptolemaic and the Copernican, in order to show that all arguments had been maturely considered and that the two doctrines stood in need of a higher decision, which was the Pope's. That decision had already been written and given to Galileo to be printed at the end of his discussion as the solution and "medicine of the end."

A remark of George Kennan's about the Oppenheimer case seems to strike to the heart of the Galileo case too: "You might just as well have asked Leonardo da Vinci to distort an anatomical drawing as that you should ask Robert Oppenheimer to . . . speak dishonestly." Galileo, an experienced courtier and man of the world, knew perfectly well that he could write rings around the authorities and cheat them with the greatest of ease, leaving the last laugh to his fellow scientists. But he didn't choose that course; because he rashly thought that his ecclesiastical superiors were also rational beings, he wanted them to think along with him, trusting to their good sense. His main concern, as he revealed covertly in the Preface, was to extricate them from the impasse their incompetence had gotten them into. To do that he had to break the rules. He had to show that his cosmological discoveries demanded a philosophical revision, even a theological one, and that conventional theories, seen in the light of a larger universe, turn out to be "hardly respectful of divine majesty."

At the end of his searching discussion, he dutifully tacked on the Pope's preordained conclusion; it wasn't his fault if it looked silly there. But making the Pope look foolish was a dangerous thing to do.

The indictment of the Preliminary Commission was quite clear about Galileo's failings. He had exposed the official school texts to ridicule (Point 5); he had not treated his own opinion with proper disbelief, but instead had indicated some belief in it (Points 3 and 4); he had not followed the papal directive with proper enthusiasm (Point 2).

In all this, Galileo was certainly being "less than candid." He had been intellectually honest, at his own risk. He had also been scrupulously legal, having his text twice revised and approved before publication. But he knew all along, ever since he had submitted the project, that he wasn't really doing what the Pope intended. Of course he hadn't lied about Cardinal Bellarmine's injunction. But in obediently endorsing an untruth by professing his orthodox belief in the immobility of the earth, he had surely been less than candid with the authorities. And some of his answers to the court were certainly evasive. Toward the end of the first session he said that he had really tried to show the weaknesses of the Copernican system. But by that time he was thoroughly scared, and his signature under the protocol was made with a trembling hand. In contrast, evasiveness was not typical of Oppenheimer's testimony; he even exaggerated his own failings.

The authorities sentenced Galileo both for disregard of basic security policy ("thou has dared discuss . . .") and for lack of candor ("nor does the license artfully and cunningly extorted avail thee"). The actual charges had to be trumped up, but the conflict underlying them was valid. It had come to a showdown about "who is going to do the thinking around here," and some lack of candor was inevitable on both sides. Loyalty was reestablished at the price of humiliation. We end up exactly where the Gray-Morgan Board leaves Oppenheimer. In each case, the scientist had certainly acted imprudently according to accepted standards, but could be brought to trial only on charges of retroactive guilt.

There are some points at which the Roman authorities would seem to have been more considerate of the defendant than the Americans were. In his abjuration, Galileo was made to promise miserably, under oath and *sub poenis*, that "should I know any heretic or person suspected of heresy, I will denounce him to this Holy Office." Although there were obviously many suspects among Galileo's acquaintances, it was not held against him subsequently that he did not turn them in. It became known that he was actually corresponding with heretics and even sending them his book to translate—it was as if Oppenheimer had entered into a secret correspondence with the Moscow Academy. But the Inquisitors decided that such conduct was only human and let it go at that.

Undeniably there was a lack of candor in Oppenheimer's answers at the hearing—not about his life but about matters of high policy. And this is because there were certain aspects of his predicament that simply could not be discussed frankly. Neither side wanted to go too far.

Light is shed on this aspect of the case by the interesting deposition of General Roscoe Charles Wilson of the Air Force, who engagingly admits that he is himself a "big bomb" man, and had consequently been very worried. He gives three reasons for his concern. One is "the fact that Dr. Oppenheimer was interested in what I call the internationalizing of atomic energy, this at a time when the United States had a monopoly . . ." The fact is that Oppenheimer was interested in that "internationalizing of atomic energy" quite officially as a scientific adviser to Bernard Baruch, who had been appointed to the U.N. Atomic Energy Commission by the President to try and find a way of establishing international control. The general is told this, but it does not seem to register in his mind. He is asked by the defense attorney whether "perhaps it might be better to internationalize it while there was a chance to do so"—that is, before the Russians got it. The general's answer is remarkable: "I had never heard that argument."

The general was worried that Oppenheimer had never backed certain ideas of the Air Force like nuclear-powered planes. "I don't challenge his technical judgment, but at the same time he felt less strongly opposed to the nuclear-powered ships."

Finally, General Wilson was worried because Oppenheimer approached thermonuclear weapons with

> more conservatism than the Air Force would have liked. . . . Once again it was a matter of judgment. I would like to say that the fact that . . . he is such a brilliant man, the fact that he has such a command of the English language, has such national prestige, and such powers of persuasion, only made me nervous, because I felt if this was so it would not be to the interest of the United States, in my judgment. It was for that reason that I went to the Director of Intelligence to say that I felt unhappy.

Here is how the Florentine Ambassador set down Cardinal Barberini's explanation of why Galileo made him nervous:

> He reminded me that Galileo wrote exquisitely, and had a marvelous capacity for persuading people of whatever he wanted to, and there was a danger that through his influence some fantastic opinion might take hold among these Florentine wits which are too subtle and curious.

Like the Cardinal, General Wilson is suspicious of the defendant's "marvelous capacity for persuading people." But what really troubled both of them were the ideas behind the eloquence. Oppenheimer had definite views on military strategy. The scientist surmised that our grand system of international alliances would not be worth the paper it was drafted on if we left our allies to face the Russians with popguns. Thus, he threw all his influence behind the development of tactical weapons that could be delivered by artillery. Generals Bradley and Collins supported him, and Gordon Dean, then chairman of AEC, also supported the policy, but naturally the Strategic Air Command was not entirely pleased by his efforts to ruin its monopoly over the A- and H-bombs, just at a time when it was having a running fight with the Navy over it. Nor was the Air Force delighted by Oppenheimer's insistence on the priority of essential defensive measures. His simile about the "champion with the glass jaw" served to turn the conflict into an open feud.

The informer Lorini had said, in a denunciation accompanying a forged document, that the Galileists were good Christians, but "a little overwise and conceited in their opinions."

This background of the Oppenheimer case is widely known in Washington, but all one finds in the trial record are the unguarded remarks of David T. Griggs, an Air Force consultant, who complained passionately about the evil influence of the "Z.O.R.C. outfit" (Zacharias, Oppenheimer, Rabi, Charles Lauritsen) in frustrating Air Force desires. Dr. Gray, the chairman, evinced no curiosity, but let us—even at this late date—sketch in the details for him. The "glacial movement," as it is called, got much of its impetus from the Air Force, and then suddenly, out of the blue, William Liscum Borden emerged from his civilian meditations at Westinghouse to denounce Oppenheimer as probably the key figure of Soviet espionage. Commissioner Smyth refers in his dissenting opinion to "enthusiastic amateur help from powerful personal enemies." As a matter of fact, the job seems to have been done with a great deal of professional skill.

It is difficult to know just what was going on. But it is all very reminiscent of the way the Jesuits of the Counter Reformation identified their order with the body of the Church and set about destroying Galileo, who had threatened their monopoly on education and intellectual strategy. Galileo had been warned by a friend quite early in the game: "It would be a business of which you would never see the end if you picked a quarrel with those Fathers, for they are so strong that they could take on the whole world, and if they are wrong, they would never concede it . . . the more so as they are no friends of the new opinions." Many years later Father Grienberger, the leading Jesuit astronomer, was to remark sadly: "If Galileo had only known how to retain the favor of the Jesuits, he would have stood in renown before the world, he would have been spared all his misfortunes and he could have written what he pleased about everything, even about the motion of the Earth."

Jesuits were fully determined to encourage progress in the arts and sciences, but only in strictly isolated compartments which the Order would establish under its own philosophical supervision. Let the mathematician develop mathematics, but let him not try to mix mathematics with physics, which is a division of philosophy—and so on. All efforts were bent toward keeping social forces under the firm control of a consistent philosophical motivation. The trouble is, it didn't work. The whole structure was put under severe strain by the Galileo case.

The issue of security was hardly more than a political smoke screen in the Oppenheimer case. There are no scientific secrets about the atom bomb, only industrial secrets. In any event, leaking of information was not even among the charges against Oppenheimer. The more important issue of security in the Oppenheimer case was described by John J. McCloy, chairman of the board of the Chase Manhattan Bank, former Assistant Secretary of War and High Commissioner to Germany:

> . . . You can't be too conventional about it or you run into a security problem the other way. We are only secure if we have the best brains and the best reach of mind in this field. If the impression is prevalent that scientists have to work under such great restrictions, and perhaps under such great suspicion, we may lose the next step in this field. . . . I would accept a great deal of political immaturity, let me put it that way, in return for this rather esoteric, this rather indefinite, theoretical thinking that I believe we are going to be dependent on for the next generation.

Oppenheimer, like Galileo, had performed his assigned task faithfully. In order to reach its unfavorable verdict the board was obliged to depend upon the curiously incoherent imputation of influencing and being influenced, plus "lack of enthusiasm" and the Chevalier episode. This was considered enough for the purpose.

We come now to the final stages of the case: verdicts. For Galileo there was only one formal sentence, but as in the Oppenheimer case, the decision was reached in two stages. The preliminary stage in Galileo's case was the sensible attempt of the Commissary General of the Inquisition to settle the affair with an administrative reprimand: this official seems to have been unhappy in his awareness that the case hung on a forgery, but he was overruled at the last minute by the Pope. In each case, then, we have a distinct final decision by the top authority.

But Urban VIII seems to have played a very different role from that of Admiral Strauss. There was a faction of "hanging judges" on the board of cardinals, and the influence of the Pope may have been, for all we know, in the direction of a compromise. In the modern case, the AEC chairman himself appears as the hanging judge.

Mr. Borden had written in his original denunciation of Oppenheimer: "More probably than not, he has since [1942] been functioning as an espionage agent, and . . . has since acted under a Soviet directive in influencing United States military, atomic energy, intelligence, and diplomatic policy." After a long subterranean voyage, the idea that Oppenheimer was somehow the servant of Communism reappears as fresh as a drop of dew in the final sentence of the AEC's majority decision:

> They [Dr. Oppenheimer's early Communist associations] . . . take on importance in the context of his persistent and continuing association with Communists, including his admitted meetings with Haakon Chevalier in Paris as recently as last December—the same individual who had been intermediary for the Soviet Consulate in 1943.

Reading this solemn judicial prose, one would think the admiral and his colleagues are referring to something mentioned somewhere in the record. But there is nothing there about "persistent and continuing associations with Communists" except the "early" associations. Once again, with effortless efficiency, the case for the defense has been swept away.

There never was a Chevalier case in any relevant sense, even in 1943. Refurbished and built up into a marvelous monster in 1954, it still remains nothing. Chevalier was and has remained a political nitwit.

The AEC's judgment is obviously meant to convey in carefully equivocal language that Oppenheimer is, more probably than not, tied up with Russia, but that it might be difficult to prove. So the best thing is to brand him publicly and leave him to the Advanced Silken Cord.

The calculated restraint has paid handsome dividends. It has prevented rioting among the hired hands, i.e., the scientists, which would have been inevitable if the charge of treason had been made explicit. It has established the idea of Oppenheimer's "guilt" in the public imagination, while avoiding the inconvenience and difficulty of a legitimate trial.

In the Roman trial, the judge-extensor who wrote the sentence needed a clause invalidating the certificate Cardinal Bellarmine gave to Galileo, but he knew it was a judicial howler and cleverly tucked it away in an inconspicuous context. The Florentine Inquisitor who read the sentence to the assembled literati had strict orders from the Holy Office not to let the text out of his hands, and in fact no authentic copy of it was unearthed until a century later. The chairman of the AEC, pleased with what he had produced, released his utterance to the press.

Why has the admiral tied this millstone around his neck? If we were to read that Dr. Watson had turned on Sherlock Holmes and torn him to pieces with his bare hands, we would all realize that Holmes had said "Elementary, my dear Watson," just once too often. In this case, the fateful word may have been spoken the time the admiral went before a Congressional committee to prevent medical isotopes from being shipped to Europe on the familiar ground of military security; Oppenheimer's devastating analysis of the argument may have been the last straw for Strauss. Or there may have been a number of such occasions. Vengeance, as they say in Corsica, is a dish that is best served cold.

Here again, the authorities of three centuries ago seem to have been considerably more perceptive than the modern ones. Then as now, the basic issue was personal. The Pope had been made to look like a fool in matters of philosophy. The admiral had been made to look like a fool in matters of national security. Urban VIII, however, was not a petty man, and he gave signs of embarrassment both during and after the trial. His bent for authority and for a spectacular showdown has obliterated for posterity the merits of a man who otherwise showed himself intelligent, open-minded, and far from ungenerous. He was, as Sacheverell Sitwell calls him, the last Latin poet. Also, he recognized the strength of Galileo's intellect, even if he could not grasp his ideas.

He was the bewildered victim of a scientific revolution that was beyond his comprehension. As a result, the Catholic Church remained obdurate in her negative position for two centuries, while modern science was establishing itself around her, and inevitably against her. It was only in 1822 that the Vatican made up its mind to take the name of Galileo off the Index. And since the Roman authorities could never bring themselves to revise the trial itself, a campaign of innuendoes and absurdities has had to go on to this day. This administrative obduracy does less than justice to the role played in the affair by an important part of the Church. In 1633 there were monks, prelates, and even cardinals who fought sacrificially for Galileo's point of view and defended his good name against all denunciations. And modern Catholic historians have done outstanding work in pointing out trial irregularities.

In both cases the authorities' mistaken zeal served to weaken the institutions they were trying to defend. Father Castelli had warned the Inquisitors before the Galileo trial—and got himself banished for his pains—that "if this holy and supreme tribunal did not proceed in the manner that is due, it would work damage to the reputation and reverence owed to it, and that, if they prosecuted a man who had written so modestly, reverently, and reservedly, it would mean that others would henceforth write brutally and resolutely."

A similar "overall commonsense judgment" was expressed by Dr. Rabi:

. . . the suspension of the clearance of Dr. Oppenheimer was a very unfortunate thing and should not have been done. In other words, there he was; he is a consultant, and if you don't want to consult the guy, you don't consult him, period. Why [do] you have to then proceed to suspend clearance and go through all this sort of thing? He is only there when called, and that is all there was to it. So it didn't seem to me the sort of thing that called for this kind of proceeding at all against a man who had accomplished what Dr. Oppenheimer has accomplished. There is a real positive record, the way I expressed it to a friend of mine. We have an A-bomb and a whole series of it, ***[the asterisks indicate a "security" deletion] and what more do you want, mermaids? This is just a tremendous achievement. If the end of that road is this kind of hearing, which can't help but be humiliating, I thought it was a pretty bad show. I still think so.

The Role of Art in the Scientific Renaissance

LET ME START STRAIGHT AT THE HEART OF THE MATTER, AND TRY to pinpoint the positive technical achievements of art over the early scientific time-scale. We have then the direct contributions of art in the rendering of observed reality. There are here cases of true symbiosis, as in the team of Vesalius and Calcar, or of Brunfels the botanist and Weiditz his illustrator. In this last case indeed, art runs ahead of science, for it can draw only what it sees, and Weiditz's German plants were in ludicrous disagreement with Dioscorides' Eastern Flora. Once the gap is bridged, we have the wonderful flowering of natural history, from Leonhard Fuchs' *Historia stirpium* (1542) all the way to Gesner and Aldrovandi, where the artist often achieves the greater scientific contribution. But where does art cease, and technology begin? What then of copperplate reproduction, which makes Dürer in a way more important than Leonardo?

Erwin Panofsky has analyzed with great learning and insight the contribution of art to science in many fields. He has rightly insisted that above all the discovery of perspective, and the related methods of drawing three-dimensional objects to scale, were as necessary for the development of the "descriptive" sciences in a pre-Galilean period as were the telescope and the microscope in the next centuries, and as is photography today. This was particularly the case, in the Renaissance, with anatomy. In this field, it was really the painters, beginning with Pollaiolo, and not the doctors, who practiced the thing in person and for purposes of exploration rather than demonstration. In all this I cannot but accept Panofsky's verdict: Art, from a certain point on, provides the means of transmitting observations which no amount of learned words could achieve in many fields. For myself, I am reminded of a letter of Ludovico Cigoli, the painter, apropos of Father Clavius and his bizarre ideas of the surface of the Moon being made of something like mother-of-pearl: "This proves to me again," he writes, "that a mathematician however great who does not understand drawing is not only half a mathematician, but indeed a man deprived of sight." In such words there lives intact the spirit of Leonardo, although they were written a century later. And so there we are back at Leonardo. But I would rather avoid, at this point, being drawn into the Vincian jungle, where the historian of art meets the historian of science, at best, as Stanley met Dr. Livingstone—to get him out.

What I intend to do, in this essay, is to concentrate on the early period, which centers around Filippo Brunelleschi (1377–1446).[1] Its importance, I think, has not been sufficiently brought

[1] Filippo di ser Brunellesco di Lippo di Tura is his exact name; if the sopranym from his father had not stuck to him, he would have been Filippo Lapi, for he belonged to the ancient noble family of Lapi-Aldobrandi, and his arms were the same as theirs. His father, Ser Brunellesco, had been a notary and a judge, who had belonged to the Council

to light. We are here at the initial point where the historian has to unscramble ideas. Brunelleschi around 1400 should be considered the most creative scientist as well as the most creative artist of his time, since there was nothing much else then that could go by the name of creative science.

We must not superimpose our own image of science as a criterion for the past. It is Brunelleschi who seems to define the way of science for his generation. Who was it that gave him his initial scientific ideas? Was it Manetti or, as others suggest, Toscanelli? Or someone else, still? Under what form? A historian of art, Pierre Francastel, has some veiled reproaches against historians of science. "So little is known," he says, "about history of science in that period, that we have no bearings."[2] He goes even further; he quotes from Henry Guerlac's report to the Ninth Historical Congress in Paris, describing the as yet embryonic and fragmentary state of our discipline, to show why the historian of art is left helpless, or has to help himself out as best he may, as Focillon did concerning the relations of mathematics and art in the twelfth century.[3]

We are, then, on the spot, and we had better accept the reminder. We have not yet created our own techniques of analysis in that no man's land between art and science; we have all too few of the facts and none of the critical tools, if we except some penetrating remarks by philosophers like Brunschvicg, who indicated in this period a moving from "Mechanicism" to "Mathematicism." And even so, what do such words really mean, and in what context? My master, Federigo Enriques, used to say in a light vein that good intellectual history is made *a priori*. I would follow his advice so far as to suggest that we be allowed to characterize *a priori* the crucial issues as we see them now, and then try to see where they were effectively tackled.

Two great issues come to mind when we think of that epoch-making change. One is the rise of the modern concept of natural law over and against the medieval one which applies to society, another the intellectual "change of axes" which allowed an explanation of nature no longer in terms of form but in terms of mathematical function.

On these issues, history of science has not much to say before the time of Galileo and Descartes, except to point up the well-known scholastic attempts. Prophetic utterances are quoted, which, scattered over three centuries, fall short of conclusiveness.

---

of Ten for Defense (Dieci di Balia) and had been ambassador for the Republic several times. The family was a wealthy one, and young Filippo had been sent to a humanist school, but his disinclination towards the study of the classics prompted his father to have him apprenticed in the guild of goldsmiths, which included at the time painters and sculptors.

[2] Pierre Francastel, *Peinture et Société* (1951).

[3] Henri Focillon, *L'art des sculpteurs romans* (Paris, 1932).

We are still looking for where the thing actually *took place* in its first form.

Let us then try to make a landfall at a point where art and science, undeniably, join. Brunelleschi created his theory of perspective by experimental means. He built the earliest optical instrument after the eyeglasses. We have Manetti's description of the device, a wooden tablet of about half an ell, in which he had painted "with such diligence and excellence and care of color, that it seemed the work of a miniaturist," the square of the Cathedral in Florence, seen from a point three feet inside the main door of the cathedral. What there was of open sky within the painting he had filled in with a plate of burnished silver, "so that the air and sky should be reflected in it as they are, and so the clouds, which are seen moving on that silver as they are borne by the winds." In the front, at the point where the perpendicular of vision met the portrayed scene, he had bored a hole not much bigger than the pupil of the eye, which funnelled out to the other side. Opposite the tablet, at arm's length, he had mounted a mirror. If you looked then, through the hole from the back of the tablet at its reflection in the mounted mirror, you saw the painting exactly from its perspective point, "so that you thought you saw the proper truth and not an image."

The next step, as we see it now, is to invert the device and let in the light through the pinhole, to portray by itself the exterior scene on an oiled paper screen. This is the *camera obscura*, not quite the one that Alberti described for the first time in 1430, but its next of kin, and it took time to be properly understood. But the whole train of ideas originated with Brunelleschi, between 1390 and 1420.

We have thus not *one* device, but a set of experimental devices of enormous import, comparable in importance to that next device which came two centuries later, namely, Galileo's telescope. Galileo, it will be remembered, announced his instrument as derived "from the more recondite laws of perspective," and in their very inappositeness (at least in modern usage), the words are revealing. The new thing could be understood by opinion only as one more "perspective instrument" and indeed its earliest Latin name was *perspicillum*, whence the English "perspective glass," a name which might apply just as well to Brunelleschi's devices.

We may note that Copernicus himself, untroubled by any modern thought of dynamics, had candidly proposed his system as a proper perspective construction: "Where should the Lamp of the Universe be rightly placed except in the center?" Conversely, there is a "Copernican" spirit about perspective. People will be portrayed as small as they have to be, if they are that distant. There is nothing wrong in looking small if the mind knows the law of proportion; whereas the medieval artists had felt that change of size had to be held within the limits of the symbolic relationship and importance of the figures to the whole.

What the devices of Brunelleschi have done is in every way as significant as the achievement of the telescope. If the telescope established the Copernican system as a physical reality, and gave men an idea of true astronomical space, Brunelleschi's devices went a long way towards establishing in natural philosophy a new idea concerning the nature of light. On these effects of the *camera obscura* I need not dwell, as they have become by now a fairly well-established item in the history of science. By showing the passive character of vision, it cut the ground from under a vast set of theories, primitive and also Platonic in origin, which assume vision to be an "active function," a reaching out, as it were, of the soul. After the discovery of the formation of an image on a screen, the theorizing may well go on for some time, since it is an acquired cultural capital, but the best minds cannot participate in it wholeheartedly, and therefore it is sentenced to eventual decay and fall.

This, then, is set; I mean, all set to be worked out properly. To see the change in the period which concerns us here, we need only compare the consistency and fertility of the new outlook with the optical theories of Ghiberti, Brunelleschi's older friend and contemporary. They are really confused and uncertain footnotes to Alhazen. He sees dimly the new thing that Brunelleschi has established, but he cannot grasp it, he flounders between old and new. Here, too, he is as Frankl has described him stylistically, the last medieval. Fifty years later, with Piero della Francesca and Leonardo, we are almost wholly within the new ideas concerning light. It may take until Benedetto Castelli in 1620 to give them uncontested scientific citizenship, but that is because in philosophical theory the old is so much slower to die, the present a coexistence of many epochs.

When it comes, however, to Brunelleschi's first optical apparatus, the perspective mirror device, understanding becomes much more complex and difficult. For if our *camera obscura* is a passive instrument like the telescope, this one is meant to project correctly a work of man, the painted tablet; yet it is undoubtedly an instrument, based on the geometrical construction later expounded by Alberti, the "visual pyramid" axed on the "centric ray." It is strictly speaking a perspicil, meant to show reality as is, and the portrayed reality even meshes with the natural in the reflection of sky and clouds in the burnished silver. The sky, we realize, is not to be portrayed. (Nor is it in the second model, where it was used directly.) Why, we shall see.

Surely, here we have the beginnings of a science—a science of visive rays, as Leonardo calls it, so scientific that there is even an apparatus designed for it. But what is it for? To help us portray rightly what we see around us—essentially, to give the illusion of it. Illusionism is a strong motive, inasmuch as the most direct application is to scenographic design. This in itself is no mean thing, nor merely a way to amuse the rich. It has been proved that those monumental town perspectives—like that of the main square of Urbino by a pupil of Piero—are no mere exercises in drawing, they are actually projects for an architecture that is not yet there, and the first sketches of town planning. This is in the true line of development, for Brunelleschi himself had devised his instrument as an aid to architectural planning. But where does it leave us as far as science is concerned? George Sarton appraised it crisply in *Six Wings*, his last book on the Renaissance. After giving a brief historical summary on perspective, he concludes: "Linear perspective implied a certain amount of mathematical knowledge, but not a great deal. The best mathematical work was done in other fields, such as trigonometry and algebra." And that's that; or rather, let it stand, even if we are tempted to qualify it. The treatment that Kepler gives in his *Optics* to just such constructions, involving catoptrics, shows the thing to require no inconsiderable mathematical skill. The point remains that Sarton considers the subject not particularly important.

Yet we all agree that if the history of science is to be understood as George Sarton himself wanted it understood, a dominant cultural factor, we cannot push it off again at such a critical juncture to a couple of algebraists working in a corner. At a time when the main avenue to reality was through art, it is inconceivable that the artist should be dismissed. But Sarton also knew that beyond his curt appraisal, one would have to enter the uncertain region of interpretation, where the art critic may feel at ease, but the scientific mind finds itself desperately uncomfortable. He restrained himself according to the by-laws of his craft. Yet he knew, better than most, that it is these by-laws which kept so much of the history of science in a condition like that of Gerontion, having neither youth nor age,

> but as it were an after-dinner sleep
> dreaming of both,

caught between a blurred past and a misapprehended present. The Scientific Revolution should be seen and studied as a major intellectual mutation, which obviously started about the time when both interest and relevance seemed to have slipped out from under the scholastic system without anyone being able to say why. But the old political axiom still holds: "On ne détruit que ce qu'on remplace." Beyond the mass of heterogeneous social factors, the rise of this and the decline of that, which are strung together in the common histories, what do we know about the actual "replacing" element? The shift of opinion can be traced to the early Renaissance. It cannot be accounted for by still non-existent experimental results, nor by "industrial growth," nor, even less, by any advances in trigonometry. That is why research seems to center at present on the new interest among scholars for the mathematical "method." I submit that, valuable as it is, it is not the answer, and I hope later on to show that indeed it could provide no "replacement."

May I be allowed, then, to ignore the by-laws for once, and to enter at my own risk the region of discomfort.

Much, of course, has been written about perspective by cultural historians. It has been said, authoritatively, that Quattrocento painting places man inside a world, the real world, exactly portrayed according to physical laws, that it asserts naturalism against medieval symbolism, and thus creates the natural presupposition for science. This may be very rightly said, but one goes on feeling uncomfortable. Such a piling up of obvious factors until science is then produced out of a hat looks suspicious. Panofsky, as we quoted him, insisted on art as a tool of science, which is methodically strict. I tried to stay on the same ground with the perspective device. There are risks in going beyond. We remember Whitehead saying that the subtle logic of the scholastics was another of those necessary presuppositions for science, and it remains a most unverifiable statement. There would be, indeed, strong reason for saying the opposite, that scholastic thought was and remained a retarding factor. The ultimate proof of the pudding lies in the Galilean consummation; behind it one might see very different factors at work: the engineering and Archimedean line of thought for example. And there again we must see how that factor works. Invocations are not enough. Such a qualified scholar as Mr. Martin Johnson has insisted on the Archimedean factor in Leonardo's development, and it can be proved—Sarton has done it—that he is wrong. Archimedes is still for Leonardo a legend, a name to conjure with, he is not a set of concepts: Leonardo's thought remains utterly non-Archimedean, committed to the concepts of a biological physics of a wholly different style. Even more does it behoove us to be careful in dealing with large words like "naturalism." There is surely full-blown naturalism in Leonardo, but he expresses it mainly by being a natural philosopher: There the ambiguity is lifted. For he certainly *is* a natural philosopher.

Then what is naturalism in art? The art critic may legitimately use this term in a way which has nothing to do with natural science. Not as realism, for instance: Leonardo, the wizard of trompe-l'oeil, insisted that here could never be truth, but a *simulacro*. The new power, or shall we say the new freedom, of a Masaccio or Masolino applies to the way people *stand* inside the setting, it indicates a new canon that is plastic and visual, a new choice perhaps—not naturalistic objectivity. And certainly not a new discovery of space. That way of placing people has been maturing since the time of Giotto. I think it is safe to say that up to Leonardo, pictorial space will remain tied up with the human action in it, and that again is continuous with Giotto. If there is an evolution, we might call it a critical revision, with the help of perspective, of the "social" conception of art which belongs to the fourteenth century.

But there is a striking change nonetheless.

If we try to define what is meant, we are led to expressions like "the presence of a charged reality," a feeling of "vital autonomy" of these beings—in short, a feeling of *immanence* as against the former sacramental transcendence. These are metaphysical terms. Since we have to enter the metaphysician's den, strewn with the bones of former explorers, let me suggest a password. It will mean here simply that our attention is held, not so much by what we see, as by what we do *not* see, by what might be called, with apologies to Maxwell, a field of force.

The invisible element up to then in the paintings has been the living dispensation of God, his mysterious presence in all things: It was symbolized by the golden background which had no depth and yet suggested infinite depth. The image was strictly an intellectual symbol in the Plotinian sense. The world of things was, as it should be, an emanation of the hypostasis of Soul, it had no depth of its own. In the new representation, imagined matter becomes truly spatial, it is bodily on its own, and not only creaturely, as it were. It is surrounded by an invisible field which does not, however, escape comprehension like the other, for it is an intelligible reality, it is space itself. One, of course, may speak in terms of plastic or tactile values. But in this way, I hope to have avoided all danger of doubletalk.

What I am saying about the new painting is still interpretation. But when we come to architecture, it turns out to be the central fact itself. Brunelleschi's perspective machine is designed to place objects correctly in space, the nearest thing to a stereopticon, each thing being defined, as Alberti says, by having *uno luogo*, one place. And the reason why the sky is not represented but used directly is highly systematic: The sky does not have *uno luogo*. It cannot be brought back to measure, proportion and comparison, hence it cannot be represented in the proportional system which defines the form. It is space itself, it is of the essence of the field. It is what represents but cannot be represented.

This is not to say that from that moment on, art becomes based on field theory. It is rather of the nature of science to be led from step to step by the firm consequentiality of abstract propositions, which as soon as discovered are developed in their fullest consequences. In art many interests have to coexist which are certainly not abstract. If Brunelleschi himself had been asked to explain what he was doing, about the same time, in his submission for the famous portals of the Baptistery, he would have stated it no differently from his competitor Ghiberti, whose painstaking report shows the humility of the medieval craftsman. Those are the Bible stories, he insists, just as they are told, carefully represented, and to show it he goes through the detail of objective particulars specifying the materials used, stone and bronze and gold each in its place.

Even the man who obviously got the theoretical illumination, he who is said to have become obsessed by perspective, Paolo Uccello, can be extremely unsystematic about it in his work. His case is clearly that of a divided personality, which accounts for his being, as Schlosser put it a bit drastically, more than half a failure. The extraordinary novelty and power in his portrayal of individual figures goes with a strange helplessness in composition, a crankiness of interests, which caused him to sink into an obscure old age. And yet, when we look at those descriptive geometry studies of absurd complication, like the *mazzocchi*, we realize that here a true engineer was lost, a simple man who would have been happy designing some new radio tower or steel pylon for power lines, who would have revelled in industrial design and become a master for Freyssinet and Nervi —but who lived at a time when there was no use for such talents.

As with Uccello, so—in a measure—with Piero della Francesca and with Leonardo himself. The breakthrough of any genuine line of scientific pursuit works to the detriment of the artist's true productivity. It is not in Piero's theorems on solid geometry that his philosophical contribution lies, nor in his *Perspectiva pingendi*, it is in his sense of the mystery and power of pure geometric form and volume which shine through his composition and heighten its metaphysical import. There is a variety of meanings you can put in such a simple thing as a circle. The circles of Piero are an unmoved reminder of perfection. Those of Paul Klee look as if they were spinning. They are the symbol of a rat in a cage. Yet both are just circles to the unaided eye. And so back we are in the region of the undefinable.

It may have something to do with the elusive nature of the artist's quest, which in turn is certainly tied with the socially long undefined nature of his activity. Let us be properly hostorical about it for a moment. Let us not forget that the Middle Ages had given music a place in the Quadrivium, among the Liberal Arts, but none to painting. If we follow the scheme down into the seven Mechanical Arts which are supposed to be as it were a pallid reflection of the higher ones, we find *lanificium, armatura* (i.e., building), *navigatio, agricultura, venatio, theatrica.* Wool-carding and hunting are recognized arts, while painting and sculpture are nowhere. The figurative arts are left to a purely servile status. They are not supposed to be a freeman's activity.

This is not just forgetfulness. Hrabanus Maurus had taught long since, at the onset of the Middle Ages, the primacy of the Word. Dante himself, who admires Giotto, shows by his idealized use of sculptures in Purgatory that he considers them a kind of teaching aid, heightened maybe by divine touch into some kind of 3-D cineramic animation effect, but still subsidiary and illustrative, whereas poetry, we know, is for him a true philosophical medium, a transfiguration of the object to cosmic significance. And even Cennini, who wrote in 1390, in time for young Brunelleschi to read him, who insists on giving art a professional status beside poetry, provides for it only the old proportion rules of antique convention, plus the new and important caution that the rules do not apply concerning woman, who has no symmetry or proportions, being irrational and a pure thing of nature.

This is the intellectual state of the question at the bursting of the early Renaissance, and it derives little clarification from the first helpless and arbitrary theorizings, or even from Vitruvius whom Brunelleschi, it seems, never troubled to study. As for "science," it was held in trust by professors who cared for none of these things. How, then, can these men effect a *prise de conscience*? How does the new intellectual constellation arise?

The problem may become clearer if we think of the second stage, so much more familiar to us. Two centuries later, at the time of Galileo, the struggle between the old and the new form of knowledge is out in the open. Galileo is an acknowledged master of acknowledged science, in mathematics and in astronomy, yet he has to contend all his life with the prejudice which denies him philosophical status. He is treated as a technician and denied any capacity to deal with the true causes of things, which are of the domain of cosmology, as taught in the schools. We all remember how much persuasion he had to spend to show that when we have found a "necessary," i.e., a mathematical cause, we have as true a cause as the mind can encompass and that we need not look farther afield. We know that it took the combined effort of Galileo, Descartes, and Newton to establish the new idea of a natural philosophy.

If now we come back to 1400 instead of 1600, when the medieval frame of ideas was still an overarching and unchallenged presence, when what we call science was still a hole-and-corner affair without a character of its own, if we think of this group of men who had no connection with the universities, little access to books, who hardly even dressed as burghers and went around girt in the leather apron of their trade—then, I say, it is no use vaguely talking about genius; we have to show some concrete possibilities underlying this sudden creation of a new world of theoretical conceptions.

The period I am referring to is fairly well defined. It is the fifteenth century itself; it starts with Brunelleschi's early work; it has reached a conclusion by 1500 with Leonardo and Luca Pacioli.

The first thing was for these men to have some conception of their social role which allowed them to think legitimately. Here we can see that they found an anchoring point in the old theory, reinterpreted. For just as medicine claimed the "physics" of the schools as its patron science (hence the names "physic" and "physician"), those craftsmen had two of the mechanical arts, architecture and *theatrica*, and above those, music and mathematics. By the time of Pollaiolo, it is commonly understood that architecture is a straight liberal art.

But mark the difference. The painter remained with only a mechanical art, *theatrica*, back of him. He did in fact tie up with it, in a measure of which we would scarcely be aware if G. R. Kernodle[4] had not collected all the evidence of the connection there was, back and forth, between scenographic art with its repertory of props and the settings of the paintings. This went one way as far as town-planning, as we have seen previously, but even when it remained pure decoration, or play scenes, it shifted the accent from the *liber pictus* of devotional art to the productions and the magnificence of court and city pageants. Ghirlandaio, Benozzo Gozzoli, are names that come to mind: But even in the production of Raphael and Titian, the new "spectacular" element is stronger than the devotional occasion. The architect, instead, has something unequivocally solid to handle. He builds reality.

This leads up to the *third* factor, the new type of patronage from a new ruling class. It is significant that just about the time when Brunelleschi was called in as a consultant to the Opera del Duomo (the Works Committee for the Cathedral) its last ecclesiastical members were dropped and it became an entirely lay body: Brunelleschi on his side, once he is the executive, shows a new technocratic high-handedness in firing the master builders *en masse* for obstructionism and re-hiring them on his own terms. But he had not risen to the top without a decisive fight with the Guild of the Masters of Stone and Wood, who resisted his plans and even managed to get him, an outsider, arrested for non-payment of dues. He appealed to the Works Committee and had them clapped in jail. This was the end of the medieval power of those he called scornfully the "Grand masters of the trowel," whom the softer Ghiberti had joined believing no one could ever lick them.

Here we have, then, for the first time the Master Engineer of a new type, backed by the prestige of mathematics and of the "recondite secrets of perspective" (Galileo's tongue-in-cheek

[4] G. R. Kernodle, *From Art to Theatre, Form and Convention in the Renaissance* (Chicago, 1944).

description of his own achievements is certainly valid here), the man whose capacity is not supposed to depend only on long experience and trade secrets, but on strength of intellect and theoretical boldness, who derides and sidesteps the usual thinking-by-committee, who can speak his mind in the councils of the city and is granted patents for his engineering devices, such as that one of 1421 which describes in the somewhat casual Latinity of those circles a machine "pro trahendo et conducendo super muris Cupolae lapides, macignos et alia opportuna," or the other, of the same year, for a river lighter equipped with cranes. He is, in fact, the first professional engineer as opposed to the old and tradition-bound figure of the "master builder": He is the first man to be consulted by the Signoria as a professional military engineer and to design the fortifications of several towns: His work is the precondition of the first text-book, that of Francesco di Giorgio Martini. But still and withal, he is acknowledged to the end of his life as the great designer and artist; not only that, but as the man who masters the philosophical implications of what he is doing. Donatello may be acquainted with the Latin classics; he is still considered a craftsman. Brunelleschi is not; he stands as an intellectual. It is only a century later that the fateful distinction emerges between pure and applied art. By that time, the pure artist himself is hardly an intellectual.

Finally, we have the fact that this complex of achievements by a well-led group of great talents—Manetti, Ghiberti, Donatello, Masaccio, Uccello, Luca della Robbia, with Brunelleschi as leader—found a literary expounder of comparable talent in the person of Leon Battista Alberti (d. 1472) who gave their ideas full citizenship in the robed world of letters and humanism—something that only Galileo was able later to achieve by himself. It will have been a fragile and fleeting conjunction, no doubt. By insisting on a "science of beauty" Alberti perpetuated the rigidity of medieval disciplines with their ancient idea of "method," and their dictation of what is right. It will end up in mere academism, about the time when science breaks forth with its own idea of method and of truth. But as long as it lasted, in the period of creation, it had been a true conjunction, both in one. Alberti only paraphrases Filippo's words (we know that) when he says of the new art of architecture: "If it ever was written in the past, we have dug it up, and if it was not, we have drawn it from heaven." That "social breakthrough" that the new science of Galileo effected through the telescope, we find here in its early counterpart or rather first rehearsal. Everyone in 1450 was aware that a boldly speculative theory had preceded the complex of achievements, until the Dome of the Cathedral rose unsupported in its greatness, "ample enough," says Alberti, "to hold in its shade all the peoples of Tuscany."

We have lined up, one, two, three, four, the preconditions, or what our dialectical colleagues would call the objective possibilities for a scientific renascence, as well as, I daresay, the proper revolutionary consciousness; yet, even if we go and comb the patent records in approved dialectical style, we shall not be able to register the birth of modern empirical science. We are left with the question we started out with: "What was it? In the name of what?"

A revolution, surely. But what does that mean? Are we not reading upheavals into the past, when it is very possible that we should find, below this commotion, a sequence of slow and unnoticed alluvial effects? I suggest that it is best to be coldly phenomenological about it. Revolutionary is as revolutionarily does. Uprisings, *jacqueries*, justified as they may be, are revolts of the slighted or the oppressed; they are not revolutions. It is only when a group of individuals arises in whom the community recognizes in some way the right to think legitimately in universal terms, that a revolution is on its way. "What is the Third Estate?" said Sieyès. "Nothing. What could it be? Everything. What is it asking to be? Something." This is fair and reasonable, but that "something" has not been granted or taught from above, it is dictated to them by an inner reasoned certainty, and it is that no longer disputable certainty which makes all the difference. Here in 1789 are men whose philosophy has grown to impose itself, as it does in the calm utterances of our Declaration of Independence, men who know they can assume responsibility for the whole body social, not only in the running of its affairs, but in its decisions about first and last things. When these decisions sweep even the entrenched opposition off its feet, and move it to yield freely its privileges in the historic night of August 4th, then we know that a revolution has taken place. It is the resolute assumption of responsibility which forms the criterion.

May I insist upon this line of discrimination, as it might enable us to cut across the large amounts of indecisive data and shaded pros and cons which encumber our research.

To be sure, there had been in our case, over more than a century, a discernible trend among scholars towards the mathematical knowledge of nature; but in what spirit? Alistair Crombie's contribution to this volume, even if conducted *ex altera parte*, would provide by itself enough material for my contention, which stands as a tribute to his fairness. We read that Hugh of St. Victor and Gundisalvi pleaded for the admission of technical concerns to educational theory, because the *architector et ingeniator* is a useful figure indeed. "The science of the engines," says Gundisalvi, "teaches us how to imagine and to find a way of arranging natural bodies, etc." Why surely. But what was Gundisalvi conceding from his book-lined study that a man like

Villard de Honnecourt did not know much better by himself? What contributions did the patronizing scholars bring to the still primitive efforts at writing of men like Walter of Henley, Guido da Vigevano, or Conrad Kyeser? J. Ackerman[5] has published a case which is very much to our point, since it deals with the predicament of the Lombard masters, Brunelleschi's rivals, when it came to establishing the plans for Milan Cathedral in 1386. On one side there is the local guild commission, suggesting that geometry might be of use in some way for designing the buttresses, on the other the consultant Pierre Mignot, described as "maximus inzignierus" (or Big Injuneer as our students would call him). As he is unable to give any positive advice, he takes evasive action in a fog of doubletalk about Aristotle's principle that mathematics should not be used in the science of locomotion, and since statics as a part of mechanics belongs to that science, let's just make the buttresses doubly thick to be on the safe side. The Masters are not impressed but bow to authority. So much for the collaboration of the scholars with technology.

As the scholars cannot see beyond the immediate utility, so they cannot overcome their own school-bred respect for the raw data of observation and the commonsense physics that goes with these. More than once I find in Crombie the term "irresoluteness" which acutely characterizes their attitude either in equipping themselves with the proper knowledge of mathematics, or in their way of attempting experiment. Buridan does not really hope that nature will provide the conditions for mathematical laws to be fulfilled, although "it could happen that they should be realized by the Omnipotence of God." In other words, wouldn't it be wonderful, but only a miracle of divine benevolence could free us from the Aristotelian bondage. This is exactly the attitude of the traditionalist vs. the revolutionary. Yet Buridan is no timid spirit. His words show him to be a true rationalist, but he has to defer to long-established authority, whose dictates become akin in his mind to the deposit of the Faith or to the divine right of kings. For two centuries this kind of speculation has been going on with nothing much happening.

Here and there, the scholar can risk bold theorizing, he can intimate, adumbrate, and prophesy; but he must be prepared for an intervention of authority which tells him to drop his playthings and come back to a correct attitude. This intervention did come at last, decisively, with the anti-Copernican decree of

[5] J. Ackerman, "Ars sine scientia nihil est," *Art Bulletin*, XXXI (1949), 84–111. "Mechanics examines bodies at rest, their natural tendency (to a locus), and their locomotion in general, not only assigning causes of natural motion, but devising means of impelling bodies to change their position, contrary to their natures. In this (last) the science of mechanics uses theorems . . ." These are words not even of Aristotle, but of Pappus in his *Math. Collection*, VIII, 1.

1616. By this time, however, even if alone and abandoned by the scholars in retreat, there was Galileo. He stated in no uncertain terms that in such grave matters, his authority was fully equal to that of the Church Fathers themselves. This is what I call the assumption of responsibility. Galileo does not hesitate to denounce the authorities for playing irresponsibly with reactionary subversion. The freedoms granted by tradition, he insists, are his protection, the reason that God gave us to understand His laws is on his side. He uses all the proper language of submission, but he makes it clear by his attitude that he will not compromise, that he will not retreat, and that he will be heard.

As we know, Galileo could have gone on establishing the pure and simple science of dynamics without all this fuss. He actually did—by the time he could do nothing else. This would be enough to prove that he did not consider his thought the empiricistic outcome of industrial division of labor or advanced technology or book-keeping or whatever gadget it is that amateur sociologists have devised for his rationale. He felt he had to face the central issue: To the well-worked-out cosmos of his predecessors he opposed another cosmology, another way of knowledge whereby man has to go ahead forever in discovery, trusting Providence that it will not lead him to perdition. This Galileo maintained even when told by the Successor to Peter, the Vicar of Christ, that his doctrine was "pernicious in the most extreme degree." He alone, with very few men of his time, perhaps only Kepler and Castelli, could really know what he was doing. Even his trusted Ciàmpoli, who sacrified his career to get the Dialogue published, romantically thought that this was some novel and wondrous line of Neoplatonic speculation, in the spirit of Robert Grosseteste. Here is what I consider Galileo's assumption of responsibility for the whole body social in first and last things. It stands with us to this day.

Now that we have defined our terms, let us go back to the situation around 1400, and I daresay we can see some reason for the fog of indecisiveness which hangs over the period to the eyes of the historian of science. The gap was too wide between the world of the scholar and that of the technologist to be crossed by anything profoundly significant or fruitful. Encouraging noises were the most of it, and they can be discounted. Even in the extremities of nominalism, the world of the scholar is too well-knit, spiritually and conceptually, not to keep dangerous deviations in check. Nicole d'Autricourt is free to suggest atomism as a natural philosophy, but once the chips are down, he has to back out or become a heretic. The investigator of mathematical methods is given more latitude, but he, too, knows there is an end to his tether, hence his "irresoluteness."

Yet there is agreement among historians, as I note from both Crombie and Hall, about the highly intellectual and theoretical character of the Scientific Renaissance from its inception. No accumulation of progress in the crafts could bring it forth. Now if we search for the point of conceptual start, where the "flash-over" could take place from the world of intellect to that of the crafts, we are certainly on better methodical ground than if we juxtapose incongruous factors into a specious syncretism. The idea that I would submit for reflection is that the flashover occurred in the one art capable of receiving a high theoretical content, namely, architecture. It will not lead directly to physical science, that is obvious, but in those early years of the sixteenth century it is, in Whitehead's simile, the laboratory in which the new ideas are inconspicuously taking shape, for it provides the point at which the old dominant ideas of *form* can be resolved effectively into mathematical law. The resoluteness with which Brunelleschi carries through this transformation of intellectual axes makes of him a more decisive figure than Leonardo, who, faced with vaster problems, tends to lapse back into a medieval "irresolution." Not being a branch of philosophy, not even quite a liberal art yet in the estimation of the learned, architecture is free to assume its commitment unchallenged, and to lead it to concrete fruition and victorious achievement. There is nothing like success to establish a certain way of thinking; it is the success that had never attended the efforts of Oresme or Buridan which allows Brunelleschi and Alberti to work out their ideas meaningfully, to their far implications. That is why I have tried here to concentrate on the figure of those Founding Fathers.

Of Brunelleschi there is no question but that he stands there as the scientific-minded Innovator *par excellence*. He is that, if I may say so, from snout to tail. Take only the way he went at studying the Roman monuments in his early years, while earning his living on the side as a clockmaker (this small point, too, has its relevance). He took down "on strips of vellum" the measures of each part, written in terms of one basic measure. It may look simple enough, but it is described as a great new idea. The old master builders had never come upon it. They did not write. They took their measures, we are told, with pieces of string, and left it at that. No collaboration of practical necessity with the wisdom of the learned monks who did advise them, no interplay of scholarly thought with technology had gotten beyond this stage for centuries.

Small wonder that we find in Brunelleschi's theory, through Alberti, an analysis of proportion which leads one back to Greek mathematics at the time, say, of Theodorus. His method shows that it took one mind from start to finish to bring in with the technique of measurement the new idea of proportion, and make it work; just as it took one mind, Faraday's, to bring in from start to finish the electro-magnetic idea. He is the man, too, who could assume a commitment and maintain it in the face of opposition. What we know of him (and I do not mean the watered-down generalities to be found in Vasari) shows him as a daring leader but also a careful strategist. Witness the time when he capably withdrew and allowed his rival to try his hand at building the Cathedral Dome, but as soon as the chain-and-girder system devised by the latter had snapped, he was free of his "sickness" and ready to take on the job. The easy-going and humanistic Ghiberti provides the needed foil for his affirmative and polemic personality. When Machiavelli, in his famous preface, says that it is time to do for politics what the great artists have done in building, he has clearly in mind Filippo's way of dealing with Roman antiquities: not to stop entranced at the grandeur of them as Donatello did, but to study the joints and structure of the buildings, how the stuff was actually put together so as to stand forever. Which is just the way Galileo studied Archimedes. We have there what Vitruvius defines as invention, "the mobile vigor of the mind." In all three cases, it has to face from contemporaries the bitter old reproach, that of the cold and abstract—if not destructive—pride of intellect,[6] while the poetic and tender-minded uphold the virtues of tradition.

There is indeed in the personality of Brunelleschi much that reminds us of the other two "patricians of Florence"; his love of good company and vivid argument, his irony and sarcasm (he was, says the biographer, "most facetious and prompt in repartee"), not to mention his pranks, some of which were incredibly elaborate, and required half the town in connivance, like the one he played on Grasso the carpenter, to make him believe that he was not himself at all, but another man called Matteo, who was being looked for by the police. With the diligent help of Donatello and the police chief who had him booked, Grasso was made to lose his identity so that he went around for two days in a daze asking people "Who, then, am I?" until the friends restored him in sleep to his own bed. This climate of jokesmanship in terms of the ultimate is to me not incidental. In Machiavelli's letters, in Galileo's poems and correspondence, we realize what it stands for: Freedom of spirit, *homo ludens*, the crackling of the sharply critical and relativistic mind; the play that can go with single-minded dedication, and even with flashes of profound metaphysical poetry. If the flavor of that salt be lost, we are bereft of one of our senses in historical perception. We miss the power of strong irony and liberating wit, from Erasmus to Voltaire. There is more than one way of merriment: This one is the straight opposite to that, otherwise charming, of *mansuetudo*, and the much later reaction of a man

[6] Giovanni di Gherardo wrote against him in a sonnet which begins: "O deep and brimming wellspring of ignorance"; Cavalcanti wrote that Florence had been led astray by "their false and lying geometry," and there were many more such attacks.

caught between the two ways might show us a kind of litmus test. Magalotti is one of those men who had been under Galileo's influence, and who, like their master, had never lost their sincere concern with salvation. Late in life he entered a monastery, but had to leave it after two years of fruitless endeavor. As he writes rather shamefacedly to Cosimo III, it was not the ascetic life that drove him out, that was indeed what he had come to seek: "it was rather, I have to admit it, the good Fathers' way of having fun."

Brunelleschi is akin to Galileo in his sense both of fun and of purpose. Like Galileo, he could be bold, clear, and decisive in a way that compelled assent even in matters but dimly understood by the public. One is reminded, too, of Guicciardini's good-natured note to Machiavelli on reading the *Discourses*: "Well, here you go, *ut plurimum* paradoxical and upsetting in your conclusions, but always very notable."

What the revolution was about is less easy to define, because of the intellectually elusive quality of art. Such a theory as the Copernican will put the issue squarely, as between closed world and infinite universe. It will bring violent reactions and counter-actions beyond the bounds of reason. Averroist naturalism—or Pomponazzi's hard logic—will evoke sectarianism, condemnation and refutation without end. Whereas the artist simply projects the thing, something that stands there by itself, he brings in magically a new way of seeing, and then leaves imagination to take its course. What comes out in this case, for instance, is that when the artistic revolution is done, all the old emotions about realism and nominalism are as dead as a door nail. Something new is in the world, but the creators have gone unchallenged.

It could not happen today, granted. No combination of Picasso, Gropius, and Mies van der Rohe could sway our philosophy that much. But that is because we live in a world where modern science has taken over, and will not allow thought to be moved around beyond certain bounds. Five centuries ago, science being conceived as of forms, the appeal of a new science of forms could blot out the old one, if those forms were felt as particularly significant. The proof is such a well-known work as the *Hypnerotomachia Polyphili*, the mystic tale of a quest similar to those of the Rose or of the Grail. The symbols are no longer the ancient and medieval ones, they are drawn from architectural fantasies. Architecture, as I said earlier, seems to be the point where art and knowledge are felt to join.

It is then left to us to decide what the new thing actually *is*, and to evaluate it. This will be the subject of the last part of this paper.

It might be well to see first what they *thought* it was. The literary theorist of the movement is Leon Battista Alberti, himself an artist of sufficient stature to assure us that he understood what his friends were about. The label that he puts on it is the neoplatonic one. Neoplatonism was orthodox enough to be safe, strong and speculative enough to be new. The mathematical bent of the whole school was so marked, that such a label is hardly unexpected. Here again, we are faced with the fact so well marked by Professor Koyré, that the new thought arising against the old logic is of a necessity under the invocation of Plato, and will stay so until and after Galileo. The Galilean way in dynamics, as he points out, is to explain the real case by way of a theoretical one that can never be brought under observation, the concrete by way of the abstract, what *is* by way of what cannot be said to "be."

The theory of linear perspective might seem too simple to lend itself to such weighty thoughts, It can be kept down to a workout in elementary geometry, just as Sarton described it, and one wonders why the medievals who tried found such difficulties in relating the objects portrayed to a fixed position—if it is really a matter of drawing lines. But let us not forget that Alberti, like most theoreticians, is putting his new wine in old bottles, whence the label of Platonism. He can use only then-known, i.e., elementary terms, hence his explanation falls short of what is really the case. What we call "a system of mental representation," and "the ordering of a conventional space in depth," and so on, are things which cannot be expressed in his language but only pointed up to. The system that is being evolved is part mathematical, part symbolic and mythical; it is fully there only in the actual works of the artists. What comes out of those, we shall try to work out later. But it must be extracted from implication, it is not stated in simple words. Unless they be, by rare chance, some few poetic words of Brunelleschi's very own. We have those few words in the scornful sonnet he wrote in reply to Giovanni di Gherardo:

> Ogni falso pensier non vede l'essere
> Che l'arte dà, quando natura invola[7]

"False thinking does not see the being to which art gives birth when it steals [its secrets from] nature."

The visual space of these early theoreticians is seen as containing somehow the secrets of nature. It is not mere analytical relation as in Descartes, nor does it only express the togetherness of beings as in Gothic. The creative mind is always midway in process; so here. Geometry is used instrumentally, for unravelling that space; the business of perspective unravelling goes on for centuries to pose problems still to such a distinguished

[7] See note 6.

mathematician as Desargues in 1648.[8] Optical space tends to wriggle away from the geometric straitshirt. What is truly abstract, hence the guiding mystery throughout, is *logos*, is proportion, is number.

Now, as to Brunelleschi; how much was he, whose business after all it was to make things, aware of the intellectual implications? We know that he was very keen on theory, were it only from the passing mention that he considered Alberti a bit too simple in his thoughts. The few poetic words we have quoted of him certainly go deeper than Alberti's theorizing, but whither do they tend? We would have to know more about his background to have an exact answer. The real books of his early education, we are told, were Dante and the Bible (we read, just as in Helmholtz's autobiography, that instead of following Latin classes in school, he would draw houses and geometrical diagrams). Manetti and Toscanelli cannot be properly called his teachers, since they are younger than he. But when he decided to move from sculpture into architecture, they became his advisers and confidantes. There is some documentary evidence of their influence in his planning and thinking. And here, even with insufficient facts, we might come close enough with *a priori* inference to help M. Francastel out of his difficulties. What these men imparted was not so much the elements of geometry which were needed for perspective and graphical statics; it was a certain frame of thought connected with the subject, which had come down to them from the world of scholars. It might be said by some that it was a mantle of formal dignity intended to place them above the teachers of the hornbook and the abacus. It would be truer to describe it as the garment of their own thought, what went with education, and the "gentle soul." I have heard critics wonder how Dante could thank so tenderly and solemnly old Brunetto Latini, the dry encyclopedist and professional backroom politician, whom he finds broiling in Hell, for "having taught him time and again how man makes himself eternal."[9] But after all, if he says it, we have to believe him, who believed so much in the importance of philosophy for the "cuor gentile," hence we must conclude that even the hard-boiled Brunetto knew how to dispense more than factual information. In short, whatever his trade, this type of teacher had to communicate a philosophical understanding, it was part of the medieval style, just as the German professor of the good epoch could not but transmit his emotions about the dignity of *Geist* and *Bildung*.

All this would hardly need to be said, were it not that I fear we tend to lose the feeling of past life in our schemes of "trans-

[8] A. Bosse, *Maniere universelle de M. Desargues de pratiquer la perspective* (Paris, 1648).

[9] *Inferno*, VII, 82: "for there is ever in my mind, and still moves me deeply, the dear and good fatherly image of you, as you taught me in the world, time and again, the way in which man makes himself eternal."

mission." What did those men, then, actually transmit? The feeling of the high dignity of mathematics, for one, as vouched for by Platonic wisdom; the hope in mathematics, as revived in the preceding century by famous scholars like Bacon and Grosseteste; most of all, the beliefs and wondrous intimations to which Christian intellectual mysticism had clung through the centuries, and which expressed themselves in the "metaphysics of light."

With this body of doctrine we are fully acquainted through many expositions. It starts from the Platonic analogy of God with the sun, that is set forth in the myth of the Cave. It pursues the analogy to suggest that, as God is the life of the soul, so the physical world is held together and animated by the force of light and heat, which should turn out to be, as it were, the ultimate constituent of reality.[10] One could not express it better than Galileo does in the Third Letter to Dini in 1615.

> It appears to me that there is in nature a substance most spiritual, tenous and rapid, which in diffusing through the universe, penetrates all its·parts without hindrance, warms, vivifies and makes fertile all living things, of which power the body of the sun seems to be a principal receptacle. . . . This should be reasonably supposed to be somewhat more than the light we actually see, since it goes through all bodies however dense, as warmth does, invisibly, yet it is conjoined to light as its spirit and power, and concentrates in the Sun whence it issues fortified and more splendid, circulating through the universe, as blood does through the body from the heart. This ought to be, if I may risk a supposition, "the spirit that hovered on the face of the waters," the light that was created on the First Day, while the Sun was made only on the Fourth. . .

Later, Galileo was to insist that he believed the ultimate substrate of reality to be light itself. There is no need, after that, to weigh his explicit professions and reservations with respect to Platonism. The doctrine of light, "a principal access to the philosophic contemplation of nature," as he calls it, is the true Platonic watermark.

Should I pursue the lineage into the Cambridge Platonists and beyond? I trust the case can rest here. There are minds to whom the geometric virtues of the light ray, its sovereign diffusion and instantaneous transmission, are symbols of its closeness to creative omnipotence, and intimations of its mysterious role as a prime element. There are other minds, call them Aristotelians, to whom all these are fine and poetic thoughts, but cats is cats, and dogs is dogs, and light is best characterized as the entelechy of transparency, that is, the per-

[10] See Dionysius the Areopagite, as quoted in Galileo's letter to Dini.

fection of an attribute, not a substance, hence incapable by itself of bringing forth even the simplest squid.

We might add that there are still other kinds of minds, fascinated by the protean changes of living substance, to whom fire and warmth seem a truer essence than light. These are the Stoics, but they belong to quite another story.

Of these so different lineages, the men that concern us here belong definitely to the first. From them springs the persistent interest in optics, from Alhazen to Witelo the Pole and Johannes Kepler. From them descends the line of speculation which becomes significant in great scholastics like Grosseteste or Oresme, men who have taken to scanning the world of mathematical ideas and entities for pure schemes, like the triangle or the quadrangle, which may be superimposed on the phenomena of change as a grid to reveal their law. Such diagrams are forms still disembodied, floating around inconclusively, keys searching for their lock; nothing will happen until Galileo brings them down to mechanical reality, the only lock that will fit them. It will mean then a deep transformation of the languages and their formal content, as e.g., from "uniformly difform qualities" to "uniformly accelerated motion"; but the schemes are there already, more than pure shapes, trains of thought in mid-air, asking to be brought down to earth. Father Clark gives a striking example in the diagram that Oresme tries vainly to apply to qualities, and will appear later, with only a change of axes, as Galileo's first integral of motion.

Such were the ideas hovering around, say, in 1360 (the time of Oresme's writing). They were disembodied and yet very pregnant ideas. They had superadded themselves to the old traditional wonderings about the cosmic role of the five geometrical solids. They are the inspiration that teachers, from Toscanelli to Pacioli, communicated with passion. At this point, in these years, they hit fertile ground, with the invention of perspective by Brunelleschi and Uccello; here we are back in our story, but we may understand better all that Brunelleschi would see in his invention—if he was the intellectual that history shows him to be. We have not yet investigated Toscanelli as an individual; but we have characterized enough of his ideas to provide an adequate first answer to Francastel's query. We have reconstructed this education as safely as we would Newton's (supposing we knew nothing about it) from the fact that his educators had to be Protestant divines and classical scholars.

The documents will then tell us that Toscanelli was an intensely ascetic and spiritual man, "a physician, philosopher, and astrologer of most holy life" Landucci calls him; a man who shunned meat and held it was wrong to take the life of animals. When we see this unusual doctrine so strongly emphasized by his successor Leonardo, with an explicit and equally unusual

Pythagorean connotation, we may conclude that we know something of Toscanelli's line of thought.*

We understand better, after this, certain peculiar characteristics of Alberti's avowed Platonism. Ficino is already starting a trend, and it is natural for Alberti to "move in" on it. But what he brings is very far indeed from Ficino's *Schwärmerei*.

Says Alberti: "Great, small, high, low, light, dark, and all such which are called the accidents of things are such that all knowledge of them is by comparison and proportion . . ." Does this remind us of something we heard elsewhere? Why surely it does.

> In our speculating we either seek to penetrate the true and internal essence of natural substances, or content ourselves with a knowledge of some of their accidents. . . . But I shall discover that in truth I understand no more about the essences of such familiar things as water, earth or fire than about those of the moon and the sun, for that knowledge is withheld from us, and is not to be obtained until we reach the state of blessedness. But if what we want to grasp is the apprehension of some accidents or affections of things, then it seems to me that we need not despair of acquiring this by means springing from measurement and geometry, and respecting distant bodies as well as those close at hand—perchance in some cases even more precisely in the former than in the latter.[11]

This is Galileo writing on the sunspots, and the kinship of thought is unmistakable. Galileo is using here diplomatic restraint, for he is arguing against the authorized system. In the *Dialogue*, he will go further and suggest that what is called change of form might be nothing but a rearrangement of invariant parts; later, Robert Boyle will be forthright about it:

> This convention of essential accidents [i.e., the order of constituent particles] being taken together for the specific difference that constitutes the body and discriminates it from all other forms, is by one name, because consider'd as a collective thing, called its form.

The word is out, the essential knowledge is not of forms but of the order and position of parts. Although a very religious man, Boyle will not have to retract his words like Nicole d'Autricourt, he will take his chance with the "Epicurean error"; for it has become what we call science.

Alberti has been writing the manifesto of something that he cannot grasp in its full import, for theoreticians know in part, and they prophesy in part; but he—and Leonardo—call it a science, not an art like music, which is a daring commitment, proper science having been properly defined long ago by the authorities in the Trivium and Quadrivium. The new science of

* See "Paolo Toscanelli and His Friends," p. 33.

[11] *Discoveries and Opinions of Galileo*, tr. Stillman Drake (New York, 1957).

light and space is one of "accidents" or properties,[12] something which to the mind of the scholastic could not possibly hang together, or make sense.

Is it that they are unaware of the official stop sign? Surely not. The current language of their time would be enough to point it up unmistakably; that is why they have to work their way around the language. But they do not have to come into conflict with the philosophic doctrine, because they, the artists, are not compelled, at that point, to choose between "substance" and "accidents."

That grave choice will have to be Galileo's, who is after abstract knowledge. If he decides he cannot know the substance of things, he will have to be explicitly agnostic about it. The artist can be completely confident about the "substance" of his quest, for it is his own artistic creation and nothing else. If it does not exist yet, it is going to exist, of that he is pretty sure, or his life would be bereft of meaning.

Let us restate the thing in Alberti's simple terms. There is a science, perspective, whose aim is correct comparison and proportion, projection in a visual space (we shall see later all that this implies, but Alberti himself need not be aware of it as yet). It allows us, by way of geometric properties, to deal with the object, the substance, architecture itself, or rather *il murare*, as they say so much more concretely, the *act* of raising walls brick by brick. The right walls. If they know what they are doing, that is all they need.

We have come to a point where we can take stock of the situation. We have here a type of knowledge which refers strictly to what "we ourselves are doing," a *conversio veri et facti* which will find its theoretical development with Vico three centuries later. That future development does not concern us here, but its immediate continuity in Leonardo, the student of nature, surely does so. We cannot forget how, after his restless search on all planes for the essential forms and mainsprings of nature, a search which cannot lead to an abstract physics because it presupposes so much more, Leonardo is led at last to set limits to his understanding:

> You who speculate on the nature of things, do not expect to know the things that nature according to her own order leads to her own ends, but be glad if so be you know the issue of such things as your mind designs.[13]

This is the end of that trail; the artist has to go back to a knowledge which is not that of nature. Leonardo's attempted system breaks up and dissolves into a magic of form and color

[12] Galileo also calls them "affections," using the old scholastic term, to mark his position with respect to the past.

[13] MacCurdy translates "conceives" which is quite misleading. The original has *disegnate*. See E. MacCurdy, *The Notebooks of Leonardo da Vinci*, I (New York, 1938), 76.

that rises to the stratosphere. But no one could deny that the fallout was considerable.

By transforming the concept of substance into something which could be designed and built up through their science of proportion, the mathematical artists have crossed the otherwise unmanageable distance between Substance and Function. Any attempt at bridging it directly by philosophy would have led to an intellectual impasse, worse, to a breakdown.

This ought to be clear at least in one aspect. In the whole of medieval philosophy the "principle of individuation" had to be carefully worked out and structurally established, for we must account for a multiplicity of true individual "beings" (there would be no proper natural foundation otherwise for what we call now the "dignity of the individual"). Aquinas individualizes Aristotle's generic natures, made up of form and matter, by having them endowed with individual "existence" by God's will. Scotus, as befits his nominalistic attitude, has to sharpen the issue; he makes of the individual natures true essences, *haecceitates*.[14] This atomization of "being" may not be very convincing but it is needed. Three centuries later, in the Cartesian system, individuation has vanished as if by a conjuror's trick. This is inherent in mathematical ideation. Even in Galileo's thinking, it is no longer clearly justified. Now all of medieval and Renaissance thought is still strongly based on individual beings, on the *signatura rerum*. That is why the sorry predicament of Grasso the carpenter, who was made to lose his individuality for a while, is far from philosophically irrelevant, and shows the prankster's awareness of ultimates. But it was a prank. To remove the props from under individuation unequivocally and in a responsible manner as is done at present would have meant in that intellectual climate a psychological trauma or a revulsion. The philosophy of the artists, although it rests on such mere "attributes" of being as light and space, does bring forth out of those again a "being," the actual individual creation; it provides thus a gradual relativizing and an acceptable transition.

It took this mediation. Are the ladies in Piero della Francesca's *Queen of Sheba* substance or function? If we affirm either thing of them, or even both at once, it will always be true—on a level from which there is no way down again to scholastic common sense. This is what Tuscany had done for Galileo.

Shall we try to describe what we called the fallout, as it seeps in invisibly, all around, for generations before the birth of Galileo?

The new science around 1430 is, as we have concluded, operational in character; that is, it defines the object of its quest by what it does about it, with the difference that whereas the

[14] G. Bergmann, "Some Remarks on the Philosophy of Malebranche," *Review of Metaphysics*, X, No. 2 (Dec., 1956), 207–26.

modern object is the experimental procedure, its object is *il murare*, the building procedure. It remains now to work out its theoretical structure, which is far-ranging.

The peculiar "substance" of that quest is a system of planes and volumes rigorously thought out by way of its properties, known and understood geometrically, physically, functionally, aesthetically, and even symbolically. It imports a fullness of knowledge. The perceptual raw material, as it were, of that knowledge is provided by the past of civilization, for it is in the traditional architecture which is already around, on which judgment and criticism have been able to sharpen themselves. That is the stuff which is now going to be transformed. The huge variety and multiplicity of the pre-existent Gothic pile is a wonderful mass of decorative singularities, where the eye is led without break from the minute particular to the immensity of the whole. Ockhamism concluded, as it were. The Gothic structure, thinks Alberti, is a denial of proportion, a seething cosmos of things streaking off towards heaven; we have to bring into it a constructive law which is dictated by ratio and perspective: "*A speciebus ad rationes*," as Ficino transcribes the Platonic principle.

Let us make this a little clearer. Form, here, for the artist, has the function of *ratio* or cause of all the species, insofar as there are not really many aspects or forms, but *the* form or the Idea ("concetto"), given by draftsmanship. Perspective shows us the actual size of a thing that looks small in the distance; its position in space determines the truth and invariance of the individual object: its projection the true form abiding in it. The module and reality of the particular are shifted from the thing to geometric space. It is in this space of *ratios* that true construction takes place.

I am trying to paraphrase as best I can the actual ideas of a contemporary who thought he saw what was taking place but could perceive only a dim outline. You cannot expect it to be as clear as a theorem. But if this goes as Platonism, it is certainly not the literary variety with its fashionable uplift. We are treated to diagrams and visual pyramids, to a coördinates net on a screen. We are asked to see longitudinal perspective in terms of that other inverted pyramid ending in the flight-point placed on the infinite circle: that mathematical point at infinity in which all the forms and ratios of reality are absorbed or rather "contracted." No one could deny that we are here on Cusan territory, although there could be no question of direct influence, since Nicholas of Cusa was just having his initial ideas in 1433 when Alberti was writing. What these men have in common can only be the source, the unformulated Pythagorean element just then being transformed. Alberti is fully aware that the longitudinal perspective carries the theme of contemplation; it loses itself as

Plotinus suggests in that one flight-point.[15] In fact, it is the equivalent of the medieval golden background: But the imagined ensemble of flight points is, with respect to that sensuous gold, utterly abstract—a true intellectual construction, like that of Nicholas of Cusa, ending up on the "circle of infinite radius."

This metaphysical aspect had been fully grasped by Brunelleschi himself, as is shown by his main line of research, the inflexible endeavor pursued through his life to achieve a synthesis between the longitudinal perspective, implying transcendence, and the central perspective, which implied to him an intrinsic organization of space, or, in philosophical terms, immanence. We can follow the successive stages of this study in his great buildings, San Lorenzo, Santo Spirito, the Ospedale degli Innocenti, until the synthesis is achieved right at the time of his death (1446), with the topping of his great Dome. For the Dome is not only his most outstanding solution in static engineering (what was felt as the miracle of unsupported growth), it is also, in its "rib-and-sail" structure as it was called, the conclusive formal solution of a philosophical issue. The slowly convergent triangles are pure geometric forms leading up to infinity, as no hemispherical dome ever could. The Gothic vertical flight has been transposed into another key; it is concluded and held together by the topping Lantern.

At this moment, as if to mark the scientific inspiration of the whole, astronomy comes in with a significant note. Paolo Toscanelli, Brunelleschi's trusted consultant, and no doubt in accord with his friend's wish, had a dial device built into the Lantern as it was being terminated. It was the third novel instrument in the series: a perforated bronze plate, placed so that the sun's beams struck the pavement below along a graded strip cemented into the floor. It turned the Dome, as Lalande was to write in 1765, into the greatest astronomical instrument ever built. The beam was 240 feet long, and it allowed Toscanelli to effect his solstitial measurements of the inclination of the ecliptic reported by Regiomontanus, which gave 23° 30′. It is correct within 1′, which is probably luck, but in any case better for the time than Regiomontanus' own, 23° 28′. (It is at present 23° 26′ 40″, owing to the yearly precessional variation.)

Have I been trying, then, to read philosophy or science into art, a thing reproved both by the scientist and by the aesthetician? I trust I have not. We have only to read Alberti to realize these men's keen awareness of their intellectual quest. At a time when what *we* mean by science was still beyond the horizon, when the *name* of science was monopolized by scholastic officials, who officially denied to mathematics any link with physical reality,

[15] A. Grabar, "Plotin et les origines de l'esthétique médievale," in *Cahiers Archeol.* (Paris, 1945), 15–34.

these men had conceived of an original prototype of science based on mathematics, which was to provide them with a creative knowledge of reality, repeat—creative, and could claim the name of true knowledge in that it dealt with first and last things. There should be some proper way of placing this attempt, in its true dimensions, inside the history of science, but it has yet to be made.

The historian of art, left to himself, will help us only to a point, because he is thinking of different terms. It is characteristic that so acute a critic as Heydenreich, who contributed much to the knowledge of Brunelleschi's evolution,[16] left the Dome to one side as a technical stunt—a strictly scientific job in graphic statics, we might say, raising a vault without centering. It took the careful monograph of Sanpaolesi,[17] conducted on the archival material of budgets, notes, and sketches, to show how the remote theoretical problems never left Brunelleschi's mind.

That he was left free to undertake it is curiously tied up with very practical and economic reasons. The original plans for the Cathedral, designed by Arnolfo di Cambio two hundred years earlier, established the measures for the circular base of the dome, conceived as a hemispheric vault. Those measures were found quite proper by his successors. It turned out, however, that by 1400, architects could count no longer on the huge availabilities of timber that a conventional centering frame implied. Even the carpenters able to deal with it were scarce; the task appeared "impossible, nay more than impossible," as the chronicler puts it. This is what moved the *Operai*, a committee of conservative businessmen, to consider any suggestions for a new working solution. But that solution sprang in Brunelleschi's mind from theoretical considerations. It was a triumph of the speculative, and not only of the mechanical, mind over matter, hence we should not lose sight of that speculative element.

It has its source in the Pythagorean tradition implicit in Platonism. It is a bewildering mixture of ancient tradition and daring modernity, as the old Pythagorean mentality itself had been. In his Christian faith, in his canons, in his certainty (he said once: "Our faith should be called certainty"), Brunelleschi is profoundly a medieval. He is even older than that, for Wittkower has shown that the Renaissance canon relied on integers and rational numbers, whereas the medievals had been more open to the use of irrationals. But it is all the more strongly founded on proportion and *logos*.

It is this intellectual element, overarching that whole early Renaissance, which explains many things in the rise of the new architecture (Brunelleschi himself, as we shall see, had no inhibitions about the Golden Section, irrational though it may

[16] L. H. Heydenreich, "Spätwerke B.s," *Jahrb. d. Preuss. Kunstsamml.* (1930).

[17] P. Sanpaolesi, *La cupola di S. Maria del Fiore* (Roma, 1941).

be). It will drive Uccello and Piero deep into geometrical speculation, it will eventually find its concluding manifesto in Pacioli's *Divina Proportione*, which is expressly dedicated to Piero della Francesca, "the most worthy monarch of the art of our time." In this kind of theory, elementary abstraction has hardened and simplified much of what had been profound and original creation. But the development, we said it earlier, is as linear and rigorous as one could wish.

Whither does it lead us? To what Alberti, as essentially a man of letters, could not see, nor for that matter Pacioli (who was barely above a teacher of the abacus), but seems to be present as a deep intuition in the creative masters. We mean, to an impressive generalization of the Pythagorean system. In the original doctrine, there were only a few entities which embodied geometry, but they were felt to be enough in that they acted by participation. The circle, the cube, the Harmonic Fifth, existed as absolutes, and caused things to behave "in imitation" of them. Of such manifest imitation the cases could not but be very few, and so science was limited to the charismatic regions of music and astronomy. But if we begin to think in projective terms, then we begin to see circularity inherent in ellipses, squareness in rhomboidal shapes, and so on. The "imitation" of the Ideas turns up everywhere, even if the original forms be no longer obvious: The square becomes one of its own perspectives, the circle a conic section. In fact, what used to be "form" becomes a collection of very abstract relations whose mathematical treatment is surely not elementary—and may have been above anyone's resources at the time. What would Uccello be tormenting himself about with the absurd complication of all the perspectives of the square in his *mazzocchi*, why should he be exploring the possibilities of invariance under distortion, if he did not have some such idea at the back of his mind? This is, then, a vision of the Pythagorean system become truly universal and permeating all of reality.

What is suggested here is surely inference *a priori*. I am not aware as yet of any statement documenting it unequivocally within the fifteenth century. A check that comes to mind could be found in Maurolico's treatment of the conic sections as the perspectives of a circle. It would be a definite subject of research to look for more evidence. What I was suggesting there was not even the probability of an explicit theory along the lines mentioned above, but essentially the presence of an intuition, which allows the mind to envision a new generalized Pythagorean approach to the whole of reality. This intuition becomes then, in the image of Galileo, like a sun in which the old ideas concentrate "to issue thence fortified and more splendid" to circulate through the whole culture.

However that may be, we have brought into evidence a *fifth* factor which provides what was certainly missing, the vision, the unifying intellectual element behind the artistic revolution. It is not in direct contrast with current scholastic theory, and in fact we discern no quarrel with it in the whole contemporary Florentine Platonist trend. It merely bypasses it. But it will carry thought far into the future.

I trust it is plain by now that what is involved in this story are the great categories of scientific philosophy. Erwin Panofsky has characterized the space of classical art as "aggregative." There would have been no better way to describe the space of Aristotle himself, which is nothing but an orderly pile of containers. This commonsensical kind of space is, for a modern, utterly irrelevant. The space of the Renaissance Panofsky describes by contrast as "homogeneous." In our language we might call it a metric continuum. We have seen earlier what it can imply. It is a new potential richness that Leonardo expresses with awestruck phrases.

It is not a matter of realizing its three-dimensionality. It had been three-dimensional for everybody all along, even for the most medieval of artists; we do not hear of their bumping their heads into corners from lack of space perception. It was simply that they had not felt three-dimensionality as relevant to their art. Here it has become a subject for relevance and intense abstract imagination. No one will mind making distant figures as small as they have to be: The space which comprises them in its structure will restore and define their meaning. "Grasp firmly with thy mind the far and the near together . . ." These are the words of old Parmenides, and they stood for a great beginning already at that time. It is this firm, this creative grasp which makes all the difference.

The closed space of Aristotle is only the tidy arrangement of a simple multiplicity of things, not unlike, let us say, the shipping department of Sears Roebuck. Whichever way we understand the new space, that of Nicholas of Cusa and Brunelleschi, it is certainly not that. It is for the artist a pure space of diaphanous light articulated throughout by the central design, bringing into action the law of forms from every point of view at once. It is described by Cusanus, in his famous phrase, as "that whose circumference is nowhere and the center everywhere" and the phrase should be enough to show the whole import of the revolution, for Nicholas of Cusa has borrowed it from the description that "Hermes Thrice-Greatest" gives of the soul. Such a transfer to cosmic space of the properties of the soul, with the accent on a "central perspective" of the intellect, is something no medieval would have dared.

Space is for the new imagination a matrix for infinite potential complexities and states and tensions—a matrix awaiting total structure, rather, a manifold of structures. It is on its way to becoming what is for Newton the organ of perception of God, for Malebranche the only intelligible reality, for the theory of central forces the carrier of that incomprehensible property, action at a distance; it is rich enough to bring forth set theory, group transformations, phase spaces, the electromagnetic ether, Riemann's geometry, and the Einsteinian reduction of all reality to properties of the time-space continuum.

To sum up, this investigation seems to suggest that two of the major features of the Scientific Renaissance, namely, the change-over from Form to Function, and the rise of a "natural law" unconnected with the affairs of human society, have their origin in a specific transformation of the arts. They cannot be said to arise out of the scholar's interest in mathematics, which remains wishful, nor out of the development of the crafts per se, nor out of any statistical accumulation of small interactions between the two zones. They are coherently worked out and brought to bear at the time when the representative and building arts form a new idea of themselves, and go through a theoretical elaboration of that new idea, in such a way as to be able to bring it to grips with reality in their creation. This seems to be the moment when the actual shaping of a new operative thought takes place, and it provides some fundamental categories for nascent scientific thought.

I have barely sketched out the outline of the problem. The analytical tools have yet to be forged. The scientist and the historian of art have hardly ever met, and even then under a cloud of misunderstanding. I am only trying to enter a plea for collaboration in a subject which is still tricky and most difficult.

The Italian Novel Today— A Note on Realism

THE MAN STARTED AGAIN TO SAY: "THE WORLD IS LARGE AND BEAUTIFUL, but it is much offended" . . . Much, much offended is the world, more than we ourselves know.

These words from Elio Vittorini's "Conversation in Sicily," spoken by a humble man of the people, come to haunt the mind whenever one searches for the main themes of the Italian novel of today. Even when the tale runs demurely amid everyday happenings in a family setting, there is always a tragic undertone linked with man's condition in the universe, or whatever we may call the puzzling togetherness of things. It gives meaning to the simplest situation.

Let me state first what the American reader will *not* find in the Italian novel. It is the kind of narrative he is most used to, and finds, say, in Edith Wharton and J. P. Marquand, in the *New Yorker* stories and in a host of familiar writers: the level of well-organized, active, quietly distinguished and not insensitive society, one which knows how to judge itself and behaves accordingly. One might just call it Society, if one takes away the Social Register connotation and the "socialite" caricature. This kind of novel is really a private Anglo-Saxon affair, it does not even "travel" well, as one says of wines, and we see that what the Europeans absorb from here is essentially another kind, represented by Hemingway, Faulkner, Caldwell, and Steinbeck. In all these authors there is a tragic tension of the individual over against or away from society, written with a small s. Again, take other authors respected in Europe, Robert Penn Warren and Tennessee Williams, and the way they have of pinning down clinically their white-trash characters from high to low. When one looks at the Italian middle class through the mind of the Italian novelist, one is indeed reminded of Tennessee Williams and his marvelous hatred of the death-dealing insanities of the Southern white—as they are depicted, say, in *Streetcar* or in *Baby Doll.*

The massive body of the Italian middle class is surely more ancient and structural, and also softer, than our Southern whites, but it too is in an arrested and regressive condition. Centuries of humanistic chloroform have stabilized it, but there you have it: provincial, uncouth, unsocial, cocooned in the biological unit of the family, not psychologically complex enough to provide real novelistic developments. It can be handled by brilliant, pitiless vignettes, as in Silone, or by surgical dissection as in Moravia, or in light scintillating caricature as in Carlo Montella (one of the more promising younger writers). What is sensitive, poetic, and meaningful, the stirring of the buds, the sorrow of mature understanding, is found by the Italian novelist among the poor people. By the Italian movie director too, as our public probably knows quite well.

The postwar movie and the postwar novel are one artistic

unit. If we think of De Sica's two last great movies, *Umberto D.* and *Gold of Naples*, we see what he draws out of the middle classes: moving individual predicaments, grotesque, stark, or tragic, but never what we would call a "civilized" situation. So does Moravia with his tormented adolescents. The artist is not really choosing his material according to "taste," he is in the role of a diagnostician. Anyone can tell that certain societies are sick. Fascism in Italy or Spain, nullification in our South are merely the sores that break out for all to see. What the artist does instinctively is to search, deep down, for what kind of sickness this might be. Few situations in Faulkner's novels take place in a "civilized" setting either. But in the Italian novel the point is made with a classic-minded clarity which is denied to the American authors: this world is "offended" through the fault of those who own civilization.

This may explain why a number of Italy's outstanding writers, Elio Vittorini, Vasco Pratolini, the late Cesare Pavese, appeared on the scene after the liberation as militant Communists. It is a tribute to their perceptiveness that they soon ceased to be Communists, and that years before the Khrushchev revelations and the Hungarian crisis shook the simple believers. Most of them had seen the handwriting on the wall even before 1950. But among the single-minded appointees who run our immigration affairs, the impression remained that Italian writers, like foreign political parties, must all be Communists. The result was that when Alberto Moravia was officially invited to this country by the State Department, which knew full well that he had never had any political affiliation, the immigration authorities held up his visa again and again for over two years, much to the amusement of the foreign public and with small gain for the prestige of our Policy of Protecting Freedom Everywhere. This was under the Reign of Dulles. *A tout seigneur tout honneur.* Not that his successors are much better. But public opinion is. The reasons for the snafu were never given; it is just the way we think we can win friends and influence people. Once readmitted to these impeccable shores, Moravia showed he bore us no grudge and wrote with great sympathy about America, whereas in his subsequent trip to Russia he made clear what could annoy Italian Reds most, namely that, whatever its virtues, that country has really nothing to do with Western civilization.

Moravia, who in thought and stature is at present an established international writer, has shown in his work over thirty years that political events are to him at most a changing backdrop for the enduring drama of individual existence. *The Indifferents*, his first novel, published in 1927 when he was twenty, is prophetic for a whole generation, and is the forerunner of the crop of American novels which have centered since on that strange gasping for decision in the young man of today, on his search for any substitute for a true choice, from neurotic compulsion to degenerate drives. The author could not but have in mind what he saw around him, the degeneration of the ethical tissue of society that the smart new-type governments had tried to use in their attempts at emotional engineering. But he dealt with it not in a naturalistic or emotional vein, but rather in the light of a severe Spinozian clarification. "Here is a candle to light you to bed, here is a chopper to chop off your head." The story is strictly private; it is that of a perceptive and paralyzed young man who watches listlessly the rotting away of his wealthy family in the grip of a moneylender, and finds himself finally in connivance with him.

Twenty-five years later, we have as it were the sequel to the story in *The Conformist.* Its hero might be the younger brother of the earlier one of *The Indifferents*, but what Toynbee would call the vulgarization of the dominant minority has run its course; he is an "average" state employee with a blunted perception. Passiveness and guilt are still his, but no longer fully conscious. Having been detailed to the secret police, he agrees to play the role of Judas to a friend. The tale becomes in truth a Passion play with its symbolism transparently worked out. The tragedy brings blood and murder; in the end there even descends avenging fire from heaven under the form of American planes machine-gunning the fugitive's car on the open road. Life is present at his death, as it were, in the impassive ancient stare of the peasantry watching the scene.

Critics who have definite ideas about the modern novel were startled by the book's almost medieval texture, and promptly panned it. Moravia replied tersely: "You can't go on forever writing *Madame Bovary*."

If *The Indifferents* and *The Conformist* are to be seen as two panels of a composition, then *The Woman of Rome* falls into place as the center piece of the triptych. In this, Moravia's best-known novel, the author is visibly in sympathy with the protagonist, who is the timeless figure of woman as the power of nature, life-giving and life-destroying, a river, as it were, wending its silent way unchecked through the artificial structures and tensions of civilization. The woman of the story is a beautiful prostitute, a simple girl no better than she ought to be, who endures the sorrows of her lot and the tragedies around her that she can comprehend but dimly, giving what she has to give, receiving from those about to die the new life that she is going to tend, not even knowing whether the child to be born is the issue of the criminal she hated or the young conspirator she loved. She judges not and is not judged by her creator.

I have dwelt on Moravia because the pattern of his tales is most clearly thought out, but a very similar vein runs through the work of most other major novelists, such as Ignazio Silone and Vitaliano Brancati. There is always a feeling of the irony of fate, brilliant and sarcastic descriptions of a society snarled up in its passions and prejudices, the harsh, timeless necessity of nature holding down men's lives, and always the underdog taking the rap, the helpless one as a fall guy. A world which is far indeed from our country and what it stands for—and from its "civilized" novel. In Silone's gallery of characters there is one little man, Sciatap, who has been to America; for years he has carried the hod for a coal-and-ice merchant in Brooklyn, and all he has brought back is his nick-name, the only English word he has learned, "Shut up." The question in that world is not how to be a good liberal, or how far the creative talent may compromise with commercialism, or how to develop a well-adjusted ego. The question is, how to give an accounting of the meaning of existence? The search is not for this or that meaning, but for some meaning; not for a reconciliation with the ego, but for a reconciliation with life. The medium itself may flow into a new shape. Thus Vittorini's wonderful *Conversation in Sicily* becomes really a prose poem, akin to the Book of Job.

One sees more clearly at this point the reason for the avowed lack of sympathy with the Anglo-Saxon style of thought and fiction. It is not only far away and of another world, but it implies success. The characters in our novels, confused as they may be, can have personal problems because they live inside a society which has achieved freedom, and feels it. The same might be said of the people of Jane Austen, Thackeray, or Balzac. The Italian novel indicates the fact that Italian society is only struggling towards freedom, that it is still under the dead hand of authority and immobility, considerate of those well-off, crushing to the small and helpless. This is what colors its thought. Said the G.I. in the depths of jungle misery, as the talk was of day-dreams, of girls and juicy steaks: "When I close my eyes, I see a mule's behind. Also when I don't."

Italy is a cultural country, we have heard that many a time. But see what a predicament it makes for the Italian man of letters. The poor people look up to that so-often-misused culture with pathetic respect. The Italian writer has to feel responsible.

The Seventeenth-Century Legacy: Our Mirror of Being

BECAUSE IT ASSUMES ITSELF TO BE CONCERNED WITH THE ESSENTIAL aspects of Being, seventeenth-century science continues the line of thought leading back to antiquity. It goes on being ontological.

The aspect of Being that it has discovered is matter-in-motion. It transmits this concerned to its successors; thus we have eighteenth-century materialism. When d'Alembert suggests that natural laws, if they are really necessary truths, "should be deduced from the very existence of matter," he is epitomizing the scientific mind of the period.

But the seventeenth-century mind is more complicated than that, as some brief reminder of that era may serve to show.

There is a current and facile misapprehension which makes thought move only with science into natural law and determinism. This, of course, is not so. Any rational thought assumes regularity, and the Renaissance had stressed natural law all too much: it was the Stoic version of natural law, the universal cosmic structure acting on each part through astrological and other influences. Even the schemes of such a free, critical, and historical mind as Bodin's were greatly overdetermined.

We might say, in fact, that the Renaissance world as a whole was overdetermined. Instead of one simple cause, each event had a great number, coming from all quarters of the cosmos, at all levels, but conspiring and convergent. It takes no less than that to have a cosmology based on forms, and significant forms. It takes no less than the whole of the cosmos to bring forth its image in the microcosm called man.

Overdeterminism may sound like a dreadful constraint, but it is not. It is instead a help to humanistic and poetic feeling, as we can see in John Donne or Thomas Browne. The more richly a substance is determined or "signed" by the cosmos, the more spontaneously it can act according to its own nature; this is what makes the so complex World of Being a free republic of active entities. And those "signatures" are themselves a heritage from the prodigiously complex and over-determined cosmology of archaic civilizations, which reached us through its remnants religiously preserved from classic sources. Stoicism alone would have been a storehouse, even if debased, even if deprived of the saving virtue of mathematics.

Less than justice has been done, in the current history of science, to the enormous role played by Stoicism in the intellectual transition. By transcribing the traditional scheme into properties of strictly determined matter (weirdly conceived, infinitely varied matter, but matter none the less), the Stoic theory acts as a kind of Trojan horse which establishes inside the consensus of public opinion the plausibility of the materialistic view. It presents a common-sense, animistic matter which requires no effort of abstraction and can perform all the things that we expect of life; comfortably empirical matter which encourages experimentation and lends itself to unlimited and inconclusive chemical research; matter which carries with it in the form of "elixirs" and "quintessences" all the old "signatures" of Being.

By contrast, Galileo's endeavor gains a metaphysical superiority which is readily grasped by the better minds. Here is not ordinary "materialism," even if Democritus is lurking behind it: here is insistence on the primary, namely mathematical, properties of matter. The cosmic determinism it suggests is brought down to one dominant plane, that of mathematics, and one type of cause becomes sufficient, because it is mathematical necessity itself.

That new cause, then, is far from being simply matter: it is mathematized substance, something which will be able to dissolve into the field theory of central forces. Thus, we have a really new bearer for the cosmological structure—it is a mathematical being, and the signature of things is mathematical.

This is where Galileo and Kepler can meet—in the implied foundation of mathematical rationalism. When Kepler invokes the authority of Proclus, the master of Neoplatonic systematics, concerning the eminent dignity of numbers and of the spheres, it is not simply a devout misunderstanding. If Kepler and Proclus had met, and Proclus had been sufficiently intelligent, it is certain that Kepler could have forced Proclus to accept ellipses instead of circles in his mystical system; these two men were operating from a common base. Proclus would have been more resistant to Galileo, and yet it was Galileo who stuck desperately and unreasonably to the circles of Proclus; he acted as his representative where one would least expect it. He was possessed with what Koyré has called *la hantise de la circularité*.

In sum, these men were still operating within the Neoplatonic orbit. They simply defined more clearly the behavior of Being at the level which concerned them, which was the mathematical level. This goes all the way up to Leibniz. Their theory of cognition was also the same—namely, as Spinoza would say, the order and connection of ideas is the order and connection of things. Nature and the mind were one and the same in their order.

If the order of Nature at some point did not appear to conform to the order of the intellect, it was felt to be a tragedy. Thus Kepler searches feverishly for the architectonic principles or "archetypal laws" above the straight numeric ones. *Which* is their musical consonance and the harmony of their distances? We know how Kepler worked himself to exhaustion over the orbit of Mars—because it would not fit. He tells the story of his predecessor, Rheticus, and of his fruitless efforts to bring the orbit of Mars to order inside the Copernican system. The despair of Rheticus was such that he had finally recourse to black magic and, like Faust, called upon the evil spirit to help him. The spirit came, Kepler tells us, but instead of providing a subtle answer he grabbed Rheticus by the hair, banged his head against the ceiling, then slammed it down on the floor and departed, saying, "That is all you need to know about the orbit of Mars."

If Rheticus had asked, say, about the hidden properties of some stone or plant, the devil would have obliged. But the circles of heaven are holy; the very mention of them drives the devil to madness.

There is not only in Kepler's story, but in Kepler himself, the Faustian tension of the late Renaissance; there is, even in this most guileless of writers, much of the artiness and extravagance of mannerism. Critics of style who are impressed by the new classical poise of the baroque tend to obscure the continuity of the seventeenth century with the peculiar hyperbolic madness of the declining sixteenth. It is probably from it that the "century of genius," as Whitehead called the seventeenth, develops a certain masquelike exaggeration of mood and experience which is more than an exterior fashion. People came to feel this way; those were the days of unbridled emotions, extremes of all kinds, cynicism, cruelty, sensibility, a Spanish-style grandness in all things, and not least in metaphysics.

Both society and theoretical thought enjoyed reflecting themselves, as it were, in the godlike splendor and arbitrariness of absolute monarchy; they were discovering the wonders of centralized power, fully explicated. They accepted subjection with a will, and took its harshness not only as a matter of course, but even as a true expression of a certain side of man's nature. We could barely guess the depths of Jansenist renunciation before the recent discovery of that somber figure, Michel de Barcos.

What remains in our memory of the prose of Bossuet, or Donne, are awestruck phrases:

> Dieu seul est grand, Messieurs . . . How desperate a state art thou in . . . There is not a minute left to do it. Not a minute's sand . . . For in the wombe are we taught cruelty, by being fed with blood, and may be damned, though we be never borne. . . .

It has been said that the reign of Louis XIV, beneath its trappings of sunlike splendor, signifies the advent to power of the bourgeoisie. True. But it is only of the bourgeoisie as a new sternness and organization at the service of the sovereign will. Colbert and Boileau are two complementary aspects of it. Harshness is the common experience. It takes the practical soul of Hakluyt to be shocked by the waste of manpower which is implied in the hanging of poor people for trifling offenses, "even twenty at a clap out of one gaol." No one heeded him at the time. At the very court of Louis XIV, where the king gravely took off his hat to the servant women, Lauzun could consider it a good practical joke at a garden party to grind under his heel the hand of the Princess of Monaco, resting on the grass. Conspicuous hangings at Tyburn and the execution of La Brinvilliers were social events like today's heavyweight title bouts.

The mechanical grottoes complete with mechanical nymphs and hobgoblins built into the landscaping of Versailles and Vaux-le-Vicomte are not the *rocaille* rococo amusement they will be in the next century; nor are they a merely literary reminder of Homer's cave of the nymphs, any more than Molière's Alceste or Tartuffe are mere characters of comedy; they really exorcise an ancient set of subterranean horrors, as we may realize in reading La Mothe le Vayer's allegory on that famous cave in his *Hexaméron rustique*. In the same vein, the *Mundus subterraneus* of Fr. Kircher is already a serious contribution to geology, but it still refers to those regions as *abscondita Naturae sacramenta*. And his *Oedipus Aegyptiacus* is a daring insight into still unknown cultures. The years 1650 and 1681 are all-time highs for astrological literature in England, closely followed by France and Germany. In those years five times as many astrological titles are published as in any other year, and this has to do with comets and end-of-the-world computations.

Such random features compose in our memory into an image far from all happy mediums. Galileo's sentencing is a spectacular production worthy of being portrayed by Veronese: it wilfully brings out by contrast the utter senselessness of the whole story. Spinoza's unworldly calmness may seem to be at the other pole; still it is no less extreme in its implications than the goings-on in *Arden of Feversham*. The heroes of Marlowe, of Corneille or Lope de Vega think and live in extremes. So does Kepler. So does Newton. I mean Newton "the Magician," "the last of the Sumerians" as Keynes calls him, not the Newton of the Newtonians. And under his studied evenness of demeanor, "that Grand Secretary of Nature, the miraculous Des-Cartes," is no less hyperbolic in his affirmations than he was initially in his doubt.

Small wonder that this should have been the epoch of metaphysics in the grand manner, just as it was of the drama. The fantastic arrogance of the mind inventing the ultimate logical design of the cosmos or the rigorous theodicy was strangely coupled with a Jansenist or Presbyterian somberness in submission. Disagreement, too, in the grand manner, grandiose conflict resolved, the skies revealed, were part of the scheme—but it were better to let Sir Thomas Browne say it in his own way: "The mighty exantlation of truth, wherein, against the tenacity of prescription and prejudice, this century now prevaileth."

The scene changes completely with Newtonianism and Locke. We all know it, we feel it. A new spirit has entered science. I should like to try to identify some of the fundamental differences.

If we look back from that position, we are able to see how much the seventeenth century, in its dramatic discords, has given to all of its thinkers in common—to Galileo, Descartes, Spinoza, and Leibniz as well as to their traditional opponents. And I would say it is not only a unity of style; it is a common Greek framework to their substantialist point of view—what is technically called the *analogia entis*.

Technically, the Aristotelian Analogy of Being is not such a simple idea. In sketchy outline, it says that all intelligible discrete parts of reality are one only in reference to the finite whole which contains them. Unity and individuation presuppose the cosmos.

But I am going to use the Analogy of Being here only in its intuitive sense: the being called Man has naturally in him the ability to grasp the nature, the oneness of other beings, even as his own. Thought naturally grasps nature—for there is in the Greek word *noein* the idea of grasping—insofar as it is itself part of *natura naturans*. Hence it can provide a science which is truly a Mirror of Being, a *speculum entis*.

When Galileo in his *Dialogue* has to confront Dr. Simplicio, the obdurate Aristotelian, the amount of intellectual exchange that makes it a true dialogue comes from the area of agreement between the two. They start from what is for both incontrovertible, namely, that the universe is a whole, finite and perfect, indeed the most perfect work of art. And when Simplicio refuses the new mathematical mode of thought, Galileo can well remind him that its cognitive foundation is the same. The famous parallel that he establishes at the end of the First Day between the human and the divine mind is a transposition in a new key of Aristotle's twelfth book of *Metaphysics*: there is knowledge only because of the fundamental identity between *nous* and *noeton*, between the knower and the known, or, as Parmenides had said, "Thought and the object of thought are one and the same."

Galileo, like Aristotle, like Spinoza himself, would say that our mind is *quodammodo*, in a way, but securely, at home in the divine mind, if it will only lift itself to total rationality. He only wants to specify that the "mode" is that of the primary qualities of matter. In each man the whole of truth is present, potentially; in Simplicio, too, and that is why he can be compelled Socratically to discover what he knew already.

That is also why Galileo's conception of experiment is so little empirical; in contrast with the raucous appeal of the Aristotelian to facts and to common experience, he resorts to the thought-experiment. He uses facts only as a check, as a discriminator between necessary and wishful arrangement. But the arrangement comes first, as witness his unfortunate passion for circles: the concrete is explained by way of the abstract, what *is* by what *is not.*

The dialogue is truly alive because Galileo is forcing Simplicio to remember how much of a Platonist he, too, really is. And, however much the substance has been changed which is the carrier of reality, that substance still carries also with it the *analogia entis.* It is still, and quite properly, overdetermined. That other new departure, the biological theories on preformation, on the Chinese-box *emboîtement des germes,* expresses a preposterous faith in a once-for-all overdetermination. One has to attempt either some such notion or a geometrical arrangement superimposed on it, or, when this too has to yield, a metaphysical rule emerges which is conceived as replacing the order of forms, viz. the Principle of Least Action. A principle of economy acting on maxima and minima is not as beautiful as a formal geometric principle, but it is just as teleological, and it is a more flexible and powerful abstraction; we know all that Leibniz was able to achieve with it. Even with a fully formed mechanics, Euler sees strictly in this light the differential equations he has discovered for the motion of a particle:

> There must be a double method for solving mechanical problems: one is the direct method founded on the laws of equilibrium or of motion; but the other one is by knowing which formula must provide a maximum or a minimum. The former way proceeds by efficient causes: both ways lead to the same solution, and it is such a harmony which convinces us of the truth of the solution, even if each method has to be separately founded on indubitable principles. But it is often very difficult to discover the formula which must be a maximum or minimum, and by which the quantity of action is represented.

This "harmony" it is which allows the new substance, matter-in-motion, still inadequately conceived, to overcome the miseries of simple location and misplaced concreteness, and to be transmuted eventually into that most sophisticated of substances, the Leibnizian monad.

Leibniz is very clear about it. Substance is what he needs. It remains substance ever outside of the Aristotelian scheme: something (a *vis*) which is capable of being both active subject and passive object. As he will say most revealingly, "What I mean by substance can best be grasped by way of that substance called 'I.'" With that, the *analogia entis* is narrowed to a fine point. Substantial Being is the locus where freedom meets necessity.

Galileo's original single substance is, however, full of contradictions. On the one hand, its link with pure geometrical forms ties Galileo's thought still to the finite, and we see his obstinate resistance to the other half of his mind, which pushes on toward infinity.

Finiteness is reinforced by the appearance of that new instrument of explanation called the model. No longer is the universe mirrored in every part of itself: a section of the universe can be repeated on an arbitrary scale by means of the mechanical model. It is difficult to imagine a model not founded on the stabler and simpler qualities. There can be no model for a section of Aristotelian or Stoic or even Leibnizian nature except nature herself.

But on the other hand, if Copernicanism means anything, it means the "breaking of the Circle," it means infinity. The founders of science skirt the issue as best they can; it is left to another kind of mind to realize the consequences—I mean the full metaphysical and poetic implications. This happens with Giordano Bruno. At his death in 1600, Bruno has already gone the whole way.

The discovery of Copernicus—the "fact"—is in Bruno only the detonator of his Neoplatonic-Pythagorean mixture. Although no mathematician, he has realized the new metaphysical idea that mathematics has brought about—namely, that Being in this key (we might call it Pythagorean Being) cannot be kept down to finite size.

The device that Aristotle had found for insuring a finite world was to make one part of Being perpetually a state of potency, and the other part a state of finite actualization. That device becomes unacceptable, for what is mathematical is always "all there," wholly actualized. Hence new solutions for the rhythm of becoming and the growth of the living form have to be found. Totally actualized being can only be expressed in its invariant forms, its laws will be of the type supplied by transformation groups. That, however, is far in the future; in this time of inception, we cannot expect a clear idea of all that the change implies. Only the requirements are passionately felt.

To a mind like Bruno's, filled with Neoplatonic speculations, the change from Ptolemy to Copernicus is a theological one. God has become immanent in the universe instead of being transcendent to it, for the universe is now as infinite as God himself is. For Bruno, it appears as a logical consummation: "it is not fitting" that God, who has always been conceived as totally actualized in himself, should not inhabit a world totally actualized too. The ancient idea of the *theoprepēs*, of what befits the Deity, comes back with explosive force:

> . . . I do not demand infinite space, nor does nature have infinite space, for the dignity of corporeal dimension and mass, but for the dignity of corporeal natures and species. For the infinite excellence manifests itself incomparably better in innumerable individuals, than

in those which are numerable and finite. Therefore, it is necessary that of an inaccessible divine countenance there be an infinite image, in which innumerable worlds, such as the others above us, exist as infinite members. So in view of the innumerable grades which must represent the unfolding of the divine incorporeal excellence in a corporeal way, there must be innumerable individuals, and namely these great animate beings, of which the earth is one, our Divine Mother who has borne us and nourished us and at last will take us into her bosom. . . . I believe there is no one to persevere obstinately in the false denial that as for space it can infinitely contain, and as for the individual and collective excellence of infinite worlds that they can be contained, any less than this world which we know. Each of them has a reason for appropriate existence. For infinite space has infinite aptitude, and that infinite aptitude attains its glory in an infinite act of existence, whereby the infinite efficient is saved from being deficient, and the aptitude from being fruitless.

We see where the idea can lead of Being as a positive good, or, in classical terms, as a "perfection"—an idea which our present consciousness can approach only with misgivings. Kepler is not unaware of these implications, but, like Copernicus, like Galileo himself, he backs out. The need for a finite universe, well and warmly contained within its outer glacial limits, is stronger in him than his own adventurous imagination. Fifty years later, Pascal puts it with his usual frankness: "It will be a good idea," he writes in fragment 218, "not to go any deeper into the opinion of Copernicus."

But Bruno goes the whole way. It is in him that the two world views, the old and the new, both vividly present to his mind, come into destructive conflict. On the one hand, he still thinks in terms of forms—after all, a man cannot jump over his own shadow. He feels the need for the finite, for the sake of that restrained actualization of Being that is form, for what it grants to the thinker—the possibility of vision, of the dense intuition, of the growth of thought in contemplation.

On the other hand, that Being is now conceived as expanding beyond all limits, and in this realization the mind is torn from its anchorage, it feels, as it were, propelled into infinity. Thus the outcome is not simply pantheism and serene acceptance. The intensive thought which used to be brought to bear on finite entities, which reflected, as it were, their Being on man, is now brought to bear on what Bruno perceives can be only a continuous process, an analysis without end, a trajectory toward ever-receding horizons, in which man has to surrender the limitations of his own finite individuality. When Bruno was sentenced to the stake in 1600, he must have thought of his own prophetic image: the hunter who has come upon the deity in the dark woods and is torn to pieces by his own staghounds turned against him.

The world of Galileo and Kepler, although strained to the conceptual limit, although dangerously nominalistic, remains congruous to the universe of discourse of Dante. It does raise major problems and terrible questions within that universe; but it cannot and will not answer them, for it insists on remaining, if one may say so, metaphysically isomorph with the classical conception.

With Hobbes and Newton and Locke, we are undeniably in a very different climate of thought. That Hobbes and Locke refuse the *analogia entis* is obvious. We are moving from ideation to ideology. What concerns us here more directly is to see how it happens with Newton.

As a Cartesian, Newton cannot see gravitation as in any way deducible from the essence of matter. That is why he says, in effect, "I don't understand it, *et hypotheses non fingo*." To him gravitation is a miraculous intervention, an act of God whereby the simplest order and dynamic equilibrium are maintained in the universe. In his famous passage on God Newton writes:

> A true, supreme or imaginary dominion makes a true, supreme or imaginary God. And from his true dominion it follows that the true God is a living, intelligent and powerful Being. . . . We know him only by his most wise and excellent contrivances of things, and final causes; . . . but we reverence and adore him on account of his dominion: for we adore him as his servants; and a god without dominion, providence, and final causes, is nothing else but Fate and Nature.

This is truly the nominalistic break. This is the primacy of the Will. God is no longer a mind in which we can "find ourselves at home," as the Greeks might have put it, and as Galileo understood it. God is an impenetrable Will, and all we can do is try to understand his intentions as best we may, in order to carry out those intentions. Newton deals with God as a Grand Vizier would deal with a fearsome Sultan. He has deciphered one of his major decisions in natural philosophy: he tries in other directions too. It is usually considered a blemish on Newton's life that he spent the last twenty years working out numerology from the Scriptures, and became impatient when people asked him questions about physics. Yet we should see the logic of it. Newton was trying to discover the will of God again by way of numbers: this time his will concerning man. He did not get anywhere; but the intention is clear.

Yet what Newton has gained is not small. He has imposed the feeling of something radically novel: the discovery, on an unsuspected plane, of laws which rule the stars in their courses, the mystery of heaven at last understood: it is a new combination of intellectual pride and emotional resignation to "iron determinism." The notion of a sky henceforth silent to our prayers can fit a detachment in the Spinozian vein, or it can become a kind of Presbyterian surrender to the Law; both are represented in the new high priests of science. Absolute and simple mechanical determinism was, of course, a myth. It would have rationally led to a block universe where nothing happens. But out of the myth of necessity, a new metaphor of Being had established itself. It needed no other religion; it was a religion itself, with its basic religious paradox: a new power of the mind, a new irrelevance of man. Such is the new *speculum entis*.

Once the link between man and nature is broken, we are left fumbling as to the nature of knowledge. We get soundly practical attempts, such as Locke's, which creates the phantom of a power of objects to induce representations in the mind; a common-sense idea which will come to scientific function in our time, but one which philosophically is hardly more than nonsense. Epistemology has reared its ugly head. The Principle of Individuation does not know where to look for a new home. The Mirror is dangerously cracked.

Thus we enter the eighteenth century, the *siècle des lumières*, in a situation highly exciting but also very untidy. All sorts of startling propositions offer themselves as seemingly irrefutably empirical and invite the most diverse deductions. The century is strewn with the corpses of such theories. The conflict between Cartesian rationalism and the new empiricism creates an occluded front between the two leading countries which lasts well into the second half of the century.

In the end, a general agreement is established, under the ironical gaze of Hume, on what we might call a new type of *analogia entis*. It is a naïve materialism: man is matter too, of a freewheeling variety. So the analogy proceeds. We remember that d'Alembert still hoped to derive the laws of nature from the "essence of matter."

In fact, a new mythology of matter is arising, which will break down only in the nineteenth century. Nature, as Fontenelle presents it, is nothing but a stage set and a *trompe-l'oeil*. The real action takes place by tackle and counterweight behind the scene. "'I perceive,' said the Marquise, 'philosophy is become very mechanical.' 'So mechanical,' said I, 'that I fear we shall quickly be asham'd of it. . . . Pray, tell me, Madam, had you not formerly a more sublime idea of the Universe?'"

But the eighteenth century has an extraordinary clarity, all the same. It has the illuministic clarity, the will to light, the hope of a new reason and a new justice. This explains, of course, the social intensity of the scientific campaign—a pragmatistic intensity, surely, which develops a shameless Baconianism, but aimed at awakening a new common sense.

That such a common sense needed the new *analogia entis* goes without saying. The offensive against authority and mystery provides reassurance by way of simplicity, and the ways of matter seem to be so gratifyingly simple. There is nothing simpler than gravitation, asserts Voltaire without batting an eyelash. There is nothing so amusing as electricity, says Priestley, while pigs are roasted electrically and a chain of six hundred obliging monks are made to hold hands and jump in unison through the discharge of a condenser. This is science in action. This is fun.

The class of which Voltaire is the exponent does not serve science, nor does it superstitiously respect science for the sake of applications, as it would today. It uses science for a showdown. It is only in the eighteenth century, not in the seventeenth, that the sentencing of Galileo becomes truly a scandal and a *cause célèbre*.

The very intensity of the dialogue prevents a high philosophical level, but it makes the mediocre level effective. The Jesuit and the freethinker adopt similar references, a similar tone—they court social attention and social frivolity, they aim at entertaining and provoking. This is the obverse side of what we call the interest in science. There is no time in which social motives control so overtly the intellectual superstructure. In the mood of intellectual nostalgia which often overcomes us when we think of that so-desirable era, we say that a junction was effected then between humanistic thought and scientific awareness which has been lost since. The complaint may be justified. But let us consider, first, that intellectual life was then restricted to a small elite composed of men who had lively social intercourse with one another, few of whom were specialists in our sense; second, that much of that "philosophic" elaboration does remain on a painfully amateurish level. Misapprehensions, scientific fantasies, and frivolous systems flourish in tropical luxuriance. Fontenelle stands out like a shining light in that confusion. When the matter has to be handled seriously, we are led back to what is not our modern problem only, but had been expressed already by Kepler: "It becomes an increasing problem," he had written as early as 1609, "to write on science today. If the argument is not carried on with the proper rigor, the book is not mathematical. But if the proper rigor is observed, it becomes most difficult to read. . . ."

Thus, what Montesquieu fears as the "tyranny of geometry" is mostly an unwarranted intrusion of amateur physics in fields where experts would have feared to tread. It is in this light that we ought to read his famous pessimistic remarks of 1717, echoed later by Diderot, on the decline of the mathematical sciences: "Discoveries have become rare, it looks as if there were a kind of exhaustion in observation and in observers. . . ." Clearly, if something still held the dialogue together, it was an aesthetic tension, the irresistible element of style and composition, that all-pervading thing called *le goût*.

These qualifiers, of course, in no way reflect upon the great and real advances of the time, or on the hope, and courage, and honesty of the main enterprise. Nor, certainly, on the will to clarity, and to clarification. Present-day logical empiricism—even much more so than Comte's original positivism—is a direct offspring of the eighteenth century. It is the successor of Hume and Gibbon, it is in the line of Condillac and Lavoisier's search for a "well-made language." It is in character, too, unmistakably *dix-huitième*, the conclusion of the light-hearted and reckless charge against pompous oppression and stilted prejudice, in that same spirit which urged Voltaire to spend his best years avenging the wrong done to Calas. Not by chance was our modern movement, the "Vienna Circle," born in the last country which carried into the twentieth century the too soon extinguished echo of Mozart and Watteau.

The problem today is this: what is left to overcome? The door has opened with a crash, and we have at times the feeling of spinning dizzily forward without being able to regain our balance.

For here we notice the second crack in the Mirror of Being. Our century brings right with its beginnings (that is, in 1914) a new degree of arbitrariness in physical thinking which does provide the freedom needed for dealing with quantum phenomena, but at the price of metaphysical consistency, as Einstein has ruefully pointed out. On the literary plane at least, the change might be said to fit the "era of wonderful nonsense," as the Twenties were called, and one detects an echo of that era in the intellectual mood of the young revolutionaries of physics. The outcome is a reality which is accepted as theoretically *less* than determined. Both nature and the object of the search are seen as *underdetermined* in themselves, and the observer—or rather his choice of action—comes in to complete the picture. Man has forced his way back, and he has been widening his bridgehead ever since. But what kind of man is that? And what kind of free activity?

A complete rejection of metaphysical implications—if it were possible—might give us what used to be called the freedom of indifference. When the hypothesis is guided only by experimental consequences, when we are willing to suppose anything that will "work," when nothing is too far-fetched to try, we have surrendered choice of thought, and enter a phase which has some of the aspects of intellectual nihilism.

One need not stay forever the prisoner of Platonic circles. But when the empiricist suggests that science is a set of operational rules for changing marks on paper, he is obviously overdoing it. Science is and remains the search for some kind of being, even an elusive being like a meson, but still a real entity. Stars are real and so are subatomic particles; they are not merely marks on photographic plates. When Leverrier found Neptune "at the tip of his pen," as panegyrics said, he was not simply looking for an economic regularizing entity—he was thinking of a new planet. Fermi knew too much about the neutrino to regard it as a mere accounting device. Entities may become rarefied and still remain such. One may believe even in a vector in Hilbert space, for it is an entity conformable to our search. But supposing demons turned out to be a paying proposition in our scientific explanation, would we use demons in physical theory without further concern? I do not know what the pragmatist would answer, but to be consistent he ought to say "Yes." Infinite freedom to posit anything that pays off is like infinite freedom to move anywhere in a desert.

The fact is, scientific work does use guides even if they are usually unacknowledged. "Revision" is a word now frequently used in physical theory. It means changing our conception of what is real in the picture so that it comes to fit what we imply by reality. The unresolved mixture of science and metaphysics that we have had since the seventeenth century gives us directions about things to try. The simple directions which once guided the attack—materialism, absolute determinism, or pan-mathematism—are now points beyond the horizon, like the Islands of the Blessed, but they still influence our course.

Let us then not take science for what some of its philosophers would like it to be. Completely "intersubjective" statements from which all metaphysical shadow is banished, from which any implication or discussion of being is removed, could occur only at the point where there are no subjects left to share them. So long as it is alive and not sterile, science will remain a *speculum entis*, it will present what metaphysics did, a symbolic structure which is an essential metaphor of being, but is not the only one.

Inevitably, if science were to insist on presenting itself as an assemblage of devices for pragmatic power and economy of thought, if it were to disguise its poetic objectivity under technological wizardry, then misunderstandings would be bound to occur. Outsiders will ask whether such a program could not just as well have fitted Renaissance nigromancy, with its system of recipes. It is only too obvious to the perceptive mind that the eighteenth century spirit among us finds little left to combat which has any stature and glory, and that debunking has become a poor game.

There arises then inevitably, too, an estrangement of public feeling; and mounted on it is the counteroffensive of bewildered humanists, which is becoming, in some, a veritable paranoia leading to a most pointless battle with windmills.

Those who believe intransigently in the right of science to lead may find these difficulties irrelevant. It is, they will say, a matter of education and patience, of taking the horse to the trough again and again until he drinks, with no concession to popularizing pressures. The researcher's business is simply to go ahead. But the trouble is right here: that science has been going ahead on its straight and logical way, going fast, and thus leaving behind all the traditional involvements, including its own. The scientist has ceased taking part in the great dialogue as cultural being. The little gusts of revolt blowing through society are the kind that the statesman might find worthy of attention.

I would suggest that the instinctive reaction of the social body, of that communal sense which has an obscure wisdom of its own, shows the start of a retreat from science to prepared positions. There is no antiscientific commitment and there cannot be, except in a histrionic vein; but a choice of interests is discernible, a concentration upon a form of knowledge which takes the place held of old by speculative metaphysics, by classic tragedy, and generally by what Aristotle would call, with a trace of condescension, "the weighty testimony of the poets."

I am referring to the novel, and of course to the important novel. When even professional philosophers think they have to take that road, it is indeed a significant decision. As a form the novel is hardly more than a century old, and not coincidentally it covers the same span of time as the unscientific philosophies born of Romanticism. Like them, it brings to the consciousness a new perception of life and time and history, it draws from a new communal sense. Like them, it represents a deliberate break with eighteenth-century ideas. It is not a *conte philosophique*; it has no thesis.

We should realize the difference from the past. For Galileo or Descartes, who yet were both instinctively artistic natures, history was a repository of classical examples set out in fine style; art and literature were essentially works of high craftsmanship meant for the pleasure of the senses, a display of magnificence and taste. They were, strictly speaking, not "serious," in the way philosophy is serious, or proper worship, or the "great affairs of princes." To the modern mind, on the other hand, what looks "serious" is the flash of a true experience glimpsed in the rushing stream of time. It is from there that speculation can take its start.

What the reader searches for in the novel is, I suppose, an increase in his own range of life-experience and understanding. His interest is aesthetic but also speculative. He is having his theoretical moment, the one that science refuses to supply, and he is having it in the ancient and original sense.

On what level? I would suggest this: the novel is built on an experience of reality, but it presupposes an essential order which is beyond experience, which is rediscovered in experience, and which provides it with a meaning. Every new narrative is, in a way, a new experimental approach. The narration circumscribes, as it were, the enigma. Its invariants are less abstract than those of science, but it, too, is a search for order in a world initially experienced as chaos. The search for an enigma of order inside chaos is manifest in that weird and sometimes hellish quality of reality which, far from being the privilege of existentialism, strikes us so often in our own time: "History is a nightmare from which I am trying to escape." Translated into abstract terms, it would be quite parallel to the Platonic escape from the physical world by way of its discovered inconsistency.

This is, then, another aspect of the search for truth. It admits reality as "chance and necessity," but chance is not considered a principle of reason—or, on the other hand, a camouflage for a pre-established harmony. The attitude remains one of methodic doubt, the search for reason and for a principle of order. We see the artist using the visible forms of convention as a stage set, and insisting on the contrast between those forms and the original nature of "being" on which they try to impose their rule—the contrast which generates conflict and irony. It is the search for this "being" which provides meaning and depth. In Maxwell's classic words concerning knowledge, "It is a universal condition of the enjoyable that the mind must believe in the existence of a law and yet have a mystery to move in."

Maxwell, like all true poets, speaks in universal terms and with a measure of ambiguity. But we rediscover in his words the classic *analogia entis*. What makes the mystery "enjoyable" is the intuition of an identity of nature between the law we discern and that of our own being. As he says elsewhere, the scientific mind should be "an abandonment of wilfulness without extinction of will." Now modern science has accepted wilfulness in the pragmatistic conception of itself. However philosophically and even dialectically justified, that wilfulness is subtly present in epistemology, where it has been detected and denounced by Einstein, acting out the role of Tiresias. It is patent in the attitude toward nature, which is one of acosmism, of advance as an unending breakthrough.

The shift, then, in canons of relevance that we discern among perceptive minds outside science, the increased attention and sensitiveness to literary existentialism in its many forms, is not simply a "reactionary" movement. It is a reaction, surely, of the communal sense, but not antiscientific; it is postscientific, in that it discounts in science a philosophic interest that science itself seems to have wilfully devalued. The center of relevance has moved to the range of reality which awaits forever to be metaphysically resolved—to the *condition humaine* as such, to quote a designation used successively by Montaigne, Pascal, and Malraux. In that range of reality, we find, beyond all sociology and anthropology, an inviolate resistance of the object, which is man's nature itself, the dramatic experience, the "mystery in which to move," i.e., the intuition that the universe and the subject are of the same nature, the possibility of achieving or regaining an insight by means of art.

To that range of cosmic reality there are also other approaches. The "religious revival" of which there is now so much talk may be mostly of an irrelevant kind, but it has its high points too, and one of them leads us back to Newton with great and meaningful irony.

We remember Newton's own attempt at combining science and the humanities, I mean his previously quoted definition of the God of natural philosophy, which concluded: "We reverence and adore him because of his true dominion. . . ." This kind of God was, of course, a scientific metaphor of being, and a rather unfortunate one, which was disposed of in short order. But the live element of it (we can spot it in Laplacian determinism and ever since) was "true dominion."

In our time, we have the case of Simone Weil, herself a member of a distinguished scientific group, a freethinker reared at the *Ecole normale* in the great tradition of seventeenth-century philosophy. It is within that frame that she lived the tragic modern experience. Following her religious illumination, she looked anew at the classical Cartesian metaphor of being, namely inertial matter, and she saw it rightly as a physical myth which inside physical theory had created more difficulties than it solved. By transferring it to the other range of reality which had become her concern, she brought it to life again. It becomes there a metaphor descriptive of social humanity itself, society functioning under its own weight and inertia, *la pesanteur*. It is a determinism which rules behavior, imaginations, and desires. It creates the chain of evil and its counterpart, human "affliction," blind suffering. Wrong breeds wrong; the normal social virtues of tolerance and compromise are seen merely as lubricants for the machine. There is a pitiless realism in the way Simone Weil perceives the mechanism of affliction, which excludes from it any redeeming quality. "Affliction is anonymous above all, it makes victims into things." Here, surely, is the dominant idea, and one not unnatural in a progressive century in which already eighty to ninety million people have been killed in the name of various and novel rationales. As physics moves away from rigid mechanistic determinism, which appears now as a myth, as it projects a universe of loosely coupled systems, transient states, and limited predictability, the mechanistic symbolism finds a new habitat; "thingness" becomes evident not in things but in what men do to other men.

This intellectual vision may be compelling only to a few, but even to those who will not accept it, it will look imaginative and weirdly plausible. Affliction, as Simone Weil understands it, does not lend itself to consciousness, it empties the soul of the afflicted, "who fills it with no matter what paltry comfort he may have set his heart on." It may be scavenging in the garbage of the concentration camp, or it may be a raise in wages and a two-car garage.

Descartes' pure analytical or dissociative relationship in the *res extensa* is here given a fair parallel. The "wholly other" from this kind of matter, that which corresponds to the *res cogitans*, on this new level, is Grace, which makes the soul come alive. Thus, emerging out of an acceptance of the modern scientific universe, a theological world in the seventeenth-century style comes into being, and one that Malebranche might not have disavowed. But it carries its modern logic very far. It is known that Simone Weil never accepted formal conversion, choosing to identify herself "with the immense and unfortunate mass of unbelievers." She seems to have meant it strictly. The course of modern critical thought on all its levels, which dissolves even the notion of personality, had led her to consider religious symbols as fictions. She insisted that the real religious experience in a world of chance, necessity and automation, of force and affliction, of aspirin and antibiotics, was the absence of God. The silence, the powerlessness, the nothingness of God are the messengers of his true presence.

If God were the power behind this show, she said, taking up the words of Ivan Karamazov, then one would feel compelled to "return the ticket." But if God is not there, then his Grace becomes a reality in us by way of a metaphysical paradox; we enter a kind of gnostic theology of divine non-being.

There is no mistaking the irony of it over against the Natural Philosopher's theology: "A true, supreme or imaginary dominion makes a true, supreme or imaginary God." The answer now is: "Only a dominion which is less than imaginary, and in fact non-existent, makes the true God."

What I have been trying to do is to read the modern predicament in the light of the requirements set by that boldest of centuries, the seventeenth. What we find is an apparent scattering and alteration of factors over the whole map—in reality a richer, unpremeditated texture. In it the illuministic offensive, the "mighty exantlation of truth," is represented by the advance of science. But as the language of science moves farther away from common sense, as the scientist allows himself to be justified in the public consciousness by pragmatic results and technological wizardry, the search for the Analogy of Being, for the Mirror of Being, has to shift to other levels. Undercommitment in the way of scientific "truth" brings overcommitment to other forms of truth, until the very idea of commitment becomes starkly problematic. That is where the novel has come into its own. Metaphysics is now woven into the texture of experience itself and confronts man through his life in unexpected ways. The sentient being who finds himself existentially "thrown" into the situation has to face it and create his own system as he goes along, or be enslaved by another man's, without benefit of high abstraction. Too often, he will put the blame on "Science."

Yet, if only science avoided becoming the prisoner of its formalistic refinements or of pragmatistic roughness—if it accepted the Maxwellian definition of itself, it would find its old place in the great dialogue not simply as a structure of symbols, but as a Metaphor of Being. It does not differ in this respect from traditional metaphysics, except that the metaphor is more carefully and consistently worked out through the ordeal of experiment and the labor of generations. Its own dialectic, if deemed worthy of attention, would reveal itself tied to the dialectic of the other forms of thought, and such principles as indeterminacy and complementarity would show a value which transcended their strict operational significance.

The way for humanism to co-exist with science is neither to damn it nor to try to imitate it. Rigor and elaborateness as borrowed from science do not fit humanistic disciplines, nor do the more technical concepts, drawn from thermodynamics, information theory, psychiatry and so on, lend themselves to becoming anything but interesting metaphoric leads inside quite another system of metaphors. To take these leads literally means to develop forbidding, and indeed afflictive, contraptions of verbal machinery whose usefulness is far from proven. It means losing touch with the communal sense, clouding, too, the Mirror of Being with far less to show in return. It becomes the abstruse game for an elite, like Hermann Hesse's Bead Game in the Kingdom of Castalia—but without the corresponding elite to play it.

Science does have a universal function in that it represents the ordering capacity of thought. In the face of such chaotic situations as occur, for instance, in literary criticism, it still represents principles of order, such principles as do not come out of machines. It makes room for adequate "meta" speculation. It does have, beyond the range of controversy, a meta-physics, and that is mathematics itself. It also has a meta-mathematics, and it is willing to discuss meta-languages. In the construction and choice of theories, it is guided by principles which are ultimately aesthetic, like simplicity and symmetry.

Apart from that, it has in itself something entirely humanistic, namely its interplay of creative images, its own experiences in the search for truth, which tie up with all other forms of search. In the thought of such men as Henri Poincaré and Hermann Weyl, one finds all the levels of culture tied in with their personal speculation; not merely the bare bones of method, but the philosophical awareness, the contemplative capacity, and the dense intuition which are commonly ascribed to traditional thought. If humanists were as open to the world of scientific ideation (which has nothing to do with special results) and as comprehensive of the metaphors of science as those men were to the metaphors of literature, history, and religion, there would be little cause for the battle against windmills, and worried minds would not have to be reminded of Blake's words: "Let God me keep—from single vision and Newton's sleep." It is the monopolistic single vision, from whatever angle it may come, which is destructive of the dialogue and of the free play of critical discernment.

Thus, the metaphysical accent is never lifted, it only shifts according to time. The scientific theodicies of the nineteenth century have lapsed into oblivion, the illuministic offensive is floundering in formalism, science is in the absurd position of having to explain that "basic research" is *also* useful. It is then somewhere else that men will search for the essential; contempt of pretense, horror of non-being and of the dictatorship of banality even when dressed up in electronics, a truth which responds to their search for freedom, lightness, genuineness, in short, for a world that should make sense.

The Mirror of Being never breaks completely, it only shows in its image plane new Metaphors of Being. Science has dropped with unconcern the Platonic implications and overtones of its youth. It had once been the foundation of metaphysics; today, it professes proud indifference if metaphysics finds outside supports to negate science itself. But as it turns out that Platonism, too, and independently, is now negated on that same outside, science might well begin to wonder about this strange coincidence, and, seeing itself through alien eyes at last, begin to feel the discomfort of its displaced position.

Philolaos in Limbo, or: What Happened to the Pythagoreans?

[*This paper, written in 1950 and signed jointly by Walter Pitts and myself, had barely gone to print in* Isis *when news reached us of the sudden death of Professor Erich Frank. We expressed only too late our sorrow and regret for what might have sounded irreverent toward the figure of a highly respected master. Our somewhat acerbic irony was surely no reflection on his person, but a passionate and unguarded manifestation of open dissent from the hypercritical school, of which there are many representative. Whatever the manner, we still hold that we were right in principle.*]

THERE WAS PUBLISHED SOME YEARS SINCE A SALUTIFEROUS EDICT, WHICH for the obviating of the dangerous Scandals of the present Age, imposed a seasonable Silence upon the Pythagorean Opinion of the Mobility of the Earth.

These are the opening words of Galileo's preface to his *Dialogue on the World Systems*. One would be tempted to repeat them almost word for word today, apropos of certain contemporary philological research. The invisible edict or "trend" to which we refer has decreed that the whole development of Greek mathematics and astronomy must be condensed into a rather short interval of time around 400 B.C., so that almost all the mathematics, astronomy, and music theory of the "so-called Pythagoreans" becomes contemporary with Plato and his successors.

There are several schools which find this new viewpoint particularly congenial. One is the massed power of Platonic and Aristotelian scholarship, which tends unconsciously to see the classical landscape through the eyes of its favorite authors, and is always willing to convert a debt owed by them to one owed to them. A second one is a school of hypercritical philologists, starting with Eva Sachs[1] and continuing through Erich Frank's *Plato und die Sogenannten Pythagoreer* (1923), a book we shall presently examine in more detail, and in the last papers of the late W. A. Heidel. Finally, there is the recent school of scientific historians which has attempted to trace the connection between Babylonian and Greek mathematics. Of their work we may cite the papers of O. Neugebauer, K. Reidemeister, and B. L. van der Waerden.[2] Relying on Frank, these authors have dismissed the entire tradition about early Greek mathematics, and supplanted it either with a most improbably late transference of Babylonian mathematics to Greece in the Vth century, or else have tried to fill the gap with speculations, conceived certainly

[1] *De Thaeaeteto Mathematico*, 1910.

[2] W. A. Heidel, The Pythagoreans and Greek Mathematics, *Am. J. of Philol. 61* (1940); K. Reidemeister, Die Arithmetik d. Griechen, *Hamburg. Math. Einzelschr.*, 1939 (1940); B. L. van der Waerden, Zenon und die Grundlagenkrise d. griech. Mathematik, *Math. Ann. 117* (1940); id., Zur Pythag. Algebra, *Math. Ann. 118* (1941); id., Die Astronomie d. Pythagoreer, *Himmelswelt* 1941; id., Die Harmonielehre der Pythagoreer, *Hermes 78* (1943); id., Die Astronomie des Heraklides von Pontos, *Ber. Verh. Sachs. Ak. Wiss.*, Math.-Nat. Kl., *96* (1944); Neugebauer, Studien z. Gesch. d. ant. Algebra, in *Quellen und Studien* B, 1934–36; and his reviews of the preceding authors in *Math. Reviews*, 1940–47.

in a true and subtle mathematician's spirit, derived from conjectural traces in Euclid and Plato. Possibly they were attracted by the company of various modern philologists, who have been trapped into accepting some of Frank's destructive arguments without noticing their intimate dependence upon his unacceptable alternative. So Cherniss, on p. 386 of his *Aristotle's Criticism of the Presocratics*, says that Frank's invalidation of the fragments of Philolaos "makes it superfluous to restate the overwhelming case against them." We are led back, then, to Erich Frank as the author who carries, more than any other, the responsibility for the present hypercritical sentiment. A scrutiny of his book is therefore in order.

Frank's general thesis is this: There is no Greek science in any real sense before Anaxagoras and Democritus. "Anaxagoras was the first to formulate the principle of modern science, by distinguishing the subjective-psychological world-image in his optical investigations from the objective vision of an ideal and absolute observer" (p. 144). And where does Anaxagoras find the basis for such a feat? In the art of scenic perspective, invented by Agatharchus the painter about that time. "Without perspective, i.e. stereometry," there could be no idea of the spherical earth, nor of planetary orbits, not of practically anything physical.[3] Anaxagoras was also the first real mathematician, since the whole "Pythagorean number atomism is later than Democritus"; it is in fact only an etherealization of his atoms. The very idea of "elements" of geometry is based upon an analogy with the elements or atoms of matter; therefore the early "elements" of Hippocrates of Chios are inspired by Democritus, who invented also (for reasons best known to himself) most of the Pythagorean "tradition," including music theory, and transformed a religious revivalist of the VIth century into a master of science. It is only after 400 B.C. that Archytas inaugurates "Pythagorean" mathematics, and it is only to him and his group that Aristotle refers in quoting the "so-called Pythagoreans." The problem of the planetary system or of the spherical earth "cannot even be posed without a knowledge of the fundamental laws of mathematical mechanics. But mechanics, as we know, was founded by Archytas. One should not believe that such great truths can be found by pure speculation alone."

In this way, Frank carries to its furthest extreme a critical line which starts with Eva Sachs in 1905. In order to reach that point, however, he has to throw out most of the available evidence and stand the rest of it on its head.[4] It so happens that his

[3] Incidentally, Agatharchus did *not* invent scenic perspective. "He was the first painter to use perspective on a large scale (isolated instances occur on vases from the late VIth century B.C.)" *Oxford Class. Dict.*, 1949.

[4] One example will suffice for the way Frank handles texts. He says (p. 286) that we know from Aristotle's *Metaphysics* that the correspondence of 2 with the unlimited is

alternative account was largely ignored by historians. But the same historians who did not accept his entire thesis are now accepting the critical part of it, without noticing, apparently, that it was contrived in the interest of his positive reconstruction and depends on it. Yet Frank's work must stand or fall as a whole, since nothing short of a compelling new version of this part of mathematical history can reasonably induce us to discredit such a mass of evidence.

Now it is obvious, and has been for some time, that the historical reconstruction makes no sense at all. What has perspective in scenic painting to do with the idea of a round earth? People are normally able to think in three-dimensional space because they live in it. The capacity—and the canons—of artistic representation are quite another story. We never notice Arabs or Hindus bumping into things because their art does not use perspective. Anaximander conceived his very complicated system of vortexes and rings in space without the help of a textbook on stereometry. Frank's argument that dramatic characters first assume a "plastic personality" in the late works of Aeschylus, about the time of Agatharchus, does not make his point more perspicuous.

Another curious notion is that "elements" of geometry, meaning a systematic treatise, starting from axioms, can only have been composed after Democritus had introduced the idea of "elements" (*stoicheia*, in the sense of letters of the alphabet) in physics. No one before Democritus, says Frank, was capable of the operations of analysis and synthesis as methods of devising mathematical proofs. This is a result of something he calls the "Archaic Atmosphere" of the Vth century, which compelled people to live in a state of confusion. (Was it from this Archaic Atmosphere that Empedocles purified Akragas by enclosing it in leather bags?) As soon as the "Archaic Atmosphere" blew away, in the IVth century, there at once developed, according to Frank, a point of view that we have had in modern times only since Russell and Wittgenstein; for the very abstract analogy of atoms to logical elements (or "basic propositions") belongs to our own time, and there is good reason for that. In fact, the two ideas are poles apart. The geometrical axioms were originally "common notions," that is, universally agreed upon because intuitively evident to everybody. Geometry proceeds from them to reach notions and propositions which are continually more abstract and less obvious. The Democritan atoms, on the other

strictly Platonic, whereas the Pythagoreans made the monad unlimited. Hence "Philolaos" must have taken the idea from Plato. This is quite sufficiently startling, and would upset all we know about the Pythagoreans. If we turn, however, to *Met.* 987 *b*, we find this: "It is peculiar to him [Plato] to posit a duality instead of the single unlimited and to make the single Unlimited consist of the Great and Small." The "single unlimited" is, of course, that of the table of opposites, and not at all the monad which is the limiting principle par excellence. One does not know how to comment.

hand, are far from being everyday notions: they are the result of a long process of abstract analysis starting from the material objects of the phenomenal world. Their position in science is precisely opposite to the one held by the axioms of geometry; and it would never occur to anybody in antiquity to compare them—nor did it, as far as we know.

Frank makes free with Democritus in other respects. He wants to suppose that the Pythagorean number-atoms (their "monads having position") are mere immaterial versions of the atoms. Unfortunately, this compels him to contradict most of the firmest historical evidence about the properties of the Democritan atoms. They are not, as he would have us believe, "qualitatively indistinguishable," nor do they make up physical things merely by their number and position. Rather, they have order, position, velocity (or rather mobility) and shape. This last point is quite explicit: "No two atoms are alike." It is their shape which explains in a large measure the diversity of substances.

But Frank had to contrive a Democritus who said what he never said, because in his scheme there is no one before Democritus except Anaxagoras to share the burden of "inventing mathematics." If he did, it is strange that Eudemus, our only source, should have known nothing about it. After having described Pythagorean mathematics as "the theory of proportions and the construction of the cosmic figures," Eudemus (in Proclus' summary) goes on: "After Pythagoras, Anaxagoras touched many questions affecting geometry, and so did Oenopides, both of whom Plato mentioned in the *Rivals* as having acquired a reputation for mathematics." That is exactly all. One cannot suspect here the Neoplatonic bias with which Proclus has often been reproached. The catalogue goes on with Hippocrates of Chios, "who discovered the quadrature of the lunes and compiled Elements." This, incidentally, disposes of the idea that the quadrature of the circle that Anaxagoras is said to have "drawn" (Frank makes much of that) is anything more rigorous than Antiphon's, if it was that much. As a contemporary of Parmenides, Anaxagoras had nothing but an intuitive idea of continuity to work with. It is true that Frank credits him also with "rationally mastering and plastically transforming" the idea of the infinite, which in all previous speculation had been "a vague emotion of Dionysiac ecstasy which raised man above reality and found expression also in the dithyrambic music coming from the Orient." This rational and plastic feat Anaxagoras is supposed to have achieved by "discovering the infinitesimal," as inferred from his statement: "There is no smallest, but there is always a smaller." Certainly Anaxagoras said as much, speaking of his qualitative particles, but Zeno (whom Frank systematically ignores) said it in his "Dichotomy," probably earlier, far more clearly, and realized its implications, which have nothing obvious (except to Spengler) to do with the composition or performance of dithyrambs. This in turn disposes of the argument that Anaxagoras discovered the proportionality of the circular area to the square of the diameter, which is not presupposed in Antiphon's quadrature, although Frank says it is.[5]

Let us suppose that Frank's whole reconstruction did appear reasonable and enticing. Still, the unsolved question remains; how do we dispose of the many specific references in Aristotle to the opinions of the "so-called Pythagoreans"?[6] How about his mention of Pythagorean science at the time of Leucippus "and earlier"? How can we explain away the names and testimonials from so many other sources? For this Frank unveils his second major device (the first being the "Archaic Atmosphere"), an astonishingly ingenious one, pregnant with infinite possibilities (as Spengler would say) beyond Frank's own extensive use of it. It is simply this: Suppose *A* (e.g., Philolaos) is credited with a certain discovery by incontrovertible tradition (e.g., Aristotle). We wish to ascribe the discovery to some other later man *B* (Heraclides). We simply deny that *A* ever existed at all (except perhaps as a mere name), being merely a character in a dialogue written by *B*, in which the discovery was put into

[5] Another author has come forward recently with other ingenious reasons for disregarding Eudemus. It is W. A. Heidel (*Amer. Journ. of Philology*, *61*, 1940). His argument is as follows:

1—Tannery has made it plausible that Proclus did not take his summary directly from Eudemus, but from an abridgment of it made by Geminus.

2—The same Geminus was acquainted with the works of Posidonius, since he wrote a commentary on one of them.

3—Posidonius had no historical sense (*a*) because he believed that Parmenides discovered the five zones, and that Pythagoras invented the notion of the tripartite soul, on the strength of statements by Pythagoreans: (*b*) because he was a Stoic, and Stoics are all like that.

4—Hence, "we are fully justified in disregarding the supposed testimony on the Pythagoreans."

The line of argument is more worthy of a famous "Congressional Investigating Committee" than of a distinguished scholar. It is again a *reductio ad absurdum* of an argument started by Reinhardt in his work on Posidonius. Heidel's proposed ascription of early mathematics exclusively to the Ionians is based simply upon crediting all the historical statements in Proclus' summary *except* the ones referring to the Pythagoreans. He has evidently sawn off the limb he is sitting on. The indirect arguments he uses are rather weak ones—e.g., that Anaximander's cosmology was "essentially geometrical." It is hard to imagine a cosmology which is not.

Incidentally, Posidonius' testimonial has been accepted as valid by all other critics. See Rehm in Norden, *Einleitung*, 5. Heft, p. 12.

Our purpose here is not to cast doubt on the role of the Ionians in early Greek mathematics; we believe it was a larger one than Eudemus indicates. Our point is about method. It is not possible to employ a standard of evidence in the critical part of a paper so rigid as to dispose of all opposing testimony, and then in the subsequent constructive section, draw one's conclusions largely from evidence of the same sort as the critical standard one has rejected.

[6] Much is made of this "so-called." But Cherniss has remarked that Aristotle speaks also of the "so-called farmers," which does not mean that he doubts the existence of that honored profession.

his mouth. Since even the most reliable of the Ancients, like Aristotle and Theophrastus, had no historical sense, everybody would naturally take the dialogue for a faithful record of *A*'s actual opinions, and transmit this view to posterity, after the dialogue itself was lost. Frank applies this trick to no less than five people: Philolaos, Ecphantos and Hicetas disappear, to become characters in dialogues by Speusippus and Heraclides Ponticus; and Hippasus and Eurytos exchange earthly being for a tenebrous immortality in hypothetical lost dialogues by Archytas. Aristotle, of course, was totally unaware of this, and supposed they were real people.

It is hard to imagine that Aristotle, who was a contemporary of both Speusippus and Heraclides and knew them well as their rival in the Academy, could swallow the bait, hook, line, and sinker, and induce the careful Theophrastus to do likewise. Moreover, since the existence of Philolaic books antedating Speusippus (whatever their contents may have been) is attested not only by Aristotle and Theophrastus, but by Menon's *Iatrika*, we might wonder how Speusippus managed to sustain his forgeries among a public acquainted with the originals. But for Frank it is again quite simple: we should remember that Aristotle had no historical sense. Although not suffering from the Archaic Mentality, he is still an Ancient. "When, e.g., Aristotle quotes 'as Socrates says in the *Republic*,' or 'Aristophanes in his speech on Love,' etc., he does not mean, as a modern, critically minded reader might assume, writings of Socrates and so on, but passages in Platonic dialogues. . . . So little distinct in the consciousness of Aristotle is the historic personality of, say, Socrates from its poetic presentation in Plato or others. . . . Hence, when Aristotle tells us of the doctrines of the 'Pythagoreans,' we shall have to understand it the same way." (p. 76 and note 195, p. 360).

One wonders what kind of reader it is that would misunderstand Aristotle (or corresponding statements in modern writings), and imagine Socrates had written a book called the *Republic*. Certainly Aristotle quotes the dialogues everywhere as evidence for the opinions of Plato, not of characters in them. Indeed, Frank ought to have known that Academic opinion, far from being gullible, happened to be hypercritical as to the actual role of Socrates. Aristotle's considered judgment, not very different from that of posterity, stands in black and white: Socrates' two original contributions were induction and the determination of the concept. (*Met.* M4, 1078 *b* 27). If Aristotle, who had never known Socrates, but knew Speusippus well, was capable of taking literary inventions of that "unfriend" of his for serious references, then we may begin to suspect Frank himself of being an imaginary character in the lost dialogues of George Santayana.

The chief stumbling-block across Frank's avenging path is the fairly historical figure of Philolaos. In order to prove his main contention, that no one thought of a spherical earth before the IVth century (a contention which proved untenable[7]) he has to eradicate Philolaos from history altogether. That, in turn, compels him to inject wild confusion into a none-too-simple chapter of the history of Greek astronomy, and to subvert the few reliable bearings we had gained in it. Since the technical historians have not proved willing to follow him in his adventure, we may be excused from undertaking an elaborate refutation.[8] But there is more of Philolaos: there are the fragments, which are also about all that we have of Pythagorean literature before 400 B.C.

The authenticity of the Philolaic fragments has been put in doubt several times on serious grounds, first by Rose and Schaarschmidt, and later by Bywater, Wilamowitz and Burnet.[9] The question was carefully re-examined by Zeller and Diels, who concluded for their authenticity. Then, in 1923, Erich Frank concentrated his efforts on this particular point, which was admittedly *sub judice*, and succeeded in giving many the impression that he had provided a decisive refutation. Nobody, apparently, was willing to accept his theory that Aristotle and Theophrastus had been tricked by Speusippus, but few noticed that this curious theory was a necessary part of his argument. A point-by-point re-examination of the case has been

[7] We shall prove, in a forthcoming book, that Parmenides did have a theory of the round earth.

[8] What Frank does is to disregard (not even mentioning it) the monumental work of reconstruction of Schiaparelli and Heath. He tortures three obscure but innocent lines of Aristotle, Chalcidius and Geminus until he has wrung from them a suggestion that Heraclides attributed two movements to the earth, one of daily rotation, one of yearly rotation. This system, he says, was called for some literary reason the "Philolaic," and there was no other, "since there had been no notion of the spherical earth nor of planetary orbits before Democritus." It turns out to be a quasi-Copernican system (only with fire at the centre and the sun among the planets) and "it must have replaced the Eudoxian, which was the last word until 360," since Plato alludes to it in the *Timaeus*.

In this there are some slight initial difficulties: Plato never adopted any moving-earth system (cf. Cherniss, *Arist. Crit. of Plato*, App. VIII; see also Cornford, *Plato's Cosmology*, p. 269) and Eudoxus published his in 357. As for the idea that no one thought of a spherical earth before Democritus, it can never be held for a moment. But the real difficulty is that the theory requests us to throw out all of the explicit testimonials, which are many. We know from Simplicius and Aetius that Heraclides "put the earth at the center." We know from them and from Aristotle that the Philolaic system made the earth revolve around the central Fire in a day and not in a year. That was in fact the point of the whole system, modelled on the moon, for the earth was supposed to show always the same face to the central fire. Moreover, there was not one but several systems, as Aristotle says in *De Caelo* 293, some with more than one counter-earth. All such systems were clearly pre-Eudoxian in style, indeed pre-Archytan, and belong therefore in the Vth century, which is also the time of Philolaos. There is therefore no cause to doubt the traditional attribution of one of them to Philolaos himself.

[9] Rose, *Arist. libr. ord.* p. 2; Schaarschmidt, *Die angebliche Schriftstellerei des Philolaos*, 1864; Bywater, *J. Phil. I*, 1868, p. 21–53; Wilamowitz, *Platon* II, 93; Burnet, *E.G.P.*, 4th ed., p. 279.

recently made by Mondolfo, and we shall not go into it again.[10] But some remarks on Frank's all-too-general method seem in order.

Frank's criterion is this: whenever a word or an idea can also be found in Plato, or in his circle, it is clear that it must have been taken from Plato. He is sure that nobody before Plato used such words as εἶδος, μορφή, οὐσία, ὁλκός, συνοχή, συναρμόττειν, ἐνέργεια, ὑπεροχή, ἀποτομή, ἀνωτάτω περιέχων and so on; that nobody could possibly have thought of the oppositions ἄπειρον—πέρας or γένεσις—φθορά, or spoken of dividing a proposition, or used diaeresis, or talked of the microcosm, or distinguished between the relation of a thing to itself and its relation to other things. Now this is pernicious nonsense a priori, even apart from its being demonstrably false point by point. The last century saw a great liquidation of apocryphal texts and late forgeries. The works of many authors like Okkelos the Lucanian or Timaeus of Locri vanished into the darkness whence they had come. But the mechanical extension of the method, so as to find "Timaeographers" under every stone, leads to absurdity. It leads, in fact, to ascribing to Plato depths of scientific thought of which he was quite incapable (as Frank himself admits on p. 65), and later was to lure even great scholars into a vain chase after elusive shadows of metamathematical profundity in the Dialogues.

The *Timaeus* was no doubt the source of many imitations; but it is itself acknowledged to be practically a Pythagorean enclave in Plato's work. To anyone who reads it without preconception, it gives the impression of the enthusiastic layman trying to catch science on the wing. The science from which he drew the romantic motifs was there in its own right; it is rather difficult to imagine it without some kind of technical problems and technical language. It is quite natural that Plato should take a large part of it over for his own purposes, and this provides a perfectly simple explanation for any verbal similarities between Philolaos and the *Timaeus*. Ignoring this, Frank is led to see in Fr. 2 of Philolaos "the lumbering imitative prose of a mediocre schoolmaster devoid of ideas" (the same Speusippus who was also such a devilishly clever fellow, and who in other fragments shows his hand by a "suspicious Attic clarity of style"); whereas we do not find it hard to discern in it a careful, if quite unliterary, attempt to combine Zenonian method with Pythagorean theory. Reinhardt saw this already.

Working on independent lines, Cameron[11] seems to have come to results of the same order:

An examination of their content against Pythagorean elements in

[10] *Riv. Filol.* N. S. 15 (1937), p. 225–45, and the note on Philolaos in his edition of Zeller, vol. II, p. 367–85.

[11] *The Pythagorean background of the theory of recollection*, 1938.

Plato and Aristotle would show that the Philolaic writings are older than Plato and Aristotle. I have come to this conclusion after testing the fragments and chosen Platonic passages by the concept of Numbers as things. . . . The whole interpretation of the fragments is meaningless if put on a basis of even the least restrictive Platonic and Aristotelian definition of, e.g., form and matter.

This is the impression that anyone will have of the fragments who reads them without preconceived ideas. He may then, perhaps, proceed to look for possible rash "ameliorations" of a later date. But not so the philologists wise in the sinful condition of texts. They will suppose it less probable a priori that someone should have written something, than that somebody later should have forged the writing. Considering the nature of man, a Calvinist or a critic would say, this is sure to be more likely.

Such a somber view of things is apt to lead to less than serious results. For instance: is it really impossible, as Frank says (p. 280) to have a division of the superlunary world into Ouranos and Olympos before the idea of a spherical earth (which comes, according to him, only about the time of the Phaedo)? Very well, but then what about Parmenides, who made this distinction explicitly, and on whom Frank spends prodigious amounts of sophistry—for he needs this point very badly—to show that he believed the earth to be flat? Nor is it serious to say that there is no idea of a ἡγεμονικόν κυβερνῆτες of the world before Plato invented it, as if someone had not said two centuries earlier: "As our soul, being air, holds us together, so do breath and air surround the whole universe," (Anaximenes A2) and someone else not spoken of a δαίμων ἣ πάντα κυβερναῖ (Parmenides B 12). Or to suggest that the opposition of True and Untrue in B 11 must be due to "Speusippus' table of opposites" when we think of Alkmaion, or of all that the Goddess had to say to Parmenides on that subject, warning him also, on the side, of critics "who don't know whether they are coming or going." Or to say that the "Second Destruction" is a strictly Academic idea, as if the myths of Phaethon and Deucalion had never existed, and people since prehistoric times had not talked of "Hell and High Water." Or to state that a theory which makes the world to come out of Limit and Unlimit, whence proceed Harmony and Number, must be cribbed from the *Philebus*, just because "the result of mature Platonic thought cannot be supposed to be derived from a work a century older" (why?). Or to say that B 4 ("it is impossible to grasp anything with the mind or to recognize it without Number") is a transcendental "proof from knowledge" such as no one thought of before Plato; and then impugn B 4 and B 11 because they say that we can also know through perception and manual operation, which is again, it appears, obviously "taken from the mature thought of the *Philebus*." (p. 311) A note of comic relief is brought in when B 13, where the αἰδοῖον is said to be "the source of all things," is declared to be obviously derived from Plato's theory of the Cosmic Soul. Professor Frank seems to have been unacquainted with some very ancient facts of life, as well as with the fundamentals of Presocratic thought.

The fact that this kind of criticism could be taken seriously arises from an unspoken and half-formulated assumption which has become current among historians of philosophy: namely, that nobody can think until the proper philosophical categories are provided. Frank's philological contentions had then a strong favorable prejudice on their side, although it was easy to prove them actually untrue. This is probably how we may account for J. E. Raven's latest endorsement of Frank's criticisms,[12] in an otherwise careful study: "The strongest of all arguments against the fragments is the fact that the number of such suspicious features is unduly high." It depends on what we decide to call suspicious. An immediate *reductio ad absurdum* of this way of thinking can be seen in Raven's own conclusions: if the fragments disagree with Aristotle's statements about the Pythagoreans, they are forgeries on that account, since Aristotle had adequate means of information; and if they agree with Aristotle, they are taken from him and therefore are again forgeries. This recalls the old story about the Khalif Abu Bekr—it also opens up new vistas of doubt: Who would have taken the trouble of forging Doric fragments of Philolaos out of Aristotle alone, it being then quite unnecessary to prove that the Pythagoreans had those views since they are already in Aristotle? Frank, in his own theory, would present an answer to that. We may then combine the views of Frank and Raven into one complete reconstruction: Speusippus cribbed from Aristotle to write his book on Pythagorean numbers. Aristotle then, not recognizing his own material, excerpted from Speusippus for his work on the Pythagoreans. Speusippus then proceeded to forge from Aristotle. The result of this earliest case of literary feedback is called Philolaos. If this does not appease the hypercritical school, we do not know what will.

In the face of such positions as the above, we might feel at liberty, henceforth, to maintain an opinion which at least stems from the direct testimonial of Timon the Sillographer—certainly no slavish respecter of persons,[13] and perhaps even more critical of ancient tradition than Professor Cherniss—one which needs no "fixing" of sources, and has the endorsement of Satyrus, Hermippus, and, indeed, if we must believe Burnet, of Aristoxenus himself: namely, that Plato bought the book by

[12] J. D. Raven, *Pythagoreans and Eleatics*, 1948.

[13] A good case might be made for the contention that Timon is a much underrated source. Most of the later material is certainly as prejudiced and second-hand as his but has, nevertheless, been accepted on account of its being in the pious tradition.

Philolaos for the considerable sum of a hundred minae and proceeded frankly and openly to appropriate the contents. It would have the corroboration of many such behaviors in history, and on the part of men hardly less respected than Plato. It would explain very nicely why Plato concedes his indebtedness to men "more ancient and closer to the gods," but refers to Philolaos only once. After all, it is *the* authoritative source, Aristotle himself, who says that Plato got his system out of Heraclitus and the Pythagoreans (*Met.* 987 *b* 7):

Those entities he called Ideas and held that all sensible things are named after them and in virtue of their relations to them; for the plurality of things which bear the same name as the Forms exist by participation in them. With regard to the "Participation" it was only the term that he changed; for whereas the Pythagoreans say that things exist by imitation of numbers, Plato says that they exist by participation—merely a change of term. As to what this participation or imitation may be, they left this an open question.

Presumably Aristotle means here that the matter was not finally settled in Philolaos' book, and that therefore Plato (and we) had no answer (cf. also *Met.* 987 *b* 25 and 990 *a* 1).

We might have made this paper three times as long, and not exhausted the list of Frank's extraordinary notions. We prefer to stop at a reflexion on p. 64–66: "Since the time of the Persian wars at least, and probably still earlier in Ionia," there was a body of special sciences with which philosophers were soon unable to keep up. Each of those sciences, as Xenophon said, required a whole life-time of application; and Democritus was the last man who can be said to have encompassed the whole knowledge of his epoch. If Frank is willing to admit all this freely, one wonders what all the shooting was about; and why such a distinguished scholar and respected personality as he should have tangled himself in this web of sophistries.

Now suppose that we have adequately answered Frank. There still remains for us a problem that he did not have to face, since it was brought up by his successors: that of re-establishing a coherence between the traditional frame-work and the derivation of Greek mathematics from Babylon. In our opinion, this is best done by taking account of the evolution of van der Waerden's thought from his earlier papers to his latest. In 1941, he placed the discovery of the irrationals in the early IVth century, the time of Theaetetus. In his later work, he has come to the conclusion that a proper date should be earlier than 420, and probably 450. He suggests, in fact, that the transference from Babylon took place in the VIth century rather than in the Vth. This solution has all the merits of antecedent and historical probability. The real break between Greece and the Orient first occurs at the rise of the Achemenid Empire. The previous period was, contrariwise, exceptionally favorable. From the fall of

Nineveh in 604, the Neo-Chaldean empire under Nebuchadnezzar and his successors was one of the chief world powers, including the larger part of Syria (hence the mention in *Epinomis*); this state of affairs continued until the fall of Babylon to the Persians in 536. This is precisely the period of the traditional travels of Pythagoras, and of the great Samian technicians, Rhoikos and Theodoros, who are partly historical, partly Palamedes-like figures on whom a variety of inventions has been fathered. Let us remember also Harpalos of Miletus, of the same period, and his successor Eupalinos of Megara, whose remarkable engineering projects (and in particular the tunnel at Miletus) suggest very strongly that Babylonian mathematics, in the form of practical computing formulae, had been filtering in for a long while.

Between 536 and the Peace of Antalcidas in 386, communication between Babylon and the Greek world must have been difficult and rare; and the end of this period is commemorated by Eudoxus' voyage to Egypt.[14] It is evident that this account agrees well with the statements of the doxographers, such as they are: even Neugebauer has noted, with a poetic touch, that the legendary travels of Pythagoras might not turn out all fiction. Moreover, it does not require us to brighten the genius of the men of Plato's generation to such a blinding glare as would be involved in passing from bare computing rules to the logical problems of the continuum in one man's lifetime. Finally, in spite of van der Waerden, it admits the possibility that Zeno was already discussing the foundations of mathematics (Neugebauer says rightly that the Greeks stand in the middle of the history of mathematics; but they are at the beginning of the history of metamathematics) rather than denying puerilely what Plato first discovered how to deny transcendentally—the existence of the real world.

[14] Cf. G. de Santillana, *Eudoxus and Plato, a Problem in Chronology*, in *Isis*, Vol. 81, 1948.

Paralipomena of the Future

Although we defer to none in our respect for Antiquity, we felt we had to put our younger contemporaries on guard against an excessive reliance on classical sources and also on the learned labors of the scholars who give us the critical editions. It is in this cautionary spirit that Walter Pitts and the undersigned (re)-constructed a biography from the yet-to-be-lost Diogenes Laertius of future ages, based on the figure of a great scientist whom we both knew and loved, and who pleasantly assented to this prediction darkened and deformed in the glass of time to come. Some actual dicta of his were abandoned to the mercies of future doxographers, no wiser surely than "the greatest jackass of Antiquity," and then entrusted to the critical care of a future Diels. There shall always be a Diels.

NORBERTOS VINDOBONENSIS, ALSO CALLED WIENER OF COLUMBUS, was a mathematician and sophist who flourished in the early part of the First Century of our Era. Some writers say that he was earlier and speak of him as related to the man who discovered the Western Hemisphere. But this cannot be true, for I have seen certain verses of his where, speaking of Smith, he says "skin-flint," etc. Trofim in his *Confusion of Confounders* also quotes a pun from his *silloi*, "The bush ignited the grove but was not itself consumed," which is said to refer to Bush. It is also said that "he abused Groves but followed him."[1] Groves was a general who overcame the Japanese with firecrackers and sacrificed three scientists at the Great Games. These men are also among those mentioned in the diatribes he wrote against the doctors of alchemy and of the science of thunder (*alchymiam et tonitrualia legentes*). It is to Norbertos that Groves is reputed to have uttered his famous epigram, "Justice is what suits the stronger"; but others, with more right, make this his reply to certain members of the Congress who had reproached him with aspiring to a tyranny.[2]

As a young man he fled the oppression of the tyrant Harvardos who was ruler of Boston on the Metapontis and who wanted to enforce the cult of a new goddess called Alma Mater. He traveled east to England and Germany, and consorted with the Bonzes, who taught him a game of counters called Hilbert and the doctrine of Transmigration of Functions. After the death of the tyrant he came back to Boston and settled in nearby Antipolis, being honored by its citizens, who decreed for him a Coronal ("Cyclotron") and the title of Cybernete or governor. He wrote a book on Cybernetics or the art of ruling; in it he teaches how to deceive the people by telling them what they want to

[1] M. S. Wash *F*: "Followed him not." As *F* is the source of both *Q* and *R* we may assume the "not" was dropped by the amanuensis. But the text would then require "*and*" instead of "*but*"; the emendation is necessary, since *F* is already known to be corrupt.

[2] Nothing except this mention is known of Groves or of Bush, who must have been generals in the early wars of the Time of Troubles. Their names are not in the catalogue of Fa Hsien. The conclusion reached by recent historical criticism is that they were imaginary characters in Norbertos' dialogues.

hear, and he calls this feedback.[3] Ibrahim of Ferghana, however, maintains in his *Mirabilia* that "feedback" was the name Norbertos gave to a Hercynian beast, in his Description of Germany, which he affirmed to subsist entirely by devouring its own excrement. But I, for my part, cannot credit that so childish a fable should have been repeated by so eminent a man: for how should such a beast propagate its kind? having no access of matter whence to compound the young.

He also wrote on curved lines and harmonies and invented a new kind of mean he called Tauberian, which name he ordered should be carved on his gravestone for the instruction of posterity. In this respect, indeed, Athenagoras of Kiev mentions him as saying "Time is harmony"[4] and "Not time, but frequency." By this means he succeeded in banishing geometry from arithmetic, so as to found the theory of Primes on pure reason. The day of his death was decreed a holiday by the Academy.

He paid special honor to a goddess called Jeeby, who, he said, comes after Hebe in rank, and some explain that she was the deity of Awakening ("Morning-After"). But elsewhere he says explicitly that there is no one god, but that the world is ruled by Chance and Information and that "it befits them to move hither and thither." For such are the appellations he ascribed to the American Hermes, whom he held in peculiar reverence, inscribing on his sanctuary the apophthegm "Non Being Is." Chance, he maintained, was the same as Measure (or Temperance)[5] and the same as had earlier been worshipped under the name of the Goddess of Praeneste.

He traveled and taught ("lecturing"), preaching continence and purity and abstention from the flesh of animals who, he said, "can learn." He also invented an animal that could learn by means of a spirit infused in it. Some say, however, that he believed in Pleasure as the supreme good and wrote dialogues against the priests and oracles. On him I have written the epigram, "Naught availeth thee," etc.

Hilarion of Tula, however, in his book *On People of the Same*

[3] This would point to contradictory sources of a late date used uncritically in the recension. The sophists of the first century were essentially reformers and inventors. The tradition probably refers to N. Paraventus (see below), since it points to third-century theories on emotion engineering. The two men could have been easily confused because of their common metapontine connotation. The surname of Paraventus, borrowed from the debased *koine* of the Later Empire (cf. *Alexanemos*) is enough to show that the reputation of the later Wiener was not above reproach.

[4] Diels prefers to amend this to read "Time is money"; recalling the Vosnessensky fragments (Beazley 1–113) which are only slightly earlier, and discovering that the spelling *mony* is a well-known provincialism and legalism. It should, however, be pointed out that the latter saying is also ascribed to Bentham 973B and to Franklin. Cf. Diels, *Sophistarum antiquissimorum fragmenta quae supersunt omnia*, Samarkand ed. The GK MSS (M^3, L, Q) have an analogous corruption. (See Stackelmayr, Sitzgber. Herc. Ak. CIX, 705.).

[5] Probably an interpolation by a later moralist or scholiast.

Name, affirms that the dialogues were written by another Wiener, a mindhealer or psychoanalyst as they were called then. Besides these two, he mentions four other Wieners, of whom one was a harpsichordist, another was a friend of a philosopher called Lovejoy of Baltimore. A different Norbertos of Transpontion, which is in the Mediterranean, also known as Norbertos Paraventus, flourished two centuries later. He was a governor of the southern provinces and an emotion-engineer, and was made a companion of the order of Lenin Soter by the Marxengels of Western Eurasia. He is supposed to have introduced the cult of the divine Ancestress of the Dynasty, Aphrodite Marxa, also called Marxa Verticordia, or Marxa Pandemia.[6] He was put to death by the ruler for intensificationism or, as others maintain, for normalizationism. To him is ascribed a saying pronounced in the death-cellar: "Rulers should know their friends from their enemies." Other authors, however, say that his last words were "What a mystery-story teller dies in me!" and still others make him the originator of that well-known utterance in international West-Eurasian, "Qualis praesul pereo."

The Fragments

1. HIPPOLYTOS OF KAZAN. *Refutation of All Deviationisms:*

   (1) ". . . buffeted hither and yon, continuous, but having no derivative."

   (2) "Summable functions are pairs, yoked together by mighty Necessity; nor can both be small in the Unbounded."

   (3) "Cycle-mongering prophets, thirsty for gold, afflictors of the people, ignorant that Frequency is indivisible and continuous."

   (4) Or shall I blame Wiener who said in his oration at the centennial games of the city of Chicago, "More cows and better lanterns."[7]

2. DOUBTFUL

   "Vagrant ova found their way into cows not their own." (THEODORE OF TASHKENT, *Abominations*). Probably a late forgery, inspired by the tradition that Wiener was the discoverer of artificial insemination. But see fr. 1, 4.

[6] Early Eurasian name for the favorite deity of the Late Empire, Massa Pandemia or Massa Maxima. The attribute of Pandemia appears in the third century. Aphrodite Marxa must have been an early sky-and-earth deity, and either ambisexual or the paredra of a male god, for she appears in the early coins as a heavily bearded anguipede. She reappears later as a patroness of the plebeians, before becoming syncretically identified with the Cosmic Serpent Ouroboros as Massa.

[7] The founding legends of the cities of the Western Hemisphere were usually built around Herakles. Hence this seems to belong to a celebration of the hero's exploits against Cacus. Such forms as "bigger and better," characteristic of early sophistic rhetoric, lend a flavor of authenticity to the fragment.

3. SPURIOUS

TROFIM, 127, 2: "Our security must be the security of achievement, not the security of concealment." (From obvious considerations of style this fragment can hardly antedate the fourth century and is probably much later.)

Vico and Descartes

VICO IS COMING AT LAST INTO HIS OWN.[1] SINCE MICHELET, A century ago, dug him out of oblivion, he had been at least a name and a scheme. Today, Vico has entered English literature through *Finnegan s Wake*. The tantalizing intricacy and obscurity of Joyce's great work, revealing as they do the Viconian scheme only in flashes, are an inducement to read into it weird and apocalyptic overtones. They may none the less help effectively to shake off the Spencerian residues which are so much in evidence in our cultural world.

For more than a century, the historical consciousness of Western civilization has been split into ever-diverging streams. The current of "historicism" stemming from Hegel and Marx engulfed Germany, Italy and Russia, while the French and Anglo-Saxon cultures remained practically immune to it, cradled in solid eighteenth-century optimism.

Possibly, our intensive study of Communist tactics is bringing us nearer to an understanding of "historicism". Stalin has never read Vico, yet he is different from us in thought mainly in that he has adopted the fundamental principle brought by Vico into the world, that we never even troubled to examine until recently: the hard principle of immanence in history.

Vico is vaguely known as the man who gave a theory of history, and who believed in cycles. The first direct acquaintance of our public with him by way of Joyce may lead us into serious misunderstandings. Joyce is not a thinker, he is an artist, and a Catholic turned inside out. It is enough to him that life should move in "vicous circles". But Vico means more than that, as appears even from some of Joyce's own re-phrasings. He is a vivid assertion of the impermanence, nay of the deathly quality if preserved, of the so-called permanent values. Viewed from the viewpoint of eternity, history is bound to mean nothing. It is a "human pest cycling (pist!) and recycling (past!)". Viewed from man's own point of view, it is "the evolution of human society and the testament of the rocks from all the dead unto some of the living", the change of values which accompanies the evolution from the early stage, the divine, to the heroic and then to the civil. For this is Vico's great idea, his "law of the three states". Virtue means first piety, then honor, then duty. The inarticulate howling dark ages give way to the fabulous, and then the historical, forms of expression. Language goes from hieroglyphic to metaphorical and at last to analytical; the rise of cities is the sum of the three epochs, yet the ruins of former civilizations foreshadow the fall of cities, and preannounce the

[1] *The New Science of Giambattista Vico*, translated from the third edition (1744) by Thomas Goddard Bergen and Max Harold Fisch, Cornell University Press, Ithaca, N. Y., 1948, 398 pp.

The Autobiography of G. B. Vico, translated from the Italian by Max Harold Fisch and Thomas Goddard Bergin, Cornell University Press, Ithaca, N. Y., 1944, 260 pp.

cyclic "recurring" of civilization. The nightmare of history in nightmarish style; but who would deny that the history we are living through is a nightmare in itself? The artist alone, perhaps, can exorcise it.

Vico's personal intentions were something else again, and for those we must go to those welcome translations of the *Scienza Nuova* and of his *Autobiography*. In both books, the translators have achieved the miracle of ridding the Neapolitan of his cumbrous style and making him readable.

There is something about Vico which seems to have been obscured by his nineteenth-century admirers. The fact is that Vico did himself belong to a great constructive period, that he had no use for romantic feelings, or professorial philosophy either. His effort is, in time and intention, parallel and opposed to that of the Encyclopedists. He is the anti-Cartesian manifesto.

Vico did not understand what we mean by science. He looked, as a stranger would, at what Descartes had been doing. But this very incapacity gave him freedom to look at Descartes the metaphysician without being lured on by his scientific reasons.

As an Italian of his time he wrote Arcadian sonnets, and opposed the sterile sophistication of "marinismo"; as a philosopher he fought the "epicurean" trends of Gassendi and Bayle, and Grotius' theories. As a European, he took his place in the *querelle des anciens et des modernes*, but in a line different from that of Descartes and Fontenelle. He took the past seriously. He is the last effort of Italian culture, checked and smothered by the Counter-Reformation, to find new and deeper levels where it could be free, and commune with its tradition. The monumental historic efforts of men like Baronio, Muratori, Zeno, delving into the past, come to a conclusion in Vico's work. The strain of critical historical research that had been started by Leibniz had seemed to these men a new way to intellectual salvation. That effort was short-lived; Algarotti's *Newtonianism for Ladies*, a manifesto of transalpine trends of thought, came out in 1733, barely eight years after the first edition of the *Scienza Nuova*.

Vico is not the man of a clear orderly system. His thought does not fall into the successive paragraphs of a treatise. The best way to understand him is to go back to his early philological studies, and to his struggle with the scholars of his time, who "would have it that whatever they knew was as old as the world", as they expounded the matchless wisdom of the ancients and the complicated allegories hidden in the most uncouth tales. It came upon Vico that this was a way of disregarding the process of time and what it brings; that "the first Gentile people" must have been poets simply because they did not know how to express their thoughts except poetically, and that it was only very gradually that man's thought disentangled itself from his feeling, even as world became something different from the projection of his fancies and fears.

The first men, "stupid, insensate and horrible beasts", cannot have been capable of thought, but only of wholly "corporeal" imagination and abject terrors. The thunders and earthquakes they visualized into angry gods, and this led to the sexual taboos and to the first link in the "chain of authority". This it was that later legend represented as "the chains of the giants" forged by Jove. Actually, they were the bonds that man forged for himself in the family, which also, however, assured him of "certain" children by a "certain" (i.e. legitimate) woman. Such was certainty as it came to man, and not in the form of epistemology. This was "the first metaphysics", the way men began to "know"; and that is what knowledge stands for. In order to know the timeless truth directly, man would have to jump out of his own skin, a feat with which we could not credit even the wisest men of ancient times.

> But in the night of thick darkness enveloping the earliest antiquity, so remote from ourselves, there shines the eternal and never-failing light of a truth beyond all question: that the world of civil society has certainly been made by men, and that its principles are therefore to be found within the modifications of our own human mind. Whoever reflects on this cannot but marvel that the philosophers should have bent all their energies to the study of the world of nature, which, since God made it, He alone knows; and that they should have neglected the study of the world of nations or civil world, which, since men had made it, men could hope to know. This aberration was a consequence of that infirmity of the human mind, noted in the Axioms, by which, immersed and buried in the body, it naturally inclines to take notice of bodily things, and finds the effort to attend to itself too laborious; just as the bodily eye sees all objects outside itself but needs a mirror to see itself.

Here, then, were foundations of greater certainty than those of Descartes. The great themes had been set. But how to construct a system of providential determinism upon them? It dawned upon Vico that Leibniz, the profoundest logician of them all, was the answer to his prayers. With his "monads" which are spiritual atoms, Leibniz revived far more ancient and fundamental ideas than that "geometrical Epicurean", Descartes. He showed the way back to the intuitions of Pythagoras, and to a "re-purging of the points of Zeno from the altered relations of Aristotle." But from the very fact that he had shown the substance of the universe to be an infinity of Selves,—i.e. the monads, following their evolution through time,—Leibniz had been compelled to bring in a "pre-established harmony" to keep all those clocks running coincidently. A logical necessity, but a highly artificial contrivance. Vico thought he had the answer. The proper place for the pre-established harmony is the perfect timing by which man's bondage to his passions and his misrepresentations leads him from one situation to another in exactly the order required for the unfolding of the divine idea, as reflected in the growing orders of civil polity, and also in metaphysical understanding which in turn grows from them. This is the truly natural way in which the divine effulguration unfolds itself in living time. By the same token, the paradoxes of Cartesian occasionalism are brought to a natural solution, simply by removing it from its flat abstract plane and bringing it inside a process. For it is true that mind cannot act directly on matter, but it does not require a special continuous intervention of God to make up for that: the same course of man's nature through time is the natural occasional cause required.

Fortified by such seemingly miraculous coincidences, Vico had no doubt that he had hit upon the System of the Ages. Everything fell into place. Descartes despises fantasy and what comes to us through the senses, he discards history and tradition as a mass of popular nugacity, and believes only in the clear cold sense of the "honnête homme". He builds up nature mechanically, society atomistically. That is inevitable, since he is a mechanical abstractor, a mathematical machine producing only its own symbols. Deduction is an empty game when it is not preceded by the amplest of inductions, covering all of our experience which starts with "fantasy"—an induction such as Descartes' tyrannical precepts forbid.

What is mathematics? A true science, insofar as it operates with the concepts it has itself created. It brings in the point, then out of it constructs the line, out of the line the plane. It can order and prove its entities because it knows them truly, and it knows them because it has made them. It can, even as God can, "ad Dei instar", reach the infinite. As God knows things, so man knows his own creations. One is reminded here of Galileo's distinction between the knowledge of God, which is "extensive," and that of man which is "intensive". But then, both knowledges deal with the same essence of the universe which is mathematical. Not so with Vico. The geometrical point that man creates is his own abstraction. The point ceases to be a point as man draws it; the one, as it is multiplied, ceases to be unity and becomes units. Point and unit indicate the existence beyond themselves of the true "metaphysical point" which belongs to a higher realm of being. Mathematics can only create on its level, it is an operational science, "scienza operativa".

Before it in time, beyond it in scope, is man's total relationship with the universe. Man has been cast into the process of time, with perforce limited equipment, he stumbles along in unending action and reaction, he forges his own chains and then struggles loose from them. Memory, fantasy and will create his own world, as he emerges from the darkness of the senses. He attributes his own imaginations to things in the beginning, for "the indefinite nature of his mind leads him to making it the rule of the universe." He can never know himself: but he can realize his actions in time, and understand them in retrospect. And this, for once, is true knowledge, a confluence of myth, law, language and tradition with "reason unfolded". Here he can know the "nature of things", for it is "nothing but their coming into being at certain times and in certain fashions." "The sciences must begin where their subject matter began". The real "common sense" of all peoples is the repository of knowledge, it is the complete induction which has built into every event with which we are involved, the many causes that brought it into being; whence later the arrogant philosopher draws the simple ideas that allow him to invent one cause to account for everything.

It is then, the *science* of history, far removed from history itself, that Vico is after. The ordinary historian reconstructs events; whereas *he* is only interested in the logic of forms and relations, even as a paleontologist is.

> Our Science comes to describe an ideal eternal history traversed in time by the history of every nation in its rise, progress, maturity, decline and fall. Indeed we go so far as to assert that whoever meditates this Science tells himself the ideal eternal history only so far as he makes it, by that proof "it had, has, and will have to be" . . . Thus our Science proceeds exactly as does geometry, which, while it constructs out of its elements or contemplates the world of quantity, itself creates it: but with a reality greater in proportion to that of the orders having to do with human affairs, in which there are neither points, lines, surfaces, nor figures. And this very fact is an argument, O reader, that these proofs are of a kind divine, and should give thee a divine pleasure; since in God knowledge and creation are one and the same thing.

Here Vico has formulated his new principle of knowledge, of which he had found the first idea in Sanchez, and given it life: the equality of "truth" and "doing". The *Theses on Feuerbach* are around the corner.

The transition is easy, all too easy, to nineteenth-century immanence, to Hegel, Marx and Croce: There is nothing outside history, and therein man is actually God. So easy, in fact, that the moderns who rescued Vico from oblivion accuse him of timidity and incoherence for not having gone the whole way. That is a grievous misconception. Vico is and remains a transcendentalist; his is the last great attempt to save transcendence by integrating all of reality into its scheme, even the process of time. The guidance of the process still comes from outside, from God's providence. Even as Newton's planets revolve around the sun by virtue of intrinsic forces providentially measured to them, so the process of history rises and falls periodically, as it "runs on orders reflecting the divine attributes", and the points of the time-axis are projections on the social "certain" of eternal truths.

Vico's thought goes immediately out of focus, and can be accused of unresolved metaphysical contradictions, if we do not read in it the same thoroughgoing distinction—on a more difficult plane—that Galileo had set between our "intensive" and God's "extensive" knowledge.

It may be of interest to the historian of science to go into the technical difference between Descartes' and Vico's starting points. Fundamentally, of course, we have to do with the difference of two types of mind. We find it repeated in our times in Yeats' antagonism towards the thought of G. B. Shaw: "It seemed to me inorganic, logical straightness and not the crooked road of life, and I stood aghast before its energy." We are here at the source of that divergence. Descartes holds that knowledge (as of clear and distinct ideas) connects us directly with being: "nos idées ou notions, étant des choses réelles et qui viennent de Dieu en tout ce en quoi elles sont claires et distinctes, ne peuvent en cela qu'êtres vraies". Thus thought is not a part of the soul, it *is* the soul, independent of the body and the senses. And this thought is "intelligence", i.e. relational logic and nothing else.

Hence he will deduce metaphysically nothing but mathematical propositions, which he will endow with a physical existence; his world is pure act, wholly realized; not only nothing happens in it, but its essence is also existence—and its existence is inertial death. That is what happens when you try to equate the knowledge of man to that of angels.

The attempt by Descartes to "find" again God within his own thought is an inversion which comes close to satanic pride, it could not but lead him to make of himself an essence.

As Vico remarks sarcastically, it is not Descartes, it is Plautus' Sosia who brought up long ago the reassuring notion that if one thinks, one is quite probably around. But that can lead only to a statement of consciousness, not of any truth-content. If I were an angel, I would see all at once; if I were a clod, I would not even feel; but because I am a man, I am bound to feel and act and think.

Science is knowledge of causes. True causation can be known only in time, genetically, and known only as thinking can know, that is confusedly at first, arising from tension and interaction with the outside, from which relations are built up; not the abstract relations that can be derived discursively from a considering of magnitudes, but the real *natura*, "the way things grow".

Descartes had said it too, of course: "Leur nature est bien plus aisée à concevoir, lorsqu'on les voit naître peu à peu en cette sorte, que lorsqu'on ne les considère que toutes faites." But he had been untrue to his assumption, and had built up only a kind of Erector set, where in truth nothing grows and nothing happens, except if you make it happen, nothing comes into being, not even new physical relations. His world starts from inertia and remains inertial. His admirers say that he "dared solve the mysteries of both natures," but what is daring is his sleight-of-hand.

Larvatus prodeo. Descartes was a hard-headed physicist under the mask of a metaphysician. He did not want to "know" nature since he assumed he knew it already. What he wanted was power over nature. He wanted to know the ways in which man can construct "his own" nature, which is nothing but machines. What did his "laws" mean? The question is far from senseless, apart from the objective validity of those laws which has proved feeble. Hume and Vico both went back to human experience against that kind of deduction. But Vico tried to go deeper. Law has nothing to do with nature. "Natural law" is a later abstraction for what used to be the original "law of gods and men". It is just because law was such a creation, an *institutio*, that it had metaphysical content, that it conveyed "meaning". All attempts at abstracting a "natural law", moral, social or physical, preserved only a reflection of that meaning, and so does the whole physical universe that Descartes is trying to abstract. Law is of men, and lives only in them.

Against Descartes' laws of motion, Vico tries to conceive of a "deeper nature" of motion, what he calls the *conatus*. "What the theorists of mechanics call powers, force, impulses, are insensible motions of bodies, by which they approach their centers of gravity, as ancient mechanics had it, or depart from their centers of motion, as modern (Newtonian) mechanics has it."

Such an idea, interesting from a modern point of view, expresses a groping towards ampler concepts. But then, simple clarity would be a red danger signal in Vico's eyes. Any ideas that deal with the whole must proceed by progressive clarification, as the network of meanings is allowed to unfold itself. Vico would say with Augustine against Descartes "Fallor ergo sum," which at least is sound Christian sense.

By the definitions above proposed, men were for a long period incapable of truth or reason, which is the fount of the inner justice by which the intellect is satisfied . . . This was later reasoned out by philosophers. In the meantime the nations were governed by the certitude of authority . . . namely the common sense of the human race. So that, in this third principal regard, our Science comes to be a philosophy of authority. Of such authority account should have been taken by the three princes of the doctrine of the natural law of nations (Grothius, Selden and Pufendorf), and not of that drawn from passages in the writers. For the authority of which we speak reigned among the nations for more than a thousand years before the writers could arise, and they could have taken no cognizance of it.

This goes back to Axiom 6: "Philosophy considers man as he should be and so can be of service to but very few, who wish to live in the Republic of Plato, not to fall back into the dung-heap of Romulus." And further: "Philosophy must direct weak and fallen man, not rend his nature . . ." Whatever his cult for enlightenment, Vico remains a philosopher of authority against the partisans of methodic doubt. It is for him "the wisdom of the Romans".

Strangely enough, Vico is in agreement with Descartes about the inadequacies of ancient philosophy as still a prisoner to sensible evidence. He protests vividly against the renewed interest in Epicurean thought, and would rather have the bold abstractions of contemporary mathematical physics. The earthy common sense of Epicurean explanations, their lingering passion for "small pebbles" as the only reality,—a blind man's universe— their disdain for rigorous theory, he feels as a reversion to childish and primitive thought. Lucretius' intuition of an early feral humanity groping through the primeval forest he recognizes as true. It is a truth, however, that cannot be dominated by the materialistic mind, but rather becomes a spell that holds it down. A materialist, *contemptor matheseos*, can develop out of that truth only a theory of urges and satisfactions, unable to rise to universal norms; it is and portrays a way of being utterly enslaved to original sin. But it had to be thought, and it had to be said; it is a scientific idea, which can be saved from running wild, and put in its proper place, only within the all-embracing scheme of a *New Science*.

A continuity with the great dream of the Renaissance is here undeniable. The Florentine humanists had hoped to "save" the myths of paganism, all its cults and all its altars, by a subtile spiritualist hermeneutic; but they had only the weak instrument of literary and moral allegory at their disposal. Vico thinks he has a means of "mechanizing" that theory, as we would say today.

The fables are not a cover for an intellectual truth; they are the poetic truth, the immediate and total expression of thought, which later proceeds with astonishment to "discover" i.e. construct, the rational meaning implicit in them. Starting from the abjection of original sin, a slave to sensuous impressions, man had a hard road to travel before he could handle ideas. It was Malebranche who had said that sensible objects make all the deeper an impression on us, the less they have of being and reality. The Cartesian will understand this one way; the modern anthropologist will confirm it in another. Vico sets out on the modern way. He had, it is true, only some hints of anthropology. But he had a solid instrument in legal history. He knew early religion to have been expression of positive law: he also knew the history of law to reflect the interminable struggle of the oppressed against the oppressor in its growth into equity and reason, as the harsh bonds of greed and common interest shaped themselves slowly into the complex ties of modern society. Truly, the chanted precepts of early law were "a serious poem", and jurisprudence, "severe poetry". But the successive attainment of praetorial law which checked the aristocrats, and of the right of plebeians to full property, are no less serious, both socially and metaphysically: they are the first steps to a *recta ratio imperandi atque prohibendi*. The evolution of law is not a shifting confusion; it is reason, working itself out into intelligible propositions, it is, in fact, Divine Reason itself working its way through the passions of men into their intellect. The very hardness of oligarchic pride and prejudice and punctilio is the necessary anvil on which are hammered out the works of the spirit. War, Heraclitus had said, is the father of all things. But it is not the war beyond measure of which the atom bomb is the present symbol: it is the struggle within the bonds of common interest in which the adversaries are compelled to recognize each other. "Free peoples give their laws those meanings that they compel the powerful to read into them." Actions and passions are blind and hard, but there is the solvent of juridical argument in which reason unfolds: "Legislation considers man as he is; . . . out of ferocity, avarice and ambition, it creates the military, the merchant and the Court estates. Out of the three great vices, which could certainly destroy all mankind on the face of the earth, it makes civil happiness. This axiom proves that there is divine providence . . ."

Here Vico brings the thing to a point with one of his revealing flashes: Justice, he says, is an "imitation of violence". That is, it does not ignore the violence that goes to make up the nature of man, and which condemns the idealist to frustration; it brings it in, controlled by reason, organized into solemnity, as part of a scheme of reason. That is why justice and the social order contain the true thought of a society, as it changes and will go on changing.

Truly, this reason is "purged" of the Aristotelian scheme, according to which natures work themselves out inside the static beat of eternally repeated generations. But neither is it the Cartesian reason. To think of minds as self-contained principles of motion, going simply ahead, would be to repeat in history the seductive fallacy of rectilinear inertial motion in physics. The inertial principle requires a void, a structureless world. For Vico—as well as for Leibniz—the world, both in spirit and in matter, reveals itself an ordered plenum and all motion must go towards a providential goal. In a purely kinetic world, the mean free path of each being would be "solitary, poor, nasty, brutish and short". On the other hand, it is silly to imagine bestial cavemen or "the ferocious haughtiness of heroic senates" going in for a social contract; even if they had, they would have remained primitives. Hobbes' mechanization is a paper model.

To the humanistic delusion of a science of words by which man could equate his mind to the universe, Vico answers with a true paradox; *Homo non cognoscendo fit omnia*; man is all things *by* not knowing, and eventually becomes—only himself. But to the empiricist delusion of a *tabula rasa* on which sense-data come together nicely of their own accord, Vico opposes the primeval facts of fear and greed, creators of violent images and remorseless action, originators of an endless chain of consequences. The image of the blank tablet is inverted for him into that of a wholly written tablet, inscribed in the beginning with hieroglyphic characters of sacred potency. Man speaks at first only the inarticulate "language of the Gods," as it comes to him darkly through the noises and forces of nature; then the language of heroes, and only later the language of the polity. "Our freedom is that of doing all things that depend from the body, and through time we do them all and contain them in us."

A parallel becomes obvious, even if strange at first sight. Vico and Hume were carrying on, at about the same time, the same critique of rationalism. Hume, in a purely analytical way, was drawn to make similar distinctions about reason, fact and value, and about the role of reason in society. Both men were preparing the nineteenth-century categories of thought. But there the parallel stops. F. H. Jacobi, one of the few romantics who read Vico, rightly remarked that he had preceded Kant with his identification of creation and knowledge. One wonders what would have happened, indeed, if Kant had been awakened from his "dogmatic slumber" by Vico instead of by Hume. We might have been spared the dreary mental isolation of criticism: the artificial isolation of the spirit in its cultured void: the isolation of Progress. As we have said, it is a grievous misconception to make of Vico an announcer of that progress of the spirit in history which manifests itself by the writing of books upon the progress of the spirit in history. He had a strong cosmic sense, and could not ignore, as Hegel was to ignore as much as he could, the Copernican revolution. He thought in terms of an infinite, general and simple cause, always equal to itself. The work of spirit in man is not as it was later to become, that of abstractions, or of an ego masked in universals, for the mind is and remains dark and errant; it is the work of grace which goes on equal to itself, "were it even that from Eternity infinite worlds were to be born". History is the extension into time of the idea of the Good, which in its "circumpulsion" causes the particular wills to follow their appointed courses. A Theodicy, if we want to call it by its name, and comparable in dimensions to that of Leibniz: in Vico's words "a rational civil theology of divine providence". In both systems the idea is explicit that a sound Christian philosophy should not aggravate dualism, but solve it. There should be no absolute Necessity, no dead matter or radical Evil, no total separation between the world and a "wholly other", for in that case we would be ultimately led to such extreme conclusions of those of a Kierkegaard. If the world has to be deduced from its principle, or at least in some way to reflect it, then there cannot be a separation between the two, but there must be a Jacob's ladder, however transcendental, from one to the other. This comes straight from the Renaissance; it is still the same search for a scheme connecting all parts of the Universe, and the mind, and angels, and God. If there is no convergence and reflection of causes in God, then there is only their scattering into straight lines and atomism. From both sides of the religious barrier, Leibniz and Vico were trying to restore oecumenic Christianity, and to undo the damage that the Reformation had wrought on the one and the other side. They tried to restore the syncretistic, conciliatory, and gradualist approach which bridges the gulf between mind and matter.

Of the two, the greater logician and stricter systematic, Leibniz, proved to be the more perishable. Vico's ideas lived on, not only in reactionaries like de Maistre but in all the forms of "historicist" thought. Yet how different from themselves, in the new atmosphere of romantic emotion, or in the sensible distinctions of critical, dialectical, immanentist theory.

Our brief fancy on what might have been dissolves in the light of historical necessity. Vico could at best have checked momentarily the Newtonian and progressive fashions, but they were bound to rend his thought asunder. He had no science.

The fact is, Vico does not think much of Progress. He is not impressed by his own time, nor does he dwell on it. If he praises the "dispiegata ragione amplissima" of his own enlightened epoch, it is mainly because it has allowed such outlooks as his and Leibniz's to mature. When God is distinctly perceived as the total logical cause in every motion and in every state of being, when everything is brought back to Him by demonstrative reason, then there is nothing more to seek, not even the perfection of the Prussian state. It is a brief pinnacle. Beyond, Vico sees only increasing social individualism and atomism: "though physically thronging together, they will live like wild beasts in a solitude of spirit and will, scarcely any two being able to agree since each follows his own pleasure or caprice." It is the descent into a new dark age. Mankind being bound to time and change, its efforts to reach God are bound to fail, the wave falls back from the same movement that brought it to surge. For Vico's God is not in man's time, and were it even in an ever-receding future. He is in his own time, inaccessible to resolution by the mind, he is not a way, or a principle, or a future, he is not an ideal or a postulate, he is not the God of Hegel, he is the God of Johann Sebastian Bach; a living myth, a revealed mystery in which all contradictions cease to be. Inside the immense horizon of Vico's baroque Heaven, the pulse of our time ebbs and flows in an eternal rhythm.

That is also why Vico's attempt at scientific clarity was bound to fail. The New Science would have needed an Archimedean point outside time which was denied to it, except by way of revelation. Vico has to situate his own effort somewhere in the surge coming from the depths of the "fantastic universal", i.e. of what is common to all through the senses; it would have taken a Divine Comedy to join the depths to the heights. Analytical clarification is bound to do injustice to the whole; one can organize events, one cannot organize transcendence. That is why the whole exposition is bound to go in a circle, "recycling" past on its own tracks all the while, a reminder of Parmenides' warning: "It is the same to me where I begin, for I shall come back to the same point."

This warning having later been transgressed in the nineteenth century, the vision could not but spawn a brood of serpents. Or, to change metaphors in midstream, if the tension of the whole fabric is broken at one point, the Idea will go through time like a run in a stocking. To the writing of books there shall be no end.

For all his logical helplessness and his obscure visionary style, Vico is far more penetrating than his clever analytical contemporaries. At a time when Pope and Voltaire were turning out polished couplets which they thought to be poetry, he was able to tell them why it could not be considered poetry by any standard. At a time when political theorists believed in the noble savage and in the social contract, he was inventing sociology and comparative ethnology; at a time when the Romans were seen as high-minded characters from Plutarch, attitudinizing in plastic compositions à la David, he showed the Roman people "drowned in a sea of debts", enslaved and beaten by an obtuse aristocracy, rallying to force agrarian laws and juridical reason upon their masters.

More than all that, Vico was able to tell the illuminists that they were pulling down the house over their heads, while believing it could last for ever. Like Descartes, Vico was really a conservative, but a more consistent one. He wanted to save Christian philosophy through a supra-temporal theory of history, even as Descartes had thought he had discovered new foundations for it in mathematics. As Descartes was to lead to Robespierre, so Vico was to lead to Stalin in the end. These are the ironies of history.

This, too, is the last conclusion of the *Querelle des Anciens et des Modernes*. What the Renaissance had felt was: we are as good as the Ancients, and maybe better. In its adolescent pride, it had thought of little more than re-enacting an ancient glory, and besting its fathers as it took up their virtues. But now historical thought has come upon the scene, showing, in an interpretation which far outstrips Polybius, that the ancients belong somewhere in a scheme as a step in a given development. By the same token they are dead; they have become objects in an Institute of paleontology.

Vico has been called the Galileo of the historical sciences. But what a difference from the Florentine's clarity and poise, from his pointed wit and his assurance which combines the certainty of mathematics with the ease of the ruling bourgeoisie, to the heaviness and obscurity of the poor Neapolitan professor, stumbling in his own involved rhetoric, struggling against an ambiguous and treacherous scholarship of his time. The Vico that emerges from the Autobiography is pathetic in his uncouthness. He had never aimed at more than an average career in the humanities. As his translators remark, the decisive event in his life was his failure in the academic competition of 1723, from which he had expected an assured living. He was then 55 years of age. Frustrated in the conventional disciplines, he tried to recoup his fortunes with a great work of unconventional design, in which he would show the depth of his scholarship and confound his enemies. This was to be the *Scienza Nuova*. From then on, his life, never easy, is darkened by poverty, illness, the needs of a large family, and the capricious indifference of high-placed protectors. Vico has to pester dukes and cardinals with contorted and abject begging letters, such as the pompous gentlemen of the Spanish Vice-Regal Court expected from an obscure preceptor.

They must have seen him just as he appears in this revealing autobiography, and given stingily, carelessly, for the sake of their own grandeur, to the helpless bore. There he is, in the words of a contemporary, "with wide open staring eyes, and leaning on his walking-stick", abstracted in his fancy, buttonholing acquaintances to recount any small acknowledgment he received from foreign scholars; humbly grateful withal to his protectors, piously devout, a great believer in authority and respecter of rank, with some crabbed erudite theory about ancient law. If they had only known, a most dangerous man.

Eudoxus and Plato: A Study in Chronology

A NUMBER OF REMARKABLE WORDS HAVE COME OUT RECENTLY, investigating the relations between Plato and the contemporary mathematicians. We need only mention the names Frank, Stenzel, Becker, v. Fritz, Karpp, Solmsen, Toeplitz.[1] The Platonic period is such a crucial one for the history of thought that any new detail uncovered is apt to modify not only the actual sequence of events but essentially the genetic interpretation of the basic concepts, both in mathematics and in philosophy.

Generally speaking, it is one of the most important problems of Greek thought to know to what extent mathematical theories reacted on Plato's thought and vice versa, in what way the ideas of abstraction, definition, existentiality and the like made their way into the structure that later appeared in Euclid, as it is to know how Plato's own ideas on transcendence evolved in contact with the investigations of geometricians.

Taking only the technical problems, is it possible to suppose an actual collaboration between Theaetetus and Eudoxus? How much of the theory of Irrationals has been contributed by Theaetetus, how much by Eudoxus, to whom we owe the Euclidean formulation, what exactly is the evolution which led from the irrational to the incommensurable, what underlies the advent of the new terms with the subtle distinction between commensurability on the line and commensurability in the square, and how does the critical process involved react on logic?

These and other ideas eventually found their way into the Platonic school. On the other hand, Solmsen has tried to show the influence of the Platonic dialectic on mathematics with its insistence on the definition and the *καθ' αὑτό;* and Becker has proved that whereas the axiom of continuity in its existential form (the "Dedekind cut" as used in the Eudoxian theorem in Eucl. XII, 2) may be older than Eudoxus, the clear formulation of the concept of homogeneity connected with the exhaustion procedure, which is Eudoxus's contribution, was hardly grasped by Aristotle even in his maturity.

To take a case from another field, is the theory of homocentric spheres responsible for the development of sidereal theology in the evolution of Plato's thought, or is the traditional version of Plato's assigning the problem nearer the truth?

[1] K. v. Fritz, Die Ideenlehre des Eudoxos von Knidos und ihr Verhältnis zur platonischen Ideenlehre, in *Philologus* 82 (1927), p. 1; also, *ibid.* 87 (1930), p. 40 ff. and 136 ff; cf. by the same author the art. *Theaetetos* in Pauly-Wissowa's *Realenzyklopädie*, (1938). O. Toeplitz, Das Verhältnis von Mathematik und Ideenlehre bei Plato, in *Quellen u. Studien z. Geschichte d. Mathematik*, 1, 1 (1929), p. 3; F. Solmsen, Platos Einfluss auf die Bildung der mathematischen Methode, *ibid*, p. 93; *id*, Die Entwicklung der aristotelischen Logik and Rhetorik, Berlin, 1929; H. Karpp, Untersuchungen zur Philosophie des Eudoxos von Knidos, Würzburg-Aumühle, 1933; *id.*, Die Schrift des Aristoteles *περὶ ἰδεῶν* in *Hermes* 68 (1933), p. 384. General works: E. Frank, Plato und die sogenannten Pythagoreer, Halle 1923; Stenzel, Zahl und Gestalt bei Platon und Aristoteles, 1926; H. Hasse und H. Scholz, Die Grundlagenkrisis der antiken Mathematik, 1926 (cf. also Vogt in *Bibl. math.*, III Folge, Bd. X, 142 sqq). Eva Sachs, De Theaeteto mathematico, 1914.

Thus from only one or two instances, we can discern how intricate is the process of interreaction which characterizes this period of contact between two disciplines in statu nascendi, and the problems raised then cannot be said to be wholly solved today.

There is little doubt that the transition from intuitive to axiomatically constructed geometry must have reacted strongly on the theory of Ideas, touching as it did on the very notion of *eidos* and logical inherence. Now this transition is linked with the name of Eudoxus. And if Eudoxus really died in 355, it would mean that his theories had already been completed at the time when the *Timaeus* was written. Plato never mentions Eudoxus. Taken in itself, this would mean little, as it is rather in his manner. But apart from the *Philebus*, there is no clear evidence of his reacting to the immanentism of Eudoxus and to his critique of the idea of participation. v. Fritz, Becker, and Solmsen have tried to trace this reaction, but without reaching an agreement. Maybe the mathematical apriorism of Plato's later dialogues contains implicitly his answer, and maybe it does not. Here as before, it might be largely a question of dates.

A conclusive settlement of the chronological data would surely help to unravel many a knot. The present work is an attempt in this direction.

The official version for the chronology of Eudoxus is still that of Hultsch (Pauly-Wissowa, IX, 931, art. *Eudoxus*), and it is the one adopted by the leading textbooks on the history of mathematics. It puts the dates of Eudoxus at 408–355. It originally was worked out by Boeckh (Die vierjährigen Sonnenkreise der Alten) and confirmed by him through a very elaborate astronomical computation based on the *Octaëteris*. Cantor (Vorles. über d. Gesch. d. Math. I, 225) and Tannery (Hist. de l'astronomie) followed suit.

Boeckh's assumption, however, could be carried through only by discarding a certain number of credible data, and in 1891 G. F. Unger (*Philologus* 50, 191) took up the problem again. His suggestion was 428–375. It was based on a painstaking critique of the methods and vagaries of ancient chronology. It must be admitted, however, that his "Kombinationen" did take him very far afield, and also required some Procrustean fitting, to the point of having to deny Eudoxus the authorship of such a well-certified work as the γῆς περίοδος. Hence his dates were not generally accepted.[2] Susemihl (*Rh. Mus.*, 53, 1898, 626 sqq.) tried to bring back a sense of proportion by recalling the un-

[2] It is strange, however, to see that a distinguished scholar like A. E. Taylor still takes for granted some such date as Unger's, without going into the problem, it would seem, and merely on the strength of a word of Suidas, who calls Eudoxus a contemporary ἡλικιώτης of Plato.

disputable testimony of Eudemos, which does not allow us to set a birth date higher than 395 at most. He could base himself also on corresponding results reached independently by Helm in 1894, by starting from medical history, and tracing the succession of the doctors of the Chrysippus family, one of whom was the companion of Eudoxus. The possible life-span of this Chrysippus was the clinching argument, since the death of another Chrysippus, his son, had been definitely located by Wilamowitz about 277. But a few years later Max Wellmann, by one of his complicated pieces of puzzle-fitting in medical history, came to the conclusion that three generations of the family must have been telescoped in this one Chrysippus. A greater timespan became therefore allowable; although Wellmann himself did not avail himself of it nor suggest its adoption, and in fact put Chrysippus' voyage at a guess "in the sixties of the 4th century".

On the sole strength of those findings, however, Hultsch rather cavalierly dismissed all the other conflicting theories, apparently on the general assumption that they were not needed any more, and went back, as we said, to the original dates of Boeckh and Tannery, which have been taken as confirmed ever since. Only lately have F. Gisinger and K. v. Fritz brought up fresh grounds of dissent.

The facts that we have on the life of Eudoxus are few and not very much to the point. Apart from a few scattered indications and some inferential conclusions, the whole of the material is to be found in Diogenes Laertius. Here are the relevant passages:

Eudoxus of Cnidos, the son of Aeschines, was an astronomer, a geometrician, physician and legislator. He learned geometry from Archytas and medicine from Philistion the Sicilian, as Callimachus tells us in his Tables. Sotion in his Successions of the Philosophers says that he was also a pupil of Plato. When he was about twenty-three years old and in straitened circumstances, he was attracted by the reputation of the Socratics and set sail for Athens with Theomedon the physician who provided for his wants. Some even say that he was Theomedon's favorite. Having disembarked at Piraeus he went up every day to Athens and, when he had attended the Sophists' lectures, walked down again to the port. After spending two months there, he went home and, aided by the liberality of his friends, he proceeded to Egypt with Chrysippus the physician, bearing with him letters of introduction from Agesilaos to Nectanabis, who recommended him to the priests. There he remained one year and four months with his beard and eyebrows shaved, and there, some say, he wrote his Octaëteris. From there he went to Cyzicus and the Propontis giving lectures (σοφιστεύοντα); and he also came to the court of Mausolus. Then at length he returned to Athens, bringing with him a great number of pupils: according to some, this was for the purpose of annoying Plato, who had originally passed him over. Some say that when Plato gave a banquet, Eudoxus, owing to the numbers present, introduced the fashion of arranging couches in a semicircle. Nicomachus, the son of Aristotle, states that he declared pleasure to be the good. He was received in his native city with great honor, proof of this being the decree concerning him. But he also became famous throughout Greece as a legislator for his fellow citizens, as we learn from Hermippus. . . .

Chrysippus of Cnidos the son of Erineus attended his lectures on the gods on the world, and the phenomena of the heavens, while in medicine he was the pupil of Philistion the Sicilian. . . .

Apollodoros states that Eudoxus flourished about the 103rd Olympiad (368–364 B.C.) and that he discovered the properties of curved lines. He died in his fifty-third year. When he was in Egypt with Chonuphis of Heliopolis, the sacred bull Apis licked his cloak. From this the priests predicted that he would be famous but short-lived, so we are informed by Favorinus in his Memorabilia.

This is almost all that we know about Eudoxus' life: a pretty miserable account, by a frivolous layman, of the man who turned out to be the greatest mathematician of antiquity and one of its greatest astronomers.

Unless some new document is found, it is impossible to reach a really satisfactory reconstruction. Yet even though we have so little information, one of the main problems is to decide which part of it to reject. There are, as to the dates, two primary sources, Apollodoros and Eudemos, and they do not seem to fit; Apollodoros, as we have seen, puts the *akme* in 368–64, and as it usually means the 40th year of age, Boeckh thereupon fixed the date at 408–355. On the other hand, the capital testimony of Eudemos[3] conveys what follows:

a) Leodamas of Thasos (mentioned alongside of Archytas and Theaetetus) was just a little older than Plato: let us say his date was 430.

b) Neokleides was younger than Leodamas: say 420.

c) Leon was the disciple of Neokleides: we must suppose a minimum difference of age about 20 years (the master-and-disciple relationship was a stricter thing than today); that makes about 400.

d) Eudoxus was "somewhat younger" than Leon: that brings us down to 390; or maybe we might make it 395, but surely not more.

Independently from any such considerations, and looking only at the geographical work of Eudoxus, F. Gisinger (Die Erdbeschreibung des Eudoxos von Knidos in *Στοιχεῖα, Studien z. Gesch. d. antiken Weltbildes*, Heft 6, p. 5) pointed out recently that fr. 58 of the *γῆς περίοδος* would indicate that Eudoxus died

[3] In Proclus Comm. in Eucl. 66, 14–67, 3 Friedlein. Cf. also ib. 211, 18, and D. L. III, 24.

after, rather than before, Plato, that is, in or after 347. He therefore suggested the dates 400–347, and K. v. Fritz supported his views in *Philol.* 85 (1930), 478.

Eudoxus and Plato

These later criticisms, valuable as they are, take up one or the other element at a time, and do not claim to reconcile the new findings with the available evidence. Thus it would seem now that a systematic re-examination of the whole question might lead to some more definite conclusions.

We have two primary sources as to the dates: Apollodoros and Eudemos. Of these, Eudemos is explicit if not precise, Apollodoros precise but not explicit. There is no doubt as to what Eudemos means; but there is considerable uncertainty as to the meaning of *akme* in Apollodoros. Usually it stands for the fortieth year of age. But there is no lack of evidence that he has people "flowering" even earlier or later in life; witness his well-known statement about Anaximander, that he flourished just before his death in his sixties. A similar problem has come up apropos of Parmenides. From F. Jacoby's edition of his fragments[4] it would appear that Apollodoros often dated the *akme* by some important event in the life of a person, especially when he had no information concerning his birthdate. In Eudoxus' life we have several possible *akmes*. For he was a precocious genius and distinguished himself greatly in his early twenties:— as the first Greek astronomer who went to study in Egypt, and as the one who burst upon the attention of the Greek world with his new calendar; witness the fact that only a couple of years later he had a numerous group of disciples which followed him from the Propontis to Athens. Where would the acme be for men like Pascal, Galois, Abel, Riemann, Heisenberg, Dirac?

We might also suppose with K. v. Fritz that the date corresponds to Eudoxus' scholarchate in Athens, which is, however, not well proved (s. later); and besides, at v. Fritz's own reckoning, in 367 he would have been 33, which is exceedingly young for a scholarch in the ancient world: or we might admit, as has been done by some, that it corresponds to the announcement of his theory of homocentric spheres which was so important for the Platonic school in that it solved its problem of *σώζειν τὰ φαινόμενα;* or to his publishing the reorganized and more rigorous Elements after the discovery of the Exhaustion Lemma; or even, as Unger suggested, that it corresponds to the *ψήφισμα* with which the Cnidians honored him in his last years. All of this is almost equally plausible and equally doubtful: and in truth, when one has waded through the attempts of the scholars at sifting and reorganizing the uncouth jumble of fragments, erratic datings and obvious mistranscriptions from Sextus Africanus, Eusebius, Synkellos, Suidas and the Chronicon Paschale, one is

[4] Apollodors Chronik. Eine Sammlung der Fragmente. — *Philol. Untersuchungen* herausg. von Kiessling u. Wilamowitz, H. 16.

left with strong doubts as to the value of such terms as ἐγένετο or ἐγνωρίζετο.[5]

The best course seems, therefore, to keep an open mind as to the exact meaning of that date in Apollodoros, and to trust rather Eudemos and his Successions.

The deciding element, however, must come from outside; and we are left with two different lines of approach: one of them is the dates of Chrysippus, the other is the letter to Nectanebo.

Concerning the Egyptian voyage, the philologists seem to have been strangely inattentive or perfunctory. Probably they did not trust themselves outside their demesne. Boeckh looked up the lists of the Pharaohs, and finding that Nectanebo had a comfortably long reign (supposedly 381–363), decided that any year of those would do. Sir Thomas Heath with remarkable unconcern puts Eudoxus' visit in 381–0. In the light of present chronology, this is hardly possible. In 381 Egypt was still in a period of anarchy, out of which it emerged only after the following year under the new Sebennytic dynasty (the XXXth).[6] Nor is that all. The new king, Nectanebo of Sebennytos (Nekht hor heb), was assisted in his rise by Chabrias the Athenian, a most typical figure of those times of transition from city-state to world-state. Chabrias had been staying in Egypt since 387, had been the general and chief adviser of Akoris (Hakar) and seems to have lost nothing of his influence during the period of interregnum. For we find him holding the same position with the new king, which he does not quit until 379,[7] and even then only because he is recalled with an imperative summons by the Athenian state. In 363, we find him back again at his post. During all of that interval, there is no evidence of Spartan influence in Egypt, while we actually know that Chabrias was keeping up his Egyptian connections as far as the "King's Peace" would allow, and consistently opposing the Spartans, their allies, and their prestige.[8] We shall have to dwell on this point later on.

[5] On this subject cf. Harnack, Chronologie I; Eusebii Chronicorum I. II ed. H. Schoene 1875. 1866. Gelzer, S. Julius Africanus und die byzantinische Chronographie, 1884; Schwartz in Abh. Gött. Ges. XL 22 and in Pauly-Wissowa *s. v. Chronicon Paschale* and *Eusebios*. For an analysis of Jerome's version of the Chronicle of Eusebius cf. Schwartz in Berl. Philol. Wochenschr. 1906, 744 sqq. and Fotheringham's facsimile edition of the Bodleian Ms. 1905.

[6] In fact, Ed. Meyer (Gorschungen II, 490 sqq.) sets the date of an accession at 378, but according to Pieper in PW. 32, p. 2234 *s. v.* the end of 380 seems more probable.

[7] This unavoidable shift of at least two years in the earliest possible date for Agesilaus is enough to upset all the ingenious and apparently rigorous work of reconstruction carried out by Boeckh on the Octaëteris. But we should remember that Boeckh himself had considerable misgivings as to the degree of exactitude that could be reached. In a late study (Cf. Kleine Schriften III, 346), commenting on his "Sonnenkreise", he admits that there are some very puzzling difficulties in the dates he had previously suggested, that we cannot locate exactly the Eudoxian star positions, nor the boundaries of his celestial figures, and that the intervals given seem to be schematized.

[8] Apart from the campaigns listed by the historians, there is evidence that he had a propensity for hanging a Lacedemonian wherever he found him: cf. D. L. III, 14, apropos of the man who had sold Plato as a slave.

But if it cannot have been 382, what date appears most probable? K. v. Fritz, who avoids the chief pitfall by suggesting 378, seems to think that after that any date in the reign of Nectanebo might be considered.

Let us look into the question closely, and examine the actual interplay of political events during the youth of Eudoxus.

Knidos had more than once been on the Spartan side since the visit of Agesilaos in 395. We have evidence of it in 390 (Judeich, Kleinas. Stud. 90.102) and 387. But with 386, the peace of Antalcidas changed everything. The Spartans were handing over the cities of the mainland to their old enemy, the king of Persia. We know that Agesilaos supported the signing of the treaty. And with good reasons, too, for clearly the sacrifice of the colonies meant to him a weakening of the traditional enemy. After that, the Lacedemonian fleet and Lacedemonian influence might vanish from the Aegean, and the sea power go to Athens as her share. The Lacedemonians became in a way the regents for the Great King in Greece, having given up any activity contrary to his interests. Indeed, for Artaxerxes one of the main motives of the peace of Antalcidas had been to prevent Greek mercenaries from being recruited for Egypt, and Greek influence from being felt there.

The Cnidians, as seafaring people, must have reestablished good relations with the Athenians, and it was mainly the Athenians who kept up the connections with Egypt, albeit in a guarded way (coöperation with Euagoras, Cyprus war). It would have taken a very special convergence of circumstances to make the Cnidians go all the way to Sparta and look up Agesilaos as an intermediary. Now what was Agesilaos doing after 378? He was all involved in the critical struggle with Thebes, with heavy loss of prestige and not much leisure to carry on foreign relations. Between 376 and 371 he is gravely ill and vanishes from the scene, only to reappear in the crisis that leads up to the battle of Leuktra. After that he is hard pressed by the Thebans, has to face the revolt of the Messenians and to defend the very walls of Sparta, and turns his thoughts to Asia Minor only in 366, when the great revolt of the Satraps breaks out. There is evidence that since 367 friendly relations had been established between Sparta, Ariobarzanes and Egypt (Isocrates, Archidamos (VI) 63). Mausolos, who in the first phase of the war is on the King's side, retires after Agesilaos appears on the scene to help Ariobarzanes, and at the same time gets in touch with him and with Egypt (Xen. Ages. 2, 26). After a stay at the court of the Satrap, Agesilaos is a guest of Mausolos and receives gifts of money from him and also from Pharaoh (cf. Judeich *l. c.*, 203 n. 2). This happens in 364: in the following year we find him in Greece again, for it was the year of the battle of Mantineia, and in 362 he sails for Egypt to help king Tachos (Tzeher) in his expedition against Persia.

Here, then, we have a tolerably clear pattern. Egypt had lost contact with Greek politics through the King's Peace since 380; with the end of that treaty, Agesilaos appears on the Asiatic scene and establishes his prestige by turning the fortune of Ariobarzanes almost single-handed. This must have struck the Pharaoh's imagination, for in 362 he stipulates the old warrior's services with a following of only 30 Spartans, against enough money to recoup the fortunes of Lacedaemon. And surely this idea of Tachos must have been his own, for we cannot imagine much enthusiasm on the part of Chabrias, his chief adviser, as subsequent developments also go to prove.

Thus we have an almost complete change of situation. Before 365, to reach Egypt by way of the Taenaron would have looked an unnatural and improbable idea: and actually it is Chabrias and no one else who is called in first by Tachos in 363, to fill the post he had already held with his father eighteen years before; after all, Chabrias was still the great expert in the eyes of the Egyptians. But after 365, an introduction from Agesilaos would have appeared to a Cnidian a very desirable thing; and we have one more clue: the host of Agesilaos was Mausolus, and Mausolus is the only one who is mentioned in D. L. VIII 87 as being visited by Eudoxus.

There is, of course, a further possibility that must not be neglected: that the Nectanabis to whom the letter was addressed might be Nectanebo II (Nakht-e-nabf) to whom Agesilaos went over in 361 after betraying Tachos and leaving him and Chabrias to face the revolt of the army. Such an induction would be quite natural, and in fact was brought up by Ideler as early as 1828. But here are the facts: Agesilaos joined Nectanebo II on his very accession, and was constantly with him during the short but critical period in which they had to deal with the insurrection of Upper Egypt. As soon as the new king's power was consolidated, Agesilaos refused to stay any longer and set sail for Sparta with his 220 talents, but died on the voyage homeward in 359. There is no room anywhere in these happenings for a "letter" of introduction "borne" by Eudoxus.

We are left, therefore, with only one date at all plausible, and that is about 365.

Let us now examine the other independent line of approach, that of the dates of Chrysippus, the son of Erineus, and his rather elusive line of descendants.

This problem of the two or more Chrysippoi is one of the most confusing in a considerably confused chapter of history.

Eudoxus and Plato

It has been the object of a long-drawn-out controversy between Wellmann, Susemihl, Helm and others.[9] Briefly, Wellmann's point is that Chrysippus the son of Erineus, the friend of Eudoxus, mentioned in D. L. VIII 89, is not the same man as Chrysippus the master of Erasistratos mentioned VII 176, whose son was another Chrysippus punished by Ptolemy II about 277. To support this (which seems to him necessary if Philistion, who was master to the son of Erineus, taught about 380) he advances technical evidence from Galen and Pliny to the effect that Chrysippus got certain of his ideas from Praxagoras (which, apart from the fact that he takes the dates of Praxagoras for granted, is not at all a necessary inference, cf. e.g. D. L. III, 24); and, moreover, that the son of Chrysippus I is called Aristagoras and not Chrysippus. Now the text in D. L. is so hopelessly rambling and disconnected, that it is not even clear whether in VIII 89 it is meant that Aristagoras is the son of Chrysippus or of Eudoxus. In fact, most modern translators (R. D. Hicks, Apelt, Yonge) take *currenti calamo* the latter view. Also it would imply that in one passage (the above) Diogenes managed to forget about the first Chrysippus, in another (VII 186) about the second, which is rather improbable, even admitting that his excerpts come from different medical διαδοχαί. On the other hand, Wilamowitz (Antigonos von Karystos, 325) approaching independently the other passage VII, 186 had felt himself compelled by chronology to suggest the reading υἱωνός instead of υἱός, which would leave room for Aristagoras or another. All in all, the problem is insoluble without shifting texts around. On the face of the evidence, accepting υἱός, we would have to admit a span of 110 years between the birth of the first Chrysippus and the end of the last, which makes a father-son relationship improbable but not impossible. On the other hand, if we are to squeeze in all the generations that Wellmann seems to want, we get at most 20 years to each generation, which does seem highly improbable (Wellmann himself makes his case more difficult, as we have already noted, by setting the voyage of Chrysippus in the sixties).

Again, the key to the puzzle can only come from outside, and this time it seems provided by Jaeger's recent conclusions on Diocles of Karystos; for he has proved that Diocles has to be dated down by a generation or so, and that Praxagoras' acme shifts to about 300. For we have been given a definite and authoritative succession in the text of Celsus (prooem. 2, confirmed by Pliny): *post quem* (sc. Hippocrates) . . . *Diocles Carystius, deinde Praxagoras et Crysippus, tum Herophilus et Erasistratus.* This does not leave room for all the conflicting διαδοχαί

[9] Cf. mainly Wellmann in Fragm. d. griech. Aerzte; id., art. *Chrysippos* and *Erasistratos* in Pauly-Wissowa; also in *Hermes* XXXV (1900), p. 371; Susemihl, *Rhein. Mus.* N. F. 56 (1901), p. 313; Helm, *Hermes* XXIX, 167.

envisaged by Wellmann, which can be constructed out of the different passages of Diogenes Laertius. If Chrysippos "the pupil of Aethlios," the great contemporary of Praxagoras, had a father also named Chrysippos, this man comes to fill in the generation born about 360–350, and therefore cannot possibly be the grandson of Chrysippos *ὁ Ερίνεω*. Thus the passage D. L. VIII 89, which is already quite obviously in the wrong place and wrongly detached from the other one VIII 90 (cf. Wilamowitz, *op. cit.* 324) proves itself a hopeless mixup of diadochies, and we are left only with VII 186. Hence it appears that Jaeger's choice is actually the only way at all possible: for he takes as primary sources Sextus Empiricus *adv. math.* 657, 23 B and D.L. VII 186 (and indeed we can see that such passages as Plin. XXIX 5 and Gal. XI 171 are a muddled third hand in respect to these) and cuts the Gordian knot by assuming with Wilamowitz that there are only two Chrysippoi: one the son of Erineus and the other the contemporary of Praxagoras, who was the master of Aristogenes and died in 277. This fits beautifully with what we know of the main line of medico-philosophic transmission that leads up to Erasistratos and Straton, and leaves us with one necessary conclusion, already foreshadowed by Susemihl and Helm: viz. that Chrysippus the son of Erineus, the pupil of Philistion and the friend of Eudoxus, cannot have been born before 390, and possibly a few years later. This goes to show that the Egyptian trip cannot have been undertaken earlier than 367 at most, and that is really where the intuition of Wilamowitz had placed it at first glance.

And, finally, this date of 366 or 367 would help to solve another puzzle. Why does Sotion in D. L. VIII 86 report that Eudoxus came to Athens "attracted by the fame of the Socratics" and "to listen to the Sophists" without mentioning Plato by name? For it is only Diogenes that does and he himself seems puzzled by this omission, in view of Eudoxus' later history, and so must his informants have been, if he is only left with a bit of most improbable gossip about the astronomer having started his school in Athens as a rival of Plato "for the purpose of annoying him." Diogenes himself does not believe this; and here indeed we would have a better reason. In 366 Plato was in Sicily, and Eudoxus went to hear other masters, both inside the Academy and outside it. After all, he wanted to graduate as a Sophist. It is even possible that it may have come to a friction with the acting scholarch, and that would explain the story picked up later by the tattlers.

We have thus reached two independent confirmations of Eudemus. And, clearly, if there is an irreconcilable conflict between the two authorities, it appears by now reasonable that Apollodoros should be the one to go by the board. After all, a single date is easy enough to misspell, and we have only the one transcription of Diogenes Laertius. Let us therefore discard him, at least[10] for the moment.

Now that we have some kind of light to go by, we are in a position to explore the dank cellars of Philology, with a reasonable hope of making some interesting finds.

The dating of Apollodoros is not the only one that we have.[4] Gellius XVII, 21, 23 and Eusebius (in Jerome. 01.97, 1) bear indications which were rejected by Ideler and after him by Boeckh, as arising from third-hand or corrupt texts, and moreover at variance with each other. Unger (accepted here by Susemihl) manages to show that they do refer to the same date, the year before the fall of Rome, 391/0. But this discovery was lost on those who had no use for his main thesis. Boeckh had *a priori* reasons for neglecting the whole issue, since at that date Eudoxus was according to him only eighteen years of age. But if we in our turn ignore his prejudice, that date may again take on a significance. For it comes in Hieron. 01.97.1 as: *Eudoxus astrologus agnoscitur*, in the Chronicon Paschale as: E. ἐγνωρίζετο. Now there are many cases in which we have proof that the transcribers wrote ἐγνωρίζετο instead of ἐγένετο or ἐγεννήθη or mixed up the two meanings of ἐγένετο or γέγονε.[11] Thus a very strong case emerges through successive layers of confusion, that Eusebius and Gellius through Varro and others should have picked up the birth-date of Eudoxus as being 390, from some source other than Apollodoros.

Of course, we cannot lay too much weight on that kind of evidence. Almost anything can be read from and into these texts of a late age and corrupt transmission, of which not even a reliable canon can be established. And to give a modern example, if we think that only in the sections previously discussed of Diogenes Laertius, two creditable modern translators, Yonge and Apelt, are so careless as to translate both and quite independently μαθητής with "son" (VII, 186), we may understand how easily an exasperated hack of an amanuensis, engaged in interminably repeating a few variations on the same sentence, may have written mechanically εγνωρίσθη for ἐγεννήθη or omitted the first word in γνώριμος ἐγένετο. Even so, there are some possible checks. For instance, if the date of 390 is that of birth, we can reasonably expect, in the case of such a man as Eudoxus, to find his name mentioned again for his "flourishing" period, as happens with Plato and many others.

[10] The sacrifice, however, might even not be necessary. If we take into consideration the several possibilities mentioned at p. 253 it appears that 364 (last year of the Olympiad) might well be the date of the Octaëteris. And we know quite definitely that the Octaëteris did consecrate Eudoxus' notoriety.

[11] Cf. Unger l. c. 198, where he works out a whole list of such mistakes. A typical case is the birthdate of Plato: 01.88.4 (Kyrillos 01.88); the Armenian translator writes *Cognitus est*, while Hyeron has *nascitur* and Chron. Pasc. ἐγεννήθη. 01. 35 is the supposed birthdate of Thales, but Synkellos has ἐγνωρίζετο, the Armenian *cognoscebatur*.

And true enough, we find such a mention, not in Eusebius but in the Easter Chronicle. It is in connection with the consulate of Mamertinus and Sulla and with the earthquake that destroyed Helike and Boura in the Peloponnese—which means 357. Synkellos follows suit, independently (cf. Gelzer, *Africanus II*, 153); now Gelzer has shown that where Synkellos diverges from Eusebius, he harks back to Panodorus or Annianus, and these in turn go back to Dexippus, and through him to Apollodoros (*l. c.*, 221). Thus we would have traced our way back to another section of Apollodoros than the one quoted or misquoted by Diogenes. But whether it be Apollodoros or another (and we are not bound to the fate of Gelzer's rather controversial reconstructions), we can discern an *akme* of serious source placed at 357. And whether it refers to the theory of Homocentric Spheres or to the Exhaustion Lemma or the reorganized and rigorous edition of the Elements, 357 is a most plausible date for the crowning achievement of Eudoxus' mathematical activity.

[*P.S. (1967) This study was written in 1938, at a time when I was teaching at Harvard and could easily avail myself of the facilities of Widener Library. I was concerned at that time only with classical astronomy. It was accepted by George Sarton, for* Isis, *but as his printing plant in Bruges was overrun by the Germans, the publication had to await the year 1946. Hence the piece has had two decades of exposure to expert evaluation. It was endorsed by philologists, including the late Werner Jaeger and Erich Frank,* nemine dissentiente. *Today, it is becoming even more important to have the dates 390–337 established as valid—a shift of eighteen years beyond the current dating—since they place Eudoxus' achievement in astronomy in a period definitely later than Plato's later works, certainly later than the* Timaeus. *Plato's cosmology is shown to be pre-Eudoxian, inspired essentially by what was transmitted to him of archaic pre-Pythagorean cosmology. On the other hand, Eudoxus' study of planetary motions* (primum hos motus in Graeciam transtulit, *says Seneca) was also derived from Egyptian archaic sources, presumably from the early dynasties. The story that he wrote, "Dialogues of dogs," wildly misinterpreted by V. Bissing and others, can be restored to sense. As we see it now, it might well refer to the rich material of myths referring to celestial dogs and wolves, of which we have evidence today. It was technical talk of the archaic period (4000–3000 B.C.) of which the medieval* fabliaux *like the* Roman de Renart, *still rich in obscure astronomical allusions, appear to be the last outcome. (Cf. G. de Santillana and H. V. Dechend, "Introduction to Archaic Cosmology," 1967.)*]

"Scientific Rationalism"

Der Mensch muss bei dem Glauben verharren, dass das Unbegreifliche begreiflich sei; er würde sonst nicht forschen.—GOETHE

Introduction

THIS ESSAY DOES NOT ATTEMPT THE ANALYSIS OF A DOCTRINE but rather the life-story of an idea. The great systems of Descartes, Spinoza, and Leibniz belong to philosophy. My concern is to see what scientists did with a certain idea that runs through the systems and which belongs to science from the beginning.

"Rationalism" is a dangerous word because it is used with a variety of meanings. Colloquially, it is associated with the freethinker, which term rather vaguely connotes a gentleman of middle age who objects to people's going to church and who strenuously believes in the dictates of reason, whatever that may mean. Technically, in philosophy, it is defined as the belief in the a priori as a source of knowledge of the external world.

The present essay concerns itself with neither of these meanings. The historical meaning of the word "rationalism" is chiefly connected with the faith of men like Bayle, Condorcet, and Comte in the emancipation of human reason, or of the generation of Buckle in the rise of liberal institutions. Scientific rationalism has very strong links with these points of view. But it is nonetheless quite distinct from them, as I shall try to show. Reason in science and reason in society do work together and sometimes appear as one and the same thing, but really they are quite different in essence.

The kind of rationalism that I wish to discuss here is expressed in the simple, logical certainty of Parmenides and Wittgenstein: what is conceivable can happen. Which seems to tie up with the other certainty: that what happens is conceivable.

Galileo stated the rationalist attitude for his own time in words not to be forgotten:

> . . . The understanding is to be taken two ways, that is *intensive*,[1] or *extensive*; and *extensive*, that is as to the multitude of intelligibles, which are infinite, the understanding of man is as nothing, though he should understand a thousand propositions; for that a thousand in respect of infinity is but as a cypher: but taking the understanding *intensive*, in as much as that term imports intensively, that is, perfectly some propositions, I say that human wisdom understandeth some propositions so perfectly, and is as absolutely certain thereof, as Nature herself; and such are the pure Mathematical sciences, to wit, Geometry and Arithmetick: in which Divine Wisdom knows infinite more propositions, because it knows them all; but I believe that the knowledge of those few comprehended by human understanding equalleth the divine, as to the objective certainty, for that it arriveth to comprehend the necessity thereof, than which there can be no greater certainty.

[1] The Latin word, meaning "intensively," the same to be said of *extensive*. The passage is taken from the *Dialogue of the World Systems*; the translation is Salusbury's.

By mathematics Galileo understood implicitly the science of physics, since the book of nature "is written in mathematical characters": a belief that was later shared by Newton.

"Fortunate Newton," says Einstein, "happy childhood of science!

> Nature to him was an open book, whose letters he could read without effort. The conceptions which he used to reduce the material of experience to order seemed to flow spontaneously from experience itself, from the beautiful experiments which he ranged in order like playthings and describes with an affectionate wealth of detail.

The faith endured through many changes right into the nineteenth century—one might even say right to Einstein himself. The scientist might have become philosophically more circumspect, technically more critical; but still he kept on the same line, never assuming that he imposed reason on nature or that he was being vouchsafed its revelation; just discovering it as he worked along, and wondering how it happened, notwithstanding Professor Kant; slightly bewildered, yet doubting not in the least, and finding the whole thing rather natural: "Raffiniert ist der Herrgott, aber boshaft ist er nicht."

Any treatment of scientific rationalism, and especially in the nineteenth century, has to be unmethodical. For rationalism is never in the spotlight; it is what makes the life of method but is outside method, a persistent form of thought which creates the inner tension necessary for the progress of method. It is for the scientist what the feeling of beauty is for the artist, and hardly more communicable.

What, then, is rationalism? Surely it must be some coherent set of ideas. But if it is a system at all, it is an implicit one, a "hidden system" like those Helmholtz had to devise for his thermodynamics. Essentially, it is the scientist himself, creative science at work.

The structure of science is a well-belabored subject. There is a sufficiency of *pièces à thèse* concerning it, as well as of theories on a science of science. Let us try to forget about them.

This study is an attempt to treat science not from the outside—to view the scientist not as the technocrat, or as the laboratory artisan, or as the man in search of power over nature, or as the intellectual challenged by a difficult problem, or as the organizer building up a "well-made" language" for things; but simply as the seeker after truth.

This may be proved historically to have been the case with most of the great personalities of science; and, while social or psychological motivations may provide a fascinating field of inquiry, there is something to be said for an attempt at considering the creative scientific mind in its pristine candor and originality, to look at the scientist as a free being and a free agent.

The scientific mind, as I hope to show, is ever looking for certain forms of interpretation and a certain type of unity. Of course, the conceptualizing side of science is an aspect which finds its natural complement in the operational. The present survey will therefore have to be one sided and to appear almost partisan. Under the growing complexity of the problems of science, with the decay of the original simple clarity, a reorganization of its concepts and its language may have become a prime necessity. But there is a certain "invincible surmise" which hardly pauses at necessities and carries on with its own imaginings beyond even the bounds of the probable.

Many of the workers of science never care to consider the forms of thought and the consequences which the greater minds among them envisage. But when the wind sweeps over the wheat, the ears bend to the gusts without knowing the rhythm of the wind.

Scientific rationalism is not the only wind of that spirit. It is, as we said, a faith and an implicit doctrine. As such, it lasts until well into the nineteenth century; but it cannot continue as a body of ideas when all its philosophical props are knocked out from under it.

Its life-story is therefore really a tragedy; and my attempt to retrace it took naturally the form of a romantic biography, as it were, of a late friend.

Since this is only a rapid survey of some aspects of rationalism, I have kept to the historically central field of the physical sciences, and I had to leave out a highly interesting course of developments in mathematics, on one side, and in biology, on the other, as well as all the problems concerning classification.

The really new factor of the nineteenth century—historical rationalism—ought to have been brought in, since without it the subject loses its proper perspective; but then this essay would have become a book. For the same reason I have concentrated on the period of flowering, and I had to leave out the later crisis of rationalist ideas under the combined influence of Maxwell and Mach in physics and of Darwinism in philosophy.

The Crisis of the Eighteenth Century

The eighteenth century was rightly termed "the Newtonian era." A triumphal mood is perceptible everywhere in thought, even if the wiser minds of Berkeley, D'Alembert, and Diderot are aware of an unstable foundation. To the thinking world at large the theory of gravitation had provided proof positive that the mechanical view of Nature, the Galilean and Cartesian "new science," was objectively right. It appeared natural to believe that the world possesses a rational structure, that is to say, that reality possesses an organization coincident with the organization of the human intellect, taking this, of course, in the form of mathematical reason. The words of Galileo which we quoted in the introduction may be held as the creed of scientific rationalism. Rationalism is not simply the discovery that reason is a sound way of dealing with the outer world. As at its birth in Greece, so at its rebirth in the "century of genius," reason was not the free and irresponsible play of ideas but a radical and infrangible conviction that in astronomical thought man was in contact with an absolute order of the cosmos; it is truly a living faith in the illimitable power of the mind, but only in so far as it is admitted that mathematical reasoning releases a transcendent source of certainty which is more than our individual analytical power.

The new science is far from being only a method. The system of dynamics is a complete conceptual world. and it was present already as such in Newton's mind. Its conceptions of space, matter, force, and motion were interrelated in a whole; and, as successive epochs tended to formalize the science, they only brought out the element of high abstraction that was implicit and necessary to keep it together. The new experimental sciences that sprung from the Newtonian trunk in the eighteenth century had apparently little to do with mechanics. Yet even Lavoisier's effort, from the start, toward stripping science of its unavowed metaphysics and reducing it to a "well-made language" could not rid him of his personal presuppositions, which appeared to him a matter of sheer common sense, as they had already appeared to Condillac. Lavoisier works on the material arranged by the experimentalists who came before him. Such material inevitably implies representation, schemes, and structures; as he found out, it becomes a system "before you can do anything about it." The attempt is truly to converse in real things, like the academicians of Gulliver's Laputa; but it cannot be carried through. Reliance on the balance is not so commonsensical as it might appear, nor did the contemporary chemists, even men like Black and Priestley, admit it to be so. It is something like "flying by instruments." Lavoisier had avoided the confusion and the difficulties of the Newtonian chemists who had tried to explain by attraction the forces of affinity, but he had held fast to the fundamental idea: to explain things in terms of matter only. Not only does he leave inside his system a substantial caloric, which is actually fire matter, but, the more methodical he is, the more he accepts the essential limitations of Newtonianism. He used to say that only physicists understood what he was after. The whole of his extremely positive thought seems unified, both in what he does and in what he leaves undone, in the Newtonian definition: "All matter is heavy in proportion to its quantity, which remains forever constant." And, yet, the very substantial clarity that brings him on a common ground with his friend Laplace entices him into the forbidden realms of images. It seems natural to him to speak of bodies as made of molecules which do not ever touch each other and are kept apart by varying quantities of caloric fluid; of the gaseous state as element plus caloric. These images are not followed up with deductive rigor; but it is significant that they are found right in the creative region of his thought, where theory and experiment meet, where imagination has to deal with the fundamentals of light, heat, matter, continuity and discontinuity. The system that emerges is born of many disparate motives, of intuition, logical clarity, and operational procedure inextricably interwoven. And the thread that guides him is the Newtonian idea. When Berthollet founded chemical statics, he was consciously taking up another strain of the Newtonian system. So was Franklin, for that matter, when he accepted a principle of conservation and admired, while he refused to worship, that "wisdom which had made all things by weight and measure." Thus we see that the several sciences which are born toward the end of the eighteenth century are the result not of simple method but rather of a central, unifying inspiration proceeding from celestial mechanics and broken down into usable aspects; and that vision still provides a hidden link that will facilitate their interchanges and fusion later on. The basic images are only apparently clear; they are a mixture of quantity and quality, matter and geometry, flexible for any development. Its rigor is not the Cartesian rigor, for that is already blighted at the root, since Cartesianism insists that space is divisible and then talks of indivisible atoms, which surely cannot be. It is Newtonianism more than logic which holds the key to unity; for, if the unity sought after was still deductive, the unity that is established is really analogical, as Newton had seen it:

> For it's well known, that Bodies act upon one another by the Attractions of Gravity, Magnetism, and Electricity; and these Instances shew the Tenor and Course of Nature, and make it not improbable that there may be more attractive Powers than these. For Nature is very consonant and conformable to her self.[2]

The rationalistic postulates are redefined here in a very significant way, and that is how they are understood by Newton's successors. There never is a "strict induction" but contains a considerable amount of deduction, starting from points chosen analogically.

Strict and universal deduction, of course, is still held to be the ideal. A generation later Laplace still believed in it, even if he perceived the difficulties more clearly:

> We ought to be able to explain simply through the variety of molecular forms all the varieties of attractive forces, and thus bring

[2] *Opticks* (4th ed.; London, 1931), Query 31.

back to one general law all the phenomena of physics and astronomy. But the impossibility of knowing the shapes of the molecules and their mutual distances makes such explanations vague and useless to the progress of science.

Once research had moved beyond Newton's field of action, the vast dreams of a science unified by the "géomètres," and deduced directly from the law of gravitation, had proved no more easy of achievement that Diderot's dream at the other pole of thought, derived from Leibniz's intuition of the continuum. But we see how strictly Laplace adhered to the original canon of explaining things "par figure et mouvement." Franklin, the champion of induction, imagined the particles of electric fluid grouped in the form of triangles to "explain their compressibility." Schelling was fully justified in pointing out that the Lucretian ideal of science still held—that all its theories that tend to explain quality in substances can be reduced, except for straight analytical formulas, to attempts at "expressing qualities through figure, i.e., substituting some geometric figuration for each primordial quality."[3] Laplace's faith is all the more remarkable if we consider that fully a generation before, D'Alembert, his immediate predecessor, the man who had done most to apply analysis to mechanics, had grown to be the most skeptical of the future of this attempt:

> After having reflected for a long time on this important matter [the resistance of fluids], it has seemed to me that the small progress achieved is due to the fact that we have not yet understood the true principles according to which it must be dealt with. Therefore I sought to apply myself to seeking these principles and the way of applying, if possible, calculation to them. For these two purposes must not be confused, and modern geometricians have not perhaps paid enough attention to this point. It is often the desire to be able to make use of methods of calculation which determines the choice of principles, whereas the principles themselves should first be sought without thinking in advance to bend them forcibly to methods of calculation. Geometry which should only obey physics, when united to the latter, sometimes commands it.[4]

The Formula as Transcendent

What D'Alembert seemed to fear took place nevertheless. And, by an irony of history, he was to be among those mainly responsible. Out of the complexity of Newton's thought and background one aspect had been given special importance—the distinction between mathematical description and philosophical explanation. But it was difficult not to give to the mathematical expression, once arrived at, some causal dignity, which should be in harmony with its striking simplicity. Huygens, Euler, Le

[3] *Einleitung zu dem Entwurf, etc.*, in *Werke* (1st ser.), III, 295.

[4] *Essai d'une nouvelle théorie de la resistance des fluides* (1752).

Sage—indeed, Newton himself[5]—had insisted that a purely mechanical explanation was desirable (like ultramundane corpuscles) which should make the simplicity of the gravitational formula appear irrelevant. But the very success of Newtonianism had been too much for the out-and-out mechanists. Before Newton showed how far a simple formula could go in linking facts which were apparently disconnected, no one could have suspected that this would be possible; when philosophers realized the power of the Formula and foresaw that power extending to electricity and magnetism, an opposite movement set in through which mathematical processes were focused upon at the expense of experiment and observation and also at the expense of philosophical reasoning. D'Alembert's misgivings were ignored by his geometrical colleagues, and the mathematical formula took on something of the prestige of a cause.

This intransigent attitude resulted in an antimathematical reaction on the part of naturalists and thinkers at large, who felt that the world was too deep and varied to be written off in a formula, and one impossible of application at that. Still we should note that, when, in 1747, Clairaut suggested that it might be necessary to add a factor of correction to the Newtonian formula to make it fit the annual motion of the moon's apogee, it was Buffon who protested most loudly, for metaphysical reasons, against the infringement of the simplicity of the universe. Thus, whatever the trends of fashion, the charm of mathematics as "divine philosophy" still held sway; and the discussion of the foundations of mechanics still centred on the principle of least action as the one most likely to provide the key to the plan of the universe.

[5] Newton started by looking for a mechanical explanation of gravitation. He imagined an ether which might explain magnetic and electric phenomena as well as those of gravitation and light (Letters to Oldenburg, January 25, 1675–76; to Robert Boyle, February 28, 1678–79, and especially the fourth letter to Bentley). Having later found it more profitable to work out the mathematical consequences of the simple fact of gravitation, he abandoned his "guesses," finding, as MacLaurin says, that "he was not able, from experiment and observation, to give a satisfactory account of this medium and the manner of its operation." Thus it is pragmatic results and not a theoretical conviction that led him to distrust of hypotheses in the *Principia*. Even so, he could never bring himself to believe in action at a distance, and in the queries of the *Opticks* he reiterated a belief that the force of gravitation, like electricity and magnetism, was due to strains in the rare and subtle medium making up the extension between two bodies. The statement that gravity is as much of an experimental fact as extension and mobility and need not be further explained is of Roger Cotes (that clever heretic, as Maxwell calls him), in his Preface to the second edition of the *Principia*. And even this view which may appear positivistic actually recalls Du Bois Reymond's later "Ignorabimus." In fact, it was advocated and extended by such men as Priestley and Bernouilli. The latter wrote to Euler (February 4, 1744), referring to the ether theory: "Moreover, I believe both that the ether is *gravis versus solem* and the air *versus terram* and I cannot conceal from you that on these points I am a perfect Newtonian, and I am surprised that you adhere so long to the *principiis Cartesianis*; there is possibly some feeling in the matter. If God had been able to create an *animam* whose nature is unknown to us, He has also been able to impress an *attractionem universalem materiae*, though such is *attractio supra captum*, whereas the *principia Cartesiana* involve always something *contra captum*."

The most significant effort in this direction is that of Euler. Following his discoveries on the maxima and minima,[6] he wrote:

> There must be a double method for solving mechanical problems: one is the direct method founded on the laws of equilibrium or of motion; but the other one is by knowing which formula must provide a maximum or minimum. The former way proceeds by efficient causes, the latter by final causes: both ways lead to the same solution, and it is such a harmony which convinces us of the truth of the solution, even if each method has to be separately founded on indubitable principles. But it is often very difficult to discover the formula which must be a maximum or minimum, and by which the quantity of action is represented.[7]

At this point Euler reaches again beyond the rather cramped principle of economy of Maupertuis, the range and flexibility of Leibniz's original principle of maxima and minima. Euler's actual discovery was that the differential equations of the motion of a particle are given by the simple requirement that the integral $\int v \cdot ds$ taken over two positions of the particle should be a minimum.[8] But we are not concerned here so much with the importance of the principle in the history of mechanics. The really relevant point lies in the phrase, "both ways lead to the same solution, and it is this harmony which convinces us of the truth of the solution, even if each method has to be separately founded on indubitable principles." What appears here, more than a century after Galileo, is a still quite complex conception of the meaning of truth. It would take a miraculous adjustment and parallel development of the two ways of knowledge in one mind for an investigator to carry out correctly the program contained in that sentence. Actually, when Euler found great difficulties in extending his principle from isolated bodies to systems (which was to be achieved only by Lagrange), he unashamedly sought a short cut: "Since motions of that sort are not easy to reduce to calculation, it will be understood more easily starting from first principles."

It was D'Alembert who brought back strict scientific reason —or at least what he felt to be such:

[6] The first (and best) formulation of the principle of least action is due to Leibniz: "In a free motion, the action of the moving bodies is usually a maximum or a minimum." As deduced a priori and here formulated, it still lacks a necessary condition for its validity, viz., that energy should remain constant. Maupertuis tried to define action as mass by space and velocity, or as time by *vis viva*.

[7] *Proceedings of the Berlin Academy* (1728), p. 151.

[8] There were conditions, such as that for the velocity v should be substituted its value resulting from the principle of *vis viva* and that the theorem holds only if the principle of *vis viva* holds (and, therefore, it cannot hold for motion in a resisting medium), but Euler expected them only to be temporary limitations—and he was right.

The great metaphysical problem has been put recently: are the laws of nature necessary or contingent? To settle our ideas on this question, we must first reduce it to the only reasonable meaning it can possibly have . . . viz. whether the laws of equilibrium and motion that we observe in nature are different from those that matter would have followed, if abandoned to itself. . . . Hence this is the way the scientist should follow: first he should try to discover through reason alone which would be the laws of mechanics in matter abandoned to itself; then he should investigate experimentally what are really such laws in the universe. If the two sets of laws be different, he shall conclude that the laws of mechanics, such as those yielded by experiment, are of contingent truth, since they would appear to spring from a particular and express decision of the Supreme Being; if, on the other side, the laws yielded by experiment agree with those that could be deduced by logic alone, he shall conclude that those laws are of necessary truth: which does not mean that the Creator could not have established a wholly different set of laws, but that he did not hold it right to establish other laws than those which resulted from the very existence of matter.[9]

An attitude has been enunciated which is going to be the coherent standpoint of mechanistic philosophy from then on. Both Descartes and Leibniz had seen the laws of nature as a choice among an infinity of possibilities, arising either out of an arbitrary creative act or out of a reasoned determination in favor of the greatest variety of co-possibles. With D'Alembert, the laws of mechanics become necessary, in that they are just those which would arise simply out of the existence of matter left to itself. The divine choice is set back to a moment previous to the existence of matter—in other words, it is bowed out.[10] A new universal deduction is taking shape, with the "existence of matter" as a starting-point. But matter could hardly lend itself to the role of first principle without being lifted from its empirical status by an unnoticed regressive deduction. D'Alembert thought he had cut the ground from under metaphysics; actually, he had replaced the divine will with a not-too-clear entity called the nature of things and was resting his case upon a different, but no less remote, principle of explanation. And what did not follow from the nature of matter had to follow from the principle of sufficient reason.

The explicit recourse to this principle is among the most ancient and permanent characteristics of science. Anaximander and Archimedes made use of it. But it is more of the nature of a limiting principle than of a creative one. It has been exorcised in modern times and given a positive heuristic value in van't Hoff's scheme of stereochemistry and in Curie's principle of

[9] *Traité de dynamique* (1758), "Discours préliminaire," p. xxiv.

[10] From that time the opposition of "necessary" versus "contingent" (i.e. immanent) will mean only that the laws of nature are either rational truths, demonstrable a priori, or (which was Lazare Carnot's view) empirical truths, founded a posteriori.

symmetry. In these cases it means nothing more than a condition for the construction of models.

If for D'Alembert sufficient reason appeared such a strongly positive principle of knowledge, the reason for this should probably be sought in the social rationalism of the *philosophes*, which, having done away with all metaphysical structures, considered sufficient reason (a "good" abstraction) a norm for human relationships and hence, by an unconscious extension, an active law of nature. Scientific rationalism, however, was quite different from social rationalism; whatever its representatives may have believed, it was not dependent on such ontological abstractions as sufficient reason. Its real, though hidden, life lay rather in the "nature of matter" which to D'Alembert and Laplace appeared to belong to mere common sense. Under an inconspicuous appearance, the notion of matter, like Euler's faith in conspiring levels of truth, carried in itself a latent universe.

Formalization of Mechanics

Faith was still firm at the beginning of the nineteenth century. Laplace conceived that a universal mind would be competent to foretell the progress of nature for all eternity if only the masses of all bodies, their positions and initial velocities, were given. A dream—but not an absurd one. Matter presented no problem, and analytical mechanics had provided a scheme of incomparable economy.

On the other hand, as Mach said, no fundamental light can be expected from this branch of mechanics. The choice of a basic principle is only one of convenience. As Gauss pointed out in 1829, apropos of his own principle of least constraint, no essentially new principle could be established in dynamics: it was only a matter of new points of view; and, while a clear perception of the relativeness of the various points of view to one another might be fruitful enough, it left some serious problems unanswered. Mechanics is made by mechanicians, and in the first years of the century a very eminent one, Poinsot, voiced his misgivings apropos the principle of virtual velocities:

> We naturally believed that the science was completed, and that it only remained to seek the demonstration of the principle of virtual velocities. But that quest brought back all the difficulties that we had overcome by the principle itself. That general law, wherein are mingled the vague and unfamiliar ideas of infinity, small movements and perturbations of equilibrium, happened somehow to grow more and more obscure upon examination; and the work of Lagrange supplying nothing clearer than the progress of analysis, we saw plainly that the clouds had appeared to be lifted from the course of mechanics only because they had, so to speak, been gathered at the very origin of that science.

At bottom, a general demonstration of the principle of virtual velocities would be equivalent to the establishment of the whole of mechanics upon a different basis: for the demonstration of a law which embraces a whole science is neither more nor less than the reduction of that science to another law just as general, but evident, or at least more simple than the first, and which, consequently, would render that useless.[11]

Poinsot saw clearly, and he was resigned. But he did not like the situation as much as, perhaps, a Condillac or a Lavoisier might have liked it. Even quite positive minds may not like to be confronted with the full implications of their positiveness. The principle of least action might well have been reduced to a formal status, yet there was still some vague hope that these principles of minimum would turn out to mean *something*. "There is undoubtedly," said Heinrich Hertz later, "a special charm in such suggestions; and Gauss felt a natural delight in giving prominence to it in his beautiful discovery of least constraint. Still, it must be confessed that the charm is that of mystery; we do not really believe that we can solve the enigma of the world by such half-suppressed allusions." Poinsot, like Gauss, still felt the charm of illusions lost and could not be satisfied with the present. He already knew what Mach was to state later: that the principle of virtual velocities had its best possible foundation in the impossibility of perpetual motion, and *that*, of course, could not be merely deduced from the principle of causality. It was a fact and, what is worse, a negative fact. "One fundamental fact," warns Mach, "is not at all more intelligible than another: the choice of fundamental facts is a matter of convenience, history, and custom. . . . It is a result of a misconception to believe, as people do at the present time, that mechanical facts are more intelligible than others, and that they can provide the foundation for other physical facts."[12] This was written in 1871, but, as we see, the problem had been staring scientists in the face as far back as 1800.

Yet the whole ambition of the mathematical school had been to reduce physical reality to those mechanical, but conspicuously positive, factors for which astronomy provided the paradigm. Newton had entertained strong doubts as to the applicability of his laws to molecular dimensions; but of those doubts nothing had resulted except a riot of arbitrary assumptions and no real progress for knowledge. When Laplace, very much aware of the danger, had succeeded in deducing the laws of capillary action from the gravitational formula, all doubts and vagueness were removed.[13] With Coulomb and Ampère the law was

[11] *Elémens de statique* (10 ed.; Paris, 1861), p. 263. The statement, however, goes back to 1806 and was first published in an essay in the *Journal de l'Ecole polytechnique*.

[12] *Geschichte und Wurzel des Satzes von der Erhaltung der Arbeit*, chap. iii.

[13] *Mécanique céleste*, IV (1805), 2; cf. also *Supplément*, p. 67.

extended to electricity. Its generality appeared necessary by now, and the regressive deduction became institutionalized. As late as 1891 Kundt could still write: "We feel it difficult to step out of this circle of ideas."[14] Science had put herself under the spell of the one formula. With the discovery of Neptune as the result of pure calculation, it was clear that there was recompense for such dedication; and the "triumph of rationalism" was brought home to the thinking world. "Descend from Heaven, Urania," intoned Dr. Whewell. And he could write with simple assurance:

> We have now to contemplate the last and most splendid period of the progress of astronomy . . . the first great example of a wide complex assemblage of phenomena indubitably traced to their single, simple cause: in short, the first example of the formulation of a perfect inductive science.

Although humbly proud, he was a shade puzzled by success:

> It is a paradox that experiment should lead to acknowledged universal truths and apparently necessary ones, such as the laws of motion. The solution of that paradox is to be found in the fact that the laws are interpretations of the axioms of causality . . . our idea of cause provides the form, and experiment the matter of the laws.[15]

This is very reassuring, and we see how even Kantianism can become an armchair. Rationality obviously belonged to the scheme of things for our convenience, like many other paraphernalia of the Victorian age. But induction was the work of man; it bore the truly moral hallmark of success.

Once they felt the goal had been reached, people could ascribe it to induction or to deduction, according to their temperament. We shall have to investigate later the theoretical reasons for this permanent equivocation. But it has an important historical aspect. Good progressive minds were no longer taking rationality in the spirit of a solemn revelation or a lighthearted adventure, as they had done in the preceding centuries. Somehow, they took it for granted, and celebrated the soundness of Method, while even in mechanics the more philosophical minds, such as Gauss, Poinsot, Riemann, or Helmholtz, conceived growing doubts as to the sub-structure. The nineteenth century had brought science, and not simply reason, to the public mind. Truly it was, as it claimed to be, a scientific century. The *idées claires* in Whewell's time were—science as it stood.

Actually, the Kantian armchair of stable forms and categories was getting more and more rickety, and non-Euclidean geometry had strongly contributed to its undermining. It was proved that mind had not one "form" of space only to superpose on matter but a multiplicity of forms, flowing into one another,

[14] *Die neue Entwicklung der Elektricitätslehre*, p. 35

[15] *Philosophy of the Inductive Sciences*, I, xxvii.

and that the Euclidean one was a choice and not a necessity.[16] Riemann had seen the whole situation at a glance in the fifties.

As for the "indubitable" assumptions of mechanics, they had reached a state of dangerous abstraction which was revealed in its full extent by relativity. We need only to enumerate the chief ones:

1. Assumption of an objective local time, connected with a closed mechanical system endowed with periodicity (clock). This implies, as Einstein was to show later, an initial definition of space by means of rigid bodies.

2. Introduction of the concept of objective time for happenings over all of space: whereby local time is generalized to become the time of physical theory. To one unaware of the operational point of view, the finite velocity of light causes no difficulty; there is no need for a *Gedankenexperiment*. Empirically, events seen at the same time could well be called contemporary.

3. Concept of the material point: a bodily object which can be satisfactorily described in regard to position and movement as a point with three co-ordinates.

4. Law of motion for the material point, linking force, mass, and acceleration; which becomes the law of inertia when the components of acceleration vanish, i.e., when the point is sufficiently far from any other point.

5. Law of action between material points. These laws were provided empirically by Newton. But in Newtonian mechanics, derived from astronomy, the space K_0 comes in with a new aspect, not contained in the above-mentioned conception of space, which derives, as we have said, from rigid bodies. In this kind of space, condition No. 4 is not valid for any K_0, but only for such K_0 as we call "inertial systems".

Thus the frame of reference takes on an independent physical property which has nothing to do with geometrical space proper. This is not a theoretical refinement; it brought up grave difficulties right away, of which Newton was well aware. It was the problem of the whirling bucket, which appeared hopeless until Mach suggested that the frame of reference of mechanics might not be "absolute space" but the star system as a whole.

Scientists felt it as a disharmony that this system of abstractions should still be founded on the crudely empirical laws of force, and Laplace insisted that the inverse-square law derived a character of necessity from being linked with the very nature of Euclidean space. But, actually, Newton's law stands out among other laws that might be imagined, by reason of its success alone.

Apart from those laws, there is not much in mechanics that

[16] It is a moot question whether, space and time being not categories but *Anschauungsformen*, the Kantian critique could not have overcome this difficulty. But for most of its interpreters the system had already become a rigid thing.

might be called inductive. It has to proceed on the concept of the material point, and indeed on the concept of the unextended center of force, as systematized by Cauchy. And, since material objects almost never get anywhere near being such points, the problem is always of a resolution of the given objects into points and forces between them.[17]

It is natural to suppose those material points invariable, as well as the laws that link them. The result is a completely atomistic picture of matter. Such a picture is one of the fundamental scientific a prioris, as we hope to show in the following section. It has succeeded in providing the needed laws of matter by drawing upon celestial bodies as models of atoms. And now the theory goes back to its origins—but in the rather strange forms of materialism without matter, of causality devoid of substance. Such is the paradox of regressive deduction.

The Atomic Idea

The scientist always searches for laws, but he wants to think in terms of things. These things must be real, that is, he must be able to believe in them. Hartmann once pointed out that the scientist who should set out to describe the world in terms of objects that he knows to be untrue would admittedly belong to the lunatic asylum. Whatever the limitations and conventions attached to the words "true" or "real," it is clear that the thing which is the principle of explanation must command at least provisional belief.[18] Furthermore, as we said before in criticizing Mach's statement, it ought to be a positive and not a negative fact. It makes all the difference between the old words *scientia* and *cognitio*.

Every nascent scientific explanation will, therefore, be realistic and not nominalistic. The great theories of the nineteenth century give ample proof of this. Such a realism is not a mere fleeting overture; it accompanies them throughout the creative stage, and its struggle to survive against contradictions and to emerge from the steadily complicating network of experimental relations closing in on it is the very life-story of the theory.

There is still, in the background of all explanation, the old unsolved identity between "mechanical" and "natural." Whether it be sought in material models or in the general analytical forms of theorems on potential, there is the attempt at a true picture, and at one universally true. After D'Alembert, abstract necessity has lost its hold, science goes in for "contingency" or

[17] We have to omit the later attempts (Hertz) at a formalization of mechanics on the basis of "purely mechanical" concepts. They were bound to prove sterile, and they did.

[18] This is meant for nineteenth-century science. Modern physical theory has a vastly different aspect. Empiricism has come into its own. Yet even here it might be pointed out that both Planck and Einstein are essentially realists and rationalists of the type we are describing.

"immanence": the order of nature is supposed to express the characters of the real things which jointly compose the existences to be found in nature.[19] But in the *materia signata* of this order there are still hidden all the metaphysical characteristics that go to make an essence, as Laplace had truly called it. Simplicity, the seal of nature, is impressed on it; and so are the laws of continuity, of analogy, of identity, that are to reconstruct a unity out of the scattered pieces of the puzzle.

Theories may come and go, but this it is that makes the atomic idea a central motive of science. Atomism is the recurrent image that has dominated scientific thought for over two thousand years. If anything were more remarkable than its purely a priori origin, it would be its enduring through the ages as a strict matter of faith, its capacity for drawing new life from seemingly unrelated discoveries, and its ultimate vindication. Yet even in its principle it bears the whole drama of rationalism.

The statement of Democritus that all qualities are illusory and "in truth nothing but atoms and the void" was a decisive stroke of simplification. It showed the way both to a clear explanation of nature and to one which could be mathematized. It was the abstract belief of Democritus, as far as possible from experimental verification, which inspired Galileo, Boyle, Bernouilli, and Newton.

The appeal of the atomic idea lay in its rigorous simplicity. Yet that simplicity was deceptive. With the atom a highly complex unit had entered the stream of thought. On one side, it was a physical entity; on the other, a mathematical one. It carried with it all the implications of the Eleatic view of nature from which Democritus had sprung. Whitehead has justly if paradoxically observed that the Void of Democritus, the Space of Newton, and the God of Leibniz are one and the same thing. It is this hidden character, this concentration of properties, that made the void so terribly embarrassing to the Greek philosophers. The contrary intuitions of metaphysical plenitude and of physical void, both linked with our experience of space as a whole, have a confusing and sometimes exasperating way of exchanging aspects in a philosophical quadrille which lasts up to Leibniz and beyond.[20]

Such a permanent equivocation arises, as always, from unexpressed content. The abstract principles that we tried to outline previously must coexist with a simple faith in substance, and that substance must be matter[21]—such a matter as can be invariable and forever equal to itself, since it must represent

[19] The postulate is well expressed by Euler: "All modifications taking place in bodies have their cause in the essence and the properties of the bodies themselves."

[20] We cannot dwell on this point which ought to be qualified. It involves Plato's conception of space and Aristotle's subsequent developments (cf. *Phys.* iv. 8 and 9).

[21] For an unsophisticated statement of the requirement cf. Locke, *Essay on Human Understanding*, Book ii [ch. 27, § 3].

eternal and necessary Being itself.[22] Such is the essence of Galilean thought, and such is the stated content of the image. The decisive character of this particular conception of substantialism is the additional requirement that the location of substance should be always indubitable through the changes undergone by a system of bodies. The whole of the measuring technique is directed to ascertaining such locations in the flux of phenomena. In other words, there must be some essential system of reference. This is the hidden postulate of any geometrization of the real. The void of Democritus, although bereft of the quality of Being, is the equivalent in this of Newton's absolute space. They both express an intrinsic necessity of spatial designation or structure, which finds a correct expression at last in general relativity, as the texture of world-lines structuring the continuum.

For twenty-five centuries all this content was packed in a simple image—the atom of Democritus. It is materialized logical simplicity. It inherits the implications of Eleatic unity, but it is essentially a unit, and a unit infinitely repeated. It is substantialism reduced to small change.

Genuine realism has only one epistemological function: it refers all qualities to substance. Substance is real; phenomena are also real. All qualities are illusory which are not possessed directly by the substance itself. Mabilleau, at the close of his history of atomism, is led to a plain atomistic profession of faith: "The progress of science consists in linking the outward manifestations of matter to its internal structure, so as to establish, through the interdependence of both orders, the unity of the law without which there is no true explanation." This is practically an identification of structure and phenomenon. W. Thomson and, after him, Helmholtz both observed that atomism cannot "explain" any properties except those which are attributed gratuitously and a priori to the atom itself. In the seventeenth century the transfer is immediate and naïve. Acids have a prickly taste, so their atoms must be pointed. Still more: "Atoms constitute the immutability of elements, they cause fire to be always fire, water to be always water, and the imperceptible germs that form a man never to form a bird."[23]

The traditional atom, then, contains in itself all that the scientist needs to imagine of reality. It traverses the ages laden both with the physical and with the mathematical possibilities that wait to be developed into an explanation. But here the difficulties begin.

Let us examine them first in a strictly theoretical manner as they came up before experiment forced determinations upon them.

[22] "The necessary and the eternal always go together . . . if something exists of necessity, it is eternal, and if eternal, of necessity" (Aristotle *De gen. et corrupt.* ii. 337[b]35, 338[a]1).

[23] Voltaire, *Dictionnaire philosophique*, art. "Atome."

Rigorous and naïve substantialism leaves all the modes of substance undetermined—*in mente materiae*, if we may so put it. Substance is an absolute and ought not to bear determination from any outside factor. Why should such a substance, manifesting itself solely out of its inner power, go twice through the same modes under equal conditions or give rise to the same phenomena? If, to take Voltaire's example, fire is an unrelated absolute, why should it behave always as that which we call "fire" and not as something else? If Pierce's tychism had been there at the very start, people would have stopped trying to explain natural phenomena. Why should we look for diversity elsewhere than in protean substance itself, and why, in particular, should we look for it in outward agents which cannot influence such an autonomous substance? Unless, indeed, substance has attributes which allow for such action. In the end, if we want to build up a science and not an animism, we are left with only one choice, which is the historical one: the atom must be quite dead, its substance devoid of all spontaneity. Realism starts instinctively from a cosmos "which is itself a god" and ends in the most "thingy" thing it can conceive of. On that thing, endowed with only the primary qualities, the science of numbers and extension can operate. Galileo takes up again where Democritus left off, after many centuries of interlude in metaphysics of the soul. But to have science operate, to bring out constant laws arising from constant relations, we must break down that one Thing into so many replicas of itself. And to have that breakdown not a mere arbitrary action of our mind but an objective reality, there must be a limit to it. Only thus can the real be defined outside of our action on the phenomena. If division could be infinite, substance would become itself a veritable phenomenon and escape our analysis in the illusion of an unseizable composite. We would be sitting on one of the horns of the Eleatic dilemma: the World of Opinion. If, on the other hand, reality were one and intangible, there would be no phenomena. We would find ourselves on the other horn: a world that may be true but does not look real.

Atomism is the one way out toward a science;[24] it is a naïve materialism that has become precise so as to be amenable to mathematics.[25]

In Descartes's kinematical universe atoms are merely extension and shock. The purism of such a scheme allows them to be the subjects of only one law—that of a constant quantity of movement. But even that is so arbitrary, the idea of spontaneous movement is so obviously not contained in that of extension,

[24] Leibniz, the protagonist of the continuum, is strictly an atomist on the physical plane: "In the explanation of particular phenomena I am an out-and-out partisan of corpuscular philosophy" (Letter to Arnauld, *Philos. Schr.*, II, 58).

[25] Cf. Bachelard, *Les Intuitions atomistiques*.

that the occasionalists find it more proper to situate the laws of shock "outside." Atoms cannot even act on one another. They become a cipher, a mere pretext for the law.

Atomism is stripped to the bone; but it is stripped also of its *raison d'être*. Still, Newton has to accept the principle: the enduringness and permanence through change that distinguishes nature does not appear to him explainable otherwise than by particles "solid, massy, hard, impenetrable," coming together and separating again. But there has to be a reaction against Cartesianism, and the Newtonian reaction leads toward a richer atomic substance, endowed with both geometric figure and dynamic properties, essentially attraction; but also magnetism, electricity, affinity, even light. Thus, though against Newton's better judgment, and with much hesitation on his part, atomism was drifting back toward explanations through inherence. For chemists, such explanations were obvious because they were necessary. We have quoted Laplace's doubts on this point. Notwithstanding his doubts, Laplace was still ready to condemn the undulatory theory of Young and Fresnel because it discarded the particle.

But now, apart from vagueness, much more grave and serious difficulties arose. The finite size and the inner cohesion of the atom had never been a problem to the Cartesians, who thought in terms of "figure and movement." Form and substance went together. The atom's geometrical surface was an integrant part of its being: Cartesianism still thought, although it did not care to realize it, in substantial forms. In the Newtonian scheme, however, the atom was dynamic matter. It had properties; that is, things were supposed to happen inside it. Its cohesion had to be explained, and this meant an inner force tying its parts together. The atom was embarrassingly resolving itself into subatoms, and the question started afresh on that level. One had to attribute some kind of "absolute" hardness to those subatomic particles or to go into a regression *ad infinitum*. If scientists wanted to avoid Aristotelian types of explanation, they had to go to the limit and define the atom as a pure mathematical point, for which action by contact was unthinkable and whose only character was force, acting at a distance. Such was Boscovich's theory, the theory that Cauchy took up and extended as the fundamental picture of mechanics. The astronomical view of nature and the atomic view converged under the requirements of dynamics into a materialism devoid of matter, whose only realities were points linked by forces. It would perhaps be more accurate to say that this offshoot of the atomic idea was absorbed by the astronomic system and became formalized along with mechanics. The atomic idea of matter has culminated again in a paradox: it started with a substance that was a cause and it ends in a cause without substance.

Such a paradox is of the essence of the problem we are analyzing. We are here at the heart of the rationalist process, and we can see the form it has taken under the influence of celestial mechanics. After watching developments in the peripheral zone of the budding sciences, we are led by atomism back to the central model of explanation that had been set as the ultimate goal of *scientia*. "Understanding," said Cuvier, "that is, explaining in astronomical terms. . . ."

The unity of the understanding does not rest any longer in a deduction from abstract principles. It is based on the "essence of matter," whatever that may be, as revealed by astronomy. In other terms, the facts of celestial mechanics, organized into a scheme of matter and force-at-a-distance, are conceived as some kind of a priori. And this is hardly to be wondered at, since that particular tie of geometry with mechanics was established by Newton himself.[26] The inevitable consequence is that, once we step beyond the empirical field of validity, the scheme will not hold together. The structure of matter cannot be simply equated to a solar system; but the scientist is willing to risk any paradox at any scale of dimensions. For he thinks by now that both matter and central force are of the essence of nature.

The unity of deduction had been once replaced, at Newton's suggestion, by analogy. But the uncertain web of analogies spun over physical reality tends to converge, all difficulties notwithstanding, toward the central analogy, and that analogy tends in its turn to become an identity.

Weber, referring modestly to his contribution, says:

> After the general laws of motion had furnished a foundation, there remained in physics mainly the investigation of the laws of interaction of bodies. . . . For a long time Newton's doctrine of gravitation furnished the leading idea for nearly all theories of electricity and magnetism, till a new clue was gained through Oersted's and Ampère's discoveries regarding the equivalence of closed electrical currents with magnets. This led, first, to the reduction of all magnetic effects to the action of electrical currents; and secondly, to the enunciation of a fundamental law of interaction of two elements of electricity in motion. A third leading idea was that of reducing the interaction of all bodies to that of the mutual action of pairs of bodies.[27]

In fact, Weber had been brought to attribute to electricity something like inertia (and this was the origin of Hertz's researches). But it is only by extreme abstraction[28] that we can

[26] Cf. *Principia*, Introd.

[27] *Electrodynamische Maassbestimmungen* (1878), p. 645.

[28] Having only abstraction to guide him, Weber actually found that the constant in his law had the dimensions of a velocity, that it established the connection between

speak of electrical masses, be they one or two; of elements of current; of velocities of a something which as yet cannot be clearly defined. As Carl Neumann tried to put it safely: "Electrical matters never exist alone, but only in combination with ponderable matter." Heat was another such stuff, whose particles repelled each other. As to ponderable matter, it had no definite range of dimensions and could well carry within itself the other observed forces. Out of its very uncertainty analogy has fled into identity. An abstract substance, a projection of matter, equal unto itself in all modes: such is now the "nature of matter."[29]

The factual law, in itself a dead datum, provides the starting-point for the twofold imaginative process, converging toward identity and expanding toward generality. It is as involuntary as the rhythm of the heart. Before he knows it, the scientist has taken the decisive step; thus, when the problem of cosmic dimensions comes up in the mind of Laplace, it is settled without a doubt. A model universe, he remarks, "reduced to the smallest space imaginable, would have to offer always the same appearances to its observers."[30] Later, the more cautious Helmholtz was led to state apropos of the laws of electricity:

> If we are to consider Weber's law as an elementary law, as an expression of the ultimate cause of phenomena, and not merely as an approximately correct expression of fact within narrow limits, then we must demand that, if applied to objects of the largest imaginable dimensions, it should give results which are physically possible.[31]

In the same way Democritus, the earliest of physical rationalists, had said: "There is no reason why there should not be somewhere atoms as large as a world."

But within what range of dimensions is matter still matter? Among the many paradoxes of an infinite universe, there is also this one of the lack of absolute dimensions, which was accepted cheerfully, as it confirmed the recurrent analogy of nature suggested by Newton. But in this way an empirical law is well on its way toward becoming itself an absolute, all the more so in that it has been successively extended to the field of electricity, thence to that of electrochemistry by Berzelius, and, through sheer analytical ingenuity, to that of electromagnetism by Ampère and Weber.

---

the electromagnetic and the electrostatic system of measurements, and that it was practically the same as that for the propagation of light. Yet he passed it by as a coincidence, to which he could attach no physical meaning, although already in 1846 he was speculating about the role of the intervening medium (*ibid.*, Part I, p. 169).

[29] This went on until 1853, when Krönig and Clausius came out with the kinetic theory. For the attempts at clarification of this problem of analogy cf. C. Neumann, *Die Principien der Elektrodynamik* (1868); Weber, *op cit.*; Helmholtz, *Vorträge und Reden.*

[30] *Exposition du système du monde* (6th ed.), p. 440.

[31] *Wissensch. Abhandlungen*, I, 658.

The process of unification may take any number of ways toward its goal. Here, having to face a really unresolved multiplicity of forces, it is only natural that it should tend to ignore it and concentrate on the law itself, which is an abstraction in regard to the nongravitational forces, but only in regard to those. We are still within the frame imagined by Newton.[32] The embarrassing pictures of electrical fluids and suchlike having been abstracted out of the way, the theory stabilizes itself on the level of two seemingly intuitive representations—matter and force. The mathematical treatment is a powerful determinant in this, since it provides the accomplished mold of the equations of mechanics. Thus the substantialism inherent in science had found a resting-point: a labile one in the dialectic of rationalism, perhaps, but strong by virtue of its ancient prestige and of the highly rationalist pattern in which fact and theory were welded together. And thus the mechanics of central forces was able to weather the age of positivism and the difficulties connected with its extension to the intra-atomic field. Corrections had to be brought in; but the pattern survived, and without it science would have been utterly without a lead when it tackled the inner structure of the atom. Even today quantum mechanics has to start from the Hamiltonian equations.

When H. A. Lorentz was searching for the electromagnetic laws of the theory of the electron, he started from Maxwell's equations, that experience had shown to be well grounded, and eliminated all the quantities in which the influence of matter is revealed by material constants. He assumed that the "true" or microscopic electromagnetic field obeys these simplified harmonic laws, and he was proved to be right.

By this time the original astronomical idea of law has undergone a last and significant transformation, through which it enters modern physics. Substantialism has been reluctantly cast overboard. The exact laws of nature are linked only to atomic structure, and only from it can they derive their constants.

To recapitulate, dynamic atomism had proved intrinsically unstable. Against the wish and the imagination of its nineteenth-century supporters, it developed into a field theory, where "matter" became a substantial shadow, a counterpart set up for action. The unresolved duality provides both the pattern and the fundamental irrational. "Science," says Helmholtz, "considers the objects of the external world under two types of abstraction: on the one hand according to their mere presence,

32 "It seems to me farther, that these particles have not only a *vis inertiae* . . . but also that they are moved by certain active Principles such as is that of Gravity, and that which causes Fermentation, and the Cohesion of Bodies. These principles I consider, not as occult Qualities, supposed to result from the specifick Form of Things, but as general Laws of Nature, by which the Things themselves are form'd; their Truth appearing to us by phenomena, though their Causes be not yet discover'd" (*Opticks*, Book iii, p. 1).

and independently from their action on other objects or on our organs of sense: and this it calls matter." On the other hand, we can attribute to matter the capacity for action, and then we shall know it only through its action. "Pure matter would be indifferent to the rest of nature, for it would never be able to determine any modification in it or on our organs. Pure force would be something that has to be there and yet is not there, since we designate to-be-there as matter."

The Embarrassment of Reality

From the point of vantage of these later developments, both in mechanics and in electrodynamics, we can better survey the critical period in which "real" representations try to fight their way through progressive abstraction and the all-embracing theorems of the science of energy.

Toward the middle of the nineteenth century it was obvious that the astronomical image had worked itself into a tangle, while, on the other hand, it was becoming clear that the atomic view had a real physical foundation and must be brought back to a physical image. Maxwell was working out the kinetic theory of gases on the assumption of hard elastic particles and meeting with almost complete success. In his second paper he concluded:

> But who will lead me into that still more hidden and dimmer region where Thought weds Fact—where the mental operations of the mathematician and the physical action of the molecules are seen in their true relation? Does not the way to it pass through the very den of the metaphysician, strewed with the remains of former explorers and abhorred by every man of science?

It did. Certain inevitable discrepancies between theory and observation could not be solved—nor could the a priori element be repressed—until the advent of the quantum theory. Meanwhile, atomism groped its way through the den clad in the protective garb of Kantian criticism,[33] until it emerged safely in modern physics, where the existence of ultimate particles is established, but on a level where operational realism and axiomatic nominalism are scrambled together so as to make them foolproof against the metaphysician. The electron is no longer a coherent image; it is the support for a certain number of more or less co-ordinated behaviors revealed by experimental techniques.

[33] Given the form of our understanding, says, e.g., Lasswitz, "the science of a given epoch must end—or more exactly begin—with a given group of atomic systems that one may imagine as encased the one within the other, and such a science must start thence to explain all that is to be explained. . . ." Or, again: "There must be a phenomenal object which in itself should be immutable, impenetrable and very small, and forming the subject of all changes in Nature. But then also we have exhausted the properties to be necessarily attributed to the atom if we study it without regard to relations with other atoms. All other properties of the atom are conditioned by the connexions between atoms" (K. Lasswitz, *Atomistik und Kritizismus*, p. 62).

But to come back to the punctiform atom as imagined, let us say, about 1840. We can see how the extremely elusive concept provided by the physics of central forces was the meeting-point of several abstract lines of reasoning and, as such, was simply an intimation to science to go forward toward either a stricter analysis or a more coherent representation.[34]

The atom is postulated as an active unit. It is less the unity of a figure than the unity of a force. Still it had a substance, but no one knew what to do with it. From this mongrel being (which was to reappear in the first representations of the electron) we can either go back to substance or go forward to construct a coherent dynamic theory of matter.

Both these ways were followed, and almost at the same time. The first way, back to the physical atom, was taken by the chemists. The issue was long beclouded by the obstinate struggle of the positivists against what they considered a scientific regression; but, in its heuristic thought, chemistry, since Dalton, lived by simple belief in the substantial atom. It has been said that Dalton invented atomism only to give a convenient form to the law of multiple proportions. Lange and Kirchberger, however, have shown by the documents that Dalton was guided by the fundamental atomistic intuition of Newtonianism in organizing his research. Richter had also been looking at the same time for simple numerical proportions. "But," says Lange, "while Richter promptly jumped from the observed constancies to the most general form of the idea, and concluded that all phenomena in nature are ruled by measure, number and weight, Dalton was looking for a sensible representation, and the atomistic one came to meet him half-way."

The philosophical problems raised by Dalton's simple idea nearly smothered it in its inception. Atomism gives an additive explanation of phenomena, but it appears hardly able to explain the new properties of chemical compounds. It imagines only *Aggregatzustände*. Its implicit postulate is: what is in the whole must necessarily be in the parts—and that is just what, except for weight, the whole of chemical experience seemed to disprove. A new principle of association had to be found, less abstract and more conformable to the complexity of the real, and the first clear step toward it was, quite typically also, the reintroduction of form and figure through stereochemistry. Meanwhile, even the most imaginative were left doubtful. "I must confess," says Faraday early in his career, "I am jealous of the term *atom*; for though it is very easy to talk of atoms, it

[34] Kant, typically enough, thought that the physics of central forces provided an *ubi consistam* for theory. In the *Metaph. Anfangsgründe der Naturwissenschaft* he builds up matter out of a postulated equilibrium between attractive and repulsive forces which is necessary to explain the distribution of matter through space. Physically, the theory could not hold water without supplementary determinations.

is very difficult to form a clear idea of their nature, especially when compound bodies are under consideration."[35] But ten years later, in 1844, he added:

> The word atom, which can never be used without involving much that is purely hypothetical, is often *intended* to be used to express a simple fact. . . . There can be no doubt that the words definite proportions, equivalents, primes, etc. which did and do express fully all the *facts* of what is usually called the atomic theory, were dismissed because they were not expressive enough, and did not say all that was in the mind of him who used the word atom in their stead; they did not express the hypotheses as well as the fact.[36]

With the advent of the kinetic theory of gases, the chemical atom had become practically a certainty; yet it took long years even to give back to Avogadro's law the simple appearance of a fact under which it had been conceived, and as late as 1890 Ostwald could speak of the "rout of atomism."

Boltzmann, in his *Vorlesungen über Gastheorie*, has bitter words against his positivist friends and against the "hands off" attitude of Kirchhoff:

> On the Continent, where the theory of central forces had been generalized into a foundation of the theory of knowledge itself, and therefore a few decades ago the electrical theory of Maxwell was hardly noticed, the provisional character of any special hypothesis was again erected into a general principle, and it was concluded that even the kinetic theory of heat was bound to be discarded in time. . . . Why should the present generalization [against representations] not prove to be dangerous in its turn?[37]

The reasons for this repugnance are many, and all of them are interesting. First, of course, was the positivist taboo against figurative hypotheses; but, on the nonpositivist side, the issue was followed up half-heartedly, for it was realized by then that the material atom raised more problems than it solved. That is the recurrent drama of rationalism. Once natural philosophers had the atom, it turned out to be not quite what they wanted. The real theoretical hope, as revealed in Prout's hypothesis, had been that various elements could be shown to be formed of a condensation of the original atom of hydrogen. It was again the Cartesian ideal. Stoichiometry forbade that. The chemical atom turned out to be inconveniently multiple and circumstantial. In other words, it was a little too real. And while imagination struggled to adjust itself to the situation (e.g., with Berthollet's ideas of continuity), the kinetic theory supervened to give the *coup de grâce* to old simple schemes. It had to be admitted that the atomic radii and the masses, which could be calculated for several

[35] *Experimental Researches*, No. 869.

[36] *Ibid.*, II, 285.

[37] "Einleitung" (ed. 1895).

elements from measurements of energy and momentum in the gases, did by no means suggest constant proportion between mass and volume for all elements. In other words, the idea of a unitary matter stamped out in blocks of different size and shape or welded into aggregates was definitely dead. Each element was clearly made of its own particular stuff of a particular density.

But with this simple pluralism all the old problems that confronted the Newtonian atom came back multiplied by 92, with some fresh problems thrown in.

The rigorous equality of all atoms of a kind again inspired John Herschel to propound a direct intervention of the Creator as the only possible explanation, while all the problems of inherence came up again for the relation of the atom to its physical properties.

But there was also the new problem: once we are again on the ground of substantialism, what mechanism can we imagine which would select from the twice infinite set of substantial speres, of all possible radii and masses, only those few discrete possibilities which correspond to the actual elements? At the same time a way out was dimly perceived. The periodic system, discovered in 1847, was hailed by positivism as a satisfactory classification, but to the scientific imagination it was far more than that: the tantalizing blueprint of an as yet unrevealed unitary structure. The solution was to come only through the quantum theory, but the intimations of it were enough to give new courage to believers in the atom.

These hopes were to be fulfilled: first, through stereochemistry; then, through modern physics, matter was to find its way back to that peculiar elusive combination of substance and geometry required by rationalism.

From Mechanics to Physics

We have shown how the unextended atom of the theory of central forces was already by 1820 a dead issue and how any developments leading to new ideas had to drop one or the other of the assumptions embodied in it. One of the ways, that leading back to substantialism, we have already described. Another way led out analytically toward a mechanics of systems and ultimately toward the formalization of the science as set out previously. It simply worked out the dynamic implications of the mixed "astronomical" image. But after having originally claimed empirical matter, under its mechanical aspect, for its province, it found itself dealing with something that was matter by convention only. When Laplace found a rigorous solution of the three-body problem for the special case of an arrangement of the three bodies in an equilateral triangle, he remarked rather wistfully that this was "the only case not possible in nature." An attempt to find help in the no less abstract science of energy provided only auxiliary representations of a strictly fictitious character. Hertz was most philosophically clear-sighted on this point.

Such was the coherent ending of the daring Galilean abstraction of primary qualities and "concreteness," until it was reborn for a time with electrical instead of mechanical as subject matter.

The other possible way, and the one marked out by the rationalistic urge, was to go back to reality without yielding on generality: to find a new effective image that could fit the ample range of physical fact.

That range was rapidly extending. The theories of elasticity, heat, optics, and electricity had been organizing their inductive research around certain provisional images, like caloric fluid in heat, emission theory of light, the two-fluid theory of electricity, which had developed mathematical instruments; and these in turn, just as D'Alembert had foreseen, constrained and directed imagination. Essentially, the new developments remained within the frame of phenomenological physics, and Diderot's comments on it (see n. 51) were still valid. But the progress of mathematical technique provided wonderful bridges between domains, such as Fourier's theorem or the potential theory. The mechanics of deformable bodies set certain assumptions which allowed the science to deal with elasticity and hydrodynamics, and it became the realm of partial differential equations.

The assumptions were, of course, fictional. The mechanics of extended masses presupposed, for instance, continuous variations of density and velocity within the mass. But such concepts were linked with certain original images. Once endowed with the proper analytical apparatus, the images are adopted more boldly; they become isolated starting-points for complete deductions on the Newtonian pattern. Researchers trust their intuition and feel they are dealing with actual experimental material, whereas, of course, they are dealing with fundamental images (not yet quite models[38] in the later sense of the word) presenting the usual combination of abstraction and concreteness and, as such, able to replace the traditional forms of dynamic atomism. These new images now have captured the mind and are being belabored on all sides by imagination.

The general pattern is that of continuity. Continuous media

[38] The typical "model" in the sense of a mechanism derives from the "image" of an incompressible fluid with its vortices. MacCullagh was the first to suggest, in 1839, the replacement of elasticity by rotary motion, and in the highly mechanical imagination of W. Thomson and J. M. Rankine this gave rise to the concrete hypothesis of a gyrostatic ether. With four gyroscopes jointed in lozenge fashion one can compose a system which represents the elasticity of a spring and can well explain the rotation of the plane of polarization of light in a magnetic field. This led up to Maxwell's conception of the model as a transitory help for the imagination.

are needed to link pure mechanics not only with the theory of deformable bodies but also with "thermology" (as it was called) and optics, where the wave theory, founded anew by Young and Fresnel, was searching for adequate means of representation. There is scarcely an aspect of physics, from the planning of a steel bridge to the evanescent fringes of color exhibited by a crystal, wherein such a theory of matter does not play its part. It is, indeed, fundamental in its relations to the theory of structures, to the theory of hydromechanics, to the elastic solid theory of light, and to the theory of crystalline media.

The sort of matter imagined now is (apart from incompressible fluids) in the form of rubber bands, jellies, and suchlike substances exhibiting elastic properties and shivering behaviors, capable of shear but not of pressure, set up for the purpose of stretching, sliding, shifting, vibrating.

What is taking on a body again, from so many converging efforts of the imagination, is that old archtype of the continuum, of unity itself, the space ether.

As in the time of Huygens, Newton, and Euler, it has to be "a very subtil and elastic fluid." It is still half-substantial, still burdened with all the contradictions that smothered its theory in the first instance;[39] but this time it started on its way by definite heuristic success. Fresnel's ether was able to explain interference and double refraction. Its very success, however, added a new difficulty to those that Newton had perceived already. It vibrated transversally, which made it even harder to visualize. The time had passed for talking vaguely, as Blackmore had done in verse, of "the springy Texture of the Air." The nearest analogon would have been a jelly of surpassing rigidity. The image is not concrete enough to control the imagination, yet it is clear enough to guide research. Rowan Hamilton was able to predict conical refraction in crystals as a consequence of the mathematical fact that Fresnel's wave surface in a biaxial crystal possesses four conical points.

Such success obtained even by a first inadequate theory spurred on researchers, and so hypotheses succeeded each other, the value of which had to be estimated by the fruitfulness of their mathematical consequences. After the adynamical theory of Fresnel came the elastic solid theory of ether developed by Navier, Cauchy, Poisson, and Green, the labile ether theory developed by Cauchy and Kelvin, and the rotational ether

[39] Newton imagined ether as "filling all space adequately without leaving any Pores, and by consequence much denser than Quick-Silver or Gold." At the same time it was supposed to be so rare that "it would not offer the slightest alteration to the motion of the planet." As to this last, he reminds us of the strange "subtelty, imponderability and potency" of the electric effluvia. And, furthermore, let the objectors tell him "how the effluvia of a magnet can be so rare and subtile, as to pass through a Plate of Glass without any Resistance or Diminution of their Force, and yet be so potent as to turn a magnetick Needle beyond the Glass?" (*Opticks*, Book iii, Part I, Query 22).

theory of MacCullagh. But none of these, while constructing images and models that were often elaborate, could provide a really satisfactory entity, a *construirbare Vorstellung*.

Substantialism as a *caput mortuum* still haunted the theory. Ether was a need; it was a background; it was, as was once said, the substantive of the verb "to vibrate"; but it remained a shadowy presence. As figurations become difficult and uncertain, the analytical instrument gains predominance and all "truth value" seems to concentrate on the idea of law. The whole of French physics from Lagrange to Poincaré is permeated with a positivist spirit, even before positivitism became a doctrine. It is at best a transitional period, since it is easier to profess belief in method only than it is to get rid of all hope of an ultimate substantial representation. We have seen how this process took place even within the astronomical representation. But it was to find greater scope on a new level. A science of energy took shape after 1840, and although Faraday's intuitions, Carnot's analogies, and J. R. Mayer's metaphysical generalizations played a large part in its inception, it quickly became formalized and deflected the imagination toward a general theory of equivalence, while the embarrassing substantial substratum of all changes fell back into the shadow.[40] The great organizers of the new theory were Thomson and Helmholtz. The latter especially was to attempt a unification of science on the basis of the conservation of energy. As early as 1847 he roughly sketched out the plan of the work he was to take up twenty years later, aiming at co-ordination of the departments of mechanics, physics, and chemistry. We need not follow up these later developments. But, even here, they go from negative to positive figuration. The original principle of unification was the impossibility of perpetual motion. But the inevitable end was that energy was given a completely substantial role in the new scheme; and, when Ostwald in 1890 inveighs against the "materialism" of mechanics, it is simply that he has replaced the old stuff with a new one more to his taste.

It may be said of the science of energy, however, that in its perspicuity, economy, and ample symmetry, in its expansion and in its superordination to phenomena, it provided an almost perfect paradigm for the positivist canon of what a science should be, and such it appeared to the late positivist generation. It is a significant irony that in its beginnings Comte should immediately have taken up the cudgels against it.[41] Deriving his in-

[40] The name of "energetics" was suggested by Rankine, in 1855, as "the abstract theory of physical phenomena in general."

[41] It is also to be noted that Helmholtz's fundamental paper of 1847 was turned down for publication by Poggendorff and his committee (as Mohr's and Mayer's had been before), because, notwithstanding Joule's experimental material, the theory did not appear to live up to empirical standards. Clausius' memoir of 1855 on the kinetic theory had a similar fate.

spiration from the abstract analytical models of Lagrange and Fourier,[42] he proclaimed: "Instead of searching blindly for a sterile unity, as oppressive as it would be chimerical, in the vicious reduction of all phenomena to a single order of laws, the mind shall look at last on the different classes of events as having their own special laws."

To formulate theories concerning the "why" or the "what" of phenomena was for him the cardinal sin, which can be committed only "by minds wholly alien to the true scientific spirit." Hence a number of interdictions which today appear at least weird, among which, specifically, that we should never search for the connections between the various forms of energy.

We cannot dwell here upon the strange and important phenomenon of Comtian positivitism. But it would be easy to prove that Comte, too, is a rationalist—in fact, a classical Newtonian rationalist as far as his model of the true science is concerned. The novelty of his case is only that he is trying to apply the old model to the field which alone appears to him essential, that of sociology: all other sciences are merely ancillary and treated as such; but sociology, the all-comprising, is again supposed to provide "un miroir exact de l'ordre extérieur." Nothing is really changed; only the stress is shifted, and the reasons for the shift could be stated correctly only through a discussion of the new "historical" rationalism. That is an ample field which we cannot discuss here. Let us simply remark that the fate of Comte's doctrine is generally that of all systematizations which presuppose a closed group of primary ideas. One might extend to Comte, if one considered his fundamentally analytical and Saint-Simonian background, what Whitehead says of Stuart Mill: "His mentality was limited by his peculiar education, which gave him system before any enjoyment of the relevant experience."

The Particle and the Field

To go back to the "open" rationalism of the physicists, which goes on regardless of interdictions: a systematic treatment would mark its progressive absorption of empiricist ideas, and the successful attempts at unification which take place through the science of energy. But we wish simply to point out two fundamental historical facts which are in the strictly rationalist line and precede all formalization.

The first is the evolution of thermodynamics. As Sir J. Larmor says:

[42] "There exists a very extensive class of phenomena which are not produced by mechanical forces, but which result solely from the presence and accumulation of heat. This part of natural philosophy cannot be brought under dynamical theories; it has principles peculiar to itself, and is based upon a method similar to that of the other exact sciences" (J. B. J. Fourier, *Théorie analytique de la chaleur*, p. 13).

A science of thermodynamics leapt into being in 1824, in a fashion too novel and strange in relation to current trends of ideas to gain recognition at the time, coming from the brain of perhaps the supreme scientific genius of the last century, Sadi Carnot. . . . But the vast subject instinctively mapped out by him as regards its essential ideas could not become a progressive science until there was a basic theory of matter, on which the primary crude conception of the nature of heat, otherwise unfathomable in any exact sense, could take form in some definite way: and that arrived with sufficient precision only through the formulation of the kinetic theory of gases.[43]

Carnot had proceeded by analogy. His original image was that of heat as a waterfall. And in his short career he managed to foresee the coming form of explanation, as shown by his notebooks published only in 1878. The gap between the general idea of particle and the actual theory was abridged by Maxwell's intuitive imagination, using the technique he had developed in the study of the stability of Saturn's rings, and proceeding from assumptions which appeared sweeping to his puzzled contemporaries. Boltzmann's description of his fundamental paper likens it to a great overture; but then Boltzmann was no mean competitor:

At first are developed majestically the Variations of Velocities, then from one side enter the Equations of State, from the other the Equations of Motion in a central Field; ever higher sweeps the chaos of Formulae; suddenly are heard the four words: "put $n=5$." The evil spirit V (the relative velocity of two molecules) vanishes and the dominating figure in the bass is suddenly silent; that which had seemed insuperable being overcome as if by a magic stroke. There is no time to say, why this or why that substitution was made; who cannot sense this should lay the book aside, for Maxwell is no writer of programme music. Result after result is given by the pliant formulae till, as unexpected climax, comes the Heat Equilibrium of a heavy gas; the curtain then drops.

Through sheer acrobatic ingenuity, the particle has been found again: the phenomena of mechanics and heat are brought back to the same concrete reality, and in the end Clausius' analytical expressions, such as entropy, are given an illuminating physical meaning.

This is one of the fundamental facts. The other is the personality of Faraday.

In 1844, Faraday comes to grips with the classical atomic representation, although fully conscious of its power. He tries to overcome it. What do we know, he asks, of the atom apart from its force?

To my mind the nucleus vanishes, and the substance consists in the powers of *m* [the force]. And indeed, what notion can we form of the nucleus independent of its powers? What thought remains on which

[43] *J. C. Maxwell Commemoration Volume* (1931), p. 88.

to hang the imagination of a nucleus independent of the acknowledged force?

This view he pushes to its utmost consequences:

> It would seem to involve necessarily the conclusion that matter fills all space, or at least all space to which gravitation extends; for gravitation is a property of matter dependent on a certain force, and it is this force which constitutes the matter. In that view, matter is not merely mutually penetrable;[44] but each atom extends, so to say, throughout the whole of the solar system, yet always retaining its own centre of force.

Faraday was not as yet constructing his field theory; he was using the classical one, which says nothing more than the theory of central forces. But it was already taking a new shape. Force seemed to him an entity dwelling along the line in which it is exerted. The lines along which gravity acts between the sun and the earth seem figured in his mind as so many elastic strings; indeed, he accepts the assumed instantaneity of gravity as the expression of the "lines of weight." Such views, fruitful in the case of magnetism, barren for his time in the case of gravity, explain his efforts to transform the latter force.

The guiding thread in all of Faraday's endeavor is the search for the underlying unity of the forces of nature. Tyndall has remarked that Faraday's difficulty was at bottom the same as Newton's. But, we might add, this time the phenomena were more complicated, and, since Faraday was not a mathematician, he was not tempted to work his way out in a formula. Since 1834 he had been thinking of the correlation of chemical affinity, heat, electricity, magnetism, gravitation: "Now consider a little more generally the relation of all these powers. We cannot say that any one is the cause of the others, but only that all are connected and due to one common cause. As to the connection, observe the productions of any one from another, or the conversion of one into another." And, after examining the known transformations, he adds: "This relation is probably still more extended and inclusive of aggregation, for as elements change in these relations they change in those. . . . And even gravitation may perhaps be included." These ideas, and the electrochemical discoveries which accompanied them, prompted Joule to his experiments on the mechanical equivalent of heat. In 1849, Faraday writes again: "The exertions in physical science of late years have been directed to ascertain not merely the natural powers, but the manner in which they are linked together, the universality of each in its action, and their probable *unity in one*."

44 Faraday, as is known, had the first intuition of wave mechanics. He compares the interpenetration of two atoms to the coalescence of two distinct waves which, though for a moment blended into a single mass, preserve their individuality and afterward separate.

His certainty of an interconnection of the forces brought him (as shown in his notebooks after 1831) to the discovery of electromagnetic induction; and, through his rigorous and patient translating of experimental effects into a coherent image, the space traversed by the lines of force was drawn into the operational picture, and the electromagnetic field was evolved. At this point the astronomical view of nature had to be definitely discarded. To those steeped in the traditional doctrines there was nothing left but bitter carping about "metaphysics,"[45] or helpless wonderment. Helmholtz, still a young man, pored over Faraday's seemingly "impenetrable" statements and despaired of ever understanding what they meant.[46] So far removed was Faraday's geometric visualization from previous schemes.

But while Faraday organized his discoveries in a work which in patience, rigor, and amplitude remains possibly the greatest monument of experimental research, his dream of the unification of all forces followed him vainly to the end of his life. In 1858, aged sixty-seven, he writes in his notebooks:

> 15,786. Suppose a relation to exist between gravitation and electricity . . .—is not likely; nevertheless, try, for less likely things apparently have happened in nature.
>
> 15,805. Then we might expect a wonderful opening out of the electrical phenomena.
>
> 15,808. Perhaps almost all the varying phenomena of atmospheric heat, electricity, etc. may be referable to effects of gravitation, and in that respect the latter may prove to be one of the most changeable powers, instead of one of the most unchanged.
>
> 15,809. Let the imagination go, guarding it by judgment and principle, but holding it in and directing it by experiment.
>
> 15,814. If anything results then we shall have
>
> 15,815. An entirely new mode of the excitement of either heat or electricity.
>
> 15,816. An entirely new relation of natural forces.
>
> 15,817. An analysis of gravitational force.
>
> 15,818. A justification of the conservation of force.

The last three points are the rationalist's creed. We are reminded of Diderot's meditation (see n.51). Beyond the relations and equivalences, Faraday is still searching for the underlying one thing which will allow us to *analyze* gravitation, to *justify* the conservation of force and remove it from the positive status of a mere device of scientific accountancy.

In his quest for unity Faraday was always on the verge of the metaphysical sin, of searching for an abstraction. But what he constructed in the course of his search was his real object, the concrete unity; maybe not so universal as he hoped but leading

[45] Cf. G. B. Airy's letter to J. Barlow, February 26, 1855, and Faraday's reply thereto, in Bence Jones, *Life and Letters of Faraday*, II, 354.

[46] Cf. e.g., *Vorlesungen über Theoretische Physik*, "Einleitung."

to universality as none before it; as universal as a theory can be that is born of a creative imagination and structures the complexity of one man's thought; still, for his time the very body of experimental truth: the electromagnetic ether.

The unity thus reached could not last long. Faraday had Newton's imagination but not his mathematics. Faraday and Maxwell together might be said to compose a Newton of the nineteenth century. And Maxwell, much against Faraday's hopes and somewhat against his own, was driven to the use of purely operational models, even to a set of inconsistent ones. When he set out to translate Faraday's ideas into symbols, he tried at first to preserve his master's unity of vision. "Faraday's methods," he writes, "resemble those in which we begin with the whole and arrive at the parts by analysis, while the ordinary mathematical methods were founded on the principle of beginning with the parts and building up the whole by synthesis."

But mathematical analogies drive him far beyond any one model or figuration. He was so guarded in assuming anything about electricity that he postulated little about it beyond its name. This is not enough to enable us to visualize the part it plays in electrical phenomena. For this reason, Maxwell's system was to his contemporaries "a book with seven seals": Helmholtz said that he would be puzzled to explain what an electrical charge was in Maxwell's theory other than the recipient of a symbol. And Hertz drew the conclusion when he said that Maxwell's theory was Maxwell's equations. Thus seemingly ends the last attempt at a real figurative structure.

The Fate of Scientific Rationalism

We go back to what we said before: the search is for objects whose characters develop by necessity into the order of nature as we can see it.

For Descartes and Leibniz physics had been an extension of mathematics. Descartes discarded sensible representation and replaced it with a world which is "the object of speculative geometry." Leibniz, thinking he had found in the analysis of the infinite the means of dealing mathematically with that fugitive multitude of motions which manifests itself in sensible qualities, looked to the order of abstract truths for the discriminating principle between illusory and "well-founded phenomena." A philosophy proceeding thus from the a priori is not only called upon to justify the accord between the intelligible and the sensible but it must prove the very existence of the sensible. Newton's natural philosophy starts from a quite different point of view. The link between mathematics and physics is founded on experiment. And the value of experiment lies in bursting the too narrow frame of metaphysical evidence and in establishing types of relations to which no amount of pure reasoning could possibly have led.

After Newton, rationalism, whether scientific or not, has to admit something which is "given" beyond any argument. This, for the scientist, is matter. The problem is: What can thought do with it? For as a datum it is opaque and irrelevant, and all that counts is the program of inquiry concerning it, what Galileo called the "ordeal."

From then on thought has to forge its way ahead "in the teeth of stubborn facts," and it is a matter which is supposed to provide them out of its own fulness. It is of "the essence of matter," as Laplace would have said, that it should present an ever emergent irrational side to investigation—and, also, that the irrational side should be of one texture with the geometrical truths wrung out of reality. Not merely a shadow side of truth but a principle of opposition ever emerging and ever subdued.

How, then, are we to define the intelligible essence of this texture so that it should fulfil the scientist's myth?

First, it must have precision. That is, we must believe that whatever the growing precision of our measures, the object being measured is still more precise in its determinations, whether it be a body or a wave length.[47] In fact, the whole of physical determinism is based on the faith in a limitless precision at the heart of things.[48] This faith is what Hume had already vainly tried to undermine.

Second, the quantitative characteristics which mark objects in the scientific analysis of nature also define, under conditions marked by similar characteristics, their behavior in a wholly definite and predictable way. This is held to be a law of nature, and certain recurrences are supposed to point to invisible structures of the same type but more universal, such as forces, fields, atoms. These invisible structures then become the principle of order.

Third, the rational intellect is competent to organize sequences which are the actual functional sequences of reality. And when several explanatory constructions can be found, it is a postulate that they can be reduced to one. This is just what Hobbes and D'Alembert had doubted, but the rationalist belief goes even farther. As Einstein said in 1918:

We have always found, that among the several theoretical constructions which could be thought out, one has shown itself as uncondi-

[47] In the first half of the nineteenth century it was still an important philosophical issue to test this precision. Rigor in the equality of acceleration for all matter was seen to mark "the absence of *à peu près*" and the presence of a precise, uniform reality inside the varieties of matter, viz., mass. Bessel and Encke showed this in convergent approximation in their experiments on the pendulum. Laplace's speculations on the stability of the solar system led in the same direction.

[48] The idea of an "inherent fuzziness" in nature is quite new and of this century. But Diderot already speaks of a "fumbling" of Nature as she tries to reach her goals (*Interprétation de la nature*, §§ xii, xxxvii), and this order of ideas goes back to Plato.

tionally superior to all the rest. . . . The world of sensation determines the theoretical system in a practically universal way, even if we are denied logical access to the foundations of the theory.

There is, no doubt, an inherent contradiction in rationalism, but it is a dynamic contradiction endowed with all the characters of a dialectic. Some kind of substance, of real being, is the object of the quest. Yet, as soon as that substance appears to be reached, it shows itself to be a vain image and a stumbling block to thought.

The physical particle was no sooner found than it raised the problem of what it stood for. Tangible matter as an absolute? A metaphysics of the primary qualities? Surely not, and the simple images of Galilean rationalism had been only a mirage. The molecule had to be resolved into spatial structures; then it was the turn of the atom. The process was carried on with inflexible consequentiality, always in the same direction: toward "the core of things," as Leibniz would have said. Even after rationalism was dead as an explicit faith, after positivism and then Darwinism had knocked all the props from under it, the imagination of physicists went on working in the same line and would not be diverted into "economy of thought." The explanatory space became ever more complex, but its identification with the particle ever more precise, until at last the theory was based upon the structure of the continuum itself.

There is no inductive method that leads us to the fundamental concepts of physics. This is a recognized truth. The theoretical structures imagined are ever more removed from experience. First inertia became an obvious idea, then the absurdity of perpetual motion, then the electromagnetic field, and finally relativity. The process was already well on its way in the nineteenth century; and the lack of recognition of this fact caused considerable delay in the success of the molecular theory and of Maxwell's ideas.

For the rationalist not only is this a fact but it is a "positive" fact in that it confirms his ideal. The ideal is, and ever remains, deduction. If not simple deduction from abstract principles, then a complex deduction from the "essence of matter" as successively determined, but always going both ways: progressing toward consequences, regressing toward elementary ideas and basic structures ever more removed from experience;[49] ever alive, ever altered in the course of research by new intuitions but always seeking to embrace principles and consequences in a frame not only fitting needs but claiming absolute universality

[49] Mention should be made of Enriques's recent theory, which recognizes this fact and tends to save rationalism by what might be called the "infinitesimal a priori." There is an invariant relation, he says, between the voluntary premiss and the clarifying experiment. The premiss is the working hypothesis, which is organized and revised all the time so as to fit the requirements of rationality.

and resolved on enough strength to bear not only the present but also the future of the theory.

Hence its insistence on embodying principles of a metaphysical order, like continuity, analogy, and simplicity, the "seal of truth." These principles in turn converge toward identity.[50] But it is not tautological identity. It is a postulated identity, which is of the essence of space and denies the essence of time. The universe is what it is, has been, and shall be. "The elements," says the Critic of Königsberg, "must have that perfection which they derive from their origin"; and even so Newton refuses to conceive of "old, worn particles." Democritus had thought he was cutting the ground from under metaphysical speculation when he said: "Of what is and has been forever one should not seek the cause." But then, of course, he was admitting a "forever," and so did all scientists after him. No sooner was the disturbing fact of the degradation of energy discovered, than fantasy was started on the search for a vaster compensatory mechanism. With identity, necessity, and eternity there always goes an initial perfection, and even recent cosmogonies cannot free themselves from that canon. The unity that comes of it has the essential character of a myth; it implies "absolute" pre-existence of all that we are trying to find.

Thus, identity does not really mean tautology. Meyerson saw a fundamental paradox in the fact that science works at bringing out diversity to annul it then into unity. Historically, the paradox works out as a dialectic. But Meyerson would not even have called it a paradox if he had seen that the unity sought by the rationalist is never formal unity. He is always led and betrayed into abstraction by his analytical instrument but never resigned to it. What he searches for is the very body of truth: a unity in depth, so to speak, in which all things are subsumed without canceling out. It is this that allows a contradiction to exist within the frame without its being stultifying. The contradiction is rather felt to be significant; it points to a complexity within the unity, not to be resolved. Leibniz's "all is exact" and Diderot's "rien de précis en nature" really convey one and the same thing: we are led back to the "difficulty" of the One and the Many, to Parmenides and Heraclitus, as it was in the beginning.[51] A difficulty that could be resolved only in the pure intelligible realm of mathematics, and even there not wholly.

[50] "We know full and clearly only one law: that of constancy and uniformity. . . . When we study things that vary, it is only that we may find what is there uniform and constant. And if we find these constants becoming variable, we must take one more step, but in the same direction: it will be not the same relations, but a combination of them" (Poinsot, *Elémens de statique*).

[51] It was Diderot's idea that there must be some force or "affection" of which attraction, elasticity, magnetism, and electricity are only isolated aspects. "Lacking such a center of common correspondence, phenomena will remain isolated; all the discoveries of modern physics will tend to bring them nearer through interposition, without ever uniting them: and even if they did succeed in uniting them, it would make a continuous

"*Scientific Rationalism*"

For the scientific rationalist, that slightly imaginary quintessential character, the solution would be the Many-in-the-One. He would speak perhaps of the unity of a total system. But here, again, he finds himself at the heart of his contradiction. He is warmly convinced that he is antimetaphysical. He sets "facts" and not principles at the beginning. But it is a historical fact that in all metaphysics principles have been able to fulfil their assigned role only by being at once homogeneous with facts and superior to them in dignity. For Faraday the electromagnetic field is a reality, as the atom was for Newton. And such reality was for them not phenomenic; as little phenomenic as the "true" or "subtle" elements of the ancients. They would have answered Mach's injunction to stay on empirical ground, and to consider all facts as equivalent, by arguing that that was the way for science to get stuck in a Sargasso Sea of pointer readings and conventional entities. Yet they were as conscientously empirical as anyone could ever be. Their regressive deduction might be taken for induction at times, even by themselves. After all, were they not looking for some basic reality? Was it their fault if the theoretical frame was forever receding from empirical truth? The imagined structures looked real enough to the mind's eye. Here is the root of that permanent equivocation we mentioned apropos of Whewell's inductivism. With uncanny perception, Hegel saw and used it to denounce science as a vast tautology, which awaited an explaining principle from "elsewhere." In strict logic, he was right. How can principles account for facts, or vice versa, without some bond of communion between them? Their homogeneity is implied by empirical doctrines which claim to infer the principle strictly from the observed fact, just as much by rationalism which tries to go the inverse way. For in both cases the aim is to prove that this or that fact in nature is basically important with respect to all the rest whether it be motes in a sunbeam, or the breaking of the waves, or the silent omnipresence of cosmic space. It is only a matter of what you see in and through the thing. The true scientist has an empiricist conscience and a rationalist imagination. He may or may not see the full implications of the latter; here is all the difference between Laplace and Faraday. But so long as he remains true to the initial faith of Galileo and Newton, he is a scientific rationalist. He may at one point, from his own sociological motivations, choose to ignore the process of regressive deduction, and he will appear as an inductivist; or from other sociological and historical motivations, he may decide that what was meant by unity is

circle of phenomena where no one could tell which is the first and which is the last. A strange situation, wherein experimental physics through sheer work would have shaped a labyrinth for rational physics to wander about in endlessly; but not an impossible one" (*Interprétation de la nature*, § xlv).

just unification, and then he will be logically right, and a positivist. Or he may follow his geometrizing instinct to the bitter end, where it meets operationalism, and he will find himself in the magic circle of general relativity. At this point his rationalism will have become relatively meaningless. But only relatively.

For the unity of the rationalist is not simply logical—it is symbolic and creative. His symbol takes on an extended meaning and permeates the whole theory. In so far as he has imagination, the scientist is a metaphysician; and it is yet to be seen how long the imagination may preserve its power after the progress of inquiry has destroyed its metaphysical roots. Technically, the analytical developments of rationalism have led it to meet halfway the rise of logical empiricism, and there is no formal issue that divides the two. Vitally, it may be otherwise.

In the zone of active scientific thought there is an instinctive identification of the image with truth. A "hunch" has to become a belief if we are to work it out, and casualties do not count. It is a faith which may be forever removed from one object to another, but is not easy to destroy. The image is born out of an effort of coherent imagination; it is of one piece with all the other certainties that actuate the mind; and it is as if its truth, according to the ancient pattern, laid claim to multiple and convergent confirmation, for it is of the nature of a truth of inner experience to appear limitless in depth. Like Aristotle and Euler, so the classical scientist does not quite conceive of a simple and univocal necessity. Notwithstanding all precautionary clauses, he expects a confirmation to extend far beyond the range of his own thought and the needs of present theory; he postulates a congruence between "empiricism" and deduction, between "analysis" and "justification." Laplace gave thirteen years of work, from 1773 to 1786, to the proof of the "stability of the universe," feeling that this was necessary to dispel all doubts as to the validity of the Newtonian doctrine. No such proof was needed for the limited time requirements of Cuvier's geology; but the doctrine was expected to confirm that the universe could last forever: in other words, that both the universe and the theory were "right."

The search, to be sure, is for necessary laws, as general as possible. It is a course natural to science, away from mere figuration, toward a higher unitary formalization. But always in the dark faith that formal unity will reveal a value, a specific realm of being.

Conservative thought, as exemplified in Hegel and Comte, tends to reduce unity to abstraction and legality. But science happens not to be conservative by nature.

Since the unity as originally conceived was simple and yet complex, the symbol and epitome of all the forces of nature, the rationalist tends to expand its consequences to the infinite, to weight it with all that has been found and with what has yet to be discovered. He refuses to stop and organize the present, for he already lives in the future. He does not care to arrange what we actually have with a view to convenience or even to the necessities of the organization of thought; for the present is to him a fictitious point, dividing what has been from what will be. Therefore, also, there can be no limitation to his fancy, be it operational, theoretical, or social. The immediate goal is an admitted fiction, but beyond that there is the projection of the infinite, the eagerly awaited unforeseen, which is going to yield the illuminating miracle of unity. To the rationalist mind the miracle is only just good enough.

These are philosophical terms and perforce inadequate; for at the core of scientific thought there seems to be something alien to concepts which requires nondialectical treatment; call it an objective correlative, call it a concrete realization. It is of the nature of science to search not only for intersubjective but for objective reality. Some would define the goal as the search for power through law; such a theory is adventitious, even though it goes back to Bacon, and historically irrelevant. Through history the actual goal is the object, something that the mind's eye can see with the inner certainty that it *is* there; it is the object in turn which imposes its nature on thought and makes all philosophical terminology appear alien and fanciful by comparison. As theories expand in scope, as communities of characters and growing interdependences are discovered, all leading away from any "absolute" being, the real course of thought remains progressive concentration on the actual components of the world, the tension increases between the two levels of theory and reality; and with the tension the strength of the bond that unites them. The knowledge of a theory requires not so much clear-cut general concepts as operational acquaintance. It is the object which calls for that handling by the imagination which creates familiarity and adherence. Even today it is hard to conceive that a mere programmatic will to a coherence should produce a structure of reality; to a researcher it is rather the "feel of the thing" which imposes a coherence upon the representation. So long as the scientist can believe that in the tightening web of his theory the "thing itself" is caught, whatever it may be, so long does he preserve the certainty that he is right, that he has captured the object of his quest. Its nature is ambiguous, like all of reality, but at least it is all there; it may elude him indefinitely but not escape him, and all the limitless reserves of rationality and irrationality that go with the real are still there for him to work on. It is still the presence of the old familiar mystery with which the world faces us, and which was projected, perhaps, by ourselves: strange, consistent, and insoluble; many and, at the same time, essentially one.

Some have said that this need for unity expresses the identity of the self; others, that it stands for economy of thought. Possibly, but this is interpretation, psychologically or sociologically tinged. The need for unity is a historical fact and, as such, unresolved. It is also a symbol of science, and its myth. Science is a finely defined and articulated system of symbols; but the ultimate symbol, that of unity, can have no referent. Rather, one might say it stands for the totality of the knowable and the unknowable. A confusing situation for the scientific mind, but one it cannot escape. For the conflict at the heart of rationalism is the source of its strength, as long as it lasts.

Once the faith is lost, something else has to be found.

Under the relentless pressure of social change, with the growing operationalism of physical theory and the metaphysical devastations attendant on Darwinism, the myth of unity could no longer hold. It had to be replaced by unification. But with that the status of science is changed and also that of the scientist. The mirror of nature that reason had endeavored to build up through the ages is shattered, and we look for the first time straight out into an unknown world.

Einstein (pour le décennal de sa mort)

NOUS SOMMES EN THÈME DE COSMOLOGIE, ET VOILÀ QUE LE GRAND héros de la cosmologie moderne nous est encore tout proche, et c'est Einstein. Il est merveilleux que dans la confusion de nos temps, il se trouve être déjà un personnage légendaire et exemplaire, dramatique au sens de Sophocle. Et certes, il y a eu dans sa vie deux phases dramatiques, le héros cloué à l'irrévocable. Sa première, tout le monde la connait, c'est le rôle décisif qu'il a joué dans la bombe atomique. Sans lui, Szilard n'aurait jamais obtenu l'accès à la Maison Blanche, Roosevelt n'aurait pas pris la grande décision. Pour une fois dans sa vie, ce doux penseur fut homme d'action décisive. Et c'est justement là qu'il connut son Waterloo, puisqu'il découvrit plus tard que les Allemands n'avaient jamais été à même d'apprêter une arme atomique comme il craignait. Mais au moment où il le sut, le Japon avait déjà été foudroyé.

L'autre situation dramatique dans la vie d'Einstein se joue sur le terrain de l'esprit, et elle fait sa grandeur comme savant. Envers et contre tout, il a crée une nouvelle conception de la science. Son premier mémoire de 1905 qui fonde la Relativité Restreinte est généralement regardé comme un développement du positivisme de Mach. Il n'en est rien, et il suffirait de noter que Mach, d'abord flatté par l'hommage fait à son nom, l'attaqua avec une rare brusquerie dès qu'il comprit de quoi il s'agissait. Bien sûr, Mach avait ébranlé la foi du jeune Einstein dans la mécanique comme base de toute pensée physique. Il l'avait mis sur le chemin de la critique des fondements, mais à ce point il ne s'agissait plus de s'en tenir au strict observable, ni à l'économie de pensée. Planck avait apporté de troublants problèmes sur la nature de la radiation, qui à leur tour faisaient craquer tout l'édifice de la physique. Le dix-neuvième siècle semblait se fermer sur une voie sans issue, la bonne méthode semblait impuissante. Dans un passage célèbre, Einstein lui-même nous raconte: « Je finis par désespérer de la possibilité de découvrir les véritables lois au moyen d'efforts constructifs fondés sur des faits. Et plus je tentais, plus croissait mon désespoir, et plus j'aboutissais à la conviction que seule, la découverte d'un principe formel universel pourrait nous conduire à des résultats assurés ».

A l'aide de Mach, on avait bien taillé; à présent il fallait recoudre. Il fallait faire des sacrifices. C'est ainsi que ce fut au début « une physique du désespoir ». Mais son beau désespoir alors le secourut.

M. Gerald Holton dans une étude pénétrante vient de retracer le cheminement de la pensée d'Einstein à partir de là, et il a montré le rôle qu'y a joué la profonde meditation de la pensée de Maxwell. Mais il a montré aussi que les expériences que nous appelons cruciales, telle que celle de Michelson et Morley, comptaient pour très peu dans la naissance de la

Relativité. Bien que grand expérimentaliste, Einstein sentit n'en avoir aucun besoin. La refonte des principes était ce qui lui donnait son assurance. Aussi trouvons-nous cette phrase révélatrice dans une lettre à Lanczos de 1938: « Parti de l'empirisme sceptique de Mach, je suis devenu un rationaliste croyant, en tant que seule la simplicité mathématique me parait offrir une source de vérité ».

C'est dire qu'Einstein s'est rallié à la foi pythagoricienne, et cela lui a coûté l'appui de ceux sur lesquels au début il comptait le plus. Mais la Relativité Généralisée couronne le rêve panmathématique, puisque à travers elle la matière elle-même (« l'expérience de la dureté » dirait le P. Teilhard) se dissout en propriétés de l'espace géometrique. Parménide a triomphé. Et il n'y a point de doute qu'Einstein a éprouvé une singulière joie esthétique en retrouvant au centre de sa physique le principe métaphysique entre tous, celui de Moindre Action.

Il y a peu de renversements aussi frappants dans la carrière d'un penseur. Cuirassé désormais d'une certitude abstraite, fondée sur l'épistémologie, le grand physicien ne se soucie pas le moins du monde des démentis expérimentaux de Miller qu'on vient de découvrir et qu'on annonce à grand fracas. Il ne se donne même pas la peine de répondre, il sourit. « Cela me ferait de la peine pour le Bon Dieu — dit-il — parce que la théorie est juste ». C'est quand même à cette occasion qu'indiquant plus tard les sources probables de l'erreur (et Shankland trouva qu'il en était bien ainsi), il eut cette boutade fameuse: « Voyons, le Bon Dieu est raffiné, mais il n'est pas méchant ». Le mot n'est plaisant qu'à demi, car il révèle de la part de ce pur agnostique une foi inébranlable dans ce que Descartes appelait la « véracité de Dieu ». Il revenait souvent sur la pensée de Galilée, l'inventeur de la première Relativité. La « céleste malice » du Grand Dialogue de 1630 le remplissait de joie, et il se plaisait à troubler le repos des Gens Bien avec ses ironies à l'emporte-pièce. « J'ai pensé — dit-il une fois à un journaliste — ce que je conseillerais à un jeune homme qui doit se choisir une carrière. Je lui dirais de se faire zingueur et non savant, parce qu'un type a droit à un métier respecté.» Ceci était dit au plus fort de l'affaire Oppenheimer, où il défendait jusqu'au bout l'honneur des savants contre l'arrogance des fonctionnaires.

Nous en venons à présent à la véritable crise de la pensée einsteinienne, là où déjà en pleine possession de sa vérité, le maître doit faire face à un monde pour de bon irréconciliable, celui de ses amis et de ses pairs, qui avaient partagé la grande aventure de sa vie. Lui qui avait au début été le véritable pionnier de la théorie des quanta, il se trouva à faire face à sa propre création. Là encore, il eut une belle boutade: « Je ne me résignerai jamais — dit-il — à penser que Dieu joue aux dés avec le monde ». Pourquoi pas ? aurait dit Héraclite, dans ces dés peut bien se cacher le Logos qui nous gouverne. C'est là que prirent forme les principes d'indétermination, d'exclusion, de complémentarité, qui ont bouleversé la physique. Bohr et Einstein, on les appelait des fois les Deux Dioscures, parce qu'ils allaient toujours de concert. Aucun nuage ne troubla jamais leur amitié, mais peu à peu leur accord vint à cesser. Dans la calme lumière de l'immortalité, ces deux grands esprits, comme dans l'Ecole d'Athènes de Raphael, s'affrontent pour toujours dans des poses consacrées.

La science, disait Einstein, ne peut renoncer à être le miroir de la vérité. Bien sûr, elle est notre création, mais justement pour cela, elle veut décrire correctement, et quand ce ne serait que par des abstractions toujours plus éloignées du sens commun, les situations physiques. Elle est, comme l'a dit Hilbert dans un mot célèbre, libre invention sur un fondement de faits scientifiques. Il n'est donc point justifiable de se retrancher derrière les faits, et de refuser de parler de choses non observables. Le monde que nous avons créé n'est pas fait uniquement de choses observables. « La formulation de lois universelles — écrivait-il — implique l'usage de tous les éléments conceptuels qu'il nous faut pour mettre sur pied une description complète.» Dire qu'un certain élément (mettons, la position d'une particule dont on a observé l'accélération) n'est absolument pas observable, cela équivaut à dire qu'il n'existe pas. Et cependant, pour notre esprit, il doit bien exister.

Pourquoi? répondait-on. Pourquoi ajouter des éléments abstraits dépourvus de signification expérimentale, pure vue de l'esprit, parce que nous voulons qu'il en soit ainsi, alors que la nature nous indique péremptoirement le contraire? Quelle que soit la manière dont nous découpons la réalité — insistait-on — il manquera toujours l'un ou l'autre élément dont nous exigeons la présence. Se moque-t-on de la nature? A force de nous représenter une réalité faite d'états stables qui se prêtent à l'analyse, nous avons refusé de penser le transitoire qui seul est vrai, qui seul est réellement observable, mais se présente comme conceptuellement incomplet. Il n'y a pas de réalité extérieure observable complète au sens requis, et ce n'est pas malin, car il y manquera toujours ce qui est fourni par l'intervention de l'observateur, qu'on ne peut tout de même pas éviter. Indéterminisme, complémentarité, idées en soi très belles et philosophiques, signifient au fond ceci, qu'il n'y a pas de réalité objective qui puisse se passer de la situation et de l'intervention de l'observateur. Mais alors, peut-on la dire objective? Assurément, disent les physiciens, sans trop se soucier de la note hégélienne qu'ils portent étourdiment dans le discours. C'est ainsi que l'on définit le mot « objectif », en ce monde sinon en d'autres. « Je n'accepte pas » — disait sévèrement Einstein, et son refus était celui du contemplatif et du métaphysicien dans l'esprit classique, s'il est vrai que la métaphysique est la contemplation d'un spectacle qui nous exclut. Ce mot de Valéry est revenu nous hanter. Que le spectacle qui nous exclut puisse être, à part nous, incomplet, qu'il ne puisse être conceptuellement complet « en soi », cela lui semblait impossible, c'était une négation de sa théodicée instinctive. Dans sa jeunesse, il nous l'a raconté, alors qu'il se promenait avec Michel Besso à travers les rues nocturnes de Zurich, ils tenaient de longs propos où on évitait toujours le « trop humain », *das Allzumenschliche*. Tel était bien son instinct. Le Miroir de la Vérité ne peut qu'exclure le visage de l'homme — à moins, disait-il, qu'il ne s'agisse de Dostojevski. Sa règle du jeu se résumait pour lui en une « véracité du cosmos ». Bien entendu, il le disait à sa manière : « Ce que je n'accepte pas dans de tels raisonnements, c'est l'attitude positiviste sur laquelle ils se fondent... Ce que l'on peut dire « l'être » est mentalement construit par nous, librement posé, au sens logique. Nous n'avons pas à exiger de nos constructions, qui représentent pour nous la réalité, de dériver des sens... Leur seule justification consiste à rendre intelligible, comme nous l'entendons, ce qui nous est donné par les sens ».

Voilà bien comment il se détournait du « trop humain », de la suffisance positiviste de ses contemporains, de la science comme économie de pensée, et autres théories du même acabit. Bernard Berenson disait une fois : à vingt ans, on a une philosophie ; plus tard, on en devient prisonnier. Le vieux sceptique oubliait qu'il y a des positions qui signifient quelque chose, même « plus tard ». Il peut fort bien se donner qu'à la fin, Einstein n'ait pas à capituler. Les travaux récents de Boehm et Schwinger parlent sans embarras de l'existence de « variables cachées ». Plus tard encore, juste avant sa mort, Norbert Wiener tenta de nouveau. Pour apporter de l'ordre à la physique quantique, disait-il, il faut des variables cachées. Et cependant, on ne saurait imputer aucun préjugé métaphysique à ce grand nominaliste dans sa recherche de l'être intelligible. Mais il dut se rendre compte avec chagrin que la théorie avec laquelle il évoquait ces variables cachées les rendait du même coup strictement invérifiables. On en est là. Mais qui sait...

Quand on se trouve à avoir raison, c'est en général indirectement et d'une manière inattendue. Mais quoi qu'il en soit, cela reste le Roncevaux du vieux maître. La valeur tragique est dans le renversement des positions. Dans sa dernière bataille d'arrière-garde, il se trouva à défendre les mêmes positions que d'autres avaient tenu naguère contre lui dans sa jeunesse. Lui qui avait si audacieusement avancé en flèche sur la voie positiviste contre les tenants d'un espace et d'un temps absolus, lui le génial élève de Mach, déplorait à présent la médiocrité inhérente dans le positivisme et acceptait de défendre des positions dépassées. C'est qu'il considérait ses conquêtes passées non pas comme oeuvre de méthode (il n'osait pas le dire trop clairement) mais comme une transmutation, comme une oeuvre d'art, au sens ou l'on peut entendre le *Timée*. Après avoir géometrisé le réel, il voulait à tout prix arriver à l'unification des champs gravitationnels et électromagnétiques. Ce qui pour l'autres était mythe, comme dirait Platon, pour lui était *logos*. Il ne voulait pas voir la grande entreprise ruinée par la froide lame de l'objectivité qui avance toujours.

Après avoir dénoncé la « fausse métaphysique du probabilisme » il a dû bien se rendre compte, à un certain moment, d'avoir attaqué à vide, puisqu'en vérité, les autres n'en avaient aucune, et c'était bien ce vide qui avait induit Einstein à confesser la sienne. Mais il était tard. Avait-il lutté en vain ? Ce qu'il y a d'incompréhensible, avait-il dit une fois, c'est que l'univers puisse être compréhensible. Il avait toujours parié pour la véracité de son Dieu mathématique, pour « raffiné » qu'il pût être. Mais voilà qu'au dernier moment, la vérité se dérobait à son emprise, disparaissait sous un voile.

Seul désormais, aux prises avec la recherche actuelle, le moment doit être venu dans son grand âge où il sut regarder les choses de haut, et se réconcilier avec lui-même. C'est ainsi, comme parmi les chênes antiques du bois sacré de Colone, que se conclut une existence exemplaire.

PERMETTEZ-MOI D'ABORDER MON SUJET PAR L'ENTRÉE PRINCIPALE, le portail monumental que nous offre la Grèce à ses débuts.

Devant nous se dressera la sévère et sobre architecture des paroles d'Anaximandre vers 600 av. J-C. Sobre, elle l'est pour sûr, car nous n'avons de lui que trois ou quatre phrases:

> Ce dont naissent toutes choses est aussi la source de leur fin, *ainsi qu'il est juste*, car elles doivent se faire amende et expiation réciproque pour leur injustice mutuelle dans l'ordre des temps.

Toutes choses naissent et périssent en un rythme universel, en une loi de périodicité — voilà le premier terme de l'équation. Le second terme — et il est dit *ainsi qu'il est juste* — est le rappel de la justice immanente, l'invocation à l'ordre souverain qu'est l'Ordre du Temps. Voilà bien le début de la physique, avec ses forces en contraste, l'équilibre dynamique, qui devient tourbillon et amorce l'évolution de la vie, ainsi qu'il en est dit explicitement — idée qu'Aristote oublia depuis et qui devait renaître seulement avec Léonard de Vinci.

La substance de ce tourbillon, modèle des nébuleuses spirales, c'est *l'Apeiron*, l'Illimité. Et il est dit aussi que cette substance est le Divin et qu'elle est *l'Arché* de toutes choses — mot riche de sens s'il en fut, puisqu'il signifie primauté, pouvoir suprême, principe, commencement. Et il est dit:

> L'Illimité comprend le tout et gouverne toutes choses.

Le mot est *kybernai*, dirige, pilote. Cette gouverne est conçue non comme volontaire, mais comme action auto-régulatrice — comme cela devrait se passer dans une société bien conçue — cependant, idée réellement physique dans sa conception, bien qu'Anaximandre n'eut pas les mots pour cela; et les mots c'est contrôle automatique, cybernétique. Le terme, après tout, était déjà là.

Et voilà que d'un coup, il en sort un vrai principe physique. Pourquoi la terre ne tombe-t-elle pas? Parce qu'elle est en position symétrique par rapport à ce qui l'entoure. Il n'y a pas de *raison suffisante* pour qu'elle tombe.

C'est bien dans sa première forme le principe de *raison suffisante* que M. Oppenheimer citait à propos d'Einstein. Etrange et merveilleux départ au sein d'un monde entièrement vitaliste. Sous cet aspect particulier, négatif, c'est ce principe qui décroche la pensée des bonnes raisons à notre image et à notre petite mesure, du court-circuit sur nos fins à nous, qui la lance dans l'immense aventure de la science sans limites. Chance unique, coup de dés qui fait que ces hommes ne rêvent pas d'organisme, mais expriment leur premier modèle en termes de vent et de vapeur, de cribles et de tourbillons, empruntés à leur technologie — car c'est ce modèle qui les guide vers de nouvelles questions plus aigues, vers de nouveaux horizons — et c'est l'acuité qui a nom de *Sophia*.

Et c'est de là que naît le *rationalisme scientifique*, passion qui insiste que ce qu'on pense sans contradiction doit pouvoir être vrai, même s'il est étrange et nouveau.

C'est sur ce fondement que se dresse cette autre nouveauté éblouissante, la mathématique pythagoricienne. Cela va avec la création de l'idéal de culture que les Grecs appelaient *mousiké*, ce qui implique une union de logos, mélodie et mouvement. Nous sommes donc déjà au large de la physique toute nue, la physique matérialiste — et les vraies puissances de la nature, on les définit comme harmonie et proportion.

Le nombre est en marche, force autonome, qui n'est pas un élément comme l'air et l'eau, mais un vrai *principe* vivant de sa vie propre, et ce n'est que juste, parce qu'il représente les lois de la pensée. C'est ainsi que la physique devint elle-même *mousiké*, et l'astronomie redevint l'Art Royal qu'elle avait toujours été. Voilà bien les grands thèmes établis par la géométrie, formes pures et périodicité, qui amenèrent déjà en 270 av. J-C. Aristarque à proposer le système copernicien.

Notre cosmos est né, que Kepler chantera 2000 ans plus tard en langage de prophète :

> Voilà que la lumière m'est apparue, le soleil de la vérité — rien ne peut plus me retenir. Les dés sont jetés, j'écris pour la postérité. Le Seigneur a attendu six mille ans pour qu'on comprenne ses œuvres, je peux bien attendre aussi.

C'est son hymne à l'harmonie des sphères. Mais bientôt ciel et terre, et leur musique, seront « désaccordés », la mécanique naîtra, et Descartes démolira le cosmos. Ce sera le règne newtonien, l'univers devenu un jouet mécanique bien monté et Dieu le despote qui paraît s'amuser à ces automates.

Cela se compliquera, bien plus tard, c'est à M. Holton de nous le dire, mais c'est là que nous a mené la pensée spatiale, et elle s'affirmera philosophiquement dans la géométrisation totale d'Einstein.

Revenons donc vers les origines. Des quatre grandes phrases d'Anaximandre, deux regardent en avant, prédisent la cosmologie moderne, fondée sur l'espace, les deux autres reprennent l'idée traditionnelle que règne suprême l'Ordre du Temps. Car la quatrième (qui nous vient de Cicéron) dit que selon Anaximandre, « les dieux ont origine à de vastes intervalles à l'Orient et à l'Occident et qu'ils sont les mondes innombrables ».

Ces mots étranges, auxquels Cicéron disait n'entendre goutte, n'ont de sens que par rapport à une cosmologie presque oubliée, qui nous vient de la nuit des temps, dont il nous est resté presque uniquement des mythes et des fables, reste d'un langage technique avant l'écriture, et que nous sommes en train de reconstruire péniblement. Je vais donc revenir en arrière, chercher ce qui nous est resté des origines.

Vous voulez que je vous montre la chose à l'état brut ? Voilà un conte des Peaux-Rouges de la côte canadienne du Pacifique, un parmi des milliers, pris presque au hasard, remarqué par personne. Elle nous vient des Satlo'lq, dans le sud-est de Vancouver Island :

Il y avait une fois un homme dont la fille avait un arc et une flèche prodigieux, mais elle était paresseuse et ne faisait que dormir. Le père se fâcha et dit : « Au lieu de dormir, prends ton arc et tâche de tirer au centre de l'ombilic de l'Océan, pour qu'on aie du feu ». Or l'ombilic de l'Océan était un grand entonnoir tourbillonnant où flottaient les morceaux de bois qui servent à faire le feu. Car en ce temps-là, on n'avait pas encore de feu.

La fille prit son arc, tira, fit mouche, et les baguettes de bois bondirent sur la rive. Le vieux en fut content, il alluma un beau feu. Mais ensuite, comme il voulait le garder pour lui, il se fit une maison dont la porte se fermait de haut en bas, comme une machoire, et elle tuait ceux qui tentaient d'entrer.

Mais voilà qu'on sut que le vieux avait du feu, et le Cerf décida de voler ce feu pour les gens. Il se fourra des brins de bois résineux dans les cheveux, ensuite il lia ensemble un couple de catamarans, se fit un pont de planches, et chanta et dansa là-dessus alors qu'il se dirigeait vers la maison du vieux. Il chantait : « Ho, je vais attraper le feu ». La fille du vieux dit : « Fais-le entrer, il chante si bien ». Mais la maison se ferma. Guidé par son chant, le Cerf arriva devant la porte juste au moment où elle rouvrait, bondit dedans sans dommage. Il s'assit à côté du feu, sans cesser de chanter. Il se pencha sur le feu, comme s'il voulait se sècher, et les brindilles de bois prirent feu. Il bondit dehors, et c'est comme ça qu'il apporta le feu aux hommes.

Voilà l'histoire de Prométhée en Satlo'lq.

Mais c'est bien plus que cela. Car le Cerf n'est pas uniment notre Prométhée héroïque, celui d'Eschyle et de Shelley pour nous entendre, il est Kronos, Saturne, le plus grand des dieux planétaires, le Demiurge du Cosmos, Deus Faber. Dans la tradition hindoue, Kronos, sous le nom de Yama, a une tête de cerf, et cette tête animale s'est répandue à travers le monde archaïque. A présent, si vous allez regarder — mais on ne regarde pas — dans les hymnes orphiques, vous trouverez au n. 13 de la vieille édition Herrmann un hymne à Kronos : « O toi, dévorateur tout puissant, toujours renaissant, Kronos, grand Aiōn, vénérable Prométhée... » En grec, *Semnē Prometheū*. Ce n'est pas moi qui le leur ai fait dire.

Et le scholiaste de Sophocle, citant Polémon et Lysimachide, érudits perdus pour nous, dit que dans les jardins de l'Académie, il y avait un autel dédié à Prométhée, « premier et plus ancien » détenteur du sceptre, et à Héphaïstos deuxième et plus jeune. Or nous autres du métier nous le savons bien qu'Héphaïstos apparait comme deuxième aspect de Saturne — plus spécifiquement Demiurge, Deus Faber. Mais c'est au sombre Kronos qui sait tout, « qui a les plans », que revient la prescience prométhéenne. Nous sommes dans les sous-sols de l'antiquité grecque, et par un étrange cheminement souterrain ce sont des sauvages de la côte du Pacifique qui ont reporté notre attention sur certains textes grecs qui mettent le mythe classique en une nouvelle lumière.

Quant à l'Omphalos, l'ombilic, il y a des volumes d'études là-dessus. C'est l'île de Calypso, mais c'est aussi le Charybde de l'Odyssée, l'entonnoir du Maelstroem de la tradition indo-européenne, le *gurges mirabilis* qui transperce le globe et se termine au Séjour des Bienheureux, lequel, bien entendu, est au ciel austral, à Eridu, au Navire Argo, là où règne Kronos endormi, pour les Hindous Yama Agastya, pour les Egyptiens Osiris juge des Morts, pour les Babyloniens Ea-Enki, pour les Mexicains Quetzalcouatl — et tant d'autres. C'est là que se perdit Ulysse si nous en croyons Dante, c'est là que Gilgamesh se trouva à la « jonction des Fleuves » célestes, en quête de l'immortalité.

Pourquoi ces bouts de bois dans le tourbillon ? C'est ici de *l'autre* tourbillon qu'il s'agit, le cosmique, la Précession des Equinoxes qui était déjà connue, celle qui en 26.000 ans apporte l'Ordre du Temps. C'est à celle-là que se rapporte la figure originaire de Prométhée, Pramantha aux Indes, et les feux, non de la Saint-Jean, mais du passage du soleil équinoctial d'un signe zodiacal au prochain, tous les 2.400 ans environ : la fin d'un « monde » ou d'une ère, le début d'une autre. Permettez-moi de vous rappeler un mot de chez nous, vous le trouverez dans Agrippa d'Aubigné, et c'est bien de la fin de *ce* monde-ci qu'il s'agit :

> . . . quand les esprits bienheureux
> Dans la Voie de Laict auront fait nouveaux feux . . .

C'est à ce moment-là où, au Mexique, Tezcatlipoca allume un nouveau feu en vrillant ses bâtonnets dans le signe des Gémeaux — « et à partir de ce moment il s'appela Mizcouatl ».

Les choses se compliquent tout de suite (je vous demande un peu de patience) car le feu originaire de Mizcouatl était censé avoir eu lieu au Pôle, et il n'est pas clair pourquoi par la même occasion ce feu s'allumait dans les Gémeaux, chose attestée par plusieurs cérémonies ; mais on peut voir ici une espèce d'ambivalence, ou de bi-location du feu sacré qui consacre le colure équinoctial de ce fameux an Zéro, à partir duquel on comptait le temps, en Mésopotamie et en Chine aussi bien qu'au Mexique : le moment solennel où le soleil de l'équinoxe du printemps s'était placé dans le signe des Gémeaux, et donc aussi sur la voie Lactée, et la grande arche galactique, dressée sur l'horizon, s'était trouvée à faire figure à peu près de grand cercle ou colure équinoctial. Ceci marque bien le schéma géométrique fondamental de cette cosmogonie, tel qu'on le retrouve plus d'une fois.

Même l'élément proto-pythagoricien ne manque pas. Le rythme du Cerf chantant et dansant devient, dans un autre conte du Nord-Ouest (British Columbia, Lower Fraser River) la prouesse du petit-fils du Pivert lequel, sur le point de tirer de l'arc, entonne un chant : et dès qu'il eut trouvé le ton juste, les flèches qui partaient se fichèrent l'une dans l'autre bout à bout jusqu'à former un pont entre terre et ciel. Véritable thème orphique souvent repris, mais aussi, comme l'a remarqué Sir James Frazer lui-même, dernier souvenir de l'escalade de l'Olympe dans la Gigantomachie.

C'est à quoi on aboutit avec des histoires apparemment sans tête ni queue.

Tout de même, quelle pagaye d'idées, direz-vous. J'entends bien, n'oubliez pas que toute cette transmission était exposée aux hasards de la voieorale, à l'oubli, à l'incompréhension. Mais le désordre même ne fait qu'accentuer l'authenticité des éléments composants, l'incroyable obstination de certaines images à survivre et à se survivre, tel un dépôt sacré d'âges perdus.

Pour continuer, l'arc et la flèche se réaffirment comme images capitales, autres clés de voute de la théorie, car ils sont eux aussi au ciel ; c'est l'arc de Marduk, le Jupiter babylonien, l'arc chanté par le Poème du commencement, avec lequel il conquiert le pouvoir — et établit l'ordre universel. Mais il se trouve que c'est aussi l'arc des empereurs chinois à leur avènement. Avec cet arc, il faut dans chaque cas « atteindre » Sirius, celui, dit le grand rituel babylonien de l'Akitu, « qui mesure les profondeurs de la mer ». Il y a eu encore bien des études là-dessus. Mais les Schlegel, les Guérin, les Gundel, les grands érudits qui ont éclairci cette uranographie par leurs labeurs prodigieux, se sont souvent cantonnés chacun dans sa province, que ce fut la Mésopotamie, l'Inde, l'Egypte ou la Chine, et ont réclamé instinctivement pour leurs protégés le privilège de la découverte, laissant à d'autres le soin de jeter un pont entre des civilisations si différentes. Il y a eu aussi des astronomes illustres, qu'on ne lit pas, comme Biot et Henseling, dont l'effort comparatif s'est perdu dans le silence.

C'est cependant par des recoupements multiples qu'on a pu résoudre ces paroles énigmatiques. L'étoile de Sirius a été un objet de fascination sous bien des latitudes, et souvent l'on voit réapparaître des allusions obscures à ses liens avec la mer — jusque dans Aristote et Pline. Sirius semble avoir été une espèce de pivot pour plusieurs directions qui s'entrecroisaient, partant de différentes régions du ciel. L'alignement principal était celui qui plaçait Sirius sur la ligne joignant les Pôles, qui aboutissait au sud à Canopos, autre grande étoile fascinatrice, siège de Yama Agastya pour les Hindous, cité mythique d'Eridu, nous l'avons vu, pour les Sumériens, Suhayl-la-Lourde pour les Arabes, en tant qu'elle marquait le fond de la « mer céleste » de l'hémisphere austral. Les autres alignements joignaient Sirius aux « quatre coins du ciel », équinoxes et solstices, lesquels se déplaçaient insensiblement au cours des siècles de la Précession, et la ligne du Pôle Nord passait sur l'une après l'autre des étoiles de l'Ourse comme une aiguille sur un immense cadran.

Il apparait donc que ces mesures angulaires étaient solennellement et minutieusement vérifiées lors des grandes occasions. On concevait que par Sirius, la terre était validement « ancrée aux Profondeurs de l'Abîme » et « accrochée » au ciel septentrional; on vérifiait par lui la bonne marche de l'Univers.

Tel était, pour ce que nous pouvons deviner, le rôle mythique et cérémonial de l'Arc des dieux.

La seule originalité des Peaux-Rouges, dirait-on, c'est d'avoir mis l'arc aux mains d'une femme. Et paresseuse par-dessus le marché. Est-ce là un lointain souvenir d'Ishtar l'enjôleuse? J'aime mieux penser que le conteur indien a eu son moment de fantaisie. Il y en a si peu, de si modestes, dans cette poétique rigidement traditionnelle...

Car, pour reprendre, quant à cette étrange porte qui se ferme comme un couperet, elle est tout un avec les non moins étranges *Plangtai* d'Homère, avec les Symplégades des Argonautes, les rochers-qui-s'entrechoquent, mais encore plus loin en arrière, dans la figuration originaire, verticale, elle est l'Ecliptique qui se lève et s'abaisse sur l'horizon au cours de l'année, objet d'innombrables figurations parallèles qui s'échelonnent sur tous les continents, au moins depuis le cinquième millénaire. Alors que les sauvages, bien entendu, — on ne se fait pas faute de nous le rappeler — n'avaient aucune idée de l'astronomie. C'est bien vrai qu'ils ne l'ont plus. Et que ceux qui l'avaient n'étaient point des sauvages. Pas plus que ceux qui ont bâti Stonehenge, eux que les archéologues s'obstinaient jusqu'à l'an passé à définir comme des « howling barbarians » — jusqu'au moment où sont intervenus les ordinateurs dernier modèle de Gerald Hawkins, jeune astronome qui a su reconnaître ses anciens collègues à leurs œuvres. Sir Norman Lockyer avait déjà été lestement enterré et oublié, car les philologues ont peu de sympathie pour les astronomes, mais le voilà remis à l'honneur à présent.

Je vous ai donc offert toute une encyclopédie de thèmes en dix lignes. Je vous ai donné une de ces fleurs japonaises, ces graines de papier tassé qu'on jette dans l'eau et qui s'ouvrent en grands dessins.

La première ouverture de la fleur japonaise, on peut la trouver dans *l'Alexandra* de Lycophron, poème-grimoire du mythe archaïque; l'ouverture plus ample dans la *Bibliothèque* d'Appolodore, réservoir des mythes classiques, et aussi dans les *Fastes* d'Ovide, dans les commentaires de Proclus et de Porphyre, l'épanouissement plein ou presque dans les *Dionysiaka* de

Nonnos le Panopolite, ou dans le *Tétrabible* de Ptolémée, les vrais manuels de la mythologie archaïque.

Nous le savons bien, le fouilleur infatigable de l'antiquité pré-classique, le novateur, ce fut Sir James Frazer, mais alors qu'il eut son grand jardin aménagé, avec ses parterres de mythes, il n'y vit que du feu, je veux dire des cultes de la végétation. Il y avait bien, dans un coin, les restes d'une hutte enterrée, c'est là qu'étaient les outils et les plans, Sir James n'y fit pas attention. Car on était évolutionniste en plein et il ne pouvait donc s'agir que d'agriculture ou de magie.

Je ne veux pas diminuer les mérites de Cook, de Jane Harrison et de toute l'école, mais si on avait regardé avec moins d'idées préconçues on aurait trouvé, en plus du cycle annuel qui se traduisait couramment en végétation, d'autres cycles de 2, 4, 8, 12, 30, 52, même 60 années, qui indiquaient des périodes bien autres, et qui ne pouvaient être que planétaires. Mais voilà, on oublie beaucoup de choses dans l'élan d'une idée neuve, et le problème d'accommoder les restes ne vient que plus tard.

Je vous ai proposé un exemple de comment une langue mythique universelle venant d'avant l'écriture se trouve recouvrir une cosmologie perdue, universelle aussi, aussi universelle que la nôtre, et ce n'est pas le moindre de ces mystères que le cheminement par diffusion d'une pensée à partir de la Mésopotamie proto-historique — car c'est là que se créerent, dirait-on, les cultes planétaires qu'Aristote attribue aux *panpalaioi* les « très-anciens » et aussi le proto-pythagorisme.

Ce qui se diffusa évidemment ce ne sont pas des idées toutes faites, ce sont des schémas : c'est l'Ecliptique et ses constellations, les stations des astres, les zones, certains mythes-clefs, cette étrange urano-géographie où s'imbriquent ciel et terre, sous la domination des seigneurs planétaires au cours inexorable.

Mais c'est aussi le lien entre l'harmonie et les astres, l'harmonie et les unités de mesure, les principes souverains d'exactitude qui s'appellent *maat* en Egypte, *ṛta* ou « rite » aux Indes. « Entre la musique des pipeaux rituels et le calendrier — dit un principe chinois — l'ajustement est si exact qu'on n'y peut guère faire passer un cheveu. » Et ce fut ainsi l'Alchimie ajustée à l'Astrologie, ensuite l'astro-médecine, les plantes, les métaux, les alphabets, les jeux savants comme les échecs, les carrés magiques comme celui qui subsiste dans la *Mélancolie* de Durer, le microcosme ajusté au macrocosme. Le tout monté non comme un système logique, mais comme une fugue en musique, ainsi qu'il convient pour un véritable organisme fermé sur soi-même : monde non seulement déterministe mais surdéterminé — sur différents niveaux qui conspirent entre eux ; sursaturé de détermination, où règne la Nécessité totale qui reste, en même temps, liberté ; comme chez le Dieu de Spinoza. « Et ils disent, remarque Aristote le Moderne sans trop de bienveillance (« ils » c'est les Pythagoriciens) que l'intervalle sur les lettres de alpha à omega est le même que celui sur les notes de *l'aulos* de la plus basse à la plus haute, et que le nombre en est égal au choeur entier du ciel.» C'est ainsi que l'idée était ancrée jusque dans les temps classiques, grâce à la ferveur pythagoricienne. Il nous est resté le nombre et le rythme, l'incidence du moment unique, du temps juste, le *kairos* disaient les Grecs, qui décide entre être et n'être pas: car il y eut un temps où le juste c'était avant tout la justesse, et le péché c'était l'imprécision.

Nous autres pensons depuis Descartes en termes d'espace simple, qu'on peut dominer, où s'inscrit notre action. L'homme archaïque pensait en termes de temps, auquel tout est soumis. Et en vérité, ce qu'on persiste à considérer comme des « distances » dans son système, ce sont des mesures angulaires sujettes au temps. L'ordre spatial tel que nous l'entendons ne joue pas sinon comme entités déjà modulées: intervalles sur la corde vibrante, sphères, triangles, carrés magiques, polyèdres. Encore pour Platon, l'espace pur, ce que nous dirions l'espace isotrope newtonien, reste ce qu'il y a de plus proche au non-être. Parménide lui-même ne saurait donner un être à son Etre sinon en lui assignant une limite en forme de sphère. « Le Souverain, disait-on en Chine, règne sur l'espace parce qu'il est le maître du temps.»

C'est ainsi que l'humanité a pensé, durant des siècles aussi longs que ceux qui nous séparent de la Grande Pyramide. Pensée totalisante, si nous pouvons nous servir du terme crée par Lévi-Strauss. L'Ordre du Temps, qui était l'ordre véritable du Cosmos, portait avec lui le sort de la vie et des âmes. Il apportait non seulement une science, mais une eschatologie à ces générations sans nombre du lointain passé. Si nous tentons à présent de le retrouver, c'est aussi parce que nous aimerions que des civilisations désormais oubliées, enfouies, reprennent leur figure, que des continents entiers qu'on avait classés comme dépourvus d'histoire et qui se représentent à présent sur la scène du monde, armés de nouvelles revendications, reprennent le rôle qui leur sied dans le passé de notre race.

Nous nous sommes dit, comme Cocteau: « puisque ces mystères nous dépassent, tâchons de nous en faire l'organisateur ». Nous avons un matériel saisissant, encore à peine déchiffrable, mais notre génération a apporté des forces nouvelles, des noms comme Hartner, van der Waerden, von Dechend, Needham, Werner, Marius Schneider, forces provenant de tous les points de l'horizon intellectuel.

Il y faudrait à présent une convergence de pensées, de disciplines, de méthodes et aussi d'entendement esthétique pour débrouiller cet Art de la Fugue, pour comprendre, comme disait déjà d'Alembert, ces pères à qui nous devons tout et dont nous ne savons rien.

De Bruno à Leibniz

QU'IL ME SOIT PERMIS, POUR ÉTABLIR MES REPÈRES, DE FAIRE ÉTAT d'un texte fort connu d'ailleurs :

« Supposons qu'on fasse prendre successivement toutes les formes possibles à un lingot d'or, et qu'on ne cesse de remplacer une forme par une autre... on ne pourrait pas dire, comme si cette forme avait une existence réelle, que c'est telle ou telle figure... L'être qui contient tous les corps en lui-même est comme ce lingot d'or. Il faut toujours le désigner par le même nom, car il ne change jamais de nature. »

Ce passage, ainsi tiré de son contexte, a l'air d'une paraphrase cartésienne où le « morceau de cire » serait remplacé par du métal... Il n'en est rien, vous l'avez déjà reconnu, il vient du *Timée*, et il s'agit de Dieu. On est tenté de penser que le Dieu de Platon et la matière de Descartes se ressemblent singulièrement par un côté du moins. Ils sont tous deux, nous assurent leurs auteurs, objets de l'intellect et non des sens : ils sont ce qu'on a « découvert », le substrat intelligible, ne se prêtant à aucune opération qui puisse l'altérer ; ce substrat même que l'esprit scientifique n'a cessé de postuler, depuis le temps de Parménide. Mais l'un est transcendant, l'autre ne l'est pas. C'est au point d'inversion entre les deux que se situe à mon avis la pensée de Giordano Bruno.

On nous dit que Bruno s'évada d'abord de l'aristotélisme vers l'épicurisme, mais c'est un accident de sa carrière, une manifestation de son esprit rebelle plutôt que de sa pensée. En vérité, il charriait avec lui tout ce qu'il ramassait dans son cours, comme un fleuve impétueux, mais sa nature reste jusqu'au bout celle du néoplatonicien : c'est de là que lui viennent ses intuitions et aussi ses fureurs sacrées, si peu plotiniennes cependant : « C'est l'Un — dira-t-il dans un passage célèbre — qui commande mon amour : ce par quoi je suis riche dans la pauvreté, heureux dans le malheur, consolé dans la solitude... »

On admettra que ce ne sont pas là des sentiments épicuriens chez un homme dont on a voulu faire un matérialiste et un atomiste parce qu'il adopte les atomes. Épicure, c'est pour lui avant tout la *vivida vis animi*, c'est l'esprit qui a brisé les murailles où le monde était enfermé, les *flammantia moenia mundi*, et qui s'élance au-delà, *immensum peragrans mente animoque*. C'est Lucrèce qui l'attire, ce n'est pas la froide logique épicurienne, celle dont sait se servir Lorenzo Valla.

Mais tout cela aurait pu rester à l'état d'enthousiasme et de rêve, comme chez tant d'autres platoniciens, Pic de la Mirandole notamment, auquel Bruno ressemble par plus d'un côté, esprit lui aussi aventureux, indiscipliné, courageux, encombré de mémoire et de doctrines, dont l'élan finit par se désorganiser et sombrer dans l'impitoyable piété savonarolienne. C'est là ce qui serait peut-être arrivé à Bruno, s'il n'y avait pas eu, entre les deux, Copernic. Car c'est lui qui avait brisé une fois pour toutes, non seulement grâce à l'*animus* de Lucrèce, mais par don de géométrie, ces « murailles enflammées » qui pour l'imagination malgré tout chrétienne de Bruno n'étaient pas de feu uranien, mais bien plutôt celles de la Cité de Dis telle que la vit Dante, rougies par le feu éternel, enceinte de perdition.

Copernic fait fonction de charge explosive: c'est grâce à lui que Bruno peut passer au-delà, charriant avec lui tout un ensemble d'images et d'éléments stoïciens, épicuriens, voire aristotéliciens, la physique et les lieux communs du temps. Mais dans cet univers désormais ouvert, en état d'« explication », il retrouve celui qui l'avait prophétisé, le Cardinal de Cuse, esprit direct, platonicien de la grande espèce, et c'est cet esprit qui lui fournira les mesures de l'univers nouveau.

Esprit platonicien, avons-nous dit, mais aussi et surtout esprit pythagoricien (Nicolas de Cuse ne s'en cache pas), et c'est là que Bruno découvrira les « vérités de Salomon et de Pythagore », qu'il avait jusqu'alors cherchées confusément, « ces racines perdues, comme il dit, qui vont faire surgir à présent des rejetons vivaces, cette vérité qu'on avait obscurcie, mais qui monte désormais à l'horizon et qui va devenir lumière méridienne ». La pensée de Bruno est donc, quoi qu'on en dise, une philosophie scientifique, en tant qu'elle s'étage sur les découvertes réelles de son temps, découvertes qu'elle a su percevoir alors que la plupart des savants, des rationalistes et des hommes de bon sens, lui étaient restés fermés.

Bruno n'était pas un esprit solidement systématique, il ne comprenait guère les mathématiques dont il tentait de se servir, il prenait pour une géométrie nouvelle les élucubrations paraphréniques de Fabrizio Mordente et s'engageait à leur défense; on en a conclu que c'était au fond un pauvre homme, un hanneton de la pensée, un verbeux farfelu qui tentait de se donner une importance que les savants lui refusaient en annonçant à grand éclat la transmogrification du Tout en soi-même. C'est peut-être une réaction inévitable au personnage qu'avaient mis en pied les romantiques allemands, sage universel et voyant impassible, sinon au libertaire et au pontife de l'anticléricalisme qu'avaient inventé les libres penseurs, voire, au « premier martyr de la démocratie » — un titre qui lui sied aussi mal que possible. Mais c'est aller un peu loin dans l'autre sens que de faire de lui, comme l'a esquissé Olschki, une espèce de Victor Hugo moins le don de la poésie.

Il ne comprend pas les mathématiques, soit, mais le faute en est à sa formation de séminaire. Il n'est que de voir la pensée de ses contemporains, les censeurs de Galilée, autorités attitrées dont on tenait à dire qu'ils étaient « versés dans les mathématiques », de lire les sottises à peine croyables qui s'étalent dans les opinions écrites de ces graves consultants de la Curie. Il n'y avait que les mathématiciens jésuites dont on pût dire qu'ils y entendaient quelque chose (avec quels résultats d'ailleurs...) et quelques Pères çà et là dont on avait fait des ingénieurs, quelques esprits « de la bonne coupe » comme les appelle le Père Castelli, pour se sauver de cette nullité universelle. Bruno n'était pas de ceux-là, il était un esprit avant tout verbal, peu enclin à la sobriété mathématique, et de plus, il faut bien le dire, il était napolitain, au sens ultime et caricatural du mot, ce qui le place au-delà de l'horizon sud de Marseille. Et il était isolé.

Academico di nulla academia, detto il fastidito — c'est ainsi qu'il se présente lui-même, avec son caractère ombrageux, sa sensibilité à vif, insouffrant et insouffrable tour à tour. On ne sait jamais au juste quand il est sérieux, et quand il passe au « canular » gigantesque, dans sa polémique perpétuelle avec les pouvoirs établis. Mais à la fin, on sait à quoi s'en tenir, car il y a l'épreuve du feu que fort peu de philosophes ont affronté — et très peu d'historiens intellectuels aussi. Ce sont les flammes du bûcher qui font le départ entre ce que Bruno a pensé et ce qu'on a pensé de lui.

J'ai dit: ce qu'il a pensé; je devrais ajouter, ce qu'il a prophétisé, car la fable d'Actéon dont il fait le symbole de l'expérience philosophique (symbole intellectuellement pas très clair, nous dit Cassirer, et qu'on serait assurément tenté de mettre dans le tas de toute son imagerie maniériste) s'éclaire singulièrement à la lueur du feu de Campo dei Fiori.

Si donc il est juste de prendre au sérieux cette pensée, qu'est-ce que la *substance* telle que l'entend Bruno ? Matière, évidemment. Dans cet univers réellement physique de l'immanence, la substance est étendue infinie, sujet des dimensions et de la quantité, ingénérable et incorruptible, et de plus, atomique. Ce n'est pourtant pas la matière démocritienne, puisqu'elle est en même temps la forme, l'acte substantiel, la puissance active et la passive, l'Ame du Monde enfin. Elle est donc aussi la matière stoïcienne, et toutes sortes de choses encore. Mais lorsqu'on se trouve en face d'une terminologie aussi manifestement syncrétiste, il me semble juste de réexaminer le sens des termes, et d'en chercher la signification réelle. J'ai tenté de montrer une fois, à propos de Léonard, combien était captieuse l'identification que fait Duhem de son langage avec celui de Nicolas de Cuse; car il est bien vrai que les deux disent parfois ce qui semble être la même chose dans les mêmes termes, mais Nicolas identifie la force avec un élément spirituel, alors que Léonard, lorsqu'il parle (comme tout le monde d'ailleurs) d'un élément spirituel, entend réellement une force physique, une énergie.

Dans le cas de la matière brunienne, la confusion des termes était inévitable, puisque c'est à cette substance qu'incombe le difficile honneur d'être le Tout hors duquel il n'y a Rien. Et dire d'autre part: « rien que les atomes et le vide », est d'un réductionisme si extrême et dépouillé que seuls peuvent s'y complaire les gens qui avant tout veulent en finir avec les dieux. Leibniz nous dira que dans sa jeunesse, lui aussi avait penché pour les atomes et qu'il avait compris ensuite qu'il fallait autre chose. Pour Bruno, l'Un, qui est le Tout, est suprêmement vivant, et comme il refuse le feu subtil des stoïciens, porteur de l'esprit, cette vie doit être au tréfonds de la substance même qui constitue l'univers (remarquons qu'une idée semblable a tenté certains grands esprits scientifiques de notre temps, tels que C. S. Peirce et Schrödinger, alors qu'elle n'a aucun intérêt pour les philosophes) et donc qu'elle se trouve jusque dans la particule ultime. Ceci n'est pas fait pour faciliter les choses, ni pour éclaircir les termes. Mais si on cherche l'idée essentielle que s'est formée Bruno, on peut la trouver dans certaines de ses images. La substance, dit-il, n'a pas de détermination individuelle, non parce qu'elle est privée de détermination comme l'abîme est privé du jour, ou la glace de chaleur, mais comme la femme enceinte est encore privée de sa progéniture, parce qu'elle la recèle en elle-même. Il serait tentant de tirer de là le sens des *Mütter* dans le *Faust*, concept que Gœthe veut envelopper de mystère, mais ce serait se détacher de la pensée de Bruno, qui se tient proche de la réalité du fait vital.

La substance brunienne n'est pas un *Geist* déguisé. Elle est une réalité physique. Immortelle, incréée, ne subissant aucune détermination du dehors, cette réalité est presque exactement la *physis* d'Anaximandre, une « poussée » vers la forme (ce mot n'est-il pas étymologiquement le même ?) : ce qui, dans une Renaissance toute imprégnée de naturalisme péripatéticien et de matérialisme stoicien, en fait *aussi* puissance et acte, *aussi* le feu d'Héraclite. Mais en vérité, elle a cette invariance, cette autarchie, cette aséité contenue en elle-même et non dans les « mesures » de l'Etre intelligent, qui en font la substance d'Anaximandre, matrice et *gonimon* tout ensemble. Et le reste, il faut bien le dire, y compris les points géométriques et les atomes, est littérature. Ou du moins, à ce niveau-ci du système, il n'a pas encore lieu d'être pris en considération.

Mais c'est bien cela, le monisme véritable : matière et forme non distinctes qui n'en font plus qu'une, comme l'indique l'analogie de la femme enceinte, l'Etre Un qui est tout, et auquel on peut donner tous ces noms, en un seul hexamètre :

Mens, Deus, Ens, Unum, Verbum, Fatum, Oratio, Ordo.

Il n'y a là que des différences d'aspects, un miroitement de points de vue, il n'y a pas de distinction réelle. Et la vérité est immanente à cet Un, elle ne s'en distingue pas. Elle est « début, milieu et terme ; principe, génération et fin ». En termes gœthéens : « Wir denken, Ort zu Ort — sind wir im Innern ».

Dire que cette substance une est corporelle, cependant, ce serait pousser jusqu'au bout le langage stoïcien, et Bruno s'y refuse nettement. Sa substance est aussi incorporelle que l'Ame du Monde de Plotin, tout en étant aussi matérielle que la chose de Démocrite.

Le paradoxe est nécessaire, en bon monisme il est proprement inévitable (Newton ne manquera pas de voir toutes les difficultés de l'atome) : à vouloir tout embrasser, Bruno risque de ne rien étreindre. C'est le Cardinal de Cuse qui va le tirer de ce mauvais pas.

C'est en effet lui qui fournit à Bruno le Minimum quasiment inétendu, dans lequel se reflète en « complication » le Maximum. C'est ainsi que Bruno peut retrouver l'unité métaphysique de la Substance en chaque parcelle, et d'une manière que n'aurait pas désavouée Eddington — si nous imaginons un Bruno sachant s'expliquer avec un moderne. Dans ses propres paroles : « Une âme non distincte de l'animé, une puissance non distincte de l'acte. De telle manière que l'univers devient un premier principe qui entend soi-même... et il ne sera pas difficule d'accepter à la fin que tout, selon la substance, est un, et c'est ainsi probablement que l'entendait Parménide, qu'Aristote traite ignoblement. »

Le mot est dit, nous sommes en train de rendre à l'Etre de Parménide son contenu réel et non grammatical ; et c'est en reportant à la lumière ce qui certainement se cache dans la pensée de l'Éléate, une dialectique post-pythagoricienne. C'est grâce au Cardinal de Cuse que Bruno devient pythagoricien au sens véritable. Il n'est et ne sera jamais mathématicien, il ne peut pas être mené au pythagorisme, comme tant d'autres, par les voies de la découverte mathématique : il s'installe d'emblée au cœur du pythagorisme grâce au paradoxe du Maximum et du Minimum.

C'est une vieille histoire, et des plus compliquées, que celle du Maximum et du Minimum. Avant que le Cusain la relance métaphysiquement dans le monde moderne, les Grecs en avaient mesuré toutes les difficultés. Il y avait eu là pour eux plus qu'un divin paradoxe — il y avait une aporie des plus malencontreuses, et une pierre d'achoppement pour les sages. Les mathématiciens du IVe siècle avaient sondé les problèmes où on risquait de se perdre avec ce qui, techniquement, était l'infinitésimal en acte.

Mais le pythagoricien ne renonce pas facilement au monadisme, et du temps d'Archytas, il doit y avoir eu de très subtiles discussions sur les rapports entre la Monade et la grande Monade, qui n'est autre que l'Univers lui-même. Platon y prendra tardivement son point de départ pour ses spéculations sur l'Un ; mais au sein du Parti, il devait y avoir la plus grande réserve, car c'est là justement que la ligne générale commençait à flotter et que les déviations devenaient dangereuses. Je me sers de ces termes spéciaux parce que je pense qu'ils représentent adéquatement la situation jusqu'au temps qui précède Aristoxène. Si Aristoxène lui-même tente de donner de ces choses une image plus banale et pour ainsi dire « éclairée », c'est que les gens comme lui n'y comprenaient plus rien, et même de parti pris, car ces bigarrures primitives les gênaient chez des penseurs qui avaient inventé le mot même de « philosophie »: ils étaient, ces doctes critiques, comme ceux qui voudraient parler d'alchimie en partant des manifestes du Grand Orient de la Troisième République.

Il y a un peu de cela chez les historiens de Bruno et notamment chez Felice Tocco, lequel s'étonne à raison que Bruno parle du Maximum comme d'un Minimum multiplié un nombre infini de fois. Si le Maximum et le Minimum coïncident, comment l'un serait-il un simple multiple de l'autre? Le Cardinal de Cuse a parlé d'une « infinitation » de la quantité dans l'infini, où l'être et le néant coïncident. C'est bien autre chose. Bruno, manifestement, s'empêtre.

Mais Nicolas de Cuse était libre d'effectuer sa relance à la manière qu'il entendait, il était un métaphysicien chrétien, dégagé, allemand par-dessus le marché, alors que Bruno est un « acousmatique » de l'espèce véritable, il insiste sur l'exégèse, il veut rester à l'intérieur du Parti. Tout au plus voudrait-il moderniser ses atomes, il n'y réussit pas, d'autres auront ce souci — comme pensait déjà Copernic au sujet de ses épicycles. En tout cas, il n'entend pas se départir de la monade réelle — et par là il se retrouve pris dans les difficultés essentielles du vrai pythagorisme, de celui dont Aristote dit fort injustement qu'on ne sait pas trop ce qu'il veut. Bruno reste attaché à cette école, c'est dans son esprit qu'il interprète la doctrine cusaine. Voyez son exemple géométrique, révélateur, du Maximum et du Minimum. Prenez, dit-il, un segment quelconque AB. Ce segment en contient une infinité qui se recouvrent. Que l'un de ceux-ci se détache, entre dans l'existence, commence à tourner autour du point O situé entre A et B. Nous aurons, d'un côté, l'angle aigu minimum, auquel correspond de l'autre la naissance de l'angle obtus maximum...

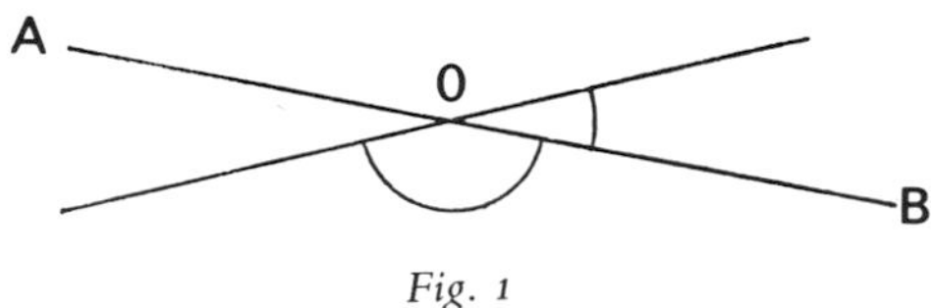

Fig. 1

On voit, à la lumière de cette lanterne, que Bruno voudrait être d'un réalisme mathématique intransigeant — en même temps que physicien de la substance Une. Il n'a, évidemment, ni la rigueur logique, ni, de loin, l'outillage technique qu'il y faudrait, son langage reste donc allusif et flottant, mais l'intuition derrière ce langage ne l'est point. Elle est totale et compréhensive. Bruno est l'homme qui « se jette à l'eau » dans l'infini et dans le principe de plénitude, il les suit aussi loin qu'ils le mènent, il étage une nouvelle morale et une nouvelle anthropologie là-dessus. C'est sa manière à lui d'être conséquent. Il va jusqu'au bout. L'allure de cette pensée, on peut la percevoir dans ce texte du *Spaccio della Bestia Trionfante*: « Et tu dois savoir encore, ô Sophie, que l'unité est dans le nombre infini, et le nombre infini dans l'unité: que l'unité est un infini implicite, et l'infini une unité explicite; que là où il n'y a pas d'unité, il n'y a pas de nombre, et partout où il y a nombre il y a unité. Celle-ci est donc la substance de celui-là: et celui qui connaîtrait non accidentellement comme les intellects particuliers, mais essentiellement à la manière de l'intelligence universelle, connaîtrait l'unité, l'un, le nombre, le fini et l'infini, la fin et terme par compression et excès du tout... Comme en substance, essence et nature sont un, de même, par la raison du nombre qu'ils assument (*subintrano*), elles encourent d'innombrables vicissitudes et espèces de mouvement et de changement... »

Voilà comment le nombre devient principe d'ordre et d'invariance dans le foisonnement de la plénitude. Il serait vain de demander à Bruno comment il va distinguer l'ordre formel de l'invariance. Il reste à l'ombre du dogme pythagoricien que « les choses sont nombres » avec toutes les possibilités d'exégèse qu'il comporte. L'apport de sa pensée propre, c'est l'effort pour ouvrir ce monde vers l'infini. Variété innombrable, « compression et excès du tout »... il ne cesse d'insister sur l'infini; et sur l'infiniment infini, comme seule réalité digne de la toute-puissance et de la fécondité divines — et c'est là aussi une théorie du *θεοπρεπὲς* d'allure nettement plotinienne. S'il y avait eu de son temps le microscope, il en aurait tiré ce qu'en a tiré Leibniz, vers l'infiniment petit, mais il l'annonce déjà, et on trouve dans ses textes la source des effrois pascaliens.

Plénitude et Raison suffisante sont tous deux des aspects du principe de Fécondité: « il n'y aurait pas plus de raison, disait déjà Métrodore, pour un seul monde dans l'espace illimité que pour un épi unique de blé dans un champ sans bornes ». Voilà le moment initial de cette axiomatique. Mais chacun des deux principes qui en dérivent tire un peu de son côté, et Bruno arrange comme il peut leur coexistence. Car le principe de raison suffisante, le plus abstrait et mathématique des deux, insiste sur les symétries du champ et sur l'uniformité. Des mondes infinis uniformément répartis pourraient bien être toujours les mêmes. De par ce principe, il faut un espace infini, de la matière partout, de la matière « comme ici », et donc la répétition représentée par l'idée même d'atome. De par le principe de plénitude, au contraire, il faut « des natures particulières infinies et innombrables », des mondes peut-être « non dissemblables » du nôtre, mais qui ne sont pas pour autant la répétition de celui-ci. Et sur ce niveau la vision n'est plus atomistique, quantitative et répétitive, démocritienne en somme, elle est pythagoricienne et qualitative, car il est de la nature du nombre pythagoricien d'être formel et qualitatif. Le monde est « le grand simulacre », où rien n'est identique à autre chose mais où tout concourt à l'unité, il est « tout ce qui peut être, selon un mode expliqué, dispersé et distinct ». Chaque élément ou individu « expliqué » ne peut pas « être tout ce qu'il peut être, mais tend à l'une ou l'autre possibilité », et c'est pourquoi « ils perdent un être pour en avoir un autre, ou les confondent entre eux, et sont ainsi insuffisants et estropiés du fait de l'incompatibilité de cet être-ci et de celui-là ».

L'univers de Bruno n'a donc pas la netteté du plan abstrait et du calcul binaire: il est encore lié au principe de plénitude sous l'aspect de la fécondité conçue au sens terrestre, c'est un foisonnement de choses qui s'amorcent et se muent: c'est pourquoi ses êtres errent à travers les formes, se coulent à travers elles, à peu près comme les premiers monstres d'Empédocle, tentant au hasard l'aventure de la *compatibilité*: celle-ci deviendra plus tard, dans le schéma leibnizien, le calcul rigoureux et anticipé des *compossibles*. Plénitude et raison suffisante seront réconciliées.

Il ne faut pas trop pousser le rapprochement: la démarche de l'esprit leibnizien n'a rien de celle de Bruno, encore tout empêtré dans la métaphysique des formes — bien que pas plus empêtré, hâtons-nous de le dire, que la philosophie de Bacon par exemple. Mais ce qu'il y a chez Bruno et ce qu'il n'y a pas chez Bacon, c'est une vision lointaine mais nette de ceux qui deviendront les principes leibniziens, et par quoi il se différencie de la tradition plotinienne tout aussi bien que de la stoïcienne: principes d'invariance, de plénitude, de raison suffisante.

Ce sont ces choses-là qui font le départ entre la philosophie naturelle de la bonne espèce et les autres. Je mets Bacon lui-même parmi les « autres », à cet égard. Les Encyclopédistes auraient trouvé cela malhonnête, et il peut être un peu paradoxal de mettre Bacon dans le même sac avec les averroïstes, les pomponazziens, Campanella et *tutti quanti*. Mais nous parlons ici de la théorie scientifique et non de la connaissance inductive. Si Galilée avait jamais lu Bruno (ce qu'il se garda de faire, certainement, car dans ces histoires d'hérésie, mieux vaut s'assurer deux fois qu'une) il n'aurait pas manqué de voir l'affinité avec ses idées à lui, même à travers le verbiage du napolitain. Kepler pour sa part, ne l'ignorait pas, et son âme pieuse en ressentait une profonde gêne, qui s'exprime dans ses rapports avec Wackher von Wakhenfels, le brunien sans inhibitions. La pensée de Bruno n'a pas de méthode, c'est entendu: mais il n'y avait pas de son temps de méthode qui valût quoi que ce soit, si ce n'est pour l'exposition. Elle n'est pas pour autant celle d'un simple confusionnaire : elle est le magma incandescent d'où va sortir une philosophie mathématique de la nature.

Quant à la mise en forme, c'est l'affaire de son successeur direct, de ce grand forgeron de la pensée qu'est Leibniz.

C'est ici que je voudrais chercher une toute petite querelle à M. Koyré, et surtout pour qu'elle me donne l'occasion de parler d'un très beau livre qu'il vient de publier récemment, *From the Closed World to the Infinite Universe*. Dans ce livre, et en début de chapitre, il pose comme chose qui va de soi que Leibniz s'intéressait en réalité bien plus à la morale et à l'homme qu'à la physique et à la cosmologie. Or il est évident qu'un personnage aussi complexe que Leibniz se prête à être lu de plusieurs manières, toutes compatibles entre elles. Il est certain aussi que la courbe intellectuelle de sa pensée part de l'homme et y revient au bout du discours, avec une insistance qui n'est pas celle du pur naturaliste. Mais ne pourrait-on pas dire de Newton lui-même que sa pensée, très presbytérienne au fond, prend son départ d'une recherche de la volonté de Dieu, et y revient en fin de carrière explicitement par ses longues spéculations sur la Bible ? On pourrait remarquer à propos de Niels Bohr que ses idées sur la complémentarité sont nées d'une méditation sur la condition humaine, ce qui est vrai, et M. Bohr n'en resterait pas moins le parfait physicien de notre temps.

Ce que je crains dans le cas de Leibniz, c'est le malentendu qui pourrait naître de ces remarques d'un historien de la science aussi connu et aussi qualifié que l'est M. Koyré ; car il est de purs philosophes, ses ex-collègues, qui ne seront que trop heureux de se prévaloir de son autorité pour ramener Leibniz dans la ligne de succession de Spinoza, dont on soutient qu'il ne s'est écarté que par politique. Et j'entends déjà d'autres encore y trouver un soutien à leurs revendications, car il est de mode à l'heure qu'il est de présenter Leibniz comme le rénovateur de la scolastique, le transbordeur de l'ontologie des formes, et pour tout dire, le restaurateur d'Aristote. On vous dit à présent, avec un peu trop d'insistance, que s'il reprend à son compte la Monade, il ne s'agit que d'un souvenir philologique, que c'est bien autre chose qu'il a dans l'esprit, et que, avec la sagesse qui le distingue, il se range sous la bannière d'Aristote au lieu de l'affronter comme le fait Bruno. C'est en somme une espèce de Leibniz-Wolff qu'on nous demande de voir comme le personnage réel, bizarre et hyperbolique, mais encore utile à l'occasion pour la thèse spiritualiste, alors que le cours de la pensée physique est censé officiellement aller de Newton au premier Kant, et de là entrer dans l'ordre de la bonne philosophie.

Il est naturel que quelqu'un soit laissé à faire les frais de cette restauration, et ce quelqu'un, il se trouve que c'est la métaphysique de la science. M. Koyré n'aimerait pas cela du tout, il n'est pas de ce parti-là, c'est pourquoi je me permets de lui signaler le danger. Quant à moi, il me semble clair que l'axe de la pensée de Leibniz, c'est une cosmologie et une théorie s'étayant sur une nouvelle physique, mais qui est une vraie physique de physicien, même s'il y est parvenu par des voies quelque peu détournées. Il me semble que si Leibniz, dans son infatigable désir d'universalité et de conciliation, s'applique à respecter la façade d'Aristote, c'est pour le mieux vider par le dedans.

Il n'est que de voir la démarche de sa pensée. Quiconque a regardé d'un peu près l'histoire de la spéculation grecque se rend compte de l'incompatibilité qui s'affirme entre les principes de raison formelle d'Aristote et le principe de Raison Suffisante (dont le véritable sens, d'Anaximandre jusqu'à Einstein, est celui d'un principe d'uniformité et de symétrie dans la distribution de l'ignorance et donc du risque raisonné dans l'hypothèse). Là où on le trouve, on sait qu'on a affaire aux gens de la *physis*. Là où il est nié, on sait qu'on est chez les idéalistes. C'est aussi tranché que le diable et l'eau bénite.

Or ce qui se passe avec Leibniz, c'est que le diable s'est mis dans l'eau bénite et la fait bouillir.

Il y faut pour cela une subtilité vraiment extra-terrestre, car Aristote sait se protéger et créer des zones d'interdiction *contra negantem principia*. Il sait contraindre l'adversaire à l'attaquer de front comme a fait Galilée. Mais Leibniz, par des voies détournées, a porté jusque dans le camp adverse la bannière de Bruno dont il est le successeur. Intelligence plus forte et plus rigoureuse que celui-ci, il ne se laisse pas entraîner par le mélange des idées, au contraire, il s'en sert avec une diplomatie consommée pour masquer sa démarche et la rendre acceptable. Avec lui, il ne faut jamais s'arrêter à la terminologie, qui peut être de pure complaisance. Il faut regarder comment va la chose.

Qu'on prenne, par exemple, cette chose fondamentale qu'est l'espace. Sur ce point, Leibniz n'a pas à faire de compromis avec les idées simplettes d'Aristote, idéalisations à peine transposées de la boîte et de la bouteille. Il se range du côté de l'espace cartésien, mais non plus comme une donnée première de l'esprit ; car on le redécouvre tel quel, insiste-t-il, au bout du raisonnement métaphysique, comme ordre des corrélations dynamiques entre monades. Mais est-ce vraiment l'espace cartésien ? Demandons-nous, pour vérifier, si un espace de Riemann, dont la géométrie même change de point en point selon certaines données contingentes et arbitrairement surimposées — si cet espace-là est encore celui que pouvaient entendre Descartes et Malebranche et Newton lui-même. En langage du XVIIe siècle, on appellerait cela non pas espace, mais matière. L'espace de Descartes est affirmé comme matière, mais il est avant tout espace euclidien, qui impose son être à la matière. L'espace de Riemann, par contre, apparaîtrait à un cartésien comme matière qui ose se prétendre espace. Or, l'espace Riemannien vient en droite ligne de Leibniz. La conciliation apparente a sauté. Ce qu'on retrouve au bout, c'est ce qu'il y avait au début — la réalité du physicien, et non l'*a priori* cartésien.

Où est Bruno dans tout cela, dira-t-on. Pas directement présent, certes, nous sommes ici sur le terrain des *solutions* originales de Leibniz. L'espace de Bruno lui-même est encore proche du sens commun. Mais il n'est pas pour autant l'espace d'Aristote, champ d'ordre soigneusement délimité, ou celui de Descartes, claire et simple nécessité de la vision géométrique. Son espace à lui, cet espace grouillant de choses, expansion d'une toute-puissance en acte, est justement celui qui invoque la solution leibnizienne de n'être qu'un schéma de l'ordre des rapports dynamiques entre monades. Comme celui de Leibniz, il exprime avant tout le principe de Plénitude. Alors que celui de Descartes, si l'on y pense, est pour ainsi dire tiré du néant avec un minimum de création, réalité simple et purement répétitive.

Je pourrais terminer ici, mais il peut être utile de montrer certaines caractéristiques générales de la pensée leibnizienne, à l'appui de mon point de vue.

Leibniz part des sciences humaines, assurément. Mais ce qui semble caractéristique de sa manière de penser, c'est qu'à partir du moment — qui est le moment parisien — où, grâce à Huygens, il découvre les possibilités de la physique, il entre résolument dedans et pense désormais en physicien. Ce qui n'est possible qu'à un homme qui raisonnait au départ et avant tout mathématiquement, et qui a découvert ici le terrain propre pour ce type de raisonnement. Il reprend à son compte la substance aristotélicienne, c'est bien vrai, mais lorsqu'on dit *substance* et qu'on entend *énergie* l'étiquette ancienne ne devrait tromper personne. Son univers n'est nullement substantiel, c'est un entrelacement serré de « points de vue » changeant vertigineusement, c'est un univers *optique*. Aristote et Descartes sont presque aussi loin de lui l'un que l'autre, il se sert de leurs techniques de langage et les imbrique en un sens tout différent. Il n'est pas, quoi qu'on dise, affilié au cartésianisme, ou plutôt, ce qu'il y a de cartésien en lui, c'est justement ce qu'ont oublié les cartésiens — l'idée d'une *ars inveniendi*; quant à la physique cartésienne, il n'y en a plus guère chez lui, et de la métaphysique non plus. Sa pensée est une physique généralisée, et Dieu la machine calculatrice qui la met en place.

Il est assurément singulier que ce physicien soit passé du côté de la gravitation newtonienne sans lui faire le moindre sort, et c'est ce qui donne son poids à la remarque de M. Koyré. Mais je voudrais tout de même vous demander de réfléchir que pour

Leibniz, la physique newtonienne basée sur la matière ne pouvait être qu'un faux départ, lourd de conséquences malencontreuses, qui allait retarder l'avènement de sa physique à lui, la physique optique; et qu'il est bien vrai que celle-ci devait rester dans l'ombre pendant deux siècles, en attendant l'électromagnétisme et la mécanique ondulatoire. Donc, point n'est besoin, même, d'invoquer la mauvaise grâce manifeste de Newton à son égard.

Or donc, si les étiquettes qu'on a voulu coller sur Leibniz s'avèrent trompeuses, qu'est-il dans le fond?

Je voudrais suggérer que sa pensée est (comme celle de Galilée d'ailleurs, M. Koyré l'a bien montré) platonicienne. C'est par là surtout qu'il se tient dans la ligne de succession de Bruno.

Il pense avoir trouvé la dialectique réelle, qui serait son *ars inveniendi* à lui; et bien plus valable que les malheureux efforts mnémotechniques de Bruno. Il pense avoir mis en forme, une fois pour toutes, la théorie des Idées. Alors que pour Aristote, il y a d'abord le concret, et le « principe extensionnel » dans la pensée — j'entends que si les objets sont les mêmes, leurs propriétés le seront aussi —, chez Platon et chez Leibniz, « le concret n'étant tel que par l'abstrait », le concret est un résultat: il se trouve à l'intersection de propriétés données. Ce qui établit le règne de l'autre principe, celui de l'Identité des Indiscernables. Chez Leibniz comme chez Platon, on ne part pas de la Substance, mais des Idées.

Ce que je viens de relever n'est pas très nouveau, je voulais seulement souligner cette forme particulière de pensée; elle a sa source dans cet aspect de la pensée grecque, que Jaeger a appelé l' « idéation mathématisante ».

Chez Leibniz, lequel veut dépasser et résoudre le stade des formes platoniciennes — et par là même le côté encore qualitatif du platonisme brunien — cela mène à la détermination purement mathématique. Et on voit pourquoi: dans un univers optique, où règne une relativité essentielle des positions et des points de vue, où tout est point de vue — un délire de points de vue se multipliant à l'infini — ce qui met en place les situations réelles, ce seront les déterminations d'extremum, les singularités effectives, c'est-à-dire les *maxima*. Il faut partout un choix unique, infiniment déterminé, pour qu'il y ait la décision du réel, et c'est cette unicité du particulier qui fait la plénitude de l'ensemble. C'est ainsi que Leibniz a pris en main et porté à terme le programme pythagoricien de Bruno, celui-là même que nous avons lu dans le texte du *Spaccio*. Derrière le platonisme de Bruno, de Galilée, de Leibniz, on retrouve le pythagorisme qui en est l'essence.

Car s'il est vrai que le pythagorisme implique toujours le nombre, il ne faut pas prendre ce mot au sens restreint. Il y a un pythagorisme « miraculeux », mythologique, qui apparaît dans les harmonies kepleriennes et aussi, bien plus tard, dans la Série de Balmer; mais l'algèbre géométrique des Grecs, le calcul binaire de Leibniz, impliquent tout aussi bien des aspects métaphysiques du nombre, et le fameux *Calculemus* l'affirme. Les constructions d'Einstein ou de Eddington seraient pythagoriciennes même sans avoir recours à des nombres universels tels que la constante *C*, le paramètre λ, ou l'étrange et peu croyable nombre 137. Chez Leibniz le départ entre le nécessaire et le contingent, l'histoire même de la monade établie pour toujours sont conçus dans un esprit pythagoricien. Il y a des « lignes d'univers » comme il y en aura chez Einstein, et ce caractère que je viens d'indiquer, cette unicité du particulier qui fait la plénitude de l'ensemble, cela est aussi einsteinien. Position et description y sont relatives, mais le choix du parcours y est uniquement déterminé.

En somme, l'univers n'a qu'un choix. Il peut être tout vide, ou tout plein. S'il est tout plein (ou disons, s'il *est*, tout court), ce « tout plein » est une géométrie intrinsèque de l'espace, ce n'est pas un mode de description qui nous le donne, c'est là le sens même de la Relativité généralisée.

Quant à toutes les explications touchant le bon et le meilleur chez Leibniz, c'est là sa manière de ramener l'univers aux préoccupations de l'homme, de l'infléchir vers l'homme ; mais l'optimum se trouve être tout uniment une détermination maximum. La téléologie y a son compte, nous restons encore dans le programme platonicien, mais elle se révèle comme un résultat, non comme un but. Et ici se marque de nouveau l'opposition entre la pensée bruno-leibnizienne et celle d'Aristote. Réduire les causes finales à des causes formelles, c'est se ranger dans le camp pythagoricien contre le péripatétique.

C'est bien cela, la suppression de tout anthropomorphisme téléologique, qui est la réalisation logique de la plénitude brunienne, de la monadologie brunienne. Car c'est dans la morale surtout qu'on voit l'aboutissement identique des deux philosophies. L'idée du Bien cesse d'être transcendante pour devenir Plénitude. Il faut de tout pour faire un monde, et l'expérience humaine. Il y faut toutes les feuilles de toutes les plantes dont aucune n'est identique à une autre (comme le montre Leibniz aux sceptiques ahuris, sur les massifs de buis du jardin de la Princesse Electrice), il y faut les vipères, et même lubriques, il y faut les païens, les spinozistes, les vicieux, les méchants, les hérétiques. Chaque chose a sa place. C'est de cette conception œcuménique du réel que vient la morale de Bruno et de Leibniz. Bruno a aimé et respecté ses hôtes protestants, mais son jugement était contre, il les a appelés « ces grammairiens de la foi qui infestent l'Europe ». Il aurait voulu les réconcilier avec le catholicisme universel, celui-là même qui se disposait à le brûler. Cela va tout de même plus loin que la morale de Descartes.

Leibniz concevait aussi son système comme une réconciliation des haines religieuses, et il a dépensé une somme énorme d'efforts à cet égard. Nous en venons là — et c'est par là seulement que je me retrouve d'accord avec M. Koyré — au caractère essentiellement moral dans lequel se rejoignent les trois grandes figures pythagoriciennes, le Cardinal de Cuse, Bruno et Leibniz. Nous retrouvons dans cette pensée un même idéal eirénique de conciliation et de coexistence dans une « diversité infinie de discrets » comme disait Bruno. C'est une physique, elle se trouve être aussi une morale, et des meilleures que je connaisse.

Les savants nous disent à présent que la science ne comporte pas de morale, pas plus que de métaphysique. Ils me font penser un peu à Frédéric II écrivant l'*Antimachiavel.* Il peut bien y avoir une attitude puriste chez quelques-uns, elle est exprimée par Wittgenstein, le monde duquel est purement pluraliste et acosmique, un ensemble de faits atomiques reliés par des rapports uniquement logiques. Les savants ne s'en contentent pas en général, ils veulent bien de quelque « philosophie » positiviste — à condition qu'elle soit là pour ne rien dire.

Les philosophes en sont réduits par conséquent à parler d'autre chose... Elle serait pourtant bien utile, encore, la philosophie, si elle ne se limitait pas à une exégèse littéraire, ou pire, à une défense d'idées meurtrières; si elle voulait affronter les problèmes d'une difficulté réelle, comme au temps de Bruno et de Leibniz. Car il s'agirait encore de rendre compte non seulement des ordres nécessaires, mais des contingents — il s'agirait encore de voir quelles entités, quels principes, quels êtres de raison, quelles assomptions logiques ont droit de cité, et dans quelles catégories fondamentales il serait juste de les encadrer: il s'agirait de faire le départ entre le contingent et ce qui ne l'est pas, et non de se renfermer dans le babillage subtil et dans les analyses du langage.

En somme, et quoi qu'elle pense, la science se prête encore à ce qu'on lui dicte des lois, et son autonomie ne devrait tromper personne. Mais on ne voit pas de Leibniz à l'horizon.

M. Fleckenstein

Il faut tenir compte du fait de la diversité des méthodes scientifiques et de la pensée entre le XVIe et le XVIIe siècle. La monadologie de Bruno représente une « mosaïque statique » de la nature; la monadologie de Leibniz représente un « réticule des relations dynamiques ». Bruno reste dans la Renaissance de la pensée antique; Leibniz au contraire est rattaché à la science moderne (calcul infinitésimal) avec sa monadologie.

M. de Santillana

Entendu, encore que le côté statique de Bruno soit l'aspect qui est justement le plus emprunté au passé. Bruno n'avait pas l'outillage intellectuel qu'il aurait fallu pour un réarrangement de fond, pour mettre son vin nouveau dans des outres moins anciennes. C'est d'ailleurs une bonne règle historique que des deux, l'outre et le vin, un pour le moins, du premier coup, ne peut être trop nouveau, au risque d'avoir un vin qui ne ressemble à rien de connu. Il est clair que tout est nouveau dans la *méthode* leibnizienne, laquelle se fonde sur la dynamique. Mais Leibniz tient à ne pas être nouveau en tout, il se présente comme le grand réorganisateur de la pensée qui le précède, à faire passer dans sa synthèse le platonisme, l'atomisme, la scolastique et Descartes par dessus le marché. J'ai tenté de montrer que l'*intuition* de Bruno tient une place capitale dans son programme de transformation. C'est pourquoi je l'ai appelé non le successeur, mais l'exécuteur testamentaire des volontés du Nolain.

Postface à Galilée ; Les Suites de l'Affaire

APRÈS SA CONDAMNATION, SE SACHANT DÉSORMAIS SANS RECOURS ni défense en Italie, Galilée avait dédié et confié au duc de Noailles, ambassadeur de Louis XIII, les *Discours sur Deux Nouvelles Sciences.* C'est aussi dans ses lettres à Diodati et à Peiresc, au cours des dernières années, qu'il livre sans crainte le meilleur de lui-même. S'en remettant à ce que son ami Sarpi avait nommé « l'ancienne et véritablement française liberté », il léguait ainsi aux « ultramontains » l'honneur de son nom et l'avenir de la Science. Mais ses amis moururent avant d'avoir pu l'aider comme ils auraient voulu, et les philosophes, en qui il avait mis tout son espoir, évitèrent sagement de se charger de sa cause et prirent bon soin, pour plus de sûreté, d'enterrer son œuvre et son souvenir.

Sans doute le personnage de Galilée échappe-t-il à toute « classification ». Les uns lui reprochaient d'avoir été catholique, les autres, de l'avoir été trop peu. Tel l'accuse de rationalisme, tel autre d'empirisme moqueur. Il a le tort de porter ombre aux inventeurs de la Méthode. Enfin, il prend fermement parti dans la controverse scientifique, mais pas au point de s'exposer aux tortures de l'Inquisition: les représentants de la Science vous expliqueront qu'il est mieux venu, dans ce cas, de pousser sa conviction jusqu'au bûcher.

Une grande part de responsabilité, il faut bien le dire, incombe à Descartes et à ses successeurs, qui entendaient déduire leurs lois physiques sans avoir à tenir compte des lois réelles que Galilée avait mises à leur disposition.

C'est bien Descartes qui écrivait à Mersenne, le 10 janvier 1634, cette lettre significative que nous avons déjà citée:

Vous savez sans doute que Galilée a esté repris depuis peu par les inquisiteurs de la foi et que son opinion touchant le mouvement de la Terre a esté condamnée comme hérétique; or je vous dirai, que toutes les choses, que j'expliquois en mon traité, entre lesquelles étoit aussi cette opinion du mouvement de la Terre, dépendoient tellement les unes des autres, que c'est assez de savoir qu'il y en ait une qui soit fausse pour connoistre que toutes les raisons dont je me servois n'ont point de force; et quoique je pensasse qu'elles fussent appuyées sur des démonstrations très certaines et très évidentes, je ne voudrois toutefois pour rien au monde les soutenir contre l'autorité de l'Église. Je sais bien qu'on pourroit dire que tout ce que les inquisiteurs de Rome ont décidé n'est pas incontinent article de foi pour cela, et qu'il faut premièrement que le concile y ait passé; mais je ne suis point si amoureux de mes pensées que de me vouloir servir de telles exceptions, pour avoir moyen de les maintenir; et le désir que j'ai de vivre au repos et de continuer la vie que j'ai commencée en prenant pour ma devise: *bene vixit que bene latuit*, fait que je suis plus aise d'être délivré de la crainte que j'avois d'acquerir plus de connoissances que je ne désire, par le moyen de mon écrit, que je ne suis fâché d'avoir perdu le temps et la peine que j'ai employée à le composer.

On a souvent voulu voir dans ces paroles l'attitude du sage. Ce n'est assurément pas ainsi que s'exprimait Galilée, même aveugle et prisonnier. Au vrai, Descartes n'était pas fâché que la disparition de son rival lui permît de développer à son aise sa propre physique, laquelle reste théoriquement et pratiquement le contre-pied de celle de Galilée. Le P. Mersenne, malgré ses scrupules, s'était risqué à résumer le *Dialogue des Grands Systèmes* pour ses *Questions*. Après un échange de lettres avec Descartes, dont celle que nous avons citée est la première en date, il renonça à son projet. Personne ne se soucia de publier, quand ce n'aurait été qu'en Hollande, une traduction même abrégée du *Dialogue*. Salusbury, le traducteur anglais, fit une remarque acérée à ce sujet en 1661: « *The affectation of novelty* », dit-il, la manie des nouveautés semble abandonner les Français dès qu'il s'agit de Galilée. Malgré les sympathies avouées de Peiresc, de Gassendi et de tant d'autres, le savant italien est discrètement « ostracisé ». C'est peut-être, comme le veut Descartes, qu'il avait « philosophé sans fondements »...

Ce n'est pas seulement une cosmologie, mais toute une philosophie naturelle qui est abandonnée, et l'héliocentrisme avec elle: car Kepler demeurant illisible et Bouillaud dédaigné, Huyghens gardant le silence (le *Cosmotheoros* ne sera publié qu'en 1687), seule la prose galiléenne prenait philosophiquement parti pour cette cause. La force et la pureté de son style auraient dû révéler des textes dignes de Bossuet. Mais, ni alors ni plus tard, la pensée de Galilée ne fut admise dans la culture française. N'étaient les récents et remarquables travaux de M. Koyré, elle serait encore de nos jours inconnue.

Serait-ce que le drame fulgurant du procès ait rejeté dans l'ombre l'homme et son oeuvre ? Il y a eu de cela au début. Et, plus tard, on s'est contenté d'exploiter cette inattention. Les hommes de l'Encyclopédie, partisans de Bacon, ont eu beau jeu de l'ignorer.

Finalement ce fut la science française qui joua perdant: l'ombre jetée par le silence et l'antagonisme froid de Descartes s'étend sur deux générations. Encore en 1657, Pascal, qui avait su pourtant rappeler aux bons Pères dans sa *Dix-Huitième Provinciale*: « Ce fut en vain que vous obtîntes contre Galilée un décret de Rome », ne doutait pas que le système de Ptolémée ne satisfît aux observations, et croyait que la variante de Tycho Brahé suffisait à tout expliquer. En faveur de Copernic, il ne connaissait pas de démonstration qui lui parût fondée sur des « observations constantes ». C'est bien là aussi le sens de sa *Réponse au P. Noël*. Ce ne sont donc pas les interdictions de l'Église qui le retenaient, lui qui avait si hardiment protesté contre les décrets de Rome en matière de foi. Pas plus que Bouillaud en 1645, ni que l'évêque Godeau en 1653, il n'aurait craint de rendre publique son adhésion au nouveau système, s'il ne s'était laissé fourvoyer par son entourage.

Le préjugé cartésien d'abord, le préjugé baconien ensuite conspirent obscurément avec la politique jésuite en un déni de justice obstiné. Il fallut l'intervention éclatante de Voltaire pour rétablir quelques simples vérités, mais celle-ci même ne suffit point. Les intérêts en jeu étaient trop grands, et s'étendaient bien au-delà des cercles purement philosophiques. En 1784, l'attaque contre Galilée fut relancée avec une efficacité nouvelle par Mallet du Pan, pamphlétaire suisse et protestant, mais légitimiste. L'origine protestante de cette offensive lui permit de trouver crédit auprès d'Anglais tels que sir David Brewster et d'autres représentants de la pensée laïque de par le monde. C'est à Mallet du Pan que l'on doit les légendes les plus injurieuses sur Galilée.

Parmi les éléments disparates que nous venons de nommer, la propagande jésuitique savait assurément le mieux ce qu'elle faisait. Point étonnant que dans ce camp-là précisément, le P. Tiraboschi et le P. Andrès aient su se distinguer par une objectivité d'autant plus méritoire qu'elle leur était plus difficile, alors que la science dite officielle, à commencer par Lalande en 1786, adoptait plutôt comme articles de foi les racontars de Mallet du Pan et de ses acolytes, en y ajoutant des inventions de son cru. Il ne leur eût rien coûté de se documenter, mais ils étaient mus par un complexe obscur dont ils ne pouvaient pas se défendre. Il est difficile d'expliquer autrement les versions accréditées par Delambre, par Arago, par Chasles, et même par Biot, qui s'était pourtant efforcé de faire lever à Rome le décret de l'Index.

Ainsi le célèbre historien de l'astronomie, Delambre, n'a donné sur Galilée que des notes prises à la hâte et avec une inexcusable négligence. Il ne fait même pas allusion aux découvertes de Galilée en physique, et va jusqu'à déclarer le *Dialogue* inutile, et ses arguments sans valeur contre Tycho Brahé. C'est bien ce qu'avait tenté de montrer le P. Riccioli en 1651 avec ses soixante-dix-sept arguments massés en batterie; mais il savait au moins, ainsi que ses collègues, pourquoi il brouillait les cartes, même au risque de s'attirer les moqueries des savants, qui ne s'en privèrent d'ailleurs pas. On ne se découragea point. On insista. Cent cinquante ans plus tard, il se trouva encore un Delambre prêt à accepter sans examen ces inepties.

Trente ans après Delambre, Arago, porte-parole officiel de la science française, se sentit en devoir de dire quelques paroles élevées, sur le « martyr » officiel de la Science, qui furent publiées en 1854 dans ses *Notices biographiques*. Il se peut qu'il ait voulu réagir contre les exagérations passionnées d'un Libri. Le fait est qu'il rabaissa, bien plus encore que Delambre ne l'avait fait, les mérites scientifiques de Galilée, qui apparaît en outre comme un personnage aigrement vaniteux, au caractère vil.

Nous avons déjà signalé comment Galilée est accusé à tort d'avoir laissé échapper l'aveu d'une basse jalousie contre William Gilbert. Or que dit Galilée en fait ? « Je loue extrêmement, j'admire cet auteur et je lui porte envie, pour cette conception merveilleuse [*du magnétisme*] qui s'est présentée à son esprit et qui avait échappé à tant de grands hommes s'occupant du même sujet. » Il y a plusieurs autres passages où Galilée est ainsi compris non de travers, mais à l'envers. Tout cela ne s'explique que d'une seule manière : c'est qu'il y a toujours des gens prêts à fournir des « résumés » et des « extraits » de Galilée. On croit en être encore au procès de 1633. L'idée de consulter les textes authentiques semble n'être venue à personne : on dirait qu'ils ont été écrits en cunéiforme.

Le malheureux savant n'a pas été mieux traité par ses défenseurs. Libri se servit de lui pour une charge à fond qui l'emporta au-delà de tout bon sens. Michel Chasles n'hésita pas, dans sa naïveté, à accréditer les papiers d'un faussaire qui attribuaient à Galilée la priorité sur Newton. Philarète Chasles écrivit en 1861 un livre sur « *Galilée, sa vie, son procès et ses contemporains d'après les documents originaux* ». Le titre semblait promettre, à la fin, une mise au point. Il n'en fut rien. Dans l'ouvrage ne figurent que les documents reproduits dans le texte de l'Allemand Reumont, c'est-à-dire peu de chose. (L'édition Albéri des *Oeuvres complètes* était pourtant terminée depuis 1856.) Le reste est invention ou répétition de vieilles histoires. Ponsard avait presque fait mieux dans sa tragédie où il attribuait une épouse à Galilée. Chasles prétend écrire une défense ; en réalité il est encore en deçà du texte de Reumont.

Évidemment, il ne s'agit pas ici d'histoire ni d'historiens au sens propre. On peut imaginer ces écrivains (il y en a bon nombre) comme des esprits sensibles, rebutés par les excès bruyants de la littérature antireligieuse qui avait fait de Galilée son cheval de bataille, le décrivant avec complaisance torturé, aveuglé par l'Inquisition, terminant ses jours dans un cachot... Ramener une histoire si ténébreuse à des proportions sensées, y révéler une frivole indiscrétion suivie d'une condamnation somme toute peu sérieuse — belle tentation pour qui voudrait se sentir au-dessus de la mêlée. L'encouragement des savants n'y manquait point...

Il a fallu attendre jusqu'en 1868 pour voir Th. H. Martin publier un ouvrage impartial et informé, où était soulevée la question de fond, et justice faite des vieilles absurdités. Mais il est frappant de constater que Martin, malgré la pénétration dont il fait preuve, se laisse induire en erreur comme tant d'autres sur un point capital, quand il admet que la condamnation de Galilée fut légalement régulière. C. I. Jagemann avait vu cependant, dès 1784, qu'il n'en était rien. M. de l'Epinois, érudit très catholique, auquel revient le mérite d'avoir enfin publié intégralement, en 1877, le dossier de l'affaire, n'était guère homme à entretenir des doutes à ce sujet. Pour lui comme pour l'abbé Bouix, ecclésiastique fort méritant d'ailleurs, l'important était de montrer que l'infaillibilité papale n'était pas en cause.

C'est en Allemagne, avec Reusch, Wohlwill et Gebler, en Italie avec Gherardi, Berti, Favaro, que la question sera reprise avec des moyens adéquats. Mais ces grands travaux même ne suffiront pas à promouvoir une version acceptée. Au vingtième siècle on réussit, une fois de plus, à enterrer la question un peu partout, avec des détours infinis.

Il y a, indéniablement, un *spiritus vertiginis* qui paraît présider à l'historique de l'affaire, et cela jusqu'à nos jours. On dirait que l'importance des intérêts en jeu interdit à la question de se résoudre d'elle-même. Chacun s'efforce de démonétiser la vérité de l'autre, de recouvrir ce qui a été découvert. Étrange politique en vérité, puisque au bout du compte s'accréditent des versions qui déconsidèrent chaque parti, bien plus sûrement que les faits dont on a si peur.

L'histoire des péripéties du dossier en témoigne à loisir. Ayant fait transporter les documents à Paris en 1812, Napoléon donna l'ordre d'en préparer la publication. Ce n'était pas par pur intérêt historique, on s'en doute. Vint la Restauration, et on se garda bien de donner cours au projet. Les papiers étaient restés pendant plusieurs années aux mains d'un érudit, M. Barbier, qui aurait pu les faire copier pour son compte. Il n'en fit rien. Il avait trouvé, dit-il, qu'ils ne présentaient qu'un médiocre intérêt. Apparemment, ils n'administraient pas la preuve que Galilée avait été torturé...

En restituant les papiers en 1845, le ministère français eut le bon sens d'exiger du Vatican la promesse de publication. Le Vatican pensa la tenir, en faisant publier en 1851, par Mgr. Marini, un opuscule apologétique serti de quelques documents arrangés et tronqués avec art. On préférait, en fin de compte, laisser libre cours aux historiettes à la Mallet du Pan.

Or, protestant, Mallet du Pan n'avait pas à se charger de certains soucis. Pour lui, l'affaire se réduit à une querelle mesquine de vanité entre Galilée et Urbain VIII, où n'est réservé au pape que le beau rôle de celui qui pardonne (et cela non plus n'était pas exact). Mais noircir l'un ne rehausse pas l'autre pour autant. Cette interprétation peu respectueuse de la dignité du trône pontifical ne permet pas davantage de « blanchir » le Saint-Office de l'erreur théologique. C'est cependant la version qui est restée sous-jacente à nombre de publications modernes. Le P. Adolf Muller S. J., ancien directeur de l'observatoire du Vatican, en fournit un exemple : dans un gros ouvrage publié en 1910, il se donne la peine de montrer que Galilée était un personnage visqueux, sans foi ni loi, de réputation très surfaite, philosophiquement dénué de sérieux, dépourvu de solides études, ne sachant pas de quoi il parlait, tant il est vrai qu'il ne savait guère le latin, et même, nous assure sans rire le bon père bavarois, pas suffisamment l'italien... Il faut en conclure que les prélats qui respectaient sa pensée étaient des sots, et peu sérieux le jugement d'Urbain VIII, son grand protecteur et ami; celui-ci était censé pourtant s'y connaître en mérite littéraire, et aussi quelque peu en hommes. Il est difficile de comprendre à quoi tout cela veut mener.

Le P. Muller aurait gagné à ne pas trop insister sur ces arguments, car ils ne sont que l'exagération jusqu'à l'absurde d'une thèse qui avait conquis désormais droit de cité dans la littérature, à force d'être répétée d'un air naturel: Galilée animé par une ridicule ambition théologique, voulant « forcer les cardinaux » à accepter son interprétation de la Bible. Il y a là un élément de fait, habilement inverti (car nous avons vu que c'est bien là le guet-apens où on avait voulu l'attirer de toute force), qui peut servir les besoins de la cause. De Maistre et Arago lui avaient donné le poids de leur autorité. Pierre Duhem en avait fourni au début de notre siècle une version neuve et ingénieuse. Non seulement Galilée n'avait pas découvert grand-chose d'original, ayant marché sur les brisées des scolastiques de Paris, mais encore il était philosophiquement dans le faux, n'ayant pas compris ce qu'est la physique positiviste; en revanche, Bellarmin représentait la saine philosophie en même temps que le magistère de l'Écriture. Ce n'est pas seulement saint Thomas qui s'exprimait à travers le cardinal, mais aussi Bacon et Ernst Mach. Il y a eu, même parmi ses collègues, des gens pour juger fondée cette thèse.

Aujourd'hui le vent a viré d'un quart: on admet l'erreur théologique — attitude d'autant plus facile que Léon XIII a formulé les nouvelles règles pour l'interprétation de l'Écriture, qui concordent mot pour mot avec celles préconisées par Galilée dans sa *Lettre à Madame Christine*. Mais, comme le disait Galilée lui-même dans son vieil âge, il est difficile de pardonner à un homme l'injustice qu'il a subie; on continue à vouloir sauver la légalité du procès et, pour ce faire, il sied que le comportement de Galilée reste, pour le moins, fâcheusement importun. En réalité, depuis la réconciliation de l'Église avec l'État italien, cette attitude n'est pas si aisée à adopter à Rome, car Galilée est une gloire nationale... Aussi M. Andrissi, astronome, a-t-il trouvé en 1953 une manière ingénieuse de réhabiliter le savant. Dans une série d'études publiées par l'*Osservatore Romano*, il le montre dupe et victime inconsciente d'une cellule de noyauteurs et de déviationnistes (qu'on nous pardonne les termes, ils sont clairement suggérés par la pensée de l'auteur), logés à Rome même, à l'ombre du Vatican et commandés par un étranger (naturellement), agent de l'Internationale platoniste hérétique, un certain Eckius. Cette clique ne serait autre que l'Académie des Lincei...

Cet exégète n'a donc rien trouvé de mieux que de livrer au déshonneur la plus illustre initiative de l'aristocratie romaine, et avec elle les noms de gentilshommes dont l'orthodoxie resta au-dessus de tout soupçon, tels que Cesi, Stelluti, Cesarini... et de nouveau, du moins à titre de dupe, Urbain VIII lui-même, membre de l'Académie et son protecteur.

Pourquoi, après plus de trois siècles, encore cet effort inlassable et proprement insensé ?

On peut, assurément, entrevoir quelques raisons spécifiques. Par exemple, un soupçon tenace au sujet de l'orthodoxie de Galilée, soupçon habilement entretenu par les autorités à l'occasion de sa mort. Le pape avait exigé qu'on n'enterrât pas le corps à l'intérieur de l'église de Santa Croce. Cela ne siérait point, disait-il, pour quelqu'un qui est mort pénitencié. Les Florentins ne manquèrent pas de s'en étonner. Galilée n'avait-il pas été absous de la suspicion d'hérésie ? Ne lui avait-on pas pardonné ? Précisément, non. Il était mort sans qu'on levât la pénitence. Le procès *de vehementi* est un procès d'hérésie : cette tache ne s'efface pas. On voulait rappeler au monde que la Sainte Inquisition n'agit jamais sans raison suffisante, et qu'elle en sait plus long qu'elle ne se soucie d'en dire. Que pensait-on en vérité ? Plusieurs juges, nous l'avons vu, gardèrent la certitude d'avoir affaire à un hérétique sournois. Aujourd'hui encore, pour les esprits soumis, l'ombre de l'Inquisition plane sur le nom de Galilée, et c'est peut-être pour que les croyants s'en souviennent, qu'on a omis d'inscrire son nom au fronton de l'Académie pontificale des Sciences, alors que celui de Léonard de Vinci y figure en bonne place. Léonard ne fut rien moins qu'un pieux catholique, on peut même se demander s'il fut chrétien ; mais il n'eut pas de démêlés avec le Saint-Office.

On peut invoquer aussi d'autres motifs ; la solidarité infrangible et immortelle de certains ordres qui se refusent à livrer tels de leurs membres — encore qu'obscurs — au verdict de l'Histoire ; une hésitation instinctive à laisser la critique pénétrer dans cette zone mal définie du pouvoir central sur quoi s'étendait, encore au siècle dernier, le reflet de l'infaillibilité pontificale... Préoccupations, inutile de le dire, joyeusement exploitées par le parti adverse, qui ne demande pas mieux que de mettre l'Église tout entière « dans le bain ».

Mais ces motifs particuliers seraient-ils prouvés qu'ils ne toucheraient peut-être pas encore au cœur du problème. Nous préférons laisser la parole à un illustre penseur et homme d'Église, aujourd'hui disparu, qui nous écrivait à ce sujet, il y a longtemps, des réflexions qu'il n'aurait peut-être pas voulu publier de son vivant:

> Je ne nie pas des explications de cette sorte, mais s'y arrêter, c'est bien minimiser la cause. L'affaire de fond me paraît beaucoup plus grave. Je l'exprimerai sommairement en disant que l'affaire Galilée est l'acte d'un refus sur lequel, à mon jugement, les responsables de l'intelligence au sein de l'Église catholique ne sont jamais encore vraiment revenus. Le refus est celui des implications philosophiques naturelles, tant au niveau méthodologique qu'au niveau cosmologique, de la pensée scientifique naissante et destinée à poursuivre la carrière que nous savons aujourd'hui. Ce refus se préparait de longue main. C'est autour de la crise de 1615–1632 qu'il s'est vraiment mué en acte, et en acte d'Église. Depuis il n'a jamais été vraiment retiré . . .

Nous n'oserions ajouter quoi que ce soit à ce jugement inspiré par une grande foi et mûri dans un silence douloureux.

Il nous semble en tout cas que les faits s'ordonnent mieux dans ce cadre que dans les autres. Pour recouvrir une iniquité, il a fallu, comme le disait déjà Galilée, faire étalage de fausse rigueur juridique: on a fini par réduire toute l'affaire à cette iniquité. Pour sauver une demi-douzaine d'obscurs prévaricateurs et trois faux témoins, on s'est employé sans répit au long des siècles à brouiller les cartes et à jeter le discrédit sur une gloire authentique de la catholicité. C'est comme si, pour sauver Cauchon, on avait accrédité la version de la *Pucelle* de Voltaire. C'est donc que l'affaire semble bien autrement actuelle et brûlante, du moins à quelques-uns. *Timuerunt ubi non erat timor.*

Que n'est-on prêt à sacrifier à cette crainte? Car enfin l'Église romaine du temps fit bien meilleure figure que ne le veulent ses apologistes modernes. On n'y manqua ni d'intérêt pour les nouvelles idées ni d'efforts passionnés, voire héroïques (souvenons-nous de Ciampoli), pour leur donner gain de cause. Urbain VIII et Bellarmin furent pris au dépourvu par une révolution intellectuelle qu'ils ne pouvaient même pas concevoir, mais ils se comportèrent toujours en grands seigneurs — ce qu'on ne peut guère dire de plus d'un chef d'État actuel, de plus d'une suprême autorité atomique. Le commissaire général de l'Inquisition lui-même fit ce qu'il put pour étouffer une affaire qu'il jugeait absurde et pour sauver Galilée *in extremis*. Mais il y a une fatalité dans les choses: ce qui a débuté comme une constellation d'intérêts particuliers et inavouables finit par se présenter comme Raison d'État. Quant à Galilée, sans parler de ses mérites scientifiques il sort de cette affaire bien plus grand philosophiquement et humainement, que ne l'ont prétendu ses défenseurs, anticléricaux ou même cléricaux: c'est bien cela qui donne à l'affaire toute sa signification.

Par-delà les erreurs et les malentendus, il s'agit d'un conflit où s'affrontent deux conceptions du monde, et aussi deux formes de vie.

Si l'on songe à l'univers de Galilée, l'image qui vient à l'esprit est celle de l'intérieur puissant et dépouillé de la chapelle des Pazzi, ce joyau de l'architecture florentine — le point de jonction du Christ et de la géométrie. Si nous voulions la peupler, ce devrait être d'une foule où se mêleraient des personnages d'Andrea del Sarto, Ghirlandajo, Caravage, — et aussi quelques gentilhommes dédaigneux empruntés au Titien ou à Bronzino, représentant les classes dirigeantes. Né en 1564, Galilée appartient au seizième siècle toscan par toute sa formation. Bien différent était le monde baroque d'Urbain VIII: c'étaient le faste des admirables palais des Barberini, les surfaces subtilement évidées et l'ample envolée des façades de Borromini, l'encadrement colossal de Saint-Pierre, le réalisme de son imagerie de martyrs aux draperies de marbre s'envolant au gré d'un vent imaginaire — la foule dans la basilique applaudissant comme au théâtre la lente, obèse et magnifique procession pontificale. A ce cadre correspondait une réelle volonté de puissance: la Rome de la contre-Réforme était une administration centrale de type moderne, d'où un immense réseau de commandes et un flot perpétuel d'émissions modulées s'étendait autour du globe. Florence faisait désormais figure de vieille ville de province, subsistant doucement dans le train coutumier, attachée aux vieux usages. Dans la confrontation de ces deux mondes, c'est Galilée qui représente l'ancien, et Urbain le nouveau.

Oui, il est vrai que Galilée a osé admonester la Curie; mais ce n'était pas en « progressiste » ou autre personnage futuriste, c'était en fils légitime de l'Église (Dante tint des propos autrement durs, et si on ne lui en a pas gardé rancune, c'est qu'on n'a pas fait de lui une victime). Galilée ne tentait même pas de leur présenter une nouvelle métaphysique, comme Descartes; il rappelait ses adversaires à la leur.

Il est vrai aussi qu'il leur força tant soit peu la main. Mais il s'en remettait avec confiance à leur pouvoir de réflexion, à leur « second mouvement ». Non pour s'imposer, mais pour les sauver d'eux-mêmes. La « céleste malice » qu'Einstein admire dans ses écrits n'était pas tournée contre eux, mais contre les Diafoirus de son époque, ceux qui rendaient le passé, et Aristote en personne, ridicules; car, loin de chercher à rompre avec le passé, il voulait le sauver, et avec lui la civilisation et la culture dont il s'était nourri — tout ce qui fut compromis par sa condamnation.

Dans la simplicité de sa foi, le personnage de Galilée franchit les siècles. A travers lui, c'est la science moderne qui se manifeste pour la première fois; mais en lui s'affirme aussi un esprit ancien bien différent de celui des prélats de la Curie — l'esprit d'une chrétienté oecuménique et conciliaire qui enseigne et exhorte avec la dignité des Pères des premiers siècles. Le contraste entre le style théologique de Galilée et celui des autorités de son temps suffirait à le montrer. Les protestations d'obéissance et d'humilité qu'il emprunte au langage poli de l'époque voilent à peine la vigueur du discours. On le sent successeur de saint Ambroise, de saint Augustin, de saint Bonaventure, morigénant des épigones dégénérés. C'est une voix qui vient du fond des âges, qui parle au nom de la communauté des fidèles, reliant ceux qui ne sont plus à ceux qui ne sont pas encore. Il n'est pas seulement l'astronome-conseil, il est cet expert en philosophie et en métaphysique qui demande à être écouté, comme il le dit, *in concilio patrum*; et ainsi qu'il le laisse entendre, si c'est la pureté des intentions et la gravité du traitement qui font autorité, il mérite qu'on lui prête la même attention que s'il était saint Thomas lui-même. En vérité, s'il y avait eu un jeune Thomas d'Aquin en face de lui, plutôt qu'un Bellarmin âgé et timoré, qui sait... Mais le temps n'était plus aux Thomas d'Aquin.

Cet aspect du drame souligne, comme nous l'avons dit dans la préface, une situation paradoxale et assez peu dialectique: à l'intérieur du cadre propre à la chrétienté d'occident, le conflit des anciens et des modernes montre Galilée, comme tous les hommes libres, recherchant l'appui de la tradition et des coutumes établies, tandis qu'Urbain, homme du pouvoir, est, sans s'en douter, le jouet des courants nouveaux qui mènent à l'étatisme et à l'autorité policière. Ce n'est qu'en nous reportant à une vue d'ensemble de l'histoire moderne que nous retrouvons la perspective habituelle: Galilée comme interprète des forces économiques montantes, « grand bourgeois » lui-même, et représentant d'une classe dirigeante avancée. Comme tel, il fut aussi l'instrument inconscient d'une ère nouvelle, ignorant l'étendue de sa propre force.

La réalité vivante du conflit, telle que l'ont perçue en son temps les observateurs perspicaces, montre que l'innovation déréglée, l'empirisme anarchisant, l'improvisation juridique et l'aventure policière se trouvèrent du côté des forces qui se croyaient vouées à la conservation de l'acquis. Il est juste d'insister sur ces points, en un siècle où l'esprit scientifique est une fois de plus en danger et où l'affaire Galilée elle-même achève presque de disparaître de la conscience publique, effacée par d'épaisses couches de blanc appliquées sans relâche. Il est désormais prouvé qu'à force de répéter une version, la foule finit par y croire. Pas seulement la foule: il faudrait dire aussi nombre d'esprits éclairés.

On peut distinguer là un fléchissement naturel, et même très compréhensible, en face d'une pression subtile et constante. On veut bien concéder quelque chose à l'adversaire qui ne peut tout de même pas avoir entièrement tort, et l'on finit par concéder précisément ce sur quoi il ne faudrait pas démordre.

Pascal avait rudement maltraité les jésuites sur le terrain théologique ; il n'en était que plus enclin à croire que leur physique des cieux était peut-être acceptable. Plusieurs esprits compréhensifs, excédés par les criailleries anticléricales, ont été tentés d'admettre que, si la Curie avait eu tort dans le domaine de la science, elle pouvait avoir eu du moins de sérieuses raisons morales ou juridiques pour agir comme elle a agi.

Ce n'est pas là le meilleur moyen de rechercher la vérité. Ni le meilleur moyen d'affronter l'avenir. Aujourd'hui, puisque l'Histoire se répète, une bonne partie du public éclairé en Amérique est en train de se dire qu'Oppenheimer était *peut-être*, après tout, dangereux. Comment expliquer autrement, qu'une commission d'enquête composée d'hommes graves, etc. On se fait une raison. Et l'on oublie que l'affaire est d'une tout autre nature, qu'elle est celle de toujours, même si l'esprit scientifique est à présent menacé non plus par ses *ennemis* mais par ses *commanditaires*. Ces procès sont ceux d'une société qui croit, comme toujours, se protéger en accablant des hommes qui lui sont nécessaires et qui lui sont néanmoins foncièrement étrangers. Au procès de Galilée, à celui des généticiens russes et à celui des physiciens américains, la tendance est constante, comme l'atteste aussi l'identité formelle dans le déroulement des événements : il s'agit toujours de contraindre l'esprit scientifique à se séculariser d'un cran ; de faire en somme du savant un ingénieur passif aux ordres d'un pouvoir qui voudrait, et ne sait comment, se servir de lui : hâte confuse, aveugle désir, commun à toute force, disait Léonard, qui est de se ruer sur le néant.

La Storia da Riscrivere

IL SOGGETTO DI QUESTO CONVEGNO — I FATTORI DI STRESS NELLA civiltà contemporanea — fa rivivere in noi molti problemi attuali. Si pensa alla civiltà che ci ha dato Amleto e Kierkegaard, alla cultura in cui mi si dice che si riscontra ancor oggi il maggior numero di suicidi. E certo quella parola di Kierkegaard persegue ogni uomo moderno: « C'è una disperazione che consiste nel non sapere che si vive disperati ». Tema in cui ci riconduce in chiave attuale proprio l'ultimo romanzo di Moravia, in cui si descrive lo sfacelo anche intellettuale a cui conduce una esistenza « inautentica » e dunque « disattenta ».

Ma come storico mi dovrei inibire queste riflessioni contemporanee. Vi sono state ben altre incertezze e certezze incerte nel corso della nostra civiltà, e massimamente, mi sembra in quel declinare dell'Impero Romano in cui si veniva facendo strada il Cristianesimo. Quella parola di Sant'Agostino, che tanti rimangono fuori che dovrebbero esserci dentro, e viceversa, ci lascia intravvedere difficoltà psichiche non piccole. E se penso, metti conto, a Proclo, personaggio di immensa dottrina, di ferma fede neoplatonica, di erudizione infaticabile, mi chiedo perchè quel suo correre di culto in culto, di rito in rito, collezionando iniziazioni e conforti in ogni dove, non come ebbe a fare il Mirandolano per tentar la grande sintesi ma per rassicurare un'anima tormentata. Non gli sembrava di aver mai abbastanza assicurazioni e contrassicurazioni. È questa già incertezza cosmopolita, nata dal conflitto di civiltà.

È questa la coscienza moderna, così ben espressa da W. H. Auden, quando fa parlare Calibano, diventato ormai personaggio culto, anzi amministratore di cultura, spirito che non sa più dove trovare l'*intellectus*:

> Deliver us, dear Spirit, from the tantrums of our telephones and the whispers of our secretaries conspiring against Man; deliver us from these helpless agglomerations of dishevelled creatures with their bed-wetting, vomiting, weeping bodies, their giggling, fugitive, disappointing hearts, and scrawling, blotted, mis-spelt minds, to whom we have so foolishly tried to bring the light they did not want; deliver us from all the litter, the terrible mess that this particularized life, which we have so futilely attempted to tidy, sullenly insists on leaving behind it; translate us, bright Angel, from this hell of inert and ailing matter, growing steadily senile in a time for ever immature, to that blessed realm, so far above the twelve impertinent winds and the four unreliable seasons, that Heaven of the Really General Case where, tortured no longer by three dimensions and immune from temporal vertigo, Life turns into Light, absorbed for good into the permanently stationary, completely self-sufficient, absolutely reasonable One.

Questa è ben la « vita particolarizzata ». Questa la « materia inerte e sofferente, che si va facendo via via più senile in un tempo pur sempre immaturo ». Sono cose che capitano quando si comincia col « concedere alla cesura la sua libertà ». E vedete come lo strepitar dei telefoni, tanto avversato dai cardiologi, venga subito in prima linea.

Vorrei riprendere qui da un caso elementare molto noto. Due scimmie in due gabbie sono « stressate », come oggi si dice, da scosse elettriche. Ma una delle scimmie ha imparato a tentare vari pulsanti nella sua gabbia, e provando e riprovando sa come affrontare il suo cimento. Una volta tanto trova il pulsante che fa cessare la scossa. Insomma si dà da fare. L'altro soggetto non può niente. Rimane lì a incassare. È il rassegnato, il paziente. In capo a tre settimane, quello che ha affrontato la sorte ha l'ulcera gastrica. Il rassegnato è rimasto sano. Se non che, naturalmente, è di molto stanco.

Questo breve apologo ci dice a che prezzo ci venga la libertà. Il prezzo è la nevrosi. Là dove si dà scelta, possibilità, esitazione, ricerca, si è anche liberi. Chi si sottomette al destino soffre, ma la sorte lo protegge. *Ibi silentium laus.*

Questo è lo schema. Ma Hans Selye, il geniale teorico dello *stress*, ci ha mostrato oggi che esso implica sempre cause molteplici e concorrenti. Come poi avviene nella vita reale, quando si tratta di fattori neurogenici. Se ora vogliamo pensar da storici, e sopra un vasto arco di tempo, alle sorti dell'umanità in travaglio, sarà bene levar di mezzo le spiegazioni correnti, che riflettono a loro volta la coscienza turbata del presente. Chi ci parla di « mentalità prelogica » e ci costruisce sopra una socio-psicologia alla Mauss si inoltra in petizioni di principio. La « mentalità logica » quale la postuliamo è un modellino preso a prestito dalla scienza, non è un campione di vita. D'altra parte, l'addentrarsi nello studio scientifico della psiche non è cosa innocente. Lo scoprire anormalità significa spesso metterle in azione. Ai tempi di Charcot regnava la Grande Isteria. Dopo, con Morton Prince, spuntarono personalità multiple come i funghi, e com'essi sparirono con lui. Oggi, chi va dallo psicanalista può sognare su ordinazione. Già, direi quasi, se ne sapeva troppo ai tempi di Kraepelin, per benemerito che fosse.

E dunque guardiamo le cose senza preconcetti. Chi sappia interrogar così gli uomini delle civiltà più antiche, come i Boscimani del Kalahari o gli Eschimesi delle zone ancora intatte, ne ricava risposte semplici e non ambigue. Non vale cercare strutture normali e normalizzanti. Le cose essendo quel che sono, come direbbe De Gaulle, la risposta viene da sé. Quei popoli accettano come cose ovvie comportamenti estremi, come fra gli Eschimesi l'infanticidio, o l'abbandono dei vecchi, imposti dal minimo vitale, che non creano complicazioni psicologiche. Peraltro è gente naturalmente gentile, buona coi bimbi, non violenta. La tensione è tutta rivolta verso la natura, nello sforzo per sopravvivere. Fra gli uomini c'è intesa, compagnia, ragione. La splendida collezione di favole dei Boscimani, in cui il protagonista è la Mantide Religiosa, il personaggio per eccellenza su cui viene trasferita l'esemplarità, definisce le situazioni tipiche: l'astuzia, la vanteria, la bravura, l'imbarazzo, il ridicolo. È quasi del Moliere. E tutto questo delinea un ordine di ragione. I giovani Boscimani che cantano fra di loro una loro varietà semplice di jazz non hanno temi o soggetti da spiegare, per loro la musica ha un senso non un significato, come direbbe il Dr. Schneider. Ma il problema di accendere il fuoco con un'asticella, come si usa da loro dall'età della pietra, quella sì è un'opera di tecnica sottile e di significato indubbio, da cui sono venute grandi teorie cosmologiche in civiltà più tarde.

Né questa gente manca di un'etica. Come altri cacciatori primitivi, sono ordinati, monogami, rispettosi fino allo scrupolo della proprietà individuale. Hanno un senso vitale della colpa, perché sanno che uccidere è un male, se pur inevitabile. Hanno riti di espiazione per gli animali che uccidono, né cercano pretesti nella brutalità o nell'incesto del bruto ignaro. Insomma qui vige il comportamento dettato da natura, con la ragione già vigile che mette la coscienza a parte. Forse sarebbe questa la proiezione marxista dell'Eden. Certo è quello che intendevano gli antichi, quando favoleggiavano dei *Saturnia regna*. Ma questa fase era già apparsa ai primi osservatori, a un Cook o ad un Livingston. Le costruzioni idilliche del nostro Settecento hanno una base: la coscienza non aggiogata al pensiero individuale.

Altrimenti stanno le cose, quando si viene alle civiltà agricole. Lì si può parlare di « prelogico », perchè quella è la feccia di Romolo. Lì si trovano i sacrifici cruenti, i prigionieri sgozzati, l'ozio alla fine concesso, l'oppressione, perchè mentre le donne grattano la terra, gli uomini possono giocare agli ossicini, o razziarsi degli schiava. Qui c'è già tempo libero, come si dice oggi con parola neutra, e su di esso si ergono le culture dette superiori. Come se queste non avessero già una base preagricola. Ma noialtri si rimane prigionieri dei nostri clichés.

Ed è così che si entra nella cosidetta storia, che non va senza regni, imperi, rapine, concentrazione di ricchezze, quindi arbitrio e soggezione, violenza e crudeltà. Ci sembrò giusto prezzo (il reale essendo, dicono, razionale, per i fatti di coscienza che ne sbocciano, poesia, fede, senso della colpa, ricerca della giustizia e della misura) l'angoscia del pensiero. E non c'è che dire, le grandi civiltà storiche conoscono bene la nevrosi. Quando cerchiamo in esse modelli di serenità e di equilibrio, troviamo tempi labili, momenti metastabili. Chi oggi accetterebbe sul serio l'Etica Nicomachea? Forse è il fatto della Rivoluzione Industriale che ha creato questa frattura in tre generazioni.

Ma oggi come oggi, stentiamo a capire come il servaggio « corvéable et taillable à merci » possa aver generato altro che psicosi; come dall'imposta sul macinato non sia venuta senz'altro la Comune. Stentiamo a capire l'inumanità normale della classe abbiente. Eppure sappiamo che alla virtù, a tante virtù, non si era insensibili, se ne parlava anche troppo. Qui appunto appare la dubbia coscienza. La bonarietà patriarcale non significa rapporto empatetico, solo costume; è pronta a mutarsi in offesa. Come il contadino picchia le sue bestie senza badarci, così il rapporto di forza poteva svelarsi a ogni momento.

Sono ormai generazioni, direi dal 1793 in poi, che la Gente Bene non fa che deplorare il « sordido materialismo e gli istinti bestiali delle masse ». Strana inversione dovuta alla paura. Mi sia permesso di ricordare ancora un detto che sentii da Paul Claudel, grande poeta cristiano: « Il problema sociale non è mai esistito. Il solo problema è combattere l'alcoolismo fra il popolo ». Questo è un ribadir le catene dei « dannati della terra », glielo avrebbe potuto dire anche il suo collega Verlaine. A gente in quelle condizioni che evasione rimaneva se non l'alcool, la violenza o il sogno rivoluzionario? Almeno, nei regimi liberi, si poteva ancora distinguere fra cristiani o bestie. Nei regimi a schiavitù, il rapporto umano era negato in partenza. Di qui tensioni a cui non si pensa, se non ci si svelano nella storia sotto l'aspetto di Spartaco, dei Bagaudi o delle Jacqueries. Ancor oggi, uno psicanalista cinese che esercita a Taiwan mi diceva che alla nevrosi in alto fa controparte la psicosi in basso. Come era da prevedersi.

Andando al limite, la comprensione ci sfugge. Che cosa poteva essere la mente azteca, questa strana nevrosi ossessiva di tutto un popolo? Nevrosi di paura certo, come si ritrova nel Basso Impero, dove ogni tentativo degli umili di sfuggire alle tasse era punito col rogo. Nel Messico, paura che il Sole si fermasse, se non gli si offrivano di continuo cuori ancor palpitanti.

Ma qui si affrontano i problemi generali della decadenza delle alte civiltà delle cosiddette « Hochkulturen ». È qui che appare il regno delle masse, nel senso vero, non in quello moderno e artefatto. È, come direbbe il Libro dei Proverbi, la terza sciagura che affligge l'umanità, lo schiavo che regna al posto del padrone: Basso Impero retto da liberti e bucellarii, il potere fiero di venire dal nulla. Quindi non più regola né remora, la sorte degli uomini affidata al mero caso. Mi sembra che questa sia anche la situazione di paralisi dell'Islam dopo il periodo Almohadico, in un caos di tiranni, regoli, usurpatori, avventurieri, mamluki, cioè, di nuovo, liberti. Un caso che viene dal nulla lo abbiamo sotto gli occhi, è quello del Congo. La prima fase, anarchia innocente. Fu bella cosa vedere queste tribù abbandonate a se stesse ritrarsi dal consorzio statale, ciascuna intenta a ritrovar in sé la linea di agnazione dei capi legittimi, insomma alla ricerca del solo ordine comprensibile. Dopo, ma solo dopo, venne la violenza e il caos.

Prendo esempi a caso per farvi sentire che alcune situazioni della storia, più le spieghiamo, e meno le comprendiamo, voglio dire dal punto di vista di chi ci stava dentro. E sia detto con ogni rispetto per Vico. Ma sto ragionando qui non di *ratio cognoscendi* bensì di *ratio essendi*, quella che concerne la coscienza del medico. Da tanti millenni che si scrive la storia, si può seguire il travaglio di coloro che la facevano, ma quasi nulla di quelli che la pativano. E anche se ci si vuole scorgere ovunque l'eccipiente della consuetudine, non si possono che indovinare quali e quante fossero le croci degli sfortunati. Le masse sommerse partecipano in superficie alle certezze e alle fedi dei reggitori. Più giù, credo che abbia parlato, una volta per tutte, in loro nome, il solo Epicuro. Era quello il razionalismo di coloro che subiscono. Ma solo il *Graius homo*, lo ha ben detto Lucrezio, avrebbe potuto aiutarli ad affrontare i terrori e gli incubi delle superstizioni. Proprio in Africa, che adesso emerge dal profondo, e può già dare qualche testimonianza letteraria di sè, si può vedere da quale moltitudine di mostri sia popolato l'inconscio delle masse. Una buona cosa la superstizione per tali masse? Lasciamolo dire a Cicerone e ai suoi colleghi d'oggi.

Per tornare su terreno più noto, pensiamo in che perpetuo subbuglio deve essere stato il nostro medioevo. La « disciplina » sempre predicata dall'alto (e come ancora la imponeva la teocrazia nel Congo) può apparire una sana direttiva. Eppure lo storico imparziale sarà sempre tentato di invertire le parti. Gli sconvolgimenti perpetui, le avventure insensate come la Crociata degl'Innocenti, le grandi eresie, le insurrezioni operaie e contadine, lo stesso satanismo, potrebbero essere interpretati come un disperato sforzo verso l'equilibrio psichico, uno sforzo sempre sostenuto dalla speranza messianica contro una pressione deformante. Dai tempi di Tanchelmo fino agli Anabattisti, è una ridda di nomi, Poverelli, Catari, Adamiti, Flagellanti, Piagnoni, Hussiti, Taboriti, Utraquisti, Fratelli del Libero Spirito, una continua ripresa degli antichi messaggi Sibillini, Joanniti, e poi Gioachimiti, senza di cui non avremmo Dante.

Tutto questo è una continua riscoperta della certezza, così del male come del bene, certezza che fa andare la gente al rogo come si rendesse a festa, esultando nella promessa della Parusìa. Non vi è solo spregio delle autorità, promessa rivelata, vi è un vecchio e tenace fondo filosofico di panteismo, l'idea di uno stato di giustizia originaria e inalienabile, che fa parte della ragion comune, così che si ritrova nelle « Coutumes de Beaumanoir » e nel « Roman de la Rose » come più tardi in Rousseau. Già nel cosiddetto vangelo di Schwester Katrei, è detta la volontà di « far risalire le cose alle origini » allo Stato di Natura. Si ritrova il mito dei *Saturnia Regna*, ma confortato dalla promessa rivelata. Così si spiegano, in una situazione di forza non tollerabile, le successive esplosioni che riportano la pressione a zero, anche a costo del rogo.

Siamo stati da sempre al limite di rottura dell *stress*.

Quello che ci manca oggi è di poter afferrare quale fosse esattamente la forzatura psichica di quei tempi, che cosa significassero allora p. es. le domande degl'Inquisitori e le risposte che si opponevano, quale fosse il senso delle parole. Perchè certo nulla ci è chiaro, se pur abbiamo i verbali. Si chiude un soggetto sospettato in una segreta al buio per cinque anni, poi lo si interroga con la tortura, lo si fa confessare e si estrae una lista di nomi. Allora si ricomincia con quelli. Che rapporto poteva avere tutto questo con la Fede, quella che salva? Ci deve essere stata una intesa misteriosa fra Inquisitore e interrogato. Ci servirebbero dei test di associazioni verbali per quei tempi come sarebbe il vecchio Kent-Rozanoff — ma non ne abbiamo. Siamo ridotti a procedere a tastoni. Benedetto Croce forse ancora era in grado di capire, lui che scrisse: « La Santa Inquisizione, veramente Santa... » Ma non ci ha spiegato.

Oggi, si è sull'altro versante della storia, quello della solidarietà empatetica diffusa, in cui non si è più noncuranti dei sentimenti e dei motivi altrui, in cui si cerca di evitare azioni ispirate a crudeltà conscia o inconscia. Pensate alla tecnica chirurgica d'oggi a raffronto con quella di un Magendie, l'operatore col cappello a tuba e il grembiulone inondato di sangue.

Basterebbe solo pensare alla psicologia nel corso di un secolo. A me sembra che se si prende il buon Ottocento — quello, mettiamo, che viveva ancora nella mente di Croce — come un punto mediano d'equilibrio, e si tenta di integrare attorno ad esso un tratto di due secoli, ci si rende conto di un capovolgimento che fa perdere alle parole il loro senso. È forse la Rivoluzione Industriale che ha creato il capovolgimento: certo dal 1760 al 1960 non ci si capisce più, malgrado la comunanza e la continuità di cultura, malgrado tuttoquello che vive in noi così naturalmente di Diderot, Goethe e Stendhal. E oggi che si dovrebbe essere in grado di capire tante cose, è proprio l'organo della comprensione che viene a mancare. Tante cose erano ancora ovvie per i nostri genitori, che a noi sfuggono. Si tratta forse solo di un allargamento della coscienza. Voglio insistere che oggi il rapporto empatetico fra uomini è divenuto normale, mentre ieri si estendeva solo a una cerchia ristretta. Le scosse sismische dei « civil rights » nella società americana ce ne danno un esempio a scatto ritardato. Ancor ieri, era naturale trattar la gente come bestie, ancor che si volesse distinguere le bestie dai cristiani, come si dice in Toscana. Da sempre era così, malgrado gli interdetti della *religio*, del timor degli dei, della legge naturale o della pietà cristiana. Nè penso solo agli oppressi, ma alla società in generale, in cui tutti si opprimono fra di loro. Che mentalità era quella delle folle, ricchi e poveri, che si precipitavano ad assistere allo squartamento di Damiens, al supplizio della Brinvilliers, alle forche di Tyburn? Che criterio era quello di condannare le proprie figlie a quello che era per talune un carcere a vita, vedi *la Religieuse* di Diderot, o la seconda figlia di Galileo? I grandi non si risparmiavano fra di loro, lo vediamo dalle *Liaisons Dangeureuses* o anche da Saint-Simon. Per loro c'era, sì, il tedio, lo *spleen*, il tetro ritiro, il lato d'ombra di una attività sociale intensamente, furiosamente diretta; ma per loro c'era anche, come sfogo, la protervia, le crudeltà, la vendetta, lo scherno; e all'altro capo, l'esibizione di generosità, la « sensiblerie », tutti moventi poderosi: poichè non c'è soddisfazione come il sentirsi pari a Dio.

Lasciamo dunque le virtù del buon tempo antico. Lasciamo la *douceur de vivre*. La prima descrizione clinica di un manicomio è quella di Arthur Haslam, che fu primario di Bedlam. Vi si vedono non solo condizioni inconcepibili, ma casi di psicosi che non hanno ricontro dei nostri manuali. Un altro mondo.

Più vicino a noi ci sono gli orrori della Prima Rivoluzione Industriale, o le condizioni dei braccianti del Mezzogiorno, a cui fu concessa la parola credo solo dai tempi di Rocco Scotellaro in qua. Non dimentichiamo l'assurdo attuale, vivente, bollato da Lorenzo Milani, lucido intelletto sociale moderno, coscienza evangelica, che le chiese d'oggi, da destra e sinistra, hanno fretta di obliterare. Già sparite le sue splendide « *Esperienze Pastorali* ». Cancellato il tentativo di Danilo Dolci.

Ma chi ha parlato per noi con giustezza originale e universale è stata Simone Weil, l'ultima grande santa, a cui si addice questo titolo anche se non poteva dirsi credente. A lei dobbiamo il concetto dell' « afflizione » che inquadra bene le masse d'oggi, ricchi o miserabili che siano. L'afflizione non si fa presente alla coscienza, in quanto vuota l'anima dell'afflitto, la quale colma il vuoto con quel che trova a portata di mano, e ciò può essere così il razzolare fra le immondizie del recinto spinato come all'altro capo la caccia alla utilitaria e all'elettrodomestico. L'afflizione è cosa anonima e senza redenzione, trasforma le sue vittime in cose. E a noi non dispiace l'equivoco italiano fra « reità » e « la cosa » che si diventa, equivoco distribuito anch'esso lungo lo spettro che va dal popolo grasso ai rei incolpevoli del mondo concentrazionario. Siamo nella pura modernità. Passati i tempi del gran sogno socialista, siamo venuti ai *lendemains qui déchantent*. È questa forse la forma moderna, statistica, subdola del *taedium* onnipresente, quello che va a colpire le coronarie? Ce lo diranno i medici. E se qui si ritrova in essenza il *taedium* moderno, allora Chiaromonte ci ha ben delineato come sul piano morale e non religioso, il *taedium* di oggi prende l'aspetto dell'*inattenzione* moraviana.

Non si può riportare tutto a forze economiche, a condizioni obiettive, come cercano di fare i progressisti che hanno fretta. Non si può negare ogni funzione di *Gestalt*. C'è una tesi recente che ci mostra le forze della storia basate sulle neurosi individuali dei capi. È un tentativo pericoloso, che mira però alla conoscenza in profondità, come anche gli studi di Stekel sul fattore sessuale. È almeno il polo opposto alla posizione di Plekhanoff.

Ma poichè vengo dall'America, la « società del futuro », ostinatamente ottimista nella sua moderna afflizione, lì dove tedio e terrore, fusione e segregazione coesistono bizzarramente, sarebbe giusto che dicessi qualcosa di questo terreno esemplare ai vostri studi. Vi si trovano nel Sud situazioni di forza che fanno rivivere l'Alto Medioevo: vi si trova altrove lo sfacelo di tanti modi di vita ereditari, e pur talvolta anche zone di Paradiso Terrestre ricostruito con civile accorgimento. Una gamma incomparabile di soggetti. In un mondo come nessun altro sciolto, mobile, mutante, si trovano da una parte i *beatniks* e i minorenni delinquenti, dall'altra gruppi fermi, giustapposti come in un *cloisonné* di gusto medioevale, gruppi altrettanto fortemente incistati come i primi cristiani, che resistono al tempo; ghetti rimasti ancora all'epoca dei *pogrom* e delle visioni messianiche, poi Amish e Mormoni; o ancora quei siciliani di « Cosa Nostra » enucleati di colpo da una chiusura millenaria, che a contatto con i mezzi moderni hanno perduto quasi sembianza d'uomo mutandosi in lupi mannari. Per tanti altri italiani, quelli che patirono, vige il nomignolo salvato da Silone, Sciatàp, cioè « shut up » — coloro a cui si impone di tacere. Quando gli è stata ridata la parola, non sanno più servirsene. Questi fenomeni traumatici dell'incomunicabile si ritrovano adesso anche in Italia, e ovunque si sia giunti di colpo da situazioni arcaiche al test psicotecnico. Qualche anno fa scrisse Ottieri di « *Donnarumma all'assalto* », oggi abbiamo Volponi col *Memoriale* e *La Macchina Mondiale*. Tanto più grave è la cosa in America, paese del trapianto, quando un portoricano o un albanese si trova a dover reagire in modo per gli altri incomprensibile a situazioni che a lui sono inconcepibili. Qui allignano le più strane psicosi. Potrei citarvi casi clinici di follia nata per opera di medici coscienziosi, ma etnologicamente ignari e sprovveduti. È fatale che la facoltà di comprensione di una cultura che si è affidata a Freud si trovi messa in scacco dagli accidenti della storia.

Ho visto da vicino gli irlandesi, quasi tutti scampati all'inferno della Grande Carestia del 1846, prodigio di crudeltà dove è gran cosa che la gente non impazzisse. È gente adesso chiusa, aggressiva, neurotizzata. Fra loro è nato il « Know-nothingism ». Ma avevano la parola, anzi il dono dell'eloquenza inglese, e così hanno vinto. Così hanno salvato il loro mito. Ora si osserva che quel loro mito vitale si fondò su un « complesso edipico » caratterizzato, sulla figura della Madre, fulcro del gruppo etnico. È quanto mai naturale per una stirpe smarrita che vive nell'immediato, che ha perduto la facoltà di pensare e prevedere. Ma con questo è svanita la figura del padre, degradato dai figlioli al loro proprio rango. Dunque l'analisi freudiana qui sarebbe illusoria. Qui forse gioverebbe Jung.

Ovunque, nel mondo cosiddetto libero, ad ogni livello, si ritrova il trauma psichico, sempre diverso, e così mi si dice anche dei paesi delle Democrazie Progressive. Sembra davvero essere il prezzo che si paga per la mobilità e la libertà.

Qualche progresso c'è stato. Sissignori. Da ogni parte si spera che il vecchio detto *homo homini lupus* sia per recedere nel passato. Ed è ben vero che con l'espandersi di quella che direi la comunione empatetica, o l'attenzione al fattore psicologico, si venga attenuando quella crudeltà sconsiderata che si potrebbe anche chiamare col nome non spregiativo di animale, che si tratti di Tamerlano o degli Ateniesi a Milo, e che si estende al contadino che picchia le bestie, al gatto col topo, al ragno con la mosca, alla vespa con l'ospite prescelto per le sue uova. Insomma al comportamento irriflessivo che caratterizzava i generali sul Carso. Si profila adesso il comportamento proprio dell'uomo, che si tratti di Stalin coi suoi « impietrati » o degli SS nei campi di sterminio. Si bada a traumatizzare, a degradare, a distruggere l'intelligenza con intelligenza, con direttive ben studiate, servendosi di persone scelte per la loro nevrosi, psicosi o altri comportamenti degeneri, frutti di una civiltà mobile e matura. *Homini humanum genus homo* è forse il programma delle magnifiche sorti e progressive, come nel bene così anche nel male. E vi è forse una vendetta poetica nel vedere come proprio quella élite fra cui si creò la psicanalisi si sia vista rifiutare di colpo la condizione umana, considerata non già come formata di schiavi o bestie, nemmeno come di vermi, ma come cosa anti-umana, da estirparsi attentamente fra tormenti studiati con intelligenza simbolica. E fra questi l'incertezza traumatizzante, la tecnica del *Nacht und Nebel* fu attuata con amorosa cura, certo da gente che aveva riflettuto al *Processo* di Kafka. Si vede perchè ho parlato, per quanto spaventoso, di un certo elemento poetico nella vendetta; fra le vittime dei campi di concentramento, cedevano e si disfacevano per primi quelli che erano « eterodiretti » o diciamo ricettivi alle influenze sociali, come vorrebbe che si sia lo psichiatra, mentre resistevano quelli che si erano forgiati una personalità centrata e chiusa all'antica, di carattere stoico.

Se così ci appare il passato vicino, o il prossimo futuro, c'è altro che possiamo scoprire altrove? Come ebbe a dire Galileo, si può avere nozione di cose remotissime da noi, e talvolta per avventura più esatta che non delle vicine. Pensava allora alle proprietà matematiche che si riscontrano nell'universo. Ma lo stesso vorrei dire, almeno per traslato, di certi aspetti dei tempi remoti della nostra storia, o piuttosto protostoria: perchè lo spirito di questa gente di cui non sappiamo quasi nulla, era stato conquistato da una invenzione meravigliosa, quella del cosmo. E dico invenzione perchè, in fondo, che ne sappiamo anche oggi dell'universo, e che cosa abbiamo a fare con esso? Ma in quella fase arcaica, l'idea viveva negli uomini, era presente in ogni momento della loro vita. Era un'idea, come dice S. Agostino, di Dio stesso, più lontana che non son le stelle, più vicina all'uomo che non è il battito del suo polso. Ad essa faceva capo ogni aspetto della vita e di ciò che ci attornia. Non posso che accennare qui a quanto i miei collaboratori e io abbiamo impreso a mostrare, ma già ci appare chiara la fisionomia di questo continente sommerso dall'-intelletto, e ci si rivela l'enorme sforzo di organizzazione intesa a chiarire i fenomeni celesti, a collegarli fra di loro e anche a noi, ancora prima che esistesse una scrittura; per cui la teoria doveva esprimersi attraverso un linguaggio tecnico che più tardi ci pervenne in forma di mito.

L'origine sembra potersi rintracciare in un cerchio ristretto di pensatori audaci, vissuti in Mesopotamia verso il 5° millennio a.C., donde l'idea si diffuse per il globo per vari itinerari, in vari modi che gli etnologi oggi conglobano sotto il nome ormai convenuto di « stimulus diffusion ». Se si pensa come lo sciamanesimo portò con se pensieri già formati attraverso la catena di tribù dell'Asia Centrale, dall'India fino in Lapponia, ci si può formare un concetto di come si trasmettessero i germi teoretici. Non stiamo a sottilizzare troppo sulle date. L'evoluzionismo inteso in senso volgare o volgarizzato vorrebbe ravvicinare tutto alle scadenze storiche, lasciando l'umanità precedente allo stato brado: ma c'è, per servirmi di un'espressione usata da Zolla, una curvatura del tempo che ci nasconde gli eventi remoti.

Nel Rinascimento greco, il pensiero a cui accenno diventò il pitagorismo, fonte di ogni metafisica, e del pensiero matematico stesso. Non ho da dilungarmi su quello che il Prof. Schneider vi può esporre con tanta autorità. Ma in tempi assai più antichi, nel periodo neolitico, si è rivelato quello direi un protopitagorismo, un insieme di concezioni cosmografiche in cui terra e cielo s'incontrano, in cui cifre, ritmi, alfabeti, giochi come gli scacchi e quadrati magici, le qualità delle cose, le proprietà degli alberi e delle piante, il destino degli uomini, i poteri degli dei e degli astri, coi miti del loro divenire, s'intrecciano e s'intricano, direbbe Rimbaud « comme un opéra fabuleux ». Mi è venuta a mente quella parola nell'analizzarli. E quel che c'è di più favoloso in quest'impresa, è il potere del pensiero organizzatore divenuto esso « un opéra fabuleux », che si costruisce storie rigorose e coerenti per organizzare gli astri, i loro rapporti e le loro guerre, che audacemente sottomette il tutto alle misure e al numero, traccia allineamenti siderali per « stabilire la terra e agganciare il cielo », secondo il testo egiziano, così che tutto venga in ordine. O, per dirla coi cinesi, far così che fra le misure celesti e i toni della siringa non ci sia lo spessore di un capello. È questo il potere della fantasia esatta, come lo chiamerebbe Leonardo.

Ma in tutto questo, l'uomo dove rimane? Si trova a essere tutto e nulla, proprio come si conviene. L'anima sua trascorre per l'universo, è della sua essenza. La persona dell'uomo invece rimane presa nel gioco del destino. Quando Marcel Griaule, che ci ha rivelato civiltà ignote nel Sudan occidentale, chiedeva ai suoi esperti del luogo di parlargli un po' della terra abitata, di dirgli quel che sapevano dei paesi lontani, si meravigliava di vederli sempre indicare il cielo. E finalmente capì che per loro la « terra abitata » significava la zona dell'Eclittica. Solo lassù vivono e si muovono i soli abitanti veri, cioè i pianeti. Poichè solo degli dei si può dire in verità che esistono e sono. L'uomo si rende ben conto di esserci, e di dover badare alle sue cose, ma si sente un po' come il sogno di un'ombra, se non attraverso gli atti rituali che lo uniscono al mondo « vero ». Vita e pensiero di selvaggi, si dirà. Ma qui si trova chiarità e pace.

Non mi viene a mente che un solo documento della nostra letteratura che ci porti a contatto con questo mondo strano. Dico « nostro » perchè insomma Platone è dei nostri. E nel suo *Timeo* c'è ancora il mondo arcaico chiaramente espresso. Platone era del nostro mondo e di quell'altro, l'ultimo degli arcaici e il primo dei moderni, essere bilingue e bifronte come il dio Termine.

Ora, se guardiamo a questo quadro del *Timeo* che si dice pitagorico ma che contiene anche elementi assai più antichi, scorgiamo un universo implacabile. Le nostre anime vengono dalle stelle, essendo della medesima natura; ma il Demiurgo nel creare il mondo le ha balestrate nel tempo. Le ha piazzate sugli « strumenti del tempo » cioè i pianeti, e lì si fa il loro addestramento all'esistenza che devono condurre una volta trapiantate in terra con l'attrezzatura di quel dato pianeta. Così la loro natura è data alle anime una volta per tutte, con le loro servitù e le loro passioni: è l'impronta iniziale da cui devono liberarsi via via per tornare pure e disposte a salire alle stelle. Come farà a riordinarsi lo sprovveduto che viene da Marte, quel pianeta violento e non calcolabile? Perchè in quel mondo di fati vi è un solo criterio del bene e del male, del giusto e dell'ingiusto. Non conta la preghiera o la speranza, non vi si tratta che di esattezza, di puntualità agli appuntamenti del *Kairos*: la periodicità giusta che vi fa cadere a posto, lì dove il fato vi attende, o altrimenti si è ripresi nella bufera del tempo. Fa pensare a quella storia di Kafka: la porta era lì, aperta per noi proprio per oggi, e adesso si richiude. Chi ha mancato all'appuntamento è perduto, deve andare errando attraverso i secoli, cercando il ritorno.

Questo sì che è un universo astronomico. Per noi, abbastanza spaventoso. Eppure è in esso che lo spirito arcaico ritrovava la sua pace; e ve la trovò per dozzine di secoli, quanti ne corrono dalla Grande Piramide fino a oggi. Non sono cose facili a capire, questa accettazione totale, questo sommettersi alle necessità, se non nelle grandi menti dei teorici che avevano formato il sistema. Ma si trattava di necessità divina. E possiamo forse comprendere il calvinista, pur così vicino a noi, che si umilia a esser inspiegabilmente dannato? O possiamo comprendere il puritano Wahhabita? La risposta è pur sempre quella: Islam, Abbandono. E pure sono proprio questi i messaggi che hanno scatenato le più grandi energie libere della storia. Energia « stressata » al massimo, quando, come nel calvinista, l'Abbandono è doppiato di un dubbio terrificante quanto al proprio destino individuale. Mentre nel sistema arcaico, non c'è capriccio sovrano della divinità, come non c'è d'altra parte da pensare a misericordia. Tutto è scienza.

Necessità ho detto, dipendente da forze divine che esse stesse non hanno libertà di scelta, che si identificano con le leggi naturali.

Tutto, la nostra sorte come quel che c'è attorno, è rigorosamente determinato; che dico, non solo determinato univocamente, come in meccanica, ma sovradeterminato su vari livelli cospiranti fra di loro, polisovrasaturo di determinazione alla scala del cosmo. Qui si scopre già il Dio di Spinoza, che comanda l'*amor intellectualis*, prima ancora che si sia formato l'intelletto astratto. Ma lì dove ci si rassegna, dove regna il Fato si ritrova la libertà inerente al personaggio tragico, la pienezza della sua forma. « Gepraegte Form, die lebend sich entwickelt ». Ed è proprio quella libertà che si rivela nei miti — linguaggio tecnico dell'inizio, ma così denso di forma e di suggestione che ha invaso la coscienza storica dei popoli, dove lo ritroviamo ancor oggi. È un caso, come direbbe Levi-Strauss, di « immaginazione totalizzante ».

Questo stato di cose arcaico, lo possiamo ancora conoscere direttamente come ho detto: perchè miracolo ha voluto che in un angolo sperso della boscaglia africana, quelle tradizioni siano rimaste intatte, se pur degradate allo stato selvaggio. Ci voleva una società pastorale non ancora formata in classi, vicina al nomadismo, e tali sono i popoli Mande, ai quali Griaule ha consacrato studi che hanno rinnovato l'etnologia. È, per così dire, preistoria conservata in recipiente sotto chiusura ermetica. Attraverso Griaule e i suoi sappiamo che cosa sia una civiltà articolata in ogni punto dai grandi temi cosmologici, ancora identificata ad essi, ben più che altre culture cosiddette primitive. E benchè questa oscura gente abbia subito il tempo, si sia anche essa trovata esposta alle razzie e alla schiavitù, pure rivela una strordinaria armonia di vita, un'assenza di tensione che la tiene lontana da quei fenomeni di frattura, d'incoerenza, di bestialità che compaiono altrove nelle culture Bantù.

È stata una riuscita non prevedibile. Si era partiti per induzione dal fondo dell'ignoto, da quegli antenati, come disse una volta D'Alembert, a cui dobbiamo tutto e di cui non sapremo mai nulla, e siamo sboccati in una situazione ancora contemporanea che, decifrata, rivela una singolare pace interiore. Come quella dei veri primitivi, i Boscimani. « Se io fossi un gatto — scriveva Albert Camus — apparterrei a questo mondo ». Ecco gente che appartiene a questo mondo, nelle dimensioni astronomiche, senza dubbi nè fratture. Non sanno nemmeno di « essere ». (Ho detto che per essi chi « è » sono gli astri sulla Eclittica), e quindi tanto più nettamente « sono ». Tutte le angoscie di Sartre nella *Nausée* non li toccherebbero per nulla. Hanno in se tanto « essere » quanto quella radice d'albero che riduce alla disperazione il protagonista. Qui davvero non si parla di *taedium*. Come non è il caso di parlarne nella civiltà tradizionale dell'India coi suoi riti e la sua *bhakti*, trasmessi anch'essi per via di meditazioni cosmologiche. Ma in quella civiltà così evoluta dobbiamo pur ammettere che si rivela il fatto grave: dall'alto in basso, mancano di *sense of humour*. Manca il « reo dolor che pensa ».

Qui insomma ci ritroviamo nel noto. Partendo dal passato remoto, ci siamo ricollegati via via a situazioni più prossime, come la vita monastica; ovunque regni la costrizione accettata, l'obbedienza assoluta. Lo sappiamo che quella è pace. Lo sanno gli psichiatri e i neurologi, quali siano i benefici dell'assenza di dubbio e di libertà, ma anche di *sense of humour*. Mi torna a mente quel che scriveva quello scontento di Magalotti al suo Granduca: era entrato in convento, aveva accettato l'umiltà e la disciplina, ma quello che non gli andava giù era il modo melenso di quei cari padri di darsi un po' di buon tempo innocente. Niente da fare, siamo degl'intossicati.

A che serve questa scorsa che non può essere che una sommaria ricognizione in terreno incerto? A dirci anzitutto quanto sia vana quella saggezza classicheggiante, che l'uomo non cambia mai. Cambia sì, e cambiano le sue afflizioni. Ben poche, direbbe Platone, sono le anime che sanno accordarsi al corso degli astri. Serve ancora a dirci che a dispetto d'ogni orgoglio dialettico, si rimane smarriti nella storia. La chiave del passato si perde, e si possono appena intuire la ferite inferte dal tempo. Per questo vorrei che ai medici, forse talvolta i veri umanisti d'oggi, si potessero aggiungere storici ed etnologi, che tentassero, in accordo con loro, una paziente inchiesta, davvero umanistica, tentando di trovare in che modo, per che verso, la gente veramente ha pensato e sofferto attraverso i tempi. Oggi, lo so, si danno certe risposte « passepartout », e la psicanalisi si presenta in molte parti come il vero umanesimo, giusta fine di una parola troppo abusata e stazzonata. Ma ricordiamo che la povera umanità comune non è nata a Viēnna, è nata in qualche parte dell'Africa.

Summary

The examination of historical events shows how much has been swept under the carpet by normal historians who may have paid attention to the economic factor but surely not to the psychic and emotional factors as we begin to understand them today. Even now History is written essentially by those who make it and not by those who suffer it, and thus a large number of events remains incomprehensible to a mind conditioned by conventional standards. The development of normal empathy which characterizes present-day civilization should move us to re-examine History with a different eye and to write it from a more understanding point of view, since today's humanist is no doubt endowed first of all with a medical awareness.

Riflessioni sul Fato

Fato Antico

L'IDEA DEL FATO PRENDE FORMA QUANDO L'UOMO NON SUBISCE come le bestie, ma cerca di rendersi conto e non accetta il dono d'origine, *le grand don de ne rien comprendre à notre sort.*

Di chi è colpa? Perché colpa ci deve essere di sicuro. Se prima della scienza sono venuti i grandi miti cosmogonici è perché l'uomo vuol rendersi conto di quel che lo riguarda, perché la causa che più lo stringe davvicino è il perché e il come dei suoi guai. Il mito del peccato originale è la spiegazione che informa la nostra civiltà, tanto da rivivere ostinatamente in Freud. Ma è un mito relativamente recente, e la causa è risolta in favore del Signore. L'uomo porta tutta la colpa e, come direbbe Platone, Dio non è responsabile.

Se non ci fermiamo al fatto strettamente religioso, possiamo scorgere più indietro gli inizi di un pensiero scientifico vero e proprio, e con essi la possibilità di una valutazione più complessa di quello che si dice il Fato. Al dilà dell'Egitto e di Babilonia, al dilà anche dei Sumeri e delle civiltà dell'Indo si comincia oggi a discernere i lineamenti colossali di una vera astronomia arcaica, quella che fissò il corso dei pianeti, che dette il nome alle costellazioni dello zodiaco, che creò l'universo astronomico — e con esso il cosmo — quale lo troviamo già pronto quando comincia la scrittura, verso il 4000 a.C.

Già una generazione addietro, il Berthelot aveva proposto per questo complesso d'idee il nome di « astrobiologia », e potremmo anche accettarlo, non fosse che l'elemento biologico rimaneva ancora troppo istintivo e animistico per essere elevato a componente scientifica. Un nome più esatto sarebbe « aritmosofia astrale », nel senso che rimaneva ancor vivo nel pensiero pitagorico. Ma ciò che ne conosciamo attraverso la Grecia era un solo aspetto, quello intellettualmente più vicino a noi. Il centro vero è più indietro nel tempo, intorno al V millennio a.C., quando molti motivi e livelli di pensiero s'intrecciavano in un tutto che aveva la sua compattezza e formava una visione unitaria del cosmo. Fu proprio questo primo pensiero filosofico a fornirci l'alfabeto, inizio per noi del tempo storico, ma che fu per esso la conclusione. E la sua prodigiosa creatività intellettuale ci è documentata altresì sul terreno della tecnologia; poiché da allora data la « rivoluzione tecnologica » che doveva fornire all'antichità i suoi mezzi di presa sulla natura, dalla coltura del grano alla preparazione dei metalli, alla tessitura, alla ceramica, alle grandi tecniche edificatorie. Sarebbe un'epoca imponente nella nostra coscienza, se avesse potuto lasciare memoria scritta di sé; dopotutto fu il « balzo in avanti » che precedette la rivoluzione industriale. Ma i suoi documenti si ritrovano nel paesaggio coltivato, nelle immagini, nel mito, nella tradizione molte volte dispersa e frammentata ma in cui si ravvisano, come i pezzi di un *puzzle*, ingegnose costruzioni narrative che si erano venute diffondendo e che, ricomposte almeno in parte, si rivelano essere il primo linguaggio scientifico.

Non è un'idea nuova questa, perché già era stata adombrata dagli storici dell'astronomia del secolo XVIII, ripresa nel secolo scorso da non pochi grandi orientalisti; ma solo adesso, grazie alle scoperte dell'etnologia culturale e alla pubblicazione di testi antichi, essa comincia a venire in giusta luce. Né mancano i riferimenti a questa tradizione nella letteratura classica, ma veniva presa dai filologi per mitografia barocchesca, come in Apollodoro, Nonno Panopolita, Licofrone, fin nei commentatori dotti come l'Ovidio dei *Fasti*, come Macrobio e Marciano Capella. Non era così facile levarsi di mezzo il Platone del *Timeo*, ma lì si faceva appello alla ben nota fantasia platonica finché le stesse idee non apparvero nei testi superstiti di altre civiltà.

Questo pensiero è stato in essenza una cosmologia. E non, come si crederebbe, una prima forma del cosmo animistico e magico del Rinascimento, ma un cosmo strettamente astrale, in cui tutto si pensa in termini di moto regolare e misurato. Tutto il reale si impernia sulle potenze stellari: chi comanda il mutamento sono i pianeti.

Che gli Dei antichi fossero in origine i pianeti, questo ce lo dice Aristotele in un passo non abbastanza rilevato della *Metafisica* (1074 b 12). Il culto solare, sul quale si è tanto architettato nel secolo scorso e che in verità sembrerebbe ben naturale, appare solo episodicamente nel tempo storico. Nei tempi arcaici o protostorici, la funzione del sole sembra essere stata di provvedere la misura assoluta di tempo, quella che in Omero riappare come la « corda aurea ». La potenza assoluta è negli Dei planetari, che si combinano in vari modi con le costellazioni per presentare le varie configurazioni del potere. Così le stelle dell'Orsa, che mai non tramontano, sono per così dire altre sedi del potere degli astri mobili.

Ben poco di primitivo in tutto questo. Le storie della creazione sono costruzioni intellettuali, come lo è il *Timeo* di Platone, ma non intendono raccontarci davvero la creazione perché non c'è creazione. Tutto è da sempre. Il Demiurgo di Platone, l'artefice, il *Deus Faber* era originariamente Saturno (un aspetto del quale era Efesto) l'antico reggitore, che da sempre « forma » il mondo nel suo lento andare e « dà le misure » agli altri là dove Giove è il potere esecutivo. E così via di seguito.

Così è nata per prima una vera scienza dei moti celesti, opera di geni ignoti, i Kepleri e i Newton di quei millenni aboliti, i quali seppero tracciare percorsi molteplici convolti e intrecciati degli astri nel cielo. Che intensità di attenzione ci volesse, che capacità di analisi, che ritentiva di memoria sono cose da non comprendersi: ma possiamo farcene un'idea dai navigatori polinesiani, giunti alle soglie dei nostri tempi ancora paleolitici e prealfabeti; i cantari di migliaia di versi che comprendono cosmogonia e astonomia tutto in uno ci sono giunti attraverso i secoli affidati alla memoria senza la minima variante, perché dovevano esprimere cose esatte.

Impresa preliminare dev'essere quella di impostare una morfologia comparata di temi mitici, fiabeschi e sacri di soggetto originariamente astronomico, che ci permetta di vedere i primi lineamenti delle idee soggiacenti.

Che cosa si può già scorgere di quel pensiero? Una visione dell'universo come un ordine rigoroso, dominata da una Necessità assoluta di natura matematica. E questa visione è già metafisica, se ebbe ragione Valéry a dire che ogni metafisica esige che l'uomo sia partecipe di uno spettacolo che lo esclude.

Nulla esiste, nel senso ontologico, se non quell'ordine che non è tanto volontà degli Dei quanto la loro natura stessa, impassibile e inesorabile, portatrice di ogni bene e di ogni male, inaccessibile alle preghiere e, come direbbe Varrone, parchissima di misericordia.

Il fattore antropomorfico della divinità umanizzata, che tiene tanto posto nel nostro pensiero storico, sembra non esistesse a quel punto. La realtà, nel senso ontologico, è una, è quella regolarità della macchina cosmica. L'idea dei freddi calcolatori arcaici è molto vicina filosoficamente a quella della fisica attuale, ma quanto più impegnativa: perché quella macchina ci comanda, assai più che non possa l'attuale realtà fisica, di cui ci sembra di poterci servire, almeno per i nostri scopi limitati. Siamo noi moderni, in fondo, più vicini alla tradizionale magia. Nelle popolazioni che hanno conservato, in un angolo sperduto della storia, quella visione antichissima, possiamo ancora vedere quanto quella visione fosse imponente e consequenziale. Quando Marcel Griaule fece per primo parlare i Dogon dell'Africa occidentale, stupì di esistenze così completamente irretite in un pensiero cosmologico dalla complicazione senza fondo. Basti una nota. Volendo esplorare il loro orizzonte geografico, cercava di discorrere della terra abitata, di quello che conoscevano del mondo che li attornia. Ma dopo un momento li vedeva tornare a puntare in alto, e a indicargli dei confini nel cielo. E capì che l'idea di « terra abitata » si riferisce per loro alla zona celeste compresa fra i tropici: una banda di 47 gradi nel cielo, disposta ai due lati dell'equatore. È la zona entro cui si muovono il sole, la luna e i pianeti lungo lo zodiaco. Sono quelli i veri, i soli « abitanti ». In linguaggio aristotelico sono essi le vere sostanze, in quanto hanno un'azione. L'uomo non *è* perché non ha decisioni da prendere. È passivo, è in certo modo un riflesso. Partecipa dell'essere, in quanto celebra i miti ed esegue i riti. È forse questa l'idea che precede la metafisica indiana.

Ma senza un essere proprio, dov'è il Fato dell'uomo? Difficile a dirsi. Certo non nella Storia, perché non c'è ancora Storia. E quando la Storia appare, con la scrittura, sono le datazioni celesti che le danno consistenza. L'enorme epopea del *Mahabharata*, col suo intrico di peripezie inverosimili, si impernia sopra la battaglia di Kurukshetra. Ma questa, a sua volta, è un mondo di eventi che si distendono nel tempo. È come la guerra di Troia, ma niente della semplicità omerica, se pur vi siano strane coincidenze come la morte accidentale di Krishna per una freccia al tallone. Negli episodi sono impegnate forze celesti, e nella battaglia è interpolata la rivelazione di Krishna, il « canto del beato », ma l'insieme non ha costrutto umano. Antecedenti e generazioni si diramano interminabilmente, reami e vite sono giocati e perduti ai dadi più volte; nel pallido decotto affiorano solo a volte la tragedia e il *pathos*. Il Fato si riassume in questo, che ogni grande impresa sembra destinata in ultimo a fallire. Ma è ben poco che quadri con la nostra concezione di racconto epico. E nemmeno con quel tanto di reale che di solito traspare nel mito. Si sente che l'accento è altrove. Dobbiamo esser grati al professor Sen Gupta che ci ha fornito un filo conduttore, mostrandoci come la maggior parte degli episodi sia intesa solo a portare in gran dettaglio datazioni astronomiche sotto la forma di stazioni lunari. Si rafforza la tesi di Stucken che aveva dedotto l'origine dell'alfabeto indiano dalle stesse datazioni di stazioni lunari, e prende un senso anche quell'insistenza sui giochi d'azzardo come operatori del Fato, con i dadi falsati dagli Dei. I cosiddetti miti storici si rivelano all'analisi costruzioni astronomiche.

Dove rimane allora la libertà, elemento essenziale del Fato? Mi sia permesso di fare ricorso a Tolstoi, vero ultimo intelletto epico fra noi, il quale sembra aver afferrato questo stato d'animo arcaico. Durante l'incendio di Mosca, Pierre Bezukhov viene preso in una retata dai soldati francesi e spinto in una baracca con altri presi a caso. Il suo destino sembra segnato, poiché si vogliono degli untori da fucilare. Ed ecco che nel silenzio della notte leva gli occhi alle stelle ed è preso da pazza allegria: « Hanno messo dentro me? Chi, me? ». E si dice che tutto questo cielo è in lui, è lui — momento di catarsi che lo prepara all'incontro decisivo con Platone Karataiev, il povero contadino che ha superato la sorte.

Torniamo un secolo indietro. C'è una favola americana di colore autoctono che ancora si racconta ai bambini: è quella di Rip van Winkle, che andato a far legna al bosco si addomentò. Ed ecco che sognò di trovarsi sulla tolda della nave di Hendrik Hudson, il grande antenato navigatore, e di vedere lui e i suoi compagni giocare a bocce con grandi palle di cannone. Guardava e guardava, e poi si svegliò, e tornò al villaggio, e trovò che nessuno lo conosceva perché erano passati trecento anni.

È una fiaba che sembra nata tra i primi coloni di New York, ma quando l'etnologo scopre che ve ne sono versioni in ogni clima che vanno indietro migliaia d'anni, e diventano più chiare quanto più si va indietro, si deve pu concludere che questo è un grande mito astronomico: i numi che lanciano le loro sfere tonanti sulla tolda del cielo. E al contemplatore assorto nei calcoli mille anni diventano come un minuto. Questo era un modo di superare il Fato, passando dal tempo all'eternità, facendo della Necessità una libera creazione. È il modo dei grandi matematici d'ogni tempo. A questo si ricollega un'usanza dei Maya del Yucatan, i quali avevano in ogni loro città un grande cortile da gioco, detto il « campo di gioco delle stelle » (per gli americanisti *Star Ball Court*). In esso, in certe occasioni solenni, attori raffiguranti i Numi giocavano secondo strette regole, facendo passare la palla attraverso anelli disposti a mezzo campo; e i loro nomi indicavano solo certe datazioni del calendario astronomico. Dal racconto superstite di Sahagun, sappiamo taluni nomi: ci rimane da ricostruire il gioco.

Ecco dunque un universo di ragione, dove l'intelletto si ritrova. Ma la Ragione è affidata al Numero. È, in fondo, l'universo pitagorico, dove il Fato ultimo dell'uomo si esprime con il ritorno alle stelle (ciascuno alla sua, come è detto nel *Timeo*). Di questa visione abbiamo un'altra testimonianza, per strano che sembri, nel culto egiziano. Gli oscuri testi delle Piramidi, in quello che sembra il loro interminabile divagare, sono istruzioni di rotta per l'anima del re, morto in tali e tali situazioni astrali, perché possa trovare la sua via verso il luogo del cielo che gli sarà assegnato come eterno soggiorno. Che cosa rimane qui degli eventi umani, passata la sede del Giudizio? Non hanno storia nel senso nostro. Ma hanno una struttura, affidata a un arco di tempo molto vasto.

Tutto, vita e morte e armonia della natura, essendo compreso nell' anno, l'insistente ricerca arcaica si era sempre volta verso un anno più grande, che chiudesse non solo i cicli lunisolari ma tutti i cicli del cielo e riconducesse ogni astro al suo posto. È questo il Grande Anno accennato da Platone come già da Eraclito, e dietro di esso si asconde una scoperta che si oscurò via via attraverso i secoli, per poi tornare alla coscienza scientifica con Ipparco. Per quanto non possa dirsi ancora definitivamente provato, tutti gl'indizi ci dicono che all'inizio della Storia si conosceva già la Precessione degli Equinozi; per cui tutto lo zodiaco percorre un circolo lentissimo, di un grado ogni 72 anni, finché in 26.900 anni tutto si ritrova come prima. E mi piace di pensare che la prima misura moderna e rigorosa di questo spostamento impercettibile fu fornita da Paolo Toscanelli, servendosi del grande strumento che gli aveva costruito nel Cupolone il suo amico Brunelleschi.

In questo ciclo si iscrivono e concludono, secondo i pensatori arcaici, tutte le grandi mutazioni. È la rivoluzione massima degli orbi celesti.

Quanto è mutato il senso della parola rivoluzione da allora. Ma rimane ancora a dominare il nostro tempo. Ha ormai infranto le concezioni di innumeri pensatori, poiché la vera rivoluzione permanente che a tutto presiede è la rivoluzione industriale.

Ma in tutto il tempo moderno, rivoluzione ha significato l'irreversibile. Ha portato con sé la vera Storia. Che è poi la fuga in avanti. Pure c'è un vecchio senso che ci è ancora nascosto, noto ai rivoluzionari autentici: il ritorno alle origini. È quello a cui si è sempre pensato fin dai tempi arcaici, è la palingenesi quando anche fosse in termini di rivolgimenti multimillenari. Ogni visione apocalittica è un modo di ricongiungere la fine al principio, onde il tempo riacquisti un senso. Vi fu sempre l'idea di un Grande Anno, del rivolgimento della macchina del tempo, ad acquetare le menti. In quel tempo tutto tornava, non dico nel senso letterale dell'Eterno Ritorno, ma delle costanti dell'avventura umana, le grandi azioni, i grandi rivolgimenti di popoli, la fondazione di leggi. Le grandi crisi che scandivano il ciclo eterno si pensava avessero luogo ogni volta che il sole equinoziale entrava in una nuova costellazione, di cui ben quattro si sono succedute da che l'uomo ha coscienza del tempo. E il ciclo s'inaugurava ogni volta con un reggitore divesso, in chiave diversa.

Ripensiamo alla Quarta Ecloga di Virgilio, così diversa dalle altre, tutta quanta intonata a motivi arcaici che riaffiorano nei loro termini specifici: *Magnus ab integro saeclorum nascitur ordo...* C'è voluta una rara insensibilità filologica da parte di taluni (perfino il Norden) per farne una poesiola d'occasione. Avevano ben più ragione i medievali di farne una profezia solenne dei tempi nuovi. Il tema del ritorno di Astrea non è inteso a banale adulazione di Augusto. È un fatto astronomico (Vergine in posizione equinoziale o solstiziale) che ricorre ogni 6.000 anni o poco più: un lungo « ordine di secoli ». E non è mica inteso che verrà l'èra di Bengodi: solo che « progenie discende dal ciel nova », il fanciullo miracoloso che deve ridere alla madre, e il tempo ricomincerà: ancora una volta Ilio dovrà cadere, gli Argonauti salpare verso nuove avventure...

Così si concepivano le grandi « funzioni » del tempo come già raffigurabili, gli attori incaricati di una parte. Sul « teatro del mondo ammascherate », come direbbe Campanella, le figure si muovono secondo schemi preordinati dal Fato. Non sono a caso quelle ultime linee di Marc'Aurelio: « Ho recitato la mia parte come si deve ».

Vorrei tentare di rendere questo schema sul vivo, come si trova nell'epopea nordica. Il Crepuscolo degli Dei è la fine, ma solo la fine di *un* mondo. Questo gli interpreti romantici non lo dicono, ma lo dice per esempio Snorri Sturleson, nel *Gylfaginning* che è parte della sua *Edda* in prosa. Snorri era un poeta molto dotto in varie discipline, come lo erano allora i poeti, e avrebbe potuto scrivere il suo *Convito*. Nel passo che segue ci dice quel che succede dopo il crollo del Valhalla e la « fine del mondo »: « Gli Aesir (cioè gli Dei superstiti) si sedettero a consiglio a ricordare i racconti che già erano stati trasmessi a Gylfi, e quegli stessi nomi che erano prima stati dati li dettero agli uomini e ai luoghi di allora, al fine che quando molte età fossero passate gli uomini non avessero a dubitare che quegli stessi Aesir di cui si parlava, e quelli a cui erano dati gli stessi nomi, fossero tutt'uno. E lì Thor ebbe di nuovo il suo nome, ed era l'antico Asa Thor; ma divenne Oeku Thor, cioè il Thor del Carro, e a lui vengono ascritte le grandi imprese che Ettore compì dinanzi a Troia ».

Qui il tempo è abolito, narrativa e vaticinio si incrociano e si confondono in quello che è propriamente linguaggio sibillino. E poi altrove è detto: « I figli degli Dei uccisi che torneranno alla vita troveranno nell'erba i pezzi tutti d'oro del gioco di scacchi che fu interrotto dalla catastrofe, e siederanno a concilio e si richiameranno a mente la loro sapienza segreta ».

Non si può non pensare all'Apocalisse, alla ricostruzione della Città di Dio col regolo d'oro. Questi miti della Ripresa si trovano in diversa chiave in Messico, in India, in Cina, in Polinesia. Qui era ben chiara la funzione dell'alfabeto e dei giochi congegnati con arte come depositari della tradizione interrotta. Tanto perché Snorri non sia accusato di fantasia, il tema dei giochi riappare nel Canto della Sibilla, il *Völuspa*, dove ci è detto di più, se non più chiaramente: Asgard era costruita sul « campo del vortice », Idavöllr; lì gli Dei avevano le loro dodici case in circolo, lì si esercitavano in arti e giochi « finché non giunsero le tre vergini tremende, le figlie dei giganti di Thursenheim ».

Insomma non si esce dal sibillino, come si conviene, ma in queste faccende cosmogoniche il sibillino rimane significativo, dove che spunti. Non dimenticherò la sorpresa che ebbi quando, nello scorrere *La Création* di Agrippa d'Aubigné, mi imbatei in un altro detto sibillino. Si riferisce a « ...*Quand les esprits bienheureux / dans la voie de laict auront fait nouveaulx feux* ». Dove l'ha preso, Agrippa d'Aubigné? In quale strana trasmissione rinascimentale? Questa accensione saturnina di fuochi in cielo non fa parte, che io sappia, della tradizione europea, dove appare invece la forma volontaristica del furto di Prometeo, ma si ritrova in altri continenti. Così, nel Messico, Tezcatlipoca il Rosso accese un fuoco nella Via Lattea, dopodiché divenne Mixcouatl. Si rientra nell'ordine del Fato. È ancora ben difficile ritrovarsi. Ma in questo intrico di corsi e ricorsi, cicli e palingenesi senza principio né fine sul quadrante del tempo, dove sempre « secol si rinnova » in tutto o in parte, quel che sembra dominare è il continuo ridimensionamento del mondo e degli eventi. Il modello originario della « città quadrata » dell'Apocalisse misurata dall'angelo con la sua asta d'oro è il Paradiso Terrestre, per gli astronomi babilonesi Mul iku, che identificano col quadrato di Pegaso. E perché poi quello? Perché si trovava perfettamente inquadrato fra i punti delle Quattro Tempora, al tempo in cui i punti equinoziali si trovavano sulla Via Lattea, che sembra essere stato il momento d'origine scelto per il computo del tempo: e che fu verso il 5000 a.C. La Via Lattea diventava allora il ponte fra terra e cielo, e ai quattro capi (solstizi ed equinozi) si trovavano le quattro figure bifronti significanti immortalità: Sagittario, Gemelli, Pesci, Vergine con Spica. *Iam redit et Virgo*... Quanto non si è teneramente fantasticato di palingenesi nel Medio Evo su questa maternità cosmica. Nel miracolo di Saint Maël fin l'orsa polare tenendo il suo piccolo in braccio gli dice: « *Incipe, parve puer, risu cognoscere matrem* ».

Di là dalla leggenda cristiana, continuatrice inconscia del pensiero arcaico, si rivela nel quadrato di Eden il numero puro. *Omnia posuisti in mensura et numero*. Le piramidi a gradini di Caldea, l'arca del mito di Gilgamesh come quella di Noè, la stessa Arca dell'Alleanza erano documenti metrici intesi a conservare, oltre ogni catastrofe, i dati fondamentali che mettevano l'uomo in rapporto col divino. E che non ci fugga di vista la Torre di Babele. Non si è stati giusti con i costruttori di Etemenanki (perché questo era il suo vero nome) in quanto il racconto biblico è stato scritto dal nemico. Ma adesso che abbiamo le tavolette cuneiformi Smith possiamo capire. Era una grande piramide a gradini, come le altre *ziggurat*, e si direbbe che fu deciso di farne una somma teologica. Si voleva eternare la scienza, fermare il tempo, dominando il Fato. I maestri d'arte vollero mettere nella costruzione tutte le proporzioni, distanze e armonie planetarie, cicli e ricorrenze, le unità di misura e di musica, quadrature, poligoni e rapporti. Si volevano ricreare i dati del Quadrato fondamentale. Non è l'ultima volta che l'umanità ha cercato il Paradiso Terrestre e lo ha cercato nei modi più strani e impensati. Il problema di conciliare tanti dati in una struttura semplice sembra aver dato luogo alla « confusione delle lingue ». Il lato storico di Nimrud, che Dante mette fra i Giganti, si direbbe dunque che sia stato un primo tentativo di unificazione scientifica. E Dante stesso è un Nimrud vittorioso. La *Commedia* è un altro Etemenanki, un *tour de force* riuscito, con il suo intrico di numeri pitagorici, dati astronomici e intervalli musicali. Ma già, tutta la teoria classica dell'architettura, da Vitruvio a Villalpando, è un simile intrico che vuol chiudersi a sistema.

In verità, tra tutti questi, è Dante ancora il più vicino alla vera ispirazione arcaica, perché i dati spaziali che egli accenna rimangono una fantasia, mentre le vere misure sono portate dai *metra* del suo canto, da come esso si inquadra nel tempo. E il fattore essenziale del pensiero arcaico sono proprio le misure del tempo, da cui le unità spaziali sono ricavate. L'universo celeste è un immenso scadenzario in cui ad ogni momento si iscrivono scadenze critiche. Cicli, congiunzioni, trigoni, quadrature; tutto l'apparato della tarda astrologia che la filosofia stoica rimise in onore in Grecia, ci dice che alle scadenze delle angolature nessuno sfugge e, come solennemente insegna Manilio, *Fata regunt orbem, certa stant omnia lege.*

In questo senso, ripeto, le misure significative erano misure di tempo. Niente mi ha permesso di afferrare qualcosa della mentalità arcaica come quando compresi che le arcane armonie geometriche di punti luminosi disposti nello spazio, delle « monadi » che i pitagorici ritenevano essere fondamento del reale, non erano in origine tracciate col disegno, ma erano legate a eventi nel cielo. Mi si permetta un esempio. Cinque volte nel corso di otto anni avviene che la stella Venere si levi al momento che precede il levar del sole (quello che si chiama il sorgere eliaco, momento solenne in molte civiltà). Ora, i cinque punti così marcati sull'arco delle costellazioni, e congiunti da linee secondo l'ordine del loro succedersi, si rivelano formare un pentagramma perfetto, o quasi perfetto, perché la figura ruota di soli due gradi ogni periodo di otto anni. Questo sembra proprio un dono degli Dei agli uomini, un modo di rivelarsi. Onde i pitagorici dicevano: Afrodite si è rivelata nel segno del Cinque. E il segno è diventato magico. Ma quale intensità di attenzione e di memoria non ci volle per fermare in mente nelle loro posizioni i cinque lampeggiamenti in otto anni del pianeta che appare per poi perdersi subito nella luce del mattino — per ricostruire con l'intelletto il diagramma che essi suggerivano. Si può chiamare una capacità sinottica diversa dalla nostra, una capacità oggi perduta (come ho detto qui nel « Prologue to Parmenides »).

Questo senso ancor più che geometrico, musicale, dell'importanza del « cader giusto » nel tempo è quello che doveva andare fra i pitagorici sotto il nome di *kairós*, l'incidenza in virtù di cui la vita si scandiva nel suo flusso come nascono le misure geometriche del diagramma.

Qui ricompare la figura di Nimrud, personaggio sovrano nel mito dove si è dimenticato il suo « mal coto » e lo si ricorda solo come l'Arciere infallibile. Sovrano in quanto grande Arciere. Il perché ce lo dice per disteso la tradizione parallela cinese. L'accessione — l'investitura formale — dell'imperatore era legata all'atto del sovrano come Arciere. L'arco però era in cielo, è una configurazione di stelle che è la stessa in Cina e in Babilonia. In punta alla freccia è Sirio. Si trattava di cogliere un allineamento che non sappiamo, ma che doveva riferirsi a moti planetari. È come far passare una freccia attraverso anelli mobili. Un solo istante del tempo era l'istante giusto. Il testo antico dice concisamente: « L'imperatore deve cogliere la civetta a tre corpi. Se fallisce, pioggia di sangue dal cielo ». Non è chiaro, ma indica un brutto quarto d'ora.

Il *kairós*, l'esperienza del Fato come misura rigorosa, accompagna l'uomo anche nella morte, dove il momento della dipartita è parcamente misurato. C'è un mito diffuso dovunque, dai pitagorici alla Polinesia, che è poi quello di Dante, delle anime che si affollano in riva al mare in attesa della barca verso l'aldilà. Ma in Polinesia vi erano due soli momenti dell'anno per la partenza: quando il sole calante, il giorno dell'equinozio, sta per toccare l'orizzonte e manda una scia di luce sul mare. Quei giorni il sole era « aperto » come una porta (donde il nome classico di *Portae Solis*) perché in quei punti si trovava e sullo zodiaco e sull'equatore o, in linguaggio platonico, nei punti dove il cerchio del Medesimo coincide con quello dell'Altro. La barchetta magica andando nella scia di luce doveva raggiungerlo prima che calasse in mare, passare attraverso infilandosi dal tempo all'eternità e di lì le anime ascendevano lungo la Via Lattea verso l'ultimo soggiorno. Ma chi mancava quel momento doveva aspettare sulla riva sei mesi. L'immagine ci dice di nuovo quando quest'idea è nata. Fu quando, in virtù della Precessione, il sole equinoziale si trovava agli incroci della Via Lattea con lo zodiaco, cioè in Sagittario e Gemelli; il che avvenne nei secoli attorno al 4800 a.C.

Fin da allora, dunque, si vede che la precisione dava legge sia fisica che etica al cosmo. Chi mancava all'appuntamento del *kairós* non poteva accusare che se stesso. Quella precisione ha un simbolo espressivo nell'antico regno egiziano. È la piuma che sta ritta dietro al giudice dei morti, e si ritrova ancora come peso sul piatto della bilancia, dove si pesano le anime. Quella piuma leggera ha nome Maat, Dea della bilancia, Dea del rigore e della stretta osservanza, di quella implacabile giustezza che tien luogo di giustizia nello scompartire il bene dal male. In latino, in indoeuropeo, il suo nome è Rito, *rta*. E non fu se non logico quando Brugsch e poi Hornbostel scoprirono che il geroglifico di Maat indicava anche l'unità di lunghezza, i 33 centimetri del mattone unitario, e anche il tono fondamentale del flauto. Se l'universo è *uno*, non si possono scegliere unità arbitrarie come facciamo noi: tutte le unità di misura sono strettamente interconnesse fra loro e col tutto. Non c'è libertà, non c'è gioco ad alcun livello, tutto è come deve essere, se è.

Questo, dell'unità del cosmo, è un tema che perdura fin nel Rinascimento. Quello che gli arcaici vi hanno portato non è, come si pensa, la magia, che sempre e dovunque si trova; è una passione di misura senza pari, che fa tutto centrato sul numero e sui tempi. Ma fin da allora si erige quella incastellatura di corrispondenze, in cui i matematici ravviserebbero qualche cosa come una matrice. In alto vi saranno i numeri puri, poi le orbite del cielo, più giù le misure terrestri, i dati geodetici, poi l'astromedicina, le scale e gli intervalli musicali, poi le unità di misura, capacità e peso, poi la geometria, i quadrati magici e psefismi, poi i giochi divinatori come gli scacchi e l'alfabeto, e in fondo ci sarà l'alchimia. Tutto questo sembra essere stato oggetto di una scienza complessiva, poiché i livelli si ingranano e si spiegano fra loro, e non fa meraviglia che non se ne sia mai venuti a capo. Ma si tornava sempre all'ossatura che erano i numeri. La nostra epoca, che si fa vana di precisioni finora mai pensate, di misurare il tempo sulle vibrazioni atomiche e di telemetrare satelliti artificiali fino alla distanza di Marte, la nostra scienza insomma, quantitativa fino in fondo, non dà ancora idea di questo *furor mensurandi* dei primi tempi.

In queste condizioni che cosa può significare la libertà dell'individuo? Preso, incastrato, inscatolato da infinite forze convergenti, che cosa può essere da solo? I veri « abitanti » del mondo non siamo noi, sono le potenze stellari. E anch'esse necessitate perché sopra loro sta il Numero.

Ma qui interviene la riflessione metafisica. Non è naturale, se pur sia inevitabile, che il mondo vada come va. Che ordine perfetto è quello che costringe ogni cosa che vive a essere dolente, transeunte, mortale? Il *Timeo* platonico porta l'impronta di questo dubbio cosmogonico. Perché mai al Demiurgo, all'artefice divino piacque inclinare fra loro i due cerchi del Medesimo e dell'Altro, o come diremmo noi dell'equatore celeste e dell'eclittica? Certo, Platone lo giustifica con la necessità di un variare nel mondo, dell'alternanza delle stagioni. Ma lo si vede sempre insistere sul poco che c'è da fare col materiale caotico e amorfo che fornisce la Necessità. Nel mito del *Politico*, in quella curiosa fantasia nostalgica di un mondo che a volte rovescia l'andatura, spunta l'amaro dubbio.

L'idea più antica e più grave è che quei due cerchi incrociati siano il risultato non di un disegno ma di una disgrazia iniziale. Un tempo, si disse, il sole e i pianeti si muovevano certo lungo l'equatore celeste, non può essere che tutto non fosse simmetrico e semplice; poi lo zodiaco si sghembò da una parte, al sole toccò scendere e salire in cielo, si crearono le stagioni. La serena immutabilità dei primi tempi era finita, la vera età dell'oro; era cominciato il triste divenire. Solo in due giorni dell'anno, agli equinozi, dove i due cerchi si incrociano, il sole si ritrovava sull'equatore, il mondo tornava ad essere come all'inizio, si congiungevano tempo ed eternità. Ricordiamo che Dante inizia il suo viaggio ultraterreno all'equinozio.

Dunque, si concludeva, ci dev'essere stata una tragedia originale, un errore, qualcosa che andò fuori sesto e non ci fu più rimedio. E qui nasce l'idea di un grande conflitto dei primi tempi, in cui venne dissestata la fabbrica dell'universo. La sappiamo tutti, l'insurrezione di Lucifero, la sfida lanciata dai Titani agli Olimpi, lo sconquasso che ne venne. Ma la storia si ritrova in varie forme dovunque: lite fra i Poteri, lotta degli Assura e dei Deva nella tradizione indiana, contesa fra Kung Kung e Chuan Tzü per l'impero del mondo in Cina, caduta e dipartita di Quetzalcoatl nel Messico.

Tornando alla Grecia, si ritrova ancora in altra forma più specifica la storia di atti nefandi commessi all'inizio da personaggi di appartenenza titanesca. Il banchetto di Tieste; Tantalo e Licaone, che offrono in pasto agli Dei la carne dei propri figli, portano con sé una maledizione: gli Dei « rovesciano la tavola inorriditi », il sole si ritrae, ne segue una tragedia. La guerra dei Titani contro l'Olimpo in Grecia ha strane analogie in tutte le mitologie. Ad esempio, la caduta di Satana e la caduta degli Dei aztechi, cioè dei pianeti scaraventati dall'alto del cielo perché avevano colto i fiori proibiti; essi furono immessi in un percorso « più basso », su nuove strade, e cercarono poi continuamente di riconquistare le alte posizioni di un tempo costruendo torri e assi del mondo inclinati da una parte. Ricorre qui Babele. Ma in ognuno di questi casi c'è sempre una frattura o una inclinazione o uno sghembarsi di montagne o di colonne o di livelli, per via dei quali « il sentiero del sole recedette » oppure « il cielo si inclinò verso nord-ovest » e « il sole e la luna si spostarono ». C'è sempre implicita l'immagine della « lacerazione » di un'unità che si fraziona in vari cicli di mutamento incessante, ed essa è legata strettamente alla separazione di due poli nel cielo, all'alterna vicenda della morte e della rinascita stagionali, alla ricerca di un paradiso perduto. « Prima che arrivasse il Nemico, era sempre mezzogiorno » come dice il *Bundahishn* persiano. Quella caduta originale venne considerata la causa della fatale polarità in tutte le cose, dell'eternità e della deperibilità, del potere e della decadenza, del buio contro la luce, dell'elemento maschile e di quello femminile. Come conseguenza, abbiamo il tema dei grandi cicli universali, nei quali le configurazioni celesti tornano al loro posto e il mondo dovrebbe cominciare *ex novo*. Sulle rovine di questa grande costruzione arcaica mondiale si era posata la polvere dei secoli quando i Greci entrarono in scena.

Ma c'è di più. Se ci fu uno sregolaggio iniziale (che sembra esser stato fin dall'inizio la sghembatura del mondo, e vi si aggiunse poi la Precessione degli equinozi quando fu scoperta), la cosa irrimediabile fu il fallimento di Zeus o chi per lui nel tentare di rimetter le cose a posto. Qui interviene la *prise de conscience*, il senso dell'amara coscienza cosmica. Il reggitore tenta di rimetter ordine e così salvare anche sé dalla fine che incombe, ma non può. La profezia di Prometeo, il crudele sforzo di Zeus per strappargli il segreto ci dicono il tema. In questo tema si iscrive lo sforzo degli altri eroi cosmogonici come Maui in Polinesia, Odhin nel Nord, Quetzalcoatl in Messico, che hanno cercato di ricongiungere i cerchi, e l'opera si è infranta. Le storie sono così trasposte nella favola, fino a prendere aspetto bizzarro e insignificante, che bisogna saper scorgere le costanti morfologiche, ma non c'è da sbagliare quando si sente di questa immensa tristezza senza fondo nella quale piombano. È la tristezza di Amleto: *The time is out of joint*. Il Fato è segnato.

Dunque sono gli Dei che portano la colpa. Non per malizia, ma per limitata potenza. Sono anch'essi soggetti all'*ananke*, che è dopotutto un fatto di inerzia perversa nelle cose, le quali non consentono di esser raddrizzate.

Così nasce, credo, la chiarezza classica. Il rapporto del pensiero con la natura nei tempi classici era ben diverso dal nostro; non già ricerca di un punto di sfondamento da cui sopraffare l'avversario, ma la ricerca di un'armonia, di una proporzione, di un ritmo in cui ci si inserisce. L'uomo si concepisce come vivente in seno alla natura, non contrapposto ad essa — cittadino della grande repubblica degli Dei, degli uomini e di tutto ciò che è. Può essere un senso di focolare ritrovato, può essere disperata e grandiosa rassegnazione come in Marc'Aurelio; è sempre uno sforzo di giustificare il cosmo, di mostrarne l'ordine e la giustizia quali sono. La chiarità del vero ci salverà dal grande smarrimento, dalle orrende ambiguità che poi nel Medioevo faranno dell'uomo uno straniero al mondo. Ed è cosa da poco che il nome stesso della scienza, *episteme*, significhi « far fronte »?

Anche la determinazione è ben diversa dalla cieca necessità. Essa viene dal logo, dalla ragione ch'è tutt'uno col nostro pensiero. A quella determinazione si viene liberamente incontro come all'ordine del rituale, come al ritmo della *mousiké*. Pensiero per cui si sono perdute persino le parole. Come trovare un equivalente al termine arcaico di *mousiké*? Era un po' come dire formazione, cultura, capacità d'intendere il ritmo su cui si comincia la comprensione. Era logo, melodia, ritmo. Noialtri si viene da lunghi secoli di cultura in prosa, ma allora non c'erano che i poeti, e in essenza la « poesia seriosa » come dice il Vico. Omero e Pindaro sono un canto, la cadenza e la forma del logo. I cori delle tragedie e gli inni sono lente danze corali, il cui circuire era segnato da un breve alternarsi fra avanti e indietro, onda e pausa che facevano risaltare i liberi « numeri » del canto. Il ritmo non era sovrapposto come un battito di metronomo: parola e gesto erano tutt'uno. Quel solenne girare in metro esprimeva un'esperienza ontologica. Il modello, come dice Platone, era la « danza » dei corpi celesti, il procedere, sostare e retrocedere dei pianeti in quello che era, per usare ancora un'espressione platonica, la mobile immagine dell'eternità. È così che la *mousiké* s'intendeva: formar l'uomo poeticamente ed eticamente. Dico l'antica *mousiké* che già s'andava perdendo ai tempi di Platone, scindendosi nelle sue componenti, quella ch'egli cerca ancora di ripristinare. Armonia e ritmo, diceva Socrate, dovrebbero sostenere il « logo che si canta » e che deve esprimere il vero, così come il filosofo esige dal « logo che non si canta ».

Qui si vede quanto fosse coerente il programma pitagorico:

silenzio, musica e matematica. Silenzio per ricevere il logo non detto dal cielo, la lingua segreta degli Dei; lavoro di ricerca per inquadrarlo in ritmo, melodia, proporzioni, astronomia. La concezione arcaica rimane dunque intatta nel pitagorismo. Ma via via si sovrappone ad esso, da Maratona in poi, quello che è specificamente il principio non della nostra scienza (che è già presente) ma della nostra cultura. Coi tragici greci, il Fato si presenta sotto un aspetto che ci è familiare. È veramente un mistero che ci riguarda, dove risiedono non solo la volontà degli Dei ma gli errori e le colpe degli uomini. Goethe avrebbe detto che è lo *Schauderhafte*, quello che dà il brivido. È il tipo di tragedia che mette capo a Tucidide. Il Fato, l'uomo non ha nemmeno il diritto di invocarlo, dato che è suo e che pur non lo conosce. Si tratta di tutto ciò che egli non sa e non può in alcun modo sapere benchè gli sia attorno, che non cessa di operare e di avere effetto. Si può concepire, si, una tal quale riconciliazione, quella di Edipo. Eschilo, ne *Prometeo liberato*, l'aveva trattata ancora sul livello dei Titani e degli Dei. Quale fosse la profezia, la conoscenza che Zeus voleva strappare a Prometeo non è nel testo che abbiamo, ma ci è indicato dallo scoliasta. È il disegno arcaico, l'ordine del tempo, per cui anche Giove cadrà per aver generato chi è più forte di lui. Ma il mito ormai si sta staccando da noi, e della tragedia rimane una presa di coscienza degli uomini tra uomini.

Fato Moderno

MI SIA CONSENTITO TORNARE ADESSO A TOLSTOI, CHE HO DETTO l'ultimo grande scrittore epico, quello che riprende in linea diretta le speculazioni degli antichi sul problema di che cosa c'è di soggiacente agli eventi. « Se un'altra forza ha preso il posto degli Dei, bisogna spiegare in che cosa tale forza consiste; giacchè è in essa appunto che sta tutto l'interesse della Storia ». È questo il tema di *Guerra e pace*. In una profonda analisi del fenomeno « guerra », egli scopre che il potere è la massima dipendenza in cui ci troviamo nei riguardi del tutto. Non già, questo tutto, inteso come la « ragione » di Hegel, ma un tutto che sono gli « altri », che si potrebbe ancora dire un cosmo, un tutto infinitamente mobile e vivo. La parte, si chiami anche Napoleone, non può mai comprendere e dominare il tutto. Quanto più sale, tanto più chiaramente il potente è soggetto alla Necessità, strumento del Fato, « burattino degli Dei ». Ci ritroviamo sul vecchio terreno. Solo che non si può più capir nulla, prefigurar nulla, della volontà degli Dei. Ogni pretesa di voler immettere la ragione nella Storia è arroganza di professori.

E questa arroganza viene da lontano. Ma già Marc'Aurelio dava per scontate le loro dimostrazioni, e si diceva: i casi sono due. O ci sono gli Dei e la Provvidenza, e allora tutto è per il meglio. O non ci sono, e allora pazienza, facciamo del nostro meglio. Questi erano gli ultimi sussulti del macchinone cosmico, ormai arrugginito, dove alla precisione matematica era subentrato il molesto precisionismo morale, col suo accompagnamento di prediche, denti stretti, muso duro e il resto. Il dubbio di Marc'Aurelio gli dà la dimensione della libertà, lo porta vicino a Tolstoi.

La vera rivoluzione seria è stato il cristianesimo, in grazia del pensiero gnostico che porta in sè fin da prima delle origini. *Le soleil ni la mort ne se peuvent regarder fixement*, e altrettanto vale del Fato. Lo stoico rimaneva preso negli ingranaggi della macchina del cosmo; lo gnostico la nega e la sovverte, trasformandola in esperienza positiva del Male. L'universo tutto quanto diventa l'opera di una potenza malvagia che tiene asservito il mondo. Lucifero ha copiato lo schema delle idee eterne per i propri scopi men che raccomandabili, ha inventato la macchina del tempo e ha messo i pianeti a reggerla, come forze demoniche. Il capofila è sempre Saturno, Signore della Melanconia; ma di là dalle stesse, nell'infinito, v'è il Dio di Luce che mandò il Salvatore a liberarci, e Virgilio è profeta per aver detto che « progenie discende dal ciel nova ». Il cosmo stesso è costretto ad annunciare, attraverso spettacolosi ricorsi e congiunzioni, l'avvento di colui che deve infrangere le sue catene.

Così l'uomo è liberato. Quello che si ha da conoscere, lo dice Sant'Agostino, è Dio e l'anima soltanto, nulla più. È crollato il mondo delle stelle, e al tempo stesso il mondo della natura.

Ama et fac quod vis. La macchina tremenda è ridotta a nulla. È ormai un bell'orologio che il Signore regalò al padre Adamo per la sua nascita. La Provvidenza soprannaturale è su tutto.

Così non mi sembra strano che quando si riscopre la natura, nel Rinascimento, il Fato non pesi più. Forse perché sussiste l'idea cristiana della Provvidenza, forse perché la nuova macchina del mondo che si vien forgiando non ci incombe più addosso coi suoi tempi da essa stessa imposti, ma è cosa di leggi matematiche, di archetipi della nostra mente — insomma, di creazione intellettuale — ma certo è che si sente una leggerezza, una serenità nell'aria: proprio quando la terra si rivela piccina e insignificante, il mondo si apre verso l'infinito. Non dico per tutti. La rivoluzione copernicana è un trauma psichico per i più, in tutto il Seicento corre lo sgomento, il disorientamento, l'orrore di questo universo sferico e chiuso che si sfascia, « il circolo dell'eterno sostituito dalla retta della mortalità », il mondo ormai vecchio che « si avvia allo sfacelo ». Ma ben altra è la tempra degli spiriti magni, di Keplero, di Galileo, di Bruno, in cui l'intelletto si apre a fini che non son più limitatamente umani, e si sente di abbracciare e complettere il tutto in uno splendido *amor Fati.*

Il sarcasmo di Galileo coglie nel segno quando si appunta sulla dottrina ufficiale dei cieli cristallini e immutabili: « Questi che tanto esaltano l'incorruttibilità, l'inalterabilità, l'impassibilità eccetera parlano così, credo, dal gran desiderio che hanno di vivere a lungo, e dal timore della morte, senza pensare che, se gli uomini fossero immortali, a loro non sarebbe toccato di venire al mondo ». E quando il dottor Simplicio si scandalizza della nuova grandezza che si vorrebbe imporre all'universo, e domanda a che possa servire, Salviati lo interrompe pacatamente: « Dite piuttosto, signor Simplicio, non sappiamo che serva *per noi* ».

La serena noncuranza ci rivela che cos'è che fa aggricciare gli uomini di fronte al Fato: è l'arbitrio, l'estraneità. Se Dio è veramente « necessitato » dalle verità eterne, da quello che è identico al nostro puro intelletto, allora tutto si riconcilia, e la vita del cosmo che perpetuamente si trasforma diventa anch'essa cosa nostra. È questo « necessitare » che fa Galileo veementemente sospetto al Sant'Uffizio, che rende «abominevole » il povero Spinoza, inaccettabile Leibniz, e fa di Bruno un uomo perduto. Descartes ha capito da lontano, e scantona: « *C'est parler de Dieu comme d'un Jupiter ou Saturne, et l'assujettir au Styx et aux destinées, que de dire que ces vérités sont indépendantes de lui* ».

Le parole di Descartes, dette con verecondia quasi calvinista nei riguardi della *gloria Dei*, ci riportano come d'incanto al cuore del nostro proposto. Sì, se si percepisce un disegno arcano superiore fino agli Dei, siamo disposti a comprendere e anche a compatire. Forse possiamo indovinare che conforto derivassero i calcolatori arcaici dal loro *furor mensurandi.* Si era già visto fin dagli inizi: il vero spirito scientifico era immune dal Fato. Forse perché è già abnorme, non soggetto alle caratteristiche ordinarie della cosiddetta « umanità ». Il prosternarsi di Lucrezio di fronte all'intelligenza di quel *Graius homo*, che poi non era il « primo », ci mostra la distanza. Chi vive in ciò che è fuori del tempo non è soggetto al tempo. Però, dal Rinascimento in poi, alla serenità contemplativa dello spirito scientifico si aggiunge un estro sbarazzino, una curiosità insaziabile e incolpevole propria allo spirito moderno, che ci può condurre a precipizio nei peggiori precipizi.

Chi ne è partecipe dal difuori non è altrettanto immune; basta pensare agli spaventi calvinisti, alle tristi preoccupazioni represse dell'illuminismo, all'insincerità romantica. Ma insomma, da un certo punto in poi, la cultura è portata dall'*entrain* scientifico. « L'hoggidì overo il mondo non peggiore né più calamitoso del passato ». Quell'opuscolo scovato non so dove da Croce ci dice quanto si potesse buttare a mare della zavorra di piagnistei e sentimenti fittizi attorno alla *humaine condition*. Ci dice anche perché risulti tanto più pura per noi la musica della *Ginestra*. Si è tornati alle cose serie.

Ed è così che si è entrati nell'èra del disimpegno. La rivoluzione scientifico-industriale è cosa grave quanto la rivoluzione cristiana. Ha generato sogni di salvazione — il sogno socialista — ha tolto le catene del futuro. Nel mondo americanizzato si è voluto far scomparire ogni traccia del Fato antico, ottundere il senso della tragedia e della morte. Anche in Europa, malgrado l'attaccamento alle vecchie forme, si parla della natura trasformata in industria, del carattere naturale assunto dall'artificiale. Come erano le cose prima ? Si direbbe che certi scrittori preferiscano non ricordare. È vero che da un pezzo non le abbiamo più vissute. Si comincia davvero a pensare in termini di « magnifiche sorti e progressive ».

E si comincia anche a parlare come se l'uomo avesse superato il Fato. La Storia, dall'èra rivoluzionaria in poi, non è cosa da subire, ma da decidere (questo si sa), e i nuovi mezzi ci danno infinita potenza di fare e di decidere, di vittoria o di fallimento. Quell'aspetto predeterminato del futuro che è parte della vecchia realtà è elemento essenziale del Fato come lo si concepiva. L'ordine e il corso delle stelle prima, della natura poi, era la vera predestinazione. Il mondo industriale nega ogni futuro assegnabile, liquida la fatalità.

Ma così si entra solo nel folto dell'equivoco. Se si potesse ancora concepire una rivoluzione scientifica nel senso classico, cioè speculativo, avremmo certo un'apertura di libertà quale già apparve una volta tre secoli orsono. Ma da una parte ci siamo costituiti prigionieri della natura attraverso il darwinismo e la psicanalisi, dall'altra abbiamo lasciato che l'attività scientifica fosse presa nell'ingranaggio tecnico-industriale. Si può parlare tuttalpiù di un ridimensionamento del Fato. Ripenso al sorriso timido e schivo con cui Einstein rifuggiva dalla discussione generale: « Purché — diceva — non ci si ritrovi sempre nell'*Allzumenschliches* ». Come che volgesse il discorso, come si poteva evitare il « troppo umano » ?

Qui, come in tante altre cose, Descartes è la cerniera; perché se da una parte aveva ancora l'idea medievale di uno scibile chiuso, dell'ente che pensa, dall'altra si proponeva di portare l'umanità « al sommo della perfezione di cui è capace » attraverso una scienza impostata sulle macchine. E da troppo tempo mi sembra di sentir dire che la macchina, bene puramente strumentale, ci costringe in ogni aspetto della vita; che questo impeccabile servitore ci ha messi sotto sterzo.

Alla macchina non si pensa mai, perché sembra troppo chiara. Ma un giorno, per caso, in un'esposizione d'arte a New York, mi imbattei nelle macchine di Tinguely. Questo Tinguely è un artista svizzero il quale, divertendosi col metallo, ha costruito macchine inutili, per puro spasso estetico, e poi spero anche per dar noia. Macchine non banali, dall'aspetto complicato e solido. Ma se si mette il congegno in moto, lo si può fare una sola volta. Perché via via avvengono scoppi, scatti e sgranamenti che in buon ordine smantellano la macchina, la quale è così concepita che in un quarto d'ora è risolta nelle sue parti componenti sparse in bell'ordine per le terre. Sfasciata che è la macchina, non si può nemmeno rimontare: è distrutta.

Questa era la prima volta che avevo visto una macchina fine a se stessa. Era una feroce ironia sulla nostra concezione della macchina come un bene strumentale, che serve a noi. Non poteva non tornarmi a mente l'ingenua certezza del Vico, che se non possiamo comprendere la natura possiamo almeno comprendere la Storia, come quella che facciamo noi stessi. E ancor più facciamo e comprendiamo la macchina, e poi la macchina che fa le macchine, e poi la macchina che sa riprodurre se stessa, e poi la macchina che si modifica da sé secondo un suo pensiero proprio cibernetico, e poi quella che pensa per noi — ma fin dall'inizio, dico proprio dalla macchina a vapore, è lei che fa la Storia. E quale poi, ci stiamo domandando con un'apprensione crescente. Non avesse da essere anche quello un disegno arcano.

Non serve lasciarsi ripetere dal filosofo che la macchina è un puro e semplice fatto. Mi torna alla mente per contrasto un altro detto di Valéry, colui al quale il Nostro Filosofo ha negato ogni serietà filosofica: « Niente di più misterioso di un fatto, nulla che rassomigli di più a quei sogni regali che empivano di spavento i gran sacerdoti di Babilonia ». Non ci esce di mente quel dito misterioso che scrive sul muro della sala del banchetto: « *Mene Mene Tekel Upharsin* », parole che Daniele seppe interpretare: « Pesato, pesato sulla bilancia del tempo, e non fate il peso ». Sogno o misura? Venne il tempo che capitò anche a noi di scorgerlo. Era una ripresa di Eniwetok nel Pacifico, a una delle prime prove dell'Arma, come modestamente si chiama negli ambienti tecnici. Aspettando, mi dicevo che questa era ancora vecchia magia nera, per cui si ruba un pezzo di sole per i nostri scopi oscuri. Poi, d'un tratto, ci fu un emisfero perfetto d'un bianco abbagliante, posato per un istante sul mare. E in quell'istante, disposta sull'emisfero, un po' di lato, una coroncina di nuvolette bianche, piccola, come una ghirlandetta posata con una certa civetteria. Feci a tempo a dirmi: la nascita di Afrodite. Venere era riapparsa in bella forma geometrica come si conviene, ma non in cielo, e quanto diversa dal mito, intesa da noi stessi alla nostra distruzione. La macchina era scattata.

La vogliamo chiamare Progresso? Oppure *ananke*, la Necessità? La potremmo amare, come gli antichi avevano accettato la loro Necessità? Qui riappare evidente la superiorità del mito antico sul nostro spiegare. Non già che il mito lasci molto adito all'ottimismo. Il dolore è dovunque in esso, e la rassegnazione, da Gilgamesh all'*Edda*, e quello che ho chiamento la immensa tristezza dell'impresa mancata. Ma ogni volta che si raggiunge la vera espressione, sia nell'*epos* che nella tragedia o nel romanzo, essa si conclude in una riconciliazone significativa. Ricordiamo le parole di Tolstoi. Insomma, c'è molt'aria intorno.

Se adesso penso alla letteratura che si vuole espressiva e rappresentativa del tempo nostro, la situazione è diversa. Non posso evitare i filosofi-poeti, come si sarebbe detto nei tempi antichi, e mi ritrovo davanti Sartre e Camus, che si vogliono coscienze lucide dell'epoca nostra.

Sartre lo sa anche troppo che alla libertà di scelta oggi non si sfugge, e non finisce di rivoltare e cincischiare il concetto di libertà; ma quali siano i suoi *chemins de la liberté* lo vediamo. La sua libertà come scelta perpetua è un perpetuo ruinare a valle, sino a « Minòs che ciascheduno afferra ». Ogni istante della vita è un istante fallito di libertà entro un « progetto » fallito in partenza, un pellegrinaggio di nausea che ribatte il tema di *Huis clos*, nessuna uscita. Si riprende il tema della eterna circolarità, ma sotto l'aspetto del circolo vizioso. Alla base c'è l'acosmismo che viene dalla scienza; conseguenza e parodia del cartesianesimo. La filosofia è moderna, scientifica, o piuttosto post-scientifica, nel senso che ha scontato la scienza. Col pensiero non si torna indietro, l'io e l'essere rimangono sempre esterni a noi; la conoscenza di sé è il sé visto dagli altri. Malgrado ogni tentativo umanistico (*le regard*) si rimane dentro a una specie di solipsismo delirante che si pone al difuori di sé. Il senso privato è scomparso.

Tutto questo — come storico della scienza non posso negarlo — è conseguenza della fisica dell'« oggetto » indispensabile e fatale, dell'oggetto analitico quale lo esige la procedura scientifica. Sartre non fa che ripetere quella realtà frantumata e designificata. È ben vero che la realtà fisica per conto suo tira calci per vendicarsi dei suoi conoscitori, sparandoci in faccia una confusione di particelle elementari transeunti e mal distinte, insulto al buon senso, fra cui lo scienziato si aggira ormai come l'impallinato nella notte. Gli psicanalisti dovrebbero trovare qui di che divertirsi in modo perverso, loro che hanno così temerariamente attentato alla nostra personalità. Questo è il mondo fisico per loro, in questo universo sperimentale della fisica subatomica, dove tutto si viene spiegando in termini di momentaneità, disintegrazione, evanescenza e simili, dove — come disse recentemente un fisico — bisognerebbe creare l'unità di azione subatomica, denominata « un cataclisma ».

In Sartre, il mondo frantumato e polverizzato si ammanta di critica dialettica e di ragione sociale, ma si può andare più in là guardando al fratello nemico, artista più vero, Albert Camus. La serie dei suoi titoli ci dice già abbastanza, da *L'étranger* in poi. Un ciclo che si conclude in quel suo monologo *La chute*, in cui si imposta il personaggio dell'esule volontario che respinge tutta la sua vita di normalità e di successo per rimanersene lì nei bassifondi di Amsterdam, a urlar penitenza come un monaco medievale. Quello sì è un atto di coscienza che coinvolge tutti, ma va a creare quel nuovo personaggio contemporaneo e paradossale, il « giudice penitente », abbandonato e solo nel suo giudizio. Intorno a lui c'è l'universo morale fratturato, frantumato, che lo respinge su se stesso così che il racconto è come una spirale, ultima forma del circolo vizioso, che si richiude sul personaggio — direi quasi sulla sua maschera di ricettatore sacrilego.

Dov'è rimasto l'*amor Fati* dei creatori della scienza? Oggi ci troviamo di fronte all'inaccettabile, di cui la fusione atomica è solo un simbolo. La potremmo chiamare la Necessità delle Cose, evitando la parola materialismo che si sente sempre lamentato dalla gente bene, quasi non ne fossero loro i protagonisti. Non si tratta di un cambiamento netto, ma di uno scivolamento nei rapporti dell'uomo con la natura, dove la curiosità e il desiderio di potenza hanno preso il sopravvento. Quel rapporto ha assunto l'aspetto di una perpetua manovra di sfondamento contro un avversario mobile e irreducibile. L'armonia delle sfere è venuta meno, in fisica come in arte è subentrata la volontà non di conoscere ma di trasformare. Questa parola è divenuta un *cliché* a cui non si riflette più. Ma nelle varie forme del marxismo, dalle paurose a quelle da strapazzo, l'idea si è fatta strada, ha conquistato invisibilmente anche l'altro campo. Ammantata di una certa qual aura di scienza, la Storia si presenta come un corso forzato in cui il solo segno di virtù è l'assenso. Dicevano già gli stoici che i fati guidano i volenti e trascinano i nolenti; ma che cosa avrebbe detto lo stoico se gli si fosse domandato di trasferire il proprio assenso dall'universo e dalla Ragione universale alla più recente linea di partito ? Oggi, lacerato il manto mal rattoppato della ragione, ci ritroviamo di fronte all'Inaccettabile. Quello stesso di Kafka nel *Processo*.

Poiché non c'è filosofia che conti, mi pare giusto di domandar soccorso alla letteratura, della quale già Whitehead diceva che è rivelatrice delle idee, di quelle che sono e di quelle che non sono. Mi torna alla mente una parola di Vittorini sui « romantici tardi che hanno puntato sul socialismo come su una possibilità di restaurare il presente equilibrio naturale in seno alla natura lacerata ». Parlando non dell'utopia ma del fatto socialista, è chiaro che non restaura nessun equilibrio. La distanza dalla natura non è grave, ogni civiltà prende distanza dalla natura; ma l'assenza di un cosmo non è sostituibile dal fatto sociale. E quando il socialismo ci ha dato un libro importante, *Il dottor Zivago*, era un libro che ritrovava il cosmo e prendeva distanza dal socialismo. Tutta la letteratura che è unica o specifica del nostro tempo rivela le scuciture. Ho citato Kafka; potrei citare *Godot*, come gli oggetti che non parlano di Robbe-Grillet. Siano uomo o natura, alla nostra sensibilità gli oggetti si rivelano vagamente a una cauta esplorazione, ma rimangono altrettanto vagamente ostili. Per esprimermi con un'immagine, è un po' come se ci si vedesse attorno gente il cui tono di voce non corrisponde all'espressione del viso. Uno si tira indietro spaventato e finisce col parlare a se stesso per ristabilire una sembianza di ragione. Testimonianze simili (e mi sembra che ne vengano anche dalla pittura) non si possono rifiutare. Ci mettono sul terreno metafisico, e ognuno ne può ricavare quel che vuole.

Per riportare coerenza nel discorso, mi riferirò a una immagine fisica familiare. Immaginiamo un forno a riverbero portato all'incandescenza : si stabilisce entro di esso un equilibrio di radiazione, che i fisici chiamano quello del « corpo nero ». Gli oggetti che si trovano entro il forno, incandescenti anch'essi, diventano invisibili. Se vi si guarda dentro attraverso un foro, non si vede altro che luce. È lo stato stabile di equilibrio all'interno : forme e sagome si perdono, non si distingue più nulla. Per distinguere ci vorrebbe uno stato non stabile.

E così, direi, sembra avvenire al rapporto dell'uomo col Fato. Ci siamo dentro, ne siamo parte totalizzante, siamo tutti diventati in tutto — come diceva Tolstoi di Napoleone — « i burattini del Fato », e quindi non ci si vede più. Nel nuovo mondo autonomo, governato dalla Ragione, è come se il lume della ragione non ci fosse più per eccesso di bagliore, quello che ci fa distinguere e scegliere. C'è quest'altra riverberazione, in cui tutto si perde.

Siamo giunti così a un nuovo meccanismo del tempo, così lontano da quello antico, e pur investito di un comando assoluto. Abbiamo cercato di dargli tante forme consolanti, come ragione dialettica, forza della Storia e così via, ma il vecchio nome ottocentesco di Progresso gli si confà molto meglio, ché evoca al tempo stesso speranze ingenue e lo spavento leopardiano.

Oggi, cominciamo a vedere che cosa vuol dire. Esso non rappresenta se non la Necessità delle cose, la logica della Storia e la logica della tecnologia combinate in un solo potere. Con l'imporre mutazione ininterrotta a un ritmo sempre più veloce, questa Necessità ha fatto del tempo una continua catastrofe che non consente riti, ha reso quasi impossibile la libertà interiore e il prender distanza, ha rimosso la pietà filiale oltre l'orizzonte, nel crepuscolo della posterità. E pur impone come Moloch, a chi vuol farla parlare in dogma, il continuo sacrificio della generazione presente quale che sia a future generazioni sempre recedenti nel tempo. Essa dispensa grazie, questo sì, più d'ogni altra divintà, più d'ogni altra ci astringe alla via giusta, poiché non v'è altra via; è adorata unanimemente, ecumenicamente, a Oriente come a Occidente, e i suoi sacerdoti insegnano che è immune da ogni ombra di colpa, dismisura o deviazione, da ogni iniquità originale, poiché è la Ragione stessa in atto.

Ho cercato di delineare, in via paradossale quale si conviene a un'immagine metafisica, l'immagine del Fato quale potrebbe presentarsi a noi moderni. A noi che abbiamo inventato la libertà, il Fato può apparire davvero paralizzante — la Ragione storica in presa diretta. Una ragione ove l'intelletto non si vuol più riconoscere può diventare ancor più oscura della *ananke* antica.

Salvemini È SCOMPARSO L'ULTIMO GRANDE ITALIANO DEI NOSTRI TEMPI. Già si sente l'Italia cambiare aspetto. È come se non vi fosse più metro per misurare la consistenza degli uomini e delle idee. Molti, in Europa, avranno sentito qualcosa di simile nell'anno della morte di Voltaire. Può sembrare strano un ravvicinamento fra l'occhietto aguzzo del signore di Ferney e lo sguardo candido, il sorriso aperto dell'uomo di Molfetta (« Senti, quello che non puoi spiegare a un contadino pugliese, è inutile che tu provi a spiegarlo a me »), ma la somiglianza c'è: la ragione come una spada affilata sempre in atto a pro della chiarezza e del buon senso, una intransigenza intellettuale che nulla riesce a scalfire, il dono della parola incisiva. Questo ancora avevano in comune, i due così dissimili, di non essersi rinchiusi nei lucidi schemi della loro maestria latina, ma di essersi aperti, già passato il mezzo della vita, a intendere la civiltà anglo-sassone e diventare intrinseci ad essa, creando in se una sintesi dei due mondi. « L'eroe Salvemini dal cuore di bronzo — diceva Borgese — che ha avuto il coraggio di imparare a pensare in inglese a cinquant'anni... » Era ben detto; e lo stesso ebbe a dire una volta Rochester di Voltaire. Salvemini fu, anche lui, l'anti-Rousseau e l'anti-confusionario, fu un autentico *pamphlétaire* dell'illuminismo; la sua molteplice figura non si organizza bene che attorno a un aspetto centrale, quello del massimo pubblicista italiano. Il maestro, il teorico politico, lo storico dalla ferrea documentazione sono quasi aspetti sussidiari, perché l'insieme delle sue capacità si forgiava e sfavillava giorno per giorno in risposta ai problemi dell' oggi. Tutto il suo studio del passato non si assestava in opere « definitive » per le biblioteche, ma faceva capo alla formazione delle menti, a quel suo dono di « sorprendere » i problemi. Fu grande storico in quanto seppe essere uomo di parte (e questo si può dire di più d'uno fra i grandi storici, se pur le parti che presero furono meno apparenti). Ben lo sentiva chi aveva da temerlo: in questi ultimi anni gli onori accademici non gli furono lesinati, ma quando si parlava di fargli avere un giornale, le persone influenti, anche fra i suoi amici schietti, dicevano con aria pensierosa che il momento non era ancora maturo. Dicevano molto giusto: Salvemini ancor che ottantenne, era in vita. E finchè fu in vita, non fossero stati il *Ponte* e il *Mondo* ad accogliere i suoi scritti, la grande stampa sarebbe riuscita a soffocare la sua voce.

I suoi periodici li aveva saputi avere a suo tempo, in quanto se li fece da se. Il suo massimo contributo alla vita italiana si riassume nei nomi di *Unità* e di *Non Mollare*. Finchè vigeva la libertà, Salvemini assistito da alcuni amici, come Antonio de Viti de Marco (altro meridionale non conformista, se pur da lui diverso) Luigi Einaudi, Edoardo Giretti e anche mio padre, dette vita a una polemica inflessibile contro gli abusi della classe detentrice dello Stato. Vengono da Salvemini tanto la revisione del socialismo iniziata da Carlo Rosselli quanto quella del liberalismo di

Piero Gobetti; viene da lui, fuori ed entro la scuola italiana, lo spirito dell'educazione « laica » negli studi morali e nella vita pubblica; e una immagine di società democratica in cui i diritti del popolo fossero difesi dai suoi rappresentanti nei termini stessi delle esigenze e degli interessi dei mandanti.

Riprendendo un profondo pensiero di Ignazio Silone, vorrei dire che Salvemini rimase povero come lo sono i poveri, rimase solo come loro (e non conta che fosse attorniato e vezzeggiato, solo rimase) — e come loro disorganizzato. Rimase fuori di ogni inquadramento e da ogni « costrutto » politico in quanto il suo pensiero non voleva scostarsi da quell'« umile Italia » da cui era uscito, a cui l'inquadramento è imposto d'arbitrio, e ogni vero costrutto vietato. Povero, solo e disorganizzato come quel contadino di cui raccontava che aveva detto: « m'intendo in pancia, ma come faccio a spiegarlo? » E così, in grazia del suo genio paradossale, seppe diventare il più chiaro dei pensatori. Diceva Bertrand Russell, successor di Peano, erede degli Amberley: « Quando parlano gl'italiani colti, mi capita spesso di non capire. Salvemini non deve essere colto, perchè quello che dice lui lo capisco, e quello che pensa lo penserei anch'io ». È riapparso sulla scena Voltaire, l'universale.

Ricordo la sua gioia quando gli citai un detto di Galileo: « perchè oscuro possono scrivere molti, ma chiaro pochissimi ». Se lo appuntò in fretta sul rovescio di una busta. Il suo spirito era proprio quello, ellenico e galileiano, che in Italia è rimasto preso fra i respingenti della storia, Sud e Nord. E così, se la Puglia rimane la sua terra, Firenze fu la sua vera città. « Pensa — diceva abbassando la voce a un tragico sussurro — non fosse stata la fortuna, finivo laureato dell'università di Napoli ».

Così, Salvemini fu l'antiretorico. Diceva di aver potuto capire qualche cosa grazie a Euclide. Non voleva vedere se non problemi concreti, analisi di fondo, costruzione pezzo a pezzo di un paese di cittadini. Anche Giolitti fu l'uomo dell'antiretorica, si è detto, e fu errore storico di Salvemini il non comprendere la sua funzione salutare in quell'epoca. Ma Salvemini, e non fu il solo, vedeva in lui il manipolatore delle maggioranze, il patrono della piccola borghesia burocratica diseducatrice. « L'on. Salvemini, diceva Giolitti bonariamente, non si rende conto di essere il mio migliore alleato. Quando si leva per attaccarmi, tutta la Camera si volta contro di lui, e dimentica la mia modesta persona ». Il giudizio del grande uomo di Stato non è condanna ma definizione della parte che ebbe Salvemini nella vita nazionale. Era fuori del gioco dei politici, quindi sommamente pericoloso. La politica è arte del possibile, quella di Salvemini era scienza della responsabilità non evitabile, presenza della storia vera, quella che i dirigenti italiani hanno sempre avversato, e con ogni mezzo cercato di scansare. La sapienza di Giolitti stava nel menare avanti la barca, nel rinviare le scadenze, perchè è verissimo che strada facendo molte cose si accomodano da se. Molte ma non tutte, e le scadenze non affrontate ci hanno portato alla fine al regno dei preti. In cui, come ha osservato un cardinale in un lampo d'arguzia, qualunque problema si affronta in tre tempi: prima, lo si nega; secondo, lo si rinvia; terzo, quando si è alle strette, si fa ricorso ai santi specializzati. L'Italia vive una parodia del giolittismo.

Ricordo, verso il 1930, Mario Ferrara in un breve momento di sconforto, quando gli sembrava veder venire il momento della inevitabile sottomissione al fascismo: « Potremo almeno dire, diceva, che non siamo mai stati giolittiani ». Mi pare giusto soffermarsi su questi momenti vissuti, perchè oggi, a disfatta consumata, Giolitti è diventato simbolo, anche per i comunisti, del tempo felice. Non fu se non un episodio temporeggiatore. L'Italia rimaneva, come fu detto allora, un maso chiuso di trenta milioni amministrato da trecentomila per conto di tremila, e ogni segno di democrazia si infrangeva contro quella realtà. Salvemini conosceva il pensiero di quei tremila o più che fossero, come se se li avesse fatti; a questo serviva essere storico. Ricordava quel convegno di Sala Aragona nel 1894, nel quale i latifondisti avevano chiesto l'abolizione dell'istruzione elementare; e l'imposta sul macinato pagata da generazioni di poveri, sulla quale i teorici dell'economia avevano avuto a suo tempo poco da ridire, e i dirigenti nulla; e tante, infinite altre cose ancora, che la storia idealista dimentica. Sapeva le ragioni, non solo le parole, di Crispi, Pelloux, Salandra o Sonnino. E quindi la sua dottrina, come quella di Jefferson, era di aggressiva, implacabile vigilanza. Tanto ebbe ragione che si videro malgrado tutto i detentori del paese, con infaticabile arte di baratto, produrre nazionalismo, fascismo, qualunquismo, clericalismo, pagnottismo, gettando a mare via via tutto il « loro » Risorgimento pur di sventare la storia. Così fu che, quando ebbero alfine soppresso la Costituzione, Salvemini fondò il suo secondo giornale, creando le vie della stampa clandestina in Europa. Fu *Non Mollare*, da cui doveva formarsi l'ossatura della Resistenza.

Era cosa meravigliosa vedere come bastasse una sua domanda precisa e intempestiva, un richiamo ai fatti o alla logica (non quella crociana) per portare un biblico *spiritus vertiginis* nella compagine bene adagiata del pubblico cosiddetto colto. Andava per forza di contraggenio a tutti, ma non gli mancavano mai i giovani attorno, intendo quelli del buon taglio. Era forse perchè questo greco d'Apulia, che di Democrito aveva la dura chiarezza e il voluto semplicismo, di Socrate il taglio e l'ironia, e certo la cura delle anime, possedeva anche quella gioventù dello spirito propria alla civiltà ellenica. Era sempre visitato, come Socrate, dal suo dio interiore, che gli diceva soprattutto di no, e ancora no (si diceva già a Sparta che i Persiani erano schiavi perchè nessuno sapeva pronunciare quella paroletta *no*), mentre è noto che agli dei variopinti degl'italioti, quali e quanti che siano, si richiede di dir di sì, infaticabilmente di si, e di largir grazie a giumelle senza badare al merito della causa. Il conflitto era inevitabile.

« Professore non mi dimentichi — gli aveva detto congedandosi il suo vecchio carceriere delle Murate — speriamo che un giorno abbia ragione lei. Quell'anima santa di Lenin prega per noi dal Paradiso ». La dolce confusione dei piccoli e dell'umile Italia lo commuoveva, e pensava alla comunità evangelica del primo socialismo come al più bel tempo della sua vita. Ma alla confusione della gente di mezzo non perdonava, con la loro coltura « rampicante », diceva lui, il loro impancarsi a *élite*, i clichés che tengono luogo di un pensiero che fu. Era quello che lo rendeva tagliente, indisponente. Residui di positivismo o di marxismo, spiegavano i soliti bene informati, ma era schietto sarcasmo swiftiano, *saeva indignatio*.

Avrebbe dovuto vivere al tempo dei Comuni che aveva tanto studiato: anche la sua sensibilità artistica tendeva a rifiutare quel che viene dopo il primo Rinascimento, quello dell'Italia salvatrice. A contatto con la classe mandarina dell'Italia di oggi, era un po' come il diavolo e l'acqua santa. Pagano in fondo anche lui, ma intrinsecamente religioso e morale, si trovava di fronte una coltura amorale, politeista, ritualista, ove la furbizia largamente dispiegata nasconde una vitalità animalesca e improvvida, quella che non vuole pensieri e viceversa si infogna sempre nei guai, che riesce a fare anche del Vicario di Cristo un dorato e ingualdrappato idolone di fertilità. Come fare a intendersi? Credo che se Coluccio Salutati tornasse in vita, non si troverebbe più spaesato che lo fosse Salvemini.

L'italiano moderno mette una certa civetteria nell'inalberare un « ca' nisciuno è fesso » che ricopre poi una credulità da buon figliuolo e un sincero anelito al conformismo. Salvemini aveva la civetteria inversa di nascondere la sottigliezza del suo spirito dietro giudizi squadrati e postazioni tutte in bianco e nero. Le sue grandi semplificazioni (« È un generale? Basta ») erano intese a sganciare la mente dalle costruzioni artefatte, dagli accomodamenti che nulla accomodano, e metterle di fronte alle responsabilità immediate. All'alterigia dei rappresentanti dello Stato Etico, all'autorità esperta e indiscussa dei Maestri di Confusione e dei Dottori d'Iniquità si risponde non col solito argomentare « comprensivo » di chi vuol mostrarsi colto e civile, ma col puntare i piedi e col dare a quella gente fermamente del buffone, titolo che si può ampiamente documentare ove bisogna. Ai soprusi clericali non vedeva che una risposta ugualmente concreta del cittadino. « Bombe in Vaticano. Che vuoi che altro capiscano? La paura con quelli fa novanta. Ma lo vedi che nessuno prende l'iniziativa... » Per dar l'esempio, metteva petardi sotto gli arcivescovi e si prendeva le querele imperturbabile. I querelanti si affrettavano poi a rimetterle pur di non avere da affrontarlo, documenti alla mano. « Buffoni... » Bisognava sentire il gusto meridionale che metteva in quella parola. Se fosse vissuto ai tempi di Aristofane, avrebbe saputo farsi sentire nell'Agorà. Nella Roma dei papi e dei commendatori, dove metteva i piedi il meno possibile, si sentiva una assurdità vivente.

Dice bene Ernesto Rossi: la impopolarità che Salvemini raggiunse in certi momenti non è stata mai raggiunta da nessun altro uomo politico italiano. Dei tempi in cui era stato conclamato e vituperato come anti-italiano e vile rinunciatario per la sua politica della nazionalità, rimaneva un appiccicaticcio ricordo nella mente del pubblico, uso a sapere che tutto può andare a posto purchè ci siano i buoni sentimenti. Quello lì, si vede che non era una buona persona, ecco, eppoi gli mancava il senso storico. « Ma che senso storico, commentava Salvemini con una delle sue risate, a me mi manca il senso comune ».

Era proprio il senso comune che gli dava forza di storico. Ricordo ancora quel giorno d'inverno del 1916 (ero ragazzino allora) in cui Salvemini giunse a casa nostra in licenza dal fronte. Si scrollò di dosso la mantellina di fanteria fradicia di pioggia, si mise a tavola, e disse: « Adesso che c'è la rivoluzione in Russia, noialtri si può cominciare a dire di aver avuto ragione quando si chiese la guerra. Ed era tempo ». Era contento, sembrava sprizzasse contentezza anche la barbetta rosso-brizzolata. Glielo ricordai molti anni dopo, ed ebbe un sorriso mesto: « Bimbo mio, vedi come si spera. Ma puoi dire che avessi torto? » Il ragionamento infatti era chiaro e di buon senso. Non fu tanto, come si dice, un sentimento mazziniano (Mazzini gli dava noia) che lo spinse a sostenere una politica delle nazionalità, fu la logica indicata dagli eventi. La retorica proterva della « italianità » si ipnotizzava sulle ali tarpate della Vittoria e su fette di Dalmazia, mentre nella realtà si delineava ovunque una nuova Europa con cui si trattava di venire a patti. Pensieri per la vecchia Europa? Ne ebbe anche lui, certo più di Sonnino e dei nazionalisti, che nè prima nè dopo pensarono a niente. Più tardi, quando si nominava Francesco Giuseppe, si alzava e faceva l'inchino con comica serietà: « L'ultimo grande gentiluomo, signori ». Ma le nostalgie possono prendere consistenza nella mente di ambasciatori in ritiro, non in quella dello storico e del politico. Fu un pensiero di chiara politica nazionale quello che spinse Salvemini a chiedere un accordo con le nazioni nascenti; fu assenza totale di pensiero e autentico dispregio per il paese, se non come oggetto di declamazione, che spinse i goffi dicitori a bollarlo « rinunciatario ».

E così gli si fece il personaggio, per non aver da ragionare contro di lui. Prima rinunciatario, poi, si sa, rinnegato, sempre negatore, velenoso, amaro, antipatriota, mentalità protestantica, incapace di quella comprensione, di quel manzoniano qualcosa da cui viene calduccio e conforto. Sembra una caricatura, ma passava per giudizio maturo fra la gente cosiddetta per bene, anche quella che ha dimenticato le ubbie nazionaliste, che parla di storia e intende conformismo; su su fino ai filosofi, ai fabbricanti di nebbie, per i quali, come diceva Salvemini deridendoli, « tutto ciò che è reale è razionale e quindi va scappellato come prodotto della Storia ».

A queste *boutades* bisognerebbe sempre aggiungere come sottinteso quel che diceva di Kant: « difficile, ma non oscuro ». Il contadino pugliese non rifiutava per nulla il pensiero difficile. Quello che teneva in poco conto erano le zone dove la lama del pensiero non ha cosa da tagliare. « Hai visto che sia capitato mai nulla ai professori di archeologia romana? »

Quante volte ebbe a interrompere i nostri ragionamenti, dicendo: « Scusa, questa dev'essere filosofia, perchè non capisco più nulla ». Aveva capito benissimo. Certo non era inconscio del valore filosofico della storia, poichè ne viveva e ne traeva il suo pensiero. Spregiava il « materialonismo » dei dialettici, e gli abbiamo visto fare esegesi sottili, talvolta letterarie, dei moventi storici. Ma come Montaigne, aveva in odio gli astrattismi di comodo, le parole maiuscole e le generalità, tutto quello che si chiude in sistema e tende, come diceva, alla « fregatura intellettuale ». Voleva che l'indagine rimanesse sempre aperta, socraticamente in cammino, stringendo i fatti da presso. E come attendeva a tener duro e a rifare i conti, la gente si rifugiava nella oscura speranza che non potesse, in alcun modo, mai, aver ragione. Mi diceva un grande critico, e intendo grande davvero, mente sagace e non illusa: « Salvemini, lo vede, a ogni colpo fa padella, che vuol che conti? » Detta proprio ai tempi dell'*Anschluss*, era parola da far riflettere. Fu allora soltanto che capii come in Italia l'essere al potere, il rimanervi come che sia, significa aver avuto ragione in assoluto, perchè non comporta responsabilità. I guai, si sa, capitano a tutti, piove sul tristo e sull'innocente, ma la colpa è dell'Ingiustizia che la Storia ha fatto all'Italia, vera sorte jettata. Chi insiste a predir disgrazie è un cattivo, e per di più, siccome non gli frutta, ha fatto padella.

Mussolini per conto suo non era tanto sicuro, e pagava i suoi barzini per descrivere Salvemini come uno scritturato e un sinistro pennivendolo. Teneva lui, però, un esercito di stipendiati a fargli controbatteria all'estero, col risultato almeno di fargli sprecar tempo, perchè il vecchio, da buon cane da guardia, si perdeva a far *bau bau* appresso all'infima razzamaglia e prominentaglia dell'italoamerica. Tuonava Mussolini dallo storico balcone: « Il rinnegato Salvemini... » La gente urlava Duce. Con durissima volontà, si andava armando la prora per salpare verso il mondo.

Venne lo scontro, l'Italia si sfasciò come un barcone fatiscente, ma tutto continuò come prima, gli stessi a far lo stesso, cioè carriera col padrone dell'ora. Le triste faccie d'intrallazzatori che siedono a via Veneto e fanno legge ai Parioli lasciavano cadere negligentemente che Salvemini era un astioso e un cattivo come tutti i falliti. E poi, dicevano, che ci stava a fare in America? Ci rimanga. Passavano per le menti fugaci visioni di dollari, di quelli che non girano per Roma. In quel primo dopoguerra, con tanti corrispondenti esteri che cercavano di orientarsi nella selva politica, avevo suggerito ai miei amici il « Salvemini test » per le interviste, una specie di reazione Wassermann che si dimostrò semplice e pratica. Spiegavano i politici comecchè all'estero non si comprendeva l'Italia, si diffondevano in discorsi nobili, generosi e patetici, ma bastava far quel nome: da come reagivano si misurava subito quali e quante magagne avessero da occultare. Togliatti aveva capito, e cautamente lodava il vecchio maestro pur dicendolo « fuori della realtà ». E poi, diceva anche lui, è stato troppo in America.

È ben vero che Salvemini rimase attaccato al suo eremo di Harvard più che a qualunque altro luogo. Pagano, solare, mediterraneo quanto si vuole, fermamente ancorato nell'antica civiltà del pane e del vino — da cui, diceva, è sempre proceduto lo spirito — ma con gli anglosassoni si sentiva a casa sua, e fra loro spariva come per incanto quel lato ringhioso e difficile di cui lo perseguiva la paurosa leggenda in Italia. Non è paradosso dire che fu forse maggiore e più duratura la sua influenza dalla cattedra cantabrigense che non da quella fiorentina. In ogni università degli Stati Uniti si trovano oggi giovani storici che parlano di « Old Gaetano » come di una grande esperienza nella loro vita, che attraverso lui hanno capito non solo l'Italia, ma anche lo spirito europeo. Sono cose che avranno il loro peso nella politica dell'avvenire. Questo lo intuiva anche lui, e ne traeva coraggio. « Widener Library — diceva — gli studenti, gli amici, dodici ore di sonno filato, che vuoi di più? Sei in Paradiso ». In quello si intende che è il Terrestre, la perfezione della vita attiva. Quando si impancava di fronte alle portate di riso al burro e formaggio che gli offrivano le sue vestali per confortarlo (« Sono tanto cari, qui, ma la vedi che cosa si mangia? Sono ciechi nella bocca »), noialtri gli si diceva: « Salvemini, via sia buono, pensi al dottore, un pò di livore rinunciatario... ». Ma lui rispondeva con quel riso che mostrava la chiostra dei denti: « Non rinuncio. La Decima Musa regna in cucina ». Era un gaudente delle cose semplici e dell'amicizia. C'era qualcosa di antico e di monastico nel modo in cui assaporava il lavoro e la pace dell'anima come fini in se. La sua stanza, ovunque fosse, diventava una cella. La « documentazione » si ammonticchiava sul pavimento, disposta in ampi cerchi concentrici attorno alla sedia; erano quelle le rote magne in cui operando se ne stava contento. Gli studenti di Lowell House scorgevano a ogni ora nel vano della finestra quel cranio lucido chino su una scrivania nascosta, e dicevano in tono reverente: « Dig the Old Boy up there... ».

Lo si era avvertito che se tornava a Firenze, in case mal riscaldate, la bronchite lo avrebbe portato via. E poi che cosa lo aspettava? Lo ha detto Panfilo Gentile narrando il loro incontro con inaspettata e rivelatrice compassione: « La miseria di una stanzetta, la vecchiaia e la solitudine». Ma appena gli fu restituita la cattedra, tornò. « Senti, spiegava, quel che mi può capitare è ormai di ordinaria amministrazione. E se riesco a salvare quattro menti di giovani, sono pronto a crepare senz'altro, perchè quei quattro, non c'è rimedio, diventano quattrocento e con quelli si può salvare tutto ».

Secretosque pios, his dantem jura Catonem... Tornava a mente alle volte il verso virgiliano, nel vederlo fra i suoi giovani. Ma era soprattutto per via del contrasto. Era così poco « romano » e catoniano. Non lo si può immaginare in quella Valletta dei Giusti in Eliso, fra giuristi e filosofi del diritto. Sfascierebbe tutto dalla noia. Conviene pensarlo nelle Isole dei Beati, con gli Argonauti, Palamede, Antigone e Pentesilea, con gli eroi eponimi della gioventù del mondo, gli uccisori di mostri, quelli che infransero divieti nefandi. « Quando tu pensi all'Italia — diceva in una delle sue *boutades*, — pensa che ha dato una volta tanto l'immagine di una gioventù eterna. Pensa a Guidarello, a Ilaria del Carretto. Magari a Pisacane. Quella è una cosa che ricomincia sempre ».

Il Rovescio della Medaglia

[I conclude these essays with an open apologia (1955) about the many misunderstandings that Europeans, even friendly, harbor against the United States. Surely it will sound dated. America is today (1967) a moral shambles, created by the Masters of Iniquity and the Doctors of Confusion. But what I believed then, I still believe now, and I am grateful to Ignazio Silone for having accepted this tract in his collection for the "Freedom of Culture." History proceeds on great wavelengths, and the very agony America is going through, as it labors under a tyranny bereft of mind, shows how indestructibly it is attached to the principles that we received from her.]

I

È CAMBIATA QUANTO SI DICE, DAL 1900 AD OGGI, LA POSIZIONE morale degli Stati Uniti?

Molti americani di vecchio stampo si dolgono che non sussista più, nei rapporti con l'estero, lo spirito di cent'anni fa, quando il rude e intraprendente cittadino della Repubblica Stellata parlava e pensava come oggi il russo, con illimitato dispregio dei sistemi stranieri ancora basati sui « principi e potentati », e con quell'atteggiamento di compassione e di sfida che invitava tutti a diventare come lui.

È ben vero che il tono è cambiato, ma quegli stessi che oggi lo rilevano non sono portati a concludere che è radicalmente cambiato il loro Paese. Dicono piuttosto che le nuove responsabilità esterne lo rendono eccessivamente apprensivo. Ma anch'essi, dicendo questo, soggiacciono un po' alla stessa illusione ottica nostra. Perché in realtà non si è mai data epoca in cui l'americano abbia voluto intervenire politicamente fuori del suo continente. Fin dai primi dell'Ottocento, andava magari a sfidare i pirati di Barbaria, ma non per questo occupava Tripoli. Ha raccattato, più tardi, qua e là, delle zone divenute in fatto *res nullius*, ma anche da queste tende a ritrarsi, come nelle Filippine e perfino oggi a Portorico. Per il resto ha soltanto aspettato che cambiassero gli altri.

Cantavano i soldati nel 1945 sull'aria dolente di *Lili Marlene* (e le parole mi sembra che siano un'efficace sintesi della evoluzione storica da Annibale ai nostri tempi):

> Oh Mr Truman, why can't we go home?
> We have conquered Africa, and we have conquered Rome,
> We have subdued the Master Race
> And now they say, no shipping space.
> Oh why can't we go home?

Parole oneste, verità concrete, se pur sorprendano.

Nel 1848, al momento della patetica « rivoluzione » tedesca, circolavano ovunque, e fino a Vienna, volantini che dicevano: « Gli americani non ci abbandonano ». Nel 1945, molti europei furono presi dalla stessa speranza; e anch'essi rimasero delusi, benché gli eserciti americani fossero questa volta accampati nel loro territorio. Anzi, appunto per questo, ben più delusi.

Quindi si è detto: ipocrisia. Il pensiero si appunta sulle attuali innegabili incoerenze e collusioni con gli esponenti della reazione e del colonialismo, e vi si scorge un crollo delle posizioni morali degli Stati Uniti. Credo che sia piuttosto il caso di parlare di un cedimento parziale, perché anche oggi l'americano che rifletta non si trova in totale contraddizione con se stesso. Ci sono da sempre in lui questi due fattori: anticolonialismo da una parte, autodeterminazione e parlamentarismo borghese dall'altra, né lui pensa a rinnegarli.

Ricordo un alto funzionario di Washington, sudista per nascita e non certo tenero per le sinistre, il quale avendo assistito alla fase del « governo di Bari » non si era ancora riavuto dal suo stupore. « Pensi — diceva — l'autorità sparita, le vacanze della legalità, i carabinieri dispersi e senza scarpe, i latifondisti in fuga, e questi contadini andavano ancora col cappello in mano a portare i loro miseri soldi al gabelloto ».

« Ma se fossero passati all'azione come in Spagna — chiesi — che cosa avrebbe detto ? » Non disse nulla perché non aveva nulla da dire, ma vidi che rabbrividiva. Come aveva rabbrividito Tom Paine, l'estremista militante della Rivoluzione americana, quando nel 1792 aveva assistito dalla galleria degli invitati ai dibattiti della Convenzione francese.

In tutto questo non c'è contraddizione, c'è soltanto l'idea che i mezzi non devono essere troppo disformi dal fine. E quindi, alle volte, paralisi.

Si è spesso notato che l'Impero britannico, con tutta la sua famosa « ipocrisia », seppe sostenere nel secolo scorso l'ascesa dei partiti liberali in altri Paesi, e si è chiesto perché l'America non ha fatto altrettanto per dei partiti « americani ». Ma per l'appunto, che cosa sarebbero essi se non nuovi partiti liberali produttivisti ? E a chi appoggiarli ? (Conto per nulla i tentativi di finanziamento tramite i circoli laburisti). La penetrazione americana esiste, ma prende forme materiali perché non trova in Europa la piattaforma liberale che si cercava. Piattaforma, dico, liberale rivoluzionaria.

Gobettismo in ritardo. Niente da fare. Lo stesso pensiero gobettiano fu ai suoi tempi pensiero romantico di alcuni giovani. I più passarono all'azionismo, poi al socialismo, altri divennero quello che sappiamo. È con questo smottamento di posizioni che l'americano ha da fare. Cercava cittadini, industriali, trasformatori; trova reazionari, burocrati, dialettici, erpivori. Il dialogo diventa perpetuo equivoco.

E il nocciolo dell'equivoco sta qui: che la stessa parola capitalismo ha lì un contenuto rivoluzionario, qui un contenuto in gran parte reazionario.

L'America è rimasta sempre disponibile a qualunque possibilità di rivoluzione industriale in Europa: lo dimostra l'attuazione del Piano Marshall, lo dimostrano le sue speranze — fallite — nel Piano Monnet e simili. Dalla guerra di Corea in poi, evidentemente, quest'atteggiamento è stato offuscato dalla preoccupazione dell'attacco russo. Ma la situazione nuova si è affermata ben più qui che là. È l'Europa che ha congelato nell'estrema sinistra le sue velleità rivoluzionarie, ed ha offerto all'America una piattaforma di collaborazione unicamente reazionaria.

Avrete osservato che l'americano gioisce di qualificarsi come conservatore, anche se non lo è — né può esserlo — in termini nostri. Al più al più, sarà in realtà un liberale classico del tipo manchesteriano. Ma per lui che non ha una Destra Storica, questo è essere dell'estrema destra; mentre in Europa i più retrivi fra i reazionari sono ridotti a chiamarsi, che so, liberali indipendenti; e di lì accusano anch'essi l'americano di ipocrisia.

Qui c'è veramente una differenza di vocabolario e di mitologia. L'Europa vede la rivoluzione come un atto di volontà visionaria — un fatto di alta tensione ideologica che lancia in avanti forze nuove — salvo poi, come si sa, ad aspettarsi amaramente che il grande sforzo venga a insabbiarsi e finisca confiscato da un qualche gruppo particolare. Ma alla idea della rivoluzione amorfa, sotto la forma di Lambrette e Topolini che ti passano fra i piedi in tutte le direzioni, di jazz, televisione, elettrodomestici e potere d'acquisto — a questa rivoluzione che non everte ma pullula e man mano ricopre — a questo l'europeo non si rassegna. La trova un po' informe, questa cosa che si propaga e spunta da sé come l'insalatina. E, in fondo, per niente meritevole di essere idealizzata.

Indi l'accusa di inerzia mentale, di arretratezza e, al tempo stesso, di sfacciata diabolica penetrazione. Eppure bisognerebbe vedere che gli imperativi, semplicemente, differiscono.

Il rivoluzionario tipo nostro deve credere alla Causa — quindi a qualunque mezzo atto a quel fine — e in conclusione si trova servitore della causa, e rimane poi impegolato nella concezione di un partito fine a se stesso.

L'altro tipo deve cercare anzitutto di conservare la misura di sé, si preoccupa di serbarsi intatto attraverso il torrente della trasformazione materiale: di qui una certa rigidità intellettuale, un ritegno nelle idee, una insistenza sull'etica consuetudinaria come asse patrimoniale della sua civiltà.

Insomma, il suo insegnamento sarà schivo delle idee: tenderà a formare non l'intellettuale ma il cittadino. E così si avrà un *certa* democrazia. Non « formale », come si dice, bensì sociale anch'essa, in quanto fondata su forme di socialità intense e senza barriere di classe. Come in Inghilterra, la vita suburbana e rurale d'America è un tessuto di iniziative, di comitati, di raduni, di attività in comune. Mentre è chiaro che qui da noi la parola

« democrazia » è troppo spesso una nuova maschera del « collaborazionismo » col vincitore.

La difficoltà da parte nostra a comprendere e adattarsi mi pare che venga soprattutto da questo, che le due grandi potenze d'oggi sono realmente rivoluzionarie: due diversi aspetti della Rivoluzione Industriale. La quale, ben lungi dall'esaurirsi, si sta via via accelerando ed è entrata nella terza fase.

L'America, che le è in un certo senso consustanziale, è per lasciarla correre. La vive, diciamo così, a tiraggio libero.

I popoli di là dalla Cortina, invece, la pensano; è la rivoluzione delle aspettative crescenti, immaginata, precorsa, programmata, appassionatamente scontata.

Non è la rivoluzione che si fa da sé; è la rivoluzione romantica come l'intendiamo noi, pur ricoperta della patina grigia del collettivismo burocratico, quella cui ci si dedica con furore religioso, è il vivere del grande paradosso del *Gesta Dei per Francos*. È, insomma, la Rivoluzione Industriale a tiraggio forzato.

Quelli sono gli estremisti, mentre l'americano è il conservatore. Ma di che? Sempre della Rivoluzione Permanente.

Partendo di qui si può chairire un punto facilmente equivocabile: quell'avversione che l'americano medio prova nei riguardi delle ideologie socialiste, e che non viene, come si usa dire qui, dal timore che ha per i suoi investimenti all'estero, né dal subdolo comando di Wall Street.

Questa sarebbe una spiegazione ottima per cent'anni fa, se al posto di Wall Street si dicesse la City di Londra, perché quella veramente comandava a una politica nazionale. Ma ai tempi nostri, non sono gli untorelli di Wall Street quelli che decideranno la politica americana. L'elettore americano deride gli investimenti all'estero e rifiuta di accollarsene i rischi.

A questo punto vorrei aprire una parentesi forse superflua. I popoli pensano l'uno all'altro in termini di *clichés*, questo è inevitabile. Ed è notevole vedere come certi *clichés* delle sinistre siano entrati ormai nel patrimonio comune, a combinarsi stranamente con i soliti *clichés* delle destre.

In tutte le grandi forze ideologiche operano le immagini del loro passato creativo. C'è una *imagerie* communista come c'è una *imagerie* gesuita coi suoi santini. In questa *imagerie* comunista si ritrovano cari vecchi termini come « bonapartismo », « entrepreneur », « cricca », « lacché », « agitare la sciabola nel fodero » e tanti altri che ci sono servita dalla stampa d'oltre Cortina; termini del tempo di Nonna Speranza o magari dell'Isola dei Pinguini. Fra questi brillano oggi i termini stile « liberty » di « Wall Street » e di « piovra dei trust ». Appartengono per così dire al Seicento del marxismo, al periodo che precede la revisione Hilferding. Ma si danno volentieri in pasto al volgo. La idea del comando di Wall Street non significa più nulla, né spiega nulla. Anche il recente non bene ispirato intervento al Guatemala non è dovuto alle compagnie bananiere né alla diplomazia del dollaro, come sarebbe stato certo il caso di cinquanta anni fa. Gli Stati Uniti hanno avuto da allora, nel Sud America, una posizione direi quasi laburista, che non andava giocata così alla leggera. No, l'intervento è dovuto a una pensata politica, forse non felice, ma politica, a cui non sono state estranee le pressioni di certi governi europei.

Né la vampata del maccartismo è stata finanziata dalle casse delle banche, come fu il caso per il fascismo in Italia trent'anni fa. È stata alimentata da una nuova piccola borghesia pur ora arrivata al « colletto bianco » e alla rispettabilità suburbana, e poi ancora da quegli arricchiti di colpo che chiamerei i « tredicisti » del petrolio: gente nuova dai subiti guadagni che non ha avuto ancora il tempo di pensare più in là delle reazioni primitive, e che si vede offrire come grandi novità l'aggressione e la xenofobia da maneggioni esperti e da bande di irlandesi fanatizzati. Gente, insomma, che si è affacciata alla coscienza — e all'insicurezza sociale — solo per trovarsi alle prese con la Grande Paura.

Bisognerebbe pur che l'europeo si rendesse conto che l'America è quel Paese singolare che non ha mai conosciuto l'apprensione. Il suo passato gli ha dato finora buone ragioni per sentirsi inviolabile. Scoprire adesso che vi è una forza che lo minaccia, una forza che non è soltanto una potenza territoriale e industriale, ma un miasma sottile, un contagio incomprensibile (perché nessuno è stato mai capace di concepire la dialettica hegeliana) — qualcosa di terribile e nefando come il virus della paralisi infantile — significa una crisi di sbandamento politico senza precedenti. Ma, per l'appunto, crisi.

Quando all'eschimese si attacca il raffreddore, malattia nuova, diventa più grave di una polmonite. Poi verrà l'assuefazione.

Ho detto: crisi, e non sindrome mortale. Di questo si vedono chiari segni nello sfasamento delle azioni. Il buon McCarthy non andò, come fecero i suoi predecessori in Italia, a farsi dare camion dai prefetti e armi dai carabinieri; perché, fra l'altro, non vi erano né prefetti né carabinieri né vi era in giro l'idea di dargli armi; non si accordò con l'esercito come avrebbe fatto in Germania; ma invece caricò a testa bassa esercito e governo insieme, da quel vero tribuno populista che era, e rimase sul campo. È giusto, forse, ravvisare una misericordia speciale della Provvidenza nel fatto che in una super-potenza dove allignano simili arruffapopoli, essi non trovino da appoggiarsi a una destra nazionalista del tipo nostrano munita di Padri e Dottori, di una dottrina proterva, di una tradizione di sinistro prestigio umanistico, e di apologeti sottili quanto necessita. Creando il toro o la balena, madre Natura non ha dato loro la fame dello squalo o l'acume dello sciacallo.

Rimane, però, che l'apprensione restringe l'orizzonte mentale americano, costringe a comportamenti superstiziosi, sospettosi, meccanici, controproducenti. Fra i molti crimini di cui si sono resi colpevoli gli strateghi del Cremlino, questo mi sembra fra i più gravi, di avere in nome della ragione storica costretto un grande popolo libero, fiducioso e innocente, nella camicia di forza della paura e dell'odio, per poterlo poi additare al dispregio delle masse come una torva banda di fascisti.

Certo, da allora la politica americana ha perduto molto in generosità e dirittura. In parte questo era inevitabile, in una nazione costretta ad assumere responsabilità imperiali. In parte è contingente e patologico.

Non si può dunque negare alle accuse un contenuto di verità. Tutt'al più, si può scorgere una analogia con quello che andava dicendo Carlyle del Parlamento inglese del suo tempo, o con ciò che indubbiamente deve aver pensato un Appio Claudio della politica del Senato romano.

Ma quello che mi colpisce è che nella polemica non si mira in verità ai nuovi difetti, ma si trae occasione per colpire le virtù antiche. All'anima latina, usa da secoli a chiedere ai reggitori vastità di disegni e maestà d'imperio (pur concedendo poi, in via subordinata, che in politica non si può più di tanto e che è già segno di prodigioso accorgimento l'esser rimasti in piedi), all'anima latina, dico, questo incedere dimesso e imbarazzato di una superpotenza, questo avvertire che si intende procedere *by trial and error*, come dicono, cioè provando e sbagliando (« provando e riprovando » si diceva un tempo anche da noi, e non era un tempo di cui vergognarsi), può sembrare segno di natura incerta. Tanto più in quanto l'americano ti concede modestamente che il metodo comporta provare per l'un per cento, e sbagliare per novantanove. Peggio, sbagliare sempre allo stesso modo...

Ora questa modestia proviene per l'appunto da una vecchia virtù. È il fatto di una civiltà che non si vuol imporre, che non porta con sé volontà di prestigio. Essa si presenta come un metodo, nel senso galileiano della parola. Intendo, presenta se stessa come esponente di quel metodo, non come sua proprietaria, perché tal metodo lo suppone proprietà comune di tutti gli uomini. E in particolare, mi sia permesso ricordarlo, degli europei che l'hanno inventato qualche secolo fa.

Insomma, l'America è il Paese a cui è capitato per primo di doversi americanizzare. Se sia forza o ventura, è questione che anche lì rimane aperta.

E, ben lungi dal voler imporre forme specifiche, se le tiene per sé in modo geloso e ritroso, e accetta di essere considerata dagli altri semplicista, primitiva, infantile, indotta e quel che ne segue. In questo è l'inverso della civiltà francese, dispiegata e autoproclamantesi, che vuol sempre insegnare al mondo la sua concezione della vita e della cultura.

La civiltà americana propriamente detta invece, come si conviene alla tradizione della Nuova Inghilterra, è riservata e schiva, piena di allusioni e di modi di parlare in famiglia, di vecchie usanze, di ironie misurate, di riguardi sottili e di cerimonie scrupolose: insomma una civiltà antica e segreta, la quale ama non rendersi esplicita nemmeno a se stessa, e preferisce ammantarsi di semplicismo e di egualitarismo.

Questa non è certo l'immagine che se ne fa l'italiano medio, il quale vede l'America attraverso il cinema e i rotocalchi. Ma non è sicuro che quell'italiano non scorga soprattutto ed ovunque se stesso.

Per intenderci, prendiamo le forme della cosiddetta « società », voglio dire di quella che in tempi morigerati si chiamava *la bonne compagnie*. E non consideriamo i casi estremi, di un'Italia provinciale, ancora « piccolo mondo antico », da un lato, e dall'altro del vasto calderone del Middle West, ingorgato di masse recentemente immigrate. Mettiamo insomma a confronto entità comparabili, come Roma o Milano qui, e laggiù le grandi città della costa atlantica con tre secoli di storia.

Vedremo allora che non si può scorgere laggiù niente che corrisponda a quel vasto coagulo che si potrebbe dire « tutta-Roma » come si dice « tout-Paris ». Rispetto ad esso anche quell'incerto e sognato prototipo che è la *Cafè Society* di New York diventa un circolo chiuso. Perché, insomma, a Roma, chiunque può ragionevolmente prefiggersi di sfondare con l'aiuto dei quattrini, di un buon sarto e di un titolo qualunque, magari portato in disfida agli strali del « Falso Gotha ». Dove poi finisca, sfondando, non è chiaro, poiché si ritrova sempre entro quel vasto « malloppo » che contempla se stesso in Via Veneto nell'inerte ora meridiana. Ma, se ci tiene e fin dove scorge, può arrivare. Mentre l'ammissione alla « società » in America richiede anche oggi carte in regola. Si scrutano la nascita, la parentela, le scuole frequentate, i circoli cui si appartiene. Si richiedono contrassegni invisibili che conferisce solo una certa educazione, che non sono comunicati all'esterno, perché, lungi dal mettersi in vista, la « società » si mimetizza verso la massa così da non farsi riconoscibile, né chiede di essere riverita, ma insiste nell'essere democratica onde poter essere, per conto proprio, esclusivista. Si conoscono fra loro, e basta. È una fra le numerose autonomie di un sistema non gerarchico, bensì autonomista. E come le vere autonomie, è fortemente difesa. Per dirla in breve, mi colpisce quanto sia « vecchio mondo » la società americana in confronto a Roma. E non credo per questo che Roma sia più moderna. Sono due linee storiche diverse, e in un certo senso Roma è fuori concorso, avendo rifiutato la storia. Qualcosa di simile al presente si deve aver avuto nella Roma tardo-imperiale probabilmente in quella del IV e V secolo, quando già la sede dell'Impero era a Milano o a Costantinopoli, ma ancora le faccende della Provincia d'Italia si sbrigavano all'ombra del Palatino. Oggi come allora, il personaggio operante è il liberto.

E vedendo per le strade il notabile gallo o britanno in visita, o magari il messo di Teodorico venuto a sistemare qualche vertenza con la sede lateranense, dovevano dirsi fra di loro: « Che ci vuoi fare, *caput mundi* siamo noi, hanno da venire qui... ». Che è anche questo un modo di aver ragione della storia. Ma il centro della cultura si era già spostato, e un Rutilio era venuto solo da turista.

Così, oggi, vi sono di nuovo culture aperte più a ricevere che a dare, come l'americana, e ne viene per converso che danno molto di più di quanto ricevono, bene o male che sia, che si tratti di Hemingway, o del jazz, o della ricerca archeologica, o della scienza, o di Cinecittà. E ne viene infine che la cultura americana è oggi molto meno provinciale di certe altre le quali, conclamando senza posa la loro universalità, si ritrovano gravemente provincializzate. Questa è una legge dialettica che non perdona.

Il ritegno di cui ho parlato credo che sia peraltro alla base di quello che gli europei sono meno disposti a perdonare, cioè la insufficienza della politica estera americana. Gli Stati Uniti sono un Paese che avrebbe voluto essere una specie di Confederazione Svizzera e non può. Politiche estere non vorrebbero aver da averne. E così non c'è stata mai una vera tradizione diplomatica americana, e ai tempi quando anche le potenze balcaniche avevano le loro Cancellerie, e giocavano la Grande Politica, il presidente degli Stati Uniti doveva ancora improvvisare le sue rappresentanze, fare appello a qualche banchiere o legista di chiaro nome perché andasse a dirimere questa o quella faccenda estera sorta in modo inopinato.

A questo punto la critica potrebbe ridiventar seria. Gli Stati Uniti improvvisano un po' troppo. Per esempio, chiedono, insistono, petulano perché l'Europa si unisca, ma sembra che non riescano a vedere che razza di ridimensionamento economico e politico ci vorrebbe. Non si buttano per aria le strutture industriali di un secolo e più senza avere in vista un'altra soluzione molto concreta. Qui l'America avrebbe dovuto intervenire imperialmente, mettendo in gioco nuovi continenti, scambi triangolari, colonizzazioni e quello che ci vuole.

Ma per far cose simili ci vuole una casta di governo che costringa il popolo a pagare « finché diventino verdi » come diceva il Kaiser quando chiedeva il suo programma navale. Forse gli italiani che si lamentano della mancata politica di colonizzazione non si rendono conto che l'investimento attuale per impiantare un colono sulla terra va sui 4.000 dollari (8.000 se si tratta di un operaio). Quindi, per risistemare un solo milione di europei, ci vorrebbe un finanziamento di sei o sette miliardi di dollari; per non parlare degli altri impegni e interventi inevitabili in un simile programma di proporzioni imperiali. Gli italiani dovrebbero pensarvi, prima di lasciarsi cullare nella loro indignazione da quei notabili e altri gatti con gli stivali che un tempo imbarcavano in massa i poveri lavoratori per le « lontane Americhe » come bestiame da esportazione.

Molto si poteva fare che non è stato fatto. Questo è certo, e il tentativo recente di Mendès-France sta lì a ricordarcelo. Ma per l'appunto il popolo americano non ha una tradizione di classe dirigente e *grands services* come quella a cui faceva appello Mendès. Non riesce a pensare in grandi schemi coloniali e statali. È anche troppo che abbiano votato il Piano Marshall, e adesso si chiedono con qualche ragione dove sono andati quei soldi.

Verso l'estero, questi cosiddetti tecnocrati *U.S.* preferiscono pensare politicamente. « Datevi un governo a base larga e stabile — ripetono in ogni occasione — e la democrazia farà da se ».

È una fede ingenua, che si presta ad equivoci, ma è una fede.

Sarebbe giusto non dimenticare che quella figura molto rappresentativa che è il generale Marshall non è soltanto l'autore del Piano Marshall per l'Europa (ragion per cui gli si dà in Europa dell'imperialista proditorio e mascherato), ma fu anche iniziatore o per lo meno proponente infaticabile di un governo di coalizione in Cina con l'entrata dei comunisti, ragion per cui gli si dà oggi in America del venduto e del traditore, e McCarthy parla di lui come del capo di una mostruosa congiura per portare al trionfo le razze gialle.

Come disse un inglese che aveva dell'esperienza a un americano che ne cercava: « Dovrete imparare a sentirvi soli ».

Se l'America dovesse veramente sentirsi sola un giorno, potrebbe darsi che i figli scontino un certo peccato originale dei padri. Perché l'atto che ha costituito l'americano del passato, è stato il dir *no* alle sue radici europee. L'uomo del Nuovo Mondo ha rifiutato una volta per tutte, firmando il proprio contratto di nascita, le filosofie e le ontologie di Europa. Ha creato il suo pragmatismo aperto verso l'esterno e verso la natura, e ha riservato per sé una ontologia privata. Forte, ma privata.

L'europeo si sente a posto solo quando è inquadrato fra gli archi e le colonne di una ontologia pubblica, che procede solennemente di maiuscola in maiuscola fino ad assommarsi nelle magiche parole « Stato » e « statalità », mentre porta invece un pragmatismo estremo in quella massima e fondamentale fra le attività private che si chiama difendersi, o arrangiarsi, o tirare a campare alla meno peggio. L'americano, invece, piuttosto all'incontrario.

Ne viene anche, se abbiamo osservato, che l'americano assume senza averne l'aria quella serenità impassibile e quell'ottimismo un tantino melenso che sogliono caratterizzare il nostro retorico « volto della Patria » quando gli avviene di parlare di se stesso, e poi non sa che farsene dei panneggi ufficiali quando tratta delle cose pubbliche e della politica estera.

È ben vero, si ha voglia di dirgli, che un po' di panneggio non sarebbe tutto danno, e sotto quello qualche ferma idea strutturale.

Ci vorrebbero, non foss'altro, per attenuare quell'altro gravame serio, il più serio di tutti, e in verità inespiabile, che non è se non la realtà palese di un popolo dal reddito medio dieci volte più alto di quasi ogni altro. Fatto che mette nell'ombra la generosità pubblica e privata di questo popolo, e lo tiene in perpetuo alla sbarra degli accusati. Né vale che questa ricchezza non sia dovuta a conquista o rapina, che sia il risultato di un'attività essenzialmente innocente. Si preferirebbe in fondo che fosse colpevole, come quella di tutti, purché si manifestasse in opere di splendore e d'imperio in cui l'Occidente potesse ravvisare nuovi simboli di se stesso.

Disgrazia vuole, già l'ho detto, che un'attività innocente non consenta la presenza di forti classi dirigenti, quali sono necessarie per costringere il popolo a spendere in opere di prestigio. Tutte le immense donazioni che hanno salvato gran parte del mondo dalla malaria e dalle epidemie non conferiscono il senso di grandezza legittima che le dinastie sapevano derivare dalla Reggia di Caserta o dall'Escorial. Gli uomini sono fatti così.

È vero altresì che sarebbe nello spirito dei tempi il mettere in opera la propria potenza in grandi imprese tecnocratiche di trasformazione che si estendano a interi continenti; ma questa forma moderna di paternalismo non potrebbe mai esser disgiunta da imperialismo finanziario, che i popoli sono mal disposti a tollerare, così che appare chiaro quanto sarebbe difficile per l'America essere all'altezza della propria « missione » quale la vedono gli altri.

Sono ben piuttosto quegli « altri », se ci si pensa, i quali formulano desideri e velleità contraddittori, e sono come il malato « che col dar volta al suo dolore scherma ». Finché, sballottati da alterne reazioni all'inumano da una parte, all'informe dall'altra, l'opinione europea non veda la realtà esterna come un cosmico schiaccianoci; e indi, siccome non v'è dove sfuggire, questo rendersi passivi e neutrali, questo darsi per morti: antica e naturale mimetizzazione.

Torno dunque al mio primo proposto: è difficile guidare,

imporre, a chi crede nella spontaneità. Certo, si può indicare; dare quello che i militari anarchici nella guerra di Spagna chiamavano non ordini ma « consigli di marcia ». Si può creare un alveo. Ma se in quello poi le forze rifiutano di incanalarsi? Qui interverrebbero le grandi arti machiavelliche, gli *arcana imperii* delle nazioni use a pascere moltitudini di popoli. Ma quelli appunto l'americano non li ha. Vorrebbe poter aiutare senza intervenire...

Quante volte l'ho visto soffrire del fatto che la sua sola presenza, per quanto discreta, dava nuova forza a tendenze con le quali non voleva solidarizzare in alcun modo. E mi è toccato di ripensare a quello che diceva un celebre finanziere: « Non è che noi si abbia tanto gusto a comandare; è che tanti hanno la passione di vendersi, magari gratis ».

E così viene il rovescio della medaglia.

Può capitare che, di fronte a questa realtà insanabilmente disforme, l'americano si creda alla fine in dovere di abbandonare inutili ritegni e, quando deve intervenire, lo faccia spesso giocando di gomiti in modo inconsulto e senza riguardo per la legge non scritta della giungla politica. Basta pensare all'intervento nel Guatemala, o a quell'altro più curioso in Italia, quando fu annunciato che le commesse *offshore* sarebbero andate alle ditte che avessero il minor numero di comunisti nei comitati di fabbrica.

Sono gesti controproducenti, evidentemente. Manovre tutt'altro che diaboliche. Fanno pensare al forestiero esasperato che piglia a scapaccioni il primo scugnizzo che gli viene a tiro, pur sapendo in cuor suo che non c'è niente da fare e che vinceranno sempre gli scugnizzi e le mosche.

II

DOPO AVER TENTATO DI INQUADRARE COSÌ ALCUNI ELEMENTI DELLA situazione transoceanica, resta da vedere con quali prismi, con quali binocoli la guarda l'opinione italiana.

Molti anni fa, non dico quanti, ebbi un colloquio rivelatore con un ambasciatore americano a Roma. Quando gli dissi che venivo da Boston — il che era vero — lui si accinse con grande cortesia a spiegarmi l'Italia. E in sostanza mi disse questo: « Vedrà che non avrà difficoltà, se capisce che si tratta di un Paese diverso dal nostro come composizione. Qui non c'è che aristocrazia e popolo ».

Io rimasi lì per lì piuttosto triste. Pensavo: « Poveri noi, ecco qua come si fa la politica internazionale. Questo signore non vede la realtà più massiccia e inoppugnabile di questo Paese, il solo vero partito di massa in cui la nazione si assomma, cioè la piccola e media borghesia ».

Più tardi capii perché mi aveva parlato così. Non già che la borghesia non gli fosse proprio sotto gli occhi, ma pensando che ero semplicemente il visitatore occasionale che doveva poi raccontare qualcosa di simpatico e di allietante agli americani, cercava di attirare il mio sguardo altrove che su questa massa opaca e impenetrabile.

Entro la borghesia italiana si trova peraltro, indubbiamente, il nucleo portatore della intelligenza, della cultura e della spiritualità. In quale altra zona lo potremmo cercare?

È quindi da lì, logicamente — e non dal popolo, né dalla nobiltà — che vengono i gravami e le accuse: accuse di inintelligenza, di inciviltà, di incultura, di materialismo.

Tali accuse rimangono giustificate da parte di una aristocrazia spirituale che certamente esiste e persiste, sacrificata, arroccata su posizioni precarie. Ma il fatto è che la classe media italiana nel suo insieme fa sue queste accuse, per giustificarsi nella sua posizione di classe dirigente.

È in questo senso che parlo di una « borghesia ». Il dividere la realtà in classi astratte non può che violarne il contenuto reale. Nella « borghesia » c'è tutto. Vi si può scorgere la sostanza viva del pensiero e del costume, come vi si può scorgere il precipitato insolubile di trenta secoli di storia. Si può descrivere come la classe che ha creato le forme di ciò che si chiama civiltà italiana, e si può anche descrivere come una massa protoplasmica (« famiglia ») di comportamento ameboide, debolmente retrattile, dedita al brigantaggio alimentare.

Quando parlo qui di borghesia, mi referisco dunque specialmente alle reazioni che presenta in quanto « classe dirigente ».

(Si può chiedere perché non mi sono riferito, precedentemente, per parallelo, alla classe dirigente americana. La ragione è che gli elementi superstiti di tale classe sono stati spazzati via dalla vita politica fin dalle prime refole del maccartismo, e che si manifesta oggi la realtà, implicita fin dall'inizio, di un « popolo grasso » di ex-proletari che fa tutt'uno col Paese. I danni di un tale declassamento sono gravi e ovvi, ma c'è insomma là dentro una coerenza jeffersoniana che si è fatta strada, non vi sono pensamenti di « funzione storica ».)

Sappiamo tutti come lo sforzo di portare i paludamenti di una grande civiltà possa essere gravoso e controproducente. Perché poi, là sotto, la vita continua i suoi intrallazzi. Quegli stessi intrallazzi che l'americano per conto suo dispone alla luce del giorno, non sapendo dove altro metterli, e vi delega la categoria, ufficialmente dichiarata servile, dei *politicians*. Nel caso nostro, invece, che cosa succede? Prendiamo un caso di contatti reali.

Gli esperti e consulenti americani che hanno avuto da fare con l'industria europea sanno che di solito, quando propongono qualcosa ai dirigenti, si sentono rispondere che l'idea è ottima, però che la mentalità del personale italiano (o francese, o greco:

è sempre lo stesso) rende assolutamente impossibile la messa in opera dei nuovi metodi.

Alla fine, il consulente è indotto a chiedersi che cosa sia questa famosa mentalità. Si può definire? Si ritrovano sempre certi fattori: « non si può » perché l'operaio è abituato a far così e così; non si può perché il personale non ha quell'iniziativa che voi altri in America, beati voi, ecc. ecc.; non si può perché qui l'individualità è più marcata, il lavoro in serie non è fatto per noi, e così via.

Il che si riassume in questo: la mentalità ce l'abbiamo noi, voi non ve la sognate nemmeno. A noi la funzione storica, l'antica saggezza, la varietà dilettosa, le semplici virtù, i bassi salari di cui ci si contenta, la vita intrisa di colore e di cultura. A voi il ragionamento commerciale, la mentalità lineare, l'inesistenza.

Ora dico: possibile che l'operaio americano non abbia anche lui una mentalità? Ce l'ha sì, e reagisce abbastanza duramente contro chi cerca di violarla; e quindi si è creata tutta una diplomazia (qui, oserei proporre, sta la vera diplomazia americana) per spiegargli da pari a pari qual è l'interesse comune, per suggerire una soluzione che convenga anche a lui. Un'uscita dall'alto, come dicono. E come il famoso contadino italiano che non cambia mai e pensa e sente come una bestia (cito le parole di un gran luminare del nostro pensiero) si è dimostrato pronto a capire le nuove culture, così anche l'operaio, e magari americano, capisce...

Donde la conclusione ormai unanime dei poveri consulenti: che la famosa mentalità in questione non è quella del personale ma è quella del dirigente. Per cui si vengono piuttosto a porre problemi di gerarchia troppo rigida nell'industria, di separazione fra l'alto e il basso, di paura dei metodi nuovi, di indifferenza verso l'iniziativa, di indifferenza verso il personale, e in fondo verso tutto, perché tanto c'è lo Stato che paga.

Insomma, l'esperto scopre solo, in capo a qualche anno, e dopo che gli è stata gonfiata la testa dei soliti ragionamenti intelligentissimi che ogni commendatore crede di presentargli come nuovi e assolutamente originali, che il capitalismo italiano non è quello che si aspettava.

È un fatto abbastanza noto, che dalla querela balza prima di tutto in evidenza la mentalità del querelante.

Si può verificare subito che quella stessa categoria media che è più pronta ad arricciare il naso all'incultura transoceanica è quella che ha provincializzato la cultura italiana in questo trentennio, che non può nemmeno più leggere un romanzo francese se non tradotto, e che ha risospinto indietro le posizioni morali e culturali al più classico Seicento.

E non dico già il Seicento di Galileo, ma quel Seicento che si sbarazzò di Galileo come poteva, e cioè in malo modo.

È una maniera come un'altra, certo, di riavvicinarsi alla base, in tempi di incertezza: di ritrovare quella base astorica e stabile che si esprime in termini di questurini, diritti inconcussi, raccomandazioni, arcadie, questue, nappe, lustrini e orifiammi.

Quella base rimane. E si pensa da molte parti che se non grazie ad essa, almeno con essa, possano perdurare le virtù di una civiltà casalinga, una morale magari precettistica, una salutare prudenza, una bonaria saggezza. Ma allora non è lecito parlare, nemmeno per retorica, di « modernizzazione che s'impone ». Perché una tal base non può e non vuole lasciarsi modernizzare, si lascia solo corrompere: la modernizzazione sarà, per ben che vada, una vernice d'alluminio a spruzzo che copre vecchie magagne, più spesso e facilmente un dissolvente, e nella dissoluzione rischiano di essere trascinate anche quelle tali virtù. Tant'è vero che gli italiani, invasati oggi di modernità, di cromature e di aggeggi, sono diventati un popolo scialacquone e sbuccione più d'ogni altro (si paragoni con l'astiosa resistenza al nuovo della provincia francese) e la loro modernità d'animo si estrinseca in rotocalchi, televisione, divismo, jazz e l'ormai classico « drinchettino ».

Proprio come l'America, dal canto suo, può ricevere da noi più facilmente le camorre di Tammany Hall, oppure la nostra pittura astratta, che non i nostri valori fondamentali.

Qui forse metterebbe conto citare ad esempio di malinteso un caso illustre che ho visto l'altro giorno di collaborazione internazionale ad alto livello. Si tratta di un film che si prefigge di « far senso » per due ore di séguito e ci riesce non senza difficoltà. Non lo critico qui per l'esecuzione, condotta con maestria tecnica e artistica consumata. Ma quello che mi rese perplesso fu il testo, la sceneggiatura, in cui figuravano come autori bei nomi letterari di ambo i continenti. Dal principio alla fine, questo testo è attento a dilacerare, vilipendere e rendere assurda la figura centrale della donna, Pandora portatrice di tutti i guai. Il che può magari esser giusto, poiché così pensava anche S. Girolamo. Ma non basta l'etichetta neorealista a occultare il fatto che i nostri squisiti intendono la cosa in modo tanto meno austero quanto più avanzato. Né vale loro a scusa l'assenza totale di atmosfera erotica nel film, perché non era quella l'intenzione. Ciò che hanno in comune col Padre della *Vulgata* sembra essere solo il rifiuto di ogni *sense of humor*. E questo può essere molto significativo. Ogni civiltà ha in proprio una sua concezione del distacco, della leggerezza, del sorriso, di quel tanto di spirito con cui va condita l'esperienza della vita. Due civiltà molto diverse si direbbe — non da questo caso soltanto — che trovino un terreno d'intesa nel fare a meno di questo elemento essenziale e incomunicabile. Il che dà a riflettere. È forse così che i comunicati ufficiali dei grandi convegni diplomatici fanno ridere, appunto per non volerlo. Ma andiamo avanti.

Poiché siamo in tema di civiltà, si può osservare altresì come gli altezzosi luoghi comuni sulla Patria del Diritto siano proferiti da gente per lo più ignara o noncurante dell'ordinamento giuridico a un punto che non si ritroverebbe mai fra gli scaricatori del Nuovo Mondo — da gente per cui « legge » è divenuto da secoli sinonimo di « inghippo » e argomento di frode, così che suggerì bene quell'operaio ravennate citato da Curzio Malaparte, che converrebbe dire: patria del diritto e del rovescio.

E finalmente veniamo al materialismo. Non si può negare che l'americano parli volentieri in termini di denaro, cosa che si dovrebbe evitare nel discorso castigato, talché è raro sentir gente civile parlare di quel soggetto. Almeno, così mi si assicura.

Da quando in qua noialtri, vecchie civiltà mediterranee, ci siamo messi in testa di rinnegare uno dei nostri titoli storici più indiscutibili? Che cos'era la romanità, se non una saggezza profonda della materia fin nei suoi aspetti più cupi? Quale più chiara esplicazione del materialismo, divenuto cosa trasparente e intellettualizzata, quasi fine a se stessa, del pensiero di Machiavelli? Non esiste un vero senso materialista se non dove si svolge per contrapposto una forte dottrina del peccato inerente e inevitabile. E questo è proprio dei Paesi latini. Il modo in cui un romano sa dire *le quadrini* comunica un senso di materialità ultima, incrollabile, in cui la mente si acqueta, di fronte alla quale ogni parola anglosassone che si riferisca alla realtà monetaria diventa aerea e inconsistente, il fantasma contabile di sogni e attività senza quasi più rapporto con la materia.

Ed è pur un fatto che, nella dolorosa saggezza del nostro popolo, l'oro è il mezzo per comprare gli uomini più che le cose, lo strumento per costringerli a fare i nostri comodi (o, più in basso, la difesa contro il morir di fame); mentre per l'americano il denaro è essenzialmente un sistema metrico, magari troppo esclusivo e troppo semplice, ma che misura la capacità, l'iniziativa, la creazione dell'individuo, il suo modo di imporsi alla realtà: è la misura ingenua della sua fantasia e della sua azione, in quanto intesa per il bene di tutti. Qui si vede piuttosto quanto, in queste civiltà moderne, sia presente anche inconsciamente l'idea marxista, degli uomini inevitabilmente uniti nella loro lotta contro la natura, dell'alleanza necessaria nella grande impresa di espansione. Il cosiddetto materialismo finanziario è alla base della società più altruista del mondo moderno — della società, per dirla con gli antropologi, in cui lo scambio, a un certo livello, ha dovuto prendere la forma sistematica del dono — mentre il cosiddetto materialismo storico ha creato le più intense forme religiose di massa dell'èra contemporanea.

Si tratta sempre, in questi casi, di un'idea di materia, che serve a dare le misure all'azione. Ma la materia, ben lungi dall'essere adorata, vi è continuamente negata. Se si vuol vedere un uso mal concepito, arruffato o disforme della materia, andiamo pure a

Chicago, a Detroit, a Grand Rapids; magari, immagino, a Dniepropetrovsk. Se però si vuole vedere il materialismo allo stato puro e immediato, quintessenziale, il materialismo fatto idea platonica, quiescente in se stesso come la Bestia dell'Apocalisse, allora bisogna andare a Via Veneto.

Come nella realtà, così nell'arte. Dove trovare nel romanzo americano contemporaneo, salvo certe descrizioni del mondo del cinema, una realtà materialistica così duramente messa in luce come nella produzione di Moravia? Pensate solo al personaggio di Maria Grazia negli *Indifferenti*. Pensate ai romanzi di Brancati. Realtà archetipa, in un certo senso, che l'artista ha espresso in modo universale, così che la Palude Stigia della Canasta vi si ritrova qui o là, ovunque sia. A Hollywood, l'Urbe Sorella, dove qualche bello spirito sempre rovescia i proverbi, lo si è messo in forma: « che te ne fai della felicità, non ci puoi comprar quatrini ».

III

QUALCHE TEMPO FA UN MIO AMICO, ACUTO E SAGACE OSSERVATORE delle cose europee, mi chiese così di colpo: mi puoi dire in fin dei conti che cosa ci ha dato quest'America?

E io, preso alla sprovvista, risposi su per giù così: Mi fai pensare a quello che si diceva nel secolo scorso dell'Inghilterra, nazione di bottegai. Le stesse recriminazioni si riversano adesso sull'America, e forse a minor ragione, perché quella, allora, era la protesta veemente della vecchia Europa feudale, cavalleresca e monastica, che si vedeva minacciata dalla Rivoluzione Industriale. L'invettiva di Napoleone e di Nietzsche avrebbe voluto essere l'eco del lamento dei cavalieri catafratti di Crécy, il séguito del sirventese di Cacciaguida.

Oggi che l'Inghilterra ha perso la guerra come tutti, e che non c'è più da invidiarla, la vista sembra essersi schiarita, ed essa appare a chiunque come l'ultimo Paese che serbi l'ordinamento aristocratico; il solo, al tempo stesso, che abbia risolto la sclerosi borghese in una società nuova, in cui si contemperano i valori medioevali con la democrazia socialista.

E dunque divien chiaro che essa proteggeva i valori medievali anche allora, di fronte al continente già borghesizzato ove Napoleone l'intellettuale erigeva lo Stato prefettizio, ove il romantico Nietzsche scriveva con la mente rivolta al passato.

Così può essere che un giorno il Nord America ci appaia, sotto la maschera tecnologica, come depositario di quei valori che l'Europa si è biscazzati in quattro secoli di avventura, come una enorme riserva d'innocenza e di fede antiche le quali hanno potuto conservarsi al chiuso; che, in sostanza, abbia funzionato come una specie di cassone ideologico per tirarci su e tenerci a galla in un momento critico. I cassoni, si sa, hanno per funzione di stare a pelo d'acqua, e non sono di grande effetto estetico.

Ma anche il più bel cassone non può dare che quello che ha. L'americano, all'inverso del tedesco, è anche troppo cosciente dei propri limiti, e dell'esistenza altrui.

Venuti qua, dicevano modestamente (l'ho sentito dire): « Non potrebbe essere interessante per voi di cambiare questo sistema ereditato dal fascismo, che consacra la despotia amministrativa al posto della legge? Non si potrebbe, per esempio, tanto per fare una cosa, mettere la polizia alle dipendenze del giudiziario? Non si potrebbe tentare di fare del funzionario un delegato del cittadino e non un aguzzino dello Stato? »

Vidi i sorrisi saputi con cui venivano accolti questi discorsi, e infatti la riforma costituzionale non ne fa motto.

Il fatto è che la posa togata, i grandi paludamenti culturali non solo impacciano l'andatura, ma mettono la coscienza in stato di profondo disagio, così che si sente sempre rispondere dai competenti: « Eh già, caro lei, se noi si avesse un popolo maturo, un popolo capace di democrazia... ».

Discorsi che mi sembra aver sentiti già in altri tempi, e men democratici assai. Tant'è vero che i sullodati personaggi e gatti con gli stivali, come li chiamavo più sopra, pensano sempre allo stesso modo per esser rimasti sempre gli stessi e sempre in piedi, mentre tant'altro andava perduto.

E così, per il medio povero Cristo, la legge continua a dipendere dal questurino, e il questurino dal questore, e il questore dal ministro dell'Interno, e il ministro dallo Stato il quale è lo Stato *in aeternum* e basta.

E così l'autorità resta il Nemico, e ogni dipendente statale fino all'infimo continua a impostarsi a torvo tirannello, intento solo a far perdere tempo, pazienza e carta bollata ai cittadini. E così si hanno commissari che sfidano i giudici, Tribunali militari che sfidano Corti d'Appello, ricchi che sfidano le tasse, leggi modificate per circolare ministeriale, poliziotti che sbucano dai carri armati per verificare la lunghezza delle gonne o lo stile del costume da bagno. E così insomma si continua con la frigiobarbara stirpe dell'autorità poliziesca; e a richiamarsi alla Costituzione, come disse Calamandrei, c'è da essere schedati.

Che rimane da dire? Niente. L'americano, per la verità, avrebbe dovuto dire qualche cosa di più a suo tempo. Questo la Storia non glielo perdona. Avrebbe potuto esprimere l'*alea jacta* dei nostri tempi, magari in più dimesso linguaggio, avanzando non foss'altro l'idea a lui naturale: « Let's go places together... » Ciò facendo (sul serio) avrebbe creato di colpo il suo ormai fantomatico impero, un impero di tipo moderno. Non lo fece: ho cercato di spiegare se non di giustificare il perché. Rimane molto conforme al suo ritegno di esprimersi, che so, canticchiando fra sé e sé qualche vecchia verità: « I can't give you anything but love, baby... ». Cioè, in questo caso: « Bimbo mio, non ti posso dare che la mia affettuosa simpatia. Per il resto te la vedi tu, perché la vita ognuno finisce col risolversela da sé ».

E anche questa è dottrina a tal punto rivoluzionaria, che da molti non sembra essere stata mai afferrata.

Index